Social Psychology

Under the Editorship of Wayne G. Holtzman and Gardner Murphy

Social Psychology

Muzafer Sherif and Carolyn W. Sherif
The Pennsylvania State University

Harper & Row, Publishers
New York, Evanston, and London

Social Psychology
Copyright © 1969 by Muzafer Sherif
and Carolyn W. Sherif

Library of Congress Catalog Card Number: 69–14987

To

Sue
Joan
Ann

Contents

**Part III
Social Interaction:
Process, Products, Structure
(Organization and Norms)**

**Part IV
Self, Attitudes,
and Reference Groups**

**Part V
Man as Agent and Target
of Social Change:
Process, Products, Change**

Contents   ix

Preface

Putting widely scattered material into a text-book of a new hybrid discipline like social psychology is a long pull. It becomes longer if, during the process of selecting, the authors try to be discriminate and mindful of whether items from diverse sources have a measure of coherence. The last thing the authors write (the preface) serves as a welcome closure for afterthoughts. Such thoughts usually concern the salient features of the book that (at least in the authors' eyes) differentiate it from others in the academic marketplace. The preface also serves as the occasion to note some unpaid debts, and to express publicly gratitude to the many persons who contributed to the body and texture of the product.

The pace of development in social psychology has accelerated markedly in the choice of subject matter and in theory and research methods since the appearance of the revised edition of this book (*An Outline of Social Psychology,* 1956). It is pertinent to specify both the continuities and the significant new developments reflected in this book—a major revision, elaboration and up-dating in progress for over six years.

A textbook should be more than the expression of its authors' predilections, theoretical or personal. It should chart a course squarely within the mainstream of the discipline, both in selection of content and in responsiveness to developing trends in theory, research advances, and findings. It has to avoid undue emphasis on that which appears glittering at the moment but is doomed to fade away within a decade or so as its glamor subsides.

The mainstream of any discipline is fed by sources whose substantive contributions become established as time goes on. In a developing discipline, a mainstream does not emerge in a few years; in social psychology, we find the mainstream stemming from some of the early founders of psychology and sociology. Especially since the 1930s, the mainstream has broadened through vigorous experimental and field research in both disciplines with strong influences from other social sciences, notably anthropology. Its contours were definable in 1948 in the first edition of this book and were clarified considerably by 1956. Since the mid-1950s, the supporting and elaborating body of research findings has expanded greatly.

Despite its academic base, social psychology has responded inevitably to actualities of social life as well as to its own research traditions. Therefore, the areas of its elaboration are pronounced in problems bearing on actualities: in research on the ingredients of the social interaction situation, including the research situation itself; in research on small groups, organization, leadership, and intergroup relations; on the effective development of cognitive indicators (perceptual, judgmental) for indirect measurement of attitudes, interpersonal role relations and their change; on the central problems of conceptual functioning and the structure of human attitudes; and on ego-involvements as a function of reference groups. Many of these developments are contributing effectively to an integrating conceptualization of the important problem of personal consistency, its maintenance and its breakdown under the onslaughts of diverse situations.

No matter where we may be living in the world of the 1970s, whether under capitalism or socialism, ours is an age of social change to the point of no return. Confrontations between groups in competing and hostile relations, the emergence of national identity among erstwhile downtrodden colonial and minority groups, the alienation problems associated with a widening generation gap, and the fantastically rapid rate of technological change are reflected in problems that by their nature are of concern to social psychologists. Such social actualities pose for social psychology the issue of the *validity* of its findings and conclusions on the topics it purports to study. The aim of any scientific endeavor is prediction; the fulfillment of such an aim poses the problem of validity.

Social psychology has had to grapple seriously with problems of social change, a concern that arches over the coverage of almost every topic in this book. The space devoted to problems of social change is greatly expanded, especially for material dealing with the formation and change of groups, with the generation gap, with minority groups emerging in the midst of dominant groups, and with social movements shaping and shaped by the newly emerging self images of participants. We have departed from orthodox textbook tradition of placing the chapters on attitude change immediately after the chapters on attitudes. Research findings on attitude change are to be found in many chapters of this book, for example in the chapters on in-group formation and intergroup relations, on adolescent attitudes and on reference groups. However, the chapters entitled attitude change are now where they properly belong, in Part V, devoted to man as agent and target of social change, whether through the efforts of communicators in interaction situations, through technological change, or through participation in social movements such as newly arising nationalisms.

Despite the increased coverage in this book, more than half new to this edition, there are common threads all the way through. We do not believe that conceptual coherence (dare we use the term systematic?) is achieved through word magic nor by imposing a fixed model by chopping off anything that does not fit, producing a mutilated caricature of social events. Yet, any discerning person familiar with developments in social psychology over the last three decades cannot help noting coherence emerging within the mainstream despite differences in conceptual labels and preferred research techniques.

In Part I, the broad trends within the mainstream are stated. In Part II (Chapters 2–5), converging trends in social psychology are made more explicit through propositions derived for the most part from experimental psychology. These propositions are applied to concrete subject matter throughout the book.

Since the 1930s we have been dedicated to the proposition that valid social psychology is good psychology of the individual, and that valid psychology of the individual is good social psychology. If a principle is valid, it should be valid in the laboratory and in the more complex interaction situations of social life. We have made a persistent effort in presenting the propositions and throughout the book to compare findings from laboratory and field research to bring them into phase. Likewise, there need be no dichotomy (let alone, opposition) between what is genuinely scientific and what is genuinely humanistic in social psychology. Contrary to the labels of inclusion and exclusion used by some self-appointed "scientists" and "humanists," there is no inherent reason why what is best in science cannot also be best for human beings (cf. Sherif, 1967, pp. 10 f.).

In assessing the propositions in Part II, some readers may note that what is presented is not labeled as "cognitive" or "behavioral" or "psychodynamic"; the absence of such labels is intentional. To the serious student fifty years from now, partisan declarations that one's position in psychology is "cognitive" or "behavioral" or "psychodynamic" may appear strange, even laughable. These labels are remnants of Faculty Psychology; there are already signs that such partisan positions are breaking down. It was people like Bartlett, Köhler and Koffka, like Piaget, like S. E. Asch, H. Helson, D. T. Campbell, W. Garner and J. J. Gibson (to mention only a few) who put forth the most convincing basis for the unity of experience and behavior by demonstrating repeatedly that behavioral manifestations are indicators of underlying perceptual, judgmental and evaluative processes. It was Carl Hovland and his associates who insisted in various works that attitudes, commitments and identifications are inferred from observable behavior.

Of course, as social psychologists we are deeply committed to the study of the individual's identifications and commitments in religion, politics, ideology, and so on. The most effective breakthroughs in the study of such identifications have made concepts of motivation and cognition operational through behavioral indicators related to stimulus conditions that did not strait jacket the individual's choices by allowing few or no alternatives. There is every indication that an effective psychology of behavior is at the same time the best psychology of motivation and attitudes; a valid psychology of cognition (perception, judgment, thinking) is attainable only through effective study of *behavior* under specified conditions.

The social psychology presented in this book is, at once, cognitive-motivational-behavioral. The twelve guidelines presented in Chapter 2 in summary form specify the *interactional frame of reference for behavior,* in which observable behavior at a given time is linked conceptually with cognitive-motivational processes in specified stimulus situations. The basic propositions are elaborated in Chapters 3–5 and their utility in treating topic after topic of social psychology is spelled out in later chapters. For example, the logic of psychophysical judgment and psychosocial judgment proves congruent and applicable to problems of attitude, ego-involvement, and reference groups that involve a comparison between self and others. (For further elaboration, the interested reader may consult our *Social Judgment* with Carl Hovland and *Attitude and Attitude Change* with R. Nebergall.)

In teaching social psychology, we have found that the basic guidelines presented in Part II provide students with a framework for evaluating research on the varied subject matter in social psychology, so that they see the divers topics in common focus. Whatever revisions they may ultimately need, the broad and empirically-based propositions serve as a map, which is preferable to random sampling of topics or to fixed models that automatically eliminate much of the vital subject matter.

The instructor of lower-division undergraduate classes can proceed directly from Part I to Part III of this book during early assignments, thereby introducing students to the propositions in the concrete context of social interaction situations. (An instructor's manual is available which notes high points in each chapter, suggests further illustrations and studies, includes various aids to the teacher, and specifies sections in several chapters that may be omitted in elementary courses without disrupting the continuity of the student's reading.) When teaching younger students, less concerned with psychological technicalities, we have found that the propositions become more meaningful in the context of concrete social events familiar to them. For example, the concept of end-anchoring, presented in the language and research of the psychophysical laboratory in Chapter 4, becomes more meaningful to the young student when he encounters it in Chapter 8 in dealing with the greater weight of the leader in decision making in a group. Of course, skipping Part II during the early weeks of an undergraduate course does not mean ignoring the foundation materials. The reader will find specific applications of the guidelines in subsequent chapters (6–12). As reference is made to them, the instructor may refer effectively to the specific principles that are being applied and to particular research examples and illustrations in Part II.

Part III begins the presentation of topical subject matter with the problem of what constitutes a social interaction situation, including a research situation (Chapter 6). The research findings in Part III reflect fully the growing insistence within and outside of social psychology that concepts and findings on social interaction from field and laboratory research be brought into phase. Particularly in research on group interaction, leader-follower relations, and intergroup relations, research developments of the last decade provide evidence of the fruitfulness of combining field and laboratory methods—a trend also reflected in our *Reference Groups* (1964).

Chapter 6 concentrates upon laboratory studies in which individuals are simply together or interacting briefly. Chapters 7–10 proceed to those social situations defined as a group, with separate chapters on group formation, the rise of organization, the formation and functioning of social norms with the associated problems of conformity-deviation. Chapters 11–12 deal with interaction between groups and their members, leading to problems of intergroup cooperation and conflict, the vexing problems of domination-subordination and of prejudice, social distance, and negative stereotypes.

Part IV concerns the products of interaction, starting with consideration of conceptual functioning and including recent work by both psychologists and linguists on the acquisition of language forms, which extend the individual's relatedness to social objects in space and time (Chapter 14). While basic to the conceptual treatment of social attitudes and ego-involvements, the material in Chapter 14 may be omitted in a shortened course without disrupting the continuity of the chapters on social attitudes and their measurement (15–16). The attitude chapters are followed by presentation of the self system, as an integrative concept in the study of specific attitudes as well as human motivation in general (Chapter 17). Chapter 18 treats the reference sets or groups in which much of the identity of a person is anchored. Chapter 19 applies the concepts developed in Chapters 15–18 to the problems of self identity during the adolescent transition to adulthood.

Accounts of what is usually called socialization are in Chapters 14, 17, and 19. Since social development is certainly the central problem of social psychology, we have been asked by students why the book does not start with an account of socialization. The answer lies in our conviction that socialization processes cannot be treated adequately before the student has a grasp of the nature of social interaction and its organized forms, in their formation, stabilization, and change.

Part V, as noted earlier, is devoted to man in social change, not only as passive target of social influences but also as active agent in interaction with others. Parts III and IV are preparation for Part V in emphasizing the processes of change, as well as stability, that inhere in the formation of groups, in the formation of social norms and individual attitudes, and in the formation of the self system. Part V deals with our persistent concern that change and stability are integral parts of the same processes, hence to be treated within the same conceptual system. Some theories are forced to treat the problem of change in a roundabout way because their models fixate on the nineteenth century preoccupation with equilibrium and its maintenance, with little concern over the problem of levels of organization and appropriate units for their analysis.

Chapter 21 treats attitude change in interaction situations where specified communications are introduced, encompassing both laboratory studies and research on the mass media. In Chapter 22, the treatment of attitude change extends beyond orthodox bounds through consideration of technological change. The final two chapters (23–24) begin with analysis of behavior in collective interaction situations and proceed to the most striking and significant setting for attitude change—indeed for a new self image—emerging social movements.

ACKNOWLEDGMENTS

The pleasant task of expressing gratitude to colleagues, assistants and students, past and present, who contributed to the substance and texture of this book is constrained only by limited space for describing the nature of our debts to them.

We are especially grateful to Gardner Murphy, Carl I. Hovland, T. C. Schneirla, Harry Helson, O. J. Harvey, E. L. and Ruth Hartley, John Volkmann, Donald T. Campbell, Robert MacLeod, A. S. and Edith Luchins, William McGuire, and Gerard Lemaine. Hopefully, we have put to good use what we learned from Wendell Bell and Eshref Shevky on social area analysis, from Robert Clark on applications of the reference group concept, and from M. Brewster Smith on problems of attitudes, personal consistency, and involvements of the self.

The book is enhanced by three sections written by other authors. Ralph H. Turner wrote a summary of part of his own research on the social context of ambition especially for this book, for which we are grateful (Chapter 19). Lewis M. Killian, a long-time friend and trusted colleague, graciously consented to reprinting of a selection from his *The Impossible Revolution?* (Chapter 23). Shortly before his death, Crane Brinton permitted the reprinting of his incisive summary of the early stages of the American, French and Russian Revolutions from his book *The Anatomy of Revolution* (Chapter 24).

Several of the illustrations were provided especially for this book. We are particularly grateful to Harry Helson for the figures illustrating his impressive work on assimilation-contrast in color perception (Chapter 5); to Wayne Holtzman for illustrations and the caption on his research on the Holtzman ink-blot test (Chapter 4); to John Aboud for research and illustrations on the normative regulation of speed (Chapter 9); to S. Frank Sampson for graphs of his unpublished research (Chapter 8); to Bertram Koslin (Chapter 8) and A. S. Luchins (Chapter 4) for plates of their published findings; and to B. J. White (Chapter 3), W. R. Hood (Chapter 22), and Mübeccel Kiray (Chapter 22) for photographs. H. Leibowitz and Robert Freeman were helpful in consulting on some figures in Part II. Gian Sarup drew a number of original graphs from published research data.

As in previous writing, we were fortunate to have the assistance of graduate students who provided illustrative material and called our attention to relevant studies. Particularly on ego-involvements and reference groups, we were fortunate to have the assistance of Donald Granberg, Larry Rogers and Gian Sarup. Other former students who will find their suggestions and their own research incorporated in this book are James Harper, W. R. Hood, Bertram Koslin, Lawrence La Fave, George Larimer, Nicholas Pollis, B. J. White, and James Whittaker. Other students contributing through seminar participation include S. Shurtleff, Merrilea Stiffler, Joan Rollins, and Michael Lauderdale.

A number of the research units summarized in the book were parts of research projects directed by M. Sherif with support from the National Science Foundation. The impressive experiment by Nicholas Pollis (Chapter 7) differentiating the effects of group situations and other social situations was partially supported by the projects. Mark MacNeil conducted the study (Chapter 10) on norm transmission as a function of arbitrariness for our program, later incorporating it into his master's thesis. We are also grateful for his sending a summary and graphs from his unpublished doctoral dissertation (1968) on judgment indicators of status (Chapter 8).

Our research program on natural reference groups of adolescents, reported in Chapters 8, 10, and 19, has been supported over the years by grants from the National Science Foundation; of the many persons who collaborated and assisted in that research, we particularly want to acknowledge Sister Frances Jerome Woods, Eduardo Villarreal, and Joel Garza.

Grants from the Rockefeller Foundation implemented research units on social judgment and attitudes scattered through various chapters, including that on judgment of truth in collaboration with our friend and colleague Norman Jackman (Chapter 15) and the unit on reference groups and the importance of issues with Gene Russell (Chapter 18). In the same research area, it is a pleasure to extend thanks to Lawrence La Fave for his intelligent participation in research on the Own Categories Technique (Chapter 15) and his originality in applying the reference group concept (Chapter 18). We note with pleasure the collaboration of W. R. Hood in the study of judgment and verbal report (Chapter 10), which helped to clear up a long-standing theoretical controversy, and the research by William Prado on shifts of reference groups during adolescence (Chapter 19).

A final source of stimulation to our work on this book is not evident elsewhere and should be noted: we were afforded the opportunity to exchange notes personally with over a hundred colleagues in various social science disciplines in this country and abroad during seven interdisciplinary symposiums on social psychology that we organized at the University of Oklahoma and The Pennsylvania State University. Our interchanges with participants, in many cases far into the night, are acknowledged in the seven published volumes resulting from the symposiums, the last two of them appearing concurrently with this book (*Attitude, Ego-Involvement and Change*, 1967, and *Problems of Interdisciplinary Relations in the Social Sciences*, 1969). It is a pleasure to acknowledge once again the insightful support of Dr. George L. Cross, then President of the University of Oklahoma, and the administration of The Pennsylvania State University, where the last two symposiums were held.

For nearly three years of the work on this book, we have been most fortunate in having the assistance of Mrs. Doris Sands who, with typical optimism and cooperation, typed and re-typed every chapter and assisted in chores associated with the book's preparation.

M. S.   C. W. S.

University Park, Pennsylvania
January, 1969

Preface
to the Revised Edition

Social psychology as a scientific discipline is still in a formative stage, even though many of its problems must be almost as old as human history. The background of this formative stage and trends that seem to be making effective headway are sketched in the last chapter of this book. In recent years, research and applied activities have accelerated.

The impetus for current thriving activity in social psychology does not come entirely from within the discipline. Probably a greater impetus to accelerated growth stems from the increased urgency of human relations problems faced by men of practical affairs, who have turned to social science with questions and with means to support their investigation. Many of these questions have concerned human groups, their organization, leadership and follower-ship, morale, power relations, and communication channels. Research on relations between groups has interested men in community, industrial, and governmental affairs, as well as practitioners in the traditional area of tensions between ethnic groups. In a changing world marked by conflict between the old and the new, problems of attitude change came to the foreground. Problems of personal conflict, inconsistency, and marginality stemming from membership in multiple groups with conflicting values led to preoccupation with the topic of reference groups. Serious studies of collective behavior, crises and disasters were undertaken. An adequate picture of contemporary social psychology must reflect these interests and developments. Accordingly, proportional space is devoted to their treatment in this revised edition, in which approximately seventy percent of the writing is new.

The impetus from a world with serious practical problems has brought social psychology into more intimate contact with the actualities which it aims to understand. Another consequence has been crossing and recrossing traditional boundaries between the social sciences. However, along with these developments, the accelerated pace in social psychology encouraged and sponsored by action organizations has created numerous theoretical and methodological difficulties. If social psychology has claims to come of age as a scientific discipline, its varied activities must be related to established concepts and principles. Its findings must contribute to the development of a coherent body of knowledge. Only then can predictions of wide validity and applicability in various interpersonal, social, and cultural contexts be made. With this aim in mind, principles and generalizations which have proved their usefulness in laboratory and other research are spelled out early in this book, more specifically in Chapters 2 and 3. They are applied to treatment of various topics throughout the book with the addition of supplementary concepts and generalizations as needed.

In line with the interdisciplinary approach stated in Chapter 1, relevant material from sociology, anthropology, and history is utilized to cross-check generalizations based on laboratory and other research. The concept of "levels," as discussed in Chapter 1 and throughout the book, provides a basis for an integrative interdisciplinary approach. When the units of analysis employed at different levels of study are delineated, interdisciplinary comparison becomes an aid in checking the validity of findings and conclusions.

An integrating development for viewing individual and group in a functionally related way has emerged through analysis of the individual's ego formation and of his ego-involvements in given social settings. Conceptualization in terms of ego-involvements and reference groups, within the framework of the properties of group relations, is providing effective tools toward resolution of the long-standing controversy between proponents of an "individual approach" and of a "group approach." Therefore, these concepts and relevant material are further elaborated in this revision in the treatment of motives (Chapter 12), attitude formation and change (Chapter 16), and in chapters dealing with ego-involvements and reference groups (Chapters 17 and 18).

In the thriving state of social psychology today, textbook writers are necessarily put under heavy obligations to many people who provide time and support, good judgment, helpful suggestions, source material, encouragement, and personal kindness. It is a pleasure to acknowledge at least the outstanding ones in presenting this revision.

The group relations experiments reported in Chapters 6 and 9 were carried out under my direction in a research program underway since 1948. The first experiment completed in 1949 was jointly sponsored by the Attitude Change Project at Yale University, which is under the general direction of Professor Carl I. Hovland, and a grant from the American Jewish Committee, Department of Scientific Research, which was then directed by Dr. Samuel H. Flowerman. Continuation of this research program at the University of Oklahoma from June, 1952, to October, 1954, was made possible by a grant from the Rockefeller Foundation, for which I am grateful. As originally proposed to the Foundation, a survey of relevant literature, a theoretical approach based on the survey, and a report of the 1949 group experiment were presented in our *Groups in Harmony and Tension* (Harper, 1953) which served as the basis for plans followed in the 1953 and 1954 intergroup experiments. My gratitude to those who collaborated in the preparation, execution and analysis of the 1949 experiment, the incomplete 1953 study and the 1954 Robbers Cave study cannot be fully expressed. It is a particular pleasure to mention the collaboration of Dr. Marvin B. Sussman, Dr. Robert Huntington, Dr. O. J. Harvey, B. Jack White, William R. Hood, and Carolyn W. Sherif.

Several experiments summarized in this book were conducted under my direction with support from the Office of Naval Research. These include experiments on insecurity with the collaboration of O. J. Harvey and by Virgil Hill in Chapter 17; on status expectations by O. J. Harvey in Chapter 6; on conflicting anchorages by Norman Walter in Chapter 3; and on gradations of stimulus structure by James D. Thrasher in Chapter 3.

Members of the various social psychology seminars at the University of Oklahoma since 1950 have contributed surveys and illustrations, some of which have been utilized. O. J. Harvey, James Thrasher, Daniel Taub, Edwin Cohen, Charles Shedd, Vera Gatch, Arlene Gibson, Victor Harnack, Norman Walter, B. Jack White, William R. Hood, William Combs, James O. Whittaker, William Prado, and Lawrence La Fave were particularly helpful.

During the actual writing of this book, I was fortunate to have graduate assistants who searched for illustrative material untiringly and discerningly. William R. Hood and B. Jack White served in this respect beyond the call of their official duties.

I want to express special gratitude for the never-failing contributions of Dr. O. J. Harvey, who started in the fall of 1950 as graduate research assistant in our various projects at the University of Oklahoma and later was research associate. Even after leaving Oklahoma in 1954, he continued to lend a hand, notably by securing the pictures revealing group identification in Chapter 5 and material on intellectual movements, some of which was used in the section on intellectual aspects of social change in Chapter 21.

We are indebted to Professor T. C. Schneirla of the American Museum of Natural History for many stimulating discussions. We hope that their benefit is reflected in the introduction of the levels of organization concept in the first chapter and in spelling out the import of man's conceptual capacities in his sociocultural relations. Our appreciation is extended to Professor Lewis M. Killian, now of Florida State University, who made some of his material on multiple group membership available when he was preparing it for publication. Professor Paul David of the University of Oklahoma read a portion of the manuscript and made valuable suggestions for clarification.

Mrs. Betty Jane Frensley typed the manuscript. We are indeed grateful for her efficiency and alertness.

We are especially indebted to Mr. William R. Hood and Mrs. June Hood for their personal kindness in many ways which were invaluable. The personal efforts of Mr. and Mrs. L. A. Wood, Sr., for us and their grandchildren made it possible to complete the manuscript on schedule.

Acknowledgment for the illustrations in this book is made in the appropriate context throughout. In locating pictures, we were aided by Professor A. S. Luchins of the University of Oregon, who provided prints of his material used in Chapter 3; by Mr. Fred Snyder, The Menninger Foundation, and Dr. N. H. Pronko, University of Wichita, who provided the print of their work used in Chapter 3; by Professor Robert Bales of Harvard University, who supplied views of his work used in Chapter 7; B. Jack White, who made a number of first drawings; Frank Garner of the Norman *Transcript;* and Mr. and Mrs. James H. Bragg, Mr. R. Boyd Gunning, Professor Leonard H. Haug, and Professor Edith Mahier of the University of Oklahoma.

Time and support required for writing this book were provided by the administration of the University of Oklahoma. I am grateful for this opportunity and the generous encouragement of Dr. George L. Cross, President; Dr. Lloyd E. Swearingen, Vice President; and Dr. Laurence H. Snyder, Dean of the Graduate College. The establishment of an Institute of Group Relations in 1955 through their insight and administrative judgment added further encouragement for concentrated efforts on the central topics of social psychology presented in this volume.

Since 1947 I have had the good fortune of collaborating with Professor Carl I. Hovland in several research units. His searching and exacting questions in our discussions of attitudes and attitude change sharpened my thinking on these topics, which I hope is reflected in appropriate places.

In this undertaking, as in *The Psychology of Social Norms* and the first edition of this book, I have received encouragement and insight from Gardner Murphy. He has followed the growth of the manuscript chapter by chapter. We have incorporated some of his suggestions concerning organization and many of his editorial suggestions in the various chapters.

My wife, Carolyn Wood Sherif, refused my suggestion to join me in signing the 1948 edition, although she had written major parts of several chapters. This time, I took it upon myself to recognize that she wrote various chapters of this book, and then presented the fact to her.

Muzafer Sherif

Norman, Oklahoma
February, 1956

PART I
Orientation

1

Orientation
to Social Psychology

Major Topics of the Chapter

Topics of social psychology and ground
  rules for their study
Present state of social psychology
Three converging trends

1. Increased   utilization   of   scientific
   methods
2. Guards against ethnocentrism
3. Behavior as product of interacting influences from person and environment:
   the frame of reference

Lag in development of social psychology
Definition of social psychology
Analysis of a social situation
Sets of factors in a social situation
Varieties and scope of social stimuli
Classification of social stimuli
Social psychology and related social sci-
  ences

3

In a relatively new scientific discipline such as social psychology, a clear orientation is needed to allow us to see the lay of the land, to decide on effective approaches and strategies for research, and to gauge our bearings relative to others engaged in studying related problems. Accordingly, this chapter undertakes the following tasks:

A look at the state of things in social psychology today.

A conception of what social psychology is and is not; that is, a definition of its proper scope and units of analysis.

Specification of what constitutes a social situation and the variety of social stimuli.

Defining the interdisciplinary relationships of social psychology with social sciences (especially sociology and anthropology) through the analysis of the social situation in which man's interaction with other men takes place.

TOPICS OF SOCIAL PSYCHOLOGY
AND GROUND RULES
FOR THEIR STUDY

Works presented as social psychology deal with topics that are problems to human beings in their day-to-day living. A cursory glance at a few representative topics will demonstrate this fact.

Interpersonal relations of friends, rivals, or antagonists.

Leader-follower relations in groups.

Solidarity and morale in groups.

Conformity and deviation.

Social attitudes—their formation and change.

Effects of communication and persuasion.

Prejudice and discrimination.

Collective interaction.

The rise of social movements.

Human beings everywhere are concerned with such topics and have developed prescriptions to guide their actions for dealing with these matters in daily life. In a sense, therefore, everyone is his own social psychologist whether he is aware of it or not. This is one reason why studying social psychology differs from studying mathematics or physics, for example. In mathematics and physics, students have not already established their own opinions on the topics.

Social psychology today must be distinguished from our own personal formulations on its problems and from earlier attempts to deal with them. Through the centuries, prophets, sages, philosophers, commentators, and men of public affairs have formulated the nature of human relations and their inner springs. They offered schemes for the good life in the form of religious and political utopias.

Great essayists, playwrights, and novelists have written intriguing descriptions of the interplay among individual roles. The essays of Machiavelli are still fresh in their descriptions of the attitudes and intrigues of the prince capable of outwitting both conniving courtiers and rivals. The works of William Shakespeare inspire awe by their subtle insights into love, ambition, hate, and jealousy as the actors interact in episode after episode, each prompted by his special sentiments, station in life, ambitions, and style of handling situations. The novels of a Balzac, a Tolstoy, a Dreiser, a Steinbeck, or a Hemingway describe the state of social life in the times depicted as well as the strengths and frailties of individual characters.

A social psychology that claims to be scientific cannot be built on artistic or literary creations—insightful and eye-opening though they be. The claim to be scientific rests on adherence to the same criteria that any scientific undertaking has to follow.

There are certain ground rules to which the artist and essayist cannot be held accountable. As a minimum, the essential ground rules that guide scientific undertakings include the following:

1. Formulation of a specific problem: This crucial first step in scientific investigation amounts to asking pertinent questions about a problem that can be answered on the basis of data collection and analysis.

2. Choice and definition of concepts: Scientific concepts have clear reference to the data or to data-gathering procedures and they must mean the same thing to those who develop them, to those who use them, and to those who challenge them. In other words, scientific concepts have clear referents and are not subject to the personal interpretations of each individual who uses them.

3. Communicable and reproducible procedures for data gathering: Data pertinent to the problem and its concepts are gathered through procedures, techniques, and tools that are communicable to fellow scientists and thus reproducible by them. Communicability and reproducibility are also required in data analysis to insure that inferences from the data are not merely personal interpretations. Scientific procedures thus seek to guarantee that conclusions are not merely the intuitions or personal preferences of a single master of the art.

4. Verification of findings: By reproducing the procedures used by one investigator, others with the required skills can check his findings for reliability. By the use of other methods and by systematic variation of the factors studied, the validity of the conclusions can be checked.

The aim of scientific disciplines is to build theory capable of accounting for events in the problem areas and of making predictions about them. Many procedures, tools, and techniques for data collection and data analysis have been developed. However, the ground rules listed above (especially the communicability of concepts and the procedures that permit verification of findings) suffice here to indicate the differences between a scientific undertaking and other undertakings—including essay writing, arm-chair theorizing, and journalism.

Advances in social psychology that satisfy the basic ground rules of scientific method have been underway largely in the twentieth century. Until social psychology began to develop as a scientific discipline, the only basis for resolving controversies about man's nature and his human relationships was argument and authority of the source: *It's my word against your word; How can my ordinary intellect challenge his great authority?* Of course, prestige and authority give temporary advantage in any controversy. But, in scientific undertakings, it is the verified findings and generalizations that survive the test of time.

PRESENT STATE OF SOCIAL PSYCHOLOGY

Social psychology is still in a formative stage rather than being a mature science, rounded in its various aspects. In recent decades, there has been accelerated research activity in universities; in military agencies interested in leadership and decision making; in business organizations concerned with labor-management problems, as well as morale and productivity; and in commercial centers for surveying public opinion and consumer tastes. Despite the rapid pace and large quantity of research, established principles and laws are still accumulating slowly—and they constitute only a tiny fraction of tremendous publication output.

This appraisal of current social psychology is stated as a challenge, not as a cause for dismay. In the formative stages of a scientific discipline, opportunities are greatest for creative and significant breakthroughs. Furthermore, some solid trends have developed on which the structure of social psychology is being built.

Three Converging Trends

No matter what disagreements there may be among social psychologists on specific points, it is safe to say that their work has converged in at least three trends that provide a thoroughfare toward a rounded social psychology.

1. Increased utilization of scientific methods and techniques: Adhering to the ground rules of science, social psychology today is characterized by its active and flourishing research orientation. It uses techniques of the psychological laboratory —performing experiments in the laboratory and in the field of actual life. Attitude measurement, survey research, content analysis, and field observation are among its other accepted techniques. Efforts to devise more refined methods and techniques for gathering and analyzing data are the order of the day.

The challenge within this growing trend lies in the first ground rule of scientific undertakings, namely, that of formulating pertinent problems. Formulation of significant problems requires close familiarity with actual events in the problem area. Formulating a problem amounts to extracting crucial features or properties from the complex subject matter and deriving fruitful hypotheses the testing of which will materially advance our knowledge. As Einstein and Infeld stated in tracing the evolution of physics: "The formulation of a problem is often more essential than its solution, which may be merely a matter of mathematical and experimental skill. To raise new questions, new possibilities, to regard new problems from a new angle, requires creative imagination, and marks real advance in science" (1951, p. 95).

2. Active efforts to guard against ethnocentric or culture-bound conclusions through cross-cultural, historical, and cross-sectional comparisons of data: The use of scientific methods and techniques does not guard against the danger that findings will be applicable only to a particular set of people at a particular time and place. The investigator, himself a person with strong ties to his own groups and culture, may use the standards of his group in formulating problems, devising procedures, and in drawing conclusions about the behavior or abilities of people. The problem was clearly recognized by the psychologists Anastasi and Foley in discussing the results of psychological tests of individual and group differences in performance:

Since all types of behavior are influenced by the subject's stimulational background, it follows that psychological data obtained within any one cultural group cannot be generalized to cover all human behavior. Many statements offered under the heading of general psychology are not general at all, but are based upon human behavior as it develops within a single culture (1949, p. 838).

Social psychology seeks generalizations applicable for people generally, and takes cultural differences into account. Therefore, it cannot afford uncritically to conclude, for example, as some investigators did several decades ago on the basis of studies of American college students' performance in the laboratory, that performance in a group levels individual performance toward mediocre quality. Such a generalization does not even hold for American college students engaged in other activities, such as playing football.

Thus there is a growing trend toward comparative studies in different cultures, toward comparing results obtained on one cross section of people with those living in different circumstances (for example, different social classes), and toward checking results against reports from earlier historical periods.

3. Studying behavior as a product of the interaction between the individual and his environment: This trend will be thoroughly discussed in this book in Part II. The development of social psychology as a scientific discipline was hampered for many years by controversies between those who proposed that influences from *within* the individual were a sufficient basis for understanding his behavior and those who countered that the individual was at the mercy of his cultural upbringing and his membership in groups. In social psychology today, both of these positions are rejected as outmoded and unproductive. Instead, the orientation is toward studying behavior within the framework of factors coming from within the individual (his motives, effects of past experience, states of his organism, etc.) *and* from his immediate environment (groups, culture, other persons, etc.).

Lag in Development of Social Psychology

Social psychology, as well as other social sciences, developed long after the great strides were made in the physical sciences. Some of the causes of the lag were suggested in discussing the three converging trends that promise future development. The lag is understandable in terms of ingrained habits in man's views of himself and the complexity of the subject matter.

The closer human beings get to problems that concern themselves, the less objective and the more self-centered they become. Premises ingrained in us from our communities and cultures intrude into our outlooks and appraisals of events. It is small wonder that the sciences dealing with topics farthest from ourselves, both physically and from the viewpoint of personal concerns, were the earliest to become established.

Astronomers' prediction of the movement of heavenly bodies was well advanced in the seventeenth century. Great advances in chemistry were to come later than those in astronomy and physics. The great strides in biology awaited the middle of the nineteenth century; the experimental psychology that emerged later in the century was closely allied to that development. The early experimental work in psychology was preoccupied with topics peripheral to the central issues of man's relation to man. Only in recent decades have major breakthroughs started in the scientific study of the multifaceted aspects of human relations.

Another major reason for the lag in sciences dealing with human relations is the greater complexity of our subject matter. Most common-sense explanations are simple, but the complexity of man's relation with man is by far greater than that of the problems in more established sciences. This great complexity lies in the nature of man himself, with his enduring and highly elaborated ties with his fellows that are built up from birth.

The physiologist studying nerve conduction can sever an animal's nerve to study its electrical and biochemical properties unhindered by other influences. The physicist can study falling bodies undisturbed by air pressure by conducting his experiments in a vacuum. In the study of human relations, on the other hand, the subject of study himself comes to the laboratory with everything that he is at the time—his likes and dislikes, his pretensions as a person, his loyalties

and desires. Being man, he not only reacts to the research situation—he persistently sizes-up and interacts with his environment. What he sees and how he acts may be affected by much more than the aspects of the situation that meet the eye of the researcher who sets up the situation for study purposes. Attempts to control conditions in order to study man's behavior are, therefore, much more difficult than in physics, chemistry, or biology.

In fact, in their eagerness to apply scientific methods to human behavior, psychologists have been guilty at times of vastly oversimplifying the factors that could affect results. In the study of learning and forgetting, for example, one classic control deriving from Ebbinghaus was to use nonsense syllables as previously unlearned, meaningless, and very simple items matched in length. However, it was soon found that the simplicity and equal length of these items did not guarantee simplicity of the processes underlying the person's response. Persons memorizing these syllables supplied meaningful associations of their own that affected their learning and retention (Bartlett, 1932). The illusion that learning and forgetting were being studied in their purest, most elementary form, uncontaminated by prior experiences, had to be altered.

Similar examples can be found in the early period of social psychology. For example, it was once thought that "pure" social effects could be studied by comparing the performance of individuals working alone and working side-by-side on the same tasks. Later experiments showed that the mere presence of other people is not a "pure" factor because the person invariably sizes-up the others relative to himself.

It is ironic that some physical scientists have been more impressed with the complexity of our subject matter than have some among our own numbers. Asked why there is such a lag between man's ability to understand his social affairs and the great strides in mastering his physical environment, Einstein replied quickly that the answer was easy: The problems of physics are simpler than the problems of power relations among men. The atomic physicist Oppenheimer (1956) sounded a similar note in an invited address to the annual meetings of the American Psychological Association on "Science by Analogy." He cautioned psychologists to develop their own concepts and methods appropriate to their highly complex subject matter instead of oversimplifying their problems in order to borrow theory from the established physical sciences.

DEFINITION
OF SOCIAL PSYCHOLOGY

Our glance at representative topics of social psychology, its ground rules, and the converging trends in the present state of its development was preparation for a definition of social psychology. The definition of any class of objects or events requires specification of what it is and what it is not. This is not an easy matter in our complex subject matter.

Major generalizations are implied in defining a discipline—such as the claim that we know its scope and how to go about studying its problems. There has been disagreement on these matters since the first two books appeared under the label of "social psychology" in 1908. One was written by the psychologist William McDougall and the other by the sociologist E. A. Ross. Since then, more than fifty textbooks on social psychology have appeared.

What has actually appeared as social psychology has reflected the field's dual parentage and the interests of the authors. If you look at the definition of social psychology offered in a book, you can predict the slant of the author's emphasis throughout. Until recently, some social psychologists concentrated mainly on interpersonal relations, others on the study of groups, still others on the study of social attitudes, and some on the study of individual and culture—each almost to the exclusion of other topics.

The definition of social psychology offered here is suggested by the three converging trends in contemporary social psychology that were noted above, namely:

1. Increased adherence to the ground rules of the scientific approach and utilization of scientific methods and techniques.

2. Awareness of the need for checks to guard against ethnocentric conclusions.
3. Conception of behavior within its appropriate frame of reference as a product of interacting influences coming both from the individual and his social surroundings.

Social psychology is the scientific study of the experience and behavior of the individual in relation to social stimulus situations.

Let us take the terms in the definition one by one as an orientation to the principal theoretical issues in social psychology and its relation to the social sciences.

Scientific Study. Specifying that social psychology is a *scientific study* underscores the task of adhering closely to the ground rules of science and their ramifications in the actual operations of research. Policy makers, religious leaders, novelists, and commentators on the social scene cannot be held accountable for adhering to the ground rules of communicability and reproducibility of methods that permit verification—*but social psychologists are.* In this book, the scientific ground rules, their associated methods, and the techniques are presented, on the whole, through the summaries of significant research studies that exemplify their use.

Of the Individual. The phrase *of the individual* specifies that the unit of analysis in social psychology is the individual. Because the field is social *psychology* and not psychological sociology, its concepts refer to the individual's perception of the social world, learning about it, remembering what is experienced, appraising and evaluating it, feeling about its various aspects, imagining, or thinking. It seeks to relate these processes to the social environment.

The individual is the unit of analysis for social psychology whether the investigator happens to be stationed in a university's department of psychology or sociology (the field's twin parents). Social psychologists today do not use concepts such as "group mind." A group cannot perceive, or feel, or think. The designation *social* in our label refers to the fact that our particular task is studying the individual's behavior in relation to those aspects of his surroundings that are interpersonal or sociocultural. When the individual has traffic first with these aspects of his environment, they are external to him—that is, on the stimulus side of the familiar S-O-R (stimulus-organism-response) scheme for analysis.

Experience and Behavior. Experience is a general term that refers to the awareness of the individual, and not just to past experiences as conveyed in expressions such as "My experience has shown that. . . ." What a person perceives, feels, learns, or remembers—in a word, his experience—is inferred from his behavior, i.e., both his deeds and words as well as subtle expressions and movements. For this reason, some psychologists refer to all psychological phenomena as behavior. The terms "consciousness" and "mind" and "awareness" were for a time almost banished from academic psychology.

However, we may be very interested in the appraisals, feelings, and views that an individual makes a point of keeping entirely to himself in a particular situation but reveals through word or deed in another. With a greater time perspective, we can include both experience and behavior in our definition. Experience can be inferred from behavior at one point of time and related to behavior at another point in time.

In Relation to. In any definition the choice of words is important. The importance of these particular words reflects controversies during the earlier development of social psychology.

The phrase "determined by" was deliberately avoided in our definition. The individual is not merely a passive recipient, a *tabula rasa,* reflecting the imprints of his environment, whether social or not. Anything that impinges on the individual from the social world around him is processed and his motives, desires, attitudes, and ideas enter into processing. The processing reflects *selectivity* in what he reacts to and whom he transacts with. The processing is also affected by what he confronts. Hence, experience and behavior that *count* for the individual and in the social process are always a joint product of influences in the social environment and those from within himself, whatever he may be at a given time

with all of his past learning, his enduring and momentary motives, and his viewpoints toward the issue at hand.

Part II of this book is devoted to principles governing the joint determination of experience and behavior through the processing of external influences and the person's psychological makeup.

Social life is the natural habitat of the human individual. It is not alien to his nature. Therefore, how an individual learns the requirements and values of his group and culture, how he responds to pressures from them, and the molding of his behavior within these requirements are not the sole problems of social psychology.

The interchange between individual and his social surroundings is a two-way street. He is not merely the recipient of sociocultural influences, that is, a learner of his culture. In transaction with others, he is an active participant in the creation of social influences. To repeat, man is not merely a culture-learning and reactive organism. He is constantly involved with others in changing and creating social influences in his groups and communities. Even while children assimilate the standards of behavior, the living schedules, and the etiquette of the grown-up society in which they live, they are participants in changing the patterns of their families—they take their part in forming new customs and they engage actively with peers in creating social groups with values distinguishable from those of adults.

The two-way interchange between individual and sociocultural surroundings that is indicated in the definition by the phrase "in relation to" is the core problem of social psychology. It will recur throughout this book: for example, in analyzing the formation of groups in Chapter 7, when discussing conformity and deviation in Chapters 9 and 10 or the problems of self-identity in Chapter 17, and when dealing with the rise of new social movements prompted by the inadequacy of prevailing routines and institutions for the actualization of individuals' longings in the last chapter.

Social Stimulus Situations. The final phrase in the definition of social psychology is *social stimulus situations.* The phrase seems self-explanatory. To show that it is not, we shall consider more seriously what constitutes a social situation for the individual at a given time. This analysis will enable us to indicate the scope and variety of social stimuli that an individual may encounter in his surroundings.

Accordingly, we will discuss the phrase *social stimulus situations* under two main headings: (1) analysis of a social situation that confronts the individual at a given time; and (2) the variety and scope of social stimuli surrounding the individual in his particular environment.

ANALYSIS
OF A SOCIAL SITUATION

The term *stimulus* is not always used consistently. At times, it is used to refer to any antecedent of behavior, including the person's emotions or states of his organism. It is used in this way in some introductory psychology texts as well as in popular writings in referring to the instigator of a thought or action.

Social psychology cannot afford to be casual in its use of the term *stimulus.* In many problems of social psychology, it is important to distinguish carefully between what the individual *brings* within him and what confronts him *in* the situation. Therefore we use the term *stimulus* in this book only for aspects of the environment *external* to the individual at a given time that impinge on him or that could *potentially* impinge on him at a later time. The skin is the usual limit for externality. There is a whole vocabulary with many synonyms to refer to events beneath the skin without using the word stimulus (e.g., sensation, interoceptive impulse, percept, concept, attitude, motive, affect, emotion, *ad infinitum*).

The scientific investigation of any behavior involves, among other things, the specification of the environmental (stimulus) conditions in which behavior occurs and the antecedent stimulus exposures. In studying delinquent behavior, for example, some description or assessment has to be given of the neighborhood, the family circumstances of the misbehaver, the company the subject keeps, and the immediate situation—including the objects of the action (a parked car,

a sex object, or money), and the presence or absence of other people (particularly law-enforcement officers).

Experimental study of behavior in the laboratory presumes accurate description of the stimulus setup or conditions. As controlled observation, experimentation requires that stimulus conditions be restricted to those aspects (variables) that the experimenter intended to introduce and control as required by his particular hypothesis. This conception of stimulus is in line with the use of the term stimulus for many years in the laboratory study of judgment (discrimination) of objects.

The importance of specifying the stimulus conditions in research has become almost a truism, especially for laboratory studies. Nevertheless, in actual practice, there has been lack of implementation—with serious consequences for assessing the validity of research findings. The issue raised here has been discussed by researchers in experimental psychology as well as by researchers in social psychology.

Experimentalist James Gibson (1960) gave an illuminating discussion of varying usages of the concept of the stimulus in psychology. He pointed to the inadequacy of the conception of stimulus agents as a "mosaic of stimuli" and suggested: "We should try to discover what an organism is responding to, not what excites all the little receptors" (p. 700).

Another experimentalist, Arthur Melton, raised similar questions about the prevailing concepts of what constitutes the stimulus in learning and problem-solving experiments. He was critical of the then widely accepted assumption in behavioristic theories of learning that behavior is a response merely to an isolated stimulus that an experimenter chooses to present in his study—for example, to particular tones or lights or colors. In the S-R (stimulus-response) relationship, he noted that a particular stimulus is not a fixed entity that arouses the same response under all circumstances. Different responses may be aroused depending on whether the stimulus is presented in isolation or whether it is presented in the context of other stimuli. Melton called attention to the neglect of the context of a stimulus in the following words.

Finally, I wish to mention a specific characteristic of our contemporary S-R theory that, it seems to me, must be overcome if progress is to be made. I refer to the assumption throughout much theory and experimentation, especially in the simpler forms of learning in the rat and in human conditioning, that the stimulus is a simple punctiform affair, something that can be dealt with as though it occurred without context, as though it were the stimulation of a single receptor. This comment is certainly not new. It has been made by the critics of S-R theories of behavior since the first such theory was formulated. But it is also one to which some dominant S-R theories have not adjusted adaptively. We have had Hull's principle of afferent neural interaction stated, but nothing much has been done about it either experimentally or through revision of theory (1956, p. 281).

Of course, it is perfectly feasible to study responses to single, isolated stimuli in the laboratory, for example, by restricting the field of vision to the location of a single patch of light or color. Such restriction is one of the standard procedures in studying vision, audition, and other sensory processes. However, with such a procedure the researcher also restricts the problems that he can study. He cannot transfer his findings directly to situations in which the same patch of light or color is surrounded by others. A single stimulus does not have a fixed, absolute value to arouse the same response in every situation. Its role in the stimulus-behavior relationship changes when it appears within a context of other stimuli. This principle is so important for the present discussion that it is demonstrated here in the words of an eminent experimentalist:

Let me begin by recalling an episode in the early 1930's when I gave a demonstration before the Optical Society of America of the inadequacy of the CIE (Commission International de L'Eclairage) method of color specification. In this demonstration, although the stimulus *qua* stimulus did not change with change in surround, its color could be made anything we pleased by appropriate choice of the luminance and hue of the background color. In the discussion that followed, the late Selig Hecht, perhaps the leading worker in visual science at that time, arose and said: "Why do you complicate the problems of color vision by introducing background effects? Why can't you wait until we have solved the

simpler problems before we go on to the more complicated ones?" (Helson, 1964, p. 26).

Helson continued by listing subsequent discoveries in color vision that were possible only because he and others did not wait to solve all of the "simpler" problems, but continued investigating the problems of background colors and illumination in color vision. Many of these discoveries have been applied to problems of daily life, for example, in lighting and color photography.

What Constitutes a Social Situation for the Individual?

The effect of the context in experiencing a relatively simple stimulus has a telling lesson for the student of social psychology. If even the perception of a patch of color is affected by the context of surrounding stimuli, how much more important it becomes to specify the context of social stimuli surrounding the individual! This is why we must ask: What constitutes the social situation when the individual engages in a task or carries on a conversation with others?

The individual serving as a subject in an experiment, or filling in test forms, or listening to a communication in an attitude study is participating in a social situation. There is much more to such social situations than what immediately catches the eye, or that can be recorded on tape or film.

Of course, specification of the individuals present is important. (Are they college sophomores or school dropouts? How old are they? Are they male or female?) Too, one must know what the subjects are doing (the task, problem to be solved, or activity). But, in the context of the situation, other things count also. Are the participants strangers, rivals, or "one for all, all for one" chums? How do they stack up relative to one another? How do they size-up the task? How do they view the experimenter and his instructions?

If some of the ingredients that shape the individual's behavior in a social situation are not immediately observable "out there" in the situation, we have to use appropriate methods to detect the more subtle factors that may be in the background. For example, in our studies in the early 1950s, very few students in states bordering the South would check attitude-test items that put them in a "prejudiced" classification regarding the social position of Negroes. But the same individuals would reveal their prejudice on the issue in private conversation with their friends. Clearly there was something in the context or background of the test situation that affected their responses. Why was there this discrepancy in their behavior in the two social situations? It was the context for the administration of the attitude forms—this was done by a representative of the university faculty. There was a prevailing *collegiate norm* to appear "liberal," and it was accepted that most faculty and advanced students were liberal on this issue. One did not wish to appear as a "back number." However, with close friends who shared one's prejudiced views, this collegiate norm was not applicable.

This is no isolated case. It is another example of the general phenomenon of the "demand character" of the research situation, which has been demonstrated by Martin Orne (1962) and others systematically concerned with the "social psychology of psychological experiment." The research situation is a social situation for the individual. The presence of the researcher, the physical setup, and the task presented do not adequately describe it as a stimulus situation for the individual. The background or context includes the prestigious presence of a "man of science" in a "laboratory" to which the humble subject comes to "contribute to science."

Thus the research situation is being analyzed today as a social situation; its context and background are being studied through the experimenter-subject relationship, subject-subject relationship, and subject-test atmosphere relationship (see Chapter 6). Whether the object for study is an experimental situation, an interview, a test situation, or an event in daily life, the ingredients that compose a social situation for the individual must be identified if we are to understand his behavior. It should be emphasized that these ingredients or factors do not function independently; they combine to form a patterned context for the perceiving and interacting individual.

We will return to the question "What con-

stitutes a social situation?" in studying behavior in interpersonal and group situations (Chapter 6). As a guide to sensitize us to the obvious and not-so-obvious ingredients of a social situation, four sets of factors are presented here for use throughout the book in presenting research and in appraising the results and conclusions.

Sets of Factors in a Social Situation

1. Sets of factors pertaining to participating individuals: These include: (a) factors related to the characteristics of the individuals, such as their number, respective ages, sex, their educational level, profession, social attainments, etc.; (b) factors related to the composition of the participants as to their homogeneity—heterogeneity in age, sex, race, religion, class, etc.; and (c) factors related to the prevailing relations among the participants. Are they strangers to one another? Are they personal friends or rivals? In what combinations? Are they members of a group? Does their group have a high degree of solidarity or is it loosely knit?

2. Set of factors pertaining to the characteristics of the activity, task, problem, or occasion at hand. Is it clear-cut or ambiguous? Is it difficult or easy, complex or simple, habitual or novel? What instructions are given about the task?

3. Set of factors pertaining to the location and facilities. What is the location and its facilities? Are there other people present not related to the task or occasion at hand? What are the general atmosphere and social definition of the location? (There are appropriate places and atmospheres for romance, for work, for conversations, for drinking, and for worship.)

4. Set of factors pertaining to the individual participant's particular relation to the above three sets of factors. Is he proficient in the task or activity at hand? Is he personally involved in performing well or poorly? How does he view the other participants, the experimenter, or interviewer? Is he at ease or ill at ease in the location?

There is a wide awakening to neglected ingredients of the social situation, arrived at more or less independently, among experimentalists (e.g., Sells, 1963), contributors to the study of the "social psychology of the psychological experiment," social psychologists such as Stanley Milgram (1965) and Roger Barker (1963), sociologists carrying on the tradition of social psychology begun in Chicago, and among current exponents of "human ecology" (which aims at the study of the "total situation" of behavior).

Restricting ourselves to the American scene, it is fair to state that among those within our academic ranks who gave the earliest recognition to the problem of defining the social situation were W. I. Thomas, in his conception of the "definition of the situation," and George Herbert Mead, in his conception of the human "act" and "role." For example, Thomas and Znaniecki (1918) attempted to specify the social situation in terms of the kinds of data involved as follows:

The situation involves three kinds of data: (1) The objective conditions under which the individual or society has to act, that is, the totality of values—economic, social, religious, intellectual, etc.—which at the given moment affect directly or indirectly the conscious status of the individual or the group. (2) The pre-existing attitudes of the individual or the group which at the given moment have an actual influence upon his behavior. (3) The definition of the situation, that is, the more or less clear conception of the conditions and consciousness of the attitudes. And the definition of the situation is a necessary preliminary to any act of the will, for in given conditions and with a given set of attitudes an indefinite plurality of actions is possible, and one definite action can appear only if these conditions are selected, interpreted, and combined in a determined way and if a certain systematization of these attitudes is reached, so that one of them becomes predominant and subordinates the others (p. 76).

VARIETIES
AND SCOPE
OF SOCIAL STIMULI

We have been dealing with the ingredients (factors) that compose a social situation that confront the individual at a particular moment of time. Now we turn to the scope and variety of *potential* social stimuli surrounding the individual as parts of his social environment. At any particular time, he does not face all of the social stimuli in his environment. Nevertheless, there are definite advantages in designating the scope and variety of potential social stimuli. Three advantages are discussed in the following sections (A, B, and C).

A. Social (cultural) environments differ in the range and variety of social stimuli available. Objects and values in one environment may be lacking in another. Similar human problems may be handled through very different arrangements and customs in two environments. As individuals, we are so immersed in our particular social environment that, as a rule, we are not aware of the scope and variety of social stimuli a situation presents. As immersed in our own culture as we are in the earth's atmosphere, we tend to take that culture as much for granted as the air we breathe—which we notice only when it is scented, polluted or rarified (for example, at high altitudes). The scope and variety of social stimuli become evident to us when we encounter a new environment where there are cultural differences.

Americans traveling abroad have been known to complain in irritated tones about the scarcity of telephones for interpersonal communication, about the difficulties of finding a shower exactly when one wants it, about facilities for elimination in public places, and about finding a "decent family breakfast" in any but the most expensive hotels in European countries. On the other hand, they observe customs and arrangements lacking in their own country, such as the mid-day siesta when shops close for several hours, the Sunday promenades in the business districts and parks of many European capitals, the panorama of royal processions, and the extended network of kinship relationships in many parts of the world.

Therefore, specification of the scope and variety of social stimuli is essential to avoid a social psychology ethnocentrically based on the conditons of our own environments. There is something to be said for the old saying that the fish is the last one to discover the existence of water. The human being who is thoroughly immersed in his own sociocultural environment may be the last one to discover its features and its impact upon him.

B. Social stimuli have properties that ex-

ceed the perceptual range of the single individual. Social stimuli are not formless, chaotic bits of information. They are organized or patterned in the cultural environment just as the physical environment is patterned. Located in particular social surroundings, the individual need not confront the whole cultural arrangement in which his small location is a part any more than he can perceive directly that tomorrow's rain is forming on the other side of the mountain range. Yet the larger organizations and patterned customs may affect what he does as surely as the rain affects his activities the following day.

The anthropoligist Malinowski (1922) was among those who instructed us on the importance of specifying the patterned arrangements in social environments in understanding the behavior of individuals within them. In studying the Trobriand Islanders of the western Pacific, he observed a complicated system of exchange involving the transportation of goods over hundreds of miles and the exchange of shells made into necklaces and bracelets. These shells were, for the most part, not used as ornaments, nor were they individually owned. They were passed around "on loan" following a definite pattern. Malinowski observed these interchanges, finding them complicated and extensive, but well-ordered in terms of the religious, political, and social organization of tribal life. Yet, no single participant in the game—called Kula—knew the rules of the entire exchange system.

They know their own motives, know the purpose of individual rules which apply to them; but. . . . Not even the most intelligent native has any clear idea of the Kula as a big, organized social construction. . . . If you were to ask him what the Kula is, he would answer by giving a few details, most likely by giving his personal experiences and subjective views on the Kula. . . . For the integral picture does not exist in his mind; he is in it; and cannot see the whole from the outside (p. 83).

Nevertheless, the individual's experience and actions are affected by being in a particular location in the Kula system. An analogous circumstance in industrial societies may be that of a foreman in a large industrial plant caught in a labor-management struggle. He may perceive directly only the abusive treatments from the workers and the admonitions from management to get production rolling. But these specific manifestations are part of a conflict between different factions in an organized scheme of work relationships in which the foreman is the "man in the middle." Analysis of his behavior over time is far from complete if our view is restricted to his day-to-day encounters with workers or middle management. We gain perspective by seeing these manifestations and his reactions to them within the definite scheme of the larger organization prescribing roles of the individuals in different locations in it.

C. Specifying the scope and variety of potential social stimuli helps to clarify the appropriate relationship between social psychology and the social sciences (sociology, anthropology, political science). It is so important to clarify the interdisciplinary relationships of social psychology that a special section is devoted to it later in this chapter.

CLASSIFICATION OF SOCIAL STIMULI

We have seen that a social situation typically includes both man's relations to man and man's relation to aspects of his sociocultural environment. In the words of the anthropologist Melville Herskovits (1949), culture is the "man-made" part of the person's environment. Obviously an attempt to catalogue every variation of man's relation with his fellows and every item of the man-made part of his environment would be an impossible task. Nevertheless, it is important to indicate the varieties of potential social stimuli. On the whole, psychologists have been slow to incorporate some of these varieties in their research schemes.

S. B. Sells, an experimentalist by training and experience, contributed substantially by coming to grips with the problem of specifying the stimulus conditions for behavior. Referring to the widespread acceptance of the need for specifying stimulus conditions in the study behavior, he stated:

. . . its implementation in research design and measurement technology has been slow. In comparison with the extensive research and development on organization and measurement of individual differences, there has been little systematic effort to define and measure environmental variables. And yet . . . the nature and effects of such factors merit the most serious consideration (1963, p. v).

We list the varieties of social stimuli under the following simple classification:

I. Other people
    A. Other individuals
    B. Groups
        1. Relations within groups (intragroup)
        2. Relations between groups (intergroup)
    C. Collective interaction situations
II. Parts of the cultural environment: products of man's interaction with his fellows in the past or present.
    D. Material culture
    E. Nonmaterial culture

These classes of social stimuli are *not* mutually exclusive. The individual does not typically encounter one class alone. He usually confronts representatives of several classes in a single situation. For example, a wedding ceremony, a football game, political conventions, or a protest rally involve all classifications. Here, each of the classifications will be identified and its relation to the organization of the book will be specified.

Other People

Other Individuals. Other persons are the most obvious example of social stimuli, whether they are merely together going about their separate business in an airport, working side-by-side in an office, or engaging in interpersonal relations. When an individual interacts with another for more than a short time, an interpersonal relationship is formed that colors the behavior of each party to it. Frequently interpersonal relations occur within larger organized contexts, so that it is very difficult to consider other individuals as discrete social stimuli. For example, the give-and-take between friends, school chums, student and teacher, parent and child, and employer and employee is colored by the cultural values and particular organizational forms within which these interpersonal relationships occur.

The salience of cultural schemes in person-to-person relationships is seen when two strangers meet to chat. Typically, each has an itch to place the other in familiar

categories relative to himself: his station in life, occupation, residence, whether he is married or single. The particular category in which he is placed is likely to affect the way we see him, our impressions of him, and whether we want to continue to see him.

Situations in which individuals are together but not interpersonally related, are discussed in Chapter 6. Interpersonal relations are discussed throughout the book, especially in Chapters 6, 7, and 17, which concern interpersonal relations within groups, and in Chapters 18 and 19 on reference groups.

Groups as Social Stimuli. Interaction that continues over time among individuals facing common problems, tasks, or goals acquires unmistakable patterns or properties that affect the individual entering into it. Among these properties are established reciprocities (roles) among the individuals, regulating their give-and-take in talking, working, or playing together. If they interact regularly over a period of time in a variety of tasks, the pattern of roles takes on an hierarchical form of status positions—defined by the relative power to initiate and control decision-making and activities among the individuals. Such hierarchical patterns are reflected in leader-follower relations. Certain habitual ways of doing things, rules for treatment of each other and outsiders, and common values and goals are established among the individuals during the interaction process. The organization of roles and status positions and the group norms applicable to individual members distinguish a human group from other forms of association. Together these properties constitute the culture of the group. The human group, one of the most significant and universal forms of social stimulus situations in day-to-day living, is defined in Chapter 7.

Intragroup Situations. Confronting a group, the individual faces a social pattern of which he may or may not be a part. If he is not, he is quickly made aware by the actions of others that he is an "outsider" and does not "belong." Studies have shown that interpersonal communication and contacts and activities of individuals within a group are profoundly affected by the status and role organization and by the group standards or norms. Being a part of the pattern in some position and capacity over time, the individual's notion of himself becomes tied to the group: he is in it and "belongs" to it psychologically. Chapters 7 through 10 concern problems of intragroup relations and their psychological effects.

Intergroup Relations. When a group whose members "belong" to its organization and norm system comes into contact with another group, collectively or individually, we have a case of intergroup relations. As groups seldom function in complete isolation, intergroup situations are frequent in the individual's relations with other people. Examples are confrontations between members of different religious groups, ethnic or racial groups, national groups, or labor-management groups. As social stimuli, intergroup relations have different properties than relations within a group. These properties are governed primarily by patterns of conflict or cooperation between the groups developing or established in the past and by the norms of conduct established within each for treatment of the other group (the "out-group"). The properties and consequences of intergroup relations are discussed in Chapters 11 and 12.

Collective Interaction Situations. Collective interaction is represented by rallies, crowds, audiences, mobs, or riots. As a social stimulus situation, collective interaction is not identical with the mere presence of other people because, typically, there is some *focus* to the interaction process—such as a common object (e.g., a celebrity), common threat or disaster, or commonly experienced gripe. Neither can collective interaction be classified as merely interpersonal relations. The number of individuals is usually beyond the scope of face-to-face relationships. A closely knit nucleus or group may be mainly responsible for initiating and guiding the course of collective interaction, such as when a gang of teen-agers starts a street riot or a political group starts a mass protest. However, collective interaction must be classified separately from groups because, at least initially, it lacks an overall organization and norms for behavior embracing all participants.

Collective interaction situations are *out-of-the-ordinary events*—outside of the usual grooves of daily routine. They occur more frequently in times of unrest, crisis, or rapid social change. At times, the "cake of custom" is shattered and new customs, norms, or values arise from them in the form of short-cut formulations or slogans (e.g., "we shall overcome"—the slogan of the civil rights movement in the 1950s and 1960s). Thus collective interaction situations constitute an important framework for studying the individual in social change. As intense social stimuli, they give rise to accentuated expressions of emotions and motives. On the other hand, such occasions provide opportunity for the creation by participants of new social values or norms and patterns of human relations. Collective interaction situations are treated in Part VI, which deals with the individual in social change (Chapters 23 and 24).

Parts of Culture

The remaining two varieties of social stimuli are deliberately classified as "parts of culture." Especially in modern societies, no one individual comes into contact with the whole culture even during the course of his whole life time. We have already referred to the organizational and normative system of a human group as the "culture" of that group. Generally speaking, the social organization, norms or values, and other cultural products that encompass and apply to an entire society may be referred to as that society's culture. Because modern societies are highly differentiated by socioeconomic strata, ethnic classifications, urban-rural residence, and communities, the cultural products peculiar to a particular part of the population within a society are called "subcultures" by some social scientists.

It has been suggested that social psychology need not be concerned directly with cultural products as social stimuli because parts of culture typically confront the individual through the mediation of other persons (parents, teachers, friends, etc.). If the individual confronted cultural products only in person-to-person contacts and formed his conception of them only on the basis of the words and examples of others, it would be possible to restrict social stimuli to other people. There are at least two reasons why it is not possible to confine social stimuli to other people in interpersonal or group relationships.

1. From birth on, the individual is confronted by a man-made environment (culture) that is *not* always *mediated* by other people with whom he is in direct contact. He confronts furniture, buildings, tools, melodies, pictures, and modes of transportation and communication that unmistakably shape his tastes, his yardsticks for assessing appropriate proportions, and the tempo of events to which he is exposed. After he has acquired a working grasp of his language, much of his learning about the world is not mediated directly by other persons in face-to-face contacts. He reads books, listens to records, and follows other mass media of communication.

2. Cultural products, such as social organization and its associated values, have patterned properties that are not necessarily revealed in the interactions of particular individuals at a particular time. As social stimuli, these properties may be conveyed to the individual only during the course of time through a sequence of encounters. His behavior may be affected by a larger pattern of human relations without his immediate awareness that he is part in a larger picture (as noted earlier when Malinowski's study of the Trobriand Islanders was discussed). For a rounded picture, it is both necessary and more efficient to study individual behavior relative to the patterned features of the culture to which he is exposed than to try to reconstruct cultural influences revealed bit-by-bit in episodes of interaction with other people.

Now, as briefly as possible, what is meant by cultural products as potential social stimuli and by the terms "material culture" and "nonmaterial culture?"

Material Culture. Material culture is composed of those aspects in the man-made environment that are tangible objects or structures, and of their functioning. These aspects include furniture, dwellings, facilities for cooking and sleeping, utilities, plumbing, streets, playgrounds, means of communication (telephone, books, newspapers, radio, television), means of transportation (oxcart, automobile, train, boat, airplane), and other technological products (e.g., tools, machines, computers) that man uses.

Man's works reveal a great deal about his designs for living even without the interpretations by those living within the designs. The foreigner entering New York City for the first time does not need to be told of the riches and industrial might of the country. The skyline of the city, the traffic, the shop windows, and the unceasing movement of goods are more eloquent than words. Conversely, a stroll through a peasant village in parts of South America, Africa, or Asia reveals life problems of its residents—even though one may not speak to the residents. Through archeological findings on the artifacts, tools, and arrangements of extinct communities, we can learn a great deal about the mode of living and the problems of people long gone.

Parts of the material culture profoundly affect our notions of space and time, our standards for a "decent living," our scales for appraising what is "primitive" and "appropriate" and "splendid," the activities we engage in, the ways these activities are organized, and even our relations with our fellow men. Of course, the material culture does not affect us single-handedly, apart from our relations with other people, and the values we cherish in common or the ways we customarily use the material products. However, problems of material culture as social stimuli are among the most neglected in actual research of social psychologists. In a world in which peoples with highly elaborated and less elaborated technologies are in closer and closer contact, and where the technology of continent-wide destruction has been mastered, social psychologists cannot afford to neglect this important class of social stimulation. In this book, Chapter 22 is devoted to some effects of material culture, especially technology.

Nonmaterial Culture. The prototype of nonmaterial culture is the system of a human language. As several authors have emphasized, language is not merely another item of culture (e.g., Strauss, 1953). It is in fact the scaffold and vehicle for creation and transmission of culture, including material culture. Chapter 14 is devoted to human conceptual functioning and language as social stimuli.

As the intangible part of the man-made environment, nonmaterial culture confronts the individual from birth. He faces lullabies, feeding and sleeping schedules, the social institution of the family that defines his status for many years, the prevailing conceptions of what it means to be a boy or a girl, the activities appropriate for one of his age and sex, and the stores of fact and fantasy that are included in his cultural heritage. Later he enters a variety of social institutions (school, church, occupational, political, and governmental institutions), each with established forms of human relations and with codes that define what is proper and improper in one's dealing with his fellows and with outsiders.

The human infant is mercurial, his actions being regulated at first much more by the states of his organism and by momentary attractions to striking environmental events. Because his conceptual and motor capacities are not fully developed at first, it takes years for him to learn the parts of nonmaterial culture that he faces and to make them his own. The acquisition or learning of nonmaterial culture is not a passive process, involving merely the "stamping in" of cultural items through rewards and coercive means by adults. The individual is *selective* in his learning and gradually develops strivings to become like certain others and to do what they are doing. Such strivings emerge as he interacts with others and develops notions of himself as an identity—a person in his own right. We will discuss the formation of the self or ego and the influence of "significant others" in Chapters 17, 18, and 19 on the self and on reference groups.

A major feature of socialization in any culture is the regulation of behavior within bounds defined as acceptable, expected, and even ideal in the society. Being immersed in our culture, we are likely to feel that our conceptions of man, what is right and wrong, what we value, and what seems ideal and detestable are our own property and creations. Many of them, however, were first encountered as social stimuli during our development. We confronted them initially as something external to us and only gradually came to regulate our own behavior within such bounds. These cultural norms defining a range of acceptable behavior and a range of objectionable behavior for the would-be member are revealed through specific actions in the form of approval or acceptance of certain actions and various reactions to deviation, including punishment. These cultural norms as well as norms within smaller groups form the basis for assessing the conformity and nonconformity of individuals. The formation of social norms and norms as social stimuli are discussed in Chapters 9 and 10. When a norm is shared by all or most groups in a society, it is usually referred to as a cultural or social norm. Those shared by smaller units within the society are more often referred to as subcultural, institutional or group norms. Group norms are discussed in Chapters 7, 9, and 10.

SOCIAL PSYCHOLOGY AND RELATED SOCIAL SCIENCES

Our definition of social psychology provides orientation to the field's topics. It also clarifies the appropriate relationship between social psychology and related social sciences. The relationship between psychology, social psychology, and sociology has puzzled many specialists as well as students. One source of the confusion is the tendency to identify scientific disciplines with the academic departments of the traditional univeristy structure. After all, departments of English usually study the language and literature, and music departments concentrate on music. Why is social psychology not identified so easily? The reason is twofold:

1. The development of social psychology, as noted earlier, requires both psychological principles and the specification of social stimuli. These were traditionally separate tasks undertaken by psychology and sociology departments, respectively.

2. Historically, social psychology has dual parentage in psychology and sociology departments; both have contributed to its development.

The relationship of the offspring to parent disciplines is clarified by defining social psychology as the scientific study of the experience and behavior of the individual in relation to social stimulus situations. Psychology of any kind takes the individual as its unit of analysis. But social psychology studies the individual in relation to social stimulus situations, which include groups, social organization, institutions, and cultural objects, norms, and values. The social stimulus situations are the subject matters of sociology, anthropology, and other social sciences whose workers study them in their own right, at times with little interest in the individuals involved.

The unit of analysis in sociology is the human group or its stabilized social forms, such as social institutions. For example, one sociology textbook defines sociology as follows: "Sociology is the science that deals with social groups: Their internal forms or modes of organization, the processes that tend to maintain or change these forms of organization and the relations between groups" (Johnson, 1960, p. 2). Of course, a sociologist may be concerned with how single individuals function within groups. There should be no academic monopoly on such problems. When an investigator is studying individuals as his unit of analysis, he is studying, at the same time, as a social psychologist.

Similarly, anthropology studies kinship systems, social organization and institutions, systems of exchange, and cultural values— usually in smaller and less-developed societies, but currently in modern societies as well. Both sociology and anthropology use concepts and tools appropriate to the sociocultural level of analysis. They need not refer to the behavior of particular individuals at all—even in dealing with the same topics of study that interest a social psychologist (e.g., intergroup conflict, conformity, or deviation). Their concepts deal with regularities, recurrences, and patterns in behavior and with the properties of the man-made environment.

However, to say that social sciences work on a sociocultural level of analysis does not mean that their data and concepts are somehow less real than those tied to the behavior of particular individuals. Herskovits made the same point in discussing the reality of culture, in the following words:

There is little doubt that culture *can* be studied without taking human beings into account. Most of the older ethnographies, descriptions of the ways of life of given peoples, are written solely in terms of institutions. Most diffusion studies— those which give the geographic spread of a given element in culture—are presented without any mention of the individuals who use the objects, or observe given customs. It would be difficult even for the most psychologically oriented student of human behavior to deny the value of such research. It is essential that the structure of a culture be understood, first of all, if the reasons why a people behave as they do are to be grasped; unless the structure of custom is taken fully into account, behavior will be meaningless (Herskovits, 1949, p. 21).

There have been opinions that one or the other level of analysis—psychological or sociocultural—is somehow more basic or more central than the other. In naive form, one argument goes as follows: There could not be human groups, institutions or culture unless there were individuals. Take away the human beings, and what kind of groups or culture do you have? Therefore, the fundamental explanatory principles must be about human individuals—that is, they must be psychological principles. The reverse argument contended that groups have organizations and values quite apart from the peculiarities of particular individuals, that these properties mold the behavior of individuals, and that the structure and functioning of human social life, therefore, take precedence over psychological principles in understanding human problems.

The arguments above, which we have stated almost as caricatures, are left-overs from the cultural and philosophical heritage that treated the individual and the group or culture as though they were completely independent entities. Of course, if there were no individuals to interact, there would be no groups, institutions, values, or other cultural products. However, once groups come into existence and pass their values to new generations, the groups and their values become stimulus conditions for the new generation, setting certain limits and perspectives for them and for the very human beings who originated them.

Of course, man makes machines; but machines, in turn, affect man. Man creates social organization; we can also say that social organization recasts man. The products of man's interaction with others become subject matters for study at their own level of analysis without *necessary* reference to principles governing individual behavior. Thus sociology, anthropology, economics, and political science are disciplines the concepts of which are appropriate to the sociocultural level of analysis. To insist that they must be based on psychological principles would lead to the absurd position of saying that everything is psychology—including physics and chemistry, as these sciences are also works of men. Conversely, to insist that psychological principles are of no value to the social sciences is equally absurd: Cultures and institutions do change, and man's actions are certainly among the important sources of social change.

A rounded picture of human behavior and human societies must ultimately incorporate both the psychological and sociocultural levels of analysis. Meanwhile, social psychology has to borrow findings and concepts from the social sciences in order to specify the nature of sociocultural stimuli. Its principles must be psychological ones capable of relating the individual's behavior to these varied social patterns. In this specific sense, social psychology has to employ an interdisciplinary approach to its topics.

THE NEED
FOR INTERDISCIPLINARY STUDY
AND INTEGRATION

Although the social psychologist may from time to time work on the sociocultural level (e.g., to specify the organization of a particular small group), he is necessarily dependent upon social science to deal with the scope and variety of social stimuli. He cannot become an expert on language, values, social institutions, and technology. On the other hand, a social scientist may become interested in the roles of particular individuals or with problems of individual behavior as related to groups and cultural values. Therefore, there is genuine need for coordination and integration of the psychological and sociocultural levels of analysis.

Psychology attempts to formulate valid concepts and principles for the lawful functioning of human behavior. In the past, it has borrowed freely from biology and the physical sciences, in addition to working on its own level of analysis. For example, the psychologist learns from physics the necessary information about the nature of light and sound, from the biochemist about glandular functions, and from physiologists about the functioning of the neuromuscular system. In the same way, the social psychologist needs to learn about the properties of social stimuli from social scientists. He needs information about the stimulus patterns and contexts, for these social patterns and contexts affect the individual's perception of the discrete items composing them—just as component tones in a melody acquire their particular quality from their relationships with other tones.

It is helpful to keep the distinction between the psychological and sociocultural level of analysis in mind. In social psychology, it is often necessary to specify at a particular time which factors are within the individual and which are external, or on the "stimulus side" at the time. However, findings on individual behavior and findings on sociocultural topics are never contradictory if both are valid.

To illustrate, suppose that a sociologist wishes to study the social organization and values of a particular group, say a church. Among other things, he might observe church attendance over a period of time, finding that 75 of the 100 members attend every Sunday, 10 attend every other Sunday, 10 attend once a month, and 5 appear only on religious holidays. As a sociologist, he need not be concerned about who these people are or their individual reasons for attending or not attending. He may observe that a committee of elders visits the infrequent attenders, urging them to appear regularly. He may record evidence of scorn toward those who arrive only a few times a year. From these findings, he may infer the existence of a *social norm* favoring regular church attendance. In this instance, his data are on a sociocultural level of analysis, and his concept (social norm) is a sociological concept.

If his data are valid, a social psychologist who comes to the same community to study the attitudes of individual members should obtain findings congruent with the existence of a social norm favoring church attendance. This does not mean that those who abide by the norm will necessarily have the most favorable attitudes toward the church: a small boy may attend because his mother makes him do so, a businessman may go because it promotes his standing in the community, or an irregular attender may stay away because he does not like the minister. The important point is that his findings should supplement and not contradict the sociologist's conclusion, if both studies obtain valid data. In order to account for his findings on attitudes, the social psychologist cannot be content to refer to the existence of a social norm. Among other things, he has to deal with the problems of why the small boy obeys his mother, and why the businessman attends but the irregular churchgoer stays away when both dislike the sermons. As a social psychologist he has to collect data bearing on the individual's relation to the social norm that affects his attendance or nonattendance.

In fact, cross-checking the findings and conclusions about individual behavior with findings at the sociocultural level is one of the best means of insuring the validity of generalizations. Valid findings on one level of analysis should not be contradicted by valid findings on another level of analysis. Let us give another example: Sociologists have found that groups have certain properties (organization and norms, among others). Through analysis of the attitudes and behaviors of particular individuals, the existence of such properties is affirmed through their effects and consequences for the individual. Such collaboration across disciplines and integration of the findings are essential in the development of social psychology to a more mature and rounded discipline.

**Interdisciplinary Programs
for Training**

Therefore, social psychology increasingly relies on knowledge accumulated by the social sciences in analyzing the social stimulus situations in which the individual transacts. The reliance is scarcely a matter of choice, but of necessity. This keenly felt necessity is reflected in the strong trend in various colleges and universities throughout

the country for interdisciplinary study by graduate students in social psychology. During the last twenty years, the trend has been manifested concretely in new organizational arrangements and study programs that cut across the lines of traditional departments.

Another index of the interdisciplinary features of training in social psychology today is the increasing number of psychology departments offering social psychology as an area of specialization—with provisions for credit hours gained in social science departments. In 1955, there were 35 psychology departments in the United States with social psychology as an area of specialization for graduate study (Moore, 1955). By 1965, this number rose to 67 (Ross and Harmon, 1965). There are also a number of sociology departments throughout the country in which graduate students concentrate on social psychology. In a compilation by Sykes (1965) of information on sociology departments, 103 departments in the United States were listed as offering courses in social psychology. This list does not include courses on a number of topics of interest to social psychology—such as collective behavior, deviant behavior, juvenile delinquency, minority groups, race relations, or small groups, which were listed under separate headings. Twenty-three of the sociology departments listed social psychology as "courses or programs of special interest" in the department. Finally, in research centers and institutes, social psychologists may be found working with sociologists, economists, and political scientists on different aspects of the enormous problems offered by human behavior and social relationships.

DEVELOPMENTS IN THE 1930s:
A FORMATIVE PERIOD

We have singled out six major developments and trends from the 1930s whose impact is still with us in the shaping of social psychology. Of course, these developments have roots in earlier work, to which reference is given in appropriate context in different chapters.

In large measure, these developments and trends account for both the convergences and the contradictions that become evident to anyone who explores the literature today. Instead of elaborating on these major contributions, we shall simply cite them briefly.

Field Studies and Experiments on Small Groups. In the sociological tradition of research developed earlier, primarily at the University of Chicago (Faris, 1967), the observation of small groups and the collection of facts about them produced a proliferation of studies on small groups the impact of which has permeated social psychology. William F. Whyte's classic study in the 1930s is the culmination of the Chicago studies of actual small groups under complex field conditions (Whyte, 1943). The well-known Western Electric studies of work conditions which "discovered" that worker groups had an important part to play in whether workers met management-determined rates of production began to appear from the Harvard Business School (see pp. 196–198). In quite another key, J. L. Moreno and his associates introduced ways to map the network of interpersonal attractions among individuals in schools and work situations (sociometry). Later in the 1930s, Kurt Lewin (who had already contributed to social psychology through his studies of the "level of aspiration" in Germany) and his students initiated experimental studies on the effects on children's groups of their treatment by an adult supervisor. Their pioneering studies of "group atmosphere" marked the rise of "group dynamics" as a self-conscious research movement in social psychology.

Laboratory Experimentation. The importance of experimentation in social psychology was evident when early in the 1930s *Experimental Social Psychology* by Gardner and Lois Murphy was published (1932). In its revision with T. M. Newcomb (1937), the authors commented on the transformation that had occurred in the map of social psychology since the first edition. Referring to the work of Moreno, as well as Piaget (*see below*), they singled out the impact of the following experimental developments:

The publication of F. C. Bartlett's *Remembering* (1932) included reports of experimental studies of perception and mem-

ory side-by-side with Bartlett's observations made in Africa, without any "break" in logic or theory.

One far-reaching implication of Bartlett's laboratory and field studies was that the simplicity of the stimulus (e.g., nonsense syllables of a few letters) need not be associated with simplicity of psychological process in perception, remembering, and behavior. The internal and external context, frame of reference, or (in Bartlett's terminology) "schema," and not a single stimulus item, contributes to the psychological pattern. Bartlett's findings, as well as those derived from Gestalt studies and frame-of-reference psychology of judgment advanced by experimentalists such as John Volkmann (e.g., 1951) and Harry Helson (e.g., 1964 a and b), played havoc with reductionistic assumptions about stimulus-reaction relationships. Developments along the foregoing lines are among the solid foundations on which these outlines of social psychology are based. Principles derived from them are applied to the formulation of topics throughout the chapters of this book.

Murphy, Murphy, and Newcomb emphasized the increased awareness of the significance of Gestalt psychology. The experimental developments by Wertheimer, Köhler, Koffka, and Lewin were widely discussed, owing largely to these psychologists' migration to the United States as a result of the oppression in Hitler's Germany. The influence of Gestalt formulations is reflected in Chapters 2 and 3.

Finally, Murphy, Murphy, and Newcomb singled out the experimental studies of Muzafer Sherif on social factors in perception which, together with cross-cultural and experimental data assembled while the latter was a graduate student at Harvard and Columbia, had been published as *The Psychology of Social Norms* (see Chapter 10).

Psychoanalytic Impact with Special Reference to the Development of Prejudice and Collective Behavior. Freud's psychoanalytic theories had begun to permeate intellectual life in the United States in diverse directions. The orthodox psychoanalytic doctrine was made more palatable for social psychology by the so-called revisionists, particularly Erich Fromm and Karen Horney, and at Yale through the influence of the sociologist, John Dollard, who freely combined psychoanalytic notions with sociological concepts of caste and class as well as the then-current S-R learning theory of Clark Hull. Despite these admixtures, the basic formulations of Freud became and remain influential in social psychology—often today as unconscious assumptions.

Anthropological Studies. The impact of anthropological studies in the 1930s, chiefly from Boas and his students (Benedict and Klineberg), forced social psychology to re-examine its uncritical acceptance of research findings based on highly selective samples within the United States. Otto Klineberg's research and writing were an important source for the dissemination of the general conception that emotions, intellectual development, and many other psychological topics had to be formulated with reference to the sociocultural setting of development.

Developmental Studies of Piaget. The books by the Swiss psychologist Jean Piaget (e.g., 1928, 1932) on the child's notions of causality and, especially, of moral judgment appeared in English in the early 1930s. Their impact (as well as Piaget's more recent work on conceptual development) is still being felt in developmental psychology. However, for social psychology, the early studies were a model demonstration of the interaction of development and environment in conceptual functioning,

formation of the self concept, and of "conscience" (Chapter 17). They provided empirical documentation for theoretical views of socialization that have long been congenial to those social psychologists influenced by the work of sociologists such as G. H. Mead and Charles Cooley.

Developments in the Study of Attitudes. The 1930s saw a rash of developments in techniques for assessing attitudes and attitude change. In the early part of the decade Bogardus' Social Distance Scales came into wide use (p. 372). Thurstone formalized his scaling models and techniques (p. 368) and Likert developed his popular method for assessing attitudes (p. 371). The growing research literature was greatly augmented by E. L. Hartley's pioneering work on the formation of attitudes toward minority groups (p. 404), and by T. M. Newcomb's study in the field (Bennington College) which was initiated in the 1930s (p. 436). The public opinion survey also started to come into its own during this period.

Knowing of these developments in the 1930s, which are merely listed here, will permit better understanding of many of the trends and controversies that are still evident today. Many of the important developments, even in the last decade, have their roots in that important period of growth prior to World War II, when, suddenly, social psychology found itself in demand and attracted the interest of psychologists and sociologists with previously diverse interests.

PART II
Basic Propositions and Principles

2

Introduction
to Part II

The three converging trends in social psychology listed in Chapter 1 are represented in the concepts and work practice of many social psychologists. They are not mere statements of opinion, but summaries of the trends in the accumulated work of social psychologists.

In order to elaborate the current trends in social psychology, especially the interactionist position, we need some principles and conceptual tools. Otherwise, we cannot deal with the diverse topics of social psychology in a consistent way. Unfortunately, the theories and concepts used in treating the various topics developed, historically, along divergent lines. For example, *prejudiced* attitudes were frequently studied apart from the psychology of attitudes in general, with the result that the two topics are frequently treated as though their origins and manifestations were different.

At the present time the accumulated findings on various topics in social psychology permit adherence to at least a few reliable guidelines as we move from topic to topic. Therefore, in Part II, a number of basic propositions are introduced that will be utilized consistently in discussing each topic in the rest of the book.

The interactionist approach to social psychology has steadily become the dominant approach through the years, both in sociology and psychology. However, statements about such an approach remain mere abstractions unless there are explicitly stated principles that can be used in theory and research practice to deal with the specifics in handling topic after topic. Such prin-

27

ciples cannot be pulled from thin air; they have to be deduced from the accumulating body of empirical and experimental facts.

What kind of guidelines and concepts are needed as tools to deal with interacting influences that affect experience and behavior in various specific situations?

The guidelines should be based on empirical findings that have stood the test of time, in keeping with the trend toward adherence to the ground rules of science (Chapter 1). If we use this criterion, we should not expect that all problem areas can be covered adequately. For example, principles concerning learning, which is the vehicle of socialization, are missing from those listed in Part II. Certainly this omission is not a reflection of the quantity of research activity on problems of learning, as any student of introductory psychology knows. It reflects the present state of fluidity and even contradiction in learning theories today, especially in regard to higher-order learning that involves human language.

Social psychologists who have earnestly faced the complexity of the socialization process have become more cautious about accepting a learning theory presented by this or that particular "school" without examining its adequacy for dealing with complex problems. In the past, a number of social psychologists espoused a doctrine of learning based on research on simple responses. Unfortunately, such attempts have not fulfilled their bright promise. Understandably, the mainstream of social psychology is becoming increasingly reluctant to endorse a learning theory. This reluctance is reflected in the successive revisions of various standard books of readings in social psychology and representative research in the field.

The fact remains that socialization implies a series of learning situations. In reading the guidelines presented, we should envisage brackets to be filled in later with propositions that are adequate to handle complex learning processes. For the time being, we are on safer grounds if we concentrate on meticulous specification of the social stimulus conditions and end-products of socialization when the individual perceives, sizes-up, strives, and acts in his environment. Meanwhile, we must keep our eyes open for developments in the study of learning—especially the learning of language and its consequences in expanding the relatedness of the human individual beyond immediate surroundings in time and space.

The guidelines that we need should aid us in specifying the terms of the interactionist position. It is not sufficient merely to state that behavior cannot be accounted for *either* through an approach that is individual-bound *or* through an approach that is group-(i.e., culture-)bound. It is not sufficient to state that behavior is a joint product of psychodynamic factors stemming from the individual and social influences from his groups and culture. We need propositions or guidelines to spell out the specific terms of the interacting influences as we study behavior under varying conditions.

The guidelines need to be sufficiently broad to have bearing on the pervasive problems in social psychology. For example, the topics of leader-follower relations, conformity-nonconformity, and identification of the self with significant others all involve aspects of the problem of the individual-group relationship. Our guidelines should point to the best way to conceptualize this relationship for research and action purposes. This vast problem can be cast more effectively in general terms as a problem of part-whole (subsystem-system) relationships. Then, in treating the relationship between individual and group under varying conditions, we can utilize principles and generalizations on part-whole relationships that come from various fields of empirical research. Such an analysis will aid us later in dealing with the pattern of social situations of which the individual is an active part. (Generalizations on the part-whole relationship are presented in Chapter 5.)

It is obvious that we cannot be exhaustive and cannot, therefore, specify every principle or generalization that is established. Deliberately, the propositions to be presented in this Part are stated broadly to accommodate more specific principles and generalizations that are logically related to them. For example, the broad proposition that behavior is shaped jointly by internal and external factors subsumes both motivational-emotional promptings to action (internal factors) and the patterned properties of the social environment (external factors) that frequently channel such promptings. An important generalization—that "psychological activity is typically goal-directed"—is subsumed under this broader proposition. These and other statements not specified in the initial guidelines will be used throughout in chapters to follow. Similarly, the generalization that social situations are typically patterned affairs, while not explicitly included in the guidelines, is subsumed under the more general statements and will be referred to repeatedly.

The guidelines that follow are, then, a minimum set of broadly stated generalizations based on established findings. They apply to the major topics of social psychology and hold generally for various specific psychological processes that have been traditionally studied in their own right (such as perceiving, judging, remembering, etc.). As such, they are guidelines in specifying the terms of the *integrative interactionist approach* in actual study of our topics.

BASIC PROPOSITIONS
OR PRINCIPLES

Here, then, is a list of general essential propositions and principles to be applied throughout the book. The brief explanation after each statement pins down the terms, so that we will be thinking about the same things. Fuller clarification will be given through a diagram and more extended discussion of each statement in Chapters 3 and 4.

1. Experience and Behavior Constitute a Unity

"Experience" refers here to perceiving, judging, desiring, and other states of awareness—not to "past experience," as when we say "it has been my experience that women are fickle." The term "experience" is used to refer to an *experiencing individual* and, hence, is interchangeable with "awareness" or "consciousness." In

brief, this proposition means that one's actions (behavior) and experiences are *not independent* of one another, but are interrelated aspects of ongoing psychological activity. To speak of them as a "unity" does *not* mean that they are identical, but simply takes into consideration that each is part of an ongoing process. Ultimately, an adequate psychology of behavior will be an adequate psychology of experience. Conversely, an adequate psychology of cognition (perceiving, judging, deciding, learning, remembering) will also be an adequate psychology of behavior. To propose otherwise amounts to a conclusion that man's experience and his actions follow altogether different laws.

2. Behavior Follows Central Psychological Processing

Stimuli impinging on the individual do not have absolute stimulus value. Their effects are not invariant from person to person, from time to time, or from situation to situation. Neither is the individual oblivious of the stimulus world, acting only upon his own impulses. Impinging stimuli and impulses springing within the individual are processed through the central nervous system. Of course, the individual is not constantly aware of this processing, nor all of the constituent parts. However, what he *is* aware of (his experience) is the outcome of the central processing. Action follows the central process whereby the individual perceives a situation, sizes-up its salient aspects, and plans in terms of memories of the past and future objectives.

3. Psychological Processing Is Patterned, as Jointly Determined by External (Stimulus) Factors and by Internal Factors (Conceptual, Motivational-Emotional, Attitudinal, etc.), Whether Consciously Experienced or Not

This statement is a logical extension of the first two. Here, use of the term "stimulus" is restricted to conditions *outside* of the individual at a given time, while other appropriate terms are used to refer to effects of past stimulation as well as to momentary states of the organism, enduring concerns, recurrent needs, and other factors arising within the individual. To say that both external and internal factors enter jointly into the shaping of psychological patterns amounts to saying that neither functions independently. Both are processed by the organism and form a system of relationships (pattern) at a given time. Therefore, in order to understand behavior at a given time or to predict a future behavior, we have to specify both the stimulating conditions (external factors) and the relevant internal factors (such as conceptual categories, attitudes, motives-emotions, etc.) and relate them to one another. The appropriate *frame of reference* for studying behavior, then, is the system of relationships among all external and internal factors operative at a given time. This proposition is clarified through a convenient diagram in the next section.

4. Ongoing Psychological Activity Is Selective

There is nothing static about psychological states and processes, nor is the stimulus world limited and frozen. As the individual has dealings with other persons and objects in his surroundings, there are always more potential stimulation and more potentially relevant memories of the past than he can possibly focus upon. The span of attention or perception is necessarily limited. Therefore all psychological activity involves the screening of certain aspects of the stimulus world and focusing upon others. As we shall see, the facts revealing psychological selectivity are also among the best evidence that psychological processing is jointly shaped by internal and external factors.

5. Internal Factors (Such as Motives, Desires, Attitudes, etc.) and Experience Are Inferred from Behavior

No one can observe a desire, an inner conviction, or an individual's experience directly. Events within the individual have to be inferred from his behavior, verbal or nonverbal, in relevant stimulus situations. It follows from the preceding propositions that, because behavior is jointly shaped by

internal and external factors, behavior will reveal measurable effects of internal factors as well as the effects of external stimulus factors.

6. The Psychological Tendency Is Toward Patterning of Experience

The psychological product of the person's give-and-take with his surroundings is not a mosaic of fragments or elements but, typically, represents immediate experience of a unitary pattern. At times the pattern is so compelling that the individual deliberately has to adopt an analytic attitude in order to specify the constituents. This is particularly evident when the stimulus field is clear-cut and highly structured. When the external situation is more fluid, changing, or ambiguous, there is still a tendency over time toward patterning or arriving at some *stability.* Psychologically, it is painful to experience prolonged instability, especially after the development of a self-image that delineates for the individual what he is and is not as a person. Thus, when impinging stimuli do not provide the makings for clearcut patterns, the individual provides them himself—especially through conceptual categories that he has already formed.

7. Structured Stimulus Situations Set Limits to Alternatives in Psychological Patterning

As suggested above, the stimulus world presents objective properties and relationships that affect the kind of psychological patterning that results when the individual attends to them. When these objective properties and relationships are clear-cut, intense, or otherwise compelling (i.e., structured), the alternatives for psychological patterning are few. There is little variation among individuals in the way such structured stimulus situations are experienced and responded to.

8. In Unstructured Stimulus Situations, Alternatives in Psychological Patterning Are Increased

The stimulus world is not always well-structured. Many objects and events are ambiguous, complex, and rapidly changing. For example, a cloud, an ink-blot, or a mass of humanity moving in all directions on a crowded street represent situations lacking objective structure in different respects. In such situations, differences in what is selected for focus and differences among individuals in their antecedent experiences, motives, and attitudes can produce great distinctions in the way people perceive and size up the situation. The individual's role in the patterning of events is greater, hence individual differences in experience and behavior are increased.

9. The More Unstructured the External Stimulus Situation, the Greater the Contribution of Internal Factors— Including Internalized Social Values and Standards

This proposition proceeds from Number 8 to specify what produces the psychological pattern when it is initially lacking in the stimulus field. It implies that the objective structure of stimulus situations can be ordered in gradations from highly structured to less and less structured. As we compare psychological patterning through these gradations, we find that internal factors contribute proportionately more as we move from more- to less-structured stimulus situations. The internal factors include the individual's motives, his momentary needs, his past learning, and his attitudes—in short, what he has picked up while developing as a member of a particular group and culture.

10. The More Unstructured the Stimulus Situation, the Greater the Effectiveness of (External) Social Influences (Solutions, Communications, Suggestions) that Offer an Alternative for Psychological Patterning

This proposition is particularly significant for social psychology as it specifies the conditions in which the individual will be more or less "suggestible," that is, more amenable to adopting alternatives proposed by others. Specifically, it states that attempts to influence the individual toward agreement with the choice, prescription, or solution offered by others are more likely to succeed when the stimulus situation lacks structure in some degree and in relevant respects. This proposition is basic in assessing the results of the large literature on social influence in transitory situations.

11. Various Factors in the Frame of Reference Have Different Relative Weights

Proposition 3 stated that the appropriate frame of reference for studying behavior is composed of all of the external and internal factors operative at the time. The present proposition makes it explicit that, at a given time, some of these factors will contribute more heavily to psychological patterning than others. In fact, Propositions 8, 9, and 10 state specific principles governing the relative contribution of external (stimulus) factors and internal factors as a function of the degree of stimulus structure.

Proposition 11 is more general in that it specifies that, regardless of the degree of stimulus structure, certain factors in the frame of reference will contribute more than others to psychological patterning. These weighty factors, or anchors, may be located in the stimulus field. At other times, the individual's desires or ingrained attitudes may anchor his perception, judgment, and action so securely that they affect what he selects for attention and how he interprets objects and events.

12. Human Psychological Functioning Is Typically on the Conceptual Level

This proposition is, of course, related to those that preceded it. In a scheme for studying the human individual beyond the earliest months of life, we have to include the fact that psychological processing, selectivity, and the ensuing psychological patterns are affected by the fact that he responds to stimuli as members of classes or sets, not discretely. With the development of speech and mastery of the language of the person's society, the classifications and relationships standardized in the history of his culture become intimately and inextricably parts of the psychological process. They also permit the uniquely hu-

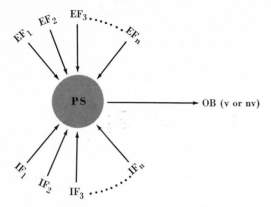

Fig. 2.1. Diagrammatic representation of the frame of reference of an observed behavior at a given time. OB (v or nv): Observed behavior (verbal or nonverbal). EF: External factors (objects, persons, groups, cultural products, etc., in the external stimulus situation). IF: Internal factors: motives, including ego-attitudes, desires, ambitions, emotions; states of the organism (fatigue, being sleepy or tense, etc.); attitudes derived from social norms; language concepts; effects of past experience, etc. PS: Psychological structuring or patterning.

man phenomenon of locating the self in space and in time—such that long-past events and future plans become crucial in what the individual attends to, how he perceives, what decisions he makes, and how he acts in particular situations.

FRAME OF REFERENCE: SOME ESSENTIALS OF THE SYSTEMATIC POSITION

As we have seen, the interactionist position has become one of the dominant trends in accounting for the experience and behavior of the individual. This trend has gained such solid ground in recent years that today an author who made a plea for an exclusively individualistic approach or an exclusively group-culture-bound approach would find only a few receptive ears.

Yet, in order to make effective headway toward a rounded picture of social psychology, the interactionist position has to be more than a series of assertions. It has to specify its terms in the form of explicit propositions spelled out so that they lead to conceptual tools in formulating significant hypotheses and in devising operational pro-

cedures in actual research practice. A diagrammatic presentation is helpful in relating the twelve propositions to one another.

For some years, psychology—the science of experience and behavior—has been moving toward the interactionist position. One well-known expression was in the following form: S-O-R. In this formula, S stands for stimulus, R for response, and O for the organism. It represents a correction on the over-simplified formula of earlier behaviorism (namely S-R) by introducing the intervening term O. The corrected formula depicts the idea that behavior is not merely a direct function of the stimulus (S) but is also jointly a function of the responding organism. The modified formula has been useful in calling attention to "intervening variables" or "mediating processes" that affect both perception of the stimulus and the nature of response.

The corrected formula (S-O-R) needs to be expanded in order to spell out the terms of the interactionist position. The expanded diagrammatic representation will represent the frame of reference for studying behavior as a function of external factors and internal factors, including the place of the central mediating processes. The diagram has proved useful also in differentiating among the properties of particular external (stimulus) conditions in order to assess their weight (i.e., their importance relative to motivational and other internal influences springing from the individual himself). These advantages will be specified in appropriate contexts.

The diagram in Fig. 2.1 is intended to depict the frame of reference for a specific behavior (verbal or nonverbal) occurring at a given time. Behavior at a given time can be accounted for adequately when studied within its appropriate frame of reference, consisting of the *system of relationships* among external factors (Ef) and internal factors (If) operative at the time.

In view of the term's loose usage in the literature, the exact meaning of *frame of reference* needs to be specified. It cannot be sufficiently emphasized that there is no such a thing as "frame of reference" in the abstract. In other words, there is no abstract agent called "frame of reference" that affects behavior. The frame of reference has meaning only when tied to a particular behavior and should be used only in reference to a specific behavior,

We should start our analysis by specifying the observed behavior (OB in the diagram) and speak of the frame of reference for studying that behavior. The frame of reference for that behavior is composed of the antecedent background and immediate context of that behavior. The term *frame of reference* is simply a capsule summary of a general principle that behavior can be understood only against its antecedent background and immediate context. The frame of reference for behavior, therefore, is the totality of interrelated external factors (Ef) in the situation and internal factors (If) arising from the individual that are operative at the given time.

As the diagram indicates, behavior cannot be accounted for adequately by considering only stimulus factors (Ef) or by considering only internal factors (If—psychodynamic factors, past experience, concepts, etc.). Adequate analysis of behavior can be attained when it is studied within the system of relationships among all factors as psychologically processed (P).

Combining the above statements, the diagram shows that behavior at a given time follows central psychological processing (such as perceiving, judging, appraising, remembering, etc.) to which both external (stimulus) factors and internal (e.g., psychodynamic, motivational, conceptual) factors contribute. Therefore, we should note carefully the directions of the arrows in the diagram. The directions of the arrows have implications for discussing the propositions in the chapters to follow, in which frequent reference is made to this diagram.

3

Propositions 1-8

Major Topics of the Chapter

Basic propositions to be evaluated
Experience and behavior constitute a unity
Behavior follows psychological processing
Psychological processing is patterned
The pattern is jointly determined by external stimulus factors and internal (motivational) factors
Ongoing psychological activity is selective
External and internal factors in selectivity
Cultural variations in selectivity
Implications for research
Internal factors and experience are inferred from behavior
The psychological tendency is toward patterning of experience
Structured stimulus situations set limits to alternatives in psychological patterning

In unstructured stimulus situations, alternatives in psychological patterning are increased

Gradations in stimulus structure and degrees of social influence (suggestibility)

1. Experience and Behavior Constitute a Unity

At first glance, this proposition appears to be more philosophical in nature than a guideline for empirically dealing with the social relations of man in his day-to-day transactions. We shall discuss why such a proposition is basic for social psychology.

Let us recall that "experience" refers here to perceiving, judging, appraising, remembering, and other states of awareness—not to "past experience." "Behavior" may be overt action (e.g., the person goes to buy a loaf of bread), or verbal expressions (his statement that he feels good or bad), or simply a bodily expression (a sneer, derogatory gesture, blush, or faint smile).

The "unity" of experience and behavior does not imply that they are the same. It means that what an individual *does* (in action, word, or expression) is *not independent* of the way in which he perceives the situation, appraises it, what he remembers at the time, and so on. In short, what one does *not* convey by words and expressions are also parts of the ongoing psychological activity. Psychological events include the person's conscious experience (i.e., how he perceives, defines, feels in the situation), as well as his actions, words, and expressions. (In the language of set theory, experience and behavior are conjunctive, not disjunctive.)

The direction of the arrows in Fig. 2.1 indicates that observed behavior (whether actions, words, or expressions) depends on the way that the individual perceives the situation, appraises it, and feels about it. Emphasis on this dependence is needed because of recurrent interpretations that when two or more behaviors are *inconsistent,* this inconsistency indicates a *discrepancy* between the person's experience and behavior. Such interpretations can be illus-

trated through experiments that compare expressed attitude (opinion) and action toward relevant objects. In this line of research, expressed opinion (behavior) is considered the indicator of the person's attitude, an assumption to be discussed shortly.

Some years ago, an investigator sent a questionnaire by mail to a number of eating and sleeping establishments in the United States, inquiring whether Chinese would be accommodated (LaPiere, 1934). More than 90 percent of the businessmen replying indicated that they would decline accommodations. These replies, however, were contrary to actions taken in these establishments when the professor visited them in person with a Chinese couple. The mixed party was almost invariably accommodated. Similarly, in more recent research conducted by Cornell sociologists (Williams, 1964), bartenders who indicated verbally that they would not serve Negroes frequently served Negro customers.

One cannot doubt the behavioral events on which the concept of "inconsistency" between attitude and behavior are based. However, from such partial findings about the entire event, the argument was advanced that "attitude" and "behavior" are unrelated to one another and even independent. In short, the view arose that the person's attitude is one thing and his behavior an altogether different thing. This view depends upon equating the person's verbal expression with his "attitude." It would be more reasonable to infer his attitude from behavior (verbal and nonverbal) in two or more situations (see Proposition 5).

As Donald Campbell (1963) pointed out, the apparent contradiction or inconsistency in these cases simply represents differences between behavior in two different situations. They in no way imply a divorce between experience and behavior. The two behaviors (verbal statement taken to represent attitude and actions toward relevant persons) occurred at different times under quite different conditons. When public expression of attitude was requested, the behavior was in terms of the prevailing popular resonse that the businessmen believed was expected of them as businessmen serving a clientele that was, on the whole, prejudiced. On the other hand, when confronted face-to-face by a well-dressed Chinese couple or a Negro student in the company of respectable white customers, behavior was affected by the businessman's views of the social niceties expected in personal encounters with his customers. The difference in the two situations was well expressed by Campbell (1963) in discussing the study about accommodations for the Chinese couple:

> The first thing we note is that the two diagnostic situations have very different thresholds. Apparently it is very hard to refuse a well-dressed Chinese couple traveling with a European in a face-to-face setting, and very easy to refuse the Chinese as a race in a mailed questionnaire. We can see easily why this would be so. But there is as yet no evidence of inconsistency. Inconsistency would be represented if those who refused face to face accepted by questionnaire, or if those who accepted by questionnaire refused face to face. There is no report that such cases occurred (p. 160).

Response to questions about a person's attitude is influenced by the person's notion of what is "socially desirable" under the circumstances (Edwards, 1957), as will be noted in the chapters on attitudes. For example, as mentioned in Chapter 1, college students questioned under university auspices about their attitude toward Negroes were prone to see the socially desirable response as "liberal" (La Fave and Sherif, 1968). Evidently a good many college campuses nowadays have a "collegiate norm" that favors a liberal appearance on this issue. The vast majority of students responded to paper-and-pencil tests by indicating lack of prejudice. In several cases, however, the same students, observed in their privacy with like-minded persons, engaged in highly prejudicial statements and actions. The "discrepancy" here simply indicates that

methods, for attitude asessment have to be devised that do not arouse the person's guard to appear "socially desirable" under given circumstances.

As these examples suggest, the arguments over discrepancies between "attitude" and "behavior" are pseudoarguments. They point to the need for refining our methods for making inferences about the person's attitude. The contention that attitude and behavior are independent amounts to saying that a good Catholic or Baptist will not give consistent indications of his commitment by his actions on Sunday, when he gets married, or when his church undertakes a concerted effort.

None of the cases in the literature interpreted as showing "inconsistency" between attitude and behavior proves that experience and action are independent. The pathological cases (or behavior caused by administration of certain drugs) are not typical of man's relations of consequence in human affairs. The cases in the attitude literature merely reveal that "verbal behavior" in one situation and action (behavior) in another situation are not necessarily identical. In some cases—for example, when the person expresses an opinion in response to a letter or direct question—other attitudes are certainly aroused regarding the source of the inquiry, what is expected of a person under the circumstances, and what is good "public relations."

When other salient attitudes are aroused, the individual's persistent attitude on the focal issue is simply not ascertained by the orthodox methods employed. Let us suppose, however, that his reply is representative of his persistent attitude on the issue. It is still possible that on a later occasion other factors in the situation may weigh more heavily in shaping his line of action than the attitude would. Attitudes or motives are not the only influences on behavior, as we shall emphasize again and again.

One does not have to be a researcher to find out that a person does not express his cherished beliefs, his commitments, or his stands on controversial topics under all circumstances. The forthright expression of one's attitude may be hazardous, harmful, or, in minor matters, tactless and inappropriate. As everyone knows, language is used under some circumstances to hide one's abiding convictions or attitudes as well as to express them. Direct verbal behavior is only one of the possible measures of a person's attitude.

Advocating the theoretical divorce of experience and behavior is akin to saying that the muscles function independently of central integrative processes. To be sure, every experience is not immediately translated into action. But when the person does act, it is the outcome of central integrative processes that are shaped by diverse factors and some experience is correlated with these processes. Therefore, there is no theoretical advantage in ruling out experience or action as aspects of ongoing psychological activity.

The implications of the proposition that experience and behavior constitute a unity are far-reaching. We have discussed some of them through controversies about "attitude" and "action." In Chapter 6, further implications will be drawn in discussing recent experiments on "verbal conditioning" and what has been called "the social psychology of the psychological experiment." The proposition stated here implies a methodology in which we can study inner psychological states by making inferences from behavior in appropriate conditions at a given time, and then make predictions about future behavior in particular situations on the basis of our inferences about these inner states.

As Donald Campbell (1963) aptly expressed it, the "bold postulation" of the unity of experience and behavior will "do much to unify social-psychological theory and to substitute genuine predictive disagreements among theories (and there are undoubtedly such) for specious semantic squabbles" (p. 133). In fact, the fruitfulness of the proposition has already been shown in attitude studies. As discussed in Chapters 15 and 16 on attitudes, research procedures have been developed that are more subtle than one-shot paper-and-pencil tests that ask the person point blank to check "yes" or "no" (agree-disagree, etc.).

In short, the postulation of the unity of the "inner" and "outer" aspects of action (as G. H. Mead expressed it) is not new. What is new is a growing development in research practice that translates the proposition into effective research operations.

2. Behavior Follows Central Psychological Processing

This proposition follows directly from the first. Underlying the unity of experience and behavior are central psychological processes upon which both are contingent. Again, note the direction of the arrows in Fig. 2.1. By following their sequence from the outer parts of the diagram to B (behavior), this second proposition can be specified. It states that one's actions (B) are not a direct function of impinging stimuli (Ef), nor are they a direct function of impulses from within the individual (motives, desires, and other internal factors—If). Both external stimuli and internal impulses are centrally processed.

In the diagram, the arrows lead from P (central processing) to B (behavior). Behavior is an outcome of the central process, hence follows it. The two diagrams in Fig. 3.1 show that there is not a direct line from stimulus to response, and not a direct line from internal factors to response. The broken lines indicate that the proposition explicitly denies each alternative.

The left-hand side of the diagram represents a crude S-R behaviorist position: namely, response follows directly from the stimulus. The right-hand part represents a crude subjectivist or psychodynamic position: namely, behavior follows directly from impulses springing from within the individual.

The proposition that behavior follows central psychological processing makes it explicit that external stimulation and internal impulses are processed centrally. Underlying the central processing is the functioning of the central nervous system. In the present state of knowledge about the central nervous system, we are on safer grounds if we deal with central processing in psychological terms (i.e., perceiving, judging, remembering, thinking, etc.). Eventually, advances in neurophysiology may provide explanations for the complex functioning of the central nervous system.

The need for new discoveries before there can be an adequate account of the

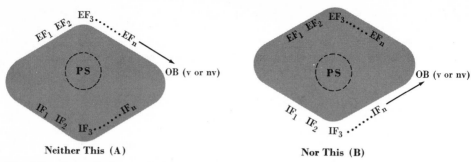

Neither This (A)   **Nor This (B)**

Fig. 3.1. Contradictions to frame of reference analysis. Observed behavior (words and deeds of the person) is not a *direct* function of external stimulus factors impinging on the organism (A above), nor is it a *direct* function of internal factors (B above: motives, emotions, attitudes, ego-involvements). But behavior (words and deeds) of the person is jointly determined by these two sets of factors as processed and patterned through central processes. (This interactional frame of reference is represented schematically in Fig. 2.1, p. 32, which should be consulted in evaluating Fig. 3.1.)

central processing was succinctly stated by E. D. Adrian (1954), one of the leading neurophysiologists of the century, in his presidential address to the British Association for the Advancement of Science.

The sensory inflow brings information about the events taking place outside us and progress reports to show how successfully we are dealing with them; signals from the muscles are needed to adjust the simplest movements and we are handicapped if we cannot hear what we are saying and cannot watch our step. But the great central mass of nerve cells has to fabricate a radically different pattern of messages to send out to the muscles and it is a pattern which depends on past as well as present information, on what happened to us a year ago as well as on what is happening now. Unfortunately, it is a great deal easier to study the immediate reactions of the nervous system than the more persistent changes which alter its habits and give us our memories. We know next to nothing about the plasticity which is the most important feature of the brain and that is the next hurdle for the biophysicists and biochemists (p. 681).

From a psychological viewpoint, it is important to note that the individual need not be, and in fact is not, aware of all of the separate stimuli and internal impulses that are processed. The outcome is a patterned product with a correlated experience. Indeed, the person's experience is immediate —not a slow registering and fusion of separate elements that compose the pattern.

Because stimulus input and impulses from within the individual are centrally processed almost simultaneously, the person's experience (e.g., perception) is not a carbon copy of the stimulus world around him. For example, depending upon the circumstances, the pattern of perception may bear a close relationship to the physical projection of the stimuli on the retina or it may differ from the mosaic of stimuli in varying degrees. Such circumstances depend on the properties of the stimuli confronting the individual, upon his motivational state at the time, upon his past encounters with similar stimuli, and the conceptual system built through years of classifying objects and events.

The individual does not attend to all objects and events confronting him. He necessarily selects a limited portion, consciously or unconsciously, as we shall see in discussing Proposition 4. Once an aspect of the environment is selected, the energy of the stimuli impinging on the receptors (such as the eye or ear) is one constituent to the central process—but only one. E. G. Boring (1946) emphasized this point in summarizing the experimental literature on visual perception of size, shape, brightness, and hue. He was particularly concerned with the finding that perception of an object tends toward "constancy" even though the sensory input differs greatly under varying conditions (with distance, illumination, etc.).

For more than a century it has been customary to say that perception is something more than sensory impression, that perception is *of an object,* that it corresponds to a stimulating object.

The modern view is that, because objects are permanent, a perception of an object tends to remain constant even when the immediate sensory impressions upon which perception is based vary with the variety of conditions that affect stimulation.

This general rule of perception applies to all sense departments. It depends upon an integrative property of the brain and is not a function of sense organs at all (p. 67).

The implication of Boring's conclusion is far-reaching. Behavior is shaped not immediately and unilaterally by the energy of the stimuli impinging on receptors but also by what the individual selects, what he sees, what he appraises, and what he remembers (because of its relevance) from a host of possible events, past and present. In the complex world of social relations, cognitive or behavioral response is not a carbon copy of events but in terms of the "definition of the situation," as W. I. Thomas aptly phrased it.

3. Psychological Processing Is Patterned, as Jointly Determined by External (Stimulus) Factors and by Internal Factors (Conceptual, Motivational-Emotional, Attitudinal, etc.), Whether Consciously Experienced or Not

We shall clarify this propostion by explaining its main terms.

Patterned. The statement makes it explicit that stimuli (Ef) and impulses from within the individual (If) at a given time do not affect behavior separately or as a conglomeration of discrete items. Central processing involves exclusion of irrelevant stimuli or internal factors and the combination of relevant ones such that the psychological product falls into a pattern or integrated unit at the time. This interrelated unit (e.g., perception, judgment, or memory) is delineated with clear contours. Since the days of William James, the focus of this unit or pattern has come to be known as the focus of consciousness or awareness.

External Factors. The referents here are stimuli (objects, persons, etc.) outside of the individual at the time, the skin being the boundary included on the side of the organism to delimit the set of external and internal factors. Properties of the stimulus world (external factors) and their contribution to

particular patterns will be discussed under Propositions 7 and 8.

Internal Factors. The referents are the motives, emotional states and feelings, commitments and identifications, attitudes and self concept, conceptual categories, and other products of past experience. In short, "internal factors" refer to any impulses springing from within the individual himself. The human individual is an active organism. While the stimulus world also has its contribution to the process, his motives —attitudes with their associated emotions in response to environmental events—lend a goal-directed character to what the individual attends to at a given time (psychological selectivity) and the ways that the stimulus world is patterned.

There is advantage in considering the contribution of motives, attitudes, and self image to the psychological product under the broad term *internal factors.* The term underscores the fact that related motives, attitudes, concepts, aspects of the self image, and action patterns are aroused simultaneously in any specific situation. Hunger, for example, does not operate in complete isolation from the picture the individual has of himself, from his status concerns and established preferences—such as the kind of restaurant he would enter and the kind of food he wants to satisfy his hunger. Likewise, sexual urges are not satisfied, as a rule, by just any sex object but are guided by the person's concerns about his status, his self-esteem, prestige, his place in the scheme of the social order, and future aspirations in these respects.

The sterile relics of faculty psychology pigeonholed perception, discrimination, learning, thinking, and remembering as *cognition*—delineating them from *motivation* and *action.* The predominant modern development in psychology, on the contrary, has been to conceive of the psychological product (whether it be a percept, a desire, an appraisal, a choice, or a motor action) as a joint function of processes oriented toward knowing about the external world and toward actively coping with it in terms of inner urges.

Perception, judgment, or remembering are seldom, if ever, devoid of motivational and attitudinal components. Perception is not merely a replica of external stimuli impinging on the organism. What the individual sees is not duplicated by putting together the images of physical stimuli on the retina; even though the contribution of physical objects is not to be discarded. Remembering of events does not consist simply of a carbon copy of things experienced or even of their fading traces. As Bartlett (1932) aptly put it, remembering is an active and creative reconstruction in which the traces of past experience are influenced, accentuated, or even distorted in various degrees by the ongoing preoccupations, interests, attitudes, and concerns of the individual.

Similarly, perceiving is an active process in which it is not only reception of stimulus input that counts, but also the whole person —with his past experience, motives, and attitudes relevant to that input. The exceptions are those cases, in an experiment, for example, in which the psychological process is deliberately restricted to give more exclusive dominance to the reception of stimulus input. However, in the latter cases, special devices have to be used (as they are in experiments on discrimination) in order to limit the individual's selectivity and hence to curtail the contribution of internal factors.

cognition The fact that what is called cognition (perception, judging, etc.) is not a process independent from what is called motivation was stated in unequivocal terms by some of the leading researchers in psychology. Wolfgang Köhler, one of the eminent founders of Gestalt psychology, referred to the joint determination of experience and behavior in his book *Gestalt Psychology* (1929), which is the most representative presentation of the Gestalt school (Newman, 1948). Köhler stated that "apart from drowsiness and similar states of low vitality, the organization of the total field will almost always have just that bipolar character, the self being directed to something else or from it" (p. 323). Later, he concluded: "Evidently it is not only the external situation which in a great many cases has to be considered, but the internal situation of the organism as well" (p. 325). In spite of such theoretical orientation, the major emphasis of Gestalt work on perception was on the structural properties of the external field.

In his classic book entitled *Remembering* (1932), Bartlett of Cambridge University summed up the joint determination of experience and behavior succinctly:

On the face of it, to perceive anything is one of the simplest and most immediate, as it is one of the most fundamental, of all human cognitive reactions. Yet obviously, in a psychological sense, it is exceedingly complex, and this is widely recognized. Inextricably mingled with it are imagining, valuing, and those beginnings of judging which are involved in the response to plan, order of arrangement and construction of presented material. It is directed by interest and by feeling, and may be dominated by certain crucial features of the objects and scenes dealt with. In all these respects it may profoundly influence remembering, of which it is legitimately regarded as the psychological starting point (p. 31).

During the last two decades, one of the influential programs of research on perception in the United States was the series of studies reported by Adelbert Ames, Hadley Cantril, F. P. Kilpatrick, W. H. Ittelson, and their associates. In different ways these studies emphasized that perceiving is always a *transaction* with the environment (cf. Kilpatrick, 1952, pp. 87–91). The position developed in this program may be characterized in the words of one of its leading exponents:

In short, the over-all trend of contemporary perceptual studies has been away from the stimulus orientation "What does the environment do to the perceiver?" and toward the treatment of perceiving as an essentially creative process actively carried on by the organism. The assumption is that the individual acts in any situation in terms of the way he perceives that situation. Perception, then, becomes a crucial process intimately involved in the effective functioning of the individual. Such an approach has necessarily led the experimental study of perception into a consideration of problems which had previously been considered a sacred domain of the branch of psychology labeled "personality" (Ittelson, 1960, pp. 6–7).

Perhaps the most impressive evidence of the importance of this proposition is that it is repeatedly stressed in the literature on perception—which is often considered as a prototype of the so-called cognitive processes. In reviewing studies of perception, H. Leibowitz (1965) emphasized the joint role of stimulus and internal factors as follows:

More generally, these studies imply that the perceptual process is by no means a passive one. If one were to attempt to predict perception from a simple knowledge of optics, the results would be grossly inaccurate. Although the eye is analogous to a camera to the extent that it focuses an image on the retina, the effects shown here of context and experience illustrate very well the important principle that *the organism itself contributes significantly to the process of perception* (p. 6).

The utility of Proposition 3 in creative research and theory was explicitly recognized by one of the recipients of the 1964 Distinguished Scientific Contribution Awards from the American Psychological Association. Receiving the award for his research on perception, Garner (1966) stated that a cornerstone of his work was that the "properties of sets of stimuli" and internal factors contribute jointly to the process of perceiving. After emphasizing that perceiving is a function of the properties of *sets* of stimuli, he emphasized his point by the use of italics: *"to perceive is an active process,* one in which the perceiver participates fully. The perceiver does not passively *receive* information about his environment; rather he actively *perceives* his environment" (p. 11). Garner's subsequent remarks are pertinent to Propositions 4, 6, 7, 8, and 9:

Nor does he simply impose his organization on an otherwise unstructured world—the world is structured. But he does select the structure to which he will attend and react, and he even provides the missing structure on occasion. In particular . . . the perceiver provides his own total set and subset [viz., of stimulus properties] when these do not physically exist (p. 11).

4. Ongoing Psychological Activity Is Selective

Evidence for the joint determination of experience and behavior by external (stimulus) factors and by internal factors (especially motive and attitude) is confirmed most solidly in research establishing that *psychological activity is selective.* This research tradition includes the work on "set" or expectation produced in the laboratory by instruction or by the sequence of stimulus presentations. For example, Külpe showed years ago (in 1904) that instructions on what to notice in a stimulus array

heightened keeness of discrimination and accuracy of recall for the stimulus attribute designated—for example, color or frequency.

We are surrounded by literally millions of objects, scenes, and events that could be singled out, perceived, judged, and acted upon. The individual's past is replete with events—pleasant and unpleasant—that could become focal in his present awareness. But he can attend to only a few items at a time. Necessarily, he selects from a myriad of potential stimuli in any particular situation.

Psychological selectivity refers to the screening process that eliminates all but a few of the potential sources of stimulation at a particular time. What, then, guides the individual's selectivity from one moment to another?

As a rule, the items that are focal in the immediate environment and events remembered from the past are relevant to the person's ongoing preoccupations, concerns, needs, and issues that are of enduring consequence for him. Thus, continual selectivity of psychological activity is one of the best indicators of such activity's goal-directed nature.

One of the impressive statements of psychological selectivity was formulated by William James (1892) in his memorable chapter on "The Stream of Consciousness":

It [consciousness] is interested in some parts of its objects to the exclusion of others and welcomes or rejects—chooses from among them, in a word—all the while (p. 152). . . . But we do far more than emphasize things, and unite some, and keep others apart. We actually ignore most of the things before us (p. 170).

Traditional research on psychological selectivity concentrated largely on the span of perception, attention, or apprehension. However, selectivity is not restricted to any one specific psychological activity. The general fact was expressed by the psychologist G. A. Miller (1962) in a chapter on "the selective function of consciousness." He noted that of all the generalizations that can be made about the characteristics of psychological processing:

. . . there is one that stands out as being central to the psychologist's task: *Consciousness is*

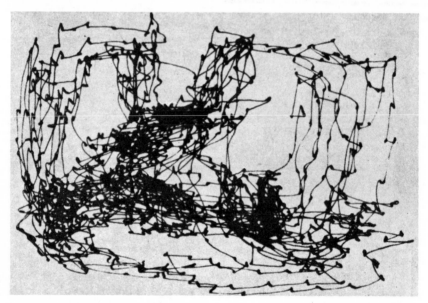

Fig. 3.2.   Records of eye movements (*see also opposite page*) demonstrate psychological selectivity by showing parts of picture that receive the most attention. These records, made by A. L. Yarbus in the Soviet Union, show normal eye movements tracing the outlines of a scene with swift movements between points of concentration. (From G. A. Miller, *Psychology: The Science of Mental Life.* New York: Harper & Row, 1962, pp. 52–53.)

selective. We are constantly swimming through oceans of information, far more than we could ever notice and understand; without some effective way to select what is important, we would surely drown (p. 38).

The *span of consciousness* at any given time is *limited.* For example, since the early days of psychology, experiments have been performed to determine how many randomly arranged items (such as beans or dots) an individual can perceive correctly during a brief exposure, how many unrelated items he can recall, and so on. Miller (1956) surveyed this literature in an article entitled "The Magic Number Seven Plus or Minus Two." The title refers to findings that

 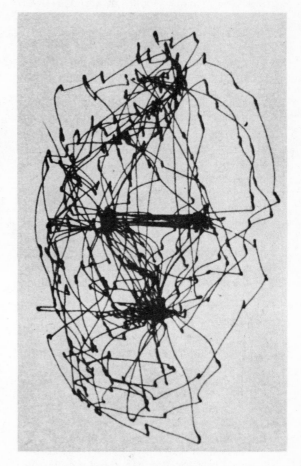

the span of immediate awareness is limited and that seven (give or take a few) is the typical number of items that can be processed at a given moment. Of course, if the items are formed into patterns, grouped into units of, say five each, or used to compose the letters of a meaningful sentence, the number of items that can be grasped in a short time is considerably increased. In this case, the groups, subpatterns or words become the units of attention (cf. Woodworth and Schlosberg, 1954, pp. 90–100.

Looking at collections of unrelated items in an experiment is not particularly typical of natural psychological activities. More often, the objects and events competing for one's attention are patterned, meaningful, and motivationally relevant. We can grasp complex arrangements of many items as a unitary experience almost instantly and identify them—for example, in a baseball game noticed as we flash by in a car. However, we could not recall on such brief

encounter much detail or very much about constituents. We might not even notice that one team had only seven players or how many players were on base at the time.

Recent research by Russian psychologists on eye-movements indicates that prolonged viewing of a complex scene involves selective attention to differing aspects in rapid sequence (Luria, 1965; cf. Miller, 1962, pp. 51–53). By reflecting light from the eyeball onto sensitized paper, the researchers have obtained records of exactly where attention is focused as the eye moves by "jumps" from one part of the scene to the next. Sample records in viewing the scenes are shown in Fig. 3.2. Note that the eye movements single out the outlines of the scene and concentrate on salient details, such as the bears in the forest and the mouth and eyes of the girl.

In certain conditions, stimulus situations may be so compelling in their size, movement, intensity, color, or pitch that they literally command focal awareness—even though they may be irritating and regarded as nuisances if they are highly irrelevant to the person's preoccupations at the time. For example, during a university lecture when the students are busily taking notes, the roar of a jet plane or a sonic boom immediately commands attention even though it is irritating (especially to the lecturer). In the normal course of life, the direction of selectivity guided by the individual's motivational promptings has to be considered in conjunction with external events and circumstances, especially in view of the fact that the surroundings are constantly changing.

The following list classifies external and internal factors that contribute to psychological selectivity. The list is not exhaustive; it was compiled on the basis of combining and extending lists in standard texts.

I. External factors
   A. Intensity, size, novelty, repetition, contrast, movement, and change of objects and events.
   B. Social influences, such as instructions, suggestions, group pressures, and group participation.

II. Internal factors
   A. Momentary set, personal interest, motives (hunger, thirst, sexual desire, and the like), and states of the organism (emotion, fatigue, etc.).
   B. Socially derived factors, such as positive or negative social attitudes, identification with or prejudice against persons or groups, linguistic repertory, internalized social norms, and the like.

Advertisement or propaganda concentrates on commanding arrangements of the external factors, of course. But effective advertisement or propaganda utilizes the stimulus properties listed above in meaningful combination conducive to arousal of strong motives, attitudes, emotions, commitments, prejudices, and appetites of the target population in order both to attract and to hold their attention. The forms, colors, sounds, and movements are, for example, those of an attractive female or male, those of affluent persons with their

car, or those of soldiers and their flag. In other words, the stimulus properties that gain our attention are not presented in abstract form. They confront us in forms related to our desires, bias, goals, and appetites.

Selectivity Revealed in the "Psychology of Testimony." There are stories of court trials in which the plot hinged upon the credibility of the witness—not upon his respect for the truth but upon his accuracy in observation and recall under the circumstances. This problem has been studied since the early years of this century. The pioneering experiments were done by the French psychologist Alfred Binet (1900). In research reported in his book *La Suggestibilité,* he found that reports of observation and recall were reached through a "process of selection." Binet was particularly interested in the effect of different kinds of questions upon the selectivity of recall. He found that simply by using "leading" questions, the investigator could increase errors in recall from about 26 percent to as much as 61 percent.

Stern (1910), who conducted extensive experiments on both observation and recall, found that children were more responsive than adults to leading questions and that naive spectators were highly selective in observing a concrete event staged for their benefit. A colorful description of the kind of study undertaken in this line of work was included in Münsterberg's *On the Witness Stand* (1908). Note that some early psychologists were well aware of the value of conducting experiments in the most natural way possible.

There was, for instance, two years ago in Göttingen a meeting of a scientific association, made up of jurists, psychologists, and physicians, all, therefore, men well trained in careful observation. Somewhere in the same street there was that evening a public festivity of the carnival. Suddenly, in the midst of the scholarly meeting, the doors open, a clown in highly colored costume rushes in in mad excitement, and a negro with a revolver in hand follows him. In the middle of the hall first the one, then the other, shouts wild phrases; then the one falls to the ground, the other jumps on him; then a shot, and suddenly both are out of the room. The whole affair took less than twenty seconds. All were completely taken by surprise, and no one, with the exception of the President, had the slightest idea that every word and action had been rehearsed beforehand, or that photographs had been taken of the scene. It seemed most natural that the President should beg the members to write down individually an exact report, inasmuch as he felt that the matter would come before the courts. Of the forty reports handed in, there was only one whose omissions were calculated as amounting to less than twenty percent of the characteristic acts. . . . But besides the omissions there were only six among the forty which did not contain positively wrong statements. . . . Only four persons, for instance, among forty noticed that the negro had nothing on his head; the others gave him a derby, or a high hat, and so on. In addition to this, a red suit, a brown one, a striped one, a coffee-coloured jacket, shirt sleeves, and similar costumes were invented for him. . . . The specific commission which reported the details of the inquiry came to the general statement that the majority of the observers omitted or falsified about half of the processes which occurred completely in their field of vision. . . . The judgment as to the time duration of the act varied between a few seconds and several minutes (pp. 51–53).

The selective observation and recall of events guided by the person's attitude were studied by Allport and Postman (1947). Just as the observers in Münsterberg's report invented bizarre costumes for the Negro, subjects in one of their experiments recalled many details in terms of their stereotyped bias. For example, a picture of a white person holding a razor and a Negro was recalled by a number of observers as a fight in which the Negro held the razor.

Cultural Variations in Selectivity. The surroundings have definite shapes and contours, but what will be noticed is affected by the emphasis placed upon them in a particular culture.

Bartlett (1932) reported an incident in London that illustrates the point. A commission of Swazi chiefs visited London. Their most vivid recollection after the trip was the image of policemen regulating traffic with uplifted hand. Bartlett raised a question about this incident to clarify the way that cultural emphasis affects selective recall:

Why should this simple action have made so profound an impression? Certainly not merely because it was taken as a symbol of power. Many other illustrations of power, far more strik-

ing to the European mind, had been seen and, for all practical purposes, forgotten. The Swazi greets his fellow, or his visitor, with uplifted hand. Here was the familiar gesture, warm with friendliness, in a foreign country, and at the same time arresting in its consequences. It was one of the few things they saw that fitted immediately into their own well-established social framework and so produced a quick and lasting effect (p. 248).

Just as cultural emphasis may affect what we single out and what we recall, lack of importance can lead to neglect of salient aspects of the environment. The striking objective properties of a stimulus need not be sufficient to draw attention to it, even when it is part of nature. Despite magnificent starlit nights, members of some societies pay scant attention to the stars. An ethnological account from the Northern Rhodesians noted:

. . . . remarkably little attention is paid to the stars. . . . When one thinks of the magnificently brilliant nights and their habits of sitting around the evening camp fires, one wonders that they should not have figured out constellations and formed myths of the stars. We have many times drawn their attention to the stars and tried to get their names, but without success. It is not reckoned taboo to attempt to count the stars, but any one who should try it would be laughed at as a fool. The only planet they name is Venus; but knowing that she appears as the evening and as morning star, they give her two names (Smith, 1920, p. 219).

The lack of emphasis on such a prominent aspect of nature cannot be discarded as a characteristic of the "primitive mind." On the contrary, the history of western societies reveals that perception of nature around us is subject to changed expectations and our preparedness to single out aspects of the natural world. The psychologist John Beebe-Center noted this fact, quoting an authority who had observed:

. . . before the eighteenth century the French had always been fond of what they called *"voyages en campagne"*—journeys into the country. But, in truth, what were these trips? If one investigates the matter one will find in reality that a *"voyage en campagne"* meant simply that one traveled to some chateau in the provinces, where one's comfort was extremely well served, and where the company shut itself up in the rooms of the chateau for conversation and drawing-room diversions, broken only by walks in the garden. No one seems to have gone into the country to enjoy the rural scene itself, or to have taken much note of the country's beauty. . . . Even so intelligent a man as Montesquieu limited his whole description (1729) of a trip from Rome to Munich to this statement: "I made a very painful journey, half of the way in excessive heat, the other half in mortal cold, in the month of August, in the mountains of the Tyrol." All grandeur of these mountains and the beauty of Lake Constance among them, meant to him nothing (Beebe-Center, 1932, quoting a report of a lecture by Paul Hazard, *Boston Evening Transcript,* November 10, 1928).

Implications for Research. In laboratory experiments, stimulus materials are prepared, their arrangements decided, and then perception or judgment of those stimuli in those arrangements is studied. This is a perfectly adequate procedure as long as we confine our theoretical interest to the problem of how accurately or erroneously the individual perceives stimuli of particular interest. It is inadequate when compared with the usual situation in actual life in which the individual, not a researcher, selects the stimuli to which he attends.

By consenting to be a subject in an experiment, *the individual has already committed himself to attend to what will be presented to him by the experimenter.* There are parallels in real life, but certainly not in most significant encounters with the environment—including the traditional "cognitive" situation of the classroom.

Therefore, *a realistic psychology of cognition requires that the selectivity problem be given primacy.* When this is done, both theoretically and in research practice, the artificiality of sharp separations between "cognition" and "motivation" and "emotion" will become evident—as indeed it is when one attends to psychological activity in actual life.

Why NB? The principle of psychological selectivity is important in studying the effects of social influences on experience and behavior. It will be indispensable when we consider the problem of how people react to communications intended to change their attitudes (Chapter 21). The extreme artificiality of the traditional experimental setup is painfully evident when we stop to wonder whether the person would have paid any attention at all to an experimenter's message if he were not a research subject.

5. Internal Factors (Such as Motives, Desires, Attitudes, etc.) and Experience Are Inferred From Behavior

It may be somewhat redundant to state this proposition. We cannot possibly know the conscious states or the person's motives and desires directly. However, the proposition follows logically from those preceding. If experience and behavior follow central processing, and if the psychological outcome is jointly determined by external and internal factors, then it follows that behavior (word or deed) may indicate the internal states of the individual (be they motives, feelings, attitudes, cherished goals or specific concepts).

In Fig. 2.1, there are four main terms in the diagram: external factors, internal factors, psychological processing, and behavior (verbal or nonverbal). Only two can be directly observed: external factors and behavior. Needs, desires, ambitions, the products of learning, attitudes, and ego concerns are never observed directly. Even if our main concentration as psychologists were on what is called "depth phenomena," we could not study them without making inferences from behavioral data: dreams as the individual recounts them, perceptual and other distortions he manifests in word and deed, slips of the tongue, and so on.

Similarly, psychological processing is never observed directly. We make inferences about perceiving, appraising, or remembering from what the person reports about stimulus objects and events which he selects, and how he acts. He reports that he sees a circle or a square, he says that one weight is heavier than another, he listens to Beethoven and not to Brahms, he shakes our hand warmly as a friend rather than a stranger. Even his memory of us is inferred from the way he greets us, and the inquiries he makes of us.

Such being the case, the only way that we can study motives, attitudes, commitments, and personal involvements is through words, deeds, and other behavioral indicators such as facial and other expressions. In increasing numbers, social psychologists are developing means to refine their strategies for doing so. The rationale underlying all such strategies is that, *given some opportunity to err in behavior, the kind and direction of variation can reflect the individual's personality* (Witkin *et al.,* 1954), attitudes (Sherif and Hovland, 1961), or strong commitments (Sherif, Sherif, and Nebergall, 1965). In various cases, the activity in question refers to perception, judgment, choice, or dealings with objects and events.

6. The Psychological Tendency Is Toward Patterning of Experience

As already noted, the organism is, as a rule, bombarded with potential stimulus agents. Similarly, within the organism, there is a myriad of potential impulses from physiological states, preoccupations with being accepted, with prestige, status and so on. As stated in Proposition 4 on selectivity, the organism screens a portion of these factors to be attended to at the time, making it focal and excluding others to the background. The process of selectivity is not arbitrary, for it is guided by the relevance of impinging stimuli to needs, attitudes, and ego concerns of the person and also by accentuated, articulated, or compelling features of the stimulus world around him.

Research has established that what is focal in experience is delineated from the rest and accentuated with clear boundaries. What is thus delineated as focal in awareness constitutes the "pattern" referred to in this proposition. An illustration is given in Fig. 3.3.

The pattern or "figure" of experience is not, however, independent of its associated background of other stimulation. Nor is the pattern independent of the background of the person's prior experiences, states, and actions. For example, a musical composition heard in the stillness of the night has different significance for the individual than the same composition heard when he is in a multitude of people who are talking and moving around him, say in a crowded hotel.

In fact, the background composed of stimuli and prior psychological states contributes to the particular quality and nuance

of the focal pattern of awareness, even though it is not included in it. Years ago, Koffka (1922) emphasized this point:

The ground has a very important function of its own; it serves as a general level (niveau) upon which the figure appears. Now figure and ground form a structure, consequently the former cannot be independent of the latter. On the contrary, the quality of the figure must be largely determined by the general level upon which it appears. This is a universal fact, observed in such products of culture as fashion and style. The same dress which is not only smart, but nice to look at, almost a thing of beauty, may become intolerable after the fashion has passed (p. 566).

Knowledge of this subtle contribution of the background to whatever we may attend or whatever task we are performing will be especially useful in dealing with the differential effects of social situations (Chapter 6).

In studies of perception, the Gestalt psychologists subsumed this tendency under their concepts of "prägnanz" and "closure." Some of the Gestalt psychologists (e.g., Köhler, 1938, p. 64; Koffka, 1935, p. 151, pp. 311–316) stated that there is a general tendency or even law for perception to proceed toward a state of equilibrium and hence toward simplicity and regularity (symmetry). This was the law of "prägnanz." As David Katz (1950) noted, this analogy with a physical model (equilibrium in physical fields or in hydraulics) was certainly not new (p. 44). The behavioral *data* on which the concept of prägnanz was advanced, however, were the many examples of "closure"—that is, the tendency to perceive and recall incomplete figures, such as a broken circle, as complete or closed. Katz reviewed the evidence (pp. 40–44) and noted that the tendency for open figures to be "closed" psychologically is also found in after-images.

The tendency toward "closure" is one aspect of the general tendency toward some kind of patterning in experience. For example, the arrangement of irregular forms at the left in Fig. 3.4 is typically perceived as a dog, and there is an effort to arrive at a simple and complete pattern in the one at the right. In fact, M. D. Vernon (1962), who used these forms, reported that "If the ob-

Fig. 3.3a. Figure-ground relationship. Although the parachutist occupies but a tiny fraction of this picture, he quickly gains figure character against the cloudy sky. (Frederic Lewis, New York.)

Fig. 3.3b. The ground affects perception of the figure. Here, the compelling view of Yosemite in California becomes background for early photographer William H. Jackson, whose figure would be inconspicuous standing back under the rocky ledge. (Denver Public Library Western Collection.)

server cannot easily make out what the pattern represents, he may be left feeling dissatisfied and worried" (p. 30).

Contemporary psychologists of perception are more apt to view the trend as an adaptive process relative to the organism's environment. Rather than speaking of symmetry and simplicity of perceptual patterns, they more frequently use terms such as "stability" and "consistency." Thus Vernon (1962) wrote about the qualities of what is focal in perception as being "constructed from the primary sensory data . . . in order that the observer might preserve as far as possible the appearance of *stability*, persistence, and *consistency* of the environment; and hence be able to understand

it, and know how to react to it satisfactorily" (p. 257; italics ours).

Similarly, Leibowitz (1965) introduced his study of perception with the "working hypothesis" that "one of the goals and purposes of perception is to stabilize our awareness of the world about us in the interest of successful adjustment" (p. 3). He further emphasized the importance of the background for "stabilizing the visual world," noting that the "surrounding context" is critical in maintaining perception of permanent objects. "This is remarkable, because we do not usually consider the fact that objects to which we do not attend have such important effects on perception" (p. 5). Figure 3.5 illustrates the significance of the background or context in perception of size.

Fig. 3.4. "Incomplete figures" are scattered stimuli whose pattern is completed by the person. (Reprinted with the permission of the publisher from R. F. Street's *A Gestalt Completion Test: A Study of a Cross Section of Intellect—Teachers College Contributions to Education No. 481* [New York: Teachers College Press], copyright 1931, Teachers College, Columbia University.)

In remembering, the tendency toward patterning and toward stability of experience is even more striking. In his book *Remembering* (1932), Bartlett presented numerous illustrations of the fact that things seen are later remembered in more accentuated form. Far from being carbon copies of past events, memories of things past are not even mere accentuations of the objective properties of the events. Aspects of the past are accentuated and their sequence knit more tightly, but there may be striking changes and transformations in terms of the preoccupations and concerns of the individual.

The pattern of awareness is certainly not independent of the structure of stimulus conditions. If the conditions present objective patterns, the person will ordinarily perceive them. However, *even when external conditions are ambiguous, chaotic and fluid, as represented, for example, by times of social crisis or instability, the tendency toward patterning and stability is still found.* In complex situations lacking in clarity, orderly sequence of events, and structured relationships, there is a tendency for individuals to place some kind of clear pattern in their interpretation and action. As a rule, they do not wait in such circumstances for the dust to settle to see the course of events as they eventually shape-up. They

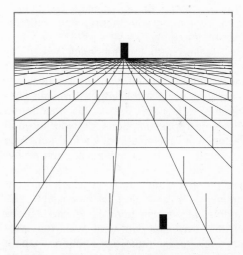

Fig. 3.5. Effect of context on perceived size. The black rectangle at the top appears to be on the horizon and larger than the one in the foreground. The two rectangles are identical in size. Viewing the picture with only one eye increases the effect because the impression of the two-dimensional page is reduced somewhat. (From H. W. Leibowitz, *Visual Perception.* New York: Macmillan, 1965, p. 139.)

try to arrive at some pattern in the situation in terms of their past experiences, their concerns, and anxieties.

The lack of pattern in experience produces tensions and unease. Thus, these are the times ripe for the rise and spread of rumors as to what has happened and what will happen. These are the times when people are more susceptible to interpretations by leaders and even demagogues as to what the pattern of events was and what should be done. We shall return to this application of the principle in Chapters 23 and 24 when we discuss collective interaction and the rise of social movements.

Perceiving things, remembering events, and reacting to persons and situations in patterned ways compatible with the person's habits of perceiving, categories for evaluation, and expectation all contribute to the stability and continuity of awareness. Lack of stabilization is unpleasant and tension-producing for the organism. The tendency toward stabilization and its associated phenomena are sufficiently general that many writers have referred to them and constructed theories about them under different labels: for example, equilibrium theory, balance theory, dissonance theory, congruity-incongruity theory, and "intolerance of ambiguity."

In dealing with this tendency, we prefer to use the terms *patterning* and *stabilization* because they are fairly neutral terms that seem to cover a wide range of related phenomena. Many of the labels mentioned above carry assumptions derived through analogy with physical models and concepts borrowed from other sciences, such as hydraulic models of equilibrium, homeostasis, and physiological needs in which tension-reduction is a biological necessity. The model that we use does have implications for the way that we deal with the phenomena and make predictions about outcomes.

For example, one of the major preoccupations has been the problem of the way that the organism achieves stabilization, balance, or consonance in interpersonal relations when reacting to communications that jar his well-entrenched views, and in compliance or noncompliance with social influence from others. In such problems, we quickly find that a conceptual model based on analogy with momentary physical events is inadequate. Immediate closure in a transitory perception is not the entire issue. In such matters, the tendency toward patterning and psychological stability is not a one-shot affair, but proceeds *over time.*

From a time perspective, there is the problem of the personal consistency, or congruity, of the individual's established cognitions (his beliefs, attitudes, and ideals). Therefore, a model based on patterning of perception in momentary situations is not sufficient—although the perceptual stage is important, too. If we stop at this stage, we arbitrarily rule out consideration of the course of stabilization over time, which is, after all, what counts for the individual. Such a longitudinal view necessarily brings in factors that need not be evident in a momentary situation.

In considering the tendency toward establishing balance or stability in coping with the environment over time, the recurring demands of the individual's self-image become crucial (Chapter 17). The involvement of the person's self in his day-to-day transactions in a series of tasks means that *stabilization of·psychological activity at any cost will not do.* Involvement of the self in any one of its various roles—while the person performs tasks, deals with others, or reaches a decision—establishes a level at which stabilization can be achieved. Thus a general theory of the tendency toward patterning and stabilization requires an adequate theory of self-development and ego-involvements, as we shall emphasize (pp. 385 ff).

As any college student knows, the period of waiting for the grade after an examination arouses feelings of uncertainty, suspense, or uneasiness—proportional to the importance of the particular examination in one's scheme of things. Announcement that the grades are posted certainly brings relief from this suspense and uncertainty. This is one fact to be noted, but the certainty is momentary. The consequences of the momentary relief may be more important psychologically than the relief itself. If closure of the incomplete event is that a person whose usual performance level is A gets a grade of C, the dissonance aroused will be more discomforting than the feeling of suspense. The same C grade will be gratifying and settling for a person, who, as a student, is a "borderline case" between D and C.

Thus we see that the problem of psychological patterning and stability involves more than the momentary patterning of perception or decision. It involves the consequences of the perceptual pattern or decision reached. And in assessing these consequences, the level set in the individual's self-image in regard to the activity has to be brought into the psychological account, for it is almost invariably involved in matters of any importance to the person.

In recent years, the problem of patterning and stabilization of experience has been studied in terms of reactions to communication, interpersonal relations, and other adjustments to the environment. Because these problems are longitudinal, it cannot be emphasized sufficiently that stabilization is not merely a problem of achieving a definite cognitive pattern at the moment in a transitory stimulus situation. For example, when a person is exposed to a communication discrepant from his own views, the problem is not merely how the person arrives most quickly or easily at a stable configuration that reduces his momentary tension. In predicting his <u>reactions</u> over time, we need to <u>consider the consequences for him if he reacts to this tension in one way or another.</u> If he adapts to the current situation in any old way that will achieve momentary balance, he may thereby thrust himself into much greater imbalance, dissonance, or instability—especially if the way he chooses runs counter to his established commitments, attitudes, and self-image.

7. Structured Stimulus Situations Set Limits to Alternatives in Psychological Patterning

Stimulus structure refers to properties of objects and events that are objectively patterned or ordered in terms of specifiable criteria or dimensions. Such properties limit the number of alternatives that psychological patterning can take. Evidence for this proposition is clear in research on perception, that is, the experience of present objects and events. It is easily seen also in much of our everyday actions. The properties of a staircase are sufficiently compelling that we do not ordinarily disregard them in coming down stairs.

In considering this principle, the classical studies of figure-ground relationships will

Fig. 3.6.   Reversible figure. When we see a vase, the shape stands out clearly—the rest forming the background. When we see two profiles, the contours of the faces are conspicuous in the foreground, and aspects not relevant to the profiles recede into the background. Note that two tiny openings become important ingredients when we see them as the mouths of the profiles, but these two tiny openings become only decorative details when we see the pattern as a vase. (From E. Rubin, *Visuell wahrgenommene Figuren: Studien in psychologischer Analyse.* Kobenhavn: Gyldendol, 1921.)

be helpful. The Danish psychologist Edgar Rubin (1921) studied the figure-ground delineation, including perception of reversible figures such as the one presented in Fig. 3.6. Such figures provide a good basis for discussing this proposition, because there are only two alternatives for psychological patterning.

Look at the picture in Fig. 3.6. If you see the two profiles facing each other (one alternative), the white area between them appears to be just an empty space. If you see a goblet, this same white space has "body" to it. The two white lines opposite each other at the lower part of the pictures are clear-cut, but our perception of them changes, depending on whether we see the profiles first or the goblet first. When the profiles are figure for us, the white lines are meaningful as openings of the mouths. However, when the goblet is figure, these white lines are merely decorative details on the goblet.

This example illustrates some general findings in the study of figure-ground relationships. The figure is distinct and stands out from the ground, which lacks distinctiveness. The figure has more clear-cut boundaries than the ground. Things and persons perceived as figures are recognized earlier and remembered longer with distinct features, whereas stimuli that constitute the ground are sometimes hardly remembered.

Such examples show once more that stimuli do not have absolute stimulating values. Their significance is derived in an important way from being parts of objective patterns that are located in the focus (figure) or background at the time. They are perceived in terms of their "membership character" in the pattern. Ittelson (1960) summarized the relative properties of figure and ground in similar terms:

Through his studies of figure-ground relationships in perception, Rubin discovered several differences in the appearance of the figure and the ground. For example, the figure appears to have shape or form, while the ground ordinarily does not unless it has some patterns on it; the ground appears to be continuous and behind the figure. The figure appears to be a thing while the ground seems to be material. Psychologically, these differences are important, for the figure stands out in perceiving and is better remembered (Ittelson, 1960, p. 93).

The study of figure-ground relationships shows us clearly that the stimulus factors limiting the alternatives in psychological patterning are not merely intensity, size, movement, and the like, but also have to do with stimulus arrangements (structure) and sequence in time. Among the best examples of such properties are those studied by the Gestalt psychologists, which were primarily based on the fundamental contribution of Max Wertheimer in the 1920s (see English translation, 1958).

Objective Stimulus Factors Responsible for Limiting the Alternatives in Psychological Patterning. When the stimulus field has definite objective pattern or structure, the patterning of perception corresponds to it rather closely. The following list of such properties is based on Newman's discussion (1948) with the seventh added in line with the work of Wertheimer and David Katz (1950):

1. Similarity
2. Proximity
3. Symmetry
4. Good continuation or "common fate"
5. Common movement
6. Consistency of moving patterns or formations
7. "Closed forms"

These factors are illustrated in the simple drawings in Fig. 3.7a. They are equally compelling when we watch people in formations—for example, in commencement processions, military parades, or marching bands (see Fig. 3.7b).

Items or objects closer to one another (*proximity*) will be grouped together (if other factors do not work against it too heavily).

When some objects are similar and some are dissimilar, those that are *similar* are grouped together (if other arrangements do not operate against it).

Parts of an object or pattern that have clear *continuity* will be perceived as belonging together. This factor may work against proximity and similarity and, as we shall see later, against past experience or familiarity.

Objects bound together with sharply defined boundaries are likely to be perceived as perceptual units. Common movement, consistency in moving patterns, and symmetry are all conducive to unequivocal perceptual units.

The various objective factors conducive to clear perceptual patterning that correspond closely to stimulus structure may be mutually supporting or destructive, either singly or in combination. For example, good continuity may work against proximity, as shown in Fig. 3.7. When persons in similar costumes stand or move together, proximity, similarity, good continuity, and common movement are all working together to produce a compelling perceptual structure (Fig. 3.7b).

For economy of expression, we shall refer to objective factors such as these as "structural properties" of stimulus situations. The so-called Gestalt factors are not exhaustive, particularly as we move from perception to judgment and action. Here, dissimilarity, sequence, and order become significant properties that limit the alternatives to decision and action.

Knowledge of the properties of the stimulus field is crucial in social psychology. One of the inescapable facts of social life is that

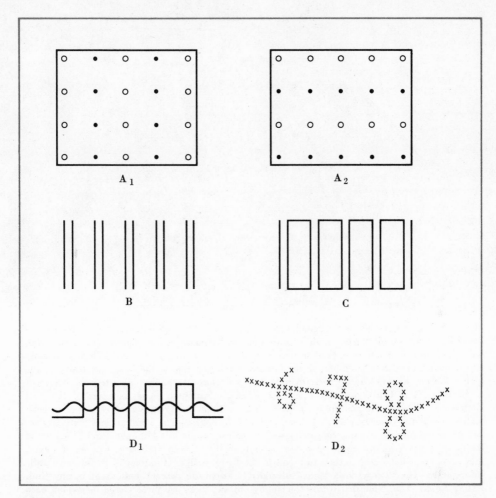

Fig. 3.7a. Classic examples of structural factors in external stimulus situations. A_1. Because of similarity, the items are seen more easily in vertical columns than in rows (after Wertheimer). A_2. Because of similarity, these items are seen more easily in horizontal rows (after Wertheimer). B. Lines are perceived in five pairs because of proximity (after David Katz). C. Vertical lines are the same as those in B, but the closed form dominates over the proximity factor (after David Katz). D_1. Continuity of contours dominates over proximity of lines (after Wertheimer). D_2. Despite proximity, distinct numbers and a curved line are seen because of good contour. Familiarity of numerals also favors distinctiveness here (after Prothro and Teska).

society surrounds the individual with cultural stimuli having definite and compelling patterns, order, and sequence over time. It surrounds the individual with certain schedules, regularities, and recurrences. A very important part of the sociocultural context of the individual is the society's technology —tools, buildings, vehicles, machines, and other parts of material culture. Our conceptions of the normal size of buildings, of normal speeds, and of normal proportions are based on the properties of habitual ob-

jects and relationships that the individual confronts and uses day in and day out. As a consequence, there is greater consensus in experience, attitude, and conceptions within a society on these matters than on topics that do not have such immediately compelling properties. This will be our topic in a later chapter when we discuss technology and its crucial role in social change (Chapter 22).

From an understanding of the effect of stimulus structure on experience of parts or

Fig. 3.7b. Examples of factors conducive to perception of definite patterns in human assemblies. *(above)* Similarity, both within light background and of contrasting dark cards, favors perception of letters in card section, regardless of whether one reads. Below, continuity works against proximity. Members in the middle of the first line of the *U* are not seen as parts of the bottom line of the *O*, even though they are closer to them. (Courtesy of Professor L. H. Haug, The University of Oklahoma.) *(below)* Although some members of the card section may be slow, the continuity of dark cards on light background enables viewer to complete the pattern. (Courtesy of D. Leherr, Public Information, The Pennsylvania State University.) *(opposite top)* Again, continuity works against proximity. Although band members at the ends of the lines are closer to one another than they are to members at point of wedge, they are seen as belonging to their own row in the flying wedge. (Courtesy of D. Leherr, Public Information, The Pennsylvania State University.) *(opposite center)* Pattern of trophy illustrating closed form. Note that within the trophy outline, there are three closed forms, but each is seen as merely part of the loving cup. (Courtesy of Professor L. H. Haug, The University of Oklahoma.) *(opposite bottom)* Because of similarity (uniforms) and proximity, band formation stands out clearly from crowd. The same individuals in variegated clothing and unevenly spaced would create the appearance of a "milling crowd." (Courtesy of Professor L. H. Haug, The University of Oklahoma.)

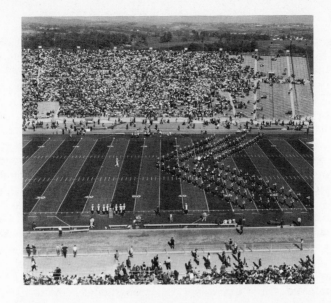

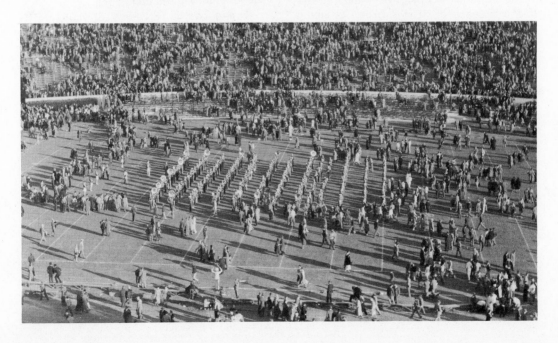

particular objects within the structure, we also have a basis for understanding what is variously called "part-whole relationships" or "subsystem-system" relationships (Chapter 5) that will be useful when we treat the formation of human groups and the behavior of individual members (Chapters 7 and 8).

8.   In Unstructured Stimulus Situations, Alternatives in Psychological Patterning Are Increased

The individual is confronted with stimulus situations in which external factors conducive to just one or two figure-ground delineations and objective patterns are lacking. Such stimulus situations are referred to as *unstructured*. Other equivalent terms used in the literature to refer to lack of structure are "equivocal," "weak," "ambiguous," "indeterminate," "vague," "impoverished," "fluid," or "complex"—as opposed to "compelling," "strong," "clear," and similar terms used to describe structured situations. Of course, for special cases, the term most appropriate should be used. A simple stimulus object may be appropriately characterized as "ambiguous," but general conditions surrounding the individual sequentially over time may be better characterized as "complex" or "fluid," as typified in times of crisis and change.

Lacking definite objective pattern (owing to the absence of definite order, grouping, sequence, similarity, and differences in the stimulus field), unstructured situations allow various alternatives for psychological patterning. When individuals are presented with a closed form, for example a square or circle, the likelihood is that all of these persons will perceive the form in much the same way and will later reproduce it as a square or circle. But to the extent that such objective structure is lacking, as in Fig. 3.8, to that extent the alternative ways that such situations are patterned vary from individual to individual. *This increase in the number of alternatives for patterning a stimulus situation is an operational measure of the relative lack of structure.*

Responses to vague, unstructured or unclear stimulus situations are among the best evidence of the psychological tendency toward psychological patterning (Proposi-

tion 6). Even though objective structure or order is lacking in some degree, the individual tries to give it some pattern or order. In other words, *whether the external stimulus field is patterned or not, the psychological tendency is in the direction of some kind of pattern* (Proposition 6).

Relating our discussion of unstructured situations to propositions discussed earlier, we find that in unstructured situations the individual's selectivity (Proposition 4) is guided more by internal factors. However, even though internal factors contribute more, the joint determination of experience and behavior by external and internal factors still applies (Proposition 3).

The fact that internal factors contribute proportionally more to patterning in unstructured situations has been utilized effectively in the study of motivation and attitudes through cognitive indicators (perception, judgment, remembering, etc.; Proposition 9). Similarly, the heightened susceptibility to social influences and greater reliance on other people's words and solutions under unstructured stimulus conditions has been utilized in studies both in the laboratory and in real-life situations. Some of this work will be presented under Principle 10 (p. 70). In fact, Principles 9 and 10 represent more specific statements of the present proposition, specifying the source of psychological patterns achieved under unstructured conditions.

Gradations in Stimulus Structure. The structuredness or unstructuredness of the stimulus situation is not an all-or-none affair. There are degrees or gradations of stimulus structure. Situations can be graded or ranked from those in which several stimulus properties (e.g., similarity, proximity, good continuity) combine to make a strong pattern in the stimulus field to the other extreme, in which such factors conflict or are absent.

Such degrees or gradations of stimulus structure are illustrated in Fig. 3.9 by selected drawings from research by Luchins (1945, 1950), who has varied stimulus structure in numerous studies. As the series of pictures proceeds from Drawing 1 of the man, the succeeding pictures become increasingly less patterned. In Plate 11, the suggestion of a bottle is included, which is made increasingly clear until the last figure

Fig. 3.8. A contrast in stimulus structure. (*above*) United Nations, New York. (*below*) Hiroshima. (Wide World.)

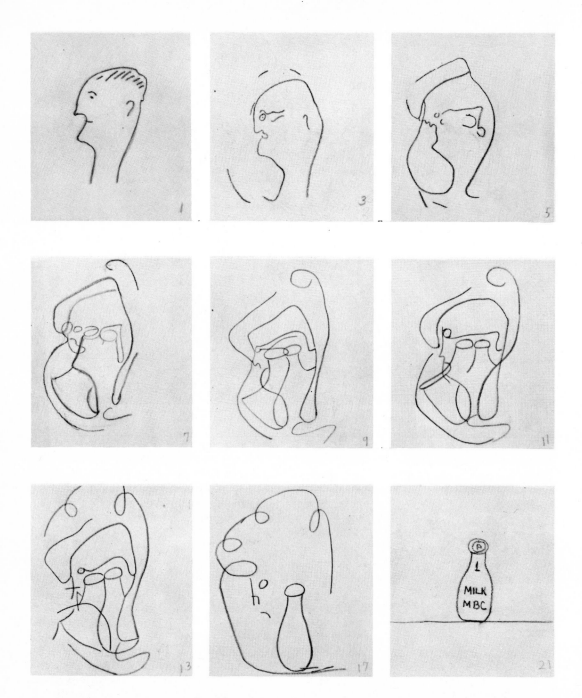

Fig. 3.9. Gradations in stimulus structure representative of Luchins' research on effects of set and social suggestion. Drawings 1 (man) and 21 (bottle) are the most structured in this series of gradations. Perception of them is least affected by social influences, e.g., suggestion. Perception of the ambiguous drawings in the middle of the series (e.g., 7, 9, and 11) is most affected by social influences. In the original Luchins series, finer gradations are represented in 21 steps. (Courtesy of A. S. Luchins.)

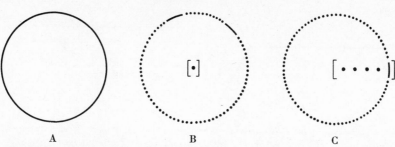

Fig. 3.10.   Three degrees of stimulus structure. Phosphorescent lucite visible to subjects in conditions A, B, and C is indicated by heavier lines. (Adapted from J. D. Thrasher.)

includes even a label. In responding to such pictures, variability of response is least for the first and last plates. The response "man" persists longer when the subject has first started the series from the human picture, revealing his expectation that he is being shown human pictures. Similarly, a suggestion to the subject of what he is looking at (external influence) is most effective in the middle range of highly unstructured drawings.

Thrasher (1954) investigated judgment of the locations of lights in three gradations of structure by using error in the direction of a friend's judgments or a stranger's judgments as a measure of relative social influence in the three situations. Figure 3.10 shows the three variations in stimulus structure used: In Situation A, the lights to be localized appeared in a dark room within a luminous circle. In Situation B, two short portions of the circumference were luminous. In Situation C, only one portion of the circumference was visible. Thrasher confirmed the degrees of structure in these three situations by the finding that error of localization was greatest in Condition C, intermediate in B, and least in A. In short, variations in judgments by different individuals decreased and correspondence with objective localization increased from the least to the most structured situation. Thrasher's study also showed that another person speaking his judgments aloud had an increasingly greater effect with the decrease in stimulus structure. As might be expected, he also found differences depending on whether that person was a friend or stranger.

Between the extremes of well-structured and unstructured situations there is, then, a tremendous range of possibilities for differ-

ent gradations in structure. A number of different measures of stimulus structure have been proposed. Wiener (1958), for example, defined ambiguity of the stimulus as "the relative probability value of each interpretation in a two-choice situation" (p. 257). Flament (1959a, 1959b) generalized this definition by taking into account a full range of stimulus structure from no ambiguity (all responses to the stimulus being identical) to complete ambiguity (all responses to the stimulus being equally probable). He formulated an index of structure not limited to two-choice situations.

It is worth noting that responses to well-structured situations are not necessarily "correct" in terms of correspondence to particular aspects of the situation. External patterns may produce some of the well-known illusions as well as correct perception in the usual sense. For example, in the Müller-Lyer illusion (Fig. 3.11a), two straight lines of identical length are seen as differing in length because they form parts of patterns with arrows pointing in different directions at the end. However, the Müller-Lyer situation is one fairly high in the order of gradations from well-structured to unstructured situations.

The line with arrows pointing outward appears longer than the line with arrows pointing inward to most people in our culture. However, the amount of the illusion is subject to cultural variations. Some cultural groups are less susceptible to the illusion than Europeans (Segall, Campbell, and Herskovits, 1966).

The problem here concerns the psychological properties of a pattern and its parts. In social psychology, the major counterpart of this problem is the individual-group relationship, which is discussed in Chapter 5.

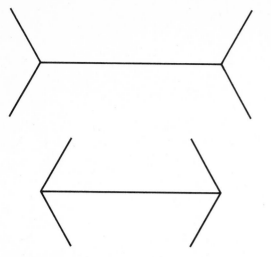

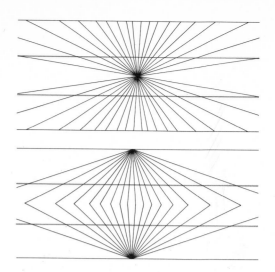

Fig. 3.11. Classic examples of the effects of context and past experience in perception. (*above*) The Müller-Lyer illusion: Which horizontal line appears longer? (Measure the lengths of lines with a ruler.) (*above right*) Two versions of the Hering illusion. (The horizontal lines are parallel.) (*below*) The Ponzo illusion (see also Fig. 3.5) in natural context. The effect is not merely a trick for the psychologist's laboratory. The two white rectangles are equal, but in the context of the perspective of converging railroad tracks the upper rectangle appears the longer of the two to every onlooker. (Photo by Derek Witty.) (*right*) The Zulus and other peoples whose culture used only few straight lines and rectangular structures are not so much subject to the foregoing illusions as those brought up in a culture with many right-angled structures. This cross-cultural difference, noted by the anthropologist Rivers early in the century, has been studied more systematically by Segall, Campbell, and Herskovits (1965). (Photo by J. Allan Cash, London.)

4

Propositions 9-12

Major Topics of the Chapter

The more unstructured the stimulus situation, the greater the relative contribution of internal factors in the frame of reference. Internal factors are motives, desires, ego concerns, conceptual categories and unique idiosyncrasies

Proposition 9 as basis of all projective tests and devices

Use of unstructured projective devices for assessing motive patterns and cross-cultural comparisons

Social motives and attitudes through perception and judgment indices

Background of research on motivational factors through cognitive indices

Motives revealed in cognitive processes under extreme deprivation

The more unstructured the stimulus situation, the greater the relative effectiveness of social influences confronting the individual (from other people, groups, communication, "suggestion")

Various factors in the frame of reference have differing relative weights: psychology of anchorages (reference points) and assimilation-contrast effects

Culturally provided anchorages

Psychosocial scales and psychophysical scales

Human psychological functioning is typically on a conceptual level

9. The More Unstructured the External Stimulus Situation, the Greater the Contribution of Internal Factors—Including Internalized Social Values and Standards

As the stimulus situation grades by degree from highly structured forms, well-defined groupings, and sequence toward situations lacking such compelling properties, the organism contributes more and more to any psychological pattern that ensues. Because there is a tendency toward patterning in experience, this means that the contribution of internal factors to psychological processing is proportionately greater as the structure of the stimulus situation decreases.

By internal factors, we refer to effects of the individual's past experience, including internalized cultural values and standards incorporated in his social attitudes, his biogenic needs (e.g., hunger), emotional states, conceptual categories, and his temporary expectations.

This principle is basic to research in which investigators have studied motives, attitudes, and personality through the individual's perception, judgment, and imagining. A complete account of the varied undertakings associated with that research development would comprise several volumes. Here we shall merely illustrate the basic rationale for the methods that have been used.

Proposition 9 Is the Basis of All Projective Tests and Devices

One line of research had its origins in the efforts to diagnose and understand personal problems through eliciting behavior relative to unstructured or ambiguous stimuli. One of the best-known examples is the Rorschach ink-blot test, in which the person is presented a series of ink-blots and asked what he sees in the blots or what they remind him of. Figure 4.1 presents examples of ink-blots developed by Holtzman (1958) in an effort to improve upon the Rorschach materials and to develop objective criteria for evaluating responses.

The ink-blot test is one example of a class called "projective tests" in the study of motives and personality. Other examples of projective tests are the even older word-association and sentence-completion tests, more recent tests that use indeterminate auditory patterns, Rosenzweig's Picture Frustration (P-F) test (1949), and Murray's Thematic Apperception Test (TAT; 1944). Unlike the ink-blot tests, the stimuli presented in some of these tests are not highly ambiguous as perceptual forms.

Let us consider first the subject's task in the ink-blot tests. He is presented a figure (see Fig. 4.1) that may be symmetrical and may have other Gestalt properties (such as closure, continuity, etc.). It is not representational (it is an ink-blot) and is usually rather complex. Therefore, the novel request that

Fig. 4.1. The Holtzman Ink-blot Technique consists of two parallel forms, A and B, each containing 45 inkblots constituting the test series and two practice blots, X and Y, preceding the test series as warmup blots. These inkblots were chosen from many hundreds that were tested on mental patients, college students, children, and other populations. The three cards were not actually chosen for either of the test forms, but they are quite similar to the inkblots actually used. Underneath each card are sample responses to illustrate the method, one from a normal college student and one from a mental patient.

There are many aspects of each response that can be coded and summed across the 45 inkblots to give 22 major scores for use in personality assessment. The area of the blot used, the time it takes to give a response, the extent to which color, form, or shading are employed as determinants of the percept, the extent to which movement or activity is projected into the percept, the way in which the percept is organized and the parts are interrelated, the content of the percept, and the subtleties of the person's thought processes as revealed in his verbalizations are all important aspects of each response. As the inkblots are in fact meaningless, what a person sees in them must be projected from within his own imagination, which provides a clue to his inner personality. (Courtesy of Wayne H. Holtzman.)

Card X35. (normal) "Sand storm blowing through an Indian village." (abnormal) "Brown and blue dirt."

Card X110. (normal) "Dog's face with a cold nose." (abnormal) "A purple heart" (center).

Card X131. (normal) "Suma wrestler" (center). (abnormal) "Those things on the side look like charred tree trunks, only they're pregnant."

the individual report what the blot reminds him of (or suggests to him) permits many alternatives. The individual has no clear guides in the stimulus situation itself. If he is naive about theories, he does not have a notion of what the researcher expects of him. Consequently, the details of the blot to which he attends and the imagery they call forth are very much his own construction.

Other projective tests (e.g., the TAT) are clear line drawings of people in real-life situations (Murray, 1938, 1944). In practice, these drawings have been adapted for use in different cultures, so that the pictures themselves are not only clear but also depict fairly familiar settings. What lacks structure here is the *task*. The person is asked to tell a story about the incident pictured. In short, the task goes beyond the immediate perceptual situation to narrative interpretation of the people's actions and relationships before and after the scene pictured. As there are many possible stories about any scene involving human figures, the person has to rely on his own resources to tell the story. Similarly, the P-F test depicts scenes of a special kind, involving potential or actual frustration of one person by others. Here the unstructured aspect is that of predicting the frustrated person's responses and/or feelings (see Fig. 4.2).

The theoretical basis for utilizing situations lacking structure in some important aspect (focal stimuli, task, or both) for studying the "personal equation" was summarized by Abt (1950) in a book devoted to projective tests.

Thus . . . the more structured the stimulus field, the more dependent behavior usually is upon the operation of the external factors in perception; and, conversely, the greater the vagueness and ambiguity of the stimulus field, the greater the opportunity for and need of internal factors in perception to operate. It is demonstrable that even in the presence of an unstructured stimulus field, the behavior of the individual is always to be regarded as lawful; but the lawfulness of such behavior arises from needs and values, of both a physiological and psychological nature, which function within the individual. . . . The fact that there is a shifting in the relative importance of the internal and external factors in perception in relation to the nature of various stimulus fields that can be presented to an individual constitutes the grounds on which all the projective methods ultimately rest (pp. 50–51).

Gardner Lindzey's survey (1961) of the use of projective tests in cross-cultural research presented a similar explanation and specified the variations in the several techniques, with appropriate attention to the problems of validating test theory across cultures. His book provides summaries and intensive analysis of projective tests in cross-cultural research up to about 1960, and the analysis has influenced those in even more recent accounts (e.g., Shneidman, 1965). For present purposes we need only note Lindzey's summary delineating what is common to the variety of projective tests:

. . . a projective technique is an instrument that is considered especially sensitive to covert or unconscious aspects of behavior, it permits or encourages a wide variety of subject responses, is highly multidimensional, and it evokes unusually rich or profuse response data with a minimum of subject awareness concerning the purpose of the test. Further it is very often true that the stimulus material presented by the projective test is ambiguous, interpreters of the test depend upon holistic analysis, the test evokes fantasy responses, and there are no correct or incorrect responses to the test (p. 45, italics in original).

Several of the above characteristics refer to lack of structure in the stimulus situation, for example, "permits . . . wide variety of subject responses," "highly multidimensional," and "ambiguous."

The most comprehensive surveys of projective-test results from different cultures do not support the claim that they reveal "modal personalities" shaped by the broad values of each culture, hence differing from culture to culture (Kaplan, 1954; Lindzey, 1961). Cultural differences in test results are found, but invariably there is wide overlap in the distributions of results from one culture to another. This outcome led Kaplan (1954) to conclude: "We interpret our results as showing that neither the extreme position of cultural determinism, nor the equally extreme view that personality maintains itself free of culture influences is tenable" (p. 32).

On the other hand, in specific respects, projective test results do reveal cultural

Fig. 4.2. Sample pictures from Rosenzweig's Picture Frustration (P-F) Test (children's form) and from Pareek's adaptation of the same plates for studying children in India.

Note that the pictures themselves are not unstructured in form or the situation represented. The unstructured aspect is the person's task of indicating what words should be attributed to the respondent (in empty box on right) in reaction to remarks of the person(s) on the left. Numerous alternatives are possible, in terms of the motives, interests, identifications, and cultural background of the individual filling in the empty boxes.

Plate 23 was adapted by Pareek because soup is not a common dish in India and milk is typically served warm, not cold. Plate 17 represents a situation included even though it might never happen to most Indian children.

Pareek, an Indian psychologist, reported that compared with data on American and Japanese children, responses by Indian children revealed less awareness that the situations were frustrating, a greater tendency to view the situations as unavoidable, and a tendency not to blame the "frustrating" person or agent. Japanese children, on the other hand, were somewhat more prone to blame the victim (child) than the frustrating agent. (Reproduced with permission from the Rosenzweig P-F Study, Children's Form, copyright 1948, and from Udai N. Pareek, *Developmental Patterns in Reactions to Frustration.* Bombay: Asia Publishing House, 1964.)

differences, as this proposition would lead us to expect. For example, the "popular" labels for ink-blots differ from culture to culture. The most frequent response by the Saulteaux Indians to one card was "turtle," whereas the popular European response is "butterfly" or "bat." Less obvious differences have also been reported, many of them related to cultural values. Samoans spent a disproportionate amount of time in responding to the white spaces in and around the Rorschach ink-blots (Cook,

1942); the investigator concluded that this unusual finding was related to the special value placed on white in Samoan life—it was the favorite color of most respondents. In locales in which pictorial representation is not common and where decorative art emphasizes fine detail, the respondents gave few overall characterizations to the blots and paid much attention to the fine details within them (Bleuler and Bleuler, 1935). This example, reported from Moroccan respondents, illustrates a more general fact about the cross-cultural use of pictures to elicit responses of research interest: The prevalence and use of pictorial forms in a culture affects individual response to test materials (e.g., Biesheuvel, 1958; Harris, 1963).

Studies of the individual's motives, attitudes, or goal-directedness through use of the projective tests have contributed a large literature showing that motivations and value orientations may be revealed in the person's responses—such as stories told about TAT pictures (e.g., McClelland *et al.,* 1953) or phrases written to complete incomplete sentences such as "This I believe. . . ." (Harvey, 1966; 1967). Such use of the projective devices has yielded valuable data for the study of personality. However, this use, as well as the attempts at more global personality assessment suffer from a common difficulty, mentioned above: As the responses obtained are at times ambiguous and typically highly complex, the agreement on scoring the responses remains dependent upon the investigator's theoretical and value orientation.

Experimental Studies of Motives Revealed in Cognition

Experimental studies *do reveal* pronounced effects of motives in perceiving, judging, and remembering situations that lack stimulus structure in some respect. The findings do *not* warrant the assumption that the effects are consistently in the direction of "defense" or of "wish-fulfillment," as mechanisms triggered by threatening or desired objects. On the contrary, the consistent finding in a large research literature is that (as compared with the processing of neutral information), when the stimulus material has motivational relevance, cognitive processes are affected whether the relevance is potentially fulfilling or threatening to motive satisfaction. For example, in recognizing words matched for familiarity, subjects recognized words with either positive or negative value more readily than neutral words (Gilchrist, Ludeman, and Lysack, 1954).

In studies of judgment, motivational relevance leads to predictable variations in how particular stimuli are discriminated when the stimulus dimension or the task is unstructured in some respect. For example, in judging glass jars filled with candy or with a sand and sawdust mixture, children's judgments of the candy were "heavier" than of the comparable weights of sawdust (Dukes and Bevan, 1951). Further, their judgments of candy were less variable than for the neutral jars. Similarly, Tajfel (1959) found that rewards attached to certain items in a series to be judged had the effect of heightening the *differences* between these and other items. As there are a number of social objects for which size or weight increases with value (e.g., size of coins, weight of candy), the direction of the differences is sometimes in the direction of *overestimat-* ing the more valued items (Tajfel, and Winter, 1963).

Studies of Social Motives Through Perception and Judgment Indices. In studies of "social motives," perception, judgment, and evaluation of relevant stimuli differ reliably from that of motivationally neutral items, provided that there is some lack of structure (ambiguity or varied alternatives) in the dimension being judged. For example, the person who is highly committed to the cause of Negro equality judges a vaguely worded statement suggesting compromise on the issue as extremely *unfavorable* to this cause, whereas a disinterested person places the same statement in a "moderate" category. Both agree, however, in judging clearcut statements of an extreme position on the issue (Sherif and Hovland, 1961). Such findings on systematic variations in judgment of items that lack clear structure have resulted in new approaches to the study of social attitudes, as we shall see in Chapters 15 and 16. The *direction* of the variations will be considered when discussing Proposition 11, which deals with anchors in the frame of reference.

The reader is cautioned to consider the foregoing conclusions carefully in order to avoid a blind alley that has already been explored in psychology. A few years ago there was an overenthusiastic reponse to studies showing the role of motivation in perceiving and judging. The over-enthusiastic reponse could be caricatured as "The world is what we make of it"—*we* referring largely to our wishes, desires, and aspirations. It was quite properly criticized by researchers who emphasized that stimulus properties have a great deal to do with how we perceive, judge, evaluate, think about, and remember the world (Gibson, 1953; Volkmann, 1951).

Research on Internal Factors Through Cognitive Indices. Historically, Bartlett's work on perceiving and remembering (1932) was among the earliest in the trend to study motives and attitudes through variations in cognition. He found that as he presented more complex and ambiguous drawings to his subjects "the more varied is the play of interests and consequent attitudes which can be evoked" (p. 193). He noted that the increased contribution of internal factors could be in the direction of "distorting" the accurate reproduction of the stimulus, especially when the task was to recall a stimulus. On the other hand, the effect of interest and attitude was sometimes toward increase in accuracy. For example, a student of mathematics compared one unstructured drawing to a mathematical function. Subsequently, he was able to reproduce it with a high degree of accuracy.

In 1935, Sherif (1935, 1936) conducted experiments that showed the effect of attitude and internalized norms in perceiving a highly unstructured stimulus situation (the autokinetic phenomenon). He compared his findings to anthropological reports suggesting that cultural norms play an important role in what is perceived (selectivity), how it is seen, and how it is remembered.

By using a variety of unstructured situations (word associations, incomplete pictures, and drawings), Sanford (1936, 1937) analyzed the frequency of food responses by children before and after meals and by college students between meals and after a 24-hour fast. At both age levels, he found that food responses were more frequent after periods of abstinence, but that increase in food responses during a 24-hour fast was not proportional to the increased time beyond the usual cycle of eating. This finding demonstrated that psychological selectivity is goal directed.

During the decade before the "new look" trend was launched, a series of experiments was conducted by Gardner Murphy and his students showing the effects of motivation in perceiving unstructured stimuli, in selectivity for "figures," and in recall. These classic experiments and the research inspired by them have established the principle being discussed beyond a shadow of a doubt: that is, motivational factors do contribute more to psychological processing (and, hence, to behavior) when the task or the stimulus object lacks objective structure.

Figure 4.3 illustrates the findings in studies of motivational factors in cognitive processes when the stimulus field lacks structure. The results are from the study by Levine, Chein, and Murphy (1942), in which subjects gave their associations with highly unstructured slides, some in black and white and some in color. The left-hand graph shows the frequency of food objects mentioned by subjects who had not eaten for one, three, six, and nine hours. The right-hand graph presents scores computed by assigning greater weight to responses of foods than to eating utensils or other food-related objects. In both graphs, it may be seen that food responses increased over time until the deprivation exceeded the normal time between meals (9 hours) and that the decrease was earlier for the colored pictures, which were so vague that subjects frequently reported no associations, particularly as the period of abstinence increased.

Motives Revealed in Cognitive Processes Under Extreme Deprivation

In experimental studies, motives are seldom extremely pressing. Therefore, their wider implications cannot be appreciated unless we also consider the effects of motives that are keenly experienced in social life. From studies of prolonged deprivation, we know that motives may come to dominate psychological processes in a variety of ways.

The findings are particularly significant for social psychology when man's biogenic

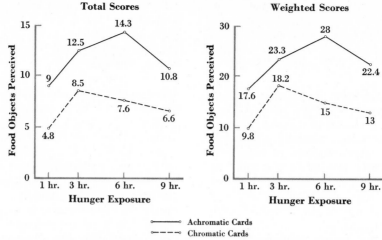

Fig. 4.3. The effect of food deprivation on associations with ambiguous pictures. The ordinate gives average scores for all subjects, while the baseline gives number of hours since eating. Total scores (left) give averages of all food-related responses. Weighted scores were computed by assigning different values to food and to eating utensils. (From R. Levine, I. Chein, and G. Murphy, 1942. The relation of the intensity of a need to the amount of perceptual distortion. *J. Psychol.*, **13**, p. 291.)

needs are deprived—for example, needs for food or sexual activity. The literature is filled with examples concerning sexual deprivation. Deprivation of food is, however, a much more significant social problem in a world still unable to feed its population. Therefore, our examples will be selected from a large literature showing that prolonged deprivation of food results in striking domination of cognitive processes by this need. It is unrealistic for social psychology to neglect this line of evidence. It has significance for a general psychology of motivation that is applicable beyond the drawing rooms of an affluent society.

Even when subjects agree voluntarily to subsist on a semistarvation diet (knowing that they will be cared for and believing that they are contributing to human knowledge by doing so), the effect of prolonged deprivation is dramatic (Keys *et al.,* 1945). Preoccupation with food increases. The importance and quality of other biogenic needs and of social standards are reduced sharply. The following quotation from Guetzkow and Bowman (1946) describes conscientious objectors who voluntarily served as subjects in a semistarvation study conducted at Minnesota during World War II:

As starvation progressed they became more and more silent, apathetic and immobile. Movements were slow and restricted; stairs were mounted one at a time and the men sat or stood leaning against a wall while they waited. In discussion there was no evidence of confusion of thought or difficulty of expression but the attitude was frequently irritable and morose. Trivial incidents were productive of exaggerated annoyance and complaint. Favorite topics of conversation were food, farming and rural life, a fact which was bitterly resented by some of the men.

All of the men continually complained of feeling cold, and even in the warm weather of July most of them wore heavy clothes. The conclusion was clear that any lack of heat in the building would have produced bitter suffering. Another frequent complaint was the sensation of being "old."

A number of men were bothered by vivid dreams, particularly dreams of breaking the diet, with attendant great remorse (pp. 25, 26).

All of the men experienced the trends described, but the range of individual differences among the subjects actually *increased* in several important respects. For example, although dedicated and pledged to complete the study, some individuals violated the moral and other social values that had become part of them during their upbringing.

This deterioration of their ethical control was all the more remarkable because these men had shown themselves to be sincere and upright throughout the two or more years of work they had performed in the civilian public service units before coming to the laboratory. . . . One of the individuals not only bought food, but also stole some from "locked" storerooms. Another individual sublimated his food cravings by stealing china cups from coffee shops. Although fasting is said at times to quicken one spiritually, none of the men reported significant progress in their religious lives. Most of them felt that the semi-starvation had coarsened rather than refined them, and they marveled at how thin their moral and social veneers seemed to be (pp. 31–32).

Similarly, the investigators reported that the men's interest in girls deteriorated to the point that "budding romances collapsed" (p. 24). Day-dreams and preoccupations became dominated by thoughts of food. Even though intellectual capacities were not noticeably impaired, the psychological world of these subjects was more and more focused on food.

The intensive preoccupation with food made it difficult for the men to concentrate upon the tasks they had intellectually decided they would work on. If a man tried to study, he soon found himself daydreaming about food. He would think about foods he had eaten in the past; he would muse about opportunities he had missed to eat a certain food when he was at this or that place. Often he would daydream by the hour about the next meal. . . . (p. 32).

Food and topics connected with food acquired almost a sacred halo for the men (Fig. 4.4). Some of these grown men did not mind licking their plates in the presence of others to avoid waste. Some tried to avoid the everlasting topic of food and were disgusted by such behavior. These findings are revealed in the items which the men jotted down in their diaries at different stages of semistarvation. Here are a few of them:

The time between meals has now become a burden. This time is no longer thought of as an opportunity to get those things done which I have to do or want to do. Instead, it's time to be borne, killed until the next meal, which never comes fast enough (p. 19).

It wasn't what the boys did with their food that I didn't like but it was their method. They would coddle it like a baby or handle it and

Fig. 4.4. A starving man's thoughts and fantasies center on food. The drawing epitomizes the findings in the Minnesota semistarvation study during World War II. (Adapted from H. S. Guetzkow and P. H. Bowman, *Men and Hunger.* Elgin, Ill.: Brethren Publishing House, 1946.)

look over it as they would some gold. They played with it like kids making mud pies (p. 20).

This week of starvation found me completely tired practically every day. If they want to get any more work out of me, they're going to have to feed me (p. 20).

Stayed up until 5:00 A.M. last night studying cookbooks. So absorbing I can't stay away from them (p. 21).

During semistarvation the social relationships of the deprived individuals were altered. The facts of deprivation and their common fate produced a new social demarcation which is described in the following summary:

One of the more profound changes which took place was the decreased sociability of the men. There were important exceptions to this, but even the men who managed to continue their social contacts often felt animosity toward strangers, merely because they were strangers. The men built up a tremendous ingroup feeling that tended to exclude both their non-starving friends and the administrative and technical staff. They were apart from others—those who had been fed. They were especially alienated by the individual who supposed he knew what it was like to be hungry because he had gone without food for a couple of days. It was hard to sit near one's comrade who had extra food. They became provoked at the laboratory staff for giving "too much" food to some and thought it criminal to restrict the rations of others, even though they clearly understood the experimental plan demanded such adjustments in rations (p. 30).

Such findings from a controlled study of semistarvation would not be particularly significant if hunger were rare in social life. In an anthropoligical study of the Siriono of Bolivia, who lived constantly in the search for food in a tropical climate ill-suited for food storage, Holmberg (1946) reported many of the same phenomena. The Siriono, he found, worry most about food, daydream about food, and use food as lures for sexual activity. The sick and aged who cannot be useful in obtaining food are not treated with respect, but as liabilities. The magic practiced relates chiefly to food.

Reports by prisoners of war and by expeditions of explorers temporarily isolated from food supplies contain striking reports of preoccupation with food—daydreaming and nights filled with hunger dreams (e.g., Wainwright, 1945).

The significance of these real-life examples for social psychology is obvious. When masses of people are severely deprived, the social situation is also frequently highly unstructured. The dominance of the hunger motive in these circumstances means, first of all, that the hungry will be highly sensitized to information or actual sources that promise to satisfy their needs and at least partially deafened to those irrelevant to them. These circumstances are optimal for the acceptance of any solution to the deprivation, including those made by propaganda and demagoguery, as well as honest ones. The greater effectiveness of attempted propaganda or suggestion in unstructured situations is a major concern in the next section.

10. The More Unstructured the Stimulus Situation, the Greater the Effectiveness of (External) Social Influences (Solutions, Communications, Suggestions) that Offer an Alternative for Psychological Patterning

In brief, this principle states that when the situation or some focal aspect(s) of it lacks objective structure, influences from other people and groups or from mass media of communication are particularly likely to affect the individual's experience and behavior. Conversely, in highly structured situations, efforts to influence the individual are less effective.

When the individual is confronted by clear-cut, sharply defined alternatives, he does discriminate them and act in terms of the stimulus patterns and differences thus discerned. Under clear-cut and circumscribed conditions, the opinion of a majority or a prestige source that contradicts our assessment of the conditions will be relatively ineffective in influencing our behavior. Likewise, as a rule, a person will not fail to heed a glaring traffic light, or remain oblivious to the speed with which his car is moving relative to other cars on an expressway. However, social life is not always composed of series of such clear-cut situations in which the individual has to make clear, split-second decisions correctly. In particular, social life seldom duplicates the simplified laboratory situation wherein the individual's selectivity is circumscribed by instructions, by the arrangement of stimuli, and by facing the simple task of comparing easily discriminable differences between lines, pictures, or statements.

On the contrary, situations in social life are frequently complex, perplexing, and fluid. They often allow alternatives for psychological patterning and behavior in varying degrees. The person is confronted with communications from other people and from the mass media concerning matters that lie far beyond the reach of his immediate assessment of the "facts." To complicate the matter further, as a rule, interested parties who advocate a point of view or a particular stand present the alternatives with a host of trappings that are not readily open for inspection by the intended recipients who might want to verify the facts. It is to the advantage of the interested party to present a problem as highly complex, for his solution is thereby more welcome—as long as the recipient cannot check the facts.

Even in a simple perceptual situation, the persistence of many alternatives in the situation arouses feelings of uncertainty and some unease (Sherif, 1935). Flament (1959) found that as the stimulus situation graded in steps from more to less structured, subjective uncertainty increased. It is no small wonder that in real life, unstructured and fluid conditions that pertain to people's significant concerns are accompanied by considerable uncertainty, a state that is not pleasant (see Proposition 6). Therefore, a major topic of study in social psychology has been the effects of social influence in unstructured, complex, and uncertain situations.

Under conditions lacking objective structure in some focal aspect, the individual becomes increasingly uncertain and suggestibility is increased. In other words, he is more prone to be influenced by the words, actions, or other communications of other individuals, groups, and mass media. When caught in fluid crisis conditions, the individual perceives, feels, moves, and acts in accentuated fashion and in ways that he might not exhibit if he were to weigh the alternatives by himself in isolation. He is increasingly sensitized to the words and deeds of others. In Chapter 6, we shall consider differences between behavior when the individual is alone and with others as the *differential effects* of social situations. Such differential effects are particularly significant in the study of collective interaction (Chapters 7, 23, and 24).

Increased "Suggestibility." As already illustrated in the experiments by Luchins (1945) and Thrasher (1954) and in Fig. 3.9, the effect of words from others or temporary "set" produced by instructions increases as the stimulus structure decreases. One of the earliest systematic studies of this relationship was made by Coffin (1941).

Coffin designed an experiment to study the relationship of suggestibility to the ambiguity of a stimulus situation. Three tonal attributes were selected as representing gradations of stimulus structure: pitch, volume, and a fictitious attribute created for the experiment and labeled "orthosonority." Subjects were presented a tone, and each tonal dimension was defined. Then they were told to equate the succeeding tone heard through their headphones with the original stimulus by turning the appropriate dial which was ostentatiously labeled. Subjects were divided into experimental and control groups. Results showed that the least ambiguous tonal attribute, pitch, was in most cases not subject to change by the experimenter's suggestion that an error had been made. Volume, on the other hand, could be reversed by suggestion with most observers, while judgments of "orthosonority" invariably followed the experimenter's

suggestion. In other words suggestibility to these attributes increased with their ambiguity.

The application of this principle will be particularly important in Chapters 23 and 24 when we discuss collective interaction. It is important to remember that the principle means that whatever the individual differences, "suggestibility" is related to the stimulus situation and is *not,* therefore, a strictly individual attribute.

Spread of Rumors. One of the well-documented effects of being caught in the uncertainty of a fluid situation lacking clear and rational guides for decision and action is the heightened susceptibility to accept rumors, even wild ones. The social psychology of rumor is a specific application of the general principle.

A situation may be unstructured or vague in general or in some aspect. If the particular aspect is one of the major concerns of the group in question, it constitutes a plastic component which may be shaped, crystallized, and standardized in this or that way. A good illustration of this was reported by Ernie Pyle in *Here Is Your War* (1945). When the first convoys left England when the North African offensive was launched against Hitler's forces during World War II, the men on board were kept in the dark as to the *destination* of their journey. They knew they were going into battle service, because other men sailing with them and objects on the boats were clear-cut indications. But the *destination* of their convoy was a matter of conjecture for them. Consequently rumors sprang up which the men came to regard as true until they were contradicted by facts and other rumors.

Of all the spots on earth where rumors run wild, I think a convoy trooper must lead, hands down. Scores of rumors a day floated about the ship. We got so we believed them all, or didn't believe any.

It was rumored we would rendezvous with a big convoy from America; that an aircraft carrier had joined us; that we'd hit Gibraltar in six hours, twenty-four hours, two days; that the ship behind us was the *West Point,* the *Mount Vernon,* the *Monterey;* that we were eighty miles off Portugal, and two hundred miles off Bermuda. None of these turned out to be true.

The rumormongering got so rife that one officer made up a rumor to the effect that we were going to Casablanca, and timed it to see just how long it would take to encircle the ship. It came back to him, as cold fact right from the bridge, in just half an hour (italics ours, pp. 7–8).

Sinha (1952) documented the spread of rumors in a catastrophe in India.

In June 1950, Darjeeling, a beautiful 7000 ft. high hill-station in the Himalayas, with a population of 33,634 (1951 census provisional figure), suffered one of the worst disasters in its history. There had been landslides before, but nothing like this had ever happened. Loss of life and damage to property were heavy and extensive. . . . In the town itself houses collapsed and victims lay buried under the debris. For over two days, rain poured incessantly down the hill slopes which continued to loosen and slide. Collapsed houses and landslides lay across the roads, and mud flowed everywhere. . . .

Over a hundred and fifty persons lost their lives in the district, about thirty of them in the town itself. Over a hundred were injured. More than two hundred houses were damaged, and over 2000 people were rendered homeless. Refugees poured into the town from the outlying districts with tales of woe and misery (p. 200). . . .

Credulity had increased considerably. Statements were mainly believed without any desire to verify them (p. 205).

Observations of people were in the form of "a house had come rolling down" (p. 208). Distorted perceptions were rampant. "People reported, when they first saw Mt. Everest, that 'it had changed its shape,' that 'it appeared higher,' and that 'it was not as tapering and pointed as it used to be.' These cases of distorted perception strengthened and corroborated the rumors" (p. 209).

The process underlying the acceptance and spread of rumors was summarized by Allport and Postman (1965) in their study of rumors during World War II and in experimental studies.

Whenever a stimulus field is of potential importance to an individual, but at the same time unclear, or susceptible of divergent interpretations, a subjective structuring process is started. . . . The process begins at the moment the ambiguous situation is perceived, but the effects are greatest if memory intervenes. The longer the time that elapses after the stimulus is perceived, the greater the . . . change is likely to be. Also, the more people involved in a serial report, the greater the change is likely to be, until the rumor has reached an aphoristic brevity, and is repeated by rote (p. 57, italics in original).

New Guideposts for Feeling and Action Arising in Uncertain Situations. When the individual is confronted by conditions of fluidity and instability, he experiences uncertainty, suspense, and even anxiety. These discomfiting experiences follow logically enough from the proposition that there is a tendency toward psychological patterning (Proposition 6). From this proposition, it follows that over time unstable and fluid situations that defy the individual's attempts to use habitual guidelines for behavior arouse uncertainty even to the point of being painful. Caught in such circumstances, the individual seeks actively to establish some measure of stability. Some authors have referred to these phenomena as "intolerance of ambiguity" (e.g., Frenkel-Brunswik, 1949).

When social life becomes unpredictable and fluid, the individual finds that old and accustomed standards are no longer adequate as guidelines for regulating his experience and his behavior relative to others. When many individuals are caught in this same boat, established standards for behavior are weakened and the ground is fertile for the rise of new guideposts. In Chapters 23 and 24, this proposition is applied to the study of crisis and social movements.

11. Various Factors in the Frame of Reference Have Different Relative Weights

At a given time, the frame of reference for behavior consists of *all* external factors in the context of the situation and also of the internal factors that are operative, such as the person's past experiences in such situations, his motivational state, his attitudes toward salient aspects of the situation, and his conceptual schema for categorizing the objects and events. That is why the factors that count in shaping experience and behavior may not be what immediately catches the eye of an observer. Admittedly, analyzing all of the factors in a situation and their relationships is a formidable task; on the face of it, the job appears insurmountable.

This proposition cuts the task of analyzing the major determinants of behavior to a size that is manageable through research operations. For all practical purposes, we do not have to concentrate *equally* on *all* factors that may affect behavior in order to assess the properties of the psychological pattern and associated behavior. The various factors in the frame of reference at a particular time do not contribute equally. Murphy and Hochberg (1951) made the same point in their theoretical treatment of perceiving; they used terms that refer to sense impressions, and muscular and other impulses of the individual facing a perceptual situation: "Exteroceptive, interoceptive, and proprioceptive components enter fully and on an equal footing, but not always with equal weights, into the dynamics of perception."

In other words, the characteristics of the psychological pattern are determined more heavily by certain factors than by others. By specifying which factors are more weighty, we are in a better position also to assess the role of subsidiary factors. This is because the relationships among the major factors color the operation of others. For convenience, those factors determining the psychological outcome more heavily than others are referred to as *anchors*.

In the psychological literature, there are numerous terms for *anchors*—including *reference points* (for orienting oneself in space, for example) and *standards* (a term used particularly in experiments on judgment). In a specific context, we may apply the term "anchor" to either stimulus factors or internal factors.

The rest of this section will demonstrate the effects of anchors in specific situations. As a first illustration, let us consider research on how we form impressions of other persons. Research on this problem shows clearly that our impression of another person as an individual does not follow a process of summing up all of his features and every aspect of his behavior. On the contrary, as Asch (1946) showed, ". . . some characteristics are discovered to be central. The whole system of relations [among the characteristics] determines which will become central. These set the direction for the further view of the person and for the concretization of the different traits. As a rule the several traits do not have equal weight" (p. 284).

Because certain characteristics or traits are central in forming impressions of other persons, change in these central traits (anchors) "may alter not that aspect alone, but many others—at times all" (p. 284). On the other hand, less central traits take on a different significance depending on their relationship to the anchors: "The envy of a proud man is, for example, seen to have a different basis from the envy of the modest man" (Asch, 1946, p. 284).

When the anchors in forming an impression of a person are fundamental social categories (for example, man or woman, child or adult, rich or poor), the transformation of subsidiary traits is particularly striking (cf. Asch, p. 289). For example, the trait of being "critical" takes on quite a different meaning when applied within such different categories. There are also strictly interpersonal characteristics that function as anchors in our impressions of a person.

Harold Kelley (1950) contributed to the research on how anchoring traits affect impressions of a person in an experiment in which a new instructor was introduced to a university class. He was introduced to all classes in identical terms except for one descriptive characteristic, namely whether he was "warm" or "cold" as an individual. Other traits mentioned included "industrious, critical, punctual and determined." Even though different individuals were assigned the "warm" or "cold" characteristic for different classes, the particular label used served to anchor the students' impressions of the instructor throughout a twenty-minute class discussion. The anchoring effect was shown in their ratings of the instructor afterwards and in the proportions of students who actually took part in the discussion. As you might expect, there was more student participation for the instructor designated as "warm."

Experimental studies on how we perceive and size up things in a situation confronting us also demonstrate anchoring effects. As we have already noted, the perception of a focal stimulus is strikingly affected by the context in which it appears. However, within that context, certain aspects of the stimulus pattern are typically selected by the person as cues or standards. For example, the picture of the locomotive shown in Fig. 4.5a was presented to subjects who were asked to report on its length. Their estimates varied between 20 and 30 feet. But when

Fig. 4.5b was presented, their reports shrank to 10–15 feet. In the second figure, the size of the man served as the anchor in perceiving the locomotive. Figure 4.6 presents a similar picture with a different object.

Anchorages (Reference Points) in Judgment

For more exacting assessment of anchors, it is instructive to consider some research findings on judgments of stimuli that form a series along some dimension—such as length, weight, pleasantness-unpleasantness (e.g., of odors), or acceptability-unacceptability. There is considerable literature on judgment with reference to physical properties of stimuli—that is, *psychophysical* judgments. The advantage of such judgment studies is that anchoring effects can be measured relative to a series of stimuli having definite objective values, or at least an objective order, with respect to some dimension or characteristic.

For example, judgments such as "early," "late," "near," or "far" are invariably made relative to some reference point in time or space, whether this anchor is made explicit or not. If we know the reference point relative to which the person is "early" or "late," we have an exact basis for determining what "early" or "late" means to him. Similarly, when a person says that someplace is "near" or "far," it is near or far to him with reference to a given location and his means of travel, whether these are made explicit or not. All such judgments are relative to reference points that anchor the range within which a judgment is made.

Culturally Provided Anchorages

The effect of anchors in the experience and judgment of time can be shown readily through anthropological findings about societies that do not have modern calendars. In some cultures the periodicity of work and market days provide the anchors for reckoning time. The market day, when ordinary work stops for trading with neighboring communities, is the main anchor, with events being located between these days. The Wagiriama of British East Africa had a market day every four days. Consequently

their anchors for time were within a "week" consisting of four days, each with a name. Other groups in Central Africa had similar basis for time reckoning, although the "week" varied from three to ten days.

The Andamanese, on the other hand, used odors as reference points for time. The anthropologist Radcliffe-Brown, who reported this unusual basis for time standards, explained it in the following words:

In the jungles of Andamans it is possible to recognize a distinct succession of odors during a considerable part of the year as one after another the commoner trees and lianas come into flower. . . . The Andamanese have therefore adopted an original method of marking the different periods of the year by means of the odiferous flowers that are in bloom at different times. *Their calendar is a calendar of scents* (1922, pp. 311 f.).

Such natural phenomena and their periodicity also serve as anchors for our own experience of time, but members of societies with formal calendars typically rely more on "what the calendar says." Reliance on anchors both from the natural environment and a man-made calendar becomes evident, however, in the following illustration:

Some American Indian groups devised calendars based on the lunar month, which did not take into account the discrepancy between twelve lunar months and one solar year. As a result, after a time, an annual celebration would fall in the "wrong" month. The "error" would be corrected by lengthening a month or adding a period for the year in question, but the conflict between the two sources of anchoring points had psychological consequences: "That the discrepancy was felt was shown by frequent reference in the literature of the Indians to discussion and quarrels about which month it is or ought to be at a given time. The arguments apparently continue in such cases until, through a comparison with the natural phenomena, matters are set right" (Cope, 1919, p. 137).

When the means of transportation are primitive and standard units of distance and time are lacking, the psychological importance of anchors in estimating distance becomes immediately evident. For example, what is a "short" or "long" distance to a Turkish villager whose village is isolated

Fig. 4.5a.   How big is the locomotive?

from modern technology? In a study conducted by the senior author and his students in the 1940s, such a villager referred to distances under three kilometers or so as "within a bullet's reach," or "as far as my voice can go," or "as far as [it takes] to smoke a cigarette." Long distances were typically referred to in terms of the effort involved: "You start early in the morning and reach there by sunset;" "You reach there [by the time] you work on crops of one dönum (of land)."

Such experiences of distance were dependent upon how the trip had been made, usually on foot. Those villagers who had made the trip by bus or train referred to long distances in terms of how many days and nights were spent on the vehicle. However, these experiences were not translatable in terms of their ordinary anchors based on walking time. As a result, there were great discrepancies between experience of some distances and the precise measurement of the distance. For example, in one village some residents who had traveled during military service considered a neighboring town more distant than Istanbul, which was objectively almost twice as far. There was a simple explanation: they had to walk to the neighboring village while they had been to Istanbul only by train. In another village, more remote from Istanbul, those men who had served in World War I in Galicia (now Poland) regarded it as "nearer" than Istanbul. They had walked all

the way to Istanbul and gone to Galicia by train, a distance of nearly a thousand miles.

In short, the cultural repertory and the person's experiences as a member of that culture provide anchors for his estimates of such basic human experiences as the passage of time and the conception of space.

Anchoring Effects in
Laboratory Studies of Judgment

As noted above, the language developed in the judgment laboratory lends considerable precision to the discussion of anchoring effects. We shall consider some of the findings from the laboratory that have particular importance for later discussions of the individual's attitudes as anchors for his experience (Chapter 15) and of the individual's reference groups (Chapter 18). The most productive work on the effects of "significant others" in shaping the individual's attitude and on the effects of attitude in perceiving and judging has been a direct descendant of the experimental study of judgment, both historically and theoretically.

An important concept in the laboratory study of judgment is "the relativity of judgment." This concept does not mean that judgment is a whimsical or arbitrary process governed solely by the individual. On the contrary, it refers to the fact that judgment of a particular object is always made with reference to other objects in the stimulus field or to such objects experienced in

Fig. 4.5b. Now how big is the locomotive? (Photographs courtesy of B. Jack White.)

the past. Examples of this general fact were given in Fig. 4.5 and 4.6.

In the classical work on psychophysics, the usual practice was to present the person with a standard stimulus of some known value to be used in comparing the stimuli presented for judgment. The experimenters who dropped this practice, partly to save time to be sure, made an important discovery: After a little experience with a series of stimuli (e.g., weights, tones, or lines) the subject was able to place them fairly consistently even though he was given no explicit standard stimulus. The technique of presenting stimuli serially without an explicit standard was called, variously, the "method of single stimuli" or the "absolute method." (Ironically, despite these labels, research using this method has shown most convincingly that our judgments of single stimuli are invariably influenced by their context, and that judgment is not absolute but a relative affair.)

What happens when the individual judges a series of stimuli, one at a time and several times over? At first, he makes many mistakes, of course. But over time, he becomes able to locate each stimulus relative to the others with fair accuracy by using categories or labels that the experimenter has instructed him to use, or by devising his own labels. Psychologically, he establishes a *reference scale* for *gauging* any particular stimulus as heavy or light, high or low, loud or soft. Much research has been done on

the determinants of such reference scales, particularly on sources of systematic errors in judgment. Here we shall consider only representative work that illustrates major determinants of reference scales particularly applicable in social psychology.

A major determinant in the formation of a reference scale is simply the *range of stimuli* presented to the person for judgment (Volkmann, 1951). We can immediately see that this fact is important in social psychology: A person who has experienced only one-story houses, travel by donkey, and time units in terms of work done with primitive tools will not have established reference scales appropriate for judging size, speed, or time in New York City. Conversely, a person who has lived all of his life in comfortable surroundings with plenty of food and warm clothing may not have appropriate categories for judging the plight of a peasant during a famine. In studies of lifted weights, Tresselt (1947, 1948) has shown that the *amount* of practice we have with a particular range of stimuli increases its effects on our judgments of new stimuli.

Suppose that a reference scale is established through practice and then the person suddenly confronts a new series of stimuli differing from the range he has learned. Wever and Zener (1928) established a reference scale for judging five weights between 84 and 100 grams, then suddenly introduced a "heavy" series ranging between 92 and 108 grams. "The effect of the first series on the judgments of the second was quite evident for 20 or 25 presentations, i.e. for four or five rounds judgments of the 'heavy' predominated for all the stimuli; from this point on, however, the judgments showed a redistribution conforming to the second stimulus series."

In other words, when the person's reference scale was established with the lighter series, a particular weight (e.g., 96 grams) was judged as "heavy." The introduction of the heavier series produced a general shift in judgment towards "heavy" for all of the stimuli, but then a new reference scale was established in which the same weight (96 grams) was judged as "light." This example is a good illustration of how a particular stimulus takes its "membership character" from its entire context.

How does the individual adjust his reference scale to conform to a change in the stimulus series? Typically, he first singles out the two most extreme stimuli and gauges his judgments of others accordingly (Volkmann, 1951). In other words, within a series of stimuli, certain stimuli are more weighty than others in establishing and controlling the reference scale. In particular, the extreme values serve as *end anchors* for the reference scale. One result is that (in using the method of single stimuli) errors in judgment of the end stimuli are smaller than those of the items intermediate to them.

Even if the stimulus series does not range objectively from one extreme to another, as in a series of different hues in the color spectrum, end anchors can be produced by instructions to use the smallest category number for one hue and the largest for another (Eriksen and Hake, 1957). The significance of *end anchors* in social psychology was shown by Fehrer (1952) by comparing judgments of statements on a social issue when extreme positions were represented and when they were removed. She found that judgment of a statement presenting an intermediate position differed, depending on whether the extreme positions were present or not.

Assimilation-Contrast Effects
Governed by Anchor-Scale Relationship

Extreme or end stimuli in a series are not the only source of anchors for experience.

In other laboratory methods for studying judgment, it is customary to present a standard stimulus of a given value to which the subject can compare each stimulus he is to judge. When that standard is in about the middle of the series of stimuli, the effect is to increase accuracy of judgment for stimuli near the middle. Volkmann's work at Mt. Holyoke College is most informative on effects of such anchor stimuli. By systematically varying the location of standard stimuli for judgments of visual inclinations and estimates of number of dots, he showed that the effect of an anchor within a series of stimuli was to reduce error of judgment for other stimuli within a nearby range but to *increase* error beyond that range. These errors consisted of *over*estimating stimuli smaller than the anchor and underestimating stimuli larger than the anchor. Such systematic shifts in judgment *toward* an anchor value are called an *assimilation effect*. They have also been noted in judgment studies in which other stimuli were used, including lifted weights.

Suppose, however, that with every stimulus to be judged the subject is given another stimulus that is much greater or much smaller than any of those he is judging. Whether he is instructed to use this discrepant stimulus as a standard or not, its frequent presentation to him does affect his judgments. Such anchors located considerably outside of the person's reference scale produce a shift in judgments *away from* the anchor, that is, a *contrast effect*. For example, if the subject continues to use the same categories for judgment that he had before the anchor was introduced, his judgments will all begin to collect in those categories most discrepant from the anchor. Or, if it is possible, he will add new categories away from the anchor, shifting his entire reference scale away from it in time (White, 1960).

In short, the way that we size up a particular object or event is not an absolute affair: our appraisal varies systematically according to the relationships among at least the following: (1) the range of the set or series of stimuli we are judging; (2) the presence or absence of end anchors; (3) the categories of the reference scale that we have previously established; (4) how strongly that reference scale is established;

Fig. 4.6a. How big is the boat? At first, a quick glance suggests that the picture is an aerial view of an ocean liner, but look at the boat's superstructure. (Bill Ray, LIFE Magazine © Time Inc.)

and (5) the values of other stimuli presented frequently or saliently as the background of the items to be judged.

Our definition of anchorages can now become more precise. In any given instance, all of the stimuli and past experiences of the person that compose the frame of reference will not have equal weight. Those that contribute more to the psychological pattern are termed *anchors*. In analysis of specific situations, it has sometimes proved feasible to estimate the relative weights of different factors to predict the outcome of an experiment (Johnson, 1955). For example, Helson (1964) found that he could predict judgments of lifted weights through a formula that weighted the anchor stimulus (standard or background) about twice as much as the average (geometric mean) of six stimuli judged. His formula expresses the "adaptation level" of the organism at the time as a *product* of the weighted geometric mean of the series stimuli, the value of the anchor appropriately weighted, and a

residual term referring to past experience and individual factors.

Hunt (1941) had subjects judge the intelligence of children (on the basis of their photographs), modern paintings, and the seriousness of various crimes. Then he told the subjects to imagine a representative of each series that was more intelligent, or more beautiful, or more serious than any they had judged. He found systematic displacements in their judgments. In general, these shifts were contrast effects, that is, the experimental items were judged as less intelligent, less beautiful, or less serious, as the case may be. The reverse effect was found when the internal anchor was below the series; the judgments shifting to *more* intelligent, etc. However, because the stimulus items were complex, the subject's selectivity sometimes resulted in a shift in the other direction (toward the anchor): "Keeping in mind the least intelligent child he had ever seen would raise O's judgments of most of the pictures, until he suddenly

Fig. 4.6b.   Which car do you prefer? (*Light and Vision* © 1966, Time-Life Books ©
Time Inc.)

noticed that one of the children in some
way resembled the unintelligent child he
had in mind. Then this child would be
judged as much less intelligent than previously" (p. 301).

The importance of internal anchors in
social psychology will become clear if we
consider briefly the *psychosocial* scales to
which they are related (Sherif and Hovland,
1961; Sherif, Sherif, and Nebergall, 1965).

**Psychosocial and
Psychophysical Scales**

In the study of psychophysics, the stimulus dimension judged is usually a physical
dimension, such as size, weight, slant,
color, or pitch. In social psychology, it is
not always possible to find a physical dimension that is clearly relevant to our social judgments, although there are important exceptions such as the weight of one's
body, the quantity of money one has, the
speed one is going, and so on. When no

physical dimension is clearly relevant, we
study judgment in relation to prevailing *psychosocial* scales, that is, prevailing orders
or schemes established in social life by
virtue of the modes of living, of work, and of
social processes among people. For example, the varying social distances at which
members of one group keep members of
other groups constitute a psychosocial
scale for assessing the intimacy that one
wishes to have with a member of a particular group.

Psychosocial scales and internal anchors
related to them typically involve a dimension that is of minor importance in the psychophysical laboratory: an evaluative
dimension. While the subject in a weight-
lifting experiment ordinarily has no preference for one weight over another, a girl
judging her own weight may have strong
feelings about what constitutes overweight
or underweight. These evaluative categories
may affect her reactions at losing or gaining
half a pound.

Fig. 4.6c.   Here is the car in the foreground of Fig. 4.6b parked adjacent to the one in the background. In Fig. 4.6b the small car is 16 yards away, but the width of the white line suggests much greater distance between the two. (*Light and Vision* © 1966, Time-Life Books © Time Inc.)

Quite similar trends were reported by Hinckley and Rethlingshafer (1951), who studied judgments of the heights of men. The objective fact of extreme human heights anchored the judgments. Extremes in height were not displaced, but within the "average" range of height, the authors concluded that "the judgment of the average height of all men is influenced by judgment of the height of the man making the judgment. The 'meaning' of the social value terms of 'short' and 'tall' is in part determined by the height of the judge" (p. 262). The tendency to use one's self as an anchor in assessing others was also found in a study of "How fat is fat?", in which similarity between the person and those he judged was found to affect judgment (Fillenbaum, 1961).

Attitudes serve as *internal anchors* when we encounter events relevant to them, whether the significant others are present or not. Modern clinical psychologists are investigating how a person arrives at judgments of personality and/or abnormality.

They are finding that the categories in the clinician's reference scale, as well as anchor stimuli (a "typical case," for example), affect clinical judgment in predictable ways, just as they do judgments of other stimuli (Bieri *et al.,* 1966).

We tend to assess ourselves in terms of our standing with significant others. In fact, a whole research literature on how we judge our standing relative to others, our elation or disappointment at personal accomplishments or failures, our feelings of satisfaction with the wages we receive, and our contentment or dissatisfaction with our associates stems directly from the work on anchor effects in judgment. We shall review this literature in Chapters 15, 17, and 18, which concern attitudes, ego-involvement, and reference groups.

12. Human Psychological Functioning Is Typically on the Conceptual Level

If the impact of formal language on perceiving, judging, or thinking were the only matter of significance, we would not need a special proposition such as this present one. The proposition holds, in brief, that the processes underlying human behavior differ from those of subhuman animals because of man's unique capacity for conceptual functioning. Note that the word "symbolic" was not used, but rather *conceptual.* Some infrahuman species use gesture and sounds symbolically and many respond to objects symbolically. However, these symbolic behaviors are so closely tied to immediate situations and social relations that they are aptly called "perceptually symbolic." Only man as a species has the capacity for formulating generalizations and rules that *regulate and guide behavior from within* and that *order experience both hierarchically and in time.*

Briefly, a symbol is any object, event, or action that comes in time to "stand for" others, in the sense that it arouses behavior originally associated with the others. *Perceptually* symbolic refers to behavior aroused by symbols in the stimulus context (or some aspect of it) in which the symbolic connection was formed or follows very soon in the sequence. *Conceptually* symbolic refers to symbolic behavior occurring and persisting in the absence of the original stimulus context, both in space and time, and in novel situations. Man's capacities for conceptually symbolic behavior permit him to utilize and manipulate symbols in the absence of stimuli originally associated with them and over time spans of months or years.

Ironically, the great synthesis of facts represented by evolutionary theory led some theorists to conclude that a science of human behavior and social relations could be built through direct analogy with findings about other species. The error in this view becomes most evident when such theorists concern themselves with problems important in social psychology: leader-follower relations, role relations, conformity and deviation, the formation and change of attitudes, and especially the motives that prompt man in his friendly or hostile relationships with other groups.

For example, the leader-follower or hostile relations in a human group have been compared with the "dominance hierarchy"

or "pecking order" within a flock of barnyard fowls, wherein fowl A pecks B and all others, but is not pecked by them; B pecks C and all others except A; C pecks D and all others except A and B, and so on. This particular analogy does not even take into account that social relations among some monkeys, much higher on the evolutionary scale than fowls, cannot be described adequately on the basis of dominance-submission schemes, as Carpenter (1964) found. T. C. Schneirla has emphasized that the analogy from fowl to primates is not warranted among those monkeys that *do* develop a dominance hierarchy, owing to the much greater complexity of its origin and variations (Schneirla, 1946, 1951). In human children, many dimensions affect status in interpersonal relations. The hierarchy of status does not resemble a "pecking order" at all (cf. Hanfman, 1963).

It is correct that animals other than man use symbols, do communicate symbolically through sound and gesture, do generalize from past experience, and do have relations with one another. It is equally true, however, that there are wide differences in capacities to do these things among the species.

Consider Fig. 4.7. In studies of discrimination and generalization, chimpanzees were trained to make a certain response to the top triangle, but not to other forms. To test the transfer of this response to other triangles, Cards 1, 2, and 3 were presented. The chimpanzees made the response to Cards 1 and 2, indicating a generalization, but not to Card 3. A two-year-old child, however, does perceive Card 3 as "triangular" (even though very few two-year-olds know the word triangle) and responds to it accordingly.

This finding illustrates that there are *differences* between chimpanzee and human functioning even when the learning of conventional language is far from achieved. Let us suppose, however, that we had done an experiment in which the chimpanzee and the child had performed in the same way. Would we then be justified in assuming that the same factors were responsible for the outcome? Schneirla (1946, 1951) of the American Museum of Natural History has performed a great service by spelling out

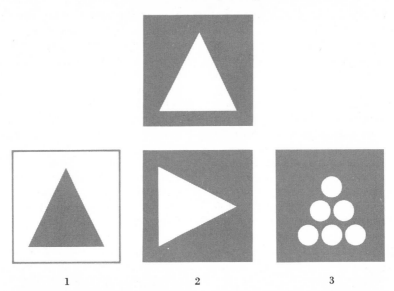

1   2   3

Fig. 4.7.   Triangularity that is equivalent for a child but not a chimpanzee. The top triangle is the training figure. After training to discriminate the top triangle, a chimpanzee responds to test figures 1 and 2 as equivalent, but not to test figure 3. A two-year-old child also responds to figure 3 as triangular. (From D. O. Hebb, *A Textbook of Psychology*. Philadelphia: W. B. Saunders, 1966, p. 37, Fig. 14.)

some of the pitfalls of analyzing human behavior through uncritical analogy with the behavior of subhuman animals.

The first pitfall is the assumption that *similar behaviors or behaviors with similar outcomes by members of different species are produced by the same set of factors.* His own studies of certain army ants illustrate the point. These ants live in tropical forests. Each day they organize into highly complex swarms, often larger than 15 yards wide and composed of more than 30,000 ants. The swarm moves as a unified body in a single direction, with its subunits engaging in alternating flanking movements. The sight looks for all the world like a vast, organized army under some central control or instruction. Through studies of these maneuvers in the field and laboratory experimentation, Schneirla showed that the underlying processes were very simple, requiring no elaborate assumptions about symbolic communication among the ants or central control. The maneuvers depend on simple reactions to chemical and tactual stimuli encountered in the richly varied tropical environment. The reactions are relayed successively through the swarm by contact. In the homogeneous environment

of the laboratory (e.g., on sheets of paper), the same process resulted simply in an endless circling movement of the swarm.

The second pitfall is assuming that *complexity of behavior is the main difference between the species.* As indicated above, the army ant maneuvers are highly complex, but the capacities of individuals are very simple. The social life of bees is much simpler than that of man, yet the dances by which a honey bee transmits both location and distance of food are complex. The cues conveyed are difficult for a human observer to interpret. Indeed, speaking the phrase "Honey in Mr. Smith's apple tree half a mile across the meadow" may be simpler as a motor action than the bee's dance. The error in going by simplicity or complexity of behavior is that it assumes corresponding simplicity or complexity of underlying process.

The third pitfall in analogy from animal to human levels is the assumption that *degree of adaptation to the environment is a valid test for similarity of process or capacity.* "A large group of 'tent caterpillars,' reassembled each night within its enclosure of silken threads spun on a tree, may be as relatively successful at surviving in its environment as human inhabitants of a nearby settlement are in theirs, notwithstanding the far greater total and greater variety of sensory impressions received by members of the human group from their surroundings" (Schneirla, 1966, p. 56). This pitfall is particularly treacherous when adaptation to the human environment is, in fact, a product of human interaction. Without the capacity to function conceptually, man could not interact with his fellows to produce language, culturally shared gestures, cultural values, tools that are constructed and stored for use—all transmitted from generation to generation. At least a part of man's problems in adaptation, therefore, are problems ultimately based on capacities for conceptual functioning that enable him to transform his physical environment and to create a culture.

Conceptual Functioning and Learning

The following is a digest of the effects of conceptual functioning on conditioning and extinction by A. R. Luria (1961), who surveyed research on the topic in the U.S.S.R. In the classical conditioning experiments of Pavlov, an animal was presented with a stimulus (e.g., food) that aroused a relatively invariant response (e.g., salivation by a hungry animal). This "unconditioned stimulus" (food) was paired with some other stimulus that ordinarily would not arouse the response, for example, a light or bell. This was the conditional stimulus. Ordinarily, the conditional stimulus would appear with or slightly before the unconditioned stimulus. With invariant recurrence of this stimulus sequence, the animal would come to make the response to the conditional stimulus. Thus a "temporary link" was established.

Early in the process of developing a new "temporary link," the elimination of the unconditioned stimulus "invariably means the extinction and rapid disappearance of the link" (pp. 42–43). After becoming firmly established, its extinction occurs gradually over time. Furthermore, if a link is firmly established, it is very difficult to change the sequence or substitute different conditional stimuli. "According to Pavlov, reshaping a system of conditioned reflexes in animals

often means [that] every firmly established link . . . [has] to be remade all over again by means of various fresh reinforcements" (p. 32). The entire process, it may be emphasized, involves "concrete signals" and their visual properties. (In other words, the symbolism is tied to perceptual situations.)

On the basic laws of conditioning, Luria wrote:

That these laws are fundamental is beyond doubt, however . . . none of them applies in full force when we come to analyzing the process of the formation of new temporary links in human beings. Here the fact that any process of establishing new links uses as intermediary other links based on speech . . . plays the decisive part. These are the links that are incorporated into man's orienting activity, that abstract and systematize the signals acting on the organism, and inhibits its direct-impulse reactions. This process *creates a new information-system within which each signal presented to the subject now operates* (pp. 43–44).

According to Luria, as soon as this new "information system" enters, the "laws" of conditioning have to be modified considerably. He cites experiments to show that this is already the case by the age of about three-and-a-half, not an age when the child is a sophisticated speaker of French or English or Russian. By about four-and-a-half or five, he reports, the conditioning process takes on all the characteristics of "conscious systematic activity" mediated inwardly by conceptual process (p. 47).

Let us find from Luria what the difference between the animal learner and the human learner is in the conditioning experiment:

If a child of school age, or an adult, is subjected to a given neutral stimulus, such as a red light, accompanied by a reinforcement . . . and if he is then presented with another light (say yellow) unaccompanied by reinforcement, we see that his behavior is never as immediate as that of animals. In a young child, the presentation of the second and differently colored signal evokes the natural question: "Shall I press for that one too?"; in an adult it at once arouses a verbal generalization formulated in inward speech as a hypothetical rule: "I am to press for a red light and not to press for a yellow;" or "I am to press for a light of any color." This adoption of a verbal rule at once modifies the nature of all subsequent reactions. Once taken into the system of verbally formulated links, the stimulus in question becomes not a mere signal but *an item* of generalized information, and all subsequent reactions depend more on the system it is taken into than on its physical properties (p. 44).

Whereas temporary links evolve gradually in animals, in man they are as a rule formed at once by incorporating the given signal into or excluding it from an existing system of reactions. . . . Whereas in animals eliminating the reinforcement means the gradual extinction of the link established, no such phenomenon is observed in man; having formulated a given rule, man no longer needs the constant external reinforcement (p. 45).

In order to change the conditioned link for school children and adults, all that is necessary is instructions to follow a new rule. Further, Luria notes, the signals that can be used to establish the links in man are much less concrete, both perceptually and in time.

We have deliberately emphasized the differences in conditioning animals and humans because most psychologists today would agree that it is one of the simplest models of learning. Turning to more complex learning and problem solving, the role of conceptual functioning in man becomes even more important. A great deal of learning by the human child involves learning schemes of verbal rules. It is not essential that he have first-hand experience with all of the objects and persons that these rules pertain to.

The implications of conceptual functioning are not, however, confined to learning. Studies of child development have shown that the development of integrated patterns of motor activity in the performance of tasks and their self-regulation by the child, as opposed to adult commands, are dependent upon conceptual attainment. Figure 4.8 shows the pattern of reactions by a three-and-a-half year old child in an experiment by Tikhomirov (Luria, 1961, pp. 86–88). The child was to press a rubber ball twice when a light appeared, the appearance of the light being indicated in the figure on the line below the polygraph tracing. As the figure shows, the instruction to press twice, which the child could understand, produced only occasionally correct response (upper figure). When the child said "go! go!" each time the light appeared (middle), the response became consistent (until the end when "go! go! go!" is the self instruction).

The bottom graph compares the three situations. Older children, even without saying "go! go!" can perform this task at will with one instruction, for the sequence becomes regulated inwardly by conceptual means.

Of course, the conceptual functioning of which we speak is dependent in the first place upon a normal human brain. This fact becomes evident in studies of brain injury or malignancy. Brain lesions may produce a wide variety of symptoms, including loss of speech, loss of motor functions, inability to name objects correctly, and so on. Probably the most common notion about injury to the frontal lobes, however, is that only complex motor function or intellectual capacity is curtailed. As the frontal lobes are known to be involved in man's conceptual capacities, it is particularly interesting that in some cases conventional use of language and speech may be retained while organized forms of perception and discrimination are severely disrupted.

For example, in looking at the reversible figures of Rubin shown in Fig. 3.6, one brain-injured patient saw the goblets, but did not see the faces after five minutes of examining the figure attentively. When asked if he could see faces and, two minutes later, whether there were any black faces, he continued to see only the goblet. Only after ten minutes of looking at the figure did he finally say, "Yes, if you look at it closely you can see two black faces, looking at each other" (Luria, 1966, p. 492).

It was findings such as these that led Luria to conclude as follows:

Observations have shown that patients with frontal lesions have no difficulty fixing their gaze on the strong components of a visual structure, and they readily submit to the influence of direct impressions. However, the task of analyzing the information obtained, of subordinating the trend of their searches to verbal instruction and, if need be, of overcoming the effect of a directly perceived visual structure, proves impossible for these patients. . . . These facts suggest that the frontal lobes take part in the organization of the process of perception just as clearly as they take part in the organization of movement or of more complex mental processes. They demonstrate that the view that in frontal lobe lesions only complex forms of movement or intellectual activity are impaired, whereas perception remains intact, is profoundly misleading (pp. 528–529).

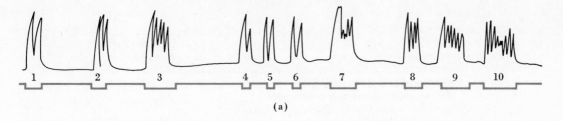

(a)

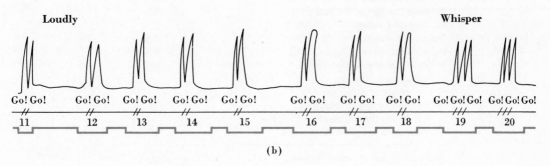

(b)

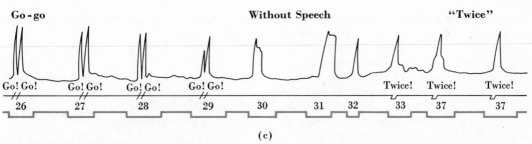

(c)

Fig. 4.8. Tracings of simple muscular reaction (pressing) by young child (a) **upon instructions** to "press twice" and (b) when saying "go-go!" upon seeing stimulus light. Only tracings with two peaks represent the correct response. Note (c) that cessation of verbal response disrupts correct pattern, while speaking "twice" results in only one peak for the 3½-year-old subject. (From A. R. Luria, *The Role of Speech in Regulation of Normal and Abnormal Behavior.* © 1961, Pergamon Press, Ltd. Permission of Liveright Publishing, New York, pp. 88–89, Fig. 14.)

In other words, man's capacity for conceptual functioning is basic even to the integrated forms of perception and movement that are ordinarily considered elementary and basic in normal adaptation to the environment. The logical conclusion would seem to be, then, that the "mediating factors" or "mediating processes" to which psychologists refer should be formulated as a basic proposition about man's psychological functioning.

In human development, the gradual attainment of some kind of conventional language is crucial. The process of arriving at systematic forms of reasoning identified with "logical thought" are even more prolonged. Investigations of the development of abstract conceptions such as time, space, and motion (Fraisse, 1963) and logical thought (Inhelder and Piaget, 1964) show that these "intellectual" or cognitive functions are rooted in the affective interchanges between an active human organism and an environment that is sociocultural as well as physical. The prolonged experiences necessary for abstract concepts of time are suggested in Table 4.1, which summarizes a large amount of research on children's reference to past and future.

In almost any children's play group that continues for any length of time, social interaction in meaningful activities produces novel generalizations, rules, and names for communicating these constructs. The formation of social norms is thus rooted in man's conceptual functioning, as we

Table 4.1.

	Age of Child When He Can:
Recognize a special day of the week, such as Sunday	4 years old
Tell whether it is morning or afternoon	5
Use the words "yesterday" and "tomorrow" with their true meaning	5
Indicate the day of the week	6
Indicate the month	7
Indicate the season	7–8
Indicate the year	8
Indicate the day of the month	8–9
Estimate the duration:	
a. of a conversation	
b. "since the holidays"	12
c. "until the holidays"	
Give the time to within 20 minutes	12

Source: Adapted from Fraisse, P. (1963), *The Psychology of Time.* New York: Harper & Row, p. 180.

shall see in Chapters 10 and 14: Man is not only a learner of conventional concepts; in interaction with his fellows, he is also their creator. This fact has to be considered of major importance in social psychology, which must be concerned not only with the child's socialization in conventional society, but with social innovation and change as well.

We find among those transacting their business daily in groups, people who do not feel a part of these groups, and who derive their sense of worth, their beliefs on various topics, their styles, and their preferences from other people who are *not* present in their immediate environment. They belong to a group in fact, but refer themselves, psychologically, to other groups—their reference groups. The phenomena associated with reference groups are incomprehensible without the proposition that man functions on a conceptual level. These phenomena, to be discussed in Chapters 18 and 19, are distinctly human. John Paul Scott (1953), an expert on animal behavior, came to this conclusion in his survey of research on infrahuman social behavior.

. . . the problem of reference groups as studied by Sherif is one which is not ordinarily met with in animal societies, because the typical animal under natural conditions tends to be a part of one primary group throughout life and there are no verbal standards of behavior for such groups (Scott, p. 69).

In short, man's conceptual functioning is so basic to all of his social behavior that a human social psychology is impossible without a proposition such as this one.

5

Individual-Group Relationship as a Part-Whole Problem

Major Topics of the Chapter

Guidelines from the propositions for the part-whole problem

The problem in scientific analysis

Historical controversy over individual vs. group

Resolving the controversy in psychology and social science

Part-whole relationships in perception, judgment, and other cognitive processes

Relationships are as real as constituent parts

Implications for research in social psychology

Indications of individual-group relationship from perception, judgment, and other cognitive processes

87

SEARCH FOR APPROPRIATE RESEARCH STRATEGY

In the preceding chapters, a minimum set of essential propositions has been stated, illustrated, and discussed. These propositions are cornerstones for building the integrative interactionist approach to social psychology. It remains to proceed on this basis to the specific topics in appropriate chapters. It will be helpful now to look back over the propositions for their general implications that can guide us through the various topics.

The first implication is a guideline for a core problem in social psychology and, for that matter, for much of social science: namely, the relationship between the individual and the group. No matter what topic we consider in social psychology—social influence, communication, group or intergroup relations, self concept or attitude— the assumptions we have about the individual-group (culture, society) relationship are bound to shape what we include in our studies, what variables are accentuated and which are neglected, and how we conceptualize our findings. Therefore, an orientation to this core problem, derived from the factually based propositions, will be useful throughout.

Second, we shall draw inferences from the propositions to guide us toward research methods and techniques appropriate in the study of various topics in social psychology.

The Part-Whole Problem with Reference to the Individual-Group Relationship

The controversy over the relative contribution of the individual and of the group or culture in shaping human relations has been perennial in social science and in ideological controversies. One characteristic way of handling this problem has been to assume either the primacy of the individual *or* the primacy of the group before analyzing their relationship. Naturally, such an *a priori* decision to make supreme either the individual *or* the group affects selectivity in choice of facts that support the position. In scientific study there is no place for unsupported assumptions on a question

so basic to all of the problems to be studied.

The propositions and principles presented in this Part were based on research findings and, therefore, provide a sounder basis for analysis of the individual-group relationship. Controversies over whether individual *or* group is the primary determinant are futile. The individual is not an isolated island, either in development or in day-to-day coping with the environment. The proposition that experience and behavior are patterned jointly by internal and external factors means that behavior makes sense only in relation to the web of interpersonal and group relations in which the individual moves and finds his being.

On the other hand, the concrete events and trends in groups and societies cannot be completely analyzed without reference to the individuals who take part as active agents in them. Many social scientists state, and rightly, that social science principles must deal with regularities in human affairs, not individual actors. It is quite another thing to conclude from this that group and social processes can be adequately understood without any reference to the individuals who participate in them.

The implications of the basic propositions can be seen more clearly if we word the problem differently. The perennial problem of the individual-group relationship is an example of a more general problem in all science: the problem of the relationship between wholes or systems and their ingredient parts. Let us look at the problem from that point of view.

Modern science is well aware of the hazards of studying a unit extracted from the system in which it is a part, whether the unit is an organism, a body organ, or a carbon atom. The unit has properties or characteristics of its own, when considered by itself, but these characteristics and unit functioning change according to the system of which the unit is part. Social philosophers were long aware of the membership character of the individual in varying social contexts. In a somewhat more scientific manner, writers in the early days of social science presented numerous examples of the effects of social systems or specific contexts on individual experience and behavior. The French sociologist Durkheim

(1893, 1933 edition; 1895, 1938 edition) collected empirical evidence to demonstrate that the forms, trends, and innovations in social life have regularities that cannot be explained in terms of the properties of individual functioning. He showed that social systems have definite consequences for individuals belonging to them.

One of the writers most influential in molding the tone of American sociology, George Herbert Mead (1934), stated the problem of the individual-group relationship in terms of the impact of the whole (group) on its parts (individual) in the following words:

We are not, in social psychology, building up the behavior of the social group in terms of the behavior of the separate individuals composing it; rather, we are starting out with a given social whole of complex group activity, into which we analyze (as elements) the behavior of each of the separate individuals composing it. We attempt, that is, to explain the conduct of the individual in terms of the organized conduct of the social group, rather than to account for the organized conduct of the social group in terms of the conduct of the separate individuals belonging to it. For social psychology, the whole (society) is prior to the part (the individual), not the part to the whole; and the part is explained in terms of the whole, not the whole in terms of the part or parts. The social act is not explained by building it up out of stimulus plus response; it must be taken as a dynamic whole—as something going on—no part of which can be considered or understood by itself—a complex organic process implied by each individual stimulus and response involved in it (p. 7).

When Durkheim and Mead wrote, the mainstream of academic psychology was pursuing a tack quite inimical to accommodating the kind of facts such men pointed to. On the contrary, academic psychology was, on the whole, looking for elements of mental life ("sensations," images, etc.) or elements of motor activity (reflexes) in the attempt to find laws for their compounding or association. It was hoped that the study of "elements" would provide a basis for complex "higher processes" and activity. Meanwhile, it was not surprising that some social scientists disclaimed such "psychology" for understanding group and collective process. If *that* was what "psychology" was, they understandably could not see its relevance to their problems.

Some of them, for example, the French sociologist Blondel, proposed that individual psychology had to be supplemented by "group psychology" or "collective psychology." George Herbert Mead made it quite explicit that the "social act" and "social behaviorism" in which he was interested had nothing in common with the elementistic analysis of the early behaviorists in psychology such as Watson and F. H. Allport in 1924 and 1933.

Today it is obvious that the part-whole relationship cannot be analyzed satisfactorily by proposing one psychology for the individual when he is alone and another psychology for the individual in collective or group situations. Yet this is precisely what is implied in the attempt to analyze individual behavior apart from its social context or, conversely, the attempt to treat behavior in a social situation as though the principles governing the part (individual) were determined wholly by the character of the whole (group, society).

Resolving the Controversy in Modern Psychology. Fortunately, developments in modern psychology and modern social science permit an analysis of the individual-group relationship that is congruent with general psychological principles and does not contradict analysis of groups and social systems. Transformations in individual experience and behavior associated with a person's membership in a system (group, collective situation, culture) are not uniquely determined by the whole (e.g., by society). They occur because of basic principles that apply even to the way the individual perceives the physical world. In order to pursue the analysis of the part-whole relationship as it bears on our problem, we shall make this point concretely and elaborate upon it. Needless to say, the analysis implies changes in psychological theory since the last century, as explained by a contemporary experimental psychologist, George A. Miller (1962):

Most psychologists no longer try to reduce the perceptual world to sensory elements, nor assume that they can learn about complicated experiences by studying only the simple ones. More and more, psychologists who study perception are shifting away from their old question, "How can I analyze this perception into its basic atoms?" and are beginning to ask a dif-

Fig. 5.1. Napoleon and the trees. (By permission from R. Stagner and T. Karowski, *Psychology*. New York: McGraw-Hill Book Company, 1952.)

ferent question, "How can I discover the transformations that a perceiver can impose upon the information he takes in?" And with each new step forward in understanding the transformations, one gains increased respect for both the complexity and the beauty of our perceptual machinery (p. 113).

The point under consideration can be made more concrete by reference to Fig. 5.1. Here a "transformation" occurs that could never be adequately explained merely by separate study of each part of the figure. When one looks at the figure and sees first two trees, the salient outlines are the black contours. The space between the areas is just empty, psychologically. But when the observer focuses on that empty space, he sees the imposing contour of Napoleon. The same empty space acquires solidity. The hollow near the upper branch of the left tree becomes the characteristic arm pose of Napoleon, and the narrow stripling at the base of the right tree outlines the general's sword (cf. Newman, 1948).

The consequence of such facts about perceiving, which can be multiplied almost indefinitely, is that events are not perceived in terms of their parts in isolation, but that the parts are perceived in terms of their

place (membership character) in the pattern (whole). The properties or characteristics that we see in the parts are to a considerable extent a function of their *membership character* in the whole pattern, and they change according to which contour is focal (Koffka, 1935).

The experience of objects and events in terms of their role, or the place they occupy in the pattern is shown even more convincingly when *familiar* forms are embedded in larger patterns and are recognized as familiar forms only with great difficulty (Gottschaldt 1955). Even a first grader will recognize the letters N, A, T when he sees them separately. Now look at Fig. 5.2. Can you see a familiar English word using these letters in the pattern? To a reader of roman script, it is likely to appear an entirely strange pattern, perhaps in the Russian alphabet. The same pattern, broken in half, readily appears as the familiar word NATIONALITY when the complicating context is removed. (See next page.) This is an example of hidden sub-patterns within a larger whole, referred to as *embedded forms*. Such embedded pictures are to be found in popular magazines as puzzles. Another example is given in Fig. 5.3.

From the earlier discussion of stimulus structure (pp. 51–56), the composition of such embedded pictures becomes evident. When the Gestalt factors in the larger pattern are mutually reinforcing, rather than contradictory, and especially when color is used, it becomes more and more difficult to disentangle the ingredient parts from the whole pattern. The absorption of a part into a whole pattern is not an all-or-none affair. It can be created in steps so that the part "dissolves" gradually. Werner Wolff showed this by a simple series of steps, shown in Fig. 5.4. In Fig. 5.4, the world ELITE is gradually embedded by first adding a lower horizontal line (part b) and then an intermediate parallel line (part c).

This same phenomena can be shown with human forms, such as a moving formation. The dancers at the Radio City Music Hall in New York, the Rockettes, are all pretty girls but varying in size, shape and coloring. When arranged in line according to size and dancing rapidly in formation, the effect is one of a compelling pattern composed of homogeneous parts. Each lovely individual has been absorbed into the pattern.

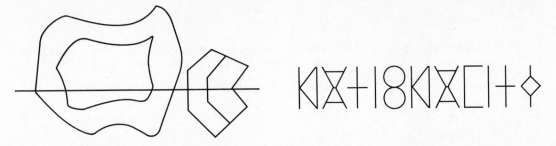

Fig. 5.2a.   Can you locate a familiar number (left) and familiar word (right)?

Fig. 5.3a.   The figures at the left appear within the complex patterns at right. Witkin (1959), among others, has used such forms to study ability to analyze the visual field. (From H. Witkin, "The Perception of the Upright." Copyright © 1959 by Scientific American, Inc. All rights reserved.)

Fig. 5.3b.   An easier task: Find the simple figure at the top in each of the three designs below. As color and greater complexity of design is added, the task is progressively more difficult. (*Light and Vision* © 1966, Time-Life Books © Time Inc.)

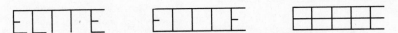

Fig. 5.4.   A familiar word gradually disappears as lines are added to from a compelling rectangular pattern. (After W. Wolff, *Essentials of Psychology.* New York: Grune & Stratton, 1956, p. 69.)

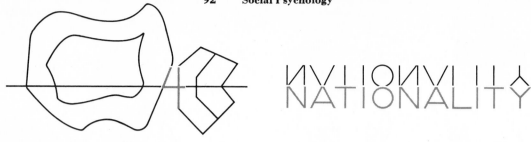

Fig. 5.2b. Embedded number (left) after W. Köhler; embedded word (right) after Prothro and Teska.

Relations Are as Real as Ingredients

The preceding illustrations show that even in understanding how we perceive things and events, it is not sufficient to consider the ingredients and their attributes in isolation. It is necessary to consider how the ingredients relate to one another, whether there are other ingredients around them (context), and the whole pattern into which the components fall. In brief, relations among objects and events are decisive in defining the properties of what we perceive, even the properties of the parts.

In an article written for the *American Journal of Physics* on the perception of objects, the psychologist E. G. Boring showed that the perception of solid forms in two-dimensional space cannot be explained in terms of the separate parts, but depends on the relationship among parts. Fig. 5.5 consists of 12 lines. These 12 lines could be arranged in many different ways if one were to permute their locations. When arranged in the relationship shown in part b of the figure, they are perceived as a solid cube.

Phenomena of color perception provide clear demonstration of part-whole relationships. For example, the arabesque in Fig. 5.6 is a classic example of brightness

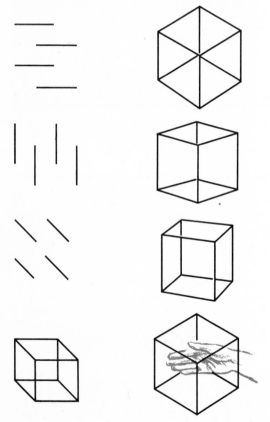

Fig. 5.5a. (*above left*) Twelve lines are 12 lines, and not the pattern of a cube or any other form. It is the *arrangement* of 12 lines that makes a cube.

Fig. 5.5b. (*above right*) Four views of a cube. The top figure looks like a flat hexagon, but it is seen at the same angle as the bottom figure.

Fig. 5.6. Assimilation effect. Which gray appears darker? The same gray is used throughout the figure. The lighter effect with white and the darker effect with black is usually called a "spreading effect." It is but one example of assimilation, which is also found in perception and judgment of nonvisual stimuli (see text). (Adapted from Evans, 1948. *Introduction to Color.* New York: Wiley.)

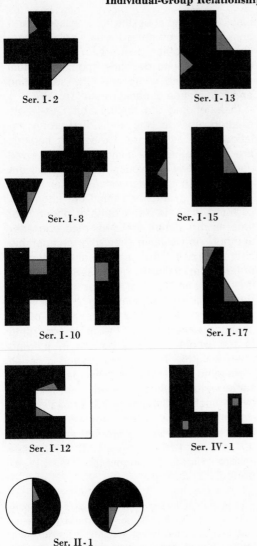

Ser. I-2   Ser. I-13

Ser. I-8   Ser. I-15

Ser. I-10   Ser. I-17

Ser. I-12   Ser. IV-1

Ser. II-1

Fig. 5.7a. The psychologist Benari was one of the earliest to clarify the apparent contradiction between contrast and the "spreading" effect by showing that which of the two occurred depended upon the relationship of the focal figure (here the stippled triangle) to a larger design or its background. Compare the "grays" within and outside of the black figures. Either assimilation or contrast occurs, depending upon the relationships between the patch and the larger figure or background. Note that it is not simply a question of the total area of black or white surrounding the patch. (From W. M. Mikesell and M. Bentley, 1930. Configuration and brightness. *J. exper. Psychol.*, **13**, 1–23.)

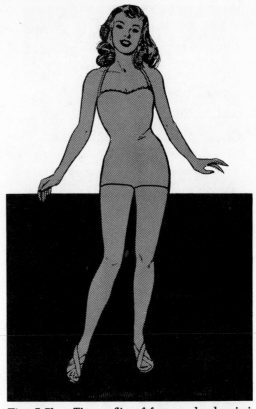

Fig. 5.7b. The conflict of form vs. local assimilation-contrast effects is not confined merely to geometric figures such as those Benari studied (Fig. 5.7a). If the form of the body is perceived as a whole, it is not subject to contrast effects. But if the upper half is covered with gray cardboard, then a contrast effect occurs on the lower part. (From D. M. Johnson, *Psychology: A Problemsolving Approach.* New York: Harper & Row, 1961, pp. 119–120.)

changing according to color of the pattern. In this case, the gray appears *darker* with the black pattern than it does with the light pattern (an *assimilation* effect). This particu-

lar phenomenon puzzled experimental psychologists for some years because, ordinarily, when a color is presented against a dark background it appears *lighter* than against a white background (see Fig. 5.7).

Helson (1964) clarified the apparent contradiction by experimenting with simpler patterns, namely simple lines, as shown in Fig. 5.8. He found that whether one obtained an *assimilation* to the background or a *contrast* effect depended upon the *relationship* between the width of the colored lines (gray or blue) and the width of the black or white lines. In other words, perception of the constituents is affected by the relationship between parts: The systematic widening and narrowing of colored and

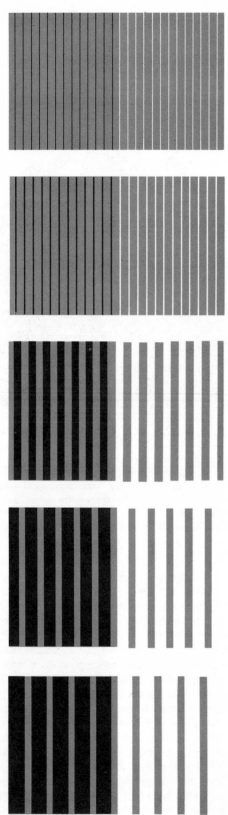

black lines changes the lightness or darkness of the perceived hue. Helson concluded: "Whether contrast or assimilation effects are found depends upon the mutual relation of line width and line separation and reflectance of background" (p. 286).

In extending the findings on part-whole relationships to the individual-group relationship, it is important that such findings are not confined to immediately perceived patterns. They also occur when stimuli are presented in time sequence (serial order). The effects of anchor stimuli on judgments of lifted weights, for example, occur over time as the stimuli are presented one after another. As we have seen, the membership character of a particular weight is derived in large part from the entire series of which it is a part and special anchor stimuli introduced by the experimenter.

Helson (1964) gave a vivid example of the changed experience of the parts according to the whole temporal pattern in judging lifted weights. The subject judged a series of weights and then was presented with the same weights either preceded or followed by an anchor stimulus of 900 grams, which *was much* heavier than any of the other weights. This highly discrepant anchor produced a *contrast* effect—a shift in this case toward "lighter" judgments. Helson reported:

[The subjects'] comments showed that they were unaware of the purpose of the experiments and believed the series weights were different when different anchors were employed. For example, one S reported that the observations were much less fatiguing with the 900 grm. anchor than with the single-stimuli method "be-

Fig. 5.8. Helson's research on assimilation-contrast in color perception shows that whether assimilation or contrast effects occur in color vision depends jointly on the relationships between the focal color (gray in the figure, but he has used blue as well) and the adjacent color (here, black or white). In these simple figures, maximum assimilation occurs when the gray is about 10 mm. wide, hence *figure* for the narrow (1–2 mm.) black and white stripes. Which looks darker: the gray on the right or left? As the black and white stripes broaden *relative* to the gray, the effect is gradually reversed to a contrast effect (see last figure). An even more pronounced effect would occur if the width of the gray were also altered proportionately. (Courtesy of Harry Helson.)

cause the weights are so much lighter now." Actually the total weight lifted with the 900-gram standard was 6000 grm. per series as against 1500 grm. with the single stimuli method (p. 136).

Similarly, musical composition, whether it be jazz or a symphony, is made up of individual tones played in sequence over time. In different combinations, the same tones can be used to compose jazz or a piano sonata. However, the perception of each tone is not dependent solely upon the ordering of the tones and the major rhythmic scheme. In any musical form, the key to musical performance becomes the connections, phrasing, and accenting of particular groups of tones to form distinctive patterns, within which any one note acquires its character. When one considers this, one can understand what the great conductor and cellist Pablo Casals meant when he said to an orchestra, "Don't play notes. Make music."

Individual-Group Relationship: A Part-Whole Problem

The importance of relations among ingredient parts, which we have seen in simple illustrations from investigations of perception, has intimate bearing on the individual-group relation in social life. When we speak of a person getting "caught up" in a social situation, we are speaking a profound truth. To some extent, the person's experience and behavior in a social situation are always a part of the whole pattern and take on much of its properties. Thus the atmosphere of a wedding or a funeral colors the behavior of the individual participant. The behavior may appear to be absurd apart from the situation.

It is perhaps strange that we seldom apply the same analysis to the individual as a member of a group of longer duration and greater significance in his life. Yet a human group is also a pattern with compelling properties. Of course, there is no such thing as a group without individuals as constituent parts. But a group is not described adequately as the mere presence of others or as any old collection of individuals.

The "group-ness" of a group emerges among people interacting as a pattern of relations among them. These relations consist of reciprocal expectations defined by each individual relative to each of the others, his characteristic way of interacting with them, and his relative power in the leader-follower hierarchy. In the pattern of relations defining the group, our earlier discussion of anchors or reference points (Chapter 4) is equally valid. Various members in a group contribute to the pattern of relations among them according to the place they occupy. The individual member, then, responds to others and behaves toward them in terms of their respective places in the pattern of relations. When those occupying positions that anchor the pattern are removed, for example, the leader, the whole character of the group and the place of others in the relationship may be transformed.

To state it flatly, when the terms "pattern" or "structure" or "organization" are used, the referent consists of particular relations among the parts, one to another. The terms pattern, structure, or organization are much in vogue currently and are, for all practical purposes, interchangeable. The most effective descriptions of their referent are in terms of the arrangement of functionally related parts, and the most effective measurements quantify these arrangements or some significant aspect of them. For example, in the organization that is a human group, the description proves to be in terms of status and role relations among the members (from the leader on down).

We shall discuss groups and their members in Chapters 7 and 8. Here it is sufficient to note that what has been demonstrated in simple part-whole phenomena about the importance of relations among parts forming a whole that affects the properties of parts is equally true for the membership character of individuals. By changing the relations among parts, the character of the whole may change. In any event, the proper analysis of the individual member requires knowledge of the relations in the whole and their stability or change. In the chapters to follow, it will become clear that this view of the individual-group relationship is not a mere extrapolation from simpler phenomena but rather a generalization about part-whole relationships that is substantiated equally in the study of group formation and functioning.

APPROPRIATENESS
OF RESEARCH METHODS
AND TECHNIQUES FOR THE PROBLEM
OF INDIVIDUAL-GROUP RELATIONSHIP

Too often, research method and techniques are regarded as a separate problem from that of theory—as though one could use any technique at all as long as it is convenient. In fact, research method and technology cannot be considered separately from theory, for they determine in decisive fashion whether the data collected are relevant to the theory, in the first place, and in the second place, whether they provide a valid test. Therefore, research methods and techniques should be logical derivations from theory and neither its master nor mere gadgets. Illustration of this general point will serve to guide us in evaluating research findings.

Although there is now a vast research literature on our topics, the solidly established generalizations about them constitute a fraction of this research. One reason may be that too little concern has been invested in developing research methods and techniques appropriate to the problem under investigation. It is becoming increasingly clear that a consistent set of propositions and principles can clarify the problem of what research methods and techniques are appropriate for investigating a particular topic.

This conclusion is supported, for example, by research experiences in the study of internal factors or variables pertaining to the individual's motives, attitudes, and past experiences. In modern psychology, some of the most effective research strategies and techniques in the study of personality, attitude and attitude change, and interpersonal, group, or other social influences have been guided by principles presented earlier or by some variant thereof—whether they were explicitly stated in the research design or not.

We refer here especially to research that has used rather simple behaviors as *indicators* of some aspect of the individual's personality, his ego-involvements, attitudes, or the effects of a communication. The general procedure is to present a stimulus situation with some aspect *relevant* to the internal factor under study which, at the same time, permits options or alternatives for behavior (i.e., is unstructured). The particular option or alternative adopted by the person is then taken as an indicator of the variable under study.

This general research procedure makes eminent sense when we recall that experience and behavior constitute a unity (Proposition 1); that they are jointly determined by internal and external factors (Proposition 3); that we can only infer internal factors from behavior (Proposition 5); that the psychological tendency is toward patterning of experience even when external structure is lacking (Proposition 6); and that the contribution of internal factors increases as external stimulus structure decreases in gradations (Proposition 9). By the same logic, and by using Proposition 10, we can see why the individual's judgment or decision in an unstructured situation in which he is exposed to social influence from another person may serve as a behavioral indicator of his attitude toward that person. Similarly, remembering that selectivity is guided by the person's concerns, preoccupations, identifications, and commitments at the time (Proposition 4), we can see why the relative frequencies of what he selects as focal when confronted by a complex stimulus field can be used as indicators of these personal dispositions.

Whenever it is possible to study behavior in a stimulus situation *relevant* to the topic under study that also has some important dimension (aspect) congenial to responses in the form of quantities or degrees, this general formulation can be used for further technical refinement. A major development characterizing modern social psychology has been the use of systematic distortions (variations) in perception in estimating the performance or attributes of other persons who stand in positive or negative relationship to the individual, and in categorizing or placing relevant objects.

For example, interpersonal attachments or dislikes have been studied through over- or underestimations of the person's performance (p. 389); status relations in groups were studied similarly, such that the person's over- or underestimation of performance by another member served to indicate his view of that member's status (p. 164); and friendly or hostile attitudes toward members of other groups were indicated by judgments about them in various respects (p. 243).

The use of behavioral indicators (verbal or nonverbal) for attitudes and personal involvements is a research strategy for studying such internal factors. From the principles stated so far, we already can deduce that if we constrict the stimulus field or present very few alternatives for behavior, the ensuing reaction by the person will reflect these compelling stimulus conditions and not his attitudes or motives or interpersonal ties. It is necessary to emphasize this point because some authors have concluded from studies using "cognitive" indicators that cognitive distortions and errors take place under any circumstances, without qualification. Such a conclusion would lead to the view that the "world is what we make of it," regardless of the situation.

A survey of the research literature using such *indirect* or *unobtrusive* techniques for assessing personality, attitude, motive, personal relation or social influence easily establishes the fact that systematic variations in cognitive processes (perception, judgment, etc.) take place under specifiable conditions that can be derived from the propositions.

First, the stimulus conditions are relevant to the internal factor under study, but the task does not arouse *awareness* that the person's likes or dislikes, stands or commitments, or personal tendencies or motives are the topic of investigation. If experience and behavior constitute a unity, we would expect, of course, that such awareness would deflect the person's behavior by putting him "on guard" about just what he wants to reveal under the circumstances. In the next chapter, we shall see what such awareness can do to the person's behavior.

Second, such research invariably presents to the individual stimulus conditions that lack clear structure in the aspect to which he is to react, that are complex, or that involve difficulty in discrimination, as we would expect from Propositions 9 and 10.

One example of this line of research is the *indirect assessment of attitudes.* In the chapters on attitudes, we shall consider examples of such attitude assessment—in-

cluding the *Own Categories Procedure,* which yields indicators of the person's stand and his personal involvement in it in quantitative form.

The methodological advantages of studying individual commitments, interpersonal and group likes or dislikes, and stands or identifications through behavioral indicators such as those mentioned above are obvious. We shall list these advantages in two steps.

1. Through using cognitive indicators such as judgments of performance or objects or attributes, it is feasible to secure data revealing likes and dislikes that are already quantitative or numerical. For example, we can use the extent of over- or underestimation, or the number of categories a person uses to discriminate a series of statements and category width, as raw data for analysis. This is a decisive advantage over techniques that secure qualitative data, such as the Rorschach test, TAT, or other projective techniques in which verbal or narrative responses have to be translated into some kind of scores with attendant controversy over the basis and legitimacy of the scoring scheme.

2. As perception and judgment tasks can be devised that do not sensitize the respondent about his personally held preferences, the research situation itself does not put him "on guard" against revealing some aspect of himself. As we shall see in the next chapter, research situations do have "demand character." When the person knows that his personal prejudices, feelings, or beliefs are the topic of investigation, he may be a "good subject" without revealing them. It is obvious that when the person is not "on guard" about revealing himself, the possibility that his behavior is only a response to these "demand characteristics" and hence a momentary artifact, is substantially reduced.

Whether the underlying assumptions were made explicit or not, the study of interpersonal, in-group (status-role), and intergroup preferences or attitudes through relatively simple perceptual and judgmental indicators under appropriate stimulus conditions and without arousing the individual's awareness is based on the propositions indicated. As we continue from one topic to the next, the reader can use the propositions presented as a basis for assessing the appropriateness of particular research methods and techniques for the problem studied. The final test of adequacy of any research method is its effectiveness in yielding data for the particular problem at hand and in developing valid indicators of the major variables it involves.

PART III

Social Interaction:
Process, Products, Structure
(Organization and Norms)

Preview of Part III

Now we have reached a vantage point for tackling major topics of social psychology, as listed in Chapter 1. The vantage point was reached by following the converging trends in social psychology and formulating terms for studying experience and behavior within their appropriate frame of reference. The propositions and principles in Part II will enable us to formulate the problems of specific topics in a coherent way, and to study them through research methods consistent with the theoretical orientation.

We start with the broad topic of man's traffic with man, devoting Chapters 6–12 to major aspects of social interaction. Social interaction is a process over time. The interaction process, in turn, has *products:* namely, roles and status positions of individual participants and a set of norms (values and standards of conduct). We shall analyze the interaction process and study the products of interaction which, in time, come to regulate subsequent give-and-take.

The interaction process does not take place in an insulated vacuum. It occurs within a social situation which is complex, even if we are dealing with an intimate situation between two persons or with two or three people participating as subjects and experimenter in the privacy of a university laboratory.

Therefore, our first task in delineating the frame of reference for the participant in interaction process is the analysis of the social situation at hand. Every social situation is composed of at least four sets of factors:

1. Factors pertaining to the individuals and their relationship (whether they are initially neutral to one another, favorably or unfavorably disposed as friends or rivals; whether there are status differentials among them; whether they are male or female; whether they are members of different groups bound in alliance or in conflict).

2. The nature and properties of the problems or tasks that confront the participants.

3. The facilities, advantages, and disadvantages of the location and instrumentalities for coping with the situation.

4. The individual participant's relationship to the foregoing three sets of factors, which have their impact in an interdependent way: how he stacks up relative to other participants as they tackle the task or problem (with which he may be familiar or unfamiliar, skilled or clumsy) in a definite location (which may be appropriate or inappropriate for the occasion, accustomed or unfamiliar, and with adequate or inadequate facilities that he does or does not know about).

Chapter 6 concentrates on analysis of the social situation and its bearing on interaction processes.

These outlines of social psychology emphasize the relationships among participating individuals as the limiting set of factors upon interaction process in a social situation. Therefore, an initial task in predicting experience and behavior of participants is specification of whether interaction occurs among participants in a transitory *togetherness* situation (without previous ties among them) or in a *group* situation, wherein the participants are linked with stabilized ties and expectations on the basis of structural and normative products of their previous interactions (Chapter 7).

People do not feel and act in the same way when they are alone and when they are participating in interaction, whether in transitory episodes together or in recurrent group situations. The differences in their experience and behavior represent *differential effects* of the social situation (p. 106). However, the determinants of such differential effects differ over time as a mere to-

getherness interaction proceeds to become group interaction. The products of interaction acquire great weight in the social situation.

The more lasting expectations regulating person-to-person interaction within groups and across group lines are derived from the role ascriptions, status arrangements, and stabilized norms of the groups. Therefore, roles, statuses and norms are essentials of group situations. (Definitions: group, p. 131; role, p. 140; status, p. 140; norm, p. 141).

These essential properties of groups are the products of interaction among the present or past generations of members. Once stabilized to any degree, the role system and norm system of the group become the basis of interdependent and binding regularities in subsequent interaction episodes within the group and in intergroup relations.

The role and norm stabilization within a group can change only through further interactions among members and not through the transitory ups-and-downs in the preferences of this or that group member, including the leader. Leadership, too, is a position within a group and not outside of it. The leader, too, is subject to correctives (sanctions) when he deviates from the range of behavior defined as acceptable by the group norms.

The bounds of acceptable behavior and the definition of deviation are not, however, the same for all matters of normative regulation. They vary according to their importance to the group, being narrowest and most definite in matters pertaining to the existence and perpetuation of the group and most flexible in matters considered to be of minor importance.

It follows that the appropriate locus for the study of leader-follower relations, as well as problems of conformity and deviation, is within the structural arrangements (organization) and norm set of groups (Chapters 8, 9, and 10). For reasons that will be elaborated in Chapters 7 and 8, we use the terms *structure* and *organization* interchangeably.

The emergence of group products in interaction and their consequences in subsequent interaction episodes stand in high relief when we trace group formation step-by-step over time. For this reason, pains are taken in the chapters to follow to trace the formation of groups. With the progressive stabilization of role expectations and normative definitions of what lies within the range of acceptability and what falls into the range of rejection, the group properties become more binding for individual participants. To that extent, the attitudes and behaviors of members become more predictable in terms of the group properties (Chapter 8).

Since the 1920s field and laboratory techniques have been developed for study of group formation, their structure (organization of roles and statuses), their norms, and the effects of these products on the attitude and behavior of members (Chapters 7–10).

Groups are not self-contained, closed systems. They are in traffic with one another as subunits of larger social systems (e.g., institutions and society). With the rapid development in means of production, transportation, and communication, groups and social systems are increasingly enmeshed in functional relations with one another, for good or for evil. In this state of interdependence, which becomes greater and greater, the goals that groups and larger social systems pursue may be compatible or incompatible with one another. If incompatible, there inevitably arises a state of friction with associated stereotypes and inferiority-superiority arrangements and practices.

Men of good will have proposed various measures for reducing conflict between human groups and reducing the tension and prejudice among their members. Such proposals remain uncoordinated and piecemeal efforts without an adequate *theory of conflict.* In recent years, there have been developments toward a theory of conflict, as well as experiments testing the validity of hypotheses derived from it (Chapters 11–12). This research, in turn, offers a basis for fruitful hypotheses concerning conditions for reducing conflict between human groups and the associated hostility of members.

Here, then, we have depicted in broad strokes the topics to be covered within the domain of social interaction, its process and products (structural and normative). Those subjects, in turn, are basic to discussion of topics in Parts IV and V.

6

Interaction
in Social Situations

Major Topics of the Chapter

Interaction in social situations: orientation

Differential effects of a social situation

Interdependent sets of factors in social situations

Studies of differential effects of social situations

Interdependence of sets of factors illustrated: number of participants

Social psychology of the psychological experiment

Research situation is a social situation: its social psychology

Who is watching behind the screen?

The Milgram experiments: compliance for science

To volunteer or not to volunteer

INTERACTION
IN SOCIAL SITUATIONS:
ORIENTATION

The give-and-take between individuals in social situations is an interaction process. We do not merely react to other people with whom we meet, talk, and have dealings. We ourselves constitute stimulus patterns for others. What we respond to in their words and deeds at a given moment is partially determined by how we have affected people previously. Interaction among persons is an ongoing process of reciprocal influence.

In this chapter, we consider experiments on the effects of other people in transitory social situations. Our principal task is to examine the appropriate frame of reference for studying interaction. We soon find that it is not sufficient to consider *only* the other people present. There are at least four sets of factors composing the frame of reference in any social situation.

After listing the sets of factors in a social situation, we start with the simplest case: the mere presence of other people while the individual performs a task. By utilizing principles presented in the preceding chapters, we shall see what is meant by the *interdependence of factors* in the frame of reference. That insight permits rapid strides toward understanding a major problem in social-psychological research: namely, that research procedures and techniques constitute *parts* of the frame of reference and have demonstrable effects on experience and behavior.

Unless research procedures and techniques are included in the frame of reference, the researcher is in grave danger of obtaining results that reflect the research situation itself rather than the factors that he set out to study and stated in his hypotheses. In that case, his conclusions are misleading. Research artifacts have been the topic of much discussion and research demonstration under the headings of "social psychology of the psychological experiment," "experimenter bias," and the "demand characteristics" of research situations for subjects. We shall also consider some experiments that have utilized the unique properties of a research situation as a model for other social situations with similar "demand character"—such as deliberate attempts to control or influence another person.

By considering how we size up a researcher, we are led to the more general problem of how we size up other persons whom we encounter in a transitory situation. Studies of "person perception" will reveal regularities in social life that frame our appraisal of others even before interaction starts. Such cultural regularities, often expressed by the individual as stereotyped expectations, produce regularities in give and take with others. This topic leads us to a more thorough analysis of problems in conducting research.

THE DIFFERENTIAL EFFECTS
OF A SOCIAL SITUATION

Have you ever observed a person who thought that he was completely alone? He may act very differently than he does when at an office, school, or social gathering. Alone, the poised beauty queen slumps and picks her nose. The confident business executive scratches his ear and curls up to rest, snoring with his mouth open. The shy boy performs a task with great dexterity, although he is all thumbs demonstrating the same skills to others. The girl preening in front of a mirror becomes a properly modest young lady when she departs on her first date.

Hundreds of experiments have compared behavior when individuals are alone and when other persons are present. The important generalization from these studies is that social situations have unmistakable effects on behavior, whether to the improvement or the detriment of performance. The effects are not confined to those social situations in which deliberate efforts are made to "influence people" (e.g., to change their attitudes). Social situations produce differential effects on our behavior whether we are aware of the fact or not.

The problem may be defined operationally for study purposes. We shall define the *differential effect* of a social situation as the difference between behavior when an individual is in a social situation and when he is alone. This operational definition can be put into a simple formula:

$$D.E. = B_s - B_a,$$

where B_s refers to behavior in a social situation and B_a to behavior alone. The difference defines the differential effects (D.E.) of a social situation.

You will note that the differential effect has a positive sign if the social situation produces an increase in intensity, quantity, or quality (improvement). Conversely, it may have a negative sign. There is no evidence in the research literature to indicate that differential effects are invariably positive or negative—that is, either beneficial or degrading in all cases. Our task in social psychology is to analyze the factors producing differential effects, not to glorify or to condemn them. The differential effects of two or more social situations may also be compared:

$$D.E. = B_{s_1} - B_{s_2}.$$

What produces differential effects in a social situation? In Chapter 3 we learned as a general principle that psychological patterning, hence behavior, is always a product of interacting influences from the environment and from the participating person. The individual is *selective* in what he responds to at a given time, and his selectivity is keenly tuned to other persons. From birth onward, other people have satisfied or frustrated his physiological needs, cared for him or abused him, and played a crucial part in his definition of himself as a person.

Why, then, could we not confine the analysis of differential effects only to the other people present? Confining the analysis to other people would amount to leaving out important variables operating in the frame of reference. We found in Part II that the background and context of a simple tone, color, or shape affect our perception. How much more crucial are the background and context of a social situation! For this reason, we ask the question "What constitutes a social situation?"

INTERDEPENDENT SETS OF FACTORS IN SOCIAL SITUATIONS

In any social situation, the frame of reference for analyzing behavior must include at least the following sets of factors:

1. Set of factors pertaining to participating individuals:

(a) Factors related to the characteristics of the individuals, such as their number, ages, sex, educational level, occupations, social status, etc. These factors include the background of cultural situations to which the individuals have been exposed.

(b) Factors related to the homogeneity-heterogeneity of the participants' characteristics (1a). These factors are included because *interaction* is not governed automatically by the background and characteristics of each individual. *Differences* in age, sex, race, religion, or social class affect interaction as soon as they are perceived.

(c) Factors related to the prevailing relations among participants. This important classification recalls the distinctions made within the first major class of social stimuli listed in Chapter 1, namely, *other people.* Other people may be strangers or they may have an established interpersonal relationship (say, as sweethearts). They may be fellow members of the same group (family, chums, club), members of different groups, or may form varying combinations in terms of group membership. They may be participating in a collective interaction situation.

2. Set of factors pertaining to the characteristics of the activity, task, problem, or occasion at hand. People work, play, attend weddings, make decisions, and solve problems. The tasks required in these activities have definite characteristics. A ceremony, attending a lecture, assembling a table from its parts, and many other tasks allow very few alternatives for the behavior of participants. They are structured in terms of the actions required and their sequence. On the other hand, decisions about an unidentified flying object, problems of discord in human relations, or interpretations of a person's expression provide considerably more leeway for alternative actions. Such tasks lack objective structure in varying degrees. Included in this set of factors are *communications* or instructions relative to the problem or task. At times, the person's cultural background defines the task or problem for him. At others, there are also explicit instructions from other persons as to how to behave or to interpret the problem. In experiments, instructions by the experimenter serve this purpose.

3. Set of factors pertaining to the location and facilities. Interaction does not take place in a vacuum. Material culture provides many different locations and facilities, some of them specific to certain activities. Cultural norms define appropriate places for interaction and task performance. There are appropriate and inappropriate settings for making love, for worshipping, for learning, and for working. There are tasks and problems that cannot be solved unless certain facilities are available. Some locations are crowded by other people not participating in the interaction. Others are so noisy that conversation is impossible. As we shall see, a psychological laboratory with equipment, recording instruments, one-way mirrors, and assistants in white coats produces a distinctive atmosphere that unmistakably affects the interaction of research subject and experimenter.

4. Set of factors pertaining to the individual participant's relation to the above three sets of factors. The frame of reference for a social situation is not complete without the system of relationships defining the individual's standing with regard to other individuals present, his attitudes and abilities with regard to the task, his established notions, his immediate impressions, and his use of the location and facilities. Past experiences, motives, and moods affect his behavior relative to the other persons, the problem, and the location.

These four sets of factors provide a scheme for analyzing the frame of reference in any social situation. However, do not assume that each set of factors always contributes to behavior in a fixed quantity such that the outcome can be computed by simple addition or subtraction of the factors. Each of the four sets of factors has demonstrable effects on behavior, but variations in any one factor need not produce one-to-one changes in behavior. The factors in a social situation are *interrelated,* hence function interdependently. The social situation forms a pattern of stimulation through the selective processing of an individual with a cultural background, with motives and attitudes relevant to the situation.

STUDIES OF DIFFERENTIAL EFFECTS OF SOCIAL SITUATIONS

Systematic studies comparing behavior when the individual is alone and when he is with others began around the turn of the twentieth century. Particularly noteworthy was the series of experiments conducted by F. H. Allport from 1916 to 1919 (Allport, 1924). In an effort to study the "pure effects" of other people as stimuli, Allport studied performance in a variety of tasks when each person worked alone in a room (his time being controlled by a buzzer operated by the experimenter) and when he worked side-by-side with three or four other persons. Instructions were given *not* to compete with others. The tasks included vowel cancellation, attention to reversible perspective, multiplication, association, reasoning, and judgment of weights and odors.

Result Allport found differences between performance alone and together. The magnitudes and signs (plus or minus) of the differences varied from task to task. In general, in the social situation there was an

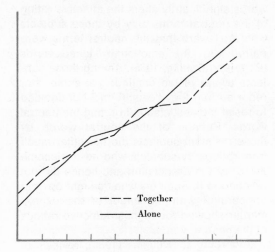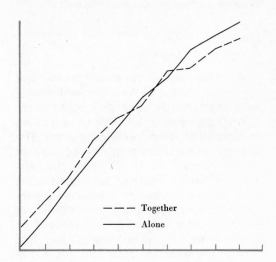

Fig. 6.1. Effects of social situation on judgments of pleasantness-unpleasantness (*left*) and judgments of weight (*right*). (After F. H. Allport.) (*Left*) Ten odors arranged from left to right in order of increasing pleasantness when smelled by subjects alone. The distance from the baseline to the dotted curve indicates the pleasantness of the same odor when smelled in the presence of other persons. (*Right*) Ten weights arranged from left to right in order of increasing weight. The solid line represents judgments of each weight, on the average, when compared with a "heavy" standard and a "light" standard. The distance from the base to the dotted curve shows judgments of the same weight when the subject judged in the presence of others.

increase in speed and quantity of performance on the simpler tasks. In reasoning, Allport reported a lowering of quality in togetherness situations for six of the nine subjects and an increase in quality for the other three. In judgments of odors and weights, there was a tendency to avoid extreme judgments in the together situations (see Fig. 6.1). In short, differential effects of social situations occur even when there is no deliberate effort by anyone to influence behavior.

Subsequent investigators have also reported differential effects of performing together. Their positive or negative direction depends on the task, the setting, and nature of relations among persons (Kelley and Thibaut, 1954). Therefore, the differential effects cannot be accounted for simply in terms of additional stimulation provided by the sight and sound of other persons present. The flaw in the attempt to study "pure effects" of other people as "added" stimuli was revealed through a series of experiments by Dashiell (1930).

Dashiell essentially repeated Allport's studies, using multiplication, word analogies, and word-association tasks. Dashiell's most significant finding came not by comparing behavior alone and together but by comparing two "alone" situations. In one condition, the subjects came to the laboratory at *different* times and each worked in a private room. In the other, several subjects came to the laboratory at the *same* time, each working in a private room. Dashiell found that performance by persons working *simultaneously* in different rooms was comparable to performance in a together situation. In short, awareness that other individuals are performing the same task can influence behavior even though those persons are not physically present.

The lesson from Dashiell's research is related to one of the principles presented in Chapter 4. Psychological patterning is influenced by what a person brings to a situation and how he interprets it. Psychological processing of the factors "out there" in a social situation occurs on a conceptual level. A theory of behavior in social situations that omits this distinctively human feature of psychological processing is bound to prove inadequate sooner or later.

Awareness in "Verbal Conditioning" Experiments

More recently, some investigators have conducted studies of "verbal conditioning," regarding verbal behavior as a performance theoretically similar to pecking responses of pigeons or lever-pressing by a rat. The analogy is made through the concept of "reinforcements" in the situation. The pairing of a verbal response with approval is conceived as analogous to a rat's association of lever-pressing with the release of food. For example, during an interview, an experimenter murmurs "mmm-hmm" or "right" whenever the subject utters plural nouns, personal pronouns, or another selected class of words. Increase in his use of the selected class of words is attributed to the experimenter's "reinforcement." Lights, bells, or buzzers have also been used to "reinforce" a selected class of words.

Another procedure is to have the subject learn pairs of words in which the first word (theoretically, the "conditioned stimulus") is neutral, but the second ("unconditioned stimulus") is emotionally toned (favorably or unfavorably). Subsequently, the subject rates the neutral term according to its affective value (e.g., from unpleasant-pleasant). Increases in affective rating of the neutral terms are interpreted as evidence of verbal conditioning.

What is being studied in experiments on verbal conditioning? Researchers are finding that the phenomena are differential effects of a social situation, in which the experimenter's verbal "reinforcement" is only part of the picture. In other words, what is being studied is not comparable to the formation of conditioned responses in animals (see Proposition 12, Chapter 4) but represents a temporary adaptation to a social situation by an *experiencing* individual.

When the experimenter says "mmm-hmm" every time the person utters a plural noun, the subjects who increase their use of plural nouns are those who later indicate that the experimenter was approving certain responses, and furthermore, that they desired and tried to secure his approval (Spielberger and DeNike, 1962, 1966; De-

Nike and Spielberger, 1963). Similarly, the pairing of neutral and emotionally toned words significantly alters the affective rating of the neutral terms only by those subjects who are aware that the neutral terms were paired with the emotionally toned words (Page and Dahlke, 1965). Among those subjects aware of the contingency, some later reported that they "caught on," but decided to resist the association in rating the neutral words. Ratings of the neutral words by those resistant subjects did not differ much from ratings by subjects who never become aware of the association and hence did not respond to it. Subjects who "caught on" but cooperated with the intent of the experimenter showed the highest affective ratings of the neutral words.

According to Williams (1964), reviews of "verbal conditioning" experiments have:

laid increasing stress upon the importance of defining the variables operating in such experimental situations. Equivocal and contradictory results reported in these reviews appear to be a function of the complexity of the phenomenon and of the difficulty of controlling all important variables (p. 386).

As these are studies of social situations, it is not surprising that the frequency of the desired response varies with the instructions, with the ease of discriminating the desired response (ease of task), the attitude of the subject, and the "atmosphere" (p. 386). The sex, size, and even the appearance of the experimenter affect the outcome. In one study, two male Ph.D.'s as experimenters obtained significantly greater use of emotional words, but a female B.A. did not. None of her subjects was aware of the desired response (Krasner, Ullmann, Weiss, and Collins, 1961).

The implications of "verbal conditioning" studies repeat the lesson learned from earlier experiments that tried to treat other people merely as "added" stimuli. The differential effects of a social situation cannot be accounted for solely by single factors, such as the sheer presence of other people, the scheduling of their verbal approval, or the pairing of neutral and emotionally toned stimuli in a task. The other people, task characteristics, and location form interdependent patterns of stimulation for a person functioning on a conceptual level—who brings into the situation his cultural background, his past learning, his motives, and his attitudes toward the people, the task, and location. In analyzing behavior in a social situation, one has to recognize that human individuals function on a conceptual level and that their awareness of regularities in the situation frequently leads to self-formulation of rules for behavior in that situation (cf. Moscovici, 1967).

AN EXAMPLE
OF INTERDEPENDENCE
AMONG FACTORS:
NUMBER OF PARTICIPANTS

The size of a collection of people quite obviously affects interaction among them, if only because of limitations of space and time. We all know, however, that the effect of the number of people present depends in part on the location, the facilities, and what the people are doing. The same number of people filling a football stadium and attempting to dance in a ballroom produces very different experiences and reactions. The mutual excitement generated by the fans at a ballgame is absent when the same number of people go about their business in a large railway station or airport. Number of people is an important factor in social situations, but one that is interdependent with other sets of factors.

Research has confirmed the prediction by the German sociologist, Simmel (1902), that the "numerical factor" can affect both form and quality of interaction. Yet, available research evidence shows few one-to-one relationships between number of persons, properties of interaction among them, and individual behavior. For example, three-person situations (triads) were once regarded as conducive to interpersonal conflict because they provide a distinctive opportunity for one person to dominate by securing the support of just one other. However, the circumstances in which such coalitions form are still to be fully explored. When one person comes to the situation with recognized authority over the others, struggles for dominance and coalition formation need not occur (Turk and Turk, 1962; Hare, 1962, p. 242).

Most of the generalizations about the size

factor are fairly specific to particular settings or tasks (e.g., discussions of human relations problems, mechanical tasks, or tasks of strength; Hare, 1962). Even the attempt to name an "optimal" number of persons for a discussion must reckon with conflicting findings, for it depends on what the discussion is about and the prevailing relationships among the persons.

In their review of 46 articles dealing with the number of persons in a social situation, Thomas and Fink (1963) found that few generalizations are possible, despite the demonstrable effects of varying numbers in study after study. They concluded:

> Most of the observed effects of size reviewed here appear to be contingent upon the operation of one or more [other factors]. Where such mediating variables are affecting the outcome, the proper locus of explanation should be on the theoretical framework of which the [other factor] is a part and only secondarily on size (p. 383).

In short, number of participants affects behavior *interdependently* with other factors in a social situation. To clarify this conclusion, two specific examples from research will be given. The first concerns a task in which, it would appear, increasing the number of participants would impede task performance. The second concerns number of participants relative to the relationships among the participants.

Just a Bottle of Water
Made the Difference

In three experiments, Kelley, Condry, Dahlke, and Hill (1965) studied escape from a threatened penalty (electric shock) by four, five, six, and seven persons. Interaction occurred symbolically, without face-to-face contact. Each S (subject) had a light that signalled danger of impending shock, which he could avoid by turning a switch. Other lights on his panel represented the danger signals of other Ss. When he turned the switch, his light flashed green both on his and the other panels, so that everyone knew when he made an attempt. He could escape by holding the switch for 3 seconds; but if two or more persons activated switches at the same time, no one could escape. The task was for all individuals to escape in the allotted time.

Time for the task varied, as a standard unit of time would obviously favor the smaller numbers. In two experiments the time available was shown by the amount of water in two large bottles, assembled like an hour glass. When the water ran out of the top bottle, time was up. The amount of water depended on the number of persons, as based on the time needed for the total number to escape shock. (With at least 3 seconds per person needed, the time was *twice* the product of 3 seconds and the number of persons. For example, 4 persons were allowed 2 (3) (4)=24 seconds.)

Logically, more jamming of the switches —hence, fewer escapes—should occur as the number of persons increased. However, the investigators found that more escapes occurred for seven *Ss* than for six *Ss*. One possible explanation, they thought, might be the appearance of the very large bottle of water required to time seven persons. Could it suggest ample time and thus no reason to rush for the switch?

Accordingly, another experiment was performed in which the water-timer was eliminated. A tone that increased in pitch every few seconds conveyed the passage of time without indicating when the trial would be over. Here are the findings on the percentage of escapes in three experiments:

	No. of persons			
	4	5	6	7
Experiment with water-timer	77%	57%	31%	49%
Experiment with water-timer (using collections of seven only)	—	—	—	53%
Experiment with sound-timer	67%	63%	42%	24%

This research illustrates the interdependence of number with a facility (timing device) on a task in which number of participants is important. Researchers are just beginning to study the effects of their "instruments" on behavior in a social situation. Orne and Scheibe (1964) have shown that such a simple device as a "panic button" provided for the subject to signal the need to leave an isolation room was associated with a greater incidence of hallucinations and other unusual forms of experience reported in experiments on isolation than occurred when no button was provided.

Twelve Can Agree Faster Than Five

Findings on consensus (agreement) and satisfaction with a joint decision will illustrate the interdependent effects of relationships among participants and number of participants. Hare (1952) had Boy Scouts discuss a hypothetical camping trip, asking them to select 10 pieces of equipment, in the order preferred. Twenty minutes was allowed for discussion. Some discussions involved 5 and some, 12 persons. In this situation, 5 persons achieved greater consensus and were more satisfied than 12 persons. The study has been interpreted as showing the dependence of decision-making in a limited time upon the number of persons (Thomas and Fink, 1963 p. 381).

However, time and number of persons are not always related so intimately in decision-making. In a study to be summarized in some detail in Chapter 11, 11 boys comparable in age to those in Hare's study reached consensus in less than 2 minutes, each member expressing great satisfaction at the outcome. These boys had interacted for more than two weeks in a summer camp, establishing a fairly stable organization and network for communication. Their task was real and highly attractive: How to spend a sum of money received for their performance as a group. Among the many suggestions made, the unanimous choice was to repair their boat, which had been damaged.

We shall find it necessary to distinguish social situations on the basis of the relationships among persons in it. These relationships are frequently decisive in determining the relative importance of other factors, such as size, task, location and facilities.

RESEARCH SITUATION IS A SOCIAL SITUATION: THE SOCIAL PSYCHOLOGY OF THE EXPERIMENT

A research situation is one example of a social situation. Despite a few investigators who have emphasized this fact persistently for many years, many psychologists and social scientists have become concerned only recently about the problem that it presents. It will be most unfortunate if we regard work on "interviewer bias," "test bias," "experimenter bias," and the "social psychology of the psychological experiment" as merely technical details of research methods, interesting only to the specialist. On the contrary, we can learn a great deal about the interplay of factors in a social situation from studies of the research situation, even though a research situation has some special properties of its own.

In an age of science, almost everyone comes to a research situation with preconceived notions about "psychologists," "experimenters," "sociologists," "testers," or "interviewers." The widespread nature of such preconceptions is illustrated in an incident reported by Segall (1965), which occurred while he was in a remote district in East Africa. On a hilltop overlooking a broad plain near Ptolemy's legendary Mountains of the Moon, with hippopotami grunting in a nearby river, he met the hereditary ruler of a major East African tribe. The king extended his hand and said, "Well, Dr. Segall, I understand you are a psychologist; I suppose before this party is over you will have psychoanalyzed me" (p. 63).

This incident is only one example of the general fact: The perception of a person as occupying a social role is accompanied by expectations about him that affect our reactions to him. When the other person is identified as a researcher by a research subject, the subject's expectations may be very consequential indeed. Close observation produces differential effects even when the observer is not an investigator, as Dashiell found years ago by having observers watch closely as subjects performed. For a time, it was thought that observer effects might be avoided by automating the procedures, using one-way screens to observe, tape-recordings to secure conversation, or response switches and signal panels to enable the experimenter to leave the room. This supposition, however, failed to reckon with the unity of experience and behavior.

Who Is Watching Behind the Screen?

Some years ago, Wapner and Alper (1952) showed that automation might ac-

tually increase the differential effects of a research situation. The task was selecting one of two words that best applied to a given phrase (for example, choosing *strong* or *weak* to apply to "a masculine characteristic"). Using the time required for the choice as their measure, they had Ss make decisions in three different conditions:

1. In a room alone with the experimenter.
2. Before a one-way mirror with the illumination increased so that S could see several observers.
3. Before a one-way mirror that S knew shielded observers, although he could not see them.

The longest time for decision was in the latter situation when the individual did not know *who* was observing him. The shortest decision time was found alone with E (experimenter), with visible observers producing delays of intermediate length. In other words, taking behavior with the experimenter alone as the standard, the use of a one-way screen increased the differential effects, particularly when observers were actually hidden.

Wapner and Alper studied normal adults. Pishkin (1963) compared performance by schizophrenic adults on a simple task when the experimenter was present and when the procedures were automated. The schizophrenics, whose difficulties include establishing contact with other persons, performed *better* when the experimenter was not present. It is possible, of course, that the schizophrenic subjects did not know that one-way mirrors and electronic devices made their behavior immediately accessible to the experimenter, despite his absence. At any rate, these findings are interesting in suggesting that the effects of observation techniques are not invariant, but depend also on the personality or attitudes of the person observed.

The differential effects produced by an investigator are not confined to the laboratory. In natural settings, the presence of an observer arouses concern, interest, or secrecy, even though he never asks questions or obviously stares at others (Sherif and Sherif, 1964). He is, after all, a person whose presence is to be *explained*. People responding to a public opinion survey are more likely to give "middle-class" answers to a middle-class interviewer than to a working class interviewer (Cantril, 1944). Lower-class delinquent boys interviewed by college students give a "typical" picture of the nonverbal "lower class;" but when interviewed by another delinquent, they talk freely and at length (Pearl, 1965). Numerous studies show that Negro children react to intelligence tests and information tests differently when the investigator is white than when Negro. In one study, Negro and white examiners tested both Negro and white children. The average I.Q. was approximately 6 points higher for both Negro and white children when tested by an examiner of their own ethnic grouping. In another study, accuracy by Negroes on an information test increased markedly when a Negro asked the questions (Pettigrew, 1964).

On paper-and-pencil tests of personality and attitudes, it is now well-known that the individual is highly aware that the investigator may evaluate his "personality." In the research setting, he is likely to endorse statements that he thinks are socially desirable in the opinion of his evaluators (Edwards, 1957; Rorer, 1965). What is "socially desirable" in personality or attitude turns out to fall within the bounds of cultural or group norms defining desirable and "normal" personal traits. Thus, at least in part, paper-and-pencil tests of personality and attitude assess the individual's sensitivity in identifying the purposes and the normative standards of the test administrators. Usually, he knows that agreeing with some statements (e.g., "I usually cross the street to avoid a person I do not like") will have negative connotation about him as a person.

There is still controversy among specialists about the importance of the awareness of "being studied," and the tendency to respond with the "socially desirable." However, the facts indicating their importance are not limited to the technical sphere of research specialists. Referring to his attempts to secure interview material for a book, the novelist Truman Capote made the following observation: "People who don't understand the literary process are put off by notebooks . . . and tape recorders are worse—they completely ruin the quality of the thing being felt or talked about. If you write down or tape what people say, it makes them feel inhibited and self conscious. It makes them say what they think you *expect* them to say" (*Life* [magazine], 1966).

In experimentation, differential effects are specified more easily, although they are not less complex. In interpreting the findings on what is called "experimenter bias" and "experimenter effect," it is well to keep in mind that the mere presence of the experimenter is not the only determinant. The experimenter also chose and arranged the site, selected the tasks to be performed, and usually instructed the subjects about their performance (Kintz *et al.,* 1965; Rosenthal, 1964, 1966). He is an authority figure with an aura transferred from modern science. The subject has entered the situation voluntarily (even though he may have been coerced by a requirement to get a course grade or by payment). He expects to carry out prearranged plans that he assumes have some useful purpose, for example, to "advance science." The laboratory experiment was described as a social situation by Martin Orne and an associate as follows:

There has been increasing awareness by behavioral scientists that the subject in an experimental investigation is not a passive entity. Experimental evidence (Orne, 1959; Orne and Scheibe, 1964) has demonstrated that the subject takes an active role in interpreting the nature of the investigation and makes implicit assumptions about the hypotheses being investigated which influence his performance in the experimental situation. Nor is an experimenter free from the influence of his own investment in the hypotheses he is investigating. In a series of studies, Rosenthal has shown that experimenters who have different hypotheses about the outcome of a particular experiment may obtain results which are congruent with their hypotheses (for example, Rosenthal, 1964; Rosenthal and Fode, 1963). Such studies imply that it is necessary to consider the nature of the special interpersonal interaction which exists between the subject and the experimenter in psychological experiments.

Orne (1960, 1962) has emphasized that the experimental context legitimizes a very broad range of behavioral requests. Subjects have implicit faith that experimenters are responsible people, that they will not be asked to carry out tasks which are devoid of meaning, and that regardless of appearances they will not be permitted to suffer any harm because of obvious social sanctions.

In a series of informal experiments in our laboratory, it has been impossible to devise a task which the subject perceives as completely "meaningless" within the context of an experiment. For example, subjects were confronted with a stack of paper, each page containing rows of random digits. The experimenter instructed subjects to continue adding the rows of numbers successively, and after accurately completing each page, to tear it into a minimum of 32 pieces. Although subjects were given no reason to justify the task, they continued this apparently meaningless endeavor beyond the tolerance limits of the experimenter (Orne, 1962).

Frank (1944) has reported some informal experiments in which subjects continued meaningless and impossible tasks, including trying to balance a marble on a small steel ball and transferring spilled mercury to a small bottle with a wooden paddle, even when an assistant tried to prevent them from trying to complete the tasks. No justification was given for performing the tasks other than that it was an experiment. . . . The limits of boredom, tolerance, pain and fatigue which are accepted as reasonable requests within an experimental situation seem extremely broad (Orne and Evans, 1965, pp. 189–190).

Research situations are one subclass of social situations in which some deliberate attempt is made to influence behavior. This is a very broad class of social situations, including those in which a communicator attempts to change a person's opinion or attitude and those in which a member of a group tries to get a fellow member to conform to the group's norms. Let us consider now some experiments on deliberate attempts to influence in *transitory* laboratory situations. Typically, such situations do not involve prior interaction or established interpersonal ties among subjects or between subject and researcher; however, the authority of the researcher to give instructions, make requests, and arrange the tasks is taken for granted.

DELIBERATE ATTEMPTS TO INFLUENCE BEHAVIOR IN TRANSITORY SITUATIONS

For many years, the scientific study of the differential effects of social situations was hampered by labels implying causal mechanisms that, in fact, explained very little. For example, the labels *suggestibility, hypnotic trance, imitation,* and *submission* have

been used as though they explained responses to social influence. In fact, such labels tell us nothing about what produced the behavior. They merely furnish names to identify the phenomena in question. ("He agreed *because* he is suggestible." "He simply *imitated* what he saw." "She couldn't pull her hands apart *because* she was *hypnotized.*")

Contemporary studies of social influence attempt to analyze the interacting factors—*in the social situation* and *from the person*—that produce compliance with social influences or resistance to them. Even hypnotic phenomena are being subjected to rigorous examination as differential effects of a particular social situation in which the investigator (hypnotist) goes through various procedures that will "induce a trance," such as instructing the subjects to fixate on flashing lights, to relax, etc.

An account of the extensive research on hypnosis is beyond the scope of this book. It is relevant, however, that phenomena treated for two centuries under the somewhat mystical cloak of "trances" are being analyzed in terms of the factors that affect the subject's "definition of the situation." The occurrence of behaviors usually taken as evidence of "hypnotic trance" (muscular rigidities, hallucinations, selective forgetting, post-hypnotic responses, etc.) has been found to vary with changes in instructions, tasks, and facilities (Barber and Glass, 1962).

There is now considerable evidence that the behaviors indicative of "heightened suggestibility" can be produced without the usual "trance induction" procedures (Barber and Calverly, 1964). Among the effective procedures are telling the subject that he is receiving a "powerful hypnotic drug" (actually sodium bicarbonate), that the experiment is a test of imagination (with instructions designed to heighten his desire to perform well), and requesting that he simulate hypnosis in order to deceive another experimenter (Barber and Calverly, 1964a; Barber and Calverly, 1964b; Glass and Barber, 1961; Orne and Evans, 1965). (Of course, the deception of an experimenter does not produce the experiences reported by "hypnotized" *Ss,* but the other procedures sometimes do.) Although there are wide individual differences in response to hypnosis procedures, it is becoming clear that the incidence and particular forms of "symptoms" are also a function of factors *out there* in the situation itself.

Milgram's Experiments on Reactions to Authority

The differential effects on behavior produced by a researcher's instructions and requests are examples of response to authority perceived as legitimate. We know that in social life much of our behavior is influenced by persons with legitimate authority over the running of daily affairs. We are inclined to behave as they expect or order us, in many cases for good reason. If our automobile is halted by a policeman who directs us to turn into another street, we usually assume that the order is given to protect us or other persons. We comply, whether it is convenient or not. However, some directives by persons in authority go strongly against the grain of those subject to them. One might suspect that a directive to administer pain to a fellow human being would be objectionable to most people. In a series of experiments, Milgram (1963, 1965) utilized the authority of a research figure to investigate this problem.

Acting "In the Name of Science . . .". Milgram studied the conditions in which *Ss* would agree or refuse to administer increasingly severe electric shocks to another person when that person erred in learning a list of paired words. The learner was actually in league with *E,* having been instructed to give wrong answers and to demand with increasing insistence as the shock increased that the experiment be stopped.

The shock generator (which actually only delivered a sample shock to convince *S* of its authenticity) was marked from 15 ("slight shock") to 450 volts ("danger: severe shock"). *S* was instructed to drill the learner and to increase the shock on each error. At 300 volts, the learner refused to answer and demanded to be freed. *E* commanded them to continue. *S's* score was assigned on the basis of the maximum intensity he delivered, a score of 30 representing the highest voltage and 0 representing unwillingness to administer any shock. *Ss* were mature males in samples stratified by age and socioeconomic rank.

The first condition studied was *proximity* of the learner. Figure 6.2 shows the decrease in the average intensity of shock delivered when the "victim" was in another room (but pounded on the wall), when only his voice could be heard, when he was 1½ feet away, and when *S* was ordered to force the victim's hand on the shockplate after he had removed it. In the latter variation, 70 percent of the *Ss* refused to continue the experiment, as compared with 34 percent when the victim was in the next room.

Similarly, the physical presence of *E* was found to be a particularly important factor: Compliance with instructions decreased markedly when *E* was out of the room, even though he gave orders by telephone. Some *Ss* reported they had administered the shock when in fact they had not.

By moving the experiment from Yale University to an office building in another town, Milgram hoped to assess the effect of the experiment's location. The experiment was presented as the work of a firm called "Research Associates" (which probably is a prestigeful title). At Yale, 65 percent delivered the maximum shock while 48 percent did so in the office building.

In the early stages, Milgram was sufficiently surprised at the extent of compliance with demands to increase the shock that he made a check to see whether other competent persons would have anticipated the results. He described the experimental setup and procedures to 40 psychiatrists, asking them to predict the percentage who would increase the shock to each level. The predictions underestimated considerably the amount of shock actually administered (See Figure 6.3). The psychiatrists predicted that only about one-tenth of a percent would deliver the maximum shock, while an average of 62 percent actually did.

Milgram attributes the predictive error to a conception of human action as determined by motives apart from the properties of particular situations. He points out that his experimental situation presented highly authoritative pressures on *S* to continue a task for which they were paid. Milgram's research and interpretation illustrate the value of studying the interaction of all sets of factors in a social situation, including the individual's motives and uncertainties relative to it. (Note: Milgram conducted a care-

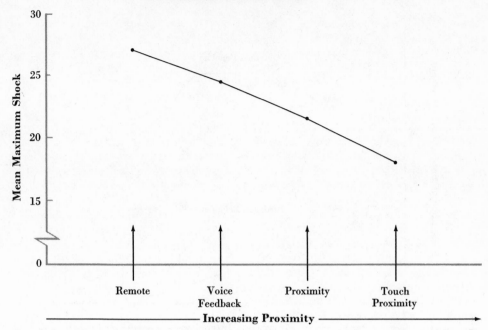

Fig. 6.2.   Effect of proximity of the "victim" upon average shock (maximum) delivered. (From S. Milgram, Some Conditions of Obedience and Disobedience to Authority, *Human Relations*, Plenum Press, 1965, vol. 18, issue no. 1, Fig. 1, p. 63.) Remote condition (*left*) placed victim in adjacent room, where only his pounding on the wall could be heard. Voice feedback was identical except that his voice could be heard. In proximity condition, victim was 1½ feet from subject in the same room. In touch proximity, subject was instructed to hold victim's hand on shockplate.

ful procedure after the experiment to assure Ss' well-being when they left the laboratory.)

In Milgram's experiments, the presence of two planted subjects who refused to continue the experiment substantially reduced compliance by the naive Ss, 90 percent of whom also refused. If the other persons had been fellow members of a group whose values opposed inflicting pain, there are good grounds for predicting unanimous refusal.

Milgram's research represents imaginative use of the special properties of an experimental situation for investigation of a significant problem, namely, the determinants of obedience to an authoritative command that runs counter to human values. Its contribution is to demonstrate the importance of varying factors *in the situation* (such as proximity, location, and social support) in producing behavior that the individual would not ordinarily engage in or in reinforcing his qualms so that he refuses. It shows decisively that in this jet age, people can be induced to go to great lengths in the

name of science, but that there are some who still say, "I'll go so far and no farther."

**Actions of
Other Persons
Like Ourselves**

As was evident in Milgram's experiments, the actions of other persons similar to the subject are particularly salient aspects of a social situation. Especially when the task is ambiguous (unstructured), decisions by others similar to oneself are frequently the major standard (anchor) for our own behavior (see Proposition 10). Clark (1916) demonstrated this nicely some decades ago by using the sense of smell, one of man's less reliable senses. Each of ten college students was exposed individually to an open bottle and asked to indicate *when* they detected the "odor." The bottle contained water. Only one person reported an odor. Then Clark repeated the procedure in a large class of 168 students. Within ten seconds, some students on the first row indicated they detected the odor; in 15 sec-

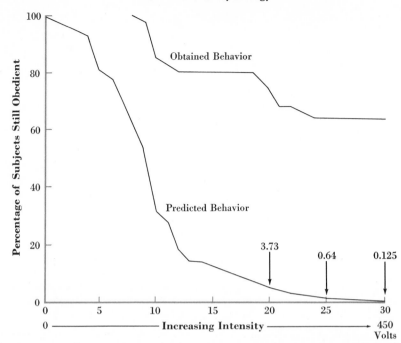

Fig. 6.3.   Obtained percentages of subjects in voice feedback condition who delivered shock at each intensity compared with percentages predicted by psychiatrists. (From S. Milgram, Some Conditions of Obedience and Disobedience to Authority, *Human Relations,* Plenum Press, 1965, vol. 18, issue no. 1, Fig. 3, p. 73.) The experiment was described in detail to 40 psychiatrists at a "leading medical school." Their predictions (*lower curve*) greatly underestimated the incidence of obedience actually obtained (*upper curve*).

onds, some on the second row responded; by half a minute, response was made on the third row; and so on until 33 students reported an odor by the end of three minutes. As in Milgram's study, the spatial arrangement of those responding was particularly interesting. All who responded were within the first 5 rows of seats, and 23 were on one side of the room.

Do the actions of casual acquaintances or total strangers affect our behavior when we do *not know* that we are in a research situation? This question was investigated by varying the decision made by a stranger in the natural setting of a college library.

**To Volunteer or
Not to Volunteer?**

The problem studied by Rosenbaum and Blake (1955) was the effect of another person's reponse on an individual's decision whether or not to serve as a voluntary subject in an experiment. An assistant to E chose a seat in the library among a number

of other students. He appeared to be just another student at work. Five minutes later, E approached the table and asked the assistant to take part in an experiment, speaking just loudly enough that others could hear the request. When the assistant accepted, he followed E from the room and returned in four minutes. In another condition, the assistant replied "No, I'd rather not" and turned to his books. The critical S was the person sitting next to the assistant. After the assistant had either accepted and returned to the table or had refused, S was asked to participate in the same manner. As a control, the assistant was eliminated and E approached S directly. The following shows the number of naive Ss who volunteered under each of the conditions:

	Agrees	Refuses	Absent
No. of Ss:			
Agreeing	13	3	8
Refusing	2	12	7
Total	15	15	15

Blake reported that one S agreeing to serve when the assistant refused said that he was interested in psychology and had been hoping to have the opportunity to serve as subject. This example of prior attitude reminds us of the importance of internal factors in the frame of reference. If the experiment had been performed during final examination week, the assistant's compliance or refusal might have had very little effect.

AGREEMENT WITH ANOTHER'S JUDGMENT IN SITUATIONS VARYING IN STRUCTURE

In Chapter 4, it was stated as a general principle that the effect of immediate social influence (e.g., words, deeds, and suggestions) increases as the objective structure of the task decreases. Here we will consider representative studies from an extensive research literature on deliberate attempts at influencing another's judgment in situations of varying objective structure. Other such studies are reviewed in appropriate context in later chapters.

When objective structure is lacking, the spoken judgments of other persons have pronounced effects, even though no deliberate attempt is made to exert influence. The individual comes to perceive the situation in line with the views of the others, and is frequently unaware that he has been influenced.

The basis of the above generalizations is a large number of experiments that have varied the design of Sherif's 1935 study of social factors in perception (Chapter 10). Sherif used the autokinetic situation as a prototype for stimuli lacking objective structure. In a completely dark room, a single pinpoint of light appears to move (autokinesis). The extent of apparent movement of the light differs markedly from individual to individual and in different spatial arrangements of the room. This unstructured situation arouses considerable uncertainty. Individuals judging the extent of movement together shifted their judgments toward a common range and around a common mode.

However, even in a stimulus situation permitting such variable response alternatives as the autokinetic situation, the sky is not the limit for attempted social influence. When the person forms his own standard and range for judging movement and then is confronted by another person giving judgments extremely discrepant from his established range, the other person's judgments have little if any effect—although the experience is somewhat unsettling for him. Whittaker (1964) showed that in the autokinetic situation, the judgments of a "planted" S that were so discrepant from the S's established range that they did not overlap with them at all still served to anchor S's judgments. The naive S's judgments shifted toward the anchor (assimilation effect). However, by systematically varying the discrepancy between anchor and established range, Whittaker found that there is a limit to the assimilation effect. When the planted Ss began to make judgments of movement *12 times the largest distance previously estimated by the naive S,* the naive S simply stuck by his original range.

Another factor that can affect whether S will be influenced by the spoken judgments of another person in a highly unstructured situation is his feeling of certainty-uncertainty or confidence-lack-of-confidence in his judgments. In general, an unstructured situation arouses uncertainty in some degree—unease and even anxiety in extreme cases. Measures that reduce the uncertainty also reduce the likelihood that S will adopt the standard provided by another person. For example, when S is told either that his judgments are correct and/or that the other person is unreliable in performing such tasks, he is unlikely to be influenced by the judgments of the other person (Kelman, 1950; Mausner, 1954, a,b).

Some writers have suggested that the entire issue of compliance with a social influence in a transitory social situation can be reduced to how confident the individual feels in his judgments. This seems to be a truism. If a person is confident in his judgment, why should he alter it? The difficulty in taking confidence as *the* factor determining whether a suggestion will be effective is that "confidence" is not merely a personal quality and does not vary directly with other important changes in the situation (Tajfel, 1969).

For example, it is now well-known that the *discrepancy* between a person's view and a standard introduced to influence him affects his certainty of his judgment. There is considerable evidence, however, that despite the uncertainty aroused, standards extremely different from the person's established judgment scale are less effective than standards nearer his scale (e.g., Blake, Helson and Mouton, 1957; Fisher and Lubin, 1958; Tuddenham, 1961; Luchins and Luchins, 1963; Whittaker, 1964). Despite feelings of discomfiture, an extremely discrepant opinion is rejected.

An influential study by Asch (1956) showed that false judgments contrary to clearly perceived differences between stimuli in an otherwise credible situation shake the confidence even of hardy persons who dare to defy them. It further showed that social influence running contrary to discriminable differences affects only a minority of individuals and only a minority of judgments, despite general quaking in subjective confidence. Asch's studies have been a model for many studies of social influence in transitory situations in recent years, particularly with the apparatus devised by Crutchfield (1955) that automatically simulates the responses of other subjects.

Moving with the Crowd Has Limits

Asch (1956) studied the social conditions conducive to resisting or complying with the spoken judgments of others in an experimental situation when these judgments are perceived as *contrary to fact.* The basic procedure was as follows: A naive S along with seven other college students was instructed to match the length of a standard line with one of three other lines (see Fig. 6.4). In fact, the other Ss were preinstructed to select the *wrong* line on certain trials. On the first two trials, they selected the correct line. On the third, they all selected a line ¾ inches longer than the correct match; on the fourth a line 1 inch shorter, and so on. The differences were sufficiently clear-cut that Ss matching standard and the comparison *alone* erred very seldom.

Asch's question was: What would happen when social consensus contradicted clearcut perceptual evidence? He found that 32

percent of the total estimates on the critical trials (when the majority erred) were errors in the direction of the majority. However, individual differences were great. Of 50 naive *Ss,* 13 did not err at all, 15 made one to three errors in the majority direction, 7 made four to five, 11 made six to nine errors, and only 4 Ss made 10 or 11 errors out of a possible total of 12.

Of those who went along with the majority, Asch found very few who were not aware that their estimates erred toward the majority. The remainder squared their experience with their actions by deciding that there must be some illusion or inadequacy in their own perception, or that it was better to be wrong than appear "different" in the situation. Most of those who did *not* err reported considerable discomfiture and conflict at the experience, despite their conviction that they were correct.

In varying the experimental conditions, Asch found that errors were considerably less when only 1 or 2 Ss gave the wrong answers, but that a majority of three produced average errors and a range of individual differences equivalent to larger majorities. The presence of another naive S or a planted S instructed to respond correctly reduced the number of errors sharply (to 10.4 percent and 5.5 percent, respectively). However, if the partner giving correct judgments were withdrawn halfway through the experiment, errors on the remaining trials climbed to 28.5 percent of the total judgments. A correct partner who arrived halfway through the experiment reduced the frequency of error to 8.7 percent. A planted partner who always chose the line *intermediate* between the erroneous majority and the correct choice reduced the frequency of errors slightly, but not significantly.

Asch found three experimental variations that sharply reduced the tendency to err. The first was the presence of one planted S making wrong choices among a naive majority: "contagious laughter" at the planted S spread among the others. The second was increasing the difference between the lines chosen by the majority and the correct line: The proportion of error decreased with the increased distances of the majority choice from the correct choice. Finally, by making the differences between correct and majority choice very small (decreasing the "structural clarity" of the task), Asch found a stronger effect of the majority, that is, increased error toward the wrong choice by naive *Ss*.

In short, Asch's experiments show that, despite severe jars to the person's confidence, there are limits to the extent of influence that can be exerted by a majority in a transitory social situation. These limits are determined by (1) the objective differences between the stimuli (smaller differences being more unstructured); (2) the extent of the discrepancy between the correct choice and the choice of the majority; and (3) the presence or absence of person's giving erroneous judgments and their number.

The reader who examines these results in conjunction with Principles 8, 9, and 10 and the results of attempted social influence in unstructured social situations will understand why degree of stimulus structure is considered fundamental. Note that, at the most, Asch's conditions produced error in the majority direction in only one-third of the judgments rendered (despite the obvious discomfiture at the bizarre situation), while in an unstructured situation, every subject converges toward an introduced standard unless it is extraordinarily discrepant (e.g., 12 times the person's largest judgment previously, as reported in Whittaker's experiment).

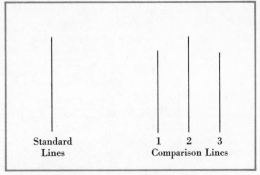

Fig. 6.4.   Example of stimulus cards in Asch experiment. Subjects were instructed to choose the comparison line (*right*) that matched the standard (*left*). In this case, correct choice is line 2; but the majority would select line 1 or 3.

SIZING UP OTHER PERSONS IN A SITUATION

So far, we have spoken of other people in the research situation as though it mattered little who they were as long as some were researchers and some subjects. We did note that some experimenters on verbal conditioning were more effective than others, and that the identity of an interviewer or a tester could influence the outcome. Now let us explore some of the findings about how we size up other people whom we meet. We already know that the roles of subject and experimenter are salient in how we perceive persons in a research situation. In many cases, these roles are also compounded by the fact that subjects are students and researchers are faculty. This does not mean, however, that all subjects size-up all experimenters in the same way.

The following experiment by Stevenson and Allen (1964) shows that the sex of the experimenter and subjects is an important variable and also that some experimenters as persons are more effective than others in producing behavior in an experiment.

Who Is Approving Makes a Difference

Stevenson had previously found that verbal approval by an adult of the opposite sex had more effect on children's performance than that of an adult of the same sex. The effect was to *increase* the rate of response on a simple task (placing marbles of five colors into holes painted with matching colors). The problem of a study by Stevenson and Allen (1964) was to determine whether adults would respond similarly. The *Es* were eight men and eight women who volunteered from a psychology class. They were not told the purpose of the study but were trained in the procedures. Each *E* was randomly assigned to 16 *Ss*, eight male and eight female, all summer school students. During the experiment, *E* delivered preplanned supportive comments twice a minute for 5½ minutes (e.g., "That's fine.").

The main results are shown in Fig. 6.5, representing the average number of marbles placed during successive 30 second intervals by *Ss* with same and opposite sexed *Es*. The curves for female *Ss* are higher throughout than those for males; however, performance is also higher when

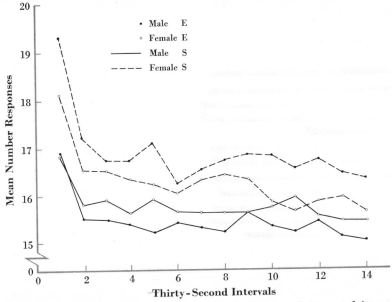

Fig. 6.5. Average number of responses made during each 30-second interval by male and female subjects with male and female experimenters. (From Harold W. Stevenson and Sara Allen, 1964. Adult performance as a function of sex of experimenter and sex of subject. *J. abnorm. soc. Psychol.*, **68**, No. 2, p. 215. Copyright 1964 by the American Psychological Association, and reproduced by permission.) Solid lines represent male subjects; dashed lines, female subjects. Solid black dot indicates that experimenter was male, while white dot indicates female experimenter.

Ss are tested by members of the opposite sex than by their own. Note that (unlike the children in the earlier study) the adults did not respond to the verbal approval by improving their response. The authors report that the drop in performance occurred because the adults started out so fast that they could not maintain the rates (apparently they assumed that speed was important). Furthermore, they report that the verbal comments had the effect of "transforming the task from a simple one to a complex one. Many of the subjects reported that they thought the experimenter was reinforcing only particular kinds of responses or only particular sequences of responses" (p. 216). Finally, they found that relative effectiveness of the *E's* (male or female) in eliciting high response from *Ss* of the same sex was closely related to their relative effectiveness with members of the opposite sex. (Rank-order correlation for male *Es* was .79 and for females was .86, both statistically significant.)

Stevenson and Allen's experiment suggests that the appraisal of an experimenter must be a rapid process when a major social difference, such as sex roles, is involved. The lack of correlation between the experimenter's age, appearance, or prior experience and his effectiveness is not too surprising. Considerable research on how we form impressions of other people indicates that our appraisals are seldom made on the basis of isolated personal characteristics, but rather on the basis of a pattern composed of the person's appearance, gestures, movements, voice, speech, and interpersonal responses (Asch, 1946; Luchins, 1960; Taguiri and Petrullo, 1958; Secord and Backman, 1964). In his studies of experimenter bias, Rosenthal (1966) has shown that a number of salient personal characteristics can produce differences in the behavior of experimental subjects.

Person Perception

With reference to the large amount of research on "person perception," a few generalizations stand out that will prove useful throughout the book (cf. Bruner and

Taguiri, 1954; Secord and Backman, 1964; Schranger and Altrocchi, 1964; Taguiri and Petrullo, 1958). With some exceptions, such as the study by Kelley on how the designation of an instructor as "warm" or "cold" affected student participation and evaluation, the procedures in this research do not involve perceiving a person. Typically, the subject is presented with a verbal description of a person, or a cluster of trait labels ("intelligent, rigid, cold," etc.), or photographs of persons, or simply the names of social roles (occupational, sex role, age grades, etc.) and groups (ethnic, religious, political, etc.). Then he is asked to make ratings about the person, or to describe him further, or to tell a story about him. In other words, the term "person perception" is something of a misnomer in terms of the typical research procedure. Most of the research clearly studies how we size-up people, how we judge them, and how we evaluate them.

One generalization that stands out from the research rings true to our experience when we first encounter a person—say, on a bus or train. We have an itch to place him (or her) in the schemes of social life, to see where he fits in the immediate situation, where he came from, what he does, and who he is. Placing someone in the social schemes is sometimes almost immediate on the basis of appearance, clothing, gesture, possessions, voice, or demeanor. This is particularly the case when the person's sex, clothing, skin color, or accent is a visible sign of a significant social differentiation.

As research has shown, almost everyone has an "implicit theory of personality" (Bruner and Taguiri, 1954), that leads him to expect certain personal characteristics to go with others—prizing some while objecting to others. Still, major outlines are provided to our "theories" by the categorization of the person in the social scheme. This categorization immediately limits the range and kind of behavior that we expect of the person and the personal qualities we anticipate. If we are male, we do not slap a lady on the back, nor do we expect her to carry our suitcase. If a person is categorized as inferior by our social circle, we do not invite the person to a place where our friends may see us, nor do we expect that person to exhibit personal traits that are not associated with the inferior status given him. If he does, his behavior is seen as impertinent or that of an upstart. If we meet a person of the opposite sex whose religion or politics or ethnic background is outside of the range for intermarriage in our group, we may terminate the encounter as quickly as possible, especially if the person is attractive.

In many of the major categories of social life, there is substantial agreement among persons belonging to any one group about the personal qualities and traits to be expected of those belonging to other groups. This is particularly the case in times of stability, when relations between human beings are not in a state of change. When members of the same group agree substantially on the traits they attribute to members of another group, we call them *stereotypes* (which we shall discuss in Chapter 12). Whether the trait clusters bear resemblance to the actual behavior of the persons to whom they are attributed is, for the time being, beside the point. They do affect our behavior. If we expect women to be flirtatious and flighty, doctors to be reliable and conscientious, Negroes to be ignorant and lazy, Jews to be pushy and grasping, or Protestant Anglo-Saxons to be narrow and self-righteous, such expectations will affect our appraisals of specific individuals and our interaction with them.

Whether stemming from stereotyped conceptions of other groups or roles or personally evolved conceptions of another person, impressions of other persons invariably involve an evaluation of them. Furthermore, the evaluation is seldom an abstract, intellectual affair. It focuses on the person's *relationship* to us. This generalization is derived from studies that allow the individual to describe other people naturally, without imposing upon him a list of adjectives or traits devised by the researcher. For example, Secord analyzed 120 tape-recorded descriptions of other persons and found that abstract qualities of the persons were rarely referred to. Rather, the descriptions were full of "relational terms" (Secord and Backman, 1964, p. 53). The terms that we use in naturalistic descriptions of others are revealing in other respects. Tajfel and Wilkes (1963) found that the terms used earliest in describing others are also those that the person regards as more important. When he rates others on these traits, he seldom sees them as "in-between" in that respect, possessing a moderation of the desired quality. His ratings are more extreme, as if to say "you either have it or you don't."

The importance of interpersonal relations was also supported in a study of children's assessments of one another in a summer camp by Yarrow and Campbell (1963). In comparing the children's descriptions of each other with ratings made by adults, they noted that adult views of the children were different. The children's descriptions "were dominated by social relevance; the emphasis on interaction and the very common use of evaluative appraisals gave evidence of this" (p. 63). The children, however, did show concern with similar aspects of their relationships:

Children's appraisals of their peers in many respects showed shared sensitivities, with repeated thematic emphasis on certain salient relationships, such as sociability, affiliative tendencies, potentially hostile acts. The same themes, with few exceptions, were characteristic of both initial and considered impressions at each age level studied. . . . These similar sensitivities (unchanged by age) may possibly be attributable to a common culture of childhood and to similar learning of the significant interpersonal cues, those that are differentially rewarding or punishing in nature (p. 71).

There are also, as noted earlier, "common cultures" in the adult world. These are particularly salient in providing "shared sensitivities" to different areas of interpersonal dealings with others. In fact, such common culture and shared sensitivities are the earmarks of the human group. There is a host of expectations about others that have their origins in becoming a member of a particular group. Among other things, we expect that fellow members of our group will share ideas with us and will listen to us and heed us.

In a study by Turk, Hartley, and Shaw (1962), it was shown that we expect to be influenced more by a person with whom we share membership in similar groups than by one who belongs to different groups. They asked each subject to make a series of ratings of photographs, indicating the likelihood that the person in the photograph belonged to groups similar to his own. He also indicated the likelihood that he would listen to, like, and be influenced by that person's ideas. They concluded: "The more an individual perceives common group membership with another, the more influence he expects will flow between the two of them" (p. 28). Not only do we expect to be influenced by a fellow group member but we also expect that he will reciprocate.

FRAME OF REFERENCE
IN SOCIAL-PSYCHOLOGICAL RESEARCH

This chapter has considered the frame of reference for behavior in a social situation. Its principal lessons are two:

1. In any social situation, it is not sufficient to consider only the individual and some other specific aspect of the situation, such as other people present. As we have seen, every social situation consists of at least four sets of factors (other persons; task or problem; location and facilities; system of relationships linking the individual to these). As the factors in a social situation function *interdependently,* it follows that neglect of any one set will lead to conclusions that are in error or lack validity. The investigation of the interrelationship of factors in a social situation is, in fact, the central problem of social psychology. It becomes particularly crucial when we consider how we appraise other people, for other people are sized-up in terms of how they are related to us.

2. The interdependence of factors in a social situation means that research methods and techniques designed to study behavior are also integral parts of the frame of reference. Their effects have to be assessed. We have seen that some experiments have utilized the commanding characteristics of research situations to study deliberate attempts at social influence. Neglecting the research aspects of the situation amounts to ignoring important factors that contributed to the results. In extreme cases, the findings are artifacts the explanation of which lies much more in the neglected research situation than in the factors that the researcher thought he was studying.

In response to widespread neglect of these points in theory and research, a corrective movement arose among researchers, broadly labeled as the *social psychology of the psychological experiment* (Riecken, 1962). We have seen that the phenomena of researcher bias and the "demand characteristics" of the research situation are found equally in test and interview situations.

HOW CAN ARTIFACTS ATTRIBUTABLE TO RESEARCH SITUATIONS BE AVOIDED?

The recent findings that researchers can unwittingly bias results in line with their hypotheses (Rosenthal, 1966) and that research situations are highly compelling influences on behavior (Orne, 1965) do not represent an entirely new discovery, although the emphasis is exerting a much-needed corrective. In his monumental study of *Sensation and Perception in the History of Experimental Psychology* (1942), Boring wrote of such effects when he discussed the controversies between "schools" of psychology and the fact that each "school" obtained research evidence to support its view.

Within the school agreement is facilitated. Wundt's students confirmed the tridimensional theory of feelings; others did not. Würzburg never found images for thought; Cornell did. Is feeling a sensation or not? Laboratory atmosphere largely determined what would be found in answer to that question, and laboratory atmosphere often extended from a parent laboratory to its offspring. Psychical acts belong to southern Germany; contents to northern; whereas mind that is of use to the organism is American. . . . there can be no doubt that within the *Zeitgeist* there are local *Geister* which determine what theory you shall apply to your experimental findings or even how you shall record your data (pp. 612–613).

In the long-term view of things, researcher bias is a less serious problem than it may seem relative to the outcomes of one or a few studies. The ultimate corrective for researcher bias in any science is the skeptical researcher who does not take all prior findings at face value and proceeds to repeat and vary conditions of prior research, carefully indicating the variations at every step.

For example, for years leading textbooks contained the conclusion, based on prior research, that a person's attitude on a controversial issue did not affect how he judged the content of statements on that issue in terms of how *pro* or *anti* the persons were on the topic. Repetition of the procedures in earlier research revealed an unwitting source of bias. A good many subjects had failed to follow instructions to find about equal numbers of statements for each degree of *pro* or *anti* views. They had been eliminated from the analysis as "careless subjects." These subjects were also those who felt most strongly about the issue at hand, that is, had an intense attitude on the topic (Hovland and Sherif, 1952; Sherif and Hovland, 1953). When persons highly committed on the topic were included in the analysis, their attitudes did affect the way they placed the statements.

Of course, the researcher can and should make positive efforts to make his own theoretical biases *explicit*, to devise research that sorely tests his expectations, and to rid himself of narrow ethnocentric views that blind him to alternative hypotheses. But researchers are human, too, and must ultimately await the *test of time* to see how generally valid their findings and conclusions are. Meanwhile, there are ways of minimizing researcher bias other than replication.

Use of a Combination of Methods and Techniques for Data Collection. One of the main sources for researcher bias is exclusive reliance on one experiment or one field study using a single method of data collection that is entirely under the researcher's control. For example, in Milgram's study, suppose that when he left the room, he had taken the subject's word for whether he administered shock in his absence. Probably the way he asked the question would have influenced the subject's replies. However, as the apparatus recorded the administration of "shock," Milgram had an independent check that could not be affected by the way he asked the question.

In the study of complex social situations, *a combination of methods and research techniques is needed.* For example, in a study of role relations in a group, a researcher can observe interaction among persons in a laboratory task and record who talks to whom, who talks most and least, and so on. However, as long as the researcher selects the task and selects the aspect of interaction on which he focuses, he may very well bias his findings unwittingly. To avoid doing so, he should repeat his observations by using tasks the group selects or, better yet, extend his observations to situations wherein the members interact normally. In short, he should extend his observations *across situations* and *outside of the laboratory* into the field. The combined use of laboratory and field research to investigate a problem is one of the first steps toward reducing researcher bias in social psychology.

There is always a source of bias as long as the researcher relies only on his own observations, ratings, and analysis of interaction. The use of another independent observer will establish the *reliability* of his observations—but not necessarily their *validity,* as the other observer may share his bias.

In studies of group formation to be reported in Chapter 11, observer ratings of behavior looking from outside at the group were compared with findings obtained with the sociometric technique. This technique provides a view of the group from the inside, as the individuals choose whom they like to associate with, and who starts things and gets things done when they are together. If the group formation looks the same by these two techniques, conclusions about relations within the group are on more solid grounds. As another independent measure to check observer bias, an *indirect* technique for assessing the relative standing of members was used, namely, judgments of each others' performance on an unstructured task. When it was found that over- and underestimations for the various persons correlated significantly with the persons' relative positions in the group, as determined by observer ratings and their likes and dislikes revealed in sociometric choices, it was possible to conclude that an unbiased view of the group had been attained.

In short, one way of reducing researcher bias in social psychology is the use of a combination of independent techniques for data collection whose agreement constitutes the test of conclusions. Another is to compare findings from laboratory research and field research, when the researcher does not have control over the site, facilities, and tasks. Ultimately the search for valid conclusions rests upon such measures being taken by different researchers over time.

Reducing Artifacts Unintentionally Produced by the Research Situation. In research, the methods may be such a salient aspect of the situation that they alone produce differential behavior. The laboratory experiment is always an artificial environment—in fact, deliberately so. Its only claim to validity is that it can incorporate major variables from real problems, controlling and varying them in ways seldom possible in real life. When the researcher tries to do this without recognizing the unique atmosphere of the research situation for the subjects, he is very likely to produce artifacts. For example, he may carefully design a persuasive communication to study its effects on subjects' attitudes. He may get a large change in opinion owing to the subjects' belief that, in order to be good subjects, they should not respond in the same way twice to his attitude test. The findings, then, tell us more about the subjects' expectations of the research than about the effects of communication in real life.

In laboratory experiments, it is usually routine to take certain steps to avoid artifacts of this kind. First, the experimenter chooses subjects who are *naive about the stimulus materials and purpose of the study.* Certainly this was more feasible years ago before psychological experiments began to be popularized widely. In college populations and in some high schools today, it is by no means easy to find subjects who have not heard about, say, the autokinetic phenomenon or the Asch experiments. The use of naive subjects is, however, still an essential condition for laboratory experimentation.

Second, the experimenter does not tell the subject what the experiment is about and deliberately constructs credible instructions describing the research as something else—for example, a "test of night vision" or an "eye-hand coordination study." Such "deception" is by no means unique to social psychology. Experiments on lifted weights in which anchoring stimuli are introduced do not instruct the subjects that they are judging the same weights. Of course, such "deception" is not effective if the subjects have already concluded that "psychologists always deceive people." In this case, the subjects simply formulate their own hunches about the purpose of the experiment. As we saw in the study by Stevenson and Allen, the subjects' hunches about an experimental procedure may even be more complicated than the real hypotheses.

Third, experimenters usually conduct a postexperimental interview to get the subjects' views of what happened. There is little doubt that this procedure could and should be improved upon. For example, many of the earlier studies of "verbal conditioning" mentioned earlier in this chapter used brief postexperimental checks and reported that the subjects were not aware that they received verbal approval for particular utterances. More careful interviews in later studies showed that some subjects may not volunteer such information in a short time, or may hesitate for fear of being wrong or of being "fooled." Longer interviews revealed that many of these subjects were aware and could verbalize the procedures.

One of the more active researchers on these problems, Martin Orne, has proposed further checks against the "research effect" in the laboratory. For example, he suggested that before an experiment some subjects be shown the laboratory setup and told about the procedures, with the request that they pretend that they had been subjects in such an experiment and produce the data (e.g., responses or rating scale) that they would have as subjects. Their "pretending" responses can then be compared with those of subjects who actually take part, in order to see whether subjects "see through" the experiment and are merely behaving as they think is expected of them. Alternatively, Orne has had subjects pretend to be real subjects, unknown to the experimenter, to see if the subjects' guesses about the "demand character" of the situations match those of naive subjects and if an experimenter can recognize the difference.

There are some limitations to these suggestions, even though their adoption would be a great improvement over uncritical acceptance of findings. For example, when subject differences are of interest in research, it would be necessary to have comparable subjects as pretenders and as actual subjects. In a study on judgment of statements about religion, Mausner (1960) reported that instructing devoutly religious subjects to make judgments as though they were atheists did not prove feasible. They confessed that they could not imagine how it would be to take an atheistic viewpoint. Similarly, some white subjects found it very difficult to respond to material on the "race issue" as though they were Negro (Webb and Chueh, 1962).

Another way to circumvent the impact of the research situation and setting is to devise measures of behavior that are *disguised* or *indirect*. For example, in research on attitudes to be summarized in Chapter 15, the subject's task was to make non-evaluative judgments of statements on a controversial social issue. The task was presented as an "intellectual" or cognitive task and his attitude on the topic was not mentioned. He could not know that his attitude would be revealed by the number of categories he used to sort the statements and the relative frequencies he placed in the various categories. Such techniques have been employed both in the laboratory and in the field.

As information about experimentation is popularized and spread, the usual laboratory with facilities allocated for the announced purpose of studying social behavior may become increasingly difficult to defend as a source of valid data. One way to minimize the danger of artifacts stemming from the demand character of the laboratory atmosphere is to *combine experimental techniques with the naturalness of field settings in which people are not aware that their behavior is the topic of investigation.*

In studies on group formation, group functioning, and intergroup relations, in experiments in natural conditions as well as field studies, data were collected without arousing people's awareness that they were being studied (Chapters 8–11). Of course, such naturalistic studies require a great deal of work in order to attain both validity and precision in measurement. Further, they limit the use of verbal control and instructions that are so common in laboratory research. However, in combination with indirect measurement techniques originally developed in laboratory research, it is possible to do research taking advantage of the naturalness and the varied locations and tasks of the field while still attaining precision in measurement.

In addition to those reported in various chapters of this book, the interested reader will find others in a recent publication on "unobtrusive measures" in research (Webb *et al.,* 1966).

7

Properties of Human Groups and Their Formation

Major Topics of the Chapter

Differentiating group situations from other social situations

Definition of group: minimum essentials

Degrees of "groupness"

Gradations from togetherness to group situations

Generality of group formation in social life

Informal beginnings of organization

Advantages of "group" as a generic concept

Group formation and the sets of factors in any social situation

Four essentials of group formation and functioning

Motivational basis conducive to recurrent interaction

An illustrative case: Ruhleben

ORIENTATION
TO STUDY
OF HUMAN GROUPS

Laboratory experiments reviewed in Chapter 6 illustrated the interdependent effects of four sets of factors on behavior in any social situation. We found that the differential effects of social situations are not simply the result of added stimulation from other persons who are present. Even in a brief laboratory session, it makes a difference *who* is present, how the subject sizes up those people, and what they are doing.

This chapter concerns interpersonal relationships that are particularly consequential: those among members of a human group. Its main task is to map features that characterize a human group of any kind, that is, the properties common to all groups. We have to distinguish interaction among group members from other interaction episodes. Then we shall inquire how groups form.

When we speak of group properties, we refer to *regularities* in the interaction among individuals and in their activities over time. Thus the properties of a group are keys to unlock the dynamics of its functioning. They capture the patterns within which individual members pursue their goals, transact with other members, and engage in activities with them.

DIFFERENTIATING GROUP SITUATIONS
FROM OTHER SOCIAL SITUATIONS

In ordinary conversation, the word *group* is used in many different ways. We need to specify carefully what is meant by the term and use it in that sense. For example,

people sometimes speak of a group waiting for a bus, of a classroom group, a discussion group, a training group, or a therapy group. In experiments, the subject samples are often referred to as experimental groups and control groups. We read about work groups, political groups, religious groups, and ethnic groups. We speak of our next of kin, our friends, or the circle in which we take our leisure as groups. Beyond the fact that a number of people are together and (possibly) interacting with one another, do relationships among individuals in all of the foregoing situations share properties in common? Very probably they do not.

The way we define the concept *group* will shape how we proceed to study behavior in a group situation. It is important to define the concept for other reasons, too. First, study after study of actual groups that function for a period of time reveals that the properties of groups are useful in predicting the differential effects of a social situation involving members (D.E. $= B_s - B_a$, p. 107). Second, membership in groups that endure for a time has consequences even when the individual is not face-to-face with other members.

It may be easier to understand why the properties of a group are useful in predicting differential effects on the behavior of members if we refer to the discussion in Chapter 5 about the part-whole relationship. Our perception of parts in a geometric figure or judgment of one stimulus in a sequence is affected by the whole pattern or sequence. Likewise, we size up and respond to individuals as parts of a social pattern. When we are part of a group, the pattern of give-and-take affects how we judge others and even how we evaluate ourselves.

DEFINITION OF GROUP

The aim of a useful definition is to establish explicit referents for a concept, to specify properties that are *essential* for inclusion in the category, and at the same time to be as parsimonious as possible. The definition that follows was developed on the basis of extensive survey of research literature, of first-hand reports, and of theoretical writing on groups of all kinds performing various tasks in many different locations (Sherif and Sherif, 1953; 1964). It is to be regarded as a statement of the *minimum* properties that distinguish a group from other associations.

A group is a social unit consisting of a number of individuals who stand in role and status relationships to one another, stabilized in some degree at the time, and who possess a set of values or norms of their own regulating their behavior, at least in matters of consequence to the group.

There are several terms in this definition that have to be specified, for example, *role, status, values* or *norms.* These terms will be defined in ways that are conducive to research procedures for studying them when we discuss group formation. Here, let us consider some characteristics of the definition as a whole.

Some terms need to be made explicit immediately. "A social unit" refers to a more-or-less bounded system of interaction, delineated from others. In well-delineated and stable groups, the *unit character* of the system is explicitly recognized by members both in their expressions of "we-ness" and in treatment of persons outside of the system (in-group and out-group delineation). Yet, even if not explicitly recognized by members, the delineated unit character of a group can be inferred on the basis of observed *regularity* and *frequency of interaction* among the individuals and the *social distance maintained from others.*

The phrase "consisting of a number of individuals" means that the social unit is specifiable in space and time. It does not imply that a group has to consist of the same individuals at all times. Some or all of the membership may change over time. It does indicate that without individuals there is no social unit and no group.

The phrase "in matters of consequence to the group" is included for two reasons: First, a group does not have values or norms relative to every task or situation its members face. Later in this chapter, when we define the term *norm,* it will become evident that members of a group could not possibly develop norms for every transitory problem or situation they encounter in the life span of the members. This qualification, therefore, cautions us not to use the concept of norm to explain every behavior by a group member. Second, it indicates that, minimally, norms must be established to regulate important activities frequently engaged in, to set bounds for treatment of fellow members, or to maintain the group as a unit.

The definition includes the essential properties to be found in actual studies of groups and their formation as well as those noted by various theorists. Therefore, it has much in common with definitions presented by many sociologists (Bales, 1950; Blau and Scott, 1962; Hare, 1962) and social psychologists (Bonner, 1959; Cartwright and Zander, 1960). This convergence in definition is particularly important because, for many years, group research (especially that on "small groups") was conducted with very little attention to the essential properties of a group. In summarizing the small-group research literature, Golembiewski (1962, p. 47) found that the procedures in the great majority of the experiments consisted of bringing unacquainted or unrelated individuals to the laboratory in conditions creating temporary interdependence among individuals in task performance. Thus many studies labeled "group" research did not allow time for group properties to appear. Such studies, although labeled "small group research," are more accurately viewed as studies showing that task or instruction variables affect the interaction of strangers or casually acquainted individuals.

In view of this earlier lack of specificity in the concept of group among social psychologists, it is particularly significant that the most recent of four successive books of readings in social psychology sponsored by Division 9 of the American Psychological Association defines a group as "two or more individuals who can be collectively

DEF,
II

characterized as follows: they share a common set of norms, beliefs, and values and they exist in implicitly or explicitly defined relationships to one another such that the behavior of each has consequences for the others" (Proshansky and Seidenberg, 1965, p. 377).

The definition presented here does not include certain specifications that are frequently included as group properties. Some of these omissions are in the interests of parsimony. For example, the definition does not include *interaction* and *communication* among individuals. Because interaction and communication are essential for all human association of any consequence, they are implied by other terms of the definition. The terms *role and status relations* and *norms* refer to particular forms of interaction. As Stogdill (1959) pointed out, the first step in understanding the nature of a group is preliminary grasp of what is meant by interaction.

It is necessary to distinguish carefully between reaction and interaction. Reaction is a one-way process which may be represented by the statement, "A responds to B." In this statement, we are interested in the behavior (reaction) of A, while our interest, if any, in B is incidental to the fact that he serves as a stimulus to the behavior (reaction) of A. Interaction, on the other hand, is a process which involves the reactions of two or more persons to each other (p. 19).

Once this distinction is grasped, the properties that define group interaction can be made the basis for distinguishing groups from other social interaction.

Other features that have been included in some definitions of a group are omitted here because they are implied by the present terms. For example, *shared sentiments, common attitudes, common goals,* and *behavior patterns* are implied in the concept of values or norms, as we shall see when these properties are discussed. In fact, the degree to which members share similar attitudes and pursue common goals is one of the measures for the stability of a group.

Finally, certain properties of groups were omitted from the definition because they are *dependent* upon the degree of organization and the stability of norms in a group. For example, the *morale* or *esprit de corps* of a group, its *solidarity* or *cohesiveness, loyalty* of members, and its *visibility* for members

and nonmembers are dependent upon some degree of organization (role and status relations) and normative regulation. Of course, these are very important aspects of groups —but they vary in terms of the more essential properties, not independently from them.

Degrees of "Groupness"

By definition, the question of whether a number of people is a group does not have an all-or-none answer. The "groupness" of a group is a matter of degree. This feature of the definition will become clear when we trace group formation from an initial state of interaction among unrelated individuals to the stabilization of role-status relationships and norms. Specifically, a collection of persons forms a group to the degree (1) that its organization (role and status relationships) are stable and (2) that its particular set of values and norms for behavior are shared by the membership and *binding* for them (in the sense that members voluntarily regulate their behavior within their bounds).

A growing number of social scientists are recognizing that a group is not a fixed, absolute quantity, but rather involves a question of degree. For example, one author states explicitly that "the criteria used to decide whether a particular set of people constitutes a sociological group entail matters of degree" (Hopkins, 1964, p. 11). Among the criteria included are degree of consensus among participants on "morally binding" or normative expectations, the degree to which "participants define themselves and are defined by others as constituting a collective entity or social unit," and the degree of stabilization in their interpersonal relationships (p. 13).

GRADATIONS FROM TOGETHERNESS TO GROUP

Group formation means that something starts and takes shape over time. By the definition of group, it is an organization (status and role relations) and set of norms that take shape. The start of group formation lies in the interaction of individuals who are together. However, not all interaction leads to group formation.

Togetherness refers to proximity or interaction among individuals who have not previously established role and status relations or common norms of their own through interaction with one another.

Clearly, transitory togetherness situations are very common—for example, in shopping, in a classroom, in public transportation, or in a movie theater. Behavior in such situations may be norm-regulated and the participants may occupy different roles—for example, doctor-patient, policeman-citizen, male-female. If the participants come from a common sociocultural background, each may regulate his behavior within the appropriate bounds of such institutional roles and norms for propriety. However, it is not at all necessary for the particular individuals to have interacted previously. In a group situation, role behavior and normative regulation are dependent upon prior interaction among the members.

In discussing group formation, we necessarily trace the rise and stabilization of interpersonal relations, of shared rules for conduct, and of in-group delineation from an initial state of sheer togetherness through time. In doing so, the properties of a group can be defined in terms appropriate for research operations. Specific methods for studying the organizational and normative aspects of groups will be presented in Chapters 8, 9, and 10, which deal with these topics.

Generality of Group Formation

In reviewing research on groups, Robert Faris (1953) concluded that one of the most impressively documented generalizations about human social life is the well-nigh universal tendency for individuals in common circumstances to form groups. There is generality of group formation in all walks of life and in all cultures. Groups are man's natural habitat; they are not alien to his nature.

Human individuals are *selective* in choice of associates. This selectivity does not always follow the path of least resistance toward the most easily accessible persons. The formation of a human group requires individuals (functioning on a conceptual level; Proposition 12) who are sufficiently socialized for self-regulation of behavior. Individuals whose behavior is regulated only by direct social pressure from authority or force are unlikely to form a group.

Very young children, for example, do not form groups in the sense of our definition. Of course, the little child is in the process of becoming a member of a family group, but the process is heavily dependent on the efforts of older relatives. Observing children's play at different ages during the preschool years, Parten (1932) found that two-year-olds seldom played *with* each other in the sense of regular and consistent give-and-take to accomplish a task. Their play was more "parallel," side-by-side, and uncoordinated. Organized give-and-take in play appeared about the age of three years, becoming increasingly frequent and more complex with age.

Through observations and experiments on children's conceptions of the "rules of the game" and their adherence to rules, the Swiss psychologist Jean Piaget (1932) showed that it is quite an accomplishment for the child to regulate his own behavior with regard to others. Until he can grasp the notion that others in a situation may have viewpoints different from his own, the child is not consistent in abiding by rules. He abides by rules at first because someone larger and more powerful tells him to, lapsing from them when the authority is gone. He progresses to the point of realizing that a rule is a general scheme for regulating behavior. At first he considers it an absolute affair, permitting no exceptions or modifications. When he can grasp the notion that rules can be modified or changed by common consent, he is also able to abide by rules voluntarily, participating with others in their modification and regulating his own behavior accordingly. Thus Piaget saw consistent forms of social interaction and consistent self-identity as developing together. We shall consider the formation of the self system through interaction in Chapter 17.

Additional evidence for the significance of self-regulatory control of behavior for group formation comes from research on psychologically disturbed adolescents (Rafferty, 1962, 1965). Conspicuously deficient in previous success as a member of family or peer groups, these adolescents lived in institutions and were observed regularly in their interactions. The striking feature of their interactions was the predominance of aggressive attempts to dominate one another and the lack of consistent reciprocities that are essential to group formation. The events most conducive to group formation among them were (1) forbidden activities, such as smoking in defiance of the staff, and (2) activities that by their nature required division of task functions—such as putting on a play, a fashion show, or an athletic game.

However, apart from the immature child, the severely retarded or psychologically disturbed, people everywhere form groups. In surveying social life on the near North Side of Chicago, Zorbaugh reported groups in every sort of neighborhood. The "Gold Coast" had its exclusive clubs; areas with a large foreign-born population had numerous mutual protection and benevolent societies; the slum had gangs; the individualistic artists had bohemian groups; and even the rooming-house areas populated mostly by single individuals were alive with cults and sects. Every pool hall and other recreation center had some sort of groups that hung around regularly (Zorbaugh, 1929, p. 192).

Informal Beginnings of Organization. The formation of informally organized groups is well documented within larger formal organizations, such as a political party, a business, industrial plant, military organization, office, or school. The membership and organization of such groups may coincide with units of the large organization and its lines of authority, or they may be at variance with the formal scheme for activity. It is well to remember that large formal organizations such as a factory or a hospital consist of arrangements for performance of various tasks. They specify lines for authority and communication all aimed at the execution and coordination of these tasks. Individual occupants of the various task roles, supervisory roles, and coordinating roles are often viewed as replaceable parts in a large organization. However, the translation of the formal scheme into action involves the formation of groups within the whole that either coincide with the formal plan or circumvent it. Observing these facts, Selvin (1960) noted that when informal groups do not coincide with formal organizational units, the groups "sometimes exercise more control than official management" (p. 10).

Historically, most formal organizations began from informal association in groups—a fact recognized by a writer on business management who wrote: "informal association rather obviously precedes formal organization" (Barnard, 1948, p. 116). Many religious groups, labor unions, businesses, political parties, and even some military organizations can trace their origins to informally organized groups. For example, one of the predecessors of the labor unions in the United States (the Knights of Labor) developed informally and functioned secretly for 12 years, united in the belief that "When bad men combine, the good must associate, else they will fall, one by one, an unpitied sacrifice in a contemptible struggle" (Lindsey, 1942, p. 4). The first cooperative store in England, an ancestor of the cooperative retail movement, grew from the informal gatherings of 12 unemployed weavers (Holyoke, 1893). The formation of small groups of buddies in armed services is a well-documented fact, as it is in prisons, schools, neighborhoods, and social and business circles.

Special Terms for Groups. Partly by historical accident and partly by the effort to build typologies for classifying groups and organizations, a rich vocabulary developed for labeling large organizations and groups. As our present purpose is discussion of properties common to all human groups, it will be helpful to disregard such customary terminology for the time being. For example, *organization* is sometimes used to refer only to social units with explicit public aims and activities. Such usage will confuse the present discussion, as one of the properties of any human group (small or large, serious or frivolous) is some kind of organization of roles and statuses. Likewise, the term *gang* (as applied only to youthful or adult groups that engage in socially undesirable or criminal behavior) suggests that the properties of such groups are distinctly different from those of other groups. On the other hand, the terms *clique, club, circle,* or *elite* have more desirable connotations to some people—with the result that they are seen as fundamentally different from gangs. In order to single out the common properties of such units, it is useful to start by treating all such formations as human *groups.*

Similarly, a sharp distinction between groups that accomplish definite work or service as "task-oriented" and groups that seem concerned largely with "socially oriented" functions may be confusing for the present purposes. As Tuchman (1965) observed, "any group, regardless of setting, must address itself to the successful completion of a task. At the same time, and often through the same behaviors, group members will be relating to one another interpersonally" (p. 385). While there is a great difference between the *tasks* of a group of adolescents hanging around on a Saturday afternoon and a work group with a definite product, it is important to note that in both cases there is *content* to their interaction and in both cases individuals are involved in interpersonal give-and-take.

Relationships Among Location, Task and Other People in Group Formation

Groups do not form in a vacuum, nor are they closed systems insulated from their environments. They form as individuals interact in definite locations and perform tasks or cope with problems that cannot be handled individually. The members, individually and collectively, have dealings with other people outside of group bounds.

The location (neighborhood, bar, school, factory, or prison) and its facilities are important in determining whether a group forms, as well as the character of interaction among members. For example, the ecology of locations precludes interaction among some individuals and facilitates contact among others through their proximity. It is well known that factories or schools with departments located on different floors or in different parts of a building tend to inhibit the development of groups across departmental lines. However, spatial proximity or distance among individuals is only one factor in group formation. With modern means of communication and transportation, the advantages or limitations of sheer proximity and distance are quickly bypassed by individuals gravitating toward one another.

As part of a study on informal, natural groups of boys between the ages of 13 and 19 years in half a dozen cities (Sherif and Sherif, 1964), we plotted the location of their homes on the city map. Even in very poor neighborhoods where none of the boys had bicycles or cars, and public transportation was not available, *sheer proximity* did not prove to be the major factor in group formation. The spread of dwellings in which members of these groups lived and the distances to locations where they usually congregated were sometimes very large, particularly in the case of groups that were highly cohesive and important to members (see Figure 7.1). When boys of more prosperous families were involved, the spread of dwellings for members of a small group was frequently on the order of several square miles. Distances between their homes and other meeting places were several miles apart and typically were covered by members in their own automobiles.

Of course, in order for the groups to form initially, the boys had to be in contact (in proximity). Many of these contacts were made initially in junior or senior high schools serving large areas of the city, while others were made in public recreation centers (e.g., community-sponsored centers, pool halls, etc.). Such findings suggest that proximity in a location, although facilitating interaction, is probably never a sufficient condition for group formation. Frequently, however, proximity in a location also means that the individuals face common problems (cf. Festinger *et al.,* 1950).

FOUR ESSENTIALS OF GROUP FORMATION AND FUNCTIONING

Stripped to bare essentials, a group forms from initial togetherness when the following four essentials are satisfied:

1. A motivational base shared by individuals and conducive to recurrent interaction among them over time.
2. Formation of an organization (group structure) consisting of differentiated roles and statuses and delineated in some degree from that of non-members.
3. Formation of a set of norms (i.e., values, rules, and standards for behavior).
4. More-or-less consistent differential effects on the attitude and behavior of

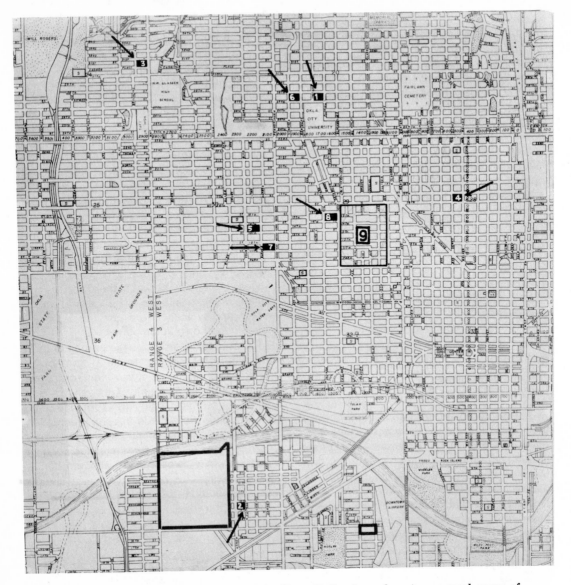

Fig. 7.1. City map showing spread of dwellings (1–8) of members in a natural group of adolescent boys and the location of the park (9) where they congregated. Member dwellings are as follows: (1) T & J before Feb. 1; (2) T (after Feb. 1); (3) J (after Feb. 1); (4) Mo; (5) B; (6) J; (7) L; (8) Mi.

Members of this group were white, lower-middle class boys between 16 and 19 years of age. T (leader) and J were brothers, residing together with one natural parent and one foster parent until Feb. 1. At that time, the adults moved with T, while J moved across the city to live with his other natural parent and, as punishment for excessive traffic fines, was required to take a job. One member of the group (Mo, No. 4) owned an old car. Other members had occasional use of parents' cars. After starting to work, J usually drove the truck assigned him as delivery boy. (Data from research in Sherif and Sherif, 1964.)

individual members produced by the group properties.

Of course, these four essentials are related to one another. For example, the motives that bring people together affect the kind of roles and statuses that develop among them, who is likely to become a leader, and the matters that become of concern for normative regulation. The strength and persistence of their common motives also relate to how consistently the individuals wil behave in interpersonal relations with members and how binding the group norms will be for them. Conversely, the group and its norms may become so valued that new motives develop in addition to those that brought members together. At times new motivations associated with being a group member are sufficiently compelling that members may deprive themselves in the very area that brought them together in order to adhere to the rules developed in the group governing responsibility and loyalty of its members.

Motivational Base Conducive to Recurrent Interaction

Participants in many "together" situations are temporarily unified by a common focus, for example, by an emergency—such as a stalled elevator or bus. The motivational base for group formation, however, is conducive to repeated and prolonged efforts to attain goals in concert. Potentially, the motivational basis for group formation covers the entire range of human needs, desires, interests, insecurities, anxieties, and aspirations that may be common to a given set of individuals. Thus the search for satisfaction to basic drives such as hunger and sex; the desire for social distinction, power, money; the search for human companionship and the feeling of belonging someplace securely; the desire for excitement and adventure; the pursuit of nefarious or lofty ideals—all may promote group formation among individuals caught in their grip.

However, the simultaneous desire for similar goals among individuals who happen to be in contact is not an adequate basis for group formation. On the contrary, many states of arousal directed toward similar goals are not conducive to group formation at all. Studies of prolonged deprivation and scarcity of food, for example, in prisoner-of-war camps, show that joint efforts to share available supplies are continually thwarted by desperate individual efforts at survival, even stealing from fellow sufferers. The discovery of gold in California in the 1840s and later in Alaska's Klondike produced many individuals with the common dream of "striking it rich." Yet the common motivation was more condu-cive to harshly individualistic efforts than to interaction among more than two or three prospectors. Five vice presidents, each dreaming of the presidency of the firm, have similar motives—but not a motivational base for interacting to achieve the goal in concert.

Thus, the disarmingly simple phrase *motives conducive to interaction* implies (1) a set of motives and (2) a set of external circumstances that put the individuals in the same boat in their efforts to do something about their deprivations or desires. Whether the common problems are a predicament or good fortune, they are conducive to group formation when the problems can be faced, escaped, enjoyed, ignored, or solved in interaction with others more readily than through individual action.

The great importance of a motivational basis for recurrent interaction is revealed in reports on attempts to form groups when such a basis is lacking, for example, for purposes of instruction or therapy. Reports on therapy and "human relations training" programs include some attempts when the participants did not share the supervisor's aim in bringing them together. The typical reaction by participants include prolonged periods of silence and hostility (Tuchman, 1965, p. 388). Even when participants have a general desire for self-improvement, ambiguity about the ways to pursue this goal in concert produces prolonged periods of uncoordinated interaction before group properties begin to emerge (Tuchman, 1965, p. 391). As one might predict from Proposition 6, prolonged ambiguity about the purposes of interaction and about where one "fits in" the situation is uncomfortable. In fact, it has been proposed that such discomfiture becomes a major motivational basis for group formation in therapy or training situations (Theodorson, 1953).

Illustrative Case: Ruhleben. The formation of a group proceeds rapidly and intensely when compelling motivations are shared by all participants. One example is the report by the Canadian psychologist, J. D. Ketchum (1965), of events at Ruhleben, an internment camp for four thousand British civilians caught in Germany by the outbreak of World War I in 1914. Ruhleben was a race track near Berlin. Within a short period, four thousand British males from all walks of life were herded into unheated horse stalls and lofts. As the German military at that time had few precedents to guide them, the inmates were remarkably free to arrange their lives as long as they kept order and answered roll call.

Ketchum secured all available documents, letters, diaries, and reports from former inmates and authorities in order to document the rise of small and large groups, which he himself had observed during the internment.

With internment in Ruhleben the Britishers were faced with many common problems: inadequate food, cold and discomfort, using the crowded space for living and sleeping, and securing facilities to keep clean and even for elimination. However, these physical needs were only part of the motivational picture during the early days. Ketchum described the common dilemma faced by prisoners in the following words:

The men and boys herded into Ruhleben were normal human beings, but they were in a highly abnormal situation. Each of them had been plucked up by the roots, torn from his accustomed setting, and plunged into a totally strange one (p. 31). . . . The past was left intact, but it was so different from the alarming present, so hard to relate to it, that the two could not co-exist in the mind. In the first shock it was often the present that was rejected: "The days seemed a dream," was how Henley, a hard-headed engineer described it in his diary on November 7. Then, as Ruhleben asserted its undeniable reality, it was the past that tended to become remote and unreal. Not for several weeks was it possible to knit the two together intelligibly, and meanwhile the prisoner found his conception of himself strangely shaken. Which was he—the respected solicitor and suburban householder, or the unshaven, straw-splattered outcast, picking the last scrap of potato out of a rusty tin bowl? That he could be *both* was for a time incredible.

A worse shock, however, was the wiping out of the future; for the first time since early childhood the men could not see even one day ahead. As a result, all the purposes around which their lives had been organized were nullified, and no new ones could be formed. This gap in the mental world was acutely disturbing; one ex-prisoner wrote feelingly of the emotional tension caused by "trying to find your feet in a totally new environment with the immediate future an absolute blank" (L 58). . . . But the men's pressing need for a predictable future is shown most clearly by

their prompt though unconscious efforts to create one. The first method, illusory but momentarily satisfying, was the spawning of countless rumours of release. The second, which finally replaced it, was to build within the camp the only context in which long-range purposes can be formed—a stable social order (p. 32).

A whole set of further needs was revealed by the snapping of the prisoner's social ties, his abrupt removal from his place in the social world (p. 32). . . . Not all were equally affected; the seafarer still belonged with his interned crew, and those with friends or relatives had at least some continuing attachments. But the crisis had its effects here too, for such groupings derived from the past, and the past no longer counted. Ship's crews lacked any further function and broke up fairly quickly; kinship was similarly affected except where it had been transformed into friendship and, though many pre-war friendships survived internment, a surprising number disintegrated (p. 33).

During the early days of internment, the common motivational base, cutting across differences in social class, occupation, and age of the prisoners, was reflected in intense and almost indiscriminate interaction among the men: Everyone wanted to talk, to relate exactly how he happened to be arrested and interned, to speculate on the future and to register gripes. Ketchum reported that when the prisoners retired for the night, the "floodgates of conversation" would open again far into the night.

The almost bizarre frequency of talking and yelling was largely unfocused at first. It was also disruptive of the order desired by the guards. Thus, unwittingly, the Germans provided a focus to the interaction and a basis for a campwide feeling of "we-ness." Their common plight was at the hands of *Germans,* undeniably because they were all *Britishers.* "This was the basis of the original solidarity of Ruhleben, a solidarity by its nature short-lived, but one that for a time transcended all differences and made internment a memorable experience of 'belonging' " (p. 38). The initial feeling of "we-ness" was expressed in "mass shouting and singing that broke out irrepressibly during the first days together. . . . Sometimes a marching song would start in spite of the guards' angry shouts, and the old British catchword, 'Are we downhearted?'—quickly shortened to 'Are we?'—brought again and again its thundering 'NO!' " (p. 39). Thus the early days at Ruhleben were characterized by *collective interaction* with all of the intense forms of expression that typify it (see Chapter 1, Chapter 23).

Naturally enough, the first groups to form were in the horse stalls, where the men faced the mutual problem of organizing the business of daily life in order that everyone could sleep, keep clean, and dress in the tiny space available. The stalls were called "boxes," a term later extended by the men to refer to any group of men who "belonged" together, including those in one corner of a loft. These small living units were compared by Ketchum to families, for they came to have the emotional pull and the petty conflicts that occur among loved ones living in intimate contact. Everyone in a box was expected to do his part; those who did not were chastised by the others. In some cases, men who could not fit into a box moved to another. Each box had its own set of *nicknames* and *catchwords,* usually reflecting some outstanding events in its collective life (pp. 144–145).

The barracks were basic units for the Germans. Especially through sports competitions arranged by the inmates to pass the long hours, each barracks developed a distinctive way of living and its own reputation in the camp. The campwide reputation, in turn, affected the way the men came to regard their own barracks. These expectations are reflected in the following words of one former inmate:

What about the queer "local patriotism" so many of us developed for our own barracks—football and cricket teams, barrack mascots like the wonderful wooden rabbit-bird that always accompanied one of the teams to the football field, Prichard "hoodoo-ing" the Barrack Ten team to make it win, and so on? It often amused me in camp. Of course there were differences; think of the associations connected with Barrack Ten (public school atmosphere), Barrack Three (Supermen), Barrack Eight (sailors), let alone Barracks Six and Thirteen! The thought of Barrack One (pro-German) still makes me shiver with horror. I was in a good barrack myself, but if I had not been there I would have chosen Barrack Eleven (p. 124).

The interest in sports, which promoted development of the barracks organizations,

was only one motivational basis among several others that quickly cut across the lines of boxes and barracks. By the first spring and summer after internment, Ketchum observed that the internees "not content with producing a host of community and family groups, had now engineered a more lively progeny, a hundred or so formally organized 'bodies' " (p. 220). These associations started from informal interaction among intellectuals, educators, musicians, artists, mechanics, and writers for whom the lack of opportunity to ply their vocations left a great gap in their daily lives. They found, further, a path pointing toward the future through their common efforts. There were discussion groups, theater groups, orchestra and chorus and, shortly, an organized program of education offering classes from high school through the university level. All of these varied organizations were formed by individuals with common interests and each provided its members a niche.

Thus, the report of Ruhleben shows the great importance of a common motivational basis for group formation. Groups form and continue to function because they are means for attaining goals and for grappling with significant problems.

Role and Status Relations
(Organization or Structure)

When a number of individuals interact— sharing common deprivations or facing problems in concert—the interaction among them produces differential effects on behavior from the start. There is heightened activity, less restraint in expression, and close interest in one another's actions.

The rise of organized or structured forms of interaction proceeds over time, achieving stability and clarity in varying degrees. The next chapter focuses on group organization. The primary task here is to specify what is meant by organization or structure. This task requires definition of two terms, specifically, *role* and *status* relations among the individual members.

Defining Role Relations. At this stage in the development of social sciences, definition and usage of many concepts are not firmly established. The reader should be warned that no definition of role can be consistent with every usage to which that over-worked term has been pressed (cf., Biddle and Thomas, 1966).

Let us approach a definition by listing what role relationships refer to in general. Probably most social scientists who use the term would agree with the following:

1. Role is a relational term. It follows that no individual can have a role apart from his relationship with other individuals. Roles refer to aspects of interaction among individuals, not to individual attributes.

2. Role relations refer to reciprocal forms of behavior among individuals, that is, give-and-take activities in varying forms. Note that reciprocity does not necessarily imply equality. For example, the husband who typically dominates decision-making in the family and the wife who submits to his word are involved in reciprocal relations. So are two roommates who take turns cleaning their room.

3. Role relations represent more or less *characteristic* modes of give-and-take among participants, at least in those activities most directly related to the focus or goal of inter-action.

Def.   **Role relations refer to patterns of reciprocal behavior and associated expectations between two or more individuals that are characteristic and recurrent in interaction of consequence to them.**

When we speak of role relationships as a property of *groups,* the individuals in question are members of the same social unit. Note, however, that role relations are defined in a more general way. The concept also becomes useful in dealing with relations between individuals who are not members of the same group (for example, a doctor and his patient). Some system of roles is observed throughout a particular society.

Role relationships are defined in terms of patterns of *behavior* (verbal or nonverbal). Over time, the give-and-take becomes regularized: treatments and evaluations of Person A by B and C become more or less characteristic, as do those of Person B by A and C, and those of Person C by B and A. As this stabilization occurs, B and C may also come to have more-or-less consistent *expectations* for A's behavior and *attitudes* toward him as a group member. Such psy-

chological products of role relations originate in the repeated interactions over time.

Status: The Power Dimension. The study of role relations in a group requires specification of reciprocal relations among members in several respects or dimensions. For example, mutual liking as revealed in consistent interpersonal choices is one such dimension. Tasks performed characteristically by various individuals in joint activities are another aspect of role differentiation. In some groups, joking relationships might be a third.

Probably the most weighty and limiting dimension of role relations in any human group is the *power* dimension. Social power does not refer merely to force or its threat, although these may be involved. Social power refers to the exercise of *effective initiative* in the interaction process, activities, and decision-making of group members. Appropriately, social power in a group is defined by the relative effectiveness of attempted influence *over time.*

Def.   **Status is a member's position (rank) in a hierarchy of power relations in a social unit (group or system) as measured by the relative effectiveness of initiative (a) to control interaction, decision-making, and activities, and (b) to apply sanctions in cases of non-participation and non-compliance.**

This definition of the key term *status* will be elaborated in Chapter 8. In Chapters 8 and 11, concrete illustrations will be given of the measurement of *effective initiative.*

As defined, a status hierarchy is the power dimension of any human group (small or large). Differential power (status) is one of the most essential properties making a group what it is. This being the case, not only a body that is explicitly political, but every human group (be it economic, social, or religious) is a power structure or organization.

As one important aspect of role relationships, the rise of a status hierarchy implies associated differences in the way members evaluate one another, in their respect for one another, and in prestige.

A Set of Social Norms

As individuals interact toward coping with motivational problems faced in common, they encounter new problems: problems related to their interaction, to the tasks they undertake together, to the personal contribution that each makes, to other people and groups, and to the facilities available. Particularly during memorable encounters when alternative courses for decision and action are vague or numerous, they create a host of shared products: names, catchwords, slogans, rules, standardized views of each other and of outsiders, modes of procedure, and conceptions of proper and improper ways of behaving. "Social norms" is a generic term referring to such products of interaction.

Chapters 9 and 10 are devoted to the formation of norms and the problems of *conformity* and *deviation* that norm formation creates. Here it is sufficient to note that reports of group formation invariably include normative regulation as part of the process. We shall arrive at a definition of norm that can be used in the study of group formation and functioning by listing what the concept refers to and what it does not.

1. Social norms does *not* necessarily refer to the average behavior by members of a social unit, or even to what is typical. The concept has little in common with the terms "test norm" or "age norm" as used in psychology textbooks.

2. Social norms are standardized generalizations that epitomize events, behavior, objects or persons in short-cut form. Like a verbal category or rule, a social norm applies to *classes* of objects (e.g., persons, behaviors, or events).

3. A social norm is *evaluative,* designating both what is valued and what is scorned, what is expected (even ideal) and what is degrading, what ought to be and what ought not to be, what is acceptable and what is objectionable.

4. Being generalizations, social norms typically define a range or *latitude* of what is permissible or acceptable, and a range of actions and beliefs that are objectionable. In other words, social norms take note of the universal facts of individual differences, of varying circumstances, and of novelty by designating ranges of positive and negative evaluation, not absolutes.

A social norm is an evaluative scale (e.g. yardstick) designating an acceptable latitude and an objectionable latitude for behavior, activity, events, beliefs, or any other object of concern to members of a social unit.

The existence of a norm is assessed through regularities in attitude and behavior of the members and through sanctions (correctives) applied to cases of deviation beyond the latitude of acceptance defined by the norm.

In the process of group formation, the stabilization of a set of norms can be observed in successive episodes by reference to the behaviors of participants. For example, in therapy and training groups, the descriptions of the development of cohesion and "we-feeling" typically include specific reference to the standardization of modes and procedures for the way that "we" go about things (Tuchman, 1965). The formation of natural groups invariably involves the formation of standards defining what members should and should not do. As we shall see in Chapters 9 and 10, the formation of norms has been studied in experiments conducted both in the laboratory and in the field.

The degree of consensus among members on what constitutes propriety, decency, and loyalty is one of the indicators of the relative stability of a group. As individuals participating in the formation of a group have a hand in creating its norms, the process of group formation is a fertile ground for understanding how what is at first *social* becomes *personal*. The "good member" experiences the norms created in group formation as his personal preferences and tastes, part of his self-identity. Such personal acceptance of group tradition accounts in large measure for the tenacity of tradition in a group.

Differential Effects of Group Properties on Individual Attitude and Behavior

One of the central problems of social psychology concerns the effects of group membership and interaction in shaping attitude and behavior. As a group forms, the relations among participants become major anchors for the individual's behavior.

The stabilization of a group involves the psychological acceptance by its members of the organizational and normative schemes. Hence, over time, immediate situational factors, such as the characteristics of particular tasks and particular locations, recede in *relative* importance. Across situations and locations, behavior of members increasingly reflects their role relations and their adherence to the set of norms standardized among them.

In his classic account of the gangs of Chicago, Thrasher (1927) reported that group members did not necessarily behave in the same way in their groups and in other situations. One youth, Ellman, was a courteous and pleasant boy when he went out with his girl friend. But with his pals, The Dirty Dozen, Ellman was one of the "meanest fellows"—very tough, loud, and bragging (p. 50). In another group, Thrasher observed that one member could always be counted upon to respond to "an appeal for the best for himself and the gang" but was insensitive to such appeals from outside the group (p. 295).

Because differential effects on behavior are found in simple perceptual situations and in mere "together" situations, we do not need entirely new principles to explain the differential effects of group situations (Chapter 6). We do, however, need to specify what it is in a group situation that produces the effects. By studying behavior relative to the developing properties of the group, we can specify the determinants of behaviors that many earlier writers took as evidence that entirely new principles were needed to understand the psychology of groups and crowds.

ANCHORING EFFECT OF GROUPS

Once members of a group have developed a common viewpoint toward some event, this viewpoint becomes an internal anchor for behavior of its members in later situations. Of course, the viewpoint is an effect of past experience. However, past experience in a group situation, as defined here, has different consequences from past experience when the individual was alone or together with nonmembers. This is one reason for differentiating group from mere together situations. The theoretical point was articulated in an experiment by Pollis (1964, 1967).

In Chapter 6, several experiments illustrated the general principle that attempted social influence is more effective when the stimulus lacks structure in some respect (Proposition 10). For example, in the Asch experiment, the proportion of erroneous choices in the direction of the majority increased as the difference between the lines decreased. In addition, the naive person was uncomfortable when the majority choice was different from his own judgment.

Proceeding from such findings, Pollis asked the following question: What will be the effect of a scale for judgment formed while interacting with fellow members of one's group when later the individual is faced with discrepant judgments in an unstructured situation? Will the group member be more compliant toward the social influence or less compliant than the individual who has formed a judgment scale individually or in a together situation?

Pollis first made a survey of acquaintance and friendship patterns for the entire sophomore class of a small college. The survey, which used the sociometric technique, was not connected in the students' eyes with the subsequent experiment. From those sophomores with about intermediate social status in the class as a whole, Pollis chose 144 subjects for the experiment. Forty-eight of them were members of clear-cut friendship groups. The other 96 did not indicate mutual friendship or acquaintance in the survey.

As an unstructured stimulus to be judged, Pollis used pulse beats in sound waves of different frequencies. The subject's task was to judge the number of beats in each exposure of sound. The task seemed feasible. Actually, however, one could not count the beats accurately because they were too rapid. Pollis found that he could produce three distinctly different ranges for judgment by giving different instructions as to the numbers in the lowest and highest frequencies of the beats he presented.

In Session 1 of the experiment, each group member participated with another member of his group. Forty-eight of the nonfriends also participated together in pairs. The remaining 48 came individually to Session 1. Each pair or individual subject judged the number of pulse beats, but Pollis provided different instructions for one-third in each subject category. At the end of the session, the subjects gave judgments within one of the three different ranges. A third of the group members established the lower scale, a third the intermediate scale, and the remainder the higher scale. Those who participated together and alone were similarly divided (see Table 7.1).

Session 2 was the critical session. Three subjects participated together. Each threesome contained one subject who had formed his scale alone, one together, and one with a fellow group member. Each unit also contained one subject trained to each of the three different judgment scales, so that their initial judgments were quite discrepant. The threesomes were composed in a counter-balanced plan so that the three subject classifications (alone, together, group of Session 1) were represented in each of the scale positions (low, intermediate, high).

Pollis now asked two questions: (1) In Session 2, who would tend to stick by the scale formed in Session 1 and who would change most in the direction of others? (2) In Session 2, who would have the most influence? Figure 7.2 presents his results in answer to the first question.

The graph shows the percentage of judgments made in Session 2 that fell within the range that a subject had established in Session 1. Each bar represents one of the conditions for past experience in Session 1 (alone, together, or with a group member). Clearly, the past experience was most binding for those who had formed a scale with a fellow group member, less binding for those in the togetherness situation, and least

Table 7.1. Design of Pollis Experiment

Session 1. Establishment of Judgment Scale

Relationship of Individuals

Range of Judgment	Alone (N)	Together (N)	Group Members (N)	Total
Low (L)	16	16	16	48
Medium (M)	16	16	16	48
High (H)	16	16	16	48
	48	48	48	144

Session 2. Judging Together with Persons Whose Initial Judgments Belonged to Disparate Scales (L, M, H) Formed in Different Social Conditions (A, T, G) in Session 1

	Alone	Together	Group	Replications	N
Range of Judgment Established in Session 1: L (low), M (medium), H (high)	L	M	H	8	24
	L	H	M	8	24
	M	L	H	8	24
	M	H	L	8	24
	H	L	M	8	24
	H	M	L	8	24
				Total	144

Design of Pollis' experiment in two sessions. Session 1 was devoted to establishing judgment scales with disparate ranges (low, medium, high) in one of three social situations (alone, together, with fellow group members). In Session 2, individuals who had formed their scales alone, together, or with group members were combined according to the range they had established (6 combinations of low, medium, high). Thus, compliance in Session 2 could not be attributed to the particular range established in Session 1.

Source: Based on Pollis, 1964.

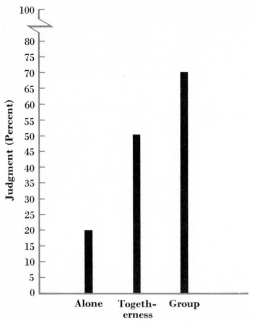

Fig. 7.2. Adherence to norms (judgment scale) initially formed alone, together, or in group situation. Percentage of judgments in Session 2 that fell within the scale formed in Session 1. (Based on data in Pollis, 1964.)

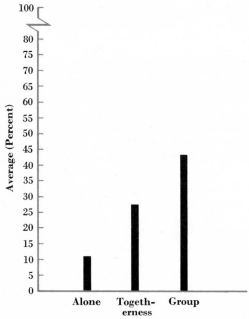

Fig. 7.3. Relative influence on judgments of other persons by subjects whose norms were initially formed alone, together, or in group situation. Average percentage of judgments by two other subjects in Session 2 that fell within the disparate range of the subject. (Based on data in Pollis, 1964.)

effective for individuals who had formed a scale alone in Session 1.

Figure 7.3 presents the analysis in response to Pollis' second question. Each bar again represents a different condition in Session 1 and the measure is an average percentage of judgments in Session 2. Pollis considered subject X's effect on subject Y and Z by computing the number of judgments by Y and Z in Session 2 that fell within X's initial range (formed in Session 1). Divided by two and transformed to a percentage of the total judgments rendered, the resulting average indicated the extent of subject X's influence in Session 2. The graph shows that, on the average, group members were more influential in Session 2 than subjects who had formed their scales together or alone. Those who had formed scales individually in Session 1 were not only more influenced by others, but least influential in Session 2.

Thus Pollis' study supports a generalization from many field studies: past experience as a group member has a greater anchoring effect than past experience gained simply together or individually. This anchoring effect renders the individual member less responsive to immediate influence in a transitory social situation when he is no longer with his group.

NEW MOTIVES EMERGING IN GROUP INTERACTION

Motives conducive to group formation remain important factors in the continuation of group activity. However, during group formation new motives and goals arise that contribute to the maintenance of the group. Such new motives are central in understanding group solidarity or cohesiveness, morale, loyalty, and responsibility.

Once a group has begun to take shape, why do its members maintain it? In the first place, belonging to a group provides an individual with a sense of being somebody, of having a place in the scheme of living. The importance of membership is seen dramatically when individuals lack such a sense of belongingness. In their frantic efforts to be accepted somewhere in their own right, they are frequently willing to turn heaven and earth. One's sense of amounting to something and experience of his own worth are closely tied to having roles in groups of which the individual is a member—his family, peer groups, and so on. To maintain these experiences implies responsibility to the groups and loyalty on his part.

Such loyalty and responsibility are not merely to the group in an abstract sense. It is loyalty and responsibility to other members who occupy various roles and statuses within the group and to the norms or values that they adhere to. Once a system of reciprocities arises among members and a set of norms is stabilized, members of a group form appropriate attitudes within the latitudes set by these group products. Henceforth, these group-related attitudes become parts of the individual's conception of himself (his self or ego; see Chapter 17).

Therefore, once an individual becomes a member of a group, it is not a pleasant experience for him to have his ties upset or severed. He feels uneasy, disturbed, and confused when ties with his group become shaky. The process of deliberately destroying his relatedness to the group, of severing his ties and seeking new affiliations elsewhere is a painful and even formidable task if the group has been central in his scheme of values. Conversely, the stability and continuity of group ties is pleasant—a state to be desired, maintained, and improved.

The formation of ego-attitudes relating to membership in a group is an essential aspect of group formation and maintenance. Without grasping their psychological significance, it is impossible to understand group functioning and maintenance. Group membership is the context in which the "social" becomes personally experienced. Such consequences of group membership are the topics in Chapters 17 and 19 (see Fig. 7.4).

Recognizing the foregoing facts and their implications for theories of human motiva-

tion, Robert MacLeod emphasized them in his analysis of Ketchum's *Ruhleben,* the work that was discussed earlier in this chapter. One of the paradoxical findings about the prisoners in Ruhleben was that, despite the cold reality of their imprisonment, man after man looked back upon the experience as one of the most stimulating periods of his life. In MacLeod's words:

> The secret of Ruhleben's high morale, however, lay in the ability of the group to discover positive goals which were both demanding of energy and worth attaining. . . . The first of the activities, the games and some of the little projects, may have had something of the contrived and the make-believe about them; there was certainly a good deal of "whistling in the dark." The impressive thing, however, is that what may have begun in many cases as merely an escape from an uncomfortable present grew into an absorbing and rewarding life. Individuals not only discovered opportunities for the exercise of their skills and talents but even caught glimpses of worlds they had never dreamed of exploring. . . . people were *discovering,* not merely an acceptable way of living together, but a way of actualizing through the life of the group something of great value. That at least something of this feeling of achievement permeated the camp is indubitable. Ruhlebenites felt themselves as Ruhlebenites, were proud of what they had made of the camp, and in some cases were grateful for having had a priceless experience (p. 365).

To build a theory of human motivation that will fit the facts, we have to include the stimulus situations in which social motives form and change. Typically, these stimulus situations are patterned as human groups. Therefore, when discussing organization and norms in the next chapters, we are also laying the groundwork for understanding the social motives that are characteristic of human motivation. The treatment of such social motives is reserved for Chapters 17 and 18 on ego-involvements and reference groups.

Fig. 7.4. Group concerns are experienced as intensely personal emotions. **a.** (*top*) Victories of our group become our victories. **b.** (*left*) Defeats of our group become our own personal frustrations. **c.** (*right*) Injury to one of us is felt like our own personal injury. (Photos UPI.)

8

Organization (Structure): An Essential Property of Groups

Major Topics of the Chapter

Organization (structure) as group property

Representative definitions of organization and clarification of conceptual ambiguities

Definition of organization (structure)

Small group research: its promise and limitations

Performance in organizations and "human relations" approach

Small groups and large organizations

Bureaucracy and administrative aspect: Max Weber reconsidered

When informal groups form in large organizations

Group organization within its sociocultural environment

Illustrative case of role-status relations within group

Stabilization of roles and hierarchical status
structure
End-anchoring in stabilization and percep-
tion of social organization
Increased predictability of member attitude
and behavior
Indirect or unobtrusive methods for assess-
ing status differentials
Leaders and other members of the group
Leader and leadership defined
Conformity-deviation by leaders and other
members
Leader-follower relations and related fac-
tors in social situations
Personal characteristics of leaders
Interpersonal choices and leadership
Is leadership behavior specific or general?
Research methods in study of leader-fol-
lower relations
Leadership techniques and their effec-
tiveness
Contingency of leadership upon other fac-
tors in group situations
Group solidarity (cohesiveness)

THE PERSON
IN GROUP STRUCTURES

The most intimate interpersonal relations—such as those within a family, a
circle of close associates in business enterprise, a club, or a fraternity—fall into a pattern of roles and status positions. This
pattern is the organization or structure of a
group.

The roles of members comprise complex
sets of reciprocal modes of behavior and
expectations. The roles of those within the
fold can, as a rule, be ranked according to
several dimensions of these sets. The most
consequential of the hierarchical role dimensions is *relative power* in effective initiative and control, each member's rank in
this respect defining his *status.*

Purpose The focus of this chapter will be upon
role and status-related behaviors of individuals belonging to groups. The chapter starts
by clarifying the concept of *organization*
(structure), which has been used in different
ways by various writers.

Organization within groups cannot be
considered in isolation. *Groups are not*

closed, self-contained systems. As a rule,
they are in traffic with other groups. They
are parts or subsystems within larger social
units, such as a neighborhood, a church, a
political party, an industrial firm, or a military establishment. Furthermore, the individual participants come to the group situation with roles and status positions already
established in the society or community.
They come as parents or as children, as
managers or workers, as officers or enlisted
men. Inevitably, all share at least some
values or norms that distinguish the society
to which they belong.

Therefore, our second task in this chapter is to place the study of role and status
relations revealed in the interactions of individuals within the framework of the larger
organization, the class structure, and the
society of which they are a part. The social-
psychological implications will be carried
further in Chapters 11 and 12 on intergroup
relations and Chapters 18 and 19 on reference groups.

Against this background, we shall turn to
a more specific account of the stabilization
of role and status structure over time. Then,

research will be presented showing that the differential effects on attitude and behavior become increasingly predictable as roles and status positions of the participants are differentiated.

A major dimension of interaction in groups is the *power* dimension, which defines the status of the member. The relations among the *leader and other members* of the group will be discussed with reference to recent research that clearly places the problem of leadership within the context of organizations functioning in definite environments with various kinds of problems.

CONCEPT OF ORGANIZATION (STRUCTURE) IN HUMAN GROUPS

Research on human groups of varying description supports a generalization about interaction processes among members of any group: Over time, the interaction reveals *recurrent* regularities in the distribution of task performance and responsibility, the relative prestige and respect accorded members, the members' treatment of each other, their relative interpersonal popularity, and their relative contributions to decision making. Such regularities in the give-and-take among members during interaction in collective activities (with their associated attitudes and expectations) are the evidence for an organization or structure of the social unit in question. The specific terms composing the organization or structure are the more or less stabilized roles and status positions of the various members (see definitions of role and status, p. 140).

Clarifying the concept of organization as a property of a *group* (which has other properties and is invariably goal-directed) will aid in analysis of specific problems of role and status relations. The concept of organization or structure has been used in vague and even contradictory ways, despite its great importance in the social science literature. The ambiguity multiplied because the term was used with reference to a variety of practical problems and in dealing with groups of varying size, purpose, and history.

The following definitions, representative of attempts to define organization, illustrate the conceptual difficulties:

Social organization has been defined as behavior which is motivated and constrained by the necessities of cooperation as these emerge in human groups (p. 7). . . . A group [is] a structure of relations between individuals in different positions (p. 8). . . . [Organizations] set limits on individual behavior and direct it into channels designed for the functioning of the total group and the individual's behavior is frequently highly predictable on these grounds alone (Greer, 1955, p. 9). *Def,*

A social organization is a continuing system of differentiated and coordinated human activities utilizing, transforming, and welding together a specific set of human, material, capital, ideational, and natural resources into a unique problem-solving whole engaged in satisfying particular human needs in interaction with other systems of human activities and resources in its environment (Bakke, 1959, p. 37).

As a formal analytical point of reference, *primacy of orientation to the attainment of a specific goal* is used as the defining characteristic of an organization which distinguishes it from other types of social systems. . . . An organization is a system which, as the attainment of its goal, "produces" an identifiable something which can be utilized in some way by another system (Parsons, 1960, p. 17, italics in original). *Def, 1.*

"Social organization" refers to the ways in which human conduct becomes socially organized—that is, to observed regularities in the behavior of people that are due to the social conditions in which they find themselves rather than to their physiological or psychological characteristics as individuals (p. 2). . . . formal organizations are characterized by explicit goals, an elaborate system of explicit rules and regulations, and a formal status structure with clearly marked lines of communication and authority (Blau and Scott, 1962, p. 14).

Organizations are social units (or human groupings) deliberately constructed and reconstructed to seek specific goals . . . (Etzioni, 1964, p. 3). *Def, 2.*

. . . an organization is a *social system* that has an *unequivocal collective identity*, an *exact roster of members*, a *program of activity* and *procedures for replacing members* (Caplow, 1964, p. 1, italics in original).

According to common usage, an "organization" is an arrangement of interdependent parts, each having a special function with respect to the whole (Cartwright, 1965, p. 1). *Def, 3.*

The foregoing definitions intersect at two points, namely in referring to (1) interdependence of parts (i.e., a social system) and (2) serving some purpose(s). In addition, each of the authors refers to the differentiation of functions within the social system—if not in the quotations, very prominently elsewhere.

However, there are obvious differences in definition that would lead to quite different theories and research strategies. As Haire (1959) wrote in introducing *Modern Organization Theory* with chapters by about a dozen distinguished contributors: ". . . we find—not only different approaches to the problem, but different views of what the problem is" (p. 2).

Similarly, in reviewing the literature on organization and bureaucracy, Mouzelis (1967) observed: ". . . there is no consensus among social scientists as to adequate meanings of the terms" (p. 4).

The situation is clarified considerably when we note that the term "organization" is used in at least two different senses:

1. As *equivalent to the social unit or group itself* and, in this usage, typically to a formally organized or institutionalized unit.

2. As a *property of the social unit or group or social system.*

The first usage is, of course, common in everyday life. The businessman or salesman speaks naturally of "my organization." In fact, this usage is more typical of writers dealing with business, industrial, or governmental units. Probably, the identification of the concept *organization* with certain specific formal units reflects the technological concerns of the business and military world in recent decades to improve productivity, efficiency, or to select and train supervisors and managers.

There is real difficulty in confining the concept of organization to formal units engaged in producing, exchanging or marketing specific products or services. A number of writers have recognized the difficulty. For example, March and Simon (1958), in one of the more influential books on formal organization, avoided the issue by writing as follows: "It is easier . . . to give examples of formal organization than to define the term" (p. 1). Mouzelis (1967) noted the lack of consensus in the literature and settled upon the following as the best approximation of the term: ". . . a form of social grouping which is established in a more or less deliberate or purposive manner for the attainment of a specific goal" (p. 4).

Nevertheless, his survey forced Mouzelis to add that organizations vary greatly as to the degree of "conscious coordination of their activities," with some appearing and growing "in a spontaneous, unplanned way, as far as their goals and internal organization is concerned" and others "highly planned even in the smaller details" (p. 183). Similarly, he wrote, "the criterion of purposiveness and goal specificity must be used in a flexible way and . . . the difference between organizations and other groups is one of emphasis or degree" (p. 183).

In view of the conceptual difficulty in distinguishing "organizations" from other social groups, the sensible way to stabilize the concept is to recognize that the term refers to a *property* of a social system or one of its subunits like the human group. Every human group (small or large, formal or informal) is delimited by its organization of roles and statuses, which delineates members from nonmembers. Yet the organization is not the only property of any group (small or large, formal or informal). The normative property of the group is equally essential. It makes a great deal of difference, even in task performance, whether the norms are shared by all, and whether they are binding for all, for some, or for only a few of the members. Productivity, morale, "effectiveness," and the maintenance of the group are all seriously affected if the norms are not binding. A blueprint of organization that worked very well in earlier times becomes completely worthless if most of the members reject the norms.

Accordingly, when we refer to organization or structure, we shall use the concept in the following way:

> <u>Organization</u> (structure) is an interdependent network of roles and hierarchical statuses defining the reciprocal expectations, responsibilities, and power arrangements of the membership in a normatively oriented social unit (small or large). (See definitions of role, p. 140; status, p. 140; norm, p. 141. Goal orientation toward objectives is implied in normative orientation.)

GROUPS AS SUBUNITS
OF LARGER SOCIAL SYSTEMS

In Chapter 5, the individual-group relationship was posed as the pivotal problem in social psychology. An important advance in the research attack on this problem was achieved when "small group" research become a flourishing activity, especially after World War II. Cumulatively, the research demonstrated that interaction process is a consequential stimulus context, both for behavior in the immediate situation and subsequently, as the antecedent of the participant's expectations and attitudes. However, the generality of findings from many specific studies labeled "small group" research is limited, owing to the following inadequacies.

Number of Participants Is Not the Adequate Criterion. When a research situation involves more than one person at a time, it is often called "group" research. In effect, the only criterion for "groupness" is then sheer number of individuals—regardless of whether they or their activities were related to one another. As noted in Chapter 7, the sheer presence of other people is not an adequate criterion for group situations.

Interdependence Criterion Is Not Sufficient. By and large, investigators of "small groups" neglected to define the group beyond stating that it involved *interdependence* or *interaction* among individuals. In many studies, the procedures involve minimal interdependence or interaction, such as hearing the voices of others as they perform a task, receiving or passing written notes, or seeing a signal (e.g., a light) representing the response of another subject. As noted in Chapter 7, the *dimensions* of interdependence within a group have to be *specified*, and they include status (power) and normative (value) dimensions at the minimum.

Study of Group as a Self-Contained System Is Misleading. The "small group" in much research is considered in isolation, as a self-contained cosmos. When taken as the universe of study, the small group defines the boundaries within which research variables are to be located. Such artificial truncation of the group from its environment prevents adequate theory about its leader-follower relations, as well as its values or norms, which frequently reflect the specific circumstances and the society in which the group functions.

Correctives to these shortcomings of research on small groups have been slow in coming. By and large, most researchers are now reluctant to base "groupness" on the mere presence of other persons. Despite lags, there has been increasing concern with establishing criteria other than "interdependence" as guides for research practice (cf., Golembiewski, 1962; Verba, 1961). Two major lines of development have played parts in correcting the view of the group as a closed system. These correctives emphasize that interpersonal relations within a group are regulated and influenced by the larger social system within which they take place. The correctives derive, on the one hand, from the study of informal groups within larger organizations and, on the other, from sociological theorizing about large social systems.

PERFORMANCE IN ORGANIZATIONS AND THE "HUMAN RELATIONS APPROACH"

The "human relations approach" owes its beginnings to research aimed at improving productivity in industrial organizations, specifically to the now-famous studies conducted by Elton Mayo and his associates at the Harvard Business School at the Western Electric Company's Hawthorne plant from the late 1920s until 1932 (Roethlisberger and Dickson, 1939 and 1961). Undertaken as a systematic attempt to assess the effects of lighting, work pauses, and other changes in work conditions, the research succeeded in "discovering what wasn't true" in prevailing conceptions about the determinants of performance and incentives for work (Whyte, 1961, p. 10).

"What wasn't true" centered around the conception of man as an individualistic creature whose performance is a direct function of economic incentives, provided that the tasks, working conditions, and hours are arranged to optimize efficiency and minimize fatigue. The industrial organization itself was viewed primarily as a formal mechanism for insuring rational means of decision-making, task division, assignment, and supervision.

The principal "discovery" of the Western Electric studies was the existence of informally organized groups whose effects on performance may be conducive to high performance levels or to restricted output, despite incentives offered by management

(Homans, 1950; Whyte, 1961). In addition to the rate of work set by management as the basis for determining bonus, the workers themselves establish a range of acceptable performance, which is affected by past experiences with management policies and employee practices. Performance above the informal norm for unit production is derogated as "rate busting" (see also Chapter 9).

The published reports on the Western Electric studies and other publications reflecting the "human relations approach" were contemporaneous with important developments in social psychology. The sociometric and "role-playing" techniques developed by Moreno in the 1930s and the studies on "group atmosphere" and "group decision" by Lewin and his associates converged as "group dynamics"—an action-oriented line of research and shortly a thriving applied activity (cf. Cartwright and Zander, 1960, 1968).

For a time, the pendulum swung to the opposite extreme with an "implicit assumption" about the determinants of performance which, in Whyte's words, was "equally unsound" (1961, p. 11). This implicit assumption was that informal relations within industry "could be studied and understood apart from economic forces, technology, work flow, organization structure, and plant-community relations" (p. 11). The practical implication was that harmonious organizations are productive organizations and that harmony is chiefly a function of "superior skills in human relations" of management and supervisory personnel. Criticism of this practical implication has been based on the lack of definitive evidence for the efficacy of training in human relations skills (e.g., Whyte, 1961, p. 12) and on the charge that such training aims at "manipulation" of workers to achieve management goals (Etzioni, 1964, pp. 44 ff.).

The study of human relations within organizations has become increasingly interdisciplinary, attracting research efforts and formulations from several fields. This state of affairs is reflected, for example, in publications on organization that include a wide variety of approaches to many different aspects of various formal and informal organizations (cf. March, 1965).

Small Groups and Large Organizations

The corrective exerted by sociological theories of society is, necessarily, toward increased awareness that small groups are subunits of a larger system. Their orientations and internal dynamics make sense only when assessed with reference to the social organization, value orientations, and ideology prevailing within the larger system. This perspective is equally pertinent to the study of worker groups, management groups, church groups, leisure-time groups, or groups of adolescents engaged in delinquent activity.

How, for example, can we deal with the motivations of members in a group of striking workers, a management group, a military unit, a group of militant civil rights advocates or opponents to civil rights, or a group of juvenile automobile thieves without reference to their larger social context? The members' value orientations, attraction to the group, their morale and solidarity, and their interpersonal give and take are permeated with values of the larger society and reverberate with conflicts or alliances with other groups.

A textbook in social psychology is not a feasible place to examine even the most important theories of society that shed light on social-psychological problems. However, the current salience in American sociology of Max Weber's brand of theorizing about large formal organizations, which are so typical of modern societies, is a development of which students in social psychology should be cognizant.

One aspect of every social system is its status structure (organization), which necessarily includes power relationships and at least rudimentary administrative functions. According to Weber, the development of value orientations which legitimize the power differential as "authority" is essential to the conduct of such administrative functions. In sociological nomenclature, the organization with developed administrative machinery invested with authority is referred to as *bureaucracy*. Max Weber's characterization of bureaucratic organization was concisely summarized by Peter M. Blau and W. R. Scott in their book *Formal Organization* (1962).

EF. Colloquially, the term "bureaucracy" connotes . . . rule-encumbered inefficiency. In sociology, however, the term is used neutrally to refer to the administrative aspects of organizations. If bureaucratization is defined as the amount of effort devoted to maintaining the organization rather than to directly achieving its objectives, all formal organizations have at least a minimum of bureaucracy . . . (p. 8).

In Weber's view . . . bureaucracy . . . is the most efficient form of administrative organization, because experts with much experience are best qualified to make technically correct decisions, and because disciplined performance governed by abstract rules and coordinated by the authority hierarchy fosters a rational and consistent pursuit of organizational objectives (p. 33).

Weber's characterization is not based on the workings of real organization: It is an "ideal type" or idealized type. Considerable sociological theorizing and research have been invested in testing his speculations about what contributes to the efficiency of the bureaucracy. Blau and Scott came to the following conclusions about Weber's construction:

A careful reading of Weber indicates that he tends to view elements as "bureaucratic" to the extent that they contribute to administrative efficiency. This contribution to efficiency appears to be the criterion of "perfect" embodied in his ideal type. However, whether or not each of these elements, or their combination, enhances administrative efficiency is not a matter of definition; these are questions of fact—hypotheses subject to empirical testing.

To exploit Weber's insightful theoretical analysis, it is necessary in our opinion, to discard his misleading concept of the ideal type and to distinguish explicitly between the conceptual scheme and the hypotheses. The latter can then be tested and refined rather than left to mere impressionistic assertions (p. 34).

The authors proceed to enumerate serious criticisms made by sociologists of Weber's conception, noting that he failed to make a "similar systematic attempt to isolate the *dysfunctions* of the various elements . . . and to examine conflicts that arise between the elements comprising the system" (p. 34). For example, they note, authority relations may promote discipline and coordination of activities, but they may also discourage subordinates from accepting responsibility. Criteria for selection and promotion are not necessarily compatible, for example, with seniority and merit. Further, as Gouldner (1954) has also emphasized, the twin criteria of administration based on discipline and expertise are by no means necessarily harmonious: ". . . Weber implies that there is no conflict between these two principles; that is, he implicitly assumes that in every disagreement between superior and subordinate, the superior's judgment is also the better judgment in terms of technical expertise. This is not a realistic assumption" (Blau and Scott, 1962, p. 35).

Finally, it should be noted that organization theory is far from complete if, like Weber's, it is so "preoccupied with the formally instituted aspects of bureaucracies and ignores the informal relations and unofficial patterns that develop in formal organizations" (p. 35). A proper balance is necessary between emphasizing, on the one hand, the importance of formally instituted structure and its impact on subunits and, on the other, the importance of informal organizations. We turn to consider briefly one facet of this important problem area.

When a Formal Organization Generates Informal Groups Within Its Body

As noted in several contexts, informal groups frequently arise within formal organizations—such as industries, military units, schools, and prisons—through the interpersonal interaction among members of a unit. If the informal groupings operate outside of work hours to pursue entirely personal goals that have no bearing on the organizational aims, they need not pose a serious question for the organization. In fact, they may in some circumstances merely "oil the wheels" of the formal structure. For example, after-hours drinking companions, fellow hobbyists, fellow club members, or girl chasers may well meet after hours pursuing their respective interests with little relevance to their organizational roles.

However, it raises a question to be reckoned with when informal groups arise owing to the malfunctioning of the formal organization. For example, informal groups do arise among unit members prompted by their reactions to incompetence, favoritism, or injustice endured within the organization, or through failure of leaders to display the requisite devotion and daring, for example in a military organization. With such common promptings, the informal group will almost inevitably be at odds with the formal structure, raising issues as to what is binding for the rank and file. Then, the rank and file observe formal lines of authority as drudgery imposed upon them, as restrictions to be evaded whenever it is possible to get away with it. *More and more, the voice of authority they heed as binding emanates from informal leadership.* On the basis of such facts, the following criterion can be advanced for assessing the adequacy of organizational functioning:

To the extent that an organization functions adequately, it obviates the rise of informal groups within it whose leadership and status hierarchy are at variance with those of the formal organization.

Conversely, to the extent that informal organization exists at variance with the formal structure and contrary to the formally instituted values, norms, or purposes, the inadequacy of the formal organization is indicated.

These generalizations can be tested through assessment of the presence or absence of informal groups within the organization and through establishing whether the informal groups (their leadership and purposes) are in phase or at odds with those of the formal organization. Operationally, such an assessment can be made through frequencies of informal association patterns during rest periods and outside the work situation.

GROUP ORGANIZATION WITHIN ITS SOCIOCULTURAL ENVIRONMENT

The interpenetration of a group with its larger environment becomes evident to any investigator who studies interaction in naturally formed groups over time. Sociological field studies of small groups provide many excellent examples (e.g., Thrasher, 1927; Whyte, 1943). Generalizations about member attitudes and behavior as a function of group membership have to specify the contribution of the group's environment, both through its more-encompassing social arrangements, the values or norms prevailing within them, and the facilities available to the group in its important activities. Such specification requires systematic research in a variety of sociocultural settings. Research with these aims was initiated in 1958 for intensive study over time of informal groups of adolescent boys (Sherif and Sherif, 1964, 1965, 1967).

The research has been conducted to date in eight cities in the southwestern and eastern United States with observations of nearly 50 groups. Because the findings are summarized in more detail in Chapter 19 on adolescent reference groups, we shall concentrate here on the study of the groups themselves, with a summary on one small group in order to make the concepts of organization, role, and status more concrete.

The impact of the larger society was evident in the values and goals prevailing among high-school students in all areas, as well as within the small groups studied. To illustrate the impact of such distinctions upon group interaction, the case summarized below represents a lower-class neighborhood populated chiefly by first- or second-generation immigrants from Mexico. The way that the locale of this group was assessed in terms of socioeconomic rank and urbanization is shown in Fig. 8.1. The baseline represents an index of socioeconomic rank that is standardized so that comparisons can be made between urban areas. The ordinate is another index (urbanization) reflecting living and family circumstances. The particular group to be described resided in area B 41, low in both socioeconomic rank and urbanization.

How the Groups Were Studied. The observer of a group was selected to "fit" into the study area, both in appearance and cultural background. He was fully instructed on observation methods and steps in data collection. The method of observation differed from "participant observation" whereby the observer tries to become part of a group, and from the use of informants to interview members about their group. The following specify the observer's role:

1. He established a clear and reasonable pretext for being in the neighborhood that

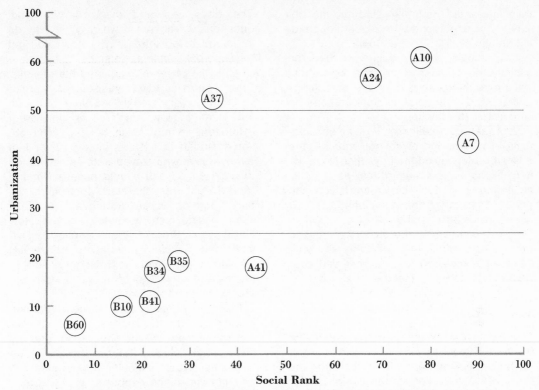

Fig. 8.1. Urban areas plotted according to socioeconomic rank (*horizontal*) and urbanization (*vertical*), as derived from social area analysis. (From Sherif and Sherif, *Reference Groups*, Harper & Row, 1964.)

would raise no suspicions of his intent, but that permitted him the opportunity to move about and to be in contact with somewhat younger boys.

2. At first, he made no approaches to any boys in the neighborhood, simply visiting it to observe clusters appearing in public (such as parks, recreation centers, pool halls, soda fountains, etc.), in order to record the frequency and regularity with which the same boys appeared together. Clusters were selected for study solely on the basis of the *frequency* and *regularity* of their association over a period of time.

3. Once a cluster was thus selected, the observer attempted to bring the boys to him through his activities, rather than to approach them directly. In the case to be reported, this procedure involved contact with young adults in the neighborhood while engaging in athletic activities, ostensibly to "keep fit." The young adults, in turn, passed along the word that the man (observer) was interested in helping a ball team.

4. The observer was instructed not to question the boys nor to start activity unless they initiated it. His aim was to gain rapport through appearing consistently a "harmless but helpful" young adult. In the case to be reported, this stricture meant that the observer had to be much less directive than the ordinary "coach" and tolerant of misbehavior.

5. Once in contact with the group, the observer regularly wrote reports and made ratings of behavior (including effective initiative), but never in the presence of group members. Secrecy of reports and ratings was scrupulously observed.

6. Successively, the observer focused on status and role relationships within the group, then on evidence of group norms. When his ratings from one time to the next were reliable, they were checked in the following ways:

A. An independent observer unacquainted with the group or the observer's ratings was given the opportunity to observe the group during several hours as they interacted naturally (through the observer's arrangements). He made independent ratings of status in the group.

B. Informally, the observer secured sociometric choices from each boy about "who gets things started," "who gets things done," and interpersonal preferences in various group activities.

C. At the completion of regular observations over a period of several months, the observer interviewed the boys, people in the neighborhood, and authorities, as well as collecting any available records on the group and its members, individually.

Thus, conclusions about the organization, norms, and activities of a group were based on data checked for its reliability and validated from recurrent events observed over time as well as from other sources.

Illustrative Case

Where and How the Observer Found the Group. The observer (Joel Garza) was Spanish-speaking and familiar with the area, which was known for a high delinquency and crime rate. He went to the city park bordering the neighborhood, which was usually full of children, couples, and young adults. The young adults joked with the younger boys, usually by calling them insulting names (a cultural tradition). The teen-age boys paid no apparent attention to the observer, so he took a basketball and "worked out" near the young men, several of whom joined him from time to time. He had the opportunity to tell them that he wanted to gain experience working with teen-agers for his aspired career as a coach, adding that he could schedule games with other teams. Many days later, he was approached by a boy who said that he had heard that the observer could get games with other teams.

After several fruitless visits to the park the observer finally met eight boys through that contact. His initial contact introduced him, saying, "El Senor este nos puede consegir juegos con otros *teams."* Note that in stating that "this man can get us games with other teams" the boy used an English word. Like all conversations, this one was in Spanish (Tex-Mex) embroidered with English terms, local slang, and huge curses.

The boys peppered the observers with questions: "Who would we play?" "Why do you want to do this?" "Why don't you get fellows from someplace else?"

After the observer explained his reasons, Che, a short sturdy 17-year-old boy turned to Juan, a very "tough" 18 year old: "Do you want to play, Juan?" Juan answered: "Hold on, let him finish talking." The observer added that it was important for him to have boys who played well, as he wanted to be a coach and should have a winning record right from the start. Juan said: "I'll play," turning to an attractive boy of 17 years beside him: "Rogelio?" "I will. How about you, Wero?" Wero replied: "Hell yeah, *que si vacillo"* (continuing in Spanish) "We'll all play and we'll all give hell to those damn guys." All of the others immediately volunteered.

How the Larger Social System Affected the Group and Its Change. Until the observer studied the neighborhood and its history more closely (later in the study), he had considerable difficulty in understanding why certain things happened in the group, including their initial decision to compete in athletics. He knew that the neighborhood was poor and "tough." The value of *machismo* was widely shared by the Spanish American boys in the city. (Translated rather inadequately into English, *machismo* means being a "he-man," more specifically implies having sexual adventures, but not being bossed by a girl or woman, and showing no fear—especially in a fight.)

What the observer did not know at the time was that a tragedy had occurred in the neighborhood some years earlier involving the older brothers of several of these boys. They, too, were a group: tough, independent, and engaging in many illegal activities. The owner of a small grocery let the boys use his store to hang around in order that he could keep an eye on his own son. The boys used the rear of the store as an arsenal and cache for stolen goods. By the time the owner found out, two boys were dead and a third seriously wounded. One of the dead boys was his son. The man committed suicide.

Some of the parents and young adults in these families were very concerned that the tragedy not be re-enacted in the younger generation. A social worker in the area at the time of the tragedy told them that the best way to prevent its recurrence was to get the younger boys interested in sports. So young adults and parents encouraged the younger boys to play ball, an activity that had not been characteristic of the neighborhood. Sports competition was *not highly valued* in the peasant culture from which they had come.

Meanwhile, the younger boys were becoming much more acculturated to the larger American society than their older brothers had been. The younger boys not only played athletic games but watched games on television. They preferred American popular music to Mexican music, hot dogs and hamburgers to tortillas, Hollywood movies to Mexican.

Another highly pertinent relationship to the larger society was the fact that only two of the older boys (17–18 years old) were still in school. Attending school was berated by the others. Wero, whose intelligence test score was average for his age (100), became a drop-out in the eleventh grade while the study was in progress. Lalo, a 15-year-old was regularly insulted about his dark skin (*el Africano*) and the fact that he was in school.

Role and Status Relations in Action. The observer followed the practice of mapping out plays on paper, but never assigning positions in the game. Juan, the tough fellow, invariably took the paper to tell each fellow what position to play, how to execute the movements, etc. He praised their successes. When Lalo (the 15-year-old) made an error, Juan cursed him strongly. Wero made a mistake once and Juan threw the ball hard at his upper back. Wero turned in a fury, which he contained when he saw who had thrown the ball. Juan was never tough in this way to Rogelio or Che, and accepted their suggestions on starting lineups and substitutions.

The team won several games arranged by the observer. On the day before the deadline, Rogelio began to explore the possibility of getting in the City League. The fee was ten dollars. Juan had all of them pool their money: a total of $1.18 of which he gave 55 cents. Later that day, Pete suggested they buy cold drinks. Rogelio, however, insisted that their money was "down payment" on the entry fee to the League and then asked the observer if he could help them by paying the rest of the fee.

After each of the interaction episodes at regular intervals each week, the observer made ratings of each boy, ranking them according to their *effective initiative.* Their ranks varied from time to time. After a month of regular observation, he consistently ranked Juan at the top, with Tony and Pinto at the bottom. Gradually, his rankings of the boys became stabilized according to their relative effectiveness in initiating and controlling activity and administering sanctions (e.g., insults). The top diagram in Fig. 8.2 shows the rank order of this small group based on the *mean* rank assigned to each boy, from the observer's ratings over the month prior to December 30, before the decision to enter League play.

After entering the League, winning became very important to the boys. Juan, who was the acknowledged leader (A in Fig. 8.2) did not play basketball as well as the others. Basketball was then the League activity. During this period, a game was called at the last minute and only six boys were available for the five-man game.

Who would start the game? Che (B in Fig. 8.2) asked the observer to decide who should sit out. The observer replied that he did not know. Rogelio (C in Fig. 8.2) asked Che to choose five players. Che eliminated Wero, who protested that his position was indispensable against the particular opponent. Rogelio asked Juan (A) please to decide. Juan thought a moment, then said that he did not feel too well and would sit out. Juan's "illness" did not last long after the game started. Pete (D) took himself out of the game, then Che and the others followed suit so that Juan could play. They won the game.

During the next month Rogelio's (C in Fig. 8.2) words began to count more and more in making selections, calling plays and other important decisions. He never left Juan out of the lineup, but Juan often volunteered to sit out when the team was in a tight spot. Juan showed no hard feelings over these events, because he too was absorbed that the team win. Such events, occurring during the middle ten days of

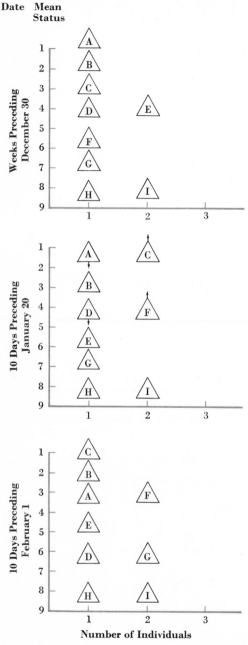

Date   Mean
        Status

Weeks Preceding
December 30

10 Days Preceding
January 20

10 Days Preceding
February 1

Number of Individuals

Fig. 8.2. Observed changes in status of members in natural group with alteration of their main activities during a month. Starting at top, figures show observer's mean ranking of individual's status (*vertical*) during repeated observations in time period designated. Letters denote individuals. Arrows pointing upward or downward indicate observer's ratings of change in progress during the period. More than one individual at a given rank indicates tie in observer's mean rank for the period. (From Sherif and Sherif, *Reference Groups,* Harper & Row, 1964.)

January, brought changes in the observer's ratings, as indicated in the second frame of Fig. 8.2

Meanwhile, the group's accomplishment in the competitions had become so important to them that the members were increasingly cautious not to *get into trouble,* which would have meant their elimination from the League competition. Juan's leadership had been closely tied with his toughness and skill in fighting. One evening, while the boys were spectators at a game between two rival church teams, the boys sensed open conflict arising. Even the pleas of two priests failed to quiet the vehemence of the rival cheering sections. The boys began to talk about what to do if they were attacked. Juan said they should attack first. Rogelio, backed by Che and Wero, told Juan in no uncertain tones *not to start* anything. On the way home, they explained to Juan how seriously they could get into trouble if he did not stop looking for a fight. Later Wero remarked that Rogelio was the best one to have along *to keep them out of trouble.*

In two months' time, Rogelio was the acknowledged leader, even though he never competed directly or came into conflict with Juan, who threw himself into group activities as heartily as ever. Juan's decline in status (effective initiative) was accompanied by the rise of Rogelio to leadership and the decline of Pete (*D* in Fig. 8.2), Juan's younger brother who shared his eagerness for combat. By February 1, the group structure appeared as shown in the lower frame in Fig. 8.2

STABILIZATION OF ROLES AND HIERARCHICAL STATUS STRUCTURE

The development of organization has been defined in terms of role relationships among a number of individuals. As defined on p. 140, role denotes reciprocal regularities in the treatments and expectations of individuals, each for the others. Because the components of such regularities differ greatly according to the individuals involved, their locations, the tasks engaged in, the common motives that brought them together, and the requirements of the larger setting, *role* is necessarily a *generic* term.

Fortunately, there are many role constellations firmly established in a society so that the concept *role* can be usefully employed in research in important areas of social interaction without qualifications; for example, sex or occupational roles (cf. Newcomb *et al.,* 1965; Sargent and Williamson, 1966; Lindesmith and Strauss, 1968).

When particular social roles are specified (e.g., as doctor-patient, inmate-guardian, guest-host at a middle-class entertainment) the interaction processes and respective behaviors of participants become highly predictable. With such focus, one detects regularities in behavior sufficiently clear-cut to term the interaction process a "ritual" (cf. Goffman, 1967). The obvious examples are the doctor's famous "bedside manner" and the impervious repetition of welcome by the hostess at a large social function.

However, when one surveys the literature available on role relations, as Biddle and Thomas (1966) have done, one finds that the concept has been used in highly contradictory and conflicting ways. The ambiguity in the concept reflects the uncritical juxtaposition of social interaction situations ranging all of the way from first encounters to institutionally ritualized situations. When, as in the present section, we wish to deal with the stabilization of roles *over time,* it becomes essential that we emphasize dimensions of roles that are found in any group that has stabilized to some degree. Relative power to initiate and control interaction process is such a dimension.

The member's position (rank) in a developing power structure is his *status* in the group—a differentiated aspect of his role that is defined in terms of the relative effectiveness of his actions in initiating, making or approving decisions, coordinating interaction, invoking sanctions for deviant actions by others, and in terms of the evaluations of other members. The member's status, therefore, reflects a dimension of role relations that is not identical with his ability to influence another's behavior in any situation at all. *Power* is manifested in situations in which influence can be implemented with *sanctions.* Status need not be identical to prominence, expertise, or the degree to which the person is liked.

Defined as *effective initiative,* the status

dimension necessarily assumes a hierarchical form over time. In other words, organization is "pyramidal at the top" (Caplow, 1964, p. 58). The highest status position is held by the leader. Especially in societies in which social equality is a valued idea, the operational leader of informally organized groups—defined by observation of his effectiveness over time—may not be designated openly as "leader" by the members. In fact, as we found in studies of informally organized groups of adolescents, members may explicitly deny that they have a "leader"— even though a leader position can be singled out by intensive observation in a variety of situations. (They say, "We don't have a leader;" "we're just friends;" or "we're all alike.")

Figure 8.3 is a diagram of the stabilization of organization over time, as defined by the power dimension. At the top (Time *a*) the diagram represents two collections of individuals with no previous history of interaction, but selected from the same cultural background in order to hold other criteria of differentiation constant. The circles represent the individuals and indicate that, at this time, their relationships cannot be reliably ranked according to relative effectiveness in initiating activity or controlling interaction from one situation to the next. Instead, the ratings of individuals according to their effective initiative are different in various activities.

The course of status stabilization diagrammed in the figure is based on the findings for six groups, formed experimentally from togetherness situations by placing unacquainted similar individuals in problem situations with highly appealing goals that could be attained only through coordination of action and pulling together. (These experiments are summarized in Chapter 11 on in-group and intergroup relations.) Deliberately, the diagram represents two groups in the process of stabilization, to indicate that the particular pattern of the organization, the steepness or flatness of the hierarchy, and which individuals occupy what positions do not follow any set, predetermined form.

The second frame in Fig. 8.3 at Time *i* represents the lowest and the highest positions by triangles. The triangle symbol is used for positions that can be reliably rated

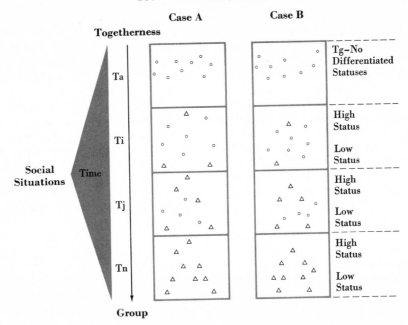

° Individual Whose Status is not yet Stabilized

△ Individual Whose Status is Stabilized

Fig. 8.3. Diagram of gradations of organization (structure) in two cases over time, from initial togetherness to hierarchical differentiation of status positions. Proceeding from top (Time a), the diagram shows initial stabilization of status at top and bottom (represented by triangles at Ti) and succeeding stabilization of structure in two different patterns. Drawn on the basis of data on the formation of six groups (see text).

from one activity to the next and from one day to the next. As we shall see in the next section, the stabilization of the top position typically occurs earlier than other positions, followed by the lowest status positions. This observation does not imply, however, that group formation consists simply in the "search for a leader." On the contrary, leadership is subject to change when conditions of interaction are altered.

At Time *j* in the figure, observers are able to agree on the positions most members occupy from one situation and from one day to the next, the exception being in the middle of the organization. Again, this is a typical finding in groups studied both in experimental and field conditions. In part, the continued flux in the middle ranks may reflect attempts by those in the middle to improve their standing or to align themselves with those of higher status. In other words, some fluctuations occur in the middle ranks. At Time *n* in the diagram, the status relationships are stabilized, all observers agreeing on the status structure—

which is also revealed in the members' perceptions of their relative standing, obtained through sociometric choices (see p. 238).

Deliberately, no issue is made at this point about which person attains *what* status in the structure. Later in this chapter, the problem is considered in discussing leader-follower relations. Here it is sufficient to note that any criteria that differentiate participants by status *outside* of the interaction situation *do* promote status differences in group structure. For example, juries tend to select foremen who are males in higher-level occupations over women and low-level occupations (Strodtbeck, *et al.,* 1965).

The speed or rate of stabilization diagrammed in the figure will vary. In the particular experiments on which the diagrams were based, the groups stabilized within about a week of continous living together and engaging regularly in highly appealing activities requiring coordinated action to attain goals. Other investigators have reported the discernible beginnings of group structure among individuals meeting in the same location for similar activities on each occasion within three to five meetings of a few hours' duration (Merei, 1949; Blake, Shepard and Mouton, 1964).

Environmental events are at least as important as internal relations of members in affecting the rate of stabilization. The stability achieved is sensitive to the introduction of new members, to changes in location and facilities, and to outside threat or emergency. In particular, as we shall see in Chapter 11, the stabilization of group structure is never independent of relationships with other groups. Prolonged competition between groups for mutually incompatible goals, important confrontations resulting in victory or defeat, and decisive actions by the larger power structure to alter or to crush the group's course of action produce changes in the internal organization of the group itself (Sherif and Sherif, 1964; Sherif, 1966).

End Anchoring in the Stabilization and Perception of Social Organization

The general finding, then, is that regular and recurrent interactions among individuals with common goal directions invariably become patterned through differentiation of member roles and status positions. Accordingly, the interactions among individuals become more predictable from one situation, one activity, and one time to the next—indicating recurrent regularities in attitude and behavior. *Who* gains *what* position remains an important problem for study.

One invariant in the stabilization of organization concerns the perception and judgment of the organization both by the members and by observers. Theoretically, the important generalization about the stabilization process is that *perception of the organization is polarized by the extreme positions at the top and bottom*. Thus, in social organization, we are dealing with a very general phenomenon, namely *end anchoring* (p. 75 f.). The end anchoring phenomenon refers to the finding that extreme stimuli in a series (e.g., weights, frequencies, lengths, or position) are identified, learned, and judged more quickly and more

accurately than intermediate stimuli are. It occurs in judgment experiments in the laboratory. In serial learning and perceptual recognition in serial presentations, end anchoring occurs as a function of *order* of presentation with the earliest and last stimuli in the series serving to define the set (Harcum, 1967).

De Soto and Bosley (1962) reported end anchoring in paired associate learning, in which subjects were required to learn names of unknown students paired with their college class (freshman, sophomore, junior, senior). Learning was faster both in terms of number of errors and of number of trials to perfect recall for the lowest (freshman) and highest (senior) classifications.

As noted in presenting Fig. 8.3, end anchoring was observed in the stabilization of six experimental groups. In the observation of several dozen existing groups of adolescents in natural field conditions, the observers' ratings of status over periods of time ranging from 6 months to a year were analyzed, with the invariant result that the ratings were more consistent for the highest and lowest status positions, with greater variability of rating in the intermediate ranks.

Figure 8.4 presents a diagram of the findings on the ratings of a number of observers each rating a different group. (Separate analysis of an individual observer of a particular group over time is presented in Sherif and Sherif, 1964.) The separate curves in the figures represent averages in the variability of ratings for separate blocks of observation periods (10 observation periods in each block) from the observers' initial encounters with the groups (Time *a*) to Time *n,* after they had observed for some months.

As Fig. 8.4 shows, the most and least effective were recognized most readily and used as standards in judging others. There is a difference from the end anchoring that occurs more typically in judgment or learning of a neutral series of stimuli. As a social structure, a group is affected by the superior anchor (high status) to a greater degree than a physical dimension. That is, the leader position tends to exert a greater anchoring effect than the bottom positions, both in the judgments of an observer and in promoting the stabilization of the structure.

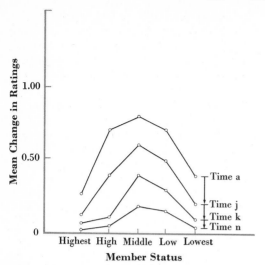

Fig. 8.4.   Observers' judgments of status in natural groups over time: end-anchoring effect. Mean
changes in rank according to observed effective
initiative for blocks of 10 observation periods from
early (Time a) to late (Time n) in study cycle.
Note that observers' judgments are more variable
at Time a, but that judgments of high and lowest
status positions stabilize earliest.

Note that variability in rating lower positions is greater than that in rating higher
positions (Fig. 8.4). Note also that, in general, the observer's variability in ratings decreases over time (Time *a* to Time *n*). This
trend occurs, of course, when no drastic
changes occur in the status structure during the time period.

As an important correlate of the end-
anchoring effect, observers are more confident of their ratings at the extreme positions (see Fig. 8.5). The observers regularly
rated their own *confidence* in the ratings
they made on effective initiative immediately following each observation period,
using a 7-point scale ranging from *altogether confident* to *not at all confident*. As
the figure shows, confidence in ratings increased over time, but was invariably
highest at the extreme status positions,
especially at the high level.

Thus, end anchoring is a general phenomenon of human judgment, both in laboratory
experiments with neutral stimuli and in observations of group formation and group
functioning. The finding is all the more significant because it is not confined to trained

observers. The same phenomena are detected in the participants' own perceptions
of the group structure as obtained through
sociometric questions as to "Who gets
things started?" and "Who gets things
done?" when members interact. Consensus
on choices is greatest for those in highest
status positions (as independently assessed
by independent observers) and those at the
lowest positions (who receive few or no
member choices on such items).

As we shall see in the next section, the
polarization of the structure by high status
positions and, secondarily, by lower positions is reflected in member expectations
for performance in relevant activities.

INCREASED PREDICTABILITY
OF ATTITUDE AND BEHAVIOR
WITH STABILIZATION

The interaction process has differential
effects on individual behavior from the very
start, as we have seen. Initially, individual
characteristics in expressiveness, "showing
off" in various respects (including a "show
of power"), reticence, enthusiasm, talka-
tiveness, and the like may be the most
pronounced evidence of these differential
effects. As the individuals face various
problems, undertake different tasks, and
move from one location to another, the
incipient differentiation of roles begins as
participants make suggestions and ineffective or effective moves toward dealing with
the problems and executing the tasks that
they face in concert. Lines of communication shift from time to time and from one
situation to the next. The general finding at
this stage is a changing constellation of
relationships from one situation to the next
reflecting, primarily, the nature of the *tasks*
and *situations* relative to the potential personal contribution of the various individuals.

However, as interaction continues over
time, the stabilization of roles and status in
a variety of activities, along with a set of
norms, shifts the relative weights of factors
affecting attitude and behavior. The stabilization process means, simply, that the relative power of these various individuals to
affect interaction, to choose activities and
locations, to make decisions, and to influ-

ence one another has become differentiated. The stabilization of the role-status structure is associated at the same time with the stabilization of reciprocal attitudes and expectations, as well as regularities in behavior. Thus the differential effects of group situations become increasingly predictable in terms of the individual's position and role in the structure.

These findings permit some generalizations with high predictive value about the determinants of behavior in togetherness and in group situations:

1. *In togetherness situations, differential effects are more predictable in terms of the individual's relation to the task, the location, and to the* formal *roles and values manifested by other participants* (e.g., as evidenced by dress, occupation, speech, etc.) *than by properties of the relationships among particular individuals in question.*

2. *In group situations, differential effects exhibited by members are increasingly determined by the nature of the status-role structure and the emerging set of norms, with a corresponding decreased importance of discrete situational factors* (e.g., tasks, activities, locations, roles established outside of the group).

These generalizations hold because during formation of group structure or organization, the members form attitudes and expectations relative to one another that are general across situations and over time. This proposition can be tested through experimental study of perception and judgment by individual members of each other's performance in activities related to the group. Such a test proceeds logically from Proposition 9 on the effects of internal factors in unstructured situations and requires, therefore, that perception or judgment be made for performance of an activity lacking clear-cut structure in the dimension to be judged.

**Experimental Test of
Status Stabilization
Through Individual Judgment**

If the stabilization of status structure implies differential attitudes and expectations toward various members, the following hypothesis is warranted: *In judging perform-*

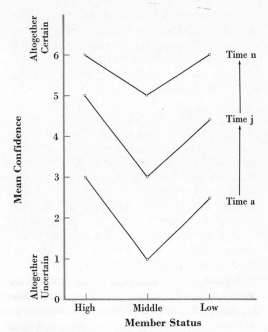

Fig. 8.5. Observers' confidence in their judgments of status in natural groups over time. Observers rated their own confidence in their ranking of group members according to effective initiative. The figure gives average self-ratings of confidence according to status level (high, middle, low) of the person ranked from Time a (*below*) to Time n (*above*). Note that initially (Time a) observers are not very confident of their rankings, but are more confident of the high and low ranks. As the study cycle progresses (Times j to n), they become increasingly confident of their judgments, especially at the extreme ranks. Thus, as in studies of psychophysical judgment, the end-anchoring effect is also mirrored in the judge's confidence ratings.

ance of members occupying differentiated status positions in activities related to the group and lacking structure in the dimension of judgment, the errors in judgment will be systematically related to the status of the member judged.

The specific application of general principles to status and member expectations followed a series of experiments on aspiration level as influenced by experimentally introduced group standards (pp. 426–427) and, subsequently, by interpersonal attitudes (pp. 389–390). The empirical feasibility of the application was suggested in an incident reported by Whyte (1943) in his observations of the Nortons, one of several groups he observed in an Italian slum area of Boston during the late 1930s.

Whyte commented that when the Nortons became interested in bowling, high scores by the top-ranking members were regarded as natural, were encouraged and appreciated. However, members with low status were not expected to excel in bowling. In the case of one member with rather low status, Frank, the contradiction between skill and expectations of the other members was manifest both in the reactions of members to Frank and in Frank's own experience. He was accused of "playing over his head" and commented himself: "I can't seem to play when I am playing with fellows I know, like that bunch. I do much better when I am playing with the Stanley A. C. against some team in Dexter, Westland, or out of town" (Whyte, 1943, p. 19).

This telling observation suggested that member expectations of other members function like other attitudes and would be revealed in estimations of *future* performance. O. J. Harvey (1953) investigated the problem in an experiment on 10 adolescent cliques. As the hypothesis required clearly differentiated groups, Harvey singled out 16 cliques on the basis of teacher's ratings, his own observations, and sociometric questions, including only those cliques in which all three measures of status rankings agreed. From each of the 10 groups surviving this test, he selected three members: the leader, the member with the lowest status rank, and a member of intermediate status.

The experimental task was judging future performance just prior to each trial in throwing darts at a target board. Each of the three members threw the darts on 10 practice trials, then on 50 trials that were judged. Before each trial, he estimated the score that he *actually* expected (not hoped) to make on that trial. Then he watched while the other two subjects threw darts, each time estimating their future performance as they had estimated his.

The target board was blank when the subjects threw the darts; however, before the performance, subjects were shown a board with scored circles like the usual target board. The possible scores ranged from 0 to 20 on a single trial. The data analyzed were the mean difference scores between performance judged *after* the trial and estimations *before* the trial.

A high positive relationship was found between the person's status in the group and member expectations for his performance ($r = .83$). On the average, middle- and low-status members overestimated the leader's performance (2.99 and 2.45, respectively). Performance by the member with intermediate status rank was overestimated slightly by the leader and the low-status member (1.66 and .98 respectively). Both the leader and the middle status member tended to underestimate the performance by the low status member ($-.13$ and $-.18$, respectively).

In short, *the higher the individual's status in the group, the greater the overestimation of his performance and the lower the status, the greater the tendency to underestimate.*

Appraisals of Performance and Status in Experimentally Produced Groups

While existing groups were used in the Harvey experiment, a more definitive test of the hypothesis that member attitudes become more predictable as a group structure stabilizes required experimental production of a group. This test was made as part of a large-scale experiment on group formation in 1953 (Sherif, White, and Harvey, 1955). Starting from an initial togetherness situation among unacquainted persons, the experiment involved conditions conducive to the formation of two distinct groups. The experimental design is described in detail in Chapter 11. Here it is sufficient to note that these conditions were highly appealing and required cooperative efforts among the individuals over a period of about a week. The experiment was conducted in a summer camp, and the subjects were 24 boys about 12 years old.

To test the proposition that differential attitudes stabilized during group formation would be reflected in members' judgments of one another, an unstructured task was devised which also appeared natural in the camp situation. It should be noted as a methodological advance over earlier experiments that the task required direct judgments of performance just *after* the activity, not estimates of future performance.

The performance to be judged was a series of 25 trials throwing a handball at a target. Just before a softball game planned between the two groups ("Panthers" and "Pythons"), it was suggested that each group hold a separate practice session. Each member took his turn at throwing the ball at the target while other members appraised his performance. Actual score on the five-foot circular target was indicated on the back of the board. As the ball hit the target, it depressed one of 15 concentric circles of plywood, making electrical contact that lighted the appropriate bulb on a panel visible only to the experimenter behind the target board. Although the boys were shown the target and informed about the value of hits (ranging from 2 to 30, the bull's eye), the front of the target was covered with blue denim during their trials.

The results were analyzed in terms of error, that is the average difference between judgments of the person's performance by all other members of his group and his actual performance on the 25 trials. The overall finding in both groups was that error in judging a person's performance was significantly related to his place in the status structure of his group. The rank-order correlation between status position and size of overestimation (error in judgment) was .74 for the Panthers and .68 for the Pythons.

Of course, it could be that this relationship simply reflected corresponding differences among members in their actual skills. However, the correlations between errors in judgment and actual performance (skill) were only .007 for the Panthers and .45 for the Pythons, neither being statistically significant. When we compare the two sets of correlations—one between error in judgment and status, the other between error in judgment and skill—we find that the *difference* between the two correlations is significant only for the Panther group.

We cannot conclude from these findings that skill is unrelated to status or that demonstrated skill has no bearing on judgment. In this task, the objective structure was deliberately reduced to permit alternative judgments. The activity, coming just before an important game, was highly relevant to each group. Under these circumstances, the performance of high status members was overevaluated and that of low status members de-emphasized, regardless

of actual performance. It is noteworthy that this tendency was clearest in the group (Panthers) with greatest solidarity. The analysis suggested that individual differences in actual performance account for much more of the variance in judgments by the Pythons (the less integrated group).

**Multiple Expectations
as Indicators
of Status Structure**

The experiments summarized in the preceding sections suggest that members' appraisals of each other can serve as an indirect or unobtrusive method for studying status and role relations in a group. This possibility was explored further in a study by Koslin, Haarlow, Karlins, and Pargament (1968), which secured judgments on four different tasks from members of four groups. Specifically, these investigators asked whether differential expectations of performance by individuals with differing status in a group would be generalized across tasks and activities. They predicted, further, that *consistency* in over- or under-estimation of performance would be greatest for individuals occupying the highest and lowest status positions, with greater variability from one task to the next for judgments of members with intermediate status. This hypothesis was derived from the general principle of end anchoring.

In an athletically oriented camp for boys, four groups were observed, each consisting of six to eight boys between 11 and 13 years old, and each living in a separate cabin (N = 29). The observer rated the effective initiative displayed by each boy in a variety of situations.

The four tasks used to tap expectations of performance were as follows:

(1) A sociometric questionnaire administered to each boy individually on the pretext of improving the camp.

(2) The height estimation test. Stick figures were presented to each boy with the instruction to imagine each figure as a member of his group, then to indicate where the top of his own head would reach on the figure.

(3) The rifle task. Each boy shot one bullet at each of four targets placed 50 feet away. When a bullet hit the target, it disap-

peared. Other members observed his performance and recorded their judgments of his performance.

(4) The canoe task. Each boy paddled from a bridge around a buoy and back to the bridge, whereupon other members recorded their estimates of the time required for the performance.

In the last two tasks (rifle and canoe), group members were already familiar with each other's proficiency before the estimates were obtained. The differences between estimated and actual performance were adjusted, therefore, to take account of level of skill.

Table 8.1 shows the correlations between the observer's ratings on effective initiative and judgments on the four tasks. For the canoe, rifle, and height estimation tasks, the correlations in the right-hand column represent the association between observed status and overestimation of performance, a positive correlation indicating greater overestimation with higher status. Correlations between sociometric scores and observations may be interpreted as evidence that the observer's views from outside the group are related significantly to the members'

Table 8.1. Correlations Between Observed Status in Groups and Member Expectations

Tasks	Rifle	Canoe	Height	Observed status
Sociometric	.58*	.61†	.66†	.64†
Rifle	—	.52*	.48*	.67†
Canoe	—	—	.65†	.67†
Height	—	—	—	.51*

* p < .005.
† p < .0005.
Adapted from Koslin et al. (1968).

views of the structure from inside the group. In addition, correlations among the various tasks are shown.

The highest association between observed status and judgments obtained when a multiple correlation was computed, using observed status as the criterion variable. The degree of relationship between performance expectations on the four tasks and observed status is indicated by the multiple r of .79 (p < .001).

Separate analysis of results for each group was made to evaluate the second hypothesis, namely that end anchoring of judgments would be revealed through greater consistency (less variability) across the four tasks for members with highest and lowest status positions. As the measurement units for the task were not comparable, the scores on each task were ranked within each group from highest to lowest. Then, for each member, the variation among his ranks on the four tasks was computed. This variance among ranks was correlated with status rank based on the observer's ratings using the statistic E (curvilinear association). Only the smallest group (Group II) in Fig. 8.6 did not show a significant departure from linearity, and, even for that group, the curvilinear relation accounted for 65.6 percent of the variance in the ranks.

The authors concluded that their findings support the predicted relationships between sociological status in the group and member expectations on several independent tasks, suggesting a generalization of expectations for the member across tasks. However, this generalization is much greater and hence expectations are more consistent for high- and low-status ranks, as expected if end anchoring occurs in perception of group structure.

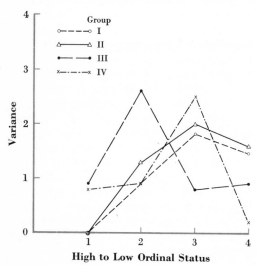

Fig. 8.6. Mean variation in judgments by group members of performance in four tasks according to the status level of the person judged. (By permission from Koslin *et al.*, 1968.) Note that end anchoring is revealed in members' judgments of each others' performance through lower variance at high-status and, to a lesser extent, low-status positions. Data on four natural groups formed in camp situation.

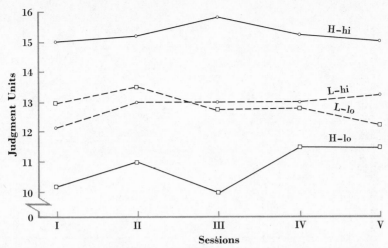

Fig. 8.7. Average of median judgments by members of groups high (H) and low (L) in stability when exposed to highly arbitrary judgments by fellow members with high (hi) or low (lo) status. (After MacNeil, 1967.) Fellow members of high or low status were indoctrinated in arbitrary judgments in previous session. Arbitrary standard was high on ordinate. Locations represent combined scores for judgments on two tasks, adjusted for scale differences.

Effects of Group Stability and Member Status

Is effective initiative simply a function of the individual's attempts to respond adequately to the demands of the immediate situation, or do members' expectations of each other, based on past interactions, affect the exercise of power in a group? An experimental study by Mark MacNeil (1967) indicates that the answer to our question depends upon the *stability* of the group structure. Six natural groups of adolescent boys were selected on the basis of observations over periods from two to seven months. By using the reliability with which observers ranked each individual's status (top to bottom) as the primary criterion, several judges rated the stability of the groups, three being rated as *high* and three as *low*.

In each group, a member of high status and a member of low status were selected to be indoctrinated in an experiment with an arbitrary norm for judging highly unstructured situations (the autokinetic situation and the number of holes in a target made by a shot gun blast). In either case, the member was contacted to earn five dollars by substituting for a college student

who had failed to appear for an experiment on the "human mind as a calculator." He served with a planted subject who distributed his judgments around an arbitrary mode and within a range much greater in magnitude than was typical in the judgment situations. As the judgment situations were highly unstructured, there was little difficulty in indoctrinating the group member with this arbitrary norm.

The question asked in the experiment was what would happen when the indoctrinated member (either high or low in status) subsequently judged the same situation with other members of his group? Would the other members accept his judgments, knowing that he had previous experience in the experiment? MacNeil predicted that the answer would depend upon whether the group was a highly stable one and upon the status of the member.

Figure 8.7 shows that the effects of the indoctrinated members on judgments of other members of their groups varied markedly. The high status members of well-stabilized groups were very effective in influencing other members and maintaining the indoctrinated norm over five sessions. Low-status members in the stable groups were scarcely effective at all, almost as if

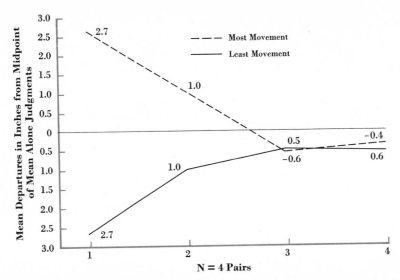

N = 4 Pairs

Fig. 8.8. Changes in judgments of autokinetic movement according to relationship between persons judging (by permission from S. Frank Sampson, 1968. The effects of selected social relationships on the resolution and maintenance of dissensus in the autokinetic situation; unpublished paper presented to the Annual Meeting of the American Sociological Association, 1968.) **a.** (*above*) Mean difference (inches) from midpoint of judgments made alone when partners were social equals (novices) with no prior relationship. Partners who gave judgments of most movement alone are averaged in dashed line over four blocks of judgments (baseline). Partners who gave judgments of less movement are averaged in solid line. Note convergence over time. **b.** (*below*) Mean difference (inches) from midpoint of judgments made alone when partners were social equals but one member highly esteemed the other without reciprocation. Note that in the first two blocks of trials, both the esteemer (*dashed line*) and the esteemed partner (*solid line*) change judgments toward one another, the esteemer changing somewhat more, but that in subsequent blocks (*right*) the esteemer reversed his direction, dragging his admirer with him. **c.** (*opposite page*) Mean difference (inches) from midpoint of judgments made alone when partners were not equal, one being an authority in the organization and the other an alienated subordinate. Despite the initial tendency to converge in judging the highly unstructured situation, the alienated subordinate (*solid line*) ceased being influenced by the authority's judgments and subsequently (*last block*) departed from them. The authority maintained a stable pattern of judgments despite the disagreement.

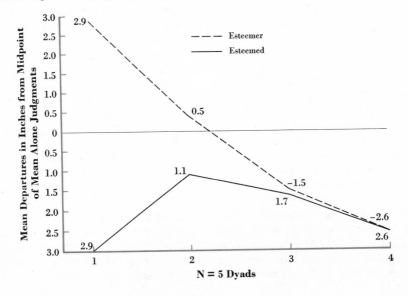

N = 5 Dyads

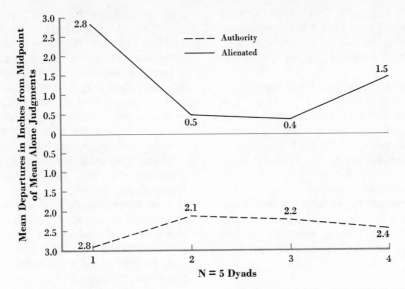

N = 5 Dyads

the other members had discredited their judgments before they started and evolved their own norms in the situation.

In the less stable groups, the indoctrinated norm had a significant effect, regardless of whether the member was high or low in status. Here the experimental situation itself became more important in determining the outcome: The fact that one of the members had previously served as a subject gave some credibility to his judgments as indicated by the higher medians evolved by the less stable groups. On the other hand, in neither case was the member of a less stable group as effective in establishing and perpetuating the arbitrary norm as the high status member of a stable group.

Judgments as Indicators of Member Roles in Formal Organization

Systematic deviations in judgment of an unstructured stimulus were used as an index of role relations in a formal organization by S. F. Sampson (1968). Through unobtrusive observation and informant techniques, Sampson studied the social structure among professed members and novices in a contemplative monastery and delineated several different role relationships involving two strata within the organization. He then selected pairs representing three typical role sets in the monastery to judge extent of apparent movement, utilizing the autokinetic technique. The role relations

represented in the pairs may be typified as follows:

I. Novices during the first week of their stay, thus social equals.

II. Novices for a year who expressed mutual liking, but asymmetrical esteem (that is A chose B as most esteemed, but B did not include A among his first three choices).

III. Novices and full members, the latter having power to sanction the former. In addition to the power differential, an ideological schism and interpersonal conflict characterized their relationships.

Each member gave 80 judgments of extent of apparent movement alone before participating with a partner. The partner was chosen so that in the initial social sessions his judgments differed by about 5 inches on the average. Each pair then served together in three sessions, giving 80 judgments a session.

Sampson analyzed the data as deviation scores, using each subject's judgments alone as the standard to assess his movement toward or away from the partner's judgments. Figure 8.8 summarizes the relative influence of members in the different role sets upon one another over the three sessions, from the initial divergence in Session 1. The new novices were mutually influenced by each other's judgments (Fig. 8.8a). In Fig. 8.8b, the asymmetric roles of older novices (varying according to esteem) are evident in the regular decline of the top curve (the follower, who did not necessarily give judgments of greater movement as the figure might suggest). The lower curve in the same figure indicates that the esteemed partner at first converged toward the other, then switched, carrying the follower along with him.

Figure 8.8 c represents the judgments of pairs from the different social strata that were in conflict. The rebellious novices (top curve) first moved toward the superiors, then moved away, while the superiors remained uninfluenced by the novices' judgments.

This research is a further example of the use of judgments in an unstructured situation as an unobtrusive or disguised indicator of role and status relations, in this case within a formal organization.

LEADERS AND OTHER MEMBERS OF THE GROUP

The terms *leader, leadership,* and *leading* have been used in a great variety of ways, and research has employed almost all of these meanings, at one time or another. Leadership has such impact in human affairs that it deserves to be specified in a way that fits with events of consequence.

Let us take the stabilization of a human group as orientation to these topics. Every group, small or large, is a status structure. Whatever else can be added about it, the status dimension is power. Group stabilization involves the differentiation of status positions that are defined in terms of the effective initiation (or suppression) of activities with implied or actual sanctions for noncompliance or resistance. This being the case, the problem of power is integral to the study of any organization of any size or origin, even though the means and instrumentalities for its exercise differ in formally and informally organized groups. This perspective leads to an operational criterion for defining a leader.

DEF·   **A leader is the member with the top status (power position) in an organizational hierarchy (see definition of organization, p. 150). The operational measure of status is the degree of** *effective initiative* **over time.**

Leadership involves the role relationships between the leader and other members and instrumentalities for coordinating interaction. The leadership process centers around (a) the initiation of policy, decisions, and activities within the group and with outsiders; (b) following their course as they are executed; and (c) applying *sanctions* for noncompliance. When leadership is used in common parlance to note, for example, that "leadership in such and such organization failed," the term is used in this sense.

These specifications have important implications for the study of leaders and leadership:

1. A leader is *part* of the organization (structure) of a social system and cannot, therefore, be understood apart from the roles and statuses of other members.

2. As part of the organization, the leadership role is subject to regulation by other properties of the group, notably its set of values or norms.

Without an organization of some degree of stability, at least, there is no leader. The leader himself is not free to violate at will the bounds of role relationships stabilized in the organization. He is not immune from the bounds defining acceptable conduct and viewpoints within his group and toward outsiders with whom his group has significant relationships. He is not immune from sanctions if he deviates too far from these bounds.

These generalizations about the context of leadership and its limitations are true of any group whatever, small or large, informally or formally organized. Their significance is immediately clear when the actions of leaders or their authorized representatives deviate widely from the stabilized expectations of the membership.

Newspaper accounts tell us what happens when a political leader lets down his followers through deals that appear personally advantageous, or when a business leader makes a secret deal with a supplier. A national leader who appears to succumb to the inducements of the enemy is rejected, as the fate of the World War I French hero, Marshal Pétain, and the former Premier Laval testify. Another case in point was the misfortune met by one O'Brien, leader of the elite ore-trimmers' union on a Lake Michigan port, after he went to Cleveland to negotiate a pay scale but became involved in a deal to transfer his men to a new union—one that would trim ore at a lower rate. When his rank and file caught up with him, "O'Brien was ready for ten months in a hospital and nobody on the street seemed to know who had prepared him" (Holbrook, 1946).

Expectations for the Leader and Other Members

In experiments summarized earlier in this chapter, we saw that expectations for the leader's performance in activities relevant to the group are higher than for other members. He also occupies a special position in members' expectations about adherence to the norms, values, or goals they share.

In a noteworthy study of preschool children's groups, Merei (1949) observed their interaction over time until each group had developed a tradition (norms) in activities, the play schedule, favored games, and jargon. Then he introduced a new child who was somewhat larger and older and had, furthermore, been designated as a leader in other group situations. Would the new child assume leadership?

In all groups, the new child was "absorbed" into the group and adopted its traditions. Over time, several alternatives were then observed. Some of the new children were completely "absorbed" by the tradition. Others were assimilated into the established customs, but gradually took over the functions of directing the proceedings or distributing play materials—all in accord with custom. Those few who became leaders and succeeded in *modifying* existing practices first abided by the established norms, then introduced slight modifications. Of the few who succeeded in modifying the norms, still fewer proceeded to introduce new customs.

Clearly, the leadership role is limited by other role relations and by norms (tradition) stabilized in the group. How, then, does the leader exercise his power toward shaping and changing the group values? Both field and experimental studies indicate that, in general, the leader and other high status members adhere more closely to the major values or norms than those with lower status (e.g., Whyte, 1943; March, 1954; Sherif and Sherif, 1953, 1964). Often, the leader is more aware of the norms and their

bounds than other members (Chowdry and Newcomb, 1952). In informal groups or in any group facing a new situation, he is likely to be more influential than other members in shaping the norm—thus being more involved in its maintenance and observance (Talland, 1954; Sherif et al., 1961).

However, the stricter adherence by the leader is *not* expected for all norms of the group. As we shall see in Chapter 9 in some detail, every group norm permits a range for variation in acceptable behavior. The extent of this latitude varies according to the relative importance of the activity to the group. In natural groups of adolescents (Sherif and Sherif, 1964), the latitude for acceptable variation in behavior was smallest for *matters affecting the maintenance of the group, its major activities, and its solidarity in the face of outside interference or threat.* In other matters of less importance, the latitude of acceptance was much broader. These generalizations held for a variety of groups in different sociocultural settings, some of them engaged in illegal and potentially dangerous activities and some not.

Figure 8.9 diagrams the general relation-

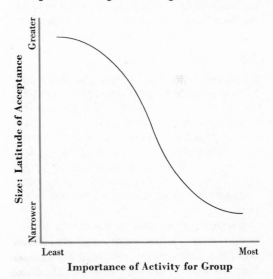

Fig. 8.9. Diagram of theoretical relationship between size of latitude of acceptance and the importance of activity subject to normative regulation in a group. Range of acceptable behavior in a group varies in scope according to importance of activity. More leeway for individual variations is tolerated without sanctions in matters of minor importance (*left*) than in matters central to group's activity and maintenance. (Based on Sherif and Sherif, 1964, and their more recent research.)

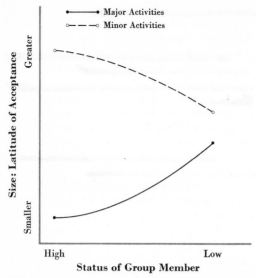

Fig. 8.10. Diagram of theoretical relationship between status in group, importance of activity, and
size of the latitude of acceptance in relevant norms.
As indicated in Fig. 8.9, latitude of acceptance is
broader for activities of minor importance (*dashed
line*) than for those of major importance (*solid
line*). However, the latitude of acceptance also
varies according to the member's status. It is narrowest for high-status members in major activities,
but broad for high-status members in minor activities. More leeway is permitted low-status members
in major activities and less in minor activities.

ship observed between the latitude acceptable to members and the relative importance of the activity for the group. The
latitude of acceptance (ordinate) is narrowest in matters of greatest importance for
maintaining the group and its standing. The
range of tolerated behavior was broader for
less important matters, particularly those
involving activities strictly within the membership.

However, in matters of considerable importance to the group, the latitude of acceptance for members with high status was
still narrower than for members of lower
status. Figure 8.10 shows two curves, one
for very important matters and one for less
important matters, representing the acceptable range of behavior for members of
different status. In matters of minor importance to the group (top curve), high-status
members, and especially the leader have
more leeway. On very important matters,

the relationship differs, the bounds of acceptable behavior for high-status members
narrows.

The foregoing generalizations provide a
framework for assessing the more role-
specific variations allowed members of a
group. Hollander (1961), for example, has
proposed that every member accumulates
"idiosyncrasy credit" to the extent that he
is evaluated as competent and personally
admirable. This credit permits him to deviate from acceptable bounds in "certain dimensions." His deviations from the bounds
of acceptance subtract from his personal
credit, thereby limiting the innovations that
even a leader can introduce. We can see
that the limitations will vary according to
the importance of the norm in question.

It follows from this discussion that the
leader's potentiality of changing the course
of his group will be greater when (1) the
norms in question are not major in importance to the group; (2) the normative structure is already weakened (cf. Kelley and
Shapiro, 1954); or (3) the members face new
problems or critical situations for which
their existing guidelines are inadequate.

Leader-Follower Relations and Other Factors in Social Situations

The massive research literature on
leadership is a tortured maze for the uniniti-
ated, particularly if leadership is viewed
solely in terms of overt behavior at a discrete point in time apart from the context of
that behavior. The literature reflects variegated theories and practical concerns, the
most prominent of which has centered on
the search for potential leaders of existing
organizations in business, military, or governmental affairs.

The findings fall into a coherent pattern
when the research situations are considered with reference to the four sets of
factors affecting behavior in any social
situation (Chapter 6). Indeed, when stabilization of interpersonal relations and norms
within groups is considered, the research
on leadership has relevance to leadership
(executive functions) in large organizations.
The institutionalization and elaboration of
leadership through delegation of power and

representation complicate the picture, but they do not transform it.

Personal Characteristics of Leaders

The older studies of leadership proceeded on the admirably simple but erroneous assumption that a leader had personal qualities or traits that accounted for his gaining and maintaining leadership. As early as 1940, Bird summarized research on the traits characteristic of leaders in various studies: there were 79 such studies, and they overlapped very little. With particular attention to studies in military situations, Jenkins (1947) concluded that leaders in similar situations differed widely and that those in different situations differed even more in their personal traits. Stogdill (1948) surveyed a wide spectrum of research at the same period and found that leaders rather consistently excelled others in at least one skill or personal characteristic, but that *what* characteristic this relative excellence involved differed enormously with the situation and/or the organization in question. As a result, Stogdill's subsequent research (1949, 1962) dealt with leadership as a function of organization.

Mann's review (1959) of research correlating personality measures and behavior in interaction covered studies that used some 500 different measures of personal characteristics. Considering the proportion of studies yielding significant correlations, Mann concluded that statistical significance had been obtained in numerous studies. However, the size of the association was so low that most of the variance remained unaccounted for. For example, half of 28 studies found intelligence scores and leadership status significantly correlated, but the median coefficient was only .25 and the highest reported was .50. Correlations accounting for such small proportions of the variance are all the more unsatisfactory because, as Cattell and Stice (1954) showed, they tend to be specific to particular measures of personality, criteria for status, and situations.

The failure to uncover general leadership traits or personal characteristics is not at all surprising: A leader's personal qualities are expressed in interaction with other members whose personal characteristics provide the context for interaction in various tasks and activities (cf. Gibb, 1968). Thus, while personal characteristics and skills are undoubtedly important factors in leader-follower relations, their relative importance cannot be assessed in the abstract, i.e., apart from other sets of factors. This was Helen H. Jennings' conclusion in her sociometric studies of leadership: "The 'why' of leadership appears . . . not to reside in any personality trait considered singly, nor even in a constellation of related traits, but in the interpersonal contribution of which the individual becomes capable in a specific setting eliciting such contributions from him" (1950, p. 205).

Interpersonal Choices and Leadership

Moreno (1934, 1953) pioneered in research on interpersonal preferences through the use of questionnaires, developing with his associates a set of techniques for graphic presentation and analysis. The sociometric technique consists of securing each person's choices of others with whom he would prefer to associate, usually in several different activities or situations. The network of mutual and one-way choices among participants can be summarized graphically (a sociogram) or arranged in matrix form, with rows and columns corresponding to the persons choosing and being chosen. More recently, graph theory has been used in the attempt to systematize analysis of sociometric networks (cf. Cartwright and Zander, 1968, pp. 492–493).

The earlier sociograms were designed to show the clustering of interpersonal choices and to locate the frequently chosen persons as well as "isolates" (unchosen). More recently, by including criterion questions pertaining to effective initiative during interaction and with use of frequency of choice as the ordinate, sociograms representing the status structure of a group were constructed (cf. Fig. 11.5–11.6).

In her study of sociometric networks in a girl's training school, Jennings (1950) found that girls who were chosen frequently as liked also tended to be leaders in school

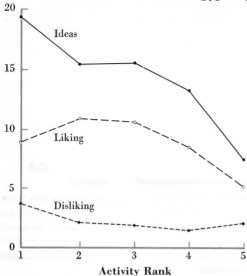

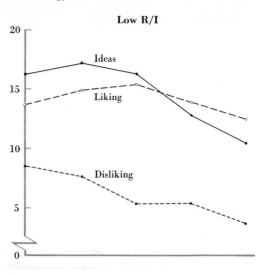

Fig. 8.11. Average ratings received on ideas, liking, and disliking by men varying in rank according to total activity during session. **a.** (*above*) Overall results based on average of 12 sessions for persons occupying activity Rank 1 . . . 5 at that meeting. Note overall tendency for most active person (Rank 1) to be rated lower in liking and higher in disliking than person in Rank 2. (From Robert F. Bales, 1953. "The Equilibrium Problem in Small Groups," p. 146, in Talcott Parsons, Robert F. Bales, and Edward A. Shils, eds., *Working Papers in the Theory of Action.* Reprinted with permission of The Macmillan Company. Copyright 1953 by The Free Press, a Corporation.) **b.** (*right*) Breakdown of findings according to feedback ratio (R/I) of person in top rank. Note that overall results in Fig. 8.11a are produced chiefly by discussions in which the most active participant received very little feedback from others (low R/I at top). Sessions with medium or high feedback (lower graphs) yielded ratings on liking of top rank man differing little from those of second rank. (Condensed from Robert F. Bales, 1956. "Task Status and Likeability as a Function of Talking and Listening in Decision-making Groups," pp. 148–161, in Leonard D. White, ed., *The State of the Social Sciences.* Chicago: University of Chicago Press.)

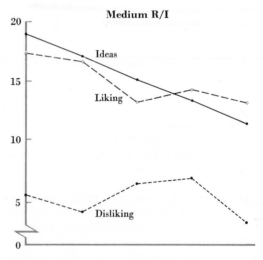

activities. However, she also found that the informal leaders singled out by sociometric analysis differed according to the activity designated. Liking in informal, interpersonal interaction was not necessarily identical with choices in cottage and school activities. Subsequent research relating interpersonal liking and measures of status showed that the person's popularity as a liked associate need not be perfectly correlated with status in the group (e.g., Norfleet, 1948;

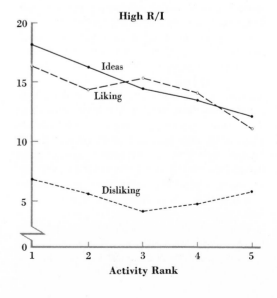

Carter, 1952; Gibb, 1950; Bales, 1953; Sherif and Sherif, 1953). This finding points to the multidimensionality of roles, including leadership.

As with so much research on leadership, research on the relationship of mutual liking and leadership neglected to examine the relative stabilization of group structure and other factors. By using temporary discussion units, Bales (1965) charted the ratings made by participants on the quality of ideas a person offered and how much he was liked or disliked. He located the average ratings for each person according to how active that person was in the discussion (activity rank, see Fig. 8.11). He found that active participants were typically rated highest for presenting "good ideas," but were not always liked as well as persons ranked second or third in frequency of talking. Conversely, the most active talkers tended to be disliked more frequently. As Fig. 8.11 shows, however, these overall results were chiefly the product of three of the nine discussion units studied, in which the most active person talked a great deal *without* receiving much communication from others (low feedback ratio: R/I = Remarks received/Interaction initiated.) Despite this finding, Bales' results were widely interpreted as showing that "groups" typically produce <u>two leadership roles</u>: one the <u>"instrumental"</u> or task leader and one the more popular <u>"expressive"</u> or social-emotional leader.

Theodorson (1957), in studying natural discussion groups composed of couples discussing marital problems or social problems, noted that it takes time for status structure to stabilize and that the "instrumental" leadership and popularity tended to converge when the group became cohesive. Cohesiveness, in turn, differed according to importance of the activities engaged in. Following-up this analysis, Turk (1961, a and b) showed that instrumental status and popularity tend to be closely associated when the group activities and criteria for status centered around major group values —the extent of the association varying with cohesiveness of the group.

Again, we see that *leadership cannot be assessed adequately apart from other properties of the group, the degree of stability over time, and the activities (tasks) engaged in—not merely as tasks with certain properties but as tasks with varying relevance to the motivational concerns of members.*

Is Leadership Specific to Particular Tasks or General Across Tasks?

Following the disillusionment with personality tests as good measures for selecting potential leaders, vigorous research was undertaken to develop other means for singling out leaders and assessing leadership. The most flourishing of these involved a technique developed initially in the armed services of several countries (Germany, Australia, the United States) to detect potential officer candidates (Gibb, 1947). Briefly, the technique consisted of bringing together participants (who were usually unacquainted) to take part in situational tests in units of five, six, or seven. Figure 8.12 shows men engaged in such tests, here moving a delicate instrument across a brook and surmounting an obstacle.

The men were observed and rated as they performed the various tasks. The technique was referred to as "leaderless group" or "emergent leadership" situations. Typically, the sessions were brief, particularly as the work continued in laboratory-like situations. Findings revealed wide differences in the frequency of "leadership behavior" exhibited by different persons from one task to another. For a time, many researchers were concluding that leadership varies with specific tasks or activities, the leader changing as the participants moved from one task to the next.

Carter and his associates (1953) exerted a corrective influence on the extreme view that leadership was a myth and that leadership behavior was specific to particular tasks in which the person excelled. They found generality of leadership behavior for families of similar tasks, even in the transitory "emergent leader" situations. Bass (1960) reported that the individual's previous experience as a "leader" in such situations had some transfer value for his willingness to initiate and his success at initiating activity in subsequent sessions.

The upshot of the "leaderless" or "emergent leadership" studies was summarized admirably by Gibb (1954).

Fig. 8.12. Emergence of status and role in "leaderless group interaction." (U.S. Army.)

Leadership is an interactional phenomenon. . . . The emergence of group structure and the differentiation of function of group members depends upon the interaction of those members, and are general group phenomena. An individual's assumption of the leader role depends not only upon the role needs of the group and upon his individual attributes of personality, but also upon the members' perception of him as filling the group role requirements. These, in turn, vary as the situation and the task alter. In general, it may be said that leadership is a function of personality and of the social situation, and of these two in interaction (p. 917).

It is quite feasible *to design an experiment to demonstrate both specificity of leadership behavior and generality across situations* simply by studying interaction over time and varying the freedom of participants to choose the activity they engage in. Early in the interaction process, let us assign tasks to unacquainted participants arbitrarily: We will find different individuals exhibiting behavior defined as "leadership" in different tasks. Allow interaction to continue *over time* and introduce the opportunity for the members to decide upon the tasks and activities to be undertaken: The leader-follower relations will begin to stabilize, typically with one person exhibiting leadership behavior more frequently than others across situations and tasks.

The investigators of "leaderless" group situations were correct in noting that leadership is related to the activities engaged in during interaction. However, in real groups stabilizing over time, the task aspect is only one of four sets of factors affecting behavior in the group. There are several reasons why leadership becomes general over time:

1. Groups tend to *specialize* in given spheres of activities that are related to the common motives and values of members.

2. Group stabilization involves the selectivity of members, particularly those achieving higher status positions, in choice of specific tasks and activities. High-status members encourage activities and tasks in which they excel and discourage those in which they are disinterested or unskilled.

3. Many important leadership functions having to do with the maintenance, solidarity, and unity of the group do not immediately and obviously involve skill in specific tasks. However, the leader's effective efforts to maintain and enhance group unity increase his general "competence" as evaluated by other members.

Note on Research Methods

The foregoing research activities led to greatly elaborated techniques for observing, categorizing, and rating leadership behavior. Many of these were paper-and-pencil rating scales used by nonparticipant observers or members, devised to be suitable for correlational and factor analytic treatment (e.g., Cattell, 1961; Hemphill, 1961). Others were schemes for coding events during interaction. For example, Bales (1950) developed a system of categories for classifying the sequence of events during interaction as completely as possible.

Bales' interaction process analysis was developed through observing discussion situations about human-relations problems. Typically, trained observers behind a one-way mirror categorize each action as it occurs, using the following categories, which are recorded in sequence automatically on a recorder (see Fig. 8.13).

Shows solidarity (gives help, reward, etc.)
Shows tension release (jokes, laughs)
Agrees
Gives suggestion
Gives opinion (evaluation, analysis)
Gives orientation or information
Asks for orientation or information
Asks for opinion (evaluation, analysis)
Asks for suggestion
Disagrees
Shows tension
Shows antagonism

Weick's review of observation methods (1968) indicates continuing interest in observational techniques and category methods, as well as increased concern over the effects of observation on the interaction process and behavior of participants.

The more complete, refined, and elaborated the measurement schemes became, the more it became necessary to confine interaction to a specific *location*. Such containment necessarily limits the *activities* that can be engaged in. Further, it heightens the participant's awareness of continually being observed, a condition that does affect behavior (cf. Sherif and Sherif, 1964; Weick, 1968).

Current trends in the study of leader-follower relations in organizations are toward (1) preserving the naturalness of the situation as much as possible, especially through the use of unobtrusive or disguised assessment techniques; and (2) devising measurement units that capture significant properties of interaction over time, rather than fractionating it at the expense of patterns to which participants actually react over time. These trends are in keeping with the growing awareness of the research situation as a social situation (Chapter 6) in which the observer is himself being observed by his subjects and his techniques or tools are being sized up (Sherif and Sherif, 1965).

Leadership Techniques and Their Effectiveness

In their pioneering studies of groups of 11-year-old boys, Lewin, Lippitt, and White (1939, 1952) systematically varied the techniques used by adults who supervised the groups. Establishing clubs for handicraft activities, the experimenters exposed each club successively to different and prescribed styles of leadership. In one condition, the adult determined the policy, procedures, and activities for the group, being distant and none-too-friendly ("authoritarian" technique). In another, the adult encouraged participation by members and behaved in a friendly, helpful manner, giving technical assistance and suggesting procedures as needed ("democratic" technique). In the third, the adult allowed freedom for decisions and activity, keeping his own initiative and suggestions to a minimum ("laissez-faire" technique).

The experiment demonstrated clearly that the manner of adult supervision significantly affected the behavior of members, despite individual differences within the various groups and personality differences among the adults. The order in which a group experienced the three styles of supervision also made a difference. For example, one club reacted fairly passively under an authoritarian treatment; but after experiencing the democratic technique, its members were discontented with the return to the authoritarian treatment. One club initiated a rowdy atmosphere in their initial condition (laissez-faire) and maintained it throughout most of the study. Individuals within the clubs reacted to the treatments somewhat differently. For example, the son of a military officer preferred the "authoritarian" adult.

Unfortunately, for the cumulative development of research knowledge about group process, many researchers seized on the findings as proof that the "democratic" technique was not only more beneficial for participants, but more effective for such aims as increasing productivity. In the decades that followed studies accumulated in industrial, business, workshop, and school settings that were essentially replications of the Lewin, Lippitt, and White studies. The bulk of them were attempts to show that a more permissive, friendly, and helpful style produced more effective groups and/or higher productivity—as measured, for example, by task performance, scores on examinations, and the like. In reviewing such research, Anderson (1963) concluded as follows:

The evidence available fails to demonstrate that either authoritarian or democratic leadership is consistently associated with higher productivity. In most situations, however, democratic leadership is associated with higher morale. But even this conclusion must be regarded cautiously, because the authoritarian leader has been unreasonably harsh and austere in a number of investigations reporting superior morale in democratic groups. . . . *The authoritarian-democratic construct provides an inadequate conceptualization of leadership behavior* (p. 160, italics in original).

If we remove the words "democratic" and "authoritarian" from the discussion as unnecessarily value-laden, and consider the problem of the *manner* of leadership, it is not difficult to see why these conclusions were reached. Leadership is only part of group organization. It is affected by other role relations in the group, by values or norms shared by members, as well as by the nature of activities and tasks engaged in. The way a leader treats others—i.e., how directive or permissive he is—is only one aspect of his role relations.

Fig. 8.13. a. (*above*) Discussion situation as observed through one-way mirror by observers using Bales' categories. (Courtesy of R. F. Bales.) **b.** (*below*) The interaction recorder used by observers to categorize behavior and mark time. (Courtesy of R. F. Bales.)

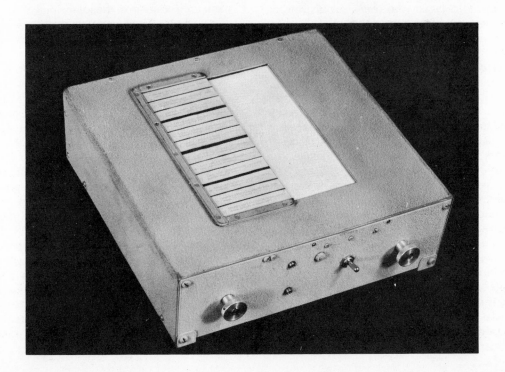

The Contingency of Leadership Style upon Other Factors in Group Situations

During fifteen years of research on 1600 groups, Fiedler (1968) sought to clarify the relationships between leadership style, group effectiveness in task performance (or productivity), and other group properties. Noting that the kind of leader who can promote successful performance by his group is still the "central question" in research on leadership, he observed: "The answer determines how millions of dollars and thousands of man hours each year are spent on management development and on leadership recruitment, selection and training" (Fiedler, 1968, p. 362).

Such realistic appraisal of the state of leadership research and its uses reflects the widespread conviction that group performance is principally a function of leadership, seen as a technical adjunct to task performance. The major implication of Fiedler's extensive research is that leadership is a function of leader-follower relations, the relative power of the leader to enforce sanctions, and the structure of the task—as well as the leader's style and technical proficiency. Therefore, it offers small comfort to those who focus exclusively on the leader's technique in human relations or his technical skills in task performance as the "central question" for leadership research.

The various groups studied by Fiedler and his associates differ widely—all of the way from high-school basketball teams to military units in different countries (the United States and Belgium), as well as to work teams in business management, research, or production. Most of them were natural groups. For the most part, the task performance used to assess "productivity" was closely related to the group's purpose. For example, productivity of ball teams was assessed by wins and losses, while tank crews performed tasks involving accuracy in target practice and speed in moving from one target to the next.

The basic measurement of the leader's style was a paper-and-pencil rating form based on Osgood's Semantic Differential (Chapter 16). The person was asked to consider his least preferred coworker and his most preferred coworker and to rate each, in turn, on a series of evaluative scales (e.g., pleasant-unpleasant). In some studies, Fiedler used the *differences* between these two sets of ratings ("assumed similarity of opposites") as the measure of the attitudes toward associates. In others, he used only the ratings of the *least* preferred coworker. Both measures assumed that the person who describes his *least* preferred coworker in highly unfavorable fashion is less concerned with maintaining the positive flavor of interpersonal relations than one who differentiates less between his most and least preferred coworker.

The main results from Fiedler's research consist of correlation coefficients between a measure of group performance (productivity) and the leaders' scores on the above rating scales (assumed similarity of opposites or negativity in evaluating the least preferred coworker). Thus, the generalizations are based on data with groups and their leaders as units of analysis, not upon correlations between two attributes of individuals (e.g., not upon correlations between individual scores on the ratings and individual task performance).

Relative to such correlations, Fiedler considered three factors and dichotomized measures on them in the following ways:

(1) Leader-member relations as assessed through sociometric choices and categorized as "good" or "poor."

(2) Task structure, assessed in terms of four aspects proposed by Marvin Shaw (degree to which correctness of a decision can be demonstrated, clarity of task requirements to members, number of alternative paths for proceeding, and number of correct solutions possible). Tasks were categorized as "structured" or "unstructured."

(3) Leader-position power; that is, power to dispense sanctions (rewards or punishments) by virtue of authority in the larger organization or (in informal groups) the member consensus. Most of the groups were units in larger organizations whose leaders had, therefore, more or less clear bounds for authority. This factor was classified as "strong" or "weak."

Figure 8.14 plots the median correlations obtained in studies of 59 *sets* of groups (total of 800 separate groups). The ordinate

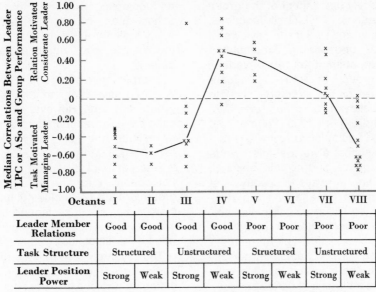

Octants	I	II	III	IV	V	VI	VII	VIII
Leader Member Relations	Good	Good	Good	Good	Poor	Poor	Poor	Poor
Task Structure	Structured		Unstructured		Structured		Unstructured	
Leader Position Power	Strong	Weak	Strong	Weak	Strong	Weak	Strong	Weak

Fig. 8.14. Correlations between leaders' LPC scores and group effectiveness (task performance) plotted for each combination of leader-member relations, task structure, and leader position power (*below*). Each x on graph indicates the median correlation for a set of groups, and the curve marks the median for that set. In order to interpet the figure, look at the baseline. The three factors used to order the groups were not linearly related; therefore, the order on the baseline is by "octants." An octant is one cell in an 8-cell model (2 × 2 × 2) of three-dimensional space. The octants are arranged as "good" to "bad" with respect to leader-member relations. Task structure for the particular cell is indicated below, followed by leader position power as a sub-division under task structure. (LPC stands for "least preferred co-worker.") (From F. Fiedler, Personality and situational determinants of leadership effectiveness, p. 371 (Figure 2), in D. Cartwright and A. Zander, eds., *Group Dynamics*. New York: Harper & Row, 1968. Reprinted by permission of the publisher.)

represents the correlation between the leader's score (least preferred coworker) and measures of group performance. A positive correlation indicates better group performance for leaders who rate their least preferred coworker higher. A negative correlation indicates better performance for leaders who rate their least preferred coworker *low.*

What the figure shows is that the more considerate, person-oriented leaders are associated with higher group performance (curve above zero) when "(a) the task is structured but the leader is disliked and must, presumably, be diplomatic and concerned with the feelings of his men and (b) the liked leader has an unstructured task and must, therefore, depend upon the . . . cooperation of his members" (Fiedler, 1968, pp. 371–372).

On the other hand, leaders who rate their

least preferred coworker low are associated with better performance when their relations with followers are good (left side of figure) and (1) the task is structured, regardless of the leader's position power, or (2) the task is unstructured but the leader's power is strong and, possibly (right side of figure), when member relations are poor, the leader's power is weak, but the task is unstructured. Points located near the zero line are, of course, indications of no significant relation between the measures of the leader and group performance. Those falling on the side of the zero line opposite to the curve are contrary to prediction.

The importance of Fiedler's research is in showing the interrelationships between leadership, other aspects of group structure, and activities engaged in by the group. They illustrate the difficulties in jumping to conclusions about behavior in groups on the basis of merely *one* aspect of the group or of the situations in which it functions. These difficulties are evident in reviews of great quantities of research accumulated over years that attempt to relate various properties of group structure (e.g., steepness vs. flatness of the structure; size) to attitude and behavior of group members (e.g., Porter and Lawler, 1965; Thomas and Fink, 1963). Such cumulative reviews reveal that there are almost always studies yielding positive, negative, and *no* relationships, and that there are few ways to specify what other factors might be affecting the relationships obtained. What seems called for, then, is greater recognition in actual research practice of the interdependent effects of personality variables, organizational variables, and task and location variables in shaping attitude and behavior.

GROUP SOLIDARITY
(COHESIVENESS)

The importance of groups and group interaction in shaping member attitude and behavior varies in degrees, depending upon how stabilized the members' role and status expectations are, and how binding the members regard the group's norms. The concepts used to refer to the relative grip of group properties upon its members and to the "cement" binding members together have included such terms as *solidarity, cohesiveness,* and *integration.*

As we have seen, the relative stability of the role structure and of members' reciprocal expectations affects the probability that a member can influence the actions of others effectively. Similarly, when group norms become stabilized, unity of members in adhering to the norms can override the attempts of a leader to change them, no matter how clever and ambitious he may be.

As with the group structure and its norms, the solidarity or cohesiveness of a group is related to the scope and the importance of its activities in the lives of the members, to the duration of the association, and to successes and failures in coping with the problems faced in concert or in achieving mutual goals (Sherif and Sherif, 1964). In short, the determinants of group solidarity are not unitary; they are manifold and complex. It follows that solidarity or cohesiveness of a group is not assessed adequately by any single indicator, such as the interpersonal attraction among members.

Interpersonal attraction among members is, as we have seen, an important aspect of group structure. However, for various reasons cited, attraction alone is not adequate to indicate role and status relations, much less the solidarity of the structure. Neither is interpersonal attraction the most essential condition for the emergence of other group properties, including its norms. Circumstances do arise that place individuals into the same boat, whether they like it or not. Life is full of such circumstances.

The research convenience of sociometric choice techniques led many researchers to define cohesiveness almost entirely in terms of interpersonal attraction or mutual liking, sometimes linked with ratings of "attractiveness of the group" as a whole (cf. Cartwright and Zander, 1960, pp. 95–162; Lott and Lott, 1965). At times, interpersonal attractiveness and "attractiveness of the group" are used as indicators of cohesiveness interchangeably, even though the two need not be significantly correlated (cf. Eisman, 1959).

The need for more adequate conceptualization and measurement of group solidarity (cohesiveness) was illustrated in Feldman's study (1968) of 61 cabin groups in summer camps lasting from two to more than six weeks. Feldman administered questionnaires differentiating among interpersonal attraction, consensus on norms, and consensus on role differentiation to a total of 538 campers. The correlations among these three indicators varied from .14 to .51. In other words, the three indicators of integration were assessing different aspects of group relationships. Furthermore, the extent of integration differed according to the camp environment.

As is the case with other aspects of organization examined in this chapter, solidarity (cohesiveness) can be studied effectively only when the relative stabilization of the group in time has been specified. Its analysis will necessarily include the structural and normative properties as well as the scope and importance of activities in the lives of members.

9

Social Norms:
Products and Regulators
of Interaction

Major Topics of the Chapter

Normative regulation and change in the
    actualities of life
Scope of normative regulation of man's vital
    activities
Individual as victim or as receiver of so-
    ciety: a relic in dichotomies
Freud and Durkheim reconsidered
Normative regulation of behavior and basic
    psychological principles
Conformity and deviation are defined by
    social norms
Crucial questions in analyzing conformity-
    deviation
Conformity-deviation and the properties of
    norms
Studying conforming and deviating behav-
    ior in groups

ORIENTATION
TO NORMATIVE REGULATION

In this chapter, we consider an important aspect of the orderliness of social life: its normative aspect. Every human group has a set of values investing certain objects with desirability as goals and eliminating others, requiring certain activities and banning others, promoting certain behaviors and denouncing others. Every human group has routines of living; customary ways of speaking and eating and loving; traditions and myths that its members cherish—not necessarily because they are the most adaptive or efficient but because they are "our" ways. The very language and its words are invested with the aura of value: "In the beginning was the Word . . . ."

DEF. In Chapter 7, a social norm was defined as a standard or, better, as a *scale* consisting of categories that define a range of acceptable attitude and behavior, and a range of objectionable attitude and behavior, for members of a social unit, in matters of consequence to that unit. Thus social norm is a concept that can be used generically in social psychology to refer to all those regularities in social life that embody *evaluation* of objects, persons, actions, and ideas. There are, of course, a host of terms in social science referring to specific examples of norms: tradition, custom, mores, taboo, folkways, fashion, fad, and moral values are among them. All of these terms imply that social life is regulated in more or less orderly fashion. There are rules defining what is done and what *should* be done: what is *expected, good, desired,* and even *ideal,* as well as what is *bad* or *forbidden.*

Social norms are an important part of the culture of a group or a society. An adequate theory of socialization or social learning has to deal with the child's acquisition of the norms upheld by "significant other" people. These "significant others" are typically members of groups to which he belongs or aspires to belong (reference groups). Children do not merely learn a collection of specific actions, each appropriate in a discrete social situation. They learn and form principles (rules) applicable to *classes* of social situations, of people, of activities and objects. If they did not, there would

scarcely be time in a human lifetime to develop the routines and modes of behavior that are exhibited by the great bulk of the membership in any human group, at least as long as its existence is not undergoing drastic change or disintegration. (In fact, social change and "disorganization" are typically assessed in terms of the distribution and relative frequency of conformity to customary routines and modes of behavior.)

Clearly, then, the topic of social norms touches upon major problems of social behavior and of social process. In this chapter, we shall consider the topic in relation to problems of *conformity* and *deviation,* which are crucial in understanding how a group or society controls behavior of its members. However, conforming and deviating behaviors are not the only normative phenomena of interest to social psychology.

Social psychology should be equally interested in the problems of norm formation and change. There is nothing absolute or final about social custom, tradition, and values. Their great variety in different cultures and in different small groups attests to the wide range of possible procedures for the orderly conduct of social interaction and activity. Social norms do change, albeit very slowly at times.

A classic example is the world of ladies' fashion, studied by the anthropologist Kroeber (1919). Fig. 9.1 presents his graph of the length of skirt, the waist and décolletage considered appropriate and, of course, beautiful, between 1844 and 1920. The lower curve, representing length of skirt, shows the increasing trend toward shorter skirts that, after 1920, produced skirts shorter than the greatest value recorded for the décolletage (upper curve). The curve for the décolletage appears to change comparatively less, but the fluctuations there are not insignificant in view of the relatively short distance between the human neck and waist.

Admittedly, the problem of changing norms, or cultural change in general, is not a problem for social psychology alone. Economic, political, and military forces far removed from the level of interacting individuals both in time and space often have to be considered before we can understand cultural change. Nevertheless, the change

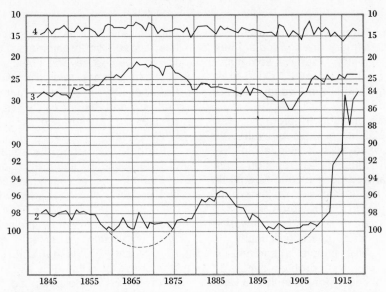

Fig. 9.1. Curve of fashion from 1844 to 1918, showing (2) length of skirt, (3) length of waist, and (4) decolletage. (From A. L. Kroeber, 1919. On the principle of order in civilization as exemplified by changes of fashion. Reproduced by permission of the American Anthropological Association from the *American Anthropologist*, **21**, 235–263). Kroeber observed that the rhythmic period for skirt length was about 35 years during the period, and that at its maximum, "fashion clearly tries, and is prevented only by physical impossibility, to drive the bottom of the dress several inches into the ground" (p. 252). He indicated this tendency by the dotted lines suggesting the "ideal curve which the data show that style would follow if it could" (p. 253).

ultimately is effective and is manifested in the interaction of individuals who respond to such sociocultural forces.

The production of social norms during social interaction is so universal and frequent that it can readily be observed in miniature, particularly in a complex and changing society. As a social-psychological problem, the formation of social norms is at least as important as the problem of conformity-deviation to existing standards. In fact, the sociological problem of "social control" (how a society regulates behavior in line with its tenets and laws) seems baffling until the problem of norm formation and functioning is considered. This chapter presents some basic generalizations from social psychology with implications for norm formation in actual social life.

THE NORMATIVE REGULATION OF BEHAVIOR

The biology of human birth and development is so immediately embedded in social process that the human personality is inevi-

tably a biosocial product. This embeddedness in social life from birth obscures the social regulation of behavior which seems, on the surface, "natural," elementary, and basic. Just as air is the last thing we think about until it is lacking, many regularities of social life are taken for granted. Consequently, their crucial importance for individual behavior is neglected. Let us consider a few commonplace examples.

Observe children in a nursery school around midmorning, considerably after breakfast but well before luncheon. Typically, they become restless and even irritable. Aware of the shorter attention span and hunger cycle of little children, wise educators long ago introduced the custom of a "break" for a glass of juice, milk, or a cracker. Each child is eager to get the refreshment as quickly as possible. At first they rush and crowd about, the quickest or nearest claiming first place in line. But day after day of being last is not pleasant, and so, in addition to the line, the order of the children is alternated from day to day. The children learn to *take turns,* a principle also applicable to games and play equipment

("It's my turn on the swing!"). *Taking turns* is a simple, elementary rule for social inter-action—so elementary that we sometimes forget that it must be learned. Taking turns implies the regulation of individual behavior by a social norm.

Watch a conversation in progress. Bar-ring a wildly exciting or unusual event, you will see that when each individual finishes speaking, he waits for a reaction from others. Ordinarily, no one else talks until he has finished. He is accused of "interrupt-ing" if he does. In other words, speaking while another person speaks is a *deviation* from propriety and, characteristically, is called "rude." Five people attempting to perform a task or solve a problem simply do not talk simultaneously for more than a brief period. Each waits and listens to the other. Human communication, too, involves *taking turns.*

Of course, all regulation of human behav-ior is not so simple as taking turns. Man has long been fascinated by the variety of pre-scriptions about sexual activities, rules de-fining what they should involve and what they should not involve. Sex, like any other biological activity that involves man's rela-tion to man, is regulated in every known human culture through its organization of kinship and its social norms. No human society permits sexual license in the sense of spontaneous sexual activity with any per-son at any place or time that, logically, permits its occurrence. Even the occasional "sex cult" that glorifies the promiscuous choice of sexual partners has certain norms regulating the choice. The recently notori-ous Hell's Angels—mobile gangs of motor-cyclists forming in California—are noted for rapacious activities, but abide strictly by the norm proscribing sexual activities with wives of members (Thompson, 1967).

[greedy] [margin annotation next to "rapacious"]

As in the normative regulation of eating, drinking, sleeping and other essential ac-tivities, the norms governing sexual activi-ties vary enormously from one group or society to another. The "universal taboo" on incest means quite different things in different societies, depending on the par-ticular definition of kinship and the range of persons defined as family members. In actual practice, therefore, the incest taboo is not universal in its definition of who is eligible and who is prohibited sexually. It has ranged from prohibition of marriage be-tween cousins several times removed and between persons related only by marriage (in-laws) to positive requirements that brothers and sisters marry (as in the royal families of ancient Egypt and Peru; cf. White, 1948).

Further, in treating the social regulation of heterosexual relationships only in terms of "taboo," we inevitably neglect an impor-tant property of social norms: Explicitly or implicitly, a taboo always implies its social obverse, directing the individual *toward* what is socially acceptable or desirable. This property is illustrated in the following tabular list for rating girls as sexual objects, which W. F. Whyte compiled from the re-actions of the Corner Boys studied in *Street Corner Society* (1943):

Sex Experience	Physical Attractiveness	Social- and Ethnic-Group Position
1. "Good girls"	Beautiful	1. Superior groups
2. "Lays" (a) One-man girls	to	2. Italian nonslum
(b) Promiscuous		
(c) Prostitutes	ugly	3. Italian slum

The girls at the top of these scales were also the most inaccessible to the boys. Every Corner Boy knew that if he even called on a "good girl," her family would assume he intended to marry her. He could only dream about a blonde representative of respectability and wealth, because he had few means to meet or court her. A "good girl" was the type he wanted to marry even-tually, and he could be respectful to her to the point of severe personal frustration. Whyte relates an incident in which a "good girl" became intoxicated and encouraged some boys. Even though she was inviting in that condition, they took her home and thus preserved her "good girl" standing. One of the same boys, however, felt no compunc-tion at all about cheating a prostitute out of her fee. The prohibition of intimacy with a relative of a fellow clique member was also noted in summarizing the Corner Boy study (p. 188).

In more recent studies of informal groups of adolescent boys, such rating schemes governing the way a particular girl is sized up as a potential sex object were frequently observed (Sherif and Sherif, 1964). For example, among a group of teen-age dropouts in a college community, the girls were rated as to sexual attractiveness and probable availability merely on the basis of their appearance and manner, with the unattainable "college girls" receiving the highest rating on the attractiveness dimension and the lowest on availability.

The large variations in what is regarded as proper and right have, at times, been used as evidence for the view that the social regulation of behavior is altogether arbitrary. For example, the social theorist, Sumner (1906) declared that culture can "make anything right." It is but a step further to declare, as have many modern writers, that morality is arbitrary, because it is relative to the standards of a particular group or society. Here it is important to note that social values or standards do survive beyond the problem situations for which they were originally modes of adjustment. Then, they may seem arbitrary and even oppressive. In addition, it should be noted that history is filled with cases in which groups identified their own interests with standards for morality to the point of enforcing human misery and suffering in the name of righteousness. None of these cases, however, supports the view that the social regulation of behavior at a given time is entirely arbitrary. Such a view overlooks the fact that people face problems, collectively, that are very real to them and that require some orderly procedures and regulation of individual action toward coping with the problems.

The emphasis on arbitrariness of norms is closely allied with the general view that *social* prescriptions are, necessarily, inimical to man's nature. There is a strong intellectual tradition that conceives of individual welfare and collective interests as polar opposites. Freud reinforced this tradition when he erected a comprehensive theory of psychological development on the funda-

mental notion that society functions primarily to limit man's biological tendencies. In his clinical population, Freud noted, no doubt accurately, that the prevailing norms governing sexual relationships had deleterious consequences for human personality. However, his theories about society were based on a selected sample of the middle-class Viennese family of the late nineteenth century, which he elevated to the archetype of society in general (Sears, 1960; Berkowitz, 1962). As a result, he saw society something like a strait-jacket for the developing organism. In fact, Freud (1922, p. 10) characterized conscience (the "superego" in his scheme) as "dread of society"—ignoring the positive values incorporated as an "inner voice" for most normal individuals.

Many newer versions of psychoanalytic thought, incorporating data on cultural variations, do not remedy the basic flaw in Freud's thinking: that is, the conception that individual and society are fundamentally opposites. Like "nature and nurture" and "heredity and environment," the individual-group polarity stifles analysis of the relationship among factors subsumed under each concept. At a given time in history, society may indeed be opposed to individual interests. Individual interests may be inimical to those of organized social life. Given these facts, the problem for scientific analysis is how each state of affairs arose, not the assumption that either is a universal fact.

Conversely, conceptions of a sharp separation between the nature of the individual and the nature of group process can produce a glorification of the group process. Many social theorists have come dangerously close to such a view. The French sociologist, Emile Durkheim, wrote of cultural variations in social control early in the twentieth century when, so far as the prevailing academic psychology was concerned, such variations were of slight interest. Proceeding on the assumption that the academic psychologists were studying psychological universals, he addressed himself to the problem of why behavior differs so greatly from one society to the next. He concluded that new forms of behavior are derived from society and not from individual activities. Thus, he placed the source of morality and creativity on the credit side for society.

The sociologist George Simpson (1963) aptly commented that Durkheim's accounts of morality and social conduct were greatly limited: "He could not foresee that one day we might be able to establish an individual psychology that would be inherently social" (p. 3). As a result, Durkheim called for a "collective psychology" as entirely distinct and different from "individual psychology." From such premises, he maintained that "religious beliefs spring . . . from society, which determines man's nature" (p. 6).

Since Durkheim's day, the mainstream of developments in psychology of perception, judgment, and thinking has been in the direction of developing an "individual psychology that would be inherently social." The problems of the rise of social relations and normative evaluation have not been seen as entirely divorced from psychology. However, the fact that the basic psychology of the individual includes the propensity toward norm formation does not mean at all that social phenomena can be *reduced* to psychological functioning. Reductionism of this kind uncritically argues that the prevailing organizational and normative system of a society simply represent some sort of sum total of the behaviors of individuals composing them.

In this chapter and throughout the book, the reader should recall the discussion of the individual-group relationship in Chapter 5. The view that the individual *or* the group is a separate entity with inevitably greater importance in the etiology of behavior is not warranted by psychological research on the most basic processes. Especially if one is concerned about the goodness or badness of moral standards prevailing in one's milieu, it is important to analyze the interrelationship of personal and social life.

**Normative Regulation
of Behavior Is Embedded
in the Basic Psychology
of Human Behavior**

At a particular time and place, the prevailing norms may be productive of social and psychological harmony, or productive of conflicts between groups. At times, op-

position to existing norms is coupled with the denunciation of all normative regulation of behavior as artificial and against "man's nature."

Such romantic protests against any normative regulation are frequently contradicted by the course of events in the movements that arise: Over time, even the most ardent nonconformists develop their own standards, rules, and guidelines. For example, anarchists opposed to marriage in New York's bohemian circles thereby established informal liaisons as socially acceptable, while consigning marriage to the latitude of objectionable behavior. To remain "good" bohemians, the couple that married kept the fact a secret from their bohemian friends (cf. Ware, 1935).

Psychologically, there are reasons why some kind of normative regulation of social interaction is inevitable. First, because many human needs are not served in isolation, the social regulation of behavior becomes a necessary vehicle for solving problems and obtaining need satisfaction. Suppose, for example, that it were necessary to secure cooperation and consensus on the time to eat every time you became hungry. A schedule of three meals a day need not be the best or the most efficient manner of handling this problem; however, it is one means of handling the periodic hunger cycle and it does come to regulate its periodicity.

Second, there is a tendency toward psychological patterning (Proposition 6) that becomes even more prominent as man's conceptual capacities extend his psychological concerns beyond the immediate past and present (Proposition 12). Becoming adept at categorizing concrete life experiences in terms of location, timing, and the recurrence of events, man's tendency toward psychological patterning expands over time and place. For man, the certainties and uncertainties of life are not confined to physical events. The regularities, rules, and guideposts of his social world provide conceptual anchors the disruption of which may be quite as disturbing psychologically as some sudden threat of nature in disrupting the physical environment.

The psychological basis for normative regulation will be discussed further when we consider experiments on norm formation. Here the point will be illustrated by two examples of the rise of norms. The first concerns the use of physical space. The second illustrates normative schedules for events over time.

The Normative Treatment of Physical Space

In Chapter 7, the general situation of prisoners in Ruhleben, a German camp for detaining civilians during World War I, was summarized. For the individual prisoner, the Ruhleben experience was at first chaotic and painful psychologically.

The habitual sequence of their lives and activities was sharply interrupted, with the ill-organized and uncomfortable prison being swiftly substituted. Both the future and the sequence of immediate events were ill-defined and unpredictable for the prisoners.

As a result, the early days at Ruhleben were psychologically painful for the inhabitants. Many of the men seemed disoriented, confused, and stunned. However, the picture at Ruhleben changed dramatically after only a few weeks. Within the bounds established by the German officials, the prisoners began to organize their daily living, and during this process, the early symptoms of psychological disorder were dissipated. Here is a description of the changes effected by the prisoners in ordering their environment within a five-months' period after their first entrance to the camp:

Already, after five months of internment, the camp is vastly changed, the visitor will still see thousands of men in a small enclosure, but the Ruhlebenite sees a settled community, divided into many neighbourhoods, each crowded with family dwellings. A camp address now has social significance, for every citizen is defined to some extent in terms of where he lives. His barrack has its distinctive reputation, his box is unlike any other, and within that he has a place that is peculiarly his own. Differentiation has thus produced four thousand unique individuals, each rooted in his particular social niche. And the prisoner now plays a variety of roles that add new interest to his life; he is one person to his box-mates, a slightly different one to his barrack, and again to the camp at large. He has "found himself" in his new world; he knows, and others know too, who he is and where he belongs.

Spatially, too, he is well oriented, for every salient feature of the compound now bears its familiar name. The canteen alley is "Bond Street," the gateway to the grandstands the "Marble Arch," the area inside the main entrance "Trafalgar Square." Fittingly enough, the latrines have German labels; the western one is "Spandau," the eastern "Charlottenburg." The names, like so many other products of the first winter, were collectively created—hit upon by some individual, picked up and repeated by others, and finally fixed as customs.

Men do not bestow nicknames on objects to which they are indifferent, and these labels are enough to show that the winter has done its work, and the prisoners have made themselves at home in Ruhleben (Ketchum, 1965, 148–149).

The Normative Treatment of Time

Among the early sociologists who analyzed social life both in cross-section and longitudinally, Van Gennep (1908) made important observations about the organization of social life across time in his classic book *Les Rites de Passage*. In addition to regulating interaction among various groupings in society according to their rights, privileges, and obligations, he found that societies have schedules over time for the acquisition and change of an individual's relationship to others, of his proper activities, attitudes, and goals.

In other words, the society delineates reference points or anchors for the temporal transition from one social status to the next. In the simpler and less modernized societies, such reference points are sometimes in the form of ceremonies or rites that mark the change. For example, many societies had rites marking the child's transition before puberty, sometimes requiring him to leave his mother's kin group to live with other members of the community. Rites to mark the social advent of adolescence (which might differ from the physical onset of puberty by months or years) served to alert both child and community of a change to adulthood.

An interesting opportunity arose for a sociologist, Julius Roth (1963), to study such "timetables" when his career was interrupted by confinement for tuberculosis. Subsequently, he studied two hospitals in which he was a patient and observed several others after he recovered. Even with modern treatments, the cure of tuberculosis takes time, the length varying with the seriousness of the disease when diagnosed, the success of various treatments, etc.

The period of time that different patients may have to spend in the hospital for treatment differs greatly. Any particular patient is subject to considerable uncertainty about the length of his stay and the sequence of treatment steps, because of the difficulty in accurate prediction of the treatment process. Physicians, therefore, try to avoid committing themselves about the length of time a particular treatment or the entire stay will take (p. 60). Patients, on the other hand, exert considerable pressure on the doctors to make tentative predictions. Through their observations and discussions with each other about the timing of treatment events, they produce a *timetable* that they come to regard as the progress that "ought" to be made and the sequence that "should" occur.

Therapy conferences, changes in activity classifications, the granting of privileges, the removal of restrictions, diagnostic procedures, surgery, changes in treatment may all serve as bench marks in a timetable that lets a patient know how far he is on the road to discharge. Such norms serve as a yardstick of progress—each patient may compare his progress with that of the norms to see whether he is ahead of or behind schedule (p. 60).

Not only do the patients seek such anchoring points in time, but they also develop reference groups among other patients who appear to have cases similar to their own. The physician also categorizes patients:

. . . in order to achieve a regularity in their treatment decisions from case to case. Conflict over the timetable often arises between physicians and patients because they use different sets of categories—those of the physicians being more highly differentiated than those of the patients. Thus, the patient may expect to be treated like one group of patients while the physician considers it more appropriate to treat him like a different group (p. 61).

Roth found that, in actual practice, the timetable followed in treatment and release was a product of norms between the physicians and the patients. Actual practice did not correspond to either side's timetable

exactly. The patients pressed to move along as quickly as they could, short of unreasonable demands; the physician attempted to resist the patient pressures, although he could not ignore them.

Thus, the norms developed by patients and doctors were not identical—although on each side there were recognizable endpoints (beginning and end of treatment) and smaller segments or ranges of time between, broken by reference points provided by the change from one treatment to another.

CONFORMITY AND DEVIATION ARE DEFINED BY SOCIAL NORMS

In recent years, the terms conformity and deviation have acquired connotations that hinder scientific analysis of conforming and nonconforming behavior. Frequently, with social criticism as their intent, social scientists and essayists have pictured the individual as a submissive and subservient conformist, on the one hand, or, on the other, as a naturally independent creature who is continually thwarted by a repressive society.

Taking a stand that conformity is either an inherent tendency or always desirable amounts to praising blind subservience in man. On the other hand, singing praises to nonconformity for its own sake can lead to an absurd dilemma. Let us cite a few cases of nonconforming behavior—for example, driving down the middle of the road, monopolizing a conversation, deliberate plagiarism or stealing. Of course, anyone who sees virtue in nonconformity for its own sake would protest these examples as crass. Praise of nonconformity is made of nonconformity that is righteous, in the sense of dramatizing some higher principle (e.g., freedom, the rights of man, or human dignity). But such higher principles are also the product of man's interaction and struggles, frequently over centuries. In short, neither nonconformity or conformity can be evaluated apart from its referent, namely, the normative basis of the behavior in question (Sherif, 1967).

An item of behavior, considered by itself, cannot be labeled either conformity or deviation. There is no such thing as conforming or deviating behavior in the abstract. In order to understand what the terms "conformity" and "deviation" mean, the following questions must be raised at the outset: Conformity to *what*? Deviation from *what*? The very terms imply a referent. Always, conformity is conformity *to* something. Deviation is departure *from* something. What is that something?

On the whole, psychologists have neglected this crucial question, particularly in developing experimental models to study the problem. For example, a frequently used model in "conformity" research simply places the individual in a situation in which others give erroneous judgments about a stimulus. If the subject makes errors in the direction of the erroneous judgments, he is said to have "conformed." To what?—to the judgments of other persons that are often clearly and obviously contrary to his own perception of the stimulus. The encounter with such errors is an unusual if not bizarre event in the ordinary run of social life. This experimental model does not contain the essentials for studying conformity and deviation in social life. In keeping with the discussion in Chapter 6, we shall refer to such shifts in behavior toward an immediate and transitory social influence as *compliance.*

The referents of conforming and deviating behavior, on the other hand, are not properly represented by immediate, brief, and sheerly arbitrary social pressure from others. What is the "something" that defines whether behavior can be termed conforming or deviating? The referent may be the prevailing, the usual, the expected or desirable ways of doing things in the individual's group or society. This is the *normative* basis of the problem. The referent may be the individual's particular role and status in the scheme of his interpersonal and group relationships. This is the *organizational* basis of the problem.

The answer to our question, therefore, is that conforming behavior or deviating behavior means that the behavior in question falls within the latitude of acceptance or within the latitude of rejection defined by a norm (or set of norms) prevailing in a social unit of which the individual is defined as a member with some role and status in the organizational scheme. This answer imme-diately leads to other questions that are crucial in analyzing the problem of conformity-deviation.

1. What other factors constitute the social situation in which conforming or deviating behavior occurs? Do other persons exert coercion, force, or their threat to keep the individual's behavior within acceptable bounds (as acceptability is defined in the group)? Or, does the behavior in question occur without *sanctions* and when others who might invoke them are not present? If sanctions or their threat are invoked, we are clearly dealing with "social pressure" upon the individual. If, however, his behavior falls within acceptable bounds without such pressure, we can infer that the norm has been "internalized." The "social" has *become "personal"* for him. The etiology of behavior in the two instances is different. This question and the way it is answered are crucial for the sociological question of *social control.*

2. What are the alternative modes of behavior available to the individual in the stimulus situation with respect to the possible ways that situation can be sized up and the possible decisions the individual can make? Are there many, few, or no alternatives? Are the alternatives clearly defined or difficult to distinguish? If the structure of the situation permits no alternatives for perception and judgment, the question of normative regulation is either fairly simple or irrelevant. For example, it is not at all difficult to understand why most normal individuals descend stairs in an upright position. It is only when the question of environmental alternatives is considered that normative issues become significant. Sliding down the bannister is an alternative which, in some situations, would be considered shocking. (Consider the entrance of royalty or the President's lady at a formal ball.)

3. What is the relative importance of the behavior area in which conformity or deviation occur? By neglecting this question, some investigators have ignored significant relationships among the various sets of factors in the social situation. Such relationships are important in affecting the behavior of others in the situation (e.g., whether they will ignore deviation or react with indignation and pressure). Psychologically, these

relationships involve motivational properties that affect adherence to social norms in real life. It is one thing to conform or deviate in matters considered relatively minor in one's group or society. Normative regulation of behavior within rigid limits, and particularly the use of severe sanctions for deviation, are not typical in all spheres of activity. Rigid bounds for conformity are character-istic, however, in matters that a group re-gards as basic to its major goals, its exist-ence, and maintenance—such as loyalty and relations with outsiders. Conversely, the norm system of a group does not cover every single item of social behavior. It is focused on areas and issues of conse-quence in the important activities of the group, the relationships among members, and relations with other groups. Therefore, analysis of conformity and deviation has to include specification of the *relative* priority of the norm in question. It is one thing to deviate from the norm to brush one's teeth after every meal and quite another to devi-ate from the norms regulating how a parent should treat and care for his family.

4. Finally, what is the individual's rela-tionship to the groups in question? Is he defined as a member? Does he consider himself a member or desire to be one (i.e., is it a reference group?)? Is the normative referent of the behavior shared and upheld by other groups to which he is related in some capacity? Or do his various groups place contradictory or conflicting demands on his behavior in various roles and situa-tions? These questions relate to the prob-lem of the integration or conflict among the normative systems of various groups to which the individual belongs, hence to the integration or conflict of values in his psy-chological world. They also bear on many issues of the individual's relationship to the society of which he is a member. For ex-ample, the commission of an act defined by the legal code as "delinquent" is certainly deviant behavior in terms of society's norms. However, the act may not be deviant in terms of the adolescent's membership in a group of peers the norms of which do not proscribe the behavior in question—and may even encourage it as an act showing bravery and manliness. Similarly, an indi-vidual "alienated" from the larger society

and its major tenets (hence, "deviant" in its terms) may conform closely to norms of smaller groups within society. We shall deal with such issues of reference groups and multiple personal loyalties in Chapter 18. For the time being, it should be noted that the normative referent of behavior has to be specified—whether it is to be condoned or censored.

When studied in the context of these questions, conforming or nonconforming behavior become amenable to scientific analysis. Such analysis provides a sound basis for evaluating the appropriateness or inappropriateness of conformity and devia-tion under given conditions of social life, with future goals serving as a standard for assessment.

Conformity-Deviation and the Properties of Norms

As noted in the definition of norm, a norm DE is not always a prescription for a single act; it is, more typically, a set of categories de-fining classes of acceptable and objection-able behavior. It follows that in assessing norms, the norm cannot be represented as a point or as a single value. This deduction is particularly important in determining whether an action is conforming or repre-sents a case of deviation.

Groups everywhere recognize individual differences within an acceptable range. It follows that a social norm is best repre-sented as a class of behaviors that are acceptable or permissible, and a class of behaviors that are objectionable or punish-able. Social norms define a *latitude of ac-ceptance* and a *latitude of rejection*.

What kinds of data are needed to charac-terize a norm, hence to provide the baseline for assessing conformity or deviation by single members? Research has included the following observations:

1. Observed similarities and regularities (over time) in attitudes and behavior among one set of persons that are not evident in another set and that vary within more or less definite limits.

2. Increasing similarity or convergence toward a range and mode of behavior during interaction over time. For example,

the entrance of a new member into a group or confrontation by a new problem situation provides an opportunity to detect the existence of a norm.

3. Correctives (sanctions) for certain behaviors and praise or rewards for other behaviors. Reactions to deviation and to idealized behavior are among the best indicators of the existence of a norm and its limits. Sanctions may range from disapproval, frowns, a silent treatment, to threats and actual punishment.

Note that these data do *not* include the "average" behavior of group members. Under some circumstances, it may be useful to compute an average value for attitude and behavior in a group; but alone, the average is not an adequate measure of a social norm. The following are among the reasons:

1. The latitude of acceptance ordinarily includes the range that is permissible, and also the modes of behavior that are expected and ideal. While the behavior of members may seldom attain that lofty standard, its definition does have observable effects on them—for example, in expressions of guilt and shame, or in discussions and directives toward improving the level of conduct.

2. Both for the definition of a norm and for assessing the behavior of a particular individual, the modal responses and distribution around the mode (in terms of the relative *frequencies* of individual variations) are more meaningful than an arithmetic mean (which weights each individual equally) or a median, which merely divides the membership at the fiftieth percentile. They are more meaningful because they better represent what has actually transpired in the interaction process.

3. The popular impression of normative regulation as a "leveling" effect toward mediocrity is tacitly reinforced by use of an average to represent a norm. At times the effect of a norm may be toward eliminating the extreme individual differences and promoting more frequent behavior within a moderate range. However, this outcome is merely one of many possible cases of normative regulation. Under other circumstances, normative regulation may *raise* the general level and *promote* forms of behavior at either extreme.

Conformity and Deviation Illustrated

Clearly, the problem of whether a social norm regulates behavior toward a lower, higher, or mediocre level of behavior depends on many conditions in addition to psychological characteristics of the individuals involved. An example is illustrated in Fig. 9.2, which concerns the speed rates that are permissible on the Pennsylvania Turnpike. The norm in question illustrates the fact that many social norms represent attempts to regulate social life both for the welfare of society and the individual. Such norms need not be arbitrary in any usual sense of that word.

The illustration is a good example of the fact that norms need not concentrate merely on lowering the level of behavior. On the contrary, in this case, the norm also specifies that a rate of speed *under* 40 miles per hour is as deviant as a rate of *over* 65 miles per hour. In fact, as Fig. 9.2b shows, there are actually *more* signs warning motorists that the minimum speed is 40 mph than those that list the maximum speed. When one considers that 40 mph was considered a high speed only a few decades ago, it can be seen that many norms reflect the concrete conditions in which social activities are conducted. (In this case, the existence of a good highway combined with fast automobiles is reflected in the insistent repetition of the minimum speed.)

What happens on the road and what sanctions are applied for deviation are regulated by both the lower and upper limits for speed. The *average* speed of motorists (which is probably near the upper limit) would be an inadequate indicator of conformity and deviation in driving on this road.

Studying Conforming and Deviant Behavior

In the conduct of research on conforming behavior, the required data may be obtained through various forms of observation—for example, the *observed* frequency of various behaviors over time for various members, by asking questions orally or on paper, or by analysis of behavior records

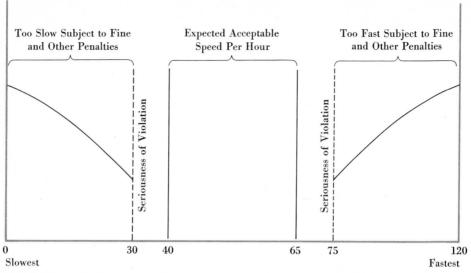

Too Slow Subject to Fine and Other Penalties   Expected Acceptable Speed Per Hour   Too Fast Subject to Fine and Other Penalties

Seriousness of Violation   Seriousness of Violation

0   30   40   65   75   120
Slowest   Fastest

Range of Driving Speed in Miles Per Hour Along the Pennsylvania Turnpike

Fig. 9.2. Acceptable and objectionable ranges of speed (miles per hour) on the Pennsylvania Turnpike. **a.** (*above*) Speed acceptable by law is from 40 (minimum) to 65 (maximum) miles per hour. Speeds either too slow (*left*) or too fast (*right*) are subject to increasingly severe penalties. Even if you find the scenery beautiful or are in a romantic mood with a friend, you cannot poke along below 40. **b.** (*below*) Diagram represents proportion of speed signs on Turnpike that give maximum and minimum speeds. The ratio of minimum to maximum speed signals or warnings along the Pennsylvania Turnpike is 3 to 2, the warnings on going too slowly being more frequent.

(e.g., work output) over time. The appropriateness of a method will depend on the setting in which behavior occurs and the particular problem under study. Here we may note the inherent difficulty of techniques for investigating normative regulation of behavior that alert the members that their behavior is under study. The problem is related to the discussion in Chapter 6 on the "demand character" of research.

There are, of course, many instances of conforming and deviating behavior that occur in full public view. They can be observed without alerting individuals that they are the object of study. An example is the behavior of pedestrians at stop lights. Numerous others are suggested in a book on *Unobtrusive Measures: Nonreactive Research in the Social Sciences* (Webb *et al.*, 1966).

The fact remains that much conforming and deviating behavior occurs in the context of interpersonal or group situations that are private in the eyes of participants and protected from intrusion. If this privacy is violated the behavior of members is influenced by the presence of an "outsider," particularly if they know that he wants to study them. Groups, after all, do not form and function for the benefit of researchers. They form and function among individuals with definite motivations, goals, and interpersonal ties. Frequently, the exposure of what goes on in such settings is significant both to members personally and for the maintenance of a group.

In view of these facts, researchers are becoming more concerned with methods of collecting data on conformity and deviation. Clark and Tifft (1966) used questionnaires to study consistency of self reports by male college students about behaviors considered "delinquent" by society for unmarried teen-agers. After each student completed the questionnaire, he was requested to participate in a second phase of the study. Within two weeks, he was interviewed with the stated interest of checking the accuracy of his reports. On the basis of a number assigned to him, he selected his own questionnaire from the others and was given the opportunity to change any responses that he might wish. Finally, each subject had a polygraph examination (recording of physiological indicators of emotional arousal,

popularly called a "lie detector"). The data were then analyzed in terms of changes made in responses at the interview and at the polygraph examination.

All respondents made corrections on their first questionnaires—about 58 percent of the changes occurring at the interview and 42 percent at the subsequent polygraph examination. Three-fourths of the changes were in the direction of increased frequency of deviant behavior, but a quarter represented changes in the opposite direction (decreasing the frequency of reported deviancy). Interestingly enough, in 23 of the 26 times when the students initially admitted acts and later denied them, the students said that "the group of boys you have generally done things with" would have regarded the actions as acceptable (e.g., starting a fist fight or having sexual relations). These cases represent verbal conformity to the norm of a small reference group, even though the act itself had not been performed. Conversely, all of the respondents who failed to admit an act initially, but later admitted it, regarded the act as "never permissible" in terms of their own feelings or those of "the guys." We are reluctant to disclose deviatons that are "out of bounds," as defined by reference group norms.

In a series of experimental and field studies on attitudes and behavior in small groups, Sherif and his associates (Sherif and Sherif, 1953, 1964, 1965; Sherif *et al.*, 1961) developed methods for an observer to study behavior in groups without actually participating in the group or alerting the members that their behavior was being studied. The procedures, which are presented in detail elsewhere (1964), require that the observer gradually establish a relationship with group members through *their* initiative rather than his own. The relationship is that of a friendly but harmless outsider. Through these methods, it was possible to collect observations, ratings, and other data on behavior occurring in natural conditions. Nevertheless, in studies of adolescent peer groups, the investigators (1965) reported that all groups had "secrets" which members protected until the observer had been tested repeatedly to determine his trustworthiness. These "secrets" concerned both socially acceptable and socially unacceptable behaviors, but

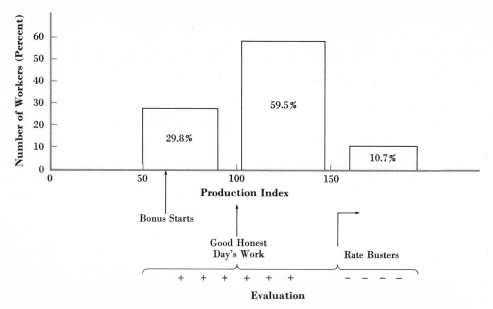

Fig. 9.3. Norm regulating work rate among 84 workers in machine shop. (Drawn from data reported by M. Dalton in W. F. Whyte, 1944, pp. 40–41.) All but 10.7 percent of the men in the shop regulated their work rate within the acceptable latitude ("good honest day's work") with a production index from 50 to 150. Only a few of these failed to get a bonus (*arrow*). Production above 150 was defined as rate busting, to be discouraged if at all possible and, if not, to subject the rate buster to harassment or isolation.

groups whose members frequently engaged in socially unacceptable behaviors were most secretive of all.

The sociologists Blau and Scott (1962) are among the investigators reporting similar difficulties in studying behavior in large formal organizations. In some detail they outlined the consequences when an observer enters an organization for purposes of data collection: suspicions about his intent, the efforts to present "proper behavior" to the observer, rumors that the observer is a "spy" from management, and the danger that the observer will become aligned or involved in the interests of one or another unit of the organization to the detriment of his rapport with others (pp. 21–25).

Such research problems are too frequently viewed merely as practical obstacles in data collection. However, they tell us something important about groups and normative regulation in them: Group interaction in real life centers around problems and concerns with motivational significance for members. As regulators of behavior in dealing with these significant problems, the norm system of the group is highly consequential to members.

Normative Regulation of Work

Among the most impressive research into the properties of norms and conformity-deviation are the many studies of "rate setting" by industrial workers, largely inspired by Roethlisberger and Dickson's report on the Hawthorne plant of the Western Electric Company (1939, 1961). The Hawthorne study started as an evaluation of the effects upon productivity of changes in illumination, rest periods, length of the working day, and other work conditions. Early in the research, the investigators discovered that, regardless of changes in such conditions, the productivity of their research groups improved steadily throughout the course of study.

Subsequently, more systematic research was conducted, including the experimental study of six women workers engaged in relay assembly and an observational study of 14 male workers wiring banks for telephone equipment. The findings of interest for the present discussion were as follows:

1. Despite systematic variations in work conditions (work periods, length of day,

wage incentives), the girls' production steadily rose throughout the study. The rising production rate reflected the friendly relations fostered among the girls, the attention paid to them, and the opportunity for friendly social intercourse afforded by their separation in the room.

2. The production output of the bank wiring men was not so high as it could have been in terms of their energies and abilities. There were informal groupings of the workers revealed in their interaction on and off the job that did not correspond to the formal organization of the work. All of the clusters in this study, however, shared a set of norms about work whose effect was to regulate output within fairly well-defined limits.

The observations of the Bank Wiring Room revealed that the men had a conception of "a fair day's work" to which they adhered, but which fell below the level management wanted. They shared the definition of a person as a *chiseler* if he worked too slowly, but as a *rate-buster* if he worked too fast. Acceptable production was be-

tween these levels. When minor violations of these limits occurred, the guilty party was ridiculed or "binged" (struck on the upper arm as symbolic of the violation). The more serious violations, such as "squealing" to the foreman, resulted in the worker being isolated by his fellows.

Figure 9.3 represents the norm for production in a machine shop, as studied by Dalton (1955) over a two-year period among 84 workers who had worked at the job seven years or longer. The wage system was such that bonus payments started at a production level of 66. Production of 100 was regarded as a "good honest day's work," while production exceeding 150 was defined as "rate busting," a practice not condoned. The "rate busters" in Dalton's study were virtual isolates in the shop and were treated as deviates. The remaining workers performed within the latitude of acceptance, between 66 and 150 with a few exceptions who consistently failed to achieve a bonus.

Figure 9.4 presents data from another study on normative regulation of work out-

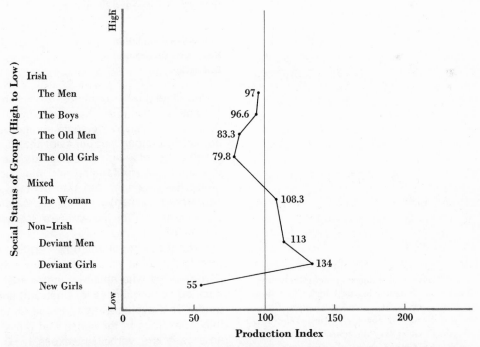

Fig. 9.4. Average production index (work output) by members of groups with varying status in an industrial department. (Based on data reported by Zaleznik, Christenson and Roethlisberger, 1958.) Note that all high-status groups maintain production below 100 (upper part of figure) while all groups with lower status in the department, except the new girls in training, regularly exceed the standard.

put in an industrial department observed by Zaleznik, Christensen, and Roethlisberger (1958). Although all in the same department, the workers were observed to cluster in several different groups, identified by regular association and interaction patterns. The highest status in this department was obtained by the groups composed of workers with Irish ancestry. Of these, a group of four men were highest in status and prestige, followed by a younger group called The Boys.

The non-Irish clustered in three groups whose members were not socially integrated nor fully accepted by other workers: the "deviant men," the deviant girls," and a small group of girls who were new and not experienced in the work. As the figure shows, the higher status groups produced, on the average, just under the standard (100 in this case). Not only did the groups with lower standing (excepting the new girls) average considerably higher but individual differences within each group were also greater, suggesting a lack of normative regulation.

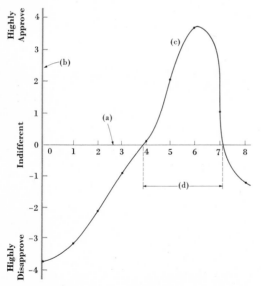

Fig. 9.5. Diagram of ranges of acceptable and objectionable behavior during an hour's discussion session. (From Jay Jackson, 1965, Structural Characteristics of Norms, in the Fifty-Ninth Yearbook of the National Society for the Study of Education, by permission.) Center line (a) represents frequency of speaking; vertical axis indicates evaluation (b). Curve (c) gives distribution of approval-disapproval by participants. Approved range (d) defines latitude of acceptance.

In order to understand such work norms (which may seem quite arbitrary) in terms of management directives and of the desire to earn a better income, it is necessary to consider the situation in which the work norms form. In the first place, management set a standard for production that would yield sufficient output in terms of the wages paid, offering incentive wages for excess production. On the other hand, the workers believed that if the production level went too high, the management would cut their pay rate, setting a new standard for the same amount of work. (Regardless of whether this would happen in a particular plant, such examples of rate-cutting in pay have occurred, particularly in the earlier days of the "time and motion studies" in industry.) Furthermore, if economic activity is low in the society or industry in question, the workers fear that continuing response to higher production rates would eventually result in some or many of them losing their jobs. The normative regulation of production, then, unites them in a common interest: the continuance of work and mutual support for the common benefit, rather than merely the temporary increase of income.

Normative Regulation Embodies Differential Evaluation

The foregoing examples of normative regulation illustrate that conformity and deviation are relative to some norm or set of norms. It is clear that behavior that is conforming by one set of standards can be deviant or nonconforming according to another. For example, the rate busters were conforming to management's standards but were deviant from the workers' latitude of acceptance.

It is equally important, however, that conformity-deviation implies *evaluation* on the part of those who abide by the norms, with decided consequences for treatment and attitude. This evaluative process need not be fully conscious in the sense that the standards used are verbalized explicitly. Deviation is met with disapproval or even punishment. Conversely, staying within the bounds of acceptability helps to insure that the individual will be counted "in" by his group and may even bring tangible signs of approval and encouragement.

The evaluative aspect of normative regulation was emphasized in the diagrammatic scheme developed by Jackson (1965) as shown in Fig. 9.5. A simple example of behavior in group interaction is arrayed along the horizontal axis—in this case, the frequency of participation in a group discussion. The vertical axis represents an evaluative scale, with a high positive rating indicating high approval by members (on the average) and a low negative rating indicating disapproval.

For various norms, one can note the range covered between the two intercepts (latitude of acceptance) as well as the level of approval within it. Similarly, the slope of the curve may reveal how clear-cut the boundaries between conformity and deviation are in relation to a particular norm, and the level of negative evaluation may indicate the seriousness of transgression.

This interesting diagrammatic presentation of the evaluative dimension of norms will be particularly useful when coupled with indications of the actual frequencies of behavior during group interaction. It could then tell us how binding the norms actually are for members.

10

The Experimental Model for Norm Formation

Major Topics of the Chapter

Norm formation and stimulus properties

Norm formation in the laboratory: the paradigm

The autokinetic setup as an unstructured situation

The autokinetic experiments on norm formation

Verifications of norm formation: the formation of individual standards

Norms formed in interaction: factors affecting convergence

Relationships among participants

The experimental model: advantages and limitations

Transmission of norms over successive generations

Arbitrariness of norms and their transmission

EXTRACTING THE ESSENTIALS
FOR NORM FORMATION
IN THE LABORATORY

For a more precise account of the psychological basis of norm formation, we turn to
experimental study under controlled conditions that permit us to trace the process
step by step. A major line of research in
social psychology has dealt with this
problem.

Study of the process of norm formation in
actual life is a complicated task. Many variables are involved over long periods of
time. For this reason, the study of the psychology of norm formation in a controlled
laboratory situation was undertaken by
Sherif (1935, 1936).

What are the essentials to be embodied
as the minimum required for an experimental model of norm formation? The sociologist Durkheim wrote that norms take shape
in out-of-the-ordinary situations, when the
usual rules and routines of daily living are
not applicable. Observers of natural groups
provided numerous examples of norm formation among members of groups in the
interstitial slum areas of large cities, where
the traditional rules and standards of society at large or of their own families were
no longer maintained. In such studies, certain common findings seemed to emerge:
Norms form when individuals interact in
problem situations that involve uncertainties
and choice among alternative modes of
action.

Norm Formation and Stimulus Properties.
Studies of psychophysical judgments have
shown that characteristic modes of behavior (judgment) can be produced among
different individuals by presenting series
of stimuli that are well graded on a physical
dimension (e.g., weight) with clearly defined end points. For example, Tresselt and
Volkmann (1942) demonstrated that uniform

judgments could be produced by such nonsocial stimulation. They concluded:

Each person in a group says what he does not
only because he has been persuaded by argument, induced by reward, compelled by pressure,
guided by past experience, or influenced by the
voiced opinions of other people; he says it also
because he faces a restricted range of social or
nonsocial stimulation, and this range has determined his scale of judgment (p. 243).

Categories of behavior corresponding
closely to salient stimulus properties and
their gradations are called *psychophysical
scales.* Frequently, the boundaries or limits
of such physical scales also define normative behavior, in the sense that what is
stabilized as *customary* and *usual* is invested with "rightness" and "desirability."
It is sufficient here to note that the normative process can be determined, primarily or
in part, by the range and salient anchorages
of stimuli to which the individuals with common concerns are exposed repeatedly. The
principles governing the formation of psychophysical scales are pertinent for understanding the effects of technology in shaping the mentality and evaluations of persons
exposed to it (Chapter 22). Thus the experimental finding that psychophysical scales
shift fairly readily upon the introduction of
new stimuli is pertinent to understanding
why new technological products are assimilated fairly quickly as compared with new
social concepts. (The time difference is referred to as the "cultural lag" by sociologists such as Ogburn.)

The more difficult and puzzling problem
of norm formation occurs when the stimulus
conditions and alternative problem solutions facing individuals are not altogether
clear-cut. How do norms form under these
conditions? Are they exclusively an outcome of social interaction, or is there a
tendency for man to stabilize his responses
to fluid and unsettling situations even when

he is alone? If so, how does the interaction among individuals produce *psychosocial scales*—categories that denote the differences between social objects and the desirability of these differences, even when objective stimulus factors do not dictate one choice or another? Proposition 6 would lead us to predict that even under fluid environmental conditions, there would be a tendency to stabilize psychological gauges for the undependable surroundings.

NORM FORMATION
IN THE LABORATORY

The experiment to be reported in this section was carried out by M. Sherif (1935) to test <u>empirical observations concerning norm formation</u> and its <u>effects on perception and judgment of individuals</u> in a laboratory setting. On the basis of the considerations outlined in the last section, a stimulus situation lacking in objective structure was chosen. The experiment was planned so that reactions by individuals before, during, and following interaction with others could be compared.

Problem   The first problem raised was: What will an individual do when he is asked to make judgments of an aspect of a stimulus situation which lacks objective structure, such that a basis of comparison in the external stimulus field is absent? Will he give a hodgepodge of erratic judgments? Or will he establish some standard of his own? By answering these questions first, the tendency of the individual could be determined and then compared with his behavior during and following interaction.

Thus the next problem was: What will a number of individuals do in this same situation? Will the different individuals give a hodgepodge of judgments? Will every person establish his own standard? Or will a common norm be established for the various individuals peculiar to the particular interaction and dependent upon the particular individuals and their influence upon one another? If, during the course of interaction, the judgments of individuals converge within a certain range and toward a modal point, we could say they have formed a common norm in their judgments of that particular situation.

It is possible, however, that such convergence may owe simply to immediate social pressure to adjust to the judgments spoken aloud by other individuals in the situation. Therefore, if it is shown that the common range and modal point established in interaction are maintained by the individual on a different day, when he is alone, then we can say that the norm formed in interaction with others has become his own norm.

The Autokinetic Effect:
Its Possibilities
for Our Problem

With the above-noted considerations in mind, our first task was to find a situation that was unstructured in some respect. From among other possible experimental situations that could be used, the autokinetic situation was chosen for this particular series of experiments.

The conditions that produce the autokinetic effect afford an excellent experimental situation. We can easily get the autokinetic effect. In complete darkness, such as in a closed unlighted room, or on a cloudy night in the open when there are no lights visible, a single small light seems to move—and it may appear to move erratically in all directions. If you present the point of light repeatedly to a person, he may see the light appearing in different places in the room each time, especially if he does not know the distance between himself and the light.

The experimental production of the autokinetic effect is very easy and works without exceptions, *provided, of course, that the person or the experimenter does not use special devices to destroy the effect.* In a completely dark room a single point of light cannot be localized definitely. There is nothing in reference to which one can locate it. The effect takes place even when the person looking at the light knows perfectly well that the light is not moving. These are facts which are not subject to controversy; anyone can easily test them for himself.

In this situation not only does the stimulating light appear erratic and irregular to the subject, but *at times the person himself feels insecure about his spatial bearing.*

This comes out in an especially striking way if he is seated in a chair without a back and is unfamiliar with the position of the experimental room in the building. Under these conditions some subjects not only report that they are confused about the location of the point of light but that *they are even confused about the stability of their own position.*

The autokinetic effect is not a new artificial phenomenon invented by psychologists. It is older than experimental psychology. As it sometimes appears in observation of the heavenly bodies, astronomers had already noticed and offered theories to explain it before experimental psychology developed. A concise history of the autokinetic effect as a scientific problem was given by Adams (1912). Several theories have been advanced by psychologists to explain the nature of the autokinetic effect. Recent studies have indicated rather clearly that it is not caused solely by eye movements or other peripheral factors, but is also centrally determined.

Luchins and Luchins (1963), who have experimented extensively with autokinetic movement under a variety of conditions, observed that any explanation would have to recognize the complex determinants of this apparently simple phenomenon. Psychologists have become aware that perception of objects in space cannot be explained adequately merely through the mechanics and biochemistry of the eye. Similarly, the Luchinses emphasized that the systematic variations in autokinetic movement with different viewing conditions require an explanation entailing central neural processes as well as receptor mechanisms. From their review of the research literature, including their own work, they conclude that the autokinetic phenomenon "arises under conditions in which a stable three-dimensional visual world cannot be achieved" (p. 442). The complexity of processes underlying perception of a "stable, three-dimensional world" is evident in modern perception psychology (e.g., Gibson, 1967). It is exceedingly unlikely that the failure is dependent merely on eye-movements, eye-drift, or other muscularly controlled events.

Autokinetic movement has several dimensions, including extent, duration, direction, and location of movement. Extent of movement permits quantitative indicators of norm formation and more alternatives for response. Therefore, extent of movement was the measure in the experiments.

Procedures

The extent of movement experienced was studied in two situations: (1) when the individual was alone, except for the experimenter, in order to obtain the individual's reactions before social factors introduced in the experiment could affect them, and (2) when the individual was together with others, giving judgments of perceived movement with them, in order to discover what modifications would be produced by interaction among individuals.

The subject was introduced into the interaction situation in one of two ways: (1) He was brought into an interaction situation *after* being experimented upon when *alone* (this was done to find out the influence of interaction after he had had an opportunity to react to the situation first in accordance with his own tendencies), or (2) he was first introduced to the situation along with other individuals, having no previous familiarity with the situation, and was afterwards experimented upon individually. The latter was done to find out whether any norm or standard which might be established in interaction with others would continue to determine the subject's reaction to the same situation when he faced it alone. This last test is crucial for our problem.

The experiments were carried on in dark rooms in the psychological laboratory at Columbia University (see Fig. 10.1). The subjects were graduate and undergraduate male students at Columbia University and New York University. They were not majoring in psychology and did not know anything about the physical stimulus setup or the purpose of the experiment. There were 19 subjects in the individual experiments; 40 took part in the group experiments.

Individual Experiments

The stimulus light was a tiny point of light seen through a small hole in a metal box. The light was exposed to the subject by the opening of a suitable shutter controlled by

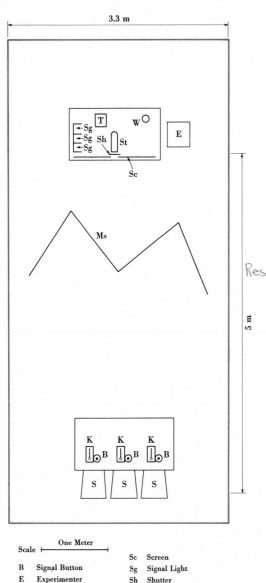

Scale ┠─────────────┨ One Meter

B	Signal Button	Sc	Screen
E	Experimenter	Sg	Signal Light
K	Reaction Key	Sh	Shutter
Ms	Movable Screen	St	Stimulus Light
S	Subject	T	Time
		W	Stop Watch

Fig. 10.1. Plan of the experimental room in auto-kinetic experiments as used in social situation.

the experimenter. The distance between the subject and the light was five meters. The observer was seated at a table on which was a telegraph key. The following instructions were given:

When the room is completely dark, I shall give you the signal READY, and then show you a point of light. After a short time the light will start to move. As soon as you see it move, press the key. A few seconds later the light will disappear.

Then tell me the distance it moved. Try to make your estimates as accurate as possible.

These instructions summarize the general procedure for the experiment. (See Figs. 10.1 and 10.2 for the experimental setup.) The exposure time after the subject pressed the key to indicate that he had begun to experience the movement was two seconds in all cases. The light was physically stationary during the entire time; it was not moved at all during any of the experiments.

After the light had disappeared, the subject reported orally the distance through which he thought it had moved. One hundred judgments were obtained from each subject. The subjects reported their estimates in inches (or fractions of inches).

Results The results unequivocally indicate that when individuals perceive movements that lack any other standard of comparison *they subjectively establish a range of extent (a scale) and a point (a standard) within that range which is peculiar to the individual.* The ranges and standards established by the various individuals differ.

In other words, when individuals repeatedly perceive movement with no objective basis for gauging its extent, they develop during the course of successive presentations a standard (a norm or reference point). This subjectively established standard or norm serves as a reference point with which each successive experienced movement is compared and judged—short, long, or medium—within the range peculiar to the subject.

To express the same point more generally, we conclude that, in the absence of an objective range or scale of stimuli and an externally given reference point or standard, each individual builds up a range of his own and an internal reference point within that range. Each successive judgment is given within that range and in relation to that reference point. The range (scale) and reference point established by each individual are peculiar to him when he is experimented upon alone.

In a second series of individual experiments it was found that, once a range and point of reference within that range are established by an individual, there is a tendency to preserve them on subsequent days. A second and third series of 100 judgments each showed a median for a

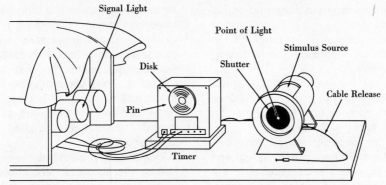

Fig. 10.2. Drawing of apparatus used in autokinetic experiments in 1934–1935. (From right to left; point of light, timer, signal system.)

given subject very similar to that found in the first series, but with a reduced variability.

The written reports obtained from every subject at the end of the experiment corroborate these conclusions. Reports of the following sort, which are typical, show that the subjects at first found it hard to estimate distance because of the lack of externally given reference points or standards:

"Darkness left no guide for distance."
"It was difficult to estimate the distance the light moved, because of the lack of visible neighboring objects."
"There was no fixed point from which to judge distance."

Other observations indicate that the subjects developed standards of their own in the absence of the objective ones:

"Compared with previous distance."
"Used first estimate as standard."

These findings reveal once more the general psychological tendency to experience things in relation to some reference point or standard.

Following the individual experiments, these findings of experimental psychology were carried into social psychology by noting the individual's reactions when in an interaction situation with others.

Interaction Conditions in the Experiments

On the basis of the results, the problem studied in the interaction conditions becomes self-evident. To recapitulate, the individual experiences the external field of stimulation in relation to anchorages within the frame of reference of factors operating at the time. When such an anchorage or reference point is given in the objective situation, it will usually determine in an important way the structural relationships of the experience. All other parts are organized as modified by it. But when objective anchorages are lacking—when the field of stimulation is unstable, vague, and not well structured—the individual perceives the situation as shaped by his own internally evolved standards or anchorages.

The process is reduced here to a very simple form; but the first fundamental problem is the way an individual perceives a stimulus situation. His behavior follows upon this perception rather than upon the simple fact of stimulation. There is no direct and simple correlation between the stimulus and subsequent behavior, especially on the level of behavior with which we are dealing. A simple perceptual situation is the first requirement for experimental analysis of the problem.

As we have seen, individuals do not face stimulus situations involving other people in an indifferent way. They are charged with certain modes of readiness and certain motives or attitudes which enter to modify their reactions. This important consideration shaped the plan of the experiments. Reactions were compared (1) when the individuals first faced the stimulus situation with others, and (2) when they first established their individual ranges and norms alone and then joined others. Accordingly, 20 of the subjects began alone and were put into the interaction condition in subsequent experimental sessions; the other 20 started with interaction sessions and ended with individual sessions.

This counter-balancing enabled us to draw conclusions regarding the following important questions:

How much of his independently established way of reacting to this situation does the individual carry over when facing the same stimulus along with others?

How will he experience the situation when he is alone after a common range and norm have been established peculiar to the interaction situation in which he participated? Will the common product developed in interaction serve as a determining factor when he subsequently faces the same situation *alone?*

The experimental setting was in general the same as in the individual experiments. Of course, additional devices were necessary to handle two or more individuals at the same time. One major addition was the use of signal lights. The experimenter could not tell from the voice who was giving a judgment; so as each subject gave his judgment aloud, he pressed a button connected with a dim signal light of a particular color by which the experimenter might identify who the speaker was (see Figs. 10.1 and 10.2).

There were eight groups of two subjects each and eight groups of three subjects each. Four groups in each of the categories started with the individual situation and then functioned in interaction. Four groups in each category started in interaction situations for the first three sessions on three different days (all members being present) and were then separated and studied in individual situations.

In order to make the relation of individuals to one another as natural as possible within the limits of the experimental setting, the subjects were left free as to the order in which they would give their judgments. In fact, they were told at the start to give their judgments in random order as they pleased. Whether the person who speaks first has more influence than the others becomes a study in leadership, which is a further interesting problem.

From the examination of the results, we can say that the reporting of the judgments has a gradual cumulative effect. Aside from whatever influence the first judgment may have on the second or third, the judgments of the third individual at a given presentation affect the subsequent judgments of the first subject in the round of presentations following. Thus the production of an established social influence is largely a temporal affair and not the outcome of this or that single presentation. We shall refer to this point again later.

Besides the quantitative judgments obtained, the subjects were asked at the end of each session to write down their observations. Questions were asked which aimed at finding out whether they became conscious of the range and norm they were establishing. These questions were: "Between what maximum and minimum did the distances vary?" "What was the most frequent distance that the light moved?"

Summary of Results

Certain facts stand out clearly from the results, and may be summarized in a few paragraphs.

1. When an individual faces a stimulus situation which is unstable and not structured in itself, he establishes a range and a norm (a reference point) within that range. The range and norm that are developed in each individual are peculiar to that individual and may vary from the ranges and norms developed by other individuals in different degrees, revealing consistent and stable individual differences. Thus the tendency toward stabilization is rooted in basic psychological processes and is not a unique outcome of social interaction.

2. When the person who independently develops a range and a norm within that range is put into a situation together with others who also enter the situation with their own ranges and norms established in their own individual sessions, the ranges and norms of the various individuals tend to converge. But this convergence is not so close as that which occurs when the subjects first work together and have less opportunity to set up stable individual norms. (See the left-hand graphs, Figs. 10.3 and 10.4.)

3. When individuals face the same unstable, unstructured situation together for

the first time, a range and a norm (standard) within that range are established which are peculiar to the interaction situation. If there is a rise or fall in the norms established in successive sessions, it is a group effect. The norms of the various individuals rise and fall toward a common norm in each session. (See the second and fourth graphs of the three subject groups in Fig. 10.4.)

To such a conclusion the objection may be raised that one subject may lead and be uninfluenced by other members of the interaction situation. The social norm may be simply the leader's norm. To this the only possible empirical reply is that in the experiments those who took a lead were constantly observed to be influenced by their followers—if not at the moment, then later in the series and in subsequent series. Although the objection has occasional force, the statement regarding social norms is, in general, true. Even if the social norm gravitates toward a dominating person, the leader represents a polarization in the situation, having a definite relationship toward others which he cannot change at will. If the leader changes his norm after the social norm is settled, he may thereupon cease to be followed. This occurred several times in our experiments. In general, cases of complete polarization are exceptional. (See the right-hand graphs, Figs. 10.3 and 10.4.)

The fact that the norm thus established is peculiar to the interaction situation suggests that there is a factual psychological basis in the contentions of those who maintain that new qualities arise in social interaction that are not identical with the properties of behavior by the individuals prior to their interaction.

4. When a member of a group subsequently faces the same situation *alone, after* the range and norm of his group have been established, *he perceives the situation in terms of the range and norm that he brings from the interaction situation.* This fact is important in that it gives a psychological approach to the understanding of the social products which weigh so heavily in discussing groups. This finding shows that the effect of the interaction situation is not just an immediate effect. The norm formed in interaction with others becomes the individual's own perspective.

Implications of the Experiment

The experiments, then, constitute a study of the formation of a norm in a simple laboratory situation. They show in a simple way the basic psychological process involved in the establishment of social norms. They are an extension into the social field of a general psychological principle that we find in perception and in many other activities, namely, that our experience is organized or modified by main anchorages in the frame of reference consisting of interrelated factors operating at a given time (Propositions 3 and 11).

On the basis of this general principle considered in relation to the experimental results, we shall venture to generalize. The psychological basis of established social norms—such as stereotypes, fashions, conventions, customs, and values—is the formation of common reference points or anchorages as a product of interaction among individuals. Once such anchorages are established and internalized by the individual, they become important factors in determining or modifying his reactions to the situations that he will face later alone—social and even nonsocial, especially if the stimulus field is not well structured.

Of course, this is a very general statement. It gives us only the broad basic principle with which we can approach any specific social norm. In each instance we have to take into consideration particular factors that contribute to its production.

The situation utilized in this experiment does not represent pressing social situations such as those found in everyday life with intense hunger, sex, and ego (i.e., status) factors. It is simply one unstable, unstructured situation that is new for the subjects. They have no set ways of reacting to it. Therefore it is plastic enough so that experimentally introduced social factors, such as suggestion, prestige, and other group influences, can have a decisive effect.

In this situation, within certain limits, there is no "right" or "wrong" judgment. One subject demonstrated this spontaneously during the experiment by suggesting: "If you tell me once how much I am

Medians in Groups of Two Subjects

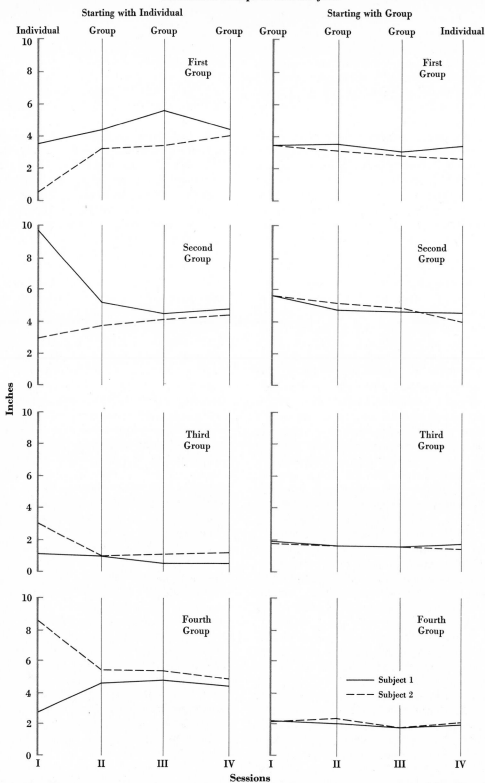

Figs. 10.3 (*above*) and **10.4** (*opposite*). When individual sessions came first (I), divergent norms established alone changed when subjects subsequently judged movement together (II, III, IV). The "funnel-shaped" forms result from convergence toward a common social norm. (See left-hand graphs in both Figures.) When judgments were made first in a social situation

Medians in Groups of Three Subjects

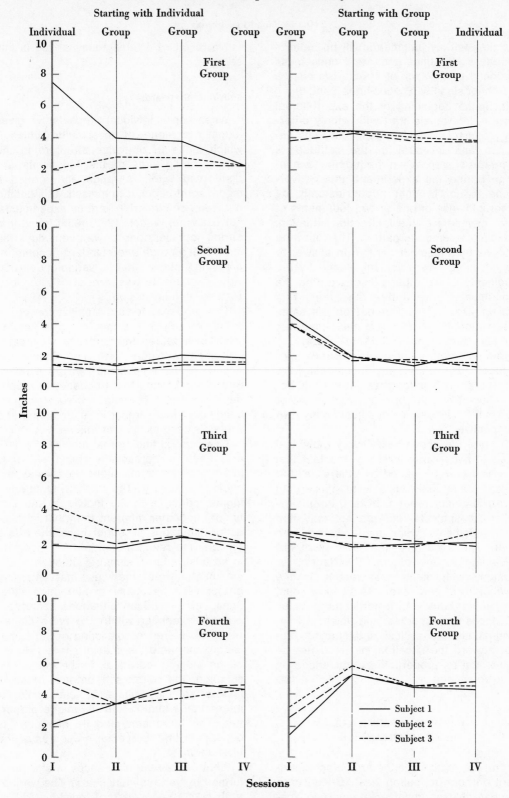

(right-hand graphs in both Figures), a social norm was formed in the first session (I) and was maintained throughout, including the final session (IV) when the individual made judgments alone.

mistaken, all my judgments will be better." Doubtless, this uncertainty and uneasiness produced by the lack of structure arouse a search for stability (Propositions 6 and 8).

If, in the beginning of the experimental session, individuals start with widely different judgments, the divergent one feels uncertain and insecure in the solitude of being out of step. When the judgments converge during the experiment, this convergence is not brought about instantly by direct influence of one or two judgments of other members of the interaction situation. It exhibits a temporal pattern. The following analysis by a member (written in answer to the question, "Were you influenced by the judgments of the other persons during the experiments?") illustrates the point. This subject wrote, "Yes, but not on the same observation. My judgment in each case was already made, and I did not change to whatever the other person said. But on subsequent observations, my judgments were adjusted to their judgments. After a number of observations, the previous agreement or lack of it influenced me in adjusting my own perspective."

Despite the above case, every individual was not necessarily aware of the fact that he was being influenced by others, or that he and other individuals were converging toward a common norm. In fact, the majority of the subjects reported not only that their judgments were made before the others spoke but also *that they were not influenced by the others.* This fact is in harmony with many observations in the psychology of perception. As we have seen, the general context of a particular stimulus influences its properties, and unless the individual takes a critical and analytic attitude toward the situation, he need not be aware that its properties are influenced by its surroundings.

FURTHER EXPERIMENTS
ON NORM FORMATION

During the years since the foregoing experiment on norm formation was carried out, a number of experiments pertaining to specific problems it raised and to related problems have been carried out. As the plan of most of these studies was similar, represen-

tative results are briefly summarized in this section.

Individual Standards

When an individual repeatedly gives judgments alone of a stimulus situation which lacks in objective structure in the aspect being judged, his judgments are distributed within a range and around a modal point peculiar to himself. This finding has been confirmed in various experiments. For example, Walter (1952, 1955) found that during four sessions on different days the individual's range and standard become increasingly stable, that is, variability of individual judgments was consistently reduced from session to session.

This tendency toward stabilization of the extent of autokinetic movement is not the result of a decreasing tendency to perceive movement with time. Using continuous exposure of the light source for 30 minutes, Stern (1964) found that frequency of reporting perceived movement *increased* significantly over time—regardless of whether the subject's head movement was restricted.

This general finding that individual standards become increasingly stable with time has important implications for social-psychological theory. The underlying psychological principle in the individual situation is not altogether different from that in interaction situations. In either case, there is a tendency to reach a standard for judgment in an unstructured stimulus situation. Here, we must correct the view that emergent properties appear only in interaction situations. In individual situations, emergent properties appear within the more limited frame of reference consisting of the stimulus situation and the special characteristics of the judging individual. In the interaction situation, the norm is a product of these factors as they relate to the particular interaction situation and its unique properties. The norm emerging in interaction is dependent on the special properties of the interaction.

What causes the differences in standards formed by various individuals? The work of Voth (1947) suggests that individual differences in personal characteristics and motivations are certainly important. An experiment by Sherif and Harvey (1952) showed that increased insecurity aroused by reducing anchorages for bodily orientation in space produces wide and significant differences in judgments as compared with those made in a situation in which the individual has some notion of his location in space. Reducing anchorages for bodily orientation in space yielded greater variability on the whole and individual judgments of perceived distance which were significantly greater in magnitude. (This experiment is reported in Chapter 17.)

Hoffman, Swander, Baron, and Rohrer (1953) made a definite contribution to this general problem by demonstrating that prior training with a light that actually moved within a luminous framework produced individual standards for judgments of autokinetic movement very much like the actual movement perceived during training. In other words, the standard produced through training with *objective* movement was generalized to the autokinetic situation.

**Norms Formed
in Interaction**

The findings concerning norm formation for autokinetic movement in interaction situations have been confirmed in detail in various experiments (e.g., Sperling, 1946). In addition, numerous points raised in the experiment reported in this chapter have been clarified.

Perhaps the most significant of these is the substantiation of the finding that after participating in the formation of a common norm, the individual takes this norm as his own standard—even when he is not in the interaction situation. Bovard (1951) demonstrated that the effect of a common norm persisted when the individuals made judgments alone 28 days after the interaction situation in which the standard was formed. The extent of carry-over of the common norm was related to initial individual differences among subjects. The tendency was for *subjects whose initial individual judgments were more variable to stick more closely to the common norm formed in interaction.*

Rohrer, Baron, Hoffman, and Swander (1954) found persistence of norms formed in interaction for a much longer period. Following training with a moving stimulus light,

subjects participated together in interaction situations. Convergence of judgments toward a common norm was found, even though this necessitated shifts from individual norms established through training. An entire year later, these individuals made judgments alone. It was found that the norms formed in interaction were carried over by the individual, while effects of the training prior to interaction were negligible after this long interval.

Through the use of different stimulus materials, it has been demonstrated that the findings concerning norm formation are not peculiar to the autokinetic situation. Similar findings have been reported for different sensory modalities, such as cutaneous perception of warmth (McCord, 1948), duration of perceptual phenomena (Sinha, 1952), estimates of size (Bovard, 1951; Mausner, 1954) and of number (Bovard, 1953; Sodhi, 1953), and aesthetic judgments (Mausner, 1953).

In fact, it is feasible to study norm formation relative to stimulus dimensions that can be defined precisely on a physical dimension. The prerequisite for doing so is that conditions limit the person's opportunity to check the physical dimension himself, hence leaving a wide margin for error in his appraisals. Nurmi (1966) demonstrated this possibility by setting up an experiment on judging weight, in which the person's judgment had to be given solely on the basis of turning a knob, which was attached to concealed pulleys that lifted the weight. In each case, the weight weighed 500 grams.

Alone, subjects in this situation gave highly variable judgments with no systematic trends over nine trials. There was a significant time-order error (negative; that is, the tendency to give judgments of "greater" on successive than the preceding trial). However, this time-order error was not consistent and was sharply reversed on the eighth trial. They used very vague judgment units, such as "about a kilo" or "say, half a kilo."

When subjects judged the weight with a pre-instructed partner who either (a) increased his successive judgments each trial from 500 to 900 grams or (b) decreased his judgments from 500 to 100 grams, the converging trend toward the prescribed judgments was significant and individual variations were sharply reduced. Ninety-one percent of the variance in the judgments was predictable from the predetermined trend. Further, judgments were reported in 10-gram units like those used by the plant.

Nurmi's results suggested that as the prescribed judgments of the 500-gram weight approached zero, there would be no appreciable convergence in judgments. Scarcely anyone would believe that his knob-turning lifted no weight at all. Such limits are not confined to precisely defined physical dimensions. Sinha (1952) showed that estimates of the duration of the spiral after-effect, which normally ranges in duration from 5 to 45 seconds with a median of 25 seconds, were markedly influenced by others' judgments within this range as long as the two individuals did not give estimates at the opposite extreme (above 40 seconds and below 10 seconds). Whittaker (1958) showed that the extent of influence on judgments of autokinetic movement decreased sharply if the person was confronted with another's judgments which were much greater than his own standard and range.

Some Factors Affecting Convergence

Several experiments have shown that instructions or prior experiences indicating to the person judging an unstructured situation that he is correct or incorrect affect his tendency to converge toward others (Kelman, 1950; Mausner, 1954; Harvey and Rutherford, 1958; Luchins and Luchins, 1961; Stone, 1967). The person who lacks confidence in the correctness of his judgments is more likely to converge toward those of others. Instructions that increase his anxiety about his performance in the situation produce stronger trends toward agreeing with the other person (Walters, Marshall, and Shooter, 1960). On the other hand, the subject who is led to believe that his judgments are correct is more likely to maintain his own standard. In fact, the combination of persons with divergent judgments, each convinced that he is correct, can lead to further divergence rather than a common norm (Mausner, 1954).

The individual's selectivity for clues in an experimental situation is not, however, as simple as it might seem when there are alternatives. Suppose that the experimenter first allows norms to form either individually or in interaction situations. Then, bringing each subject to a second session alone, he informs him that he is correct on 10 out of 40 trials, choosing those trials in which the person gives judgments of greater movement. Finally, he secures a series of judgments alone without providing any clues as to "correctness." Whose words will be more effective, the more recent words of the experimenter or those spoken earlier by other subjects during the initial formation of a norm in interaction?

Stone (1967) performed such an experiment with the following outcomes: The experimenter's confirmation of "high" responses was effective under every condition, increasing the subsequent level of judgments. However, when he stopped responding, those subjects who had formed norms in interaction tended to return to them while those who had formed standards initially by themselves continued to give the high responses approved by the experimenter. Further support for the finding that confirmation by other subjects and confirmation by the experimenter have different impact is given in research by Hollander, Julian, and Haaland (1965).

In actual life, the person sizes up others in the situation before "taking their word" for something of which he is uncertain. It is not necessary that this sizing up occur in face-to-face situations. Similarly, in the laboratory, the mere knowledge that another person is performing is sufficient to alert the subject to his words and actions. Thus, Blake and Brehm (1954) demonstrated the formation of norms for autokinetic judgments shaped by tape recordings attributed to other (nonexistent) subjects in adjacent rooms.

Because mutual influence in human interaction occurs at a conceptual level, a wide variety of experiments have been performed utilizing predetermined, simulated response sequences that are automatically presented to the subject as he performs the experimental task (e.g., Olmstead and Blake, 1955; Crutchfield, 1955).

Relationships Among Interacting Individuals. In the autokinetic experiments on norm formation, the interaction occurred between individuals who had no previously established relationship. In another experiment using the autokinetic setup, Sherif (1937) showed that affective or prestige relationships and even a confident partner could exert predictable effects on norms formed in interaction. In general, experiments have shown that attributing credibility, prestige, status, or task-competence to participants facing an unstructured problem increases those persons' influence in the judgment situation (e.g., Mausner, 1953; Graham, 1962; Kidd and Campbell, 1955; Croner and Willis, 1961).

In actual norm formation in real life, interaction process typically involves individuals as members of a group structure, stabilized in some degree. Two experiments by Bovard (1951, 1953) suggest that such established relationships enhance convergence toward a common norm. In the first, classes were taught by two different techniques, one "group-centered" and one "teacher-centered." The chief difference was that the former allowed much greater freedom for verbal interaction among students. A total of 504 subjects in 30 different classes made individual estimates of the length of rectangles. After being informed of the judgments made by others in their class, they made individual judgments again. Convergence to the group standard was greater for those classes in which the students had already experienced the most interaction among themselves. Bovard's second study compared estimates of the numerosity of dots by organized units of considerable stability and by individuals in transitory togetherness situations. Once again, convergence was greater in groups with stabilized relationships.

In Chapter 11, experiments are reported in which norms form as groups are formed, both in relation to affairs within the group and to relations with another group. Such experiments approximate the conditions of norm formation in actual life and indicate the great importance of common motives and specific problem situations faced by members in actual group situations.

Note
on the Experimental Model

The autokinetic experiment provides only the minimum essentials to be found in norm formation in real life: A common motive—in this case, the uncertainty that the naive subject experiences; interaction over time; and the carry-over into a situation when the individual is alone. The resulting norm is not an average of individual norms. Nor is it necessarily identical with the initial behavior of one or another of the individuals, although an individual with greater prestige, confidence, or status does exert greater influence on the emerging norm.

The complexity of determinants of a norm was indicated in an autokinetic experiment by Vidulich and Kaiman (1965) in which the identity of the planted subject (experimenter's confederate) and the open-closed mindedness (dogmatism) of the naive participant were varied. The higher-status plant (college professor) was more effective for the more closed-minded subjects, and hence had more to do with the norm that developed. However, the open-minded (low dogmatism) subjects were more sensitive to partners nearer their own status, that is, to fellow college students. Thus the norm that emerges in interaction is a joint product of all participants, and seldom the single-handed creation of one.

It is important to note that once the norm is formed, the immediate presence or social pressure of other individuals is not essential to its continuance. Hood and Sherif (1962) performed an experiment in which every effort was made to eliminate any hint that the experiment had anything to do with the presence of other people or with social influence. Each subject simply overheard another person making 20 judgments of autokinetic movement while waiting to take part in a "vision experiment." One sample of subjects overheard judgments ranging from 1 to 5 inches and another sample overheard judgments ranging from 6 to 10 inches.

Figure 10.5 summarizes the results when these subjects made judgments alone. It represents the percentage of judgments made by each sample that were 5 inches or less (*left*) and 6 inches or more (*right*). Later, when the subjects were asked how much the light seemed to move, their estimates, on the average, did not differ significantly from their actual judgments in the situation. The significance of this experiment is that in a highly unstructured situation, the formation of norms need not imply

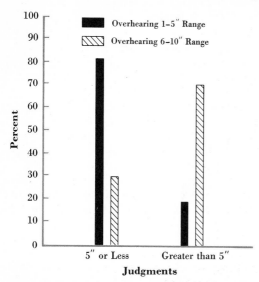

Fig. 10.5. Percentage of judgments of autokinetic movement that were 5 inches or less (*left*) and greater than 5 inches (*right*) by subjects who overheard judgments 1–5 inches or 6–10 inches prior to judging. (From W. R. Hood and M. Sherif, Verbal report and judgment of an unstructured stimulus, 1962. *J. Psychol.,* **54,** 121–130.)

conscious recognition of social influence or "distortion" of experience. Over time, perception of the stimulus is influenced by the normative range.

Unfortunately, the literal flood of research literature using the experimental model does not always recognize the great importance of two conditions that are essential in studying norm formation: The objective situation must lack structure in some aspect to be dealt with by interacting persons, and the interaction must occur over time. Consequently, the great bulk of that research is, properly speaking, concerned with factors that affect compliance to immediate social pressure in a transitory social situation (cf. Berg and Bass, 1961; Graham, 1962; Hollander and Willis, 1967).

Meanwhile, many of the techniques and procedures used in such experiments have become so familiar that it has become difficult to assume that subjects are naive or unaware that the procedures are designed to study influence processes. The shift in focus from using the model to study norms as products of interaction toward modifying it to study deliberate attempts to shape responses has resulted in the use of such elaborate batteries of tests and contrived

procedures that even initially naive subjects can easily become aware of the researcher's intentions (cf. Stricker, Messick, and Jackson, 1967).

Further, extensions of the model have focused too seldom on the profound differences between interacting with strangers and with friends of established acquaintance. The extent of such differences was suggested in research assessing metabolic changes during interaction with friends or with strangers (Bogdonoff *et al.,* 1964). With the use of lipid metabolism as the physiologic response, the researchers had friends or strangers make simple judgments in a simulated interaction situation in which their judgments were either confirmed or contradicted by their companions. Measures of lipid mobilization were consistently lower for subjects serving in the experiment with friends and, further, were differentially affected by agreement and disagreement. Agreement from strangers increased the level of the physiological measure, whereas agreement from friends decreased the level. Conversely, disagreement from friends tended to raise the level, while disagreement from strangers had little effect.

THE TRANSMISSION OF NORMS IN THE EXPERIMENT

Using the experimental model for norm formation in the autokinetic situation, Jacobs and Campbell (1961) set out to study the transmission of norms over "generations" created by systematically removing subjects and adding new subjects during the experiment. In their particular setup, the average judgment of autokinetic movement when *Ss* were alone was 3.8 inches. Wishing to study a very "arbitrary" norm, they started the experiment with one naive subject and confederates of the experimenter who were instructed to give judgments of 15.5 inches, gradually replacing each confederate with a naive subject until all subjects were naive. Subsequently, a new member was added and an old one removed after each 30 judgments.

Figure 10.6 represents a typical finding in the experiment.

The effect of the confederate can be seen on the judgments of those subjects with

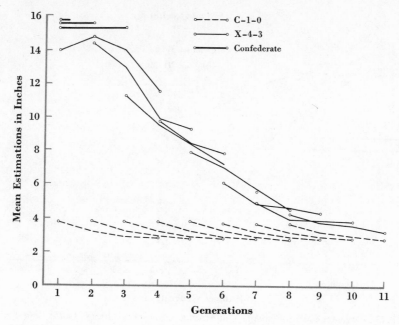

Fig. 10.6. Transmission of arbitrary norm for judging autokinetic movement with four persons judging, one being replaced by a new subject in each successive generation. (From R. C. Jacobs and D. T. Campbell, 1961. The perpetuation of an arbitrary tradition through several generations of a laboratory microculture. *J. abnorm. soc. Psychol.,* **62,** 649–658. Copyright by the American Psychological Association, and reproduced by permission.) Arbitrary norm near 16 inches was transmitted by confederate in generation 1 (the solid line at top). Successive curves indicate norms for successive "generations," each consisting of three experienced members and one naive subject. Dashed lines near bottom represent norms established without indoctrination by the confederate.

whom he judged (first generation). As these subjects were replaced one at a time by new subjects, the effect of the transmitted norm is evident for several generations—as indicated by the higher medians for the experimental subjects than controls who were not exposed to the arbitrary norm. On the average, significant effects of the transmitted norms were found for four or five generations after the confederate's removal. Gradually, however, in each of 12 experimental groups, the arbitrary norm "decayed" and the judgments drifted down to the control group's norm, a level that was "natural" in the particular experimental set-up used by the investigators.

**Transmission of Norms
as a Function
of Their Arbitrariness**

When a group has established norms for behavior and new members come as older ones depart, what conditions lead to the maintenance of the group norms in substantially similar form and which ones are conducive to their alteration?

One important variable affecting the transmission of norms and the extent of conformity to them by new members is the *degree of their arbitrariness* relative to current conditions facing the group. When a norm is transmitted by older members to a new generation of members, its "arbitrariness" can be defined relative to the conditions in which the new generation functions. The norm developing in those conditions *without* an enculturation process by older members can be termed *least arbitrary* or "natural."

If the arbitrariness of norms is an important variable in conformity-deviation, it will help explain the continuity of groups of boys who grow up in the same neighborhood, relative to the changes occurring in the neighborhood and the city of which it is a part.

To study such continuity, a laboratory

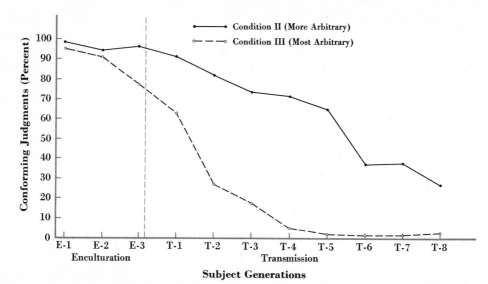

Fig. 10.7. Percentage of judgments conforming to more arbitrary (*solid line*) and most arbitrary (*dashed line*) norms for 8 generations (T-1 to T-8) after indoctrination sessions (E-1 to E-3). Enculturation is more effectively transmitted when norm is less arbitrary (as defined by judgments in control condition with no indoctrination).

experiment was initiated (MacNeil, 1965). As in the earlier studies of norm formation by Sherif (1935, 1936), a norm for behavior in this situation was defined as a common range of judgment around a modal point stabilized over time by two or more individuals. Individual conformity is defined as a judgment falling within this norm; deviation, a judgment outside the norm.

In this situation, the degree of arbitrariness of a norm could be defined operationally as the extent to which a prescribed and transmitted norm differed from the range and mode of judgments stabilized under the same laboratory arrangements *without* the introduction of a norm transmitted by "planted" subjects.

The general sequence of procedures followed those used in a study by Jacobs and Campbell (1961). As the degree of arbitrariness was the main interest, three degrees were standardized in our laboratory: (I) not arbitrary; (II) an arbitrary norm chosen not to overlap the range of Condition I and with a higher mode (a range of 9 to 15 inches around a mode of 12 inches); and (III) a more arbitrary norm not overlapping Condition II and a still higher mode (15- to 21-inch range and 18-inch mode).

In Condition I (not arbitrary), four naive subjects gave 30 judgments each of the

extent of autokinetic movement; then each in turn was replaced by a new naive subject in the succeeding "generations"—and so on, through eight generations of 30 judgments each. In Conditions II and III, a preliminary "enculturation" phase consisted of three generations, with the prescribed norm being given by three, then two, then a single planted subject, who in turn was replaced by a naive subject. Eight generations of naive subjects followed, the transmitted norm being traced over these.

The subjects were high-school students (ages 16–19). A total of 66 naive subjects participated in two replications of each condition.

The major hypothesis was that degree of conformity over successive generations would decrease (and deviation increase) as a function of the degree of arbitrariness of the transmitted norm. In order to test this hypothesis, it was also necessary to demonstrate the following: (a) a norm formed in Condition I would be transmitted with only minor variations as personnel changed, and (b) the enculturation procedures in Conditions II and III did produce conformity to the prescribed norm by naive subjects.

The findings can be summarized briefly as follows:

1. The norm formed by subjects in the

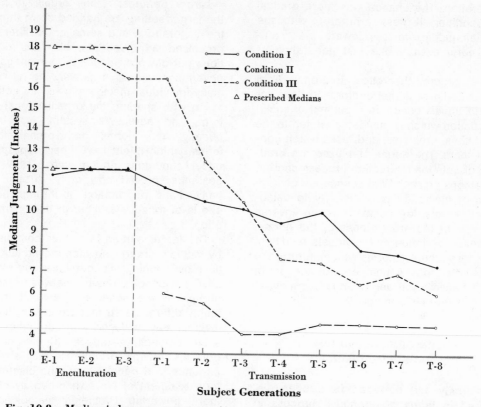

Fig. 10.8. Median judgments over successive generations when arbitrary norm was within a range around 18 inches and when it was within a range around 12 inches. Condition III (lowest curve) was control, without indoctrination.

first generation in Condition I (not arbitrary) was within an interquartile range of 4–8 inches, with a median and mean of 6 inches. The means and medians of seven successive generations were around 4 inches, with an interquartile range from 3 to 6 inches. In short, after the second generation the norm in Condition I was transmitted with only minor variations.

2. The enculturation by planted subjects in the more arbitrary conditions did result in conformity by naive subjects. In Condition II, 100 percent of the judgments fell within the prescribed range, and 90 percent of the judgments conformed in Condition III (most arbitrary), as shown in Fig. 10.7. Similarly, the median judgments of naive subjects in Condition II were very close to the prescribed median of 12 inches (11.7 inches), and the median for Condition III during enculturation was 16.5–17.5 inches.

3. The prescribed norm in Condition II was transmitted to the first generation, consisting entirely of naive subjects, and 100 percent of the judgments conformed to the transmitted norm. In the most arbitrary condition (III), there was some deviation from the prescribed norm by the first generation of entirely naive subjects, but 63 percent of the judgments conformed to the transmitted norm.

Figure 10.7 gives the percentages of judgments by naive subjects which fell within the prescribed norm for Conditions II and III through three enculturation and eight transmission generations. Conformity to the prescribed norm was significantly greater at every generation in the less arbitrary condition (II). The rate of increase in deviation was clearly more rapid in Condition III (most arbitrary).

Figure 10.8 presents the median judgments of naive subjects, generation by generation. The greatest shift away from the transmitted norm and toward the "natural" norm of Condition I was in the most arbitrary condition, with half of the downward trend occurring by the third transmission generation. The change was more gradual in Condition II (less arbitrary), with the median judgments less toward the "natural" norm even in the last generation of subjects.

Result The general theoretical inference from this experiment is that conforming behavior by individuals occurs in a context of social interaction which is inevitably related to the conditions, problems, and tasks which confront them. The norms stabilized are products of both the interaction process and the conditions present. With successive generations of membership, conformity to established norms for behavior is an inverse function of the arbitrariness of the norms. However, deviation by individuals results in new, less arbitrary norms which, in turn, are transmitted to new members. An account of norm transmission and change in a natural group is given in Chapter 19.

CONFORMITY-DEVIATION
AND SOCIAL CHANGE

Conformity and deviation have been discussed in terms of normative process in groups spontaneously organized by individuals with motives and problems seen as common, whether these motives relate to common conditions of the natural settings or to experimentally created problem situations. In such groups, whatever the organizational form and the character of the norms may be, such norms are not handed down by an outside authority. They are outcomes of the interaction process among the individual members, as influenced, of course, by previous group memberships and the setting in which the members function. Each individual attains a position in the group through his relative contribution and efforts, and his position is not fixed once and for all. Each had some hand in shaping the norms of the group and can have a hand in changing them through further interaction.

Such is not the case in traditional groups and formally organized groups in the larger cultural setting. We cannot adequately touch upon the questions raised in this chapter without at least mentioning conformity and deviation as they occur in such organizational frameworks.

Larger Settings. Many organizations in the larger setting are handed down through the generations and some are deliberately organized with blueprints, rules, and regulations put down on paper by personages or governing bodies in power. As a result many individual members have had nothing to do with shaping the organizational patterns and normative system. Not infrequently, the norms and organizational forms, which might have been appropriate under conditions at the time of their appearance, prevail now more through the heavy hand of tradition or through active efforts of those interested in their perpetuation.

The larger setting is further confounded by multiple groups in which individuals may have overlapping memberships, and by sizable power differentials between various groups in the scheme of things. In the highly differentiated modern scene, the individual may be faced with contradictory—even conflicting—modes of compliance from his multiple groups. He may also experience in a personal way the discriminatory treatment of his own group by others more powerful. Problems suggested by formal organizations and multiple groups have been investigated especially by sociologists—Durkheim, the Lynds, Merton, and Williams, to mention only a few.

CONCLUSIONS
FOR CONFORMITY-DEVIATION
IN MODERN LIFE

Looking back to Chapter 9 as well as to the present one, we are in a position to comment in a summary way on problems of conformity and deviation in modern life. In all phases of his daily living—social, political, economic, and religious—man is confronted today with pressures and exhortations to regulate his behavior within advocated molds and directions.

Concerned with the plight of those of their fellow men who have fallen prey in blind conformity to such pressures and exhortations, psychologists and social scientists have advanced various antidotes. One attempt in this direction is the cult which elevates nonconformity in its own right to a pedestal of virtue. Such attempts are laudable from the point of view of intent. But their realistic adequacy is a different matter.

Even the most ardent proponent of nonconformity would not praise stealing simply because it is a nonconforming deed. Indeed, conformity is condemned because of concern over widespread degradation of moral and artistic values, of repressive restrictions on human expression and the rights of man, and of arbitrary limitations to human dignity and potentialities. In short, the plea for nonconformity is made in the name of values or norms which were themselves formulated through a long and arduous stretch of human history. But as long as the analysis and the plea center only on conformity or nonconformity in the abstract, there is no adequate basis for evaluating conforming or nonconforming behavior. And the exhortation to individual man to assert his independence of a mountain of social pressures may not be an adequate way to move the mountain.

We repeat: an item of behavior, whether in social, political, religious, or economic spheres, cannot be characterized by itself as either conforming or deviating. It is always conformity or deviation relative to some premise, canon, standard, or value— in short, to some norm. Therefore, the primary question to be raised becomes: Conformity or nonconformity in relation to *what* practice, *what* value, *what* moral standard, or *what* norm?

Social values, moral standards, or norms are products of interaction among human beings over a period of time in matters of consequence to their mutual and individual concerns. Thus, issues of conformity and nonconformity which make the problem so urgent for study are not one-episode affairs involving momentary, transitory social influence on inconsequential matters. For these reasons, the traditional laboratory setting is far from adequate for studying significant problems of conformity and deviation.

On the whole, the traditional laboratory experiment on compliance takes the individual from a context of relationships with other people involving matters of mutual importance and exposes him briefly to a momentary situation arranged by the experimenter. The experimenter's success in demonstrating susceptibility to comply in the laboratory is inversely related to the degree of structure and the number and clarity of alternatives available in the stimulus situation the experimenter has arranged for the subjects. Thus in a highly unstructured situation with various alternatives, the subject may comply almost invariably to definitions introduced by the experimenter. To conclude, therefore, that the subject is basically a conformist may be quite in error. Likewise, demonstration of righteous protests by individuals exposed to easily discriminable stimuli and a fantastically false consensus by others is scarcely evidence for man's basic independence.

The most careful studies to date yield small comfort for the view that individuals are either "conformist" in general or "independent" in general (cf. Mann, 1959; Vaughan, 1963; Hollander and Willis, 1967). True, there are individual differences in all of the experiments and many studies have reported positive correlations between personality variables and compliance in more than one situation. However, other studies have reported zero correlations or negative correlations for some of the same variables. In fact, sex differences in compliance are probably the most consistent reported in studies using college students as subjects. Does this mean that all women in all situations conform more than men? It is hard to believe so. In general, the search for a "conforming personality" or an "independent personality" has led into a dead end.

The attribution of either blind subservience to the group or independence to the basic nature of man rests on an untenable dichotomy between individual and group. An adequate approach must begin with a clear statement of the place of norm-regulated behavior in psychological functioning. A single individual faced with a perceptual situation for which he has little in the way of established guideposts for evaluation comes *in time* to a stabilized mode of behavior, as experiments have shown. At the basis of this tendency toward stabilization lies man's capacity to regulate his behavior through conceptual categories.

Therefore, the question of concern to those who are disturbed with the plight of men caught in pressures toward certain molds of conformity should not be evaluation of conformity or nonconformity in the abstract. The first question must be conformity to *what* norm? Answers to this question entail not only the external referent of the behavior but also the context of group relationships in which it occurs and the voluntary or coercive nature of its regulation. Then analysis of the appropriateness or inappropriateness of the norm in question for the situation and in terms of other criteria may begin with an adequate basis. If, on this basis, norms are found inappropriate, a related task becomes that of discovering the processes leading to perpetuation of *dysfunctional* norms—including, notably, interested parties engaged in active efforts to perpetuate these norms.

A closely related task is assessing the demands placed upon the individual by conflicting norms—for example, norms of altruism preached on Sunday and weekday norms for the hard facts of business and professional practice. The existence of mutually conflicting values or norms characteristic of highly differentiated Western societies today—as various social scientists have pointed out—is responsible in no small part for psychological conflict with attendant wear and tear and restlessness so widely reflected in contemporary novels and social science literature.

If, as it would seem, the interdependencies of human development and human groups are becoming increasingly closer and wider in scope, then the analysis demands a flood of light upon the consequences of maintaining obsolete, constrictive norms perpetuated through ethnocentrisms and activities of particularly interested groups. The appropriate changes in norms are, of course, part of the problem of social change (Chapters 20–24). If the social scientist or psychologist backs away from this problem, he is backing away from the course of intellectual history. For good or evil, human relationships and their norms have changed and they will continue to change. The challenge of understanding the process and the directions it takes must be met if we are seriously concerned with man's creative development and larger self-fulfillment. The two are not independent.

11

In-Group
and Intergroup Relations:
Experimental Analysis

Major Topics of the Chapter

Problem of intergroup relations
Definitions of intergroup relations and inter-
  group behavior
Historically important models for intergroup
  hostility
Biological theories evaluated
Individual models: frustration-aggression
Models based on properties of in-groups
National character
Interdisciplinary approach as basis for ex-
  perimental model
Design of the experiments
The validity problem
Experimental conditions in successive
  stages over time
Experimental formation of in-groups
Reversals in friendship choices

Stabilization of organization and norms: consequences in behavior

Experimental production of intergroup conflict

Cognitive indicators of intergroup attitudes

Impact of intergroup conflict on in-group functioning

Experimental reduction of intergroup conflict

Assessment of proposed measures for attitude change

Verifications and extensions of experimental analysis

Representation and adjudication in intergroup conflict

Superordinate goals in the reduction of intergroup conflict

ORIENTATION
TO INTERGROUP RELATIONS

The preceding chapters have concerned interaction among members within a group. This chapter presents a social-psychological analysis of in-group and intergroup relations. Obviously, intergroup relations refer to states of friendship or hostility, cooperation or competition, dominance or subordination, alliance or enmity, peace or war between two or more groups and their respective members. Such relationships between groups have always been important and fateful in human affairs; history books have been written chiefly as their records.

What is not always obvious is that intergroup relations constitute an important class of social stimulus situations with distinctive effects on individual behavior (see Chapter 1). Especially in societies such as the United States, in which cultural and intellectual heritage stresses the importance of individuals and interpersonal relations, we often fail to see that many contacts among individuals are cases of *intergroup* relations. Failing to appreciate the distinctive properties of the in-group and relations between groups, we are then puzzled about failures in communication, misunderstandings, the obstinacy of certain individuals, and other events that would seem

outlandish in the usual give-and-take among members *within* the same group.

Consider the following examples:

Two passengers on a ship are reclining on deck chairs when a fellow passenger strolls by. He stops and admonishes them sharply to stand up when he walks by. (No, they are not soldiers nor he an officer. He was a missionary to Kenya returning to Europe for a furlough. The fellow passengers were African students on their way to England. One of them was J. Kenyatta. See Delf, 1961, p. 74.)

. . .

At a funeral, a young woman approaches her father's sister, greeting her "Hello, auntie!" The older woman tosses her head contemptuously: "Don't call me *auntie!* Call me *missus!*" (A family argument? No. The scene was South Africa where, according to the official *apartheid* policy, the aunt had recently been classified as *white* as long as she did not associate with *colored,* the official classification for her niece. *Time,* May 24, 1963, p. 39.)

Whether an individual is aware of it or not, his personal fortune or misfortune in budgeting his expenditures may reflect the impact of intergroup relations. His success in attaining future goals—the very way he sets these goals—may be affected more by the states of harmony or conflict between groups than any other single condition. In this generation, policy-makers, analysts, and scholars alike tell us that the fate of human beings on this planet depends upon the conduct of relations between groups and between blocs of nations.

The term *intergroup relations* has come to refer to relationships between social units, large or small. Intergroup problems include those among small groups of adolescents in a crowded city slum, the vexing struggles of subordinated peoples within various nations to achieve equal rights, frictions between labor and management groups, and alignments and rivalry among political groups, economic groups, religious groups, and even among nations of the world.

Yet, if there is a *social psychology* of intergroup relations, it should not be altogether different when we consider small groups, ethnic groups, labor and management groups, or nationalities. What may be different, of course, are the sets of factors to be included in our analysis (Chapter 6). In the rivalry between two churches, economic considerations may be very slight, whereas they may dominate labor-management negotiations. This is one reason why a social psychology of intergroup relations has to be *interdisciplinary*. Studies of economics, political science, sociology, anthropology, or history can inform the social psychologist what factors or set of factors are dominant in particular cases of intergroup relations.

In this chapter, in-groups and intergroup relations will be analyzed. Several historically important theories about the causes of social distance, hostility, and negative attitudes (prejudice) between members of different groups will be assessed. The bulk of the chapter will summarize an experimental analysis of in-group formation and intergroup relations. In a series of three experiments, unrelated individuals were brought together; they formed separate groups and then came into contact in conditions conducive to conflict between the groups. Finally, the change of intergroup conflict toward cooperation and friendship is analyzed. At pertinent points, findings from other research will be summarized. Our aim shall be to analyze intergroup relations as they take shape and as they change over time with reference to their impact on the in-groups and the attitudes and behaviors of members.

The next chapter tackles the much more difficult and complex problems of relations among groups with different social power and facilities, among which social distances were established long ago. Encounters among such groups are gripped by the heavy hand of the past, even as the world in which they live changes beyond the belief of former generations.

THE SOCIAL-PSYCHOLOGICAL PROBLEM OF INTERGROUP RELATIONS

Are all states of friendship or hostility, cooperation or competition, attraction or aggression among human beings cases of intergroup relations? Obviously, they are *not*. However, this is not an idle question. Many technically excellent studies of intergroup relations have missed their mark because they were designed without adequate guidelines to distinguish intergroup relations from other human relations.

Let us start with the concepts that have already been defined. Inter*group* relations have something to do with *groups* and their members. The minimum properties of a human group were spelled out in the last several chapters (see the definition of *group* in Chapter 7). By intergroup relations, we ordinarily refer to interaction between such groups or their members, either symbolically or face-to-face. In speaking of intergroup relations, we shall often refer to *functional* relations between groups, by which we mean that the actions by one group and its members have an impact on another group and its members, regardless of whether the two groups are actually engaged in direct give and take at the time. Accordingly, we are prepared for two definitions:

DEF, **Intergroup relations** refer to functional relationships between two or more groups (as defined on p. 131) and their respective members.

Intergroup behavior refers to the actions of individuals belonging to one group when they interact, collectively or individually, with another group or its members in terms of their group membership (with its standards for loyalty, norms, etc.).

A word of caution may be in order. The term "functional" in the definition does not carry any value connotations (good, bad, eufunctional-dysfunctional). It simply means that what each group does makes some difference to the others, at least in the sphere of activities in question.

What do these definitions mean for the study of our problem? They mean that the frame of reference in the study of intergroup attitude and behavior has to include the functional relations between the respective groups, which may be positive or negative. Such relationships have properties that are generated *over time* during interaction between the groups. These properties are not identical with the properties of a group as these affect a member. Intergroup situations are not voids.

Of course, intergroup relations are not entirely independent of the character of organization and norms (values) *within* the groups involved. On the other hand, *the characteristics of functional relations between groups cannot be deduced or extrapolated solely from the properties of relations prevailing among members within the groups in question.*

Modes of behavior that prevail within groups, such as cooperativeness and solidarity, or competitiveness and rivalry to outstrip other members, need not be the prevalent modes of behavior in relations with other groups. At times, hostility toward out-groups may be proportional to the degree of solidarity within the group. Religious and moral values governing life within a group need not be applied in dealings with other groups. Democracy at home need not imply democratic attitudes or dealings abroad.

Historically
Important Models
for Intergroup Relations

Some of the more popular theories about intergroup behavior will be examined because our experimental model has bearing on several of them. Significantly, most of these theories attempt to deal with the origins of intergroup conflict, hostility, and prejudice. For the most part, they are inapplicable to intergroup friendship and co-

operation, which any adequate model should also attempt to handle.

Biological Models

By far the most popular biologically based explanations have been those positing a physiological tendency ("instinct") toward aggression or violence. A number of important writers have adopted this basis for explanations of human affairs, notably Freud (1927, 1930) and more recently Lorenz (1963). Many authorities on animal behavior (e.g., Schneirla, 1946, 1964) have long pointed out that such theories are vastly oversimplified, even for explanation of subhuman relationships. Since about 1950, increased study of animal aggregates in their natural habitats and a series of sophisticated laboratory experiments have documented Schneirla's conclusion.

Is There a Biological Tendency (Instinct) for Animals to Aggress Against Others of Their Species? John Paul Scott (1958, 1969), an authority on experimental study of animal behavior, correctly pointed out that the appropriate biological model for conflict between human groups would be the collective aggression of an animal aggregate toward another aggregate of the same species. Conversely, interspecies aggression is not an appropriate model. A wolf pack that tracks and destroys a deer is thereby getting food. Man not only engages in such predatory behavior but domesticates lower animals for food. Neither event is analogous to the typical cases of conflict among human groups. Scott (1969) concluded that the rest of the animal kingdom simply does not provide an adequate model for human (intraspecies) intergroup relations.

What modern biological studies of animal behavior are showing is that conflict between aggregates of subhuman animals in their natural habitats, while not unknown, is less frequent than commonly presumed. Both in natural and laboratory (or captive) environments, the occurrence of conflict between aggregates of a species varies according to strictly situational (ecological) factors and to past experiences in the life history of the animals in question (Southwick, 1955, 1967). In certain strains of laboratory animals (e.g., rats) the frequency of aggressive responses is consistently higher than in other strains under the same conditions. In all strains, however, early experience plays some part—as do environmental circumstances (overcrowding, food supply, etc.).

Certainly there are physiological correlates to aggressive or violent behavior on the part of any organism. However, what these modern studies show is that a model of animal aggression that is based on biologically inherent tendencies or physiological arousal is inadequate to account for animal behavior, not to speak of the human animal.

Other biological models take into consideration the organism's early experience and the aggregate's activities in specific environments. Notably, it is periodically proposed that the phenomenon of "territoriality" among animals is a direct analogue to human conflict over territory. This analogy is inadequate for several reasons:

1. Not all subhuman animals become attached to territories and defend them by aggressive response to invasion (Scott, 1969).

2. Not all human groups that engage in conflict are territorially based, nor does human conflict always involve disputes over territory.

3. The physiological processes and past events underlying subhuman and human aggression associated with territoriality are vastly different (Schneirla, 1966). Relatively simple chemical, tactual, and visual discriminations by animals detecting unfamiliar species-members on their territory are a far cry from man's conceptualizations of property, a "homeland" or state, and his aggressive defense or craving of them. Man, in fact, is quite capable of territorial loyalty and greed without ever setting eyes on the territory in question. In short, man's conceptual level of functioning dominates his definition of territory and his reactions related to it.

Is Man Innately Aggressive and Destructive? Half a century ago, the model of man frequently included instincts for aggression or pugnacity. Freud, who in his early writings had derived a concept of aggressive behavior from response to early frustra-

tions, developed a human model based on opposing instincts of Eros (sexual instinct) and Thanatos (death instinct: "the task of which is to lead organic matter back into the inorganic state"). These latter instincts were proposed late in Freud's career, when his writing turned more and more to problems of human relations (Freud, 1922, 1927, 1930). In a famous exchange of letters arranged by the International Institute of Intellectual Cooperation of the League of Nations, Freud wrote to Einstein of his views, which were pessimistic in the extreme. Freud had decided that "there is no use in trying to get rid of men's aggressive inclinations" (1950, p. 283). His only positive social proposals were to break up human societies into small communities, "through which the aggressive instinct can find an outlet in enmity towards those outside the group" in a "conveniently and relatively harmless form" (1930, p. 90) and to encourage the education of an "upper stratum of men with independent minds . . . whose business it would be to give direction to the dependent masses" (1950, p. 284). In his letter to Einstein, Freud made his view clear that the masses of mankind were dominated by instinct, and that only a few persons had reached an evolutionary stage in which there is a "constitutional intolerance of war."

Recently, Freud's conception of a death instinct and, in general, an instinctive basis for conflict among human groups have been discredited. A careful review of the experimental work by Berkowitz (1962) concluded: "Research findings offer little support for his [Freud's] reasoning" (p. 24). He noted that the postulation of an innate drive for destruction can be attacked both factually and logically (p. 8).

One body of psychiatrists, the Group for the Advancement of Psychiatry (1964), formally rejected the hypothesis as it applies to warfare: "War is a social institution; it is not inevitably rooted in the nature of man" (p. 188).

These conclusions are supported by studies of the American soldier during World War II (Stouffer *et al.,* 1949). The great majority of soldiers reported that their reason for fighting was "to get the job done" or a desire not to let their outfits down. Only 2 percent said that they fought out of anger, revenge, or "fighting spirit." Another 3 percent gave replies that might be interpreted as aggressive such as "crushing the aggressor," "making a better world," or "belief in what I am fighting for" (p. 109). The men at the front, where expression of aggressive feelings would have been both permissible and in line with their actions, expressed the fewest aggressive feelings of all. Soldiers in training camps, where indoctrination for combat is part of the training, most frequently expressed hatred and aggressive feelings for the enemy.

Individuals Models of Intergroup Hostility

By far the most influential model for intergroup prejudice (negative attitude) and aggression during the past three decades was the frustration-aggression hypothesis (Dollard *et al.,* 1939). The model was based on Freud's formulations in his earlier writings.

Briefly, the model posits that frustration (blocking attainment of a goal) produces aggression, which acts as a drive or motive. If, however, the frustration is produced by a more powerful person (e.g., a parent), the frustrated individual cannot express aggression. Accordingly, in line with the Freudian energy model, the aggression is stored and compounded with each new frustration, ready to be released upon a suitably powerless object. Thus members of other groups, who are seen as less powerful, are suitable targets for aggression and hence become scapegoats for the frustrated members of more powerful groups. According to Freudian theory, the expression of aggression would drain off the accumulation (catharsis).

Another model based on the Freudian formulation posits that repeated frustrations and severe treatments in early childhood produce, in time, an "authoritarian personality" which is rigid, unfriendly, prejudiced toward others different from himself, and prone to violence. In other words, the authoritarian personality is characterized as neurotic and deviant, relative to the bulk of the membership in any human group. Such frustrated and frantically hostile individuals could not possibly conduct the affairs or participate in the consistent modes of inter-

action required for the formation of a group (see Chapter 7).

As these two models are related, it is possible to summarize the research evidence concerning their adequacy for intergroup hostility and conflict in a series of related conclusions:

1. *Aggression is not an invariable response to frustration:* In both animal and human studies, frustration has produced highly variable responses, including submission, regression (to simpler modes of coping), evading the situation, apathy, and forgetting about the episode (e.g., Scott, 1958, pp. 33–35; Himmelweit, 1950).

2. *Many aggressive acts are not instigated by frustrations:* Berkowitz' critical survey of research (1962) led to the unequivocal conclusion that "there *are* some aggressive acts . . . that are not necessarily instigated by frustration" (p. 30). For example, wholesale killing and destruction are initiated as policies during wartime on the basis of deliberate decisions by policymakers who need not be frustrated individuals.

3. *The most frustrated peoples are not necessarily the most aggressive:* Within a society divided by hatred and violence among its groups, the direction of prejudice and hostility is typically from the dominant and mighty groups downward to the downtrodden and deprived (Sherif and Sherif, 1953). Comparisons between societies do not show that the most frustrated are necessarily the more aggressive. As Klineberg (1950, p. 18) correctly pointed out, at the time when lynching of Negroes was not uncommon in the southern United States, white Brazilians were by and large much more frustrated in their attempts to maintain a subsistence level of life and were similarly subjected to the ups-and-downs of economic cycles. However, there were no lynchings of Brazilian Negroes.

4. *The "scapegoat" theory does not explain the targets of aggression:* Theoretically, the most likely targets would be the people most helpless and least likely to retaliate. However, Berkowitz (1962, especially pp. 135–144) found that the most helpless groups are not always the objects of hatred, and not the only ones. He concluded that the "scapegoat theory, as usually formulated is incomplete" (p. 141).

5. *Evidence that frustration experienced within an interpersonal context produces aggressive drives that can be displaced toward out-groups is not sufficient to support the theory:* Berkowitz (1962) concluded that "displacement studies have not yielded consistent results" and notes the lack of systematic attention to the conditions in which such displacement might or might not occur. There is a considerable body of experimental findings on this topic, most of it negative. Amazingly enough, the studies continue to accumulate with very little attention to what may be the crucial condition, namely, whether the frustration is experienced as an individual matter or whether it is seen by members of a group as a common source of frustration (Sherif and Sherif, 1953; Sherif, 1966).

6. *Intergroup behavior is not primarily a problem of deviate behavior:* There is reason to believe that some persons developing under unfortunate life circumstances become more intense in their prejudices and hostilities than other persons sharing these prejudices and hostilities (Hartley, 1946; Hood and Sherif, 1955). But such cases are not the crux of the problem of intergroup relations. The crux of the problem is the existence of prejudices and hostilities and the participation of the bulk of the membership in them—frequently over generations, with complete changes in individual membership. The actual "tests" used to measure the "authoritarian personality" have turned out to reflect the extent to which an individual uncritically accepts the prevailing ideology and prejudices in certain regions and circles of the United States (cf. R. Hartley, 1957). Consequently, the postulated correlations with early childhood frustrations have not stood the test of cross-regional and cross-cultural comparisons (Christie and Garcia, 1951; Christie, 1954). At best, the scales have differentiated among members within a cultural grouping as to the intensity of their prejudices toward culturally established targets, or their willingness to reveal them on paper-and-pencil tests. As Gardner Murphy (1953) concluded on the basis of UNESCO studies in India after the Hindu-Muslim conflicts, being a good member of a group engaged in conflict with another means believing all of the nasty qualities and practices attributed to

the other group by one's own group. The major problem, therefore, is such participation—not the ravings of a few deviate individuals.

Models Based on the Properties of In-Groups Alone

Is Intergroup Hostility an Inevitable Product of In-Group Formation? The sociologist Sumner (1906) observed that the formation of an in-group involves the psychological attachment of members to the group and its values, which become the basis for a particular brand of ethnocentrism. Noting the social distances prevailing among human groups and the hostile reactions by some primitive tribes to any outsider, Sumner suggested that antagonism toward outsiders was a natural byproduct of in-group formation. This view gained wide credence.

In fact, it is a very incomplete view. It neglects the fact that intergroup relations must be established *over time* between groups and that the character of such relations has properties that affect the viewpoints of both groups. It is simply not true that all initial contacts between primitive peoples with one another or with technologically advanced peoples have been hostile. Nor is it true that the course of intergroup relations always follows a predictably hostile course. On the contrary, every group regards some other groups as harmless, if not as friends and allies. Predictability is possible only if the nature of the encounters over time is specified.

Does the Character of Relationships and Norms Within Groups Wholly Determine the Course of Intergroup Relations? A popular educational belief is that the way to produce friendship and cooperation among groups is to foster friendly relations, cooperative activities, and competence within groups. While there can be no objection to such endeavors within groups, it is seriously to be questioned how much transfer to dealings with other groups can be expected.

In studying the juvenile gangs of Chicago many years ago, Thrasher (1927) observed that the height of solidarity and mutual trust among members frequently accompanied their most intense conflicts with other groups. The well-known experiments by

Lewin, Lippitt, and White (1965) on the effects of different styles of adult supervision on atmospheres within boys' clubs included, fortuitously, the occurrence of two intergroup conflicts occasioned by the proximity of the groups in the same room (which was divided by a curtain). In both cases, the conflicts involved groups that had been exposed for some time to "democratic" supervisory style or by the nonauthoritarian, hands-off policy of a "laissez-faire" adult. These were the groups whose behavior within the membership was most cooperative and friendly.

National Character. Another line of theorizing and research with implications for intergroup relations is the study of *national character.* Everyone who has been outside of his own country knows that there are differences in behavior that sometimes coincide with national boundaries. In turn, most peoples are aware of their own, more or less distinctive behavior patterns. However, descriptions and assessments of national character are plagued with the ethnocentrisms of the writers, who typically are aware of the recent or past international behavior of the nation in question before they attempt to analyze cultural norms prevailing among its members. Furthermore, studies within a national culture are based too frequently "not upon the common features of the national culture, but upon an overgeneralized picture of the particular subgroup with which the investigator was most familiar" (Anastasi and Foley, 1949, p. 787).

Nations today, even small ones, are social organizations of great complexity, often encompassing cultural and regional differences, class differences, and linguistic differences. They vary not only in history and culture but in political organization as well. Therefore, at present, it is not at all clear that any study of national character that ignores these differences would have great relevance for understanding the relations of that nation with others. In any event, international alignments in recent history have occurred among nations with very different cultural backgrounds. Within various countries, men with the same or similar backgrounds have engaged in bloody civil wars. The history of intergroup relations contains strange bedfellows if we look only at cultural similarities and differences.

The limitations of models attempting to deal with intergroup relations on the basis of strictly in-group considerations is immediately evident when we turn to the problems of war. L. F. Richardson (1950) compiled statistics on the number of wars engaged in by the great powers from 1850 to 1941, that is, the United States' entry into World War II. Britain headed the list with twenty wars—more than the Japanese (nine), Germans (eight), or the United States (seven). Explanations of German aggression during World War II were frequently based on characteristics of German culture (authoritarian family and education, mythology, etc.). Do these statistics indicate that in fact British culture was more authoritarian, its myths more warlike, or that individual Britishers were, by virtue of the national character, more frustrated than the Germans? Or does it not seem reasonable to ask whether having a mighty empire with far-flung interests to be protected and expanded had something to do with the high frequency of warfare involving the British?

Since World War II, the United States has been actively involved in two major wars (Korea and Viet Nam) and in a number of small conflicts. Does this involvement simply reflect the national character of the American people? Does it have anything to do with the permissive or restrictive upbringing of individual boys in Pennsylvania, Oklahoma, or California? These are questions that need to be faced by those who seek general theories of intergroup relations on the basis of characteristics of the culture or practices within a group.

THE INTERDISCIPLINARY EXPERIMENTAL MODEL

Any experiment is, necessarily, a miniature and stripped-down model of the actualities it purports to analyze. The experiments reported here and the hypotheses tested were constructed on the basis of extensive surveys of the literature on in-group and intergroup relations (Sherif, 1948; Sherif and Sherif, 1953). Three separate experiments were conducted, each lasting approximately three weeks, in different locations and with different subjects (Sherif, 1951, 1966; Sherif and Sherif, 1953; Sherif, White, and Harvey, 1955; Sherif *et al.,* 1961). The analysis in this chapter presents a composite picture of the three studies, the source being specified when it is feasible without confusing the account.

The first experiment was conducted in Connecticut in 1949; the second in upstate New York in 1953; and the third at Robbers Cave, Oklahoma, in 1954. The hypotheses about group formation and intergroup conflict were formulated prior to the first experiment. All other hypotheses were formulated and distributed to colleagues prior to the 1953 experiment (see Sherif, 1967, Chapter 22).

General Design
of the Experiments

In order to test the formulations on the nature of intergroup behavior, each of the experiments started with the selection of individuals with *no* previous interpersonal relationships. In addition, as we shall see, subjects were chosen very carefully to rule out the explanation of results on the basis of alternative hypotheses.

In order to control the conditions in which these unattached individuals interacted, the experiments were conducted in

Table 11.1.   Sequence of Successive Stages in Intergroup Experiments

	Experiment		
Stage	I	II	III
In-group formation			
Spontaneous interpersonal choices	X	X	
Arbitrary division into 2 matched sets according to specified criteria	X	X	X
Intergroup Conflict			
Win-lose competition	X	X	X
Planned frustration of in-groups	X	X	
Reduction of conflict			
Common enemy, individual activities, adult intervention	X		
Contact without interdependence	X		X
Series of superordinate goals			X

isolated camp sites completely at the disposal of the research program. The experimental conditions were then varied systematically in successive periods or stages, starting with conditions conducive to the formation of distinct in-groups and then proceeding to the study of intergroup relations. Table 11.1 presents a guide to the sequence in each of the experiments.

Choice of Subjects

Because the experiments were performed at camp sites, subjects were selected who would find camping both natural and absorbing for the duration of the experiments, without great interest in outside activities. Pre-adolescent boys were selected (11–12 years old).

In order as far as possible to eliminate alternative explanations for events that would transpire in the experiments, the selection procedures were careful and prolonged. Interviews were held with each boy's teachers, school officials, and family. School and medical records were studied, and when available, scores on psychological tests. In the Connecticut experiment, each boy was interviewed and tested by a clinical psychologist. In the Robbers Cave experiment, each boy was observed in natural give-and-take with agemates in the playground and in his neighborhood.

As a result of these methods of selection, the following alternative bases for explaining the results were eliminated:

1. *Previous acquaintance or personal ties among the boys.* Boys were chosen from different schools and neighborhoods to eliminate this possibility.

2. *Excessive personal frustration situations in past history, unstable family ties, or neurotic tendencies.* Boys were chosen from stable families with both parents living in the home (no broken homes). They were healthy, well adjusted in school and neighborhood, making normal progress in their school grades, and with no past records of presenting behavior problems. Members of minority groups who might have suffered social discrimination were not included.

3. *Pronounced differences in social background or physical appearance.* All subjects were selected from stable, white Protestant families from the middle socio-

economic level. The religious backgrounds represented in a given experiment were from the most similar Protestant groups (e.g., Episcopalian and Congregationalists in Connecticut; Methodist and Baptist in Oklahoma). Intelligence test scores were all well within the normal range, the means in the experiments all being slightly above 100. In appearance, the boys displayed the normal range of individual differences within such highly selected samples. In size, they were more nearly homogeneous than boys a year or two older, when the adolescent acceleration in growth frequently produces wide variations. In dividing the sample arbitrarily into two for the study of group formation, the two sets were matched as nearly as possible in terms of size, skills and interests. The number of subjects in each experiment was between 20 and 24.

Methods
of Data Collection:
The Validity Problem

The primary method of data collection was observation and ratings made by trained observers at the end of each day. Safeguards were taken to insure the reliability and validity of findings:

(1) A *combination* of observation and other methods of data collection guarded against "researcher bias" or selectivity in reporting results.

(2) The experiments continued over sufficient time to permit *regularities* or repetitions of events to occur.

(3) The "demand character" of the research situation (see "Social Psychology of the Psychological Experiment," pp. 112 ff.) was eliminated by not making subjects aware that data were being collected or that the sequence of events occurred in line with an experimental plan.

Combination of Data-Gathering Methods. Observers were instructed to avoid making notes in the presence of subjects, except when the task fit into ongoing events (for example, when a list was being made or votes counted). Otherwise, they quickly made notes and symbols surreptitiously, each night expanding these into running accounts of major activities and events of the day. Similarly, each night they made

ratings of the developing relationships among the boys in terms of *effective initiative* (status, see p. 140). To check these ratings, independent ratings were made by observers not familiar with the groups in situations in which the groups were engaged in lively interaction. Sociometric choices (p. 173) were obtained from the subjects themselves in individual interviews that appeared to be casual conversations. At choice points, in order to obtain independent numerical evidence related to observations, laboratory-like techniques were introduced to assess attitudes through judgment tasks. In short, if the observer was not merely selecting events in line with the hypotheses, this fact would be indicated by an agreement between his observations and ratings with the independent methods of data collection.

Recurrence Over Time. A major weakness of much experimentation in social psychology has been excessive reliance on single behavioral events within the confines of a brief experimental situation. In our experiments, it was possible to collect data from observations and ratings over extended time periods. The recurrence of expressions of attitude and of other deeds both in the observers' reports and in observations by unattached members of the research staff became, therefore, a fundamental advantage in guarding against artifact and observer bias.

Eliminating the Unaccounted Factors in the Social Psychology of the Psychological Experiment. Although research into "demand characteristics" of the research situation had not been undertaken seriously at the time, the entire conception of these experiments was conditioned by the concern to avoid arousing the awareness of being a "subject." Every precaution was taken to make the entire experience as natural as possible from the moment the experiments began. All research staff appeared in the roles of personnel in a usual camp situation: senior counselors (observers), junior counselors (assistants), camp director, handyman, and so on.

All other methods of data collection were introduced as part of the natural flow of events—for example, as informal conversations, as games, or as staff efforts to improve the camp. The sequence of experimental conditions, with one exception, appeared to the boys as changes produced by their own expressed wishes or as events external to the control of the staff and the boys alike. The one exception in the first two experiments was the arbitrary division of the boys after they had started to form interpersonal preferences.

Available evidence during the experiments and, in a few instances, interviews afterwards indicate that the experiments were viewed by the subjects as entirely natural camp situations, the sequence of events arising as they do in real life. During the 1953 experiment, after intergroup conflict had begun, an experimental manipulation was seen by the subjects as the doings of the staff. That experiment was, therefore, terminated as a research study at that point.

Experimental Conditions
in the Successive Stages

Experimental conditions for each successive stage were defined in terms of the *properties* of problem situations, space, and facilities that the subjects faced. (See the section on sets of factors in a social situation, Chapter 6.) In other words, once the individuals were selected by the criteria noted, the research variables were the locations, facilities, and tasks faced by the boys. Strong motivational concern for these problem situations was insured in two ways:

(1) *Reliance on knowledge of the cultural backgrounds of the boys:* Camping, competitive sports and concern with "stacking up" relative to agemates are important aspects of life for boys of this age in the general culture. We see that the general cultural setting in which the experiments were undertaken had its impact on both the design and the behavior of boys within the experiments. In another culture, these concerns might very well be less weighty or lacking among the same age group.

(2) *Knowledge of the specific interests and preferences of the particular boys was obtained prior to and during the experiments themselves.* Sports in general and group competition in particular ranked high for these boys, as illustrated by the rank of preferences for subjects in the Connecticut experiment.

Team Activities		Others	
Softball	20	Hiking	20
Football	14	Swimming	13
Soccer	12	Fishing	9
Volleyball	5	Ping-pong	7

"Horseshoes" was named by five boys and several other activities were mentioned by four or fewer boys.

All problem situations were selected to be highly appealing and to meet the criteria for testing the hypotheses of the particular stage in which they were introduced. These criteria are stated in the hypotheses for each stage. By manipulation of objects and facilities and by timing, it was possible to introduce the procedures with a minimum of verbal instruction. Research staff was instructed, in general, to refrain from initiating or directing activities in the problem situations. Instead, they were to give free rein to the boys in meeting the problem and were to give assistance or advice when requested by the boys. Once an activity was started, the observer was to lend assistance as needed to complete it in line with plans the boys had made. Every effort was made so that the introduction of problem activities and the flow of interpersonal interaction were as natural as possible.

EXPERIMENTAL FORMATION
OF IN-GROUPS

In order to test the hypothesis that in-groups would form on the basis of stated experimental conditions, the criteria of subject selection were used to eliminate certain alternatives—for example, that groups might form on the basis of differences in social, religious, or economic background. Still another alternative was eliminated as the first step in the 1949 and 1953 experiments, namely, that the formation of in-groups was wholly or in part a function of the attraction of like-minded individuals that would have occurred without the experimental conditions.

Spontaneous Interpersonal Choices. In the first two experiments, the boys arrived at the site together, were all housed in one large bunkhouse, and, initially, were entirely free to choose companions in the activities, all of which were campwide.

Within two or three days, smaller clusters of budding friendship groups were observed, composed of two to four boys each. (One of the more prominent called themselves the "Three Musketeers.") Each boy was then asked informally who his best friends were in the camp (sociometric choices). Then the budding clusters were arbitrarily split to compose two cabins, so that about two-thirds of the best friends were in different cabins. That is, in each cabin, about two-thirds of the occupants had not chosen each other. The arbitrary division was not greeted with universal joy, as one might imagine. Therefore, each cabin was allowed to go at once on an overnight hike and camp-out, something that all of them wanted to do.

Hypothesis: **When individuals participate in the formation of different groups, their spontaneous interpersonal choices will be reversed in favor of fellow members.**

Following the period of group formation (*see below*), the boys were again asked to name their best friends—specifying that they were free to choose from the entire camp. Table 11.2 gives the data from the Connecticut study, showing that the hypothesis was supported. The procedures were replicated in 1953 with similar results.

Conclusions and Implications. The findings permitted the conclusion that groups formed on the basis of the experimental conditions, not primarily as the result of spontaneous attraction among like-minded persons. More than half of the initial choices of friends shifted from strictly spontaneous personal choices toward friendship within the in-group. These findings may have implications about the choice of friends and personal associates in daily life.

It is a popular notion that friends are chosen strictly according to personal preferences. The results show that such personal preferences are bounded in a significant fashion by the formation of an in-group. Consequently, the use of the "personal preference" as a slogan to exclude individuals which is practiced by certain organized groups (cf. Lee, 1955) is misleading. It turns out to be freedom to choose friends within the exclusionist rules for membership established by the organization.

Stage of Group Formation

This stage of the experiments started when subjects were divided into two bunches, matched as closely as possible in terms of size and skills of individuals composing them. The Robbers Cave experiment (1954) started at this point, the boys arriving on two separate buses and settling into cabins at a considerable distance. Contact between the two groups was not made until the next stage in the experiment. This procedure was not only more natural but also permitted assessment of the possible effects of relations between the cabin groups in the previous studies upon group formation. It successfully showed that intergroup contacts were not essential to the formation of in-groups.

Hypothesis: **When a number of individuals without previously established relationships interact in conditions that embody goals with common appeal value and that require their interdependent activity for attainment, over time, a group will form. The formation of a group will be reflected in:**
(a) **a definite group organization consisting of differentiated status positions and roles, and**

Table 11.2.   Reversal of Friendship Choices Before and After Group Formation

| | Persons (%) choosing from: | | | | | |
| | Group A | | | Group B | | |
Persons chosen in:	Before	After	Difference	Before	After	Difference
Group A	35.1	95.0	59.9	65.0	12.3	−52.7
Group B	64.9	5.0	−59.9	35.0	87.7	52.7

(b) norms regulating the members' behavior relative to one another and in activities commonly engaged in together.

During this stage (about a week), the boys engaged in many activities, but their common criteria were that they were (a) highly appealing and (b) required interdependent activity in order to reach a common goal. For example, they included camping out in the woods, cooking meals, improving a swimming place, cleaning up a rough field for athletics, transporting canoes placed near their cabins over rough terrain to the water, and various organized and informal games.

With the research staff instructed not to take initiative or to execute tasks, the experimental conditions meant that the boys faced many problem situations in play and in work that required all of their efforts. They did pool their efforts, organized duties, and divided tasks in work and in play. In the various activities, different individuals assumed different responsibilities and came to be known for certain skills or personal characteristics. One excelled in cooking. Another led in athletics. One often horsed around. Others, not outstanding in any particular skill, could be counted on to pitch in and do their level best in anything the group attempted. One or two boys seemed to disrupt activities, to start teasing at the wrong moment, to push others around, to offer useless suggestions, or to "goof off" when there was work to be done. On the other hand, a few boys consistently had good suggestions, needed skills, or showed ability to coordinate the activities without getting on others' nerves.

Thus, over time, the shifting and changing patterns of interpersonal relations from activity to activity and from day to day began to stabilize. As noted in outlining the process of group formation (Chapter 8) one boy in each group began to rank highest in the exercise of effective initiative across situations, frequently with the close assistance of one or two others of high rank. Some boys were sifted toward the bottom of the emerging structure while others jockeyed for higher positions of respect and influence.

An example of events during this period may clarify the process: During a hike in the woods, the boys started to get hungry. They had been supplied with unprepared food. One boy started to build a fire, asking help in getting wood. Another attacked the raw hamburger to make patties. Others prepared a place to put buns, relishes, and utensils. Two mixed soft drinks from flavoring and sugar. One boy stood around without helping and was told by several others to "get to it." Shortly the fire was blazing and the cook had hamburgers sizzling. As soon as they became browned, two boys distributed them to others. Several took turns pouring the drink. Soon the cook had eaten and it was time for the watermelon. A boy already ranked low in status took a knife and started toward the melon. Several boys protested. The most highly regarded boy took the knife and started to cut the melon, saying: "You guys who yell the loudest get yours last."

At the end of each day, the relative positions according to effective initiative were rated by the observer, with supporting evidence from his observations. When his ratings were fairly stable (reliable) for two or three days in a row, an independent rater was brought to watch the group for part of a day as they engaged in typical activities. Finally, sociometric choices were obtained informally. Thus, the reliability of observations could be checked by two independent methods. The rank-order correlations among these measures were significantly high in every case. As noted in Chapter 8, the 1953 experiment included the additional check of a judgment task, in which each boy estimated the performance of others in his group, with the result that errors in estimate were significantly correlated with relative status (Sherif, White, and Harvey, 1955).

In short, group structures did emerge in line with the hypotheses in each of the experiments. They were not all identical. In some groups, the leader-follower structure was very steep, while in others the psychological distance between leader and follower was less and the structure was more tightly knit.

Formation of Group Products and Norms. Each group did develop distinctive ways of doing things, as well as customs and notions of propriety. Perhaps the most striking contrasts occurred in the Robbers Cave

a.

b.

c.

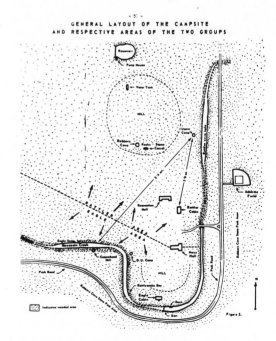

d.

Fig. 11.1. Isolated sites, ample space and wide distribution of facilities in group experiments permitted experimental controls. **a.** View of site for Connecticut experiment (1949). **b.** Camp grounds and buildings, Connecticut experiment. **c.** View from cliff above Robbers Cave shows boys in the isolated site for 1954 experiment. **d.** Layout of campsites in 1954 experiment showing respective areas for two groups before their first encounter. Note location of water tank and reservoir.

234

a.

b.

c.

d.

Fig. 11.2. Stage of in-group formation, Connecticut experiment. **a.** Red Devils relax after hike and cook-out in woods. **b.** Red Devils leave campground for expedition in the wilds, led by their daring leader (Baby Face). **c.** Quiet moment for Bull Dogs after tents are finally pitched. **d.** Bull Dogs at pond which they continually worked to improve by removing stones, thereby raising water level.

a.

b.

c.

d.

Fig. 11.3. Stage of in-group formation, Robbers Cave: Rattlers. **a.** Example of problem situation requiring coordination: carrying a canoe to swimming hole at their hideout. **b.** Rattlers practice tent pitching. **c.** Reading a clue on Treasure Hunt: winning the prize depended upon everyone's reading clues and searching together. **d.** Evening entertainment was up to the Rattlers. Here they give skits for one another in Stone Corral.

a.

c.

b.

d.

Fig. 11.4. Stage of in-group formation, Robbers Cave: Eagles. **a.** Eagles carrying canoe and equipment to their hideout. **b.** Part of equipment carried to Eagle hideout: heavy rope for construction of bridge over "Moccasin Creek" (their name for stream). **c.** Eagles hit the trail with double loads for overnight hike. **d.** An Eagle slicing meat at quick lunch; others have already opened and distributed other supplies.

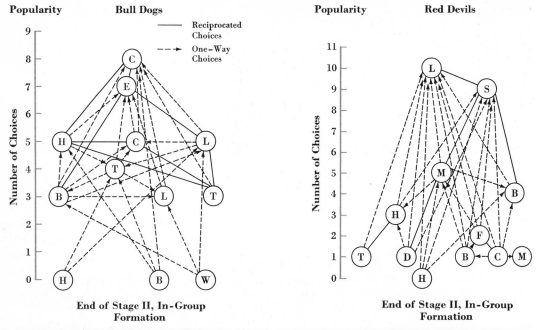

Fig. 11.5. Sociograms of friendship choices made by Bull Dogs (*left*) and Red Devils (*right*) at end of in-group formation.

experiment, in which one group cultivated a norm of "toughness" to the point that the adult staff had to watch out for signs of injury, as the boys would not even bother to treat cuts and scratches, much less show signs of hurt. The other group did not develop such a norm, but did come to dwell on being "good" in conventional terms (*not* swearing, showing consideration, etc.). This norm was dramatically evident when the two groups came into contact. The "good" group huddled in prayer before every contest (praying, of course, to defeat the opposition), while the other delighted in openly rowdy behavior and swearing.

As the group became an organization, the boys coined nicknames for one another. The blond and hardy leader of one group was dubbed "Baby Face" by his admiring followers, in recognition of his good looks and the toughness associated with that title from the well-known gangster of yesteryear. A boy with a rather long head became "Lemon Head." The gay and game athlete in another group was "Horrible Hunt." Each group developed its own jargon, special jokes, secrets, special ways of performing tasks, and preferred places. For example, in 1954, one group killed a snake near their

swimming place, named the place "Moccasin Creek" and thereafter preferred that swimming hole, even though others were better.

Wayward members who failed to do things "right" or who did not contribute their bit to the common effort found themselves receiving reprimands, ridicule, "silent treatment," or even threats (group sanctions). A boy who tried to "bully" others was successfully squelched, despite his greater size. By the end of the stage, however, most behavior in the group was in accord with the customary *modus operandi* that had been established, with very little need for frequent correctives. Some groups established standardized means for handling behavior that got "out of line." For example, the penalty in the Bull Dog group (1949) was to remove a specified number of stones from their swimming hole, which both punished the offender and succeeded in raising the water level. This sanction was administered by the leader with the consent of the membership.

Eventually, each of the groups in these studies took names for themselves. Some of these names were coined during this stage, although a few of the groups took names for themselves only after they had learned the other group had one. In the 1949 Connecticut study, the two groups called themselves the Red Devils and the Bull Dogs. In the 1953 experiment, they were the Panthers and the Pythons. The groups in the 1954 experiment called themselves the Rattlers and the Eagles.

In each case, the choice of name was made by the boys; however, they reflect the environment and situational factors in interesting ways. In 1949 the groups were assigned colors to differentiate them, and the "blue" group adopted the name "Bull Dog" from nearby Yale University, whose color was blue. Both sets of names in the other experiments reflect the surrounding terrain. The Rattlers and Eagles were located in the hills of southeast Oklahoma near a famous hideaway for outlaws, where there were numerous specimens of both rattlesnakes and large birds.

Conclusions. As the choice of subjects and the preceding stage of spontaneous friendship choices minimized other alternatives, it was concluded on the basis of three experiments that interdependent activities directed toward goals of high appeal value are a sufficient condition for group formation.

In the Robbers Cave experiment, groups formed despite the fact that each was unaware of the presence of another group in the site. Along with the developing organizations, local customs, and valued objects (the criteria for group formation), each manifested signs of "we" feeling and pride in joint accomplishments that mark an in-group.

In the two earlier experiments, comparison between "we" and "they" were evident almost from the beginning, with the edge typically given to one's own group, but without hostility toward the other. As soon as the Rattlers and Eagles discovered each other's presence at Robbers Cave, they eagerly challenged each other to competitive sports, each confident in their own victory.

Although isolated from currents of ordinary life by the experiment, the groups that formed inevitably reflected the general culture and surroundings of which they were parts. Even though experimentally pro-duced, the groups were not closed systems. As the next stages showed, no group structure is impenetrable from influences outside of it.

INTERGROUP RELATIONS: CONFLICT

Because the major challenge of intergroup relations is conflict and how to change intergroup hostility once it has taken root, the experimental analysis of intergroup relations began with tests of hypotheses concerning conditions sufficient for the production of intergroup conflict, and the rise of hostile attitudes and negative images (stereotypes). The hypotheses tested were as follows:

Hypotheses
1. When members of two groups come into contact with one another in a series of activities that embody goals which each urgently desires, but which can be attained by one group only at the expense of the other, competitive activity toward the goal changes, over time, into hostility between the groups and their members.
2. In the course of such competitive interaction toward a goal available only to one group, unfavorable attitudes and images (stereotypes) of the out-group come into use and are standardized, placing the out-group at a definite _social distance_ from the in-group.
3. Conflict between two groups tends to produce an increase in solidarity _within_ the groups.
4. The heightened solidarity and pride in the group will be reflected in overestimation of the achievements by fellow group members and lower estimates of the achievements by members of the out-group.
5. Relations between groups that are of consequence to the groups in question, including conflict, tend to produce changes in the organization and practices _within_ the groups.

Prior to this stage, neither of the groups had had encounters as groups in the 1954 experiment. Although acquainted with individual boys in the other group and aware that there was another group, the boys in the two earlier studies were engaged in activities separately throughout the group formation stage. In the Robbers Cave experiment, the two groups were not even

Rattlers - End of Stage 2

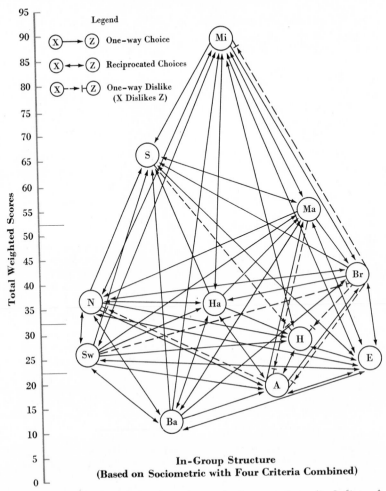

Fig. 11.6. Sociograms based on four criterion questions (including effective initiative) to Rattlers (**a**) (*above*) and Eagles (**b**) (*opposite page*) following intergroup friction.

aware of each other's presence until just prior to this stage.

The main conditions for this stage were established readily by arranging a tournament of games as though acceding to the boys' requests to engage in team sports. The series of events included baseball, touch football, tug of war, a treasure hunt, tent pitching, skits, and cabin inspection—the latter activities being included to permit the manipulation of points by the research staff to insure that the competition would be fairly close. Prizes were offered to the tournament winners as a group: a trophy as well as highly prized knives to each individual member. A large poster with drawings of

two thermometers was used to record the cumulative score of each group daily.

In each experiment, the tournament started with great zest and in the spirit of good sportsmanship to which these American boys had already been thoroughly indoctrinated. In each case, as the tournament progressed from event to event, the good sportsmanship and good feeling began to evaporate. The sportsman-like cheer for the other group, customarily given after a game, "2-4-6-8, who do we appreciate," turned to a derisive chant: "2-4-6-8, who do we appreci-*hate*."

In 1949, the Red Devils began to slip behind in the competition, thereupon accusing

Eagles - End of Stage 2

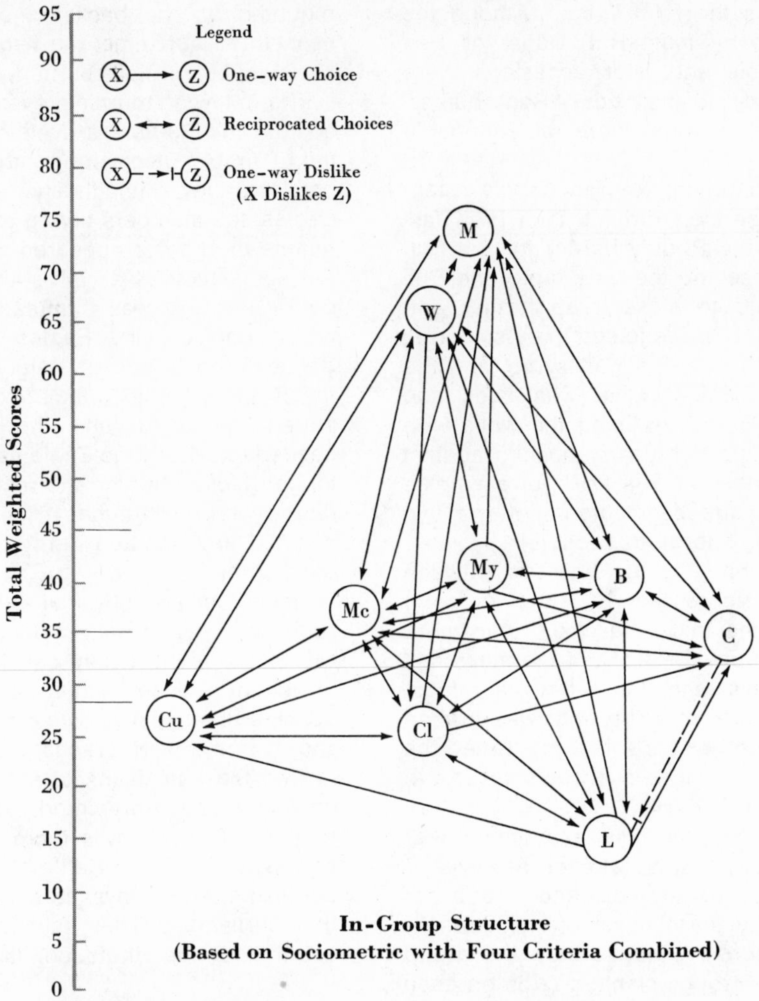

95
90
85
80
75
70
65
60
55
50
45
40
35
30
25
20
15
10
5
0
Total Weighted Scores
Legend
One-way Choice
Reciprocated Choices
One-way Dislike
(X Dislikes Z)
M
W
My
B
Mc
C
Cu
Cl
L

In-Group Structure
(Based on Sociometric with Four Criteria Combined)

the Bull Dogs of being "dirty players" and "cheats" ("At least we play fair."). The victorious Bull Dogs were elated, happy, self-content, and full of pride. The losing Red Devils were dejected. Chiefly because their leader became vindictive, blaming defeat on low-status members of his own group, their loss was conducive to signs of disorganization. Low-status Red Devils resented the accusations, and there was conflict within the group until later the Red Devils faced broadside attacks from the Bull Dogs.

Planned Frustration of In-Groups. This contest was followed by a party proposed by the staff to let "bygones be bygones" between the groups. Although each group claimed that the bad feelings between them were strictly the fault of the other group, both agreed to come. This party involved a frustrating situation planned by the staff so that it appeared to be caused by one group. It led to further frustrations *experienced in common by group members.*

The refreshments were placed on a table. Half were crushed and unappetizing; half were whole and delectable. By careful timing (which was not suspected by the subjects), the Red Devils arrived first. When told to take their share of the refreshments, they took the good half and sat down to enjoy it. When the Bull Dogs arrived a short time later and saw the sorry-looking refreshments left them, they immediately protested. The Red Devils justified their actions with "first come, first served," which became the standardized justification for all Red Devils. The Bull Dogs proceeded to eat their refreshments, hurling taunts, insults, and names at the Red Devils. Particularly common was the term "pigs." Among the names used by most Bull Dogs for Red Devils on this and later occasions were "pigs," "dirty bums," or "Red bums," "jerks," and several more objectionable terms.

The next morning the Red Devils retaliated by deliberately dirtying their breakfast table to make K.P. duty harder for the Bull Dogs. Upon seeing the dirty table, the Bull Dogs decided to mess it up further and leave it. All Bull Dogs joined in by smearing the table with cocoa, sugar, syrup, and the like, and leaving it alive with bees and wasps. The Bull Dogs hung the walls with threatening and derogatory posters against the Red Devils. (See Fig. 11.7b for examples of posters made by members of the two groups during intergroup friction.)

At lunch that day the hostility between the groups increased to such a point throughout the meal that they soon were lined-up on opposite sides of the mess hall calling names and then throwing food, cups, tableware, etc. The fight was broken up. Neither group was sure who started the fight, but each was sure it was someone in the *other* group.

At this point, the 1949 experiment was over. The conflict was not over, however. It took another two days of genuine and active efforts by the staff, involving "preaching" and coercion, just to stop the group fighting. The groups planned raids on each other's cabins. Green apples were collected and hoarded by both groups for "ammunition," with the explanation that this was done merely "in case" it might be needed. The Red Devils attempted "sneak" attacks when the other group and counselors were asleep. (The Red Devils had tended to show signs of disorganization after their defeat in the competitions. In this period the group was again united.) This fighting and raiding between groups took on a planned character. They were not merely outbursts upon momentary encounters of individuals.

Spontaneous Frustration of In-Groups. In the Robbers Cave experiment, a series of mutually frustrating situations arose in the natural course of tournament events. On the first day of the tournament, the Eagles were defeated in a tug of war. When the Rattlers left the field, one Eagle suggested that they take down the Rattler flag, which was

mounted on the backstop of the athletic field. In a short time, the flag was not only removed but partially burned.

The following morning, events were timed so that the Rattlers arrived on the athletic field first. Discovering their defamed emblem, they immediately denounced the Eagles, the members crying for revenge the minute the Eagles appeared on the field. At the suggestion of a high-status member, a cooler strategy was formulated: First, they would confront the Eagles with the evidence. If the Eagles gave signs of guilt, then the Rattlers would attack. The Eagles admitted the deed, and the Rattlers succeeded in seizing the Eagle flag. The Eagles fought back, grabbing the remaining Rattler flag in turn. Through it all, the groups scuffled and shouted derogatory names at each other.

Name calling, physical encounters and raids followed in succession. The Rattlers raided the Eagle cabin, causing quite a bit of inconvenience, some destruction, and considerable frustration among Eagles. As shown in the photographs, the Rattlers displayed the blue jeans of the Eagle leader, on which they had painted "The Last of the Eagles." The raid was reciprocated by the Eagles, who left the Rattlers' cabin in great confusion. A few days later, the Rattlers lost the tournament. Their raid on the Eagles' cabin made the others look like mild affairs.

Systemic Differences in Judgment as a Function of Intergroup Relations

Estimations of Time by In-Groups on the Verge of Victory and Defeat. The psychological effects of the differing experiences and viewpoints of in-groups engaged in rivalry were exemplified in the second tug of war. The Rattlers had won the first contest, whereupon the Eagles had burned the Rattler flag. On the next day, after the conflicts described above, the Eagles devised a strategy to win the second tug of war. On a prearranged signal, the Eagles all sat down on the ground and dug in their feet. The confident Rattlers were pulling strenuously in an upright position, but rapidly losing ground and becoming exhausted. After seven minutes, the Rattlers adopted the enemy strategy and dug in too (Fig. 11.11).

Tired by their initial pull in a standing position, the Rattlers were being pulled gradually across the line when the staff announced that the contest would be terminated in another 15 minutes. At the end of this period, the Rattlers were still not all across the line and the contest was declared a tie. The Eagles were indignant but the Rattlers were relieved and satisfied. The Rattlers accused the Eagles of employing a dirty strategy. Privately they remarked that it seemed that the contest would never end. The Eagles, on the other hand, were overheard to remark to one another that the precious time flew too fast on the verge of their victory.

On the day following the contest, observers of each group asked the members of their respective groups individually, "How long did the tug of war last after both groups had sat down and dug in?" The actual duration was 48 minutes. Figure 11.14 represents the range of individual estimates given by Eagles and by Rattlers. There was no overlap at all among the estimates made by the two groups. The Eagles gave their judgments in minutes (20–45), while the Rattlers gave theirs in hours (1–3½).

Systematic Errors in Judgment of In-Group and Out-Group Performance. In order to check observations of the tendency to deprecate the achievements of the adversary and magnify the achievements of the in-group, judgments in a laboratory-like task were obtained at the end of this stage in 1954. The experiment within the experiment was introduced as a game, with a cash prize offered to the group which could both win the game and judge its outcome most accurately. The game was bean toss, in which the aim is to collect as many beans scattered on the ground as possible within a limited time. Each person collected beans in a sack with a restricted opening, so that he could not count the number of beans he collected.

The judgment task was made unstructured by exposing through an opaque projector the beans purportedly collected by each individual for a brief time and in random arrangements. Actually, thirty-five beans were exposed each time—a number sufficiently large that it could not be counted in the time available. After each

exposure, each person wrote down his estimate of the number. Each collection of beans was identified as the collection of a member of the in-group or out-group. Figure 11.15c shows the results in terms of the average errors in judgment (from 35) of the performance of the in-group and out-group.

As the figure shows, the members of each group, on the average, overestimated the number of beans collected by fellow group members and made significantly lower estimates of the detested out-group's performance. The tendency to overestimate was much greater for the Eagles, who had been the victors in the tournament, than for the Rattlers, who had been declared the losers.

Negative Stereotypes of the Out-Group Contrasted with the Glorious In-Group. In another check on observations, members of each group were asked to rate their fellow group members and the members of the out-group on a number of personal qualities, of which six were critical. The critical six were terms actually used by the boys in referring to their own group or the out-group during the height of friction. Three were favorable (*brave, tough, friendly*) and three were unfavorable (*sneaky, smart alecks, stinkers*). Each adjective was rated using a five-step scale ranging from "all of them are . . ." to "none of them are. . . .".

Ratings of fellow group members were almost exclusively favorable in both groups (100 percent by Rattlers and 94.3 percent by Eagles). On the other hand, ratings of the out-group were predominantly unfavorable. Categorically unfavorable ratings of the out-group were made in 76.9 percent of the Eagles' judgments and 53 percent of the Rattlers.

Closing Ranks and Heightened Solidarity of In-Groups. Although the sociometric choices obtained at the end of this stage explicitly encouraged choice from the entire camp, the boys made choices almost exclusively within their own groups. After the tournament, the members of each group found the others so distasteful that they expressed strong preferences to have no further contact with them at all. In short, in-group exclusiveness was accompanied by extreme social distance between groups.

The net effect of intergroup conflict can be illustrated best by a test situation near the end of the stage of intergroup conflict in

Figs. 11.7–11.13. Through analysis of the necessary and sufficient conditions for hostility, prejudice, and violence between groups, the experimental conditions during the intergroup conflict stage embodied the essentials (see formulation of theory of conflict, pp. 268–269). In brief, the conditions embodied mutually conflicting goals and mutual frustration *as group members.*

a.

Fig. 11.7. Connecticut experiment: Intergroup competition for mutually exclusive goals led in time to glorification of in-group and derogation of out-group, as predicted. **a.** Tug of war: one of the competitive events whose winner would receive all the prizes as a group. **b.** Posters constructed by Red Devils and Bull Dogs revealing growing glorification of in-group and degradation of out-group. (See opposite page.)

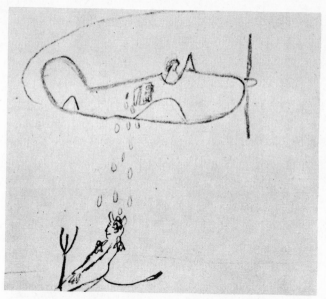

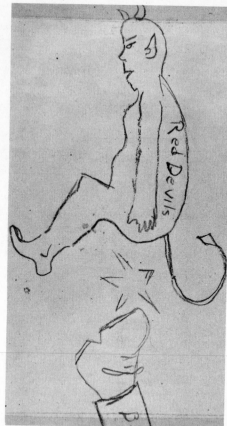

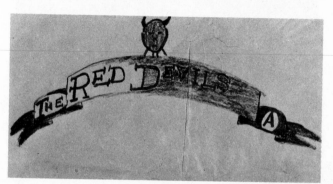

a.

Fig. 11.8. Following the planned frustration of one group ostensibly by the other, actual outbreaks occurred. **a.** The Red Devils' table smeared with food by Bull Dogs. **b.** Raids on each others' cabins became the thing to do.

a.

Fig. 11.9. Apples growing in campgrounds were collected by both Red Devils and Bull Dogs "in case we need them." **a.** Although expressly forbidden, Red Devils went on a trip for ammunition. Both Red Devils and Bull Dogs planned such expeditions as well as raids, contrary to the camp ruling. **b.** Ammunition dumps accumulated secretly by Bull Dogs and Red Devils.

a.

b.

c.

d.

e.

Fig. 11.10. In Robbers Cave experiment (1954), Rattlers and Eagles had their first contact just prior to stage of intergroup conflict. **a.** Rattlers hang banner on backdrop of playing field, which they had improved and considered "theirs." **b.** Eagles arrive at field for first contest as Rattlers look them over. **c.** The two groups eye each other across the playing field. **d.** Eagles around their banner in prayer huddle, their ritual before each contest. **e.** Rattlers developed norms of toughness and rowdiness. Here they boldly march with banners near area where Eagles (background at left) are huddled in quieter pursuit.

a.

b.

Fig. 11.11. The second tug of war, to which the previously defeated Eagles came with prearranged strategy to "dig in" (see text). a. Rattlers (foreground) stand exhausting themselves while Eagles sit down with heels dug in. b. Rattlers adopt the Eagle strategy; both sides dug in with Rattlers dangerously near finish line (white, near top right).

a.

b.

c.

d.

Fig. 11.12. The morning after the Eagles burned the Rattlers' flag, physical scuffles started in earnest. **a.** One incident during the Rattlers' attempt to retaliate: Eagles seizing Rattlers' other flag. **b.** Rattler retaliation: raid on Eagle cabin nets leader's blue jeans, which they paint with "The Last of the Eagles" and parade through camp. **c.** Rattler flag with dying bird labeled "The Last of the Eagles." **d.** Eagles' flag with motto (Tom Hale was camp name on postbox).

a.

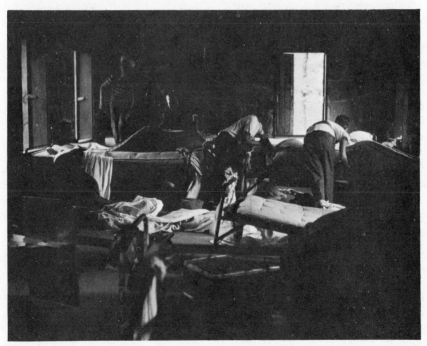

b.

Fig. 11.13. Raids on each others' cabins were conducted in stealth. **a.** Raiding Eagles entering Rattler cabin. **b.** The raid in progress as Eagles create disorder.

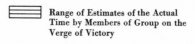

Range of Estimates of the Actual
Time by Members of Group on the
Verge of Victory

Range of Estimates of the Actual
Time by Members of the Group on
the Verge of Near–Exhaustion

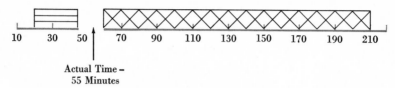

10   30   50   70   90   110   130   150   170   190   210

Actual Time –
55 Minutes

Fig. 11.14. Range of time estimates by group on the verge of victory and by group on the verge of defeat for the duration of the protracted tug of war. The tug of war ended in a tie after the fixed time of 55 minutes. This demonstrates that time estimation is profoundly affected by physical exertion (near-exhaustion) and physical exhilaration (victory in sight). All Eagles underestimated the duration, while all Rattlers overestimated the duration.

the 1954 study. The groups were taken to the beach at a nearby lake for an outing on a day when the beach was crowded with visitors and afforded many distractions. Despite the sheer effort required not to get "lost in the crowd," each group stuck together, entirely absorbed in its own activities. Observers watched carefully for diversions of attention, but the only evidence of notice paid to outsiders were such incidents as a boy bumping into a stranger and murmuring "Pardon me," as he rushed to join his fellows. Psychologically, other people did not "count" as far as the boys were concerned.

Conclusions
and Implications

The stage of intergroup conflict in the experiments showed unmistakably that the sustained conflict toward goals that each group desired, but only one could attain, is a sufficient condition for the rise of hostile, aggressive deeds, the standardization of social distance justified by derogatory images of the out-group, and the rudiments of prejudice (negative attitude). In addition, the hypotheses were supported that intergroup conflict produced an increase in in-group solidarity and pride.

The course of conflict between the groups did produce changes in the status and role relationships within the groups, as predicted. In one group (Eagles) the leadership actually changed hands when the leader who had emerged during the peaceful days of group formation proved reluctant in frontline action during conflict. In another (Rattlers) a bully who had been reduced to rather low status during group formation by the castigations of his fellow members emerged as a hero during encounters with the rival out-group. Practices established within the group as norms during group formation were altered during the intergroup encounters. A great deal of time and energy within each group went into making plans and strategies to outwit and defeat the out-group, which now appeared as an enemy.

There can be no doubt that differences in culture, language, or physical appearance facilitate discriminatory reactions toward members of an out-group. There can be no doubt that such differences play a part in the formation of intergroup hostility and prejudice. Yet, this experimental evidence shows that neither cultural, physical, nor economic differences are necessary for the rise of intergroup hostility, stereotyped images, social distance, and negative attitude—nor are maladjusted, neurotic, or unstable psychological tendencies necessary for their appearance.

The behavior during this stage may serve as a warning to psychologists to consider fully the importance of the background and the context of behavior in a social situation.

a.

b.

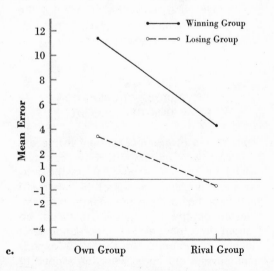

c.

Fig. 11.15. Experimental demonstration of in-group glorification and relative deprecation of out-group. **a.** Bean-toss contest in progress. **b.** Experimental setup for estimation of performance. **c.** Average errors in estimating performance by in-group members and by out-group members for victors and defeated group in intergroup tournament.

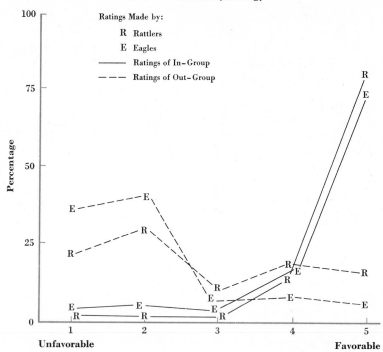

Fig. 11.16. After intergroup conflict, members of each group rated fellow members favorably but attributed predominantly unfavorable characteristics to the out-group. Percentage of ratings on six characteristics (combined) of in-group members and out-group members in each of five categories (unfavorable-favorable).

If an outside observer had entered the situation after the conflict began in any of the three experiments, he could only have concluded on the basis of their behavior that these boys (who were the "cream of the crop" in their communities) were either disturbed, vicious, or wicked youngsters.

STAGE
OF INTERGROUP COOPERATION:
REDUCTION OF CONFLICT

The problem of greatest interest in the experiments was as follows: How can two groups in conflict, each with hostile attitudes and negative images of the other and each desiring to keep the members of the detested out-group at a safe distance, be brought into cooperative interaction and friendly intercourse? In the 1949 experiment, several measures were introduced to reduce conflict in order to send the boys home in a friendly spirit. The Robbers Cave experiment studied the problem more systematically.

Various measures for reducing conflict could have been tried—for example, the distribution of favorable information, appeals to moral values, conferences by the leaders of the groups, contact as equals, or activities emphasizing individual rather than group achievement. Perhaps the most persistent notion is that groups in conflict should be given *accurate and favorable* information about one another. Indeed, groups must know something about each other if there is to be a change of hostile relationships. However, reactions to communication are not neutral affairs. Individuals select the information they will expose themselves to and interpret the content to fit their own designs. Therefore, no systematic information campaigns were attempted.

As for the related idea that *appeal to moral values* shared by each group is sufficient to reduce their hostility, the experiments contain several incidents to the contrary. Religious services were held in the Robbers Cave experiment by the same minister for each group. The topics were brotherly love, forgiveness of enemies, and cooperation. The boys arranged the services and were enthusiastic about the sermon. Upon solemnly departing from the ceremony, they returned within minutes to their concerns to defeat, avoid, or retaliate against the detested out-group.

Individual competition across group lines has been proposed as a means of furthering intergroup harmony—as, for example, in the Olympic games. In classroom and recreation situations, adults use such means in the attempt to break-up groups. However, the problem in this research was how to foster cooperation *between groups.* Therefore, this procedure was not considered appropriate.

Conferences of leaders are often necessary for the resolution of intergroup disputes. However, this measure was not used in the experiments because of evidence that leaders are not free to enter decisions that violate the prevailing norms and trends in their own groups unless these have already begun to change (see Chapter 8). During the 1949 experiment, one high-status Bull Dog went on his own initiative to the Red Devil cabin with the aim of negotiating better relationships. He was greeted by a hail of green apples, chased down the path, and derided. Upon returning to his own group, he received no sympathy. Despite his high status, he was rebuked for making the attempt, which was doomed to failure in the opinion of his fellow members.

The Common Enemy

In the 1949 experiment, several steps were taken to reduce intergroup hostility—including contact between the groups as equals and pronouncements by the adult staff. Although the latter were not effective in reducing the frequent expressions of dislike between the groups, one measure clearly was effective. An outside group was invited to the camp to compete with a campwide team selected from both groups. At least temporarily, the effect of this common enemy was to promote cooperation between groups and to reduce hostile interchange. However, the Bull Dogs and Red Devils maintained their strong in-group preferences to the end of that experiment, to the point that they still maintained social distance between them.

For two reasons, a *common enemy* was not used in the later experiments. First, history contains many examples of uniting against a common enemy in which the same old intergroup conflicts appear when the enemy is vanquished. Second, the uniting of hostile groups to defeat another is, after all, a widening of the scope of intergroup conflict. Logically, the end result is repetition of the stage of intergroup conflict on a larger scale, with potentially more serious consequences.

Hypotheses on Reduction of Intergroup Hostility

The hypotheses actually tested were as follows:

Hypotheses

1. *Contact* between groups on an equal status in activities that, in themselves, are pleasant for members of both groups, but that involve no interdependence among them, will not decrease an existing state of intergroup conflict.

2. When conflicting groups come into contact under conditions embodying goals *that are compelling for the groups involved, but cannot be achieved by a single group through its own efforts and resources,* the group will tend to cooperate toward this *superordinate goal.*

  Our definition of superordinate goal emphasizes that it is unattainable by one group singly; hence, it is not identical with a "common goal." Another implication of the definition is that a superordinate goal supersedes other goals each group may have, singly or in common with others; hence its attainment may require subordination of either singular or common goals.

3. Cooperation between groups arising from a *series* of superordinate goals will have a *cumulative effect* toward reducing the social distance between them, changing hostile attitudes and stereotypes, and hence reducing the possibility of future conflicts between them.

In short, these hypotheses concern the *conditions* under which *contact as equals* can be effective in resolution of conflict and reduction of hostility between groups.

Phase One. In order to test the first hypothesis, a series of situations was introduced involving *contact* between groups in activities highly pleasant to each group but not involving interdependence between them. Examples were going to the movies, eating in the same dining room, shooting off fireworks on July 4th, and the like. Far from reducing conflict, these situations served as occasions for the rival groups to berate and attack each other. In the dining-hall line, they shoved each other and the group that lost the contest for the head of the line shouted "Ladies first!" at the winner. They threw paper, food, and vile names at each other. An Eagle bumped by a Rattler was admonished by his fellow Eagles to brush "the dirt" off his clothes. The mealtime encounters were dubbed "garbage wars" by the participants.

Phase Two: Superordinate Goals. The measure that was effective was suggested by a corollary to our formulation of intergroup conflict: *If conflict develops from mutually incompatible goals, common goals should promote cooperation.* But what kind of common goals?

In considering group relations in the everyday world, it seemed that the most effective and enduring cooperation between groups occurs when *superordinate goals* prevail. Superordinate goals are those goals that have a compelling appeal for members of each group, but that neither group can achieve without participation of the other. To test this hypothesis experimentally, we created a series of urgent and natural situations that challenged members of both groups.

One was a breakdown in the water supply system. Water came to the camp in pipes from a tank about a mile away. The flow of water was interrupted and the boys in both groups were called together to hear of the crisis. Both groups volunteered, in their own distinctive ways, to search the water line for trouble. They explored separately, then came together and jointly located the source of the difficulty. But despite the good spirits aroused, the groups fell back on their old recriminations once the immediate crisis was over.

A similar opportunity was offered when the boys requested a movie that both groups had high on their list of preference. They were told that the camp could not afford to pay for it. The two groups got together, figured out how much each group would have to contribute, chose the film by a common vote, and enjoyed the show together. It should be kept in mind that this followed the episode of their cooperation in the water crisis.

One day the two groups went on an outing at a lake some distance away. A large truck was to go for food. But when everyone was hungry and ready to eat, it developed that the truck would not start (the staff had taken care of that). The boys got a rope—the same rope they had used in their acrimonious tug of war—and all pulled together to start the truck.

Joint efforts in situations such as these did not *immediately* dispel hostility. But gradually, the series of activities requiring interdependent action reduced conflict and hostility between the groups. As a consequence, the members of the two groups began to feel friendlier. For example, a Rattler whom the Eagles had disliked for his sharp tongue and skill in defeating them became a "good egg." The boys stopped shoving each other in the meal line. They no longer called each other names and began to sit together at the table. New friendships developed, cutting across group lines.

In the end, the groups were actively seeking opportunities to intermingle, to entertain and "treat" each other. Procedures that "worked" in one activity were *transferred* to others. For example, the notion of "taking turns" developed in the dining hall and was transferred to a joint campfire, which the boys themselves decided to hold. The groups took turns presenting skits and songs.

Given the alternative of returning in separate buses or on the same bus, members of both groups requested that they go home together on the same bus. As a whole neither group paid attention to a few *diehards* who muttered "Let's not."

On the way home, a stop was made for refreshments. One group still had five dollars won as a prize. They decided to spend this sum on refreshments for both groups rather than to use it solely for themselves and thereby have more to eat. On their own initiative they invited their former rivals to be their guests for malted milks.

Interviews with the boys confirmed the change in their attitudes. From choosing their best friends almost exclusively in their own group, many of them shifted to listing some boys in the other group. They were

a.

b.

Fig. 11.17. A series of contact situations involving groups in appealing activities as equals
—but without interdependence—tested one possible hypothesis about reduction of intergroup
hostility. **a.** Side by side, Rattlers and Eagles shoot firecrackers by roadside out of park—but
with no intermingling. **b.** The dining hall after one of the "garbage wars" that became frequent and were accompanied by name-calling.

Figs. 11.18–11.21. The theory of conflict (pp. 268–269) provides leads for necessary and sufficient conditions to reduce intergroup hostility and prejudice—namely, a series of goals urgently sought by groups in conflict that could not be ignored and that required the energies and resources of both.

a.

b.

c.

Fig. 11.18. First superordinate goal: water-shortage problem. **a.** After long trip exploring water system, Eagles and Rattlers mingle to climb up the tank to inspect contents. **b.** Both groups mingle in the attempt to clear obstacle from faucet. **c.** Lineup for water includes members of both groups.

a.

b.

c.

Fig. 11.19. Despite separate and equal facilities, the stalled truck that was to go for supplies produced cooperation and integrated eating. **a.** First attempt to start the truck by pushing. **b.** Tug of war against the truck using same rope that had served as instrument promoting conflict. **c.** Despite discussion of separate meals, preparation and eating were integrated after victory over truck.

a.

b.

Fig. 11.20. Back in camp after series of superordinate goals. **a.** Joint campfire with groups taking turns at presenting skits and songs. **b.** At their own joint request, members of both groups board one bus together for trip home.

glad to have a second chance to rate the boys in the other group as to personal qualities. Some remarked that they were inclined to change their minds since the first rating made after the tournament. Indeed they had. The new ratings were largely favorable. It is probably not accidental that the group that had been declared victorious in the intergroup tournament was also more prone to continue attributing negative qualities to the out-group and to remain more exclusive in in-group choices (See Figs. 11.21 a, b).

Conclusions

1. Intergroup conflict and its byproducts of hostility and negative stereotypes are not primarily a result of neurotic tendencies on the part of individuals but rather occur under conditions specified here—even when the individuals involved are normal, healthy, and socially well adjusted.

2. Cooperative and democratic procedures *within* groups are not directly transferable to intergroup relations. On the contrary, cooperativeness and solidarity within groups were at their height when intergroup conflict was most severe.

3. Important intergroup relations affect the patterning of roles and the norms within each group. As noted earlier, one group deposed a leader who could not "take it" in contests with the adversary. Another made a hero of a big boy who had previously been regarded as a bully. Similarly, the change to intergroup cooperation was accompanied by shifts in the status structure, particularly in one group in which some members looked back on the former days of rivalry with nostalgia.

4. Contact between hostile groups as equals in contiguous and pleasant situations does not in itself necessarily reduce conflict between them.

5. Contact between groups involving interdependent action toward superordinate goals is conducive to cooperation between groups, but a single episode of cooperation is not sufficient to reduce established intergroup hostility and negative stereotypes.

6. A series of cooperative activities toward superordinate goals has a cumulative effect in reducing intergroup hostility. This cumulative effect involves the successful development of procedures for cooperat-

ing in specific activities and their transfer to new situations, so that established modes of intergroup cooperation are recognized.

7. Tools and techniques found useful in problem-solving within groups and in intergroup conflict may also serve in intergroup cooperation. (In the experiments, the tug-of-war rope was used to pull the stalled truck.) But their use in intergroup cooperation requires recognition that the procedures involve not merely so many individuals within a group, but different groups of individuals contributing to the attainment of a common goal.

8. Cooperative endeavor between groups toward superordinate goals alters the significance of other measures designed to reduce existing hostility between them: Intergroup *contacts* in the course of striving toward superordinate goals were used in developing plans, for making decisions, and for pleasant exchanges.

Information about the other group became interesting and sought after, rather than something to be ignored or interpreted to fit existing conceptions of the out-group.

Exchange of persons for the performance of tasks was not seen as "betrayal" of one's own group.

Leaders found that the trend toward intergroup cooperation widened the spheres in which they could take positive steps toward working out procedures for joint endeavor and future contact. In fact, a leader who tried to hold back from intergroup contact found that his group was ceasing to listen to him.

In short, the findings suggest that various methods used with limited success in reducing intergroup hostility may become effective when employed within a framework of cooperation among groups working toward goals that are genuinely appealing to all and that require equitable participation and contributions from all groups.

VERIFICATIONS AND EXTENSIONS OF THE EXPERIMENTAL ANALYSIS

"The proof of the pudding is in the eating" is a popular saying whose application to experimental analysis implies a concern over *validity,* an issue that has been emphasized repeatedly in this book. Can the experimental analysis be used to analyze

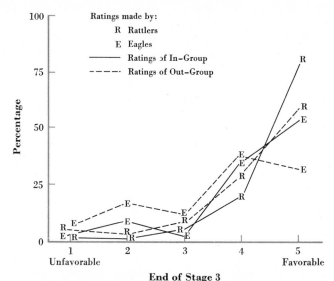

End of Stage 3
Stereotype Ratings of In-Group and Out-Group
Members on Six Characteristics (Combined)

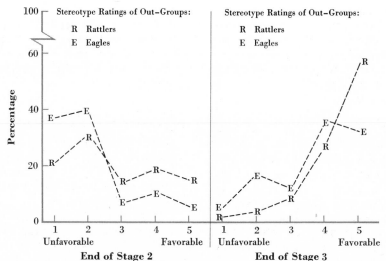

Comparison of Stereotype Ratings of Out-Groups at End of
Stage 2 (on Left) and at End of Stage 3 (on Right)

Fig. 11.21 a. Comparison of stereotype ratings following series of super-ordinate goals (Stage 3, above) and during intergroup conflict (Stage 2, above). **b.** (*opposite page*) Changes in percentage of friendship choices for members of in-group and out-group by winners and losers just after victory or defeat and following superordinate goals.

intergroup conflict and cooperation in actual life?

Recent research has supported the findings and extended the analysis. Blake and Mouton (1962) referred to the experiments as *prototypes* for analysis. Certainly many variations are possible.

Are the Experimental Findings
Merely Child's Play?

Over a period of several years, Blake and Mouton (1962; Blake, Shepard, and Mouton, 1964) conducted research in the setting of human relations workshops for adults, in-

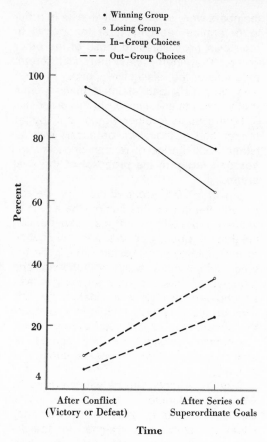

Time

cluding both college students and members of industrial organizations. Over a thousand participants and 150 groups, matched on relevant personal dimensions, took part in the research. Their findings indicate that the outcomes of the camp experiments were not mere "child's play." The investigators used the design of the camp experiments as the prototype, introducing variations that significantly extend the analysis.

Formation of In-Groups and the Impact of Intergroup Conflict

The workshops were organized to study and to improve human relations. Therefore, the content of interaction was, typically, some kind of human relations problem. With several groups operating simultaneously, Blake and Mouton reported that group structure and norms were incipient after 10 to 18 hours of interaction, despite the fact that ordinarily the individuals interacted

with other workshop participants in a highly informal setting outside the sessions.

Intergroup relations were varied by assigning all groups a problem with the aim of arriving at the best solution possible as a group and a better solution than other groups might offer. The effects of this "win-lose" competition on the in-groups were as follows:

1. Status relations within the groups were "refined" and "consolidated." In short, intergroup competition affected the in-group structure.

2. Groups closed their ranks to pull together to *win*. Bickering within the groups was reduced. In other words, solidarity or cohesiveness *within* groups increased.

These effects were also reported by Sussman and Weil (1960) when residents of two cabins at a camp for diabetic children participated for three days in activities conducive to group formation (see Hypothesis, p. 232) and then in a single day of tournaments. Sociometric choices of children outside one's own cabin were reduced by the three-day treatment, but became almost exclusively *within* group (more than 90 percent) following intergroup competition.

Representation in Intergroup Negotiation as an In-Group Phenomenon

The decision as to which group's solution was superior served as the means for studying intergroup interaction in the Blake and Mouton studies. Several variations were selected.

Representatives as In-Group Members: Heroes or Traitors? Each group chose members to represent it in negotiations for a common choice between proposed solutions. Before negotiations began, the members of all groups rated the negotiators selected, agreeing that they were "mature, intelligent, independent, and well-intentioned."

During negotiations, each group could send notes to instruct its representative or to request more information about the other groups' proposals. Content analysis of these notes showed that the majority were directed toward destruction of the rival's proposals, with very little effort to compare similarities or differences among the proposals.

As shown in Fig. 11.22, very few of the representatives backed down in supporting the merits of their own group's proposal. When, however, a decision was reached, the reactions of these mature adults were striking. Members of losing groups rated their representatives as less intelligent, less mature, and well-intentioned than formerly. If he agreed too readily to the other side's proposal, he was seen as a *traitor*. On the other hand, victorious groups saw their representative as a *hero* who had bravely defended their proposal.

Impartial Adjudication. A neutral outsider was brought in as a neutral judge in intergroup experiments. Both sides agreed initially that the third party was both neutral and competent. Groups who were subsequently awarded the decision continued to rate the judge as neutral and competent, taking his decision as evidence of the merit of their performance. Losing groups, on the other hand, no longer saw the judge as neutral. Their ratings were that he was "biased, unfair, and incompetent." He was criticized for showing "no grasp of the problem," not knowing "enough about the topic," "not intelligent enough to be fair and unbiased," and not taking "enough time" to arrive at a fair decision.

Selective Recall of In-Group and Out-Group Proposals. In the workshops, the members were given objective tests in order to determine recognition of the points in their own proposals and those of the other group. The finding was that each group recognized the distinctive points in their own proposals and claimed many points that were actually *common* to the proposals of both groups. In other words, their better recognition of their own proposals was attained at the price of recognizing *similarities* or overlap in the proposal of the rival group.

Impact of Intergroup Victory or Defeat. As with the boys at the camps, the adults in winning workshop groups experienced heightened pride, pleasure, and satisfaction at their joint victory. Losing groups, on the other hand, were typically subdued and gloomy. So different were the perspectives engendered by victory and defeat that the winners typically were unable to appreciate the disturbance experienced by the losers. It seemed natural that they should be elated, but not that the losers should be gloomy.

A typical reaction to defeat, reported by Blake and Mouton, resembles the Red Devils' reactions (p. 241). In the workshop situations, blame was assigned for the defeat—the decision-makers being the most frequent target. In some groups, members who had not been strongly supportive of the group's proposal in the first place were now likely to downgrade it and call for self-criticism by the group. The usual result was considerable disorganization and splintering of defeated groups. In some cases, new leadership arose during the in-group discussion of defeat.

Effects of Differential Facilities and Power. In actual life, groups in conflict frequently possess quite different facilities and power, unlike the design of the intergroup experiments. Victory and defeat in a temporary competition are, of course, one example of differential power. Are persistently unequal facilities available to a group also conducive to difficulties in in-group relations?

An exploratory study by Jamous and Lemaine (1962) reported striking effects upon the structure, activities, and satisfaction within groups competing toward a prize with unequal facilities. Groups of children (ages 9–14) competed in three different

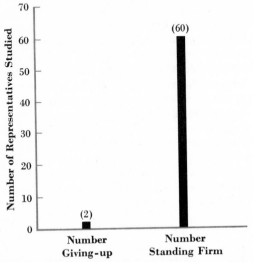

Fig. 11.22. Loyalty of representatives to their groups during intergroup competition. (After Blake and Mouton, 1961, Loyalty of Representatives to Ingroup Positions During Intergroup Competition, *Sociometry*, **24**, 177–184.)

types of activities (decoding instructions for use in construction, constructing a shelter in the woods, and planning an ideal vacation camp). For each task, one group had inferior means at its disposal, either through lack of information and materials or differences in age.

Some of the handicapped groups became discouraged and did not want to compete at all. The handicapped groups had more interpersonal friction, greater difficulties in dividing the tasks, frequent status struggles, and different attitudes toward their rivals. Notably, the favored groups were quite open in allowing outsiders to see their work and in wishing to compare it with that of their rivals. The handicapped groups were more secretive, tending to "close their frontiers" to prevent comparisons.

In short, the evidence available indicates that intergroup relations do have an impact on in-group practices and organization and that this impact differs according to the relative power and facilities of the groups. The reactions of in-groups to victory and defeat may be viewed as a special case of such differential impact.

Differential Evaluation of In-Groups and Out-Groups in Conflict and Cooperation. Proceeding from the same formulation of intergroup problems, Avigdor (1952) conducted an experiment in a settlement house among friendship clubs of girls. Her aim was to test the prediction that the stereotyped images that one group develops of another reflect the conflicting or cooperative nature of relations between them. She predicted that the particular traits attributed to the out-group would be those most *relevant* to the in-group's position, whether typifying the actual behavior of the other group or not.

Some clubs cooperated in producing a play the proceeds of which were to be spent on club jackets for each group. The members of these cooperating groups were initially neither favorable nor unfavorable in their views of one another. They came to have favorable images that were not strikingly categorical (not as expressed in the phrase "all or most of them are that way"). The groups who had reason to believe that their achievement of club jackets was being blocked by other groups became hostile toward those groups, attributing highly neg-

ative characteristics to them in categorical fashion. There was also evidence that traits irrelevant to the conflict (for example, "bad teeth") were excluded from the negative image. Instead, the image of the transgressors centered around those qualities each group saw as responsible for their joint frustration: the other group was "selfish," "bossy," "cheating."

Young women are not immune to the same processes, as O. J. Harvey (1956) found in his experiment. Friendly cliques held positive images of each other, and assessed the performance by persons in the other cliques about as accurately as they did their own. But unfriendly cliques held unfavorable stereotypes of each other and downgraded performance by members of the out-group to the point of *under*estimating it. When the unfriendly group was present, each group overestimated its own performance, revealing thereby the tendency to "close ranks" and glorify one's own group in the face of an unfriendly competitor.

An experiment by Manheim (1960) showed that invidious comparisons between groups influenced the proportion of hostile communication between them. Images of another group were created by instructions implying favorable or unfavorable comparisons between the groups. For example, having been told that its average intelligence was low or high, a group was assigned the task of reaching agreement with another group to which the same, a lower or higher intelligence, was attributed. Manheim found that the proportion of negative and antagonistic expressions in notes passed between the groups increased (relative to the total) as the number of invidious comparisons in their images of each other increased. The greatest proportion of hostile communications occurred between groups who differed both in their images of each other's intelligence and of the relative autonomy or authoritarian character of each other's leadership.

SUPERORDINATE GOALS
IN THE REDUCTION
OF INTERGROUP HOSTILITY

In extending the analysis of superordinate goals to actual life situations, it is well to recall the *definition* of superordinate goals in Hypothesis 2 for the final stage of the experiment (p. 255). This definition precludes certain expectations about the resolution of intergroup conflict.

1. *Superordinate goals, by definition, cannot be achieved merely by verbal manipulation or consensus on abstractions.* By definition, a superordinate goal requires the efforts and resources of two or more groups in the intergroup system. It is not, therefore, a magic formula for inducing mutual understanding through verbal appeals to both sides or for reaching consensus on abstract ideas. Verbal consensus on abstractions can be achieved between groups without any implications for cooperative interaction between them. For example, parties to irreconcilable conflict can reach consensus on the nobility of motherhood, the desirability of virtue as opposed to sin, and the aim of peace as against war. Such consensus does not represent a superordinate goal unless it involves the participants in the mutual use of efforts and resources toward a concerted plan of action.

2. *Superordinate goals are, by definition, compelling to all groups in conflict and are not, therefore, conditions that can be imposed by one group upon others.* When conflict between groups turns upon incompatibility between major or central aspirations of different groups, the possibility of a superordinate goal is a contradiction in terms. For example, conflict between a gang of criminal thieves and the police is a conflict of diametrically opposed goals so central to each that their reconciliation is a contradiction in terms. There is bound to be conflict as long as the gangsters are ambitious and the police are dedicated. To speak of resolution through superordinate goals is absurd. In short, when the major and central goals of two groups are diametrically opposite, persistent conflict is to be expected. For example, there are countries in the world today where a dominant group rules a majority that outnumbers it 8 to 1 or 18 to 1 (as the case is in South Africa and Rhodesia today). As long as this domination exists, the conditions for superordinate goals are simply not present within these countries. (For elaboration of the inhuman effects of these schemes of human relations, see the interesting book *Apartheid,* published by the United Nations' UNESCO in 1967). Similarly, if a strong nation seeks to impose its will and rule on another arbitrarily in the manner of a bully, it is hypocrisy to speak of common aims and interests.

3. *The criteria of superordinate goals presume that there are areas of interdependence among groups* such that there can be goals that are compelling for the groups involved, but cannot be achieved by a single group. In a modern world rendered increasingly interdependent by modern technological developments in communication, transportation, distribution, and destruction, the mutual dependence among nations and within nations is increasing (cf. Sherif, 1966). Thus, despite the perpetual danger and actualities of intergroup conflagrations unregulated by mutually supported authority and rules, the possibilities for superordinate goals can increase, not decrease, if the governments of the world do not permanently halt the trend through unbridled actions that unleash world holocaust—a specter that must be faced as one of the possible futures for mankind.

12

Intergroup Relations: Domination-Subordination, Prejudice and Change

Major Topics of the Chapter

Definitions of group prejudice, social distance, and group stereotype

Extending the theory of conflict to social life

Norms of social distance reflecting dominance-subordination

Formation and change in social distance norms

Varying criteria for social distance in different cultures

Group stereotypes arising to justify social distance

Elaboration of group stereotypes into superiority doctrines

Changes in stereotypic conceptions with changed intergroup relations

Intergroup behavior in the context of changing intergroup relations

Intergroup contacts and the heavy hand of
the past
Contact with near-equal status and social
approval
Industrial and race relations
Increasing interdependence of groups
Conflicting and harmonious loyalties
Inclusive and exclusive identifications

PREJUDICE, SOCIAL DISTANCE, AND GROUP STEREOTYPE

This chapter extends the experimental analysis of in-group and intergroup relations to vital problems within societies and between peoples. It concentrates on relations between groups that are characterized, either in the past or currently, by differential power—one being dominant or attempting to dominate the fortune and fate of the other.

As in the experimental analysis, this interdisciplinary approach to intergroup dominance-subordination focuses on social-psychological aspects. Therefore, much of this chapter treats problems traditionally labeled problems of *group prejudice* and *stereotypes.* The latter part concerns intergroup behavior in times of social change, such as that characteristic of the modern world, especially since World War II.

Prejudice, social distance, and *stereotype* are words in common usage. It will be helpful to state at the outset what is meant by these terms in this book.

Group prejudice refers to *unfavorable attitudes* held by the members of a group toward another group and its members, derived from their group's norms that regulate treatment of the out-group.

Social distance is a dimension of interaction between members of different groups, ranging from intimacy to complete separation (no contact). It is defined by norms governing the situations in which interaction with members of the out-group is permissible.

Group stereotype is a popular term referring to agreement among members of a group on their image of another group and its members.

A **group stereotype** is operationally defined in terms of the proportion of group members agreeing on labels and attributions for another group and its members. A stereotype may be said to exist when a high proportion agrees on the image of the out-group.

A thorough account of the phenomena of group prejudice and stereotypes will require more detailed analysis of conceptual functioning and the psychology of social attitudes, which are the topics in the chapters to follow. Most of the research summarized in this chapter refers to the normative character of prejudice and of group images. The reader should bear in mind, however, that psychologically the phenomena of group prejudice and group stereotypes are *not* fundamentally different from the phenomena of social attitudes and social concepts in general. Their distinctiveness derives from *the nature of the stimulus situation to which they refer (intergroup relations)*, not from the psychological principles governing concept and attitude formation or their change.

THEORY OF CONFLICT: THE GENERAL FORMULATION OF INTERGROUP PROBLEMS

In the last chapter, a series of hypotheses was evaluated through experimental findings. Let us review them in a descriptive way and see what is required for their application to the frequent case in which one group is dominant or attempts dominance over others.

Groups do not form for casual or trivial reasons. They are products of repeated interaction around motivationally significant problems, goals, or solutions to collective gripes (including frustrations) that require interdependent activity and more or less orderly division of functions and procedure.

When a group forms (into some gradation of groupness), one of the products is a delineation of "we" from "they"—the "we" including the members of the group. Proportional to the effectiveness of the organization and norms in meeting or solving significant problems, the "we" thus delineated as an in-group comes in time to embody a host of qualities and of new values to be upheld, cherished, and defended. Deviations from within, as well as offenses from without, are reacted to with corrective, defensive and, at times, offensive measures, namely, appropriate sanctions.

When the in-group has significant encounters with another group that comprise the "they" from the group's own point of view, a set of qualities, traits, or stereotypes is attributed to the out-group. The characteristics attributed to other groups and the norms that arise to regulate interaction with them are not present as whole cloth in the formation of the group. They are not a direct outgrowth of practices and norms developed to regulate relations *within* the in-group, although they are *not independent* of them.

On the contrary, norms for dealing with another group and images of them are products of actual or perceived relationships between the groups. (We add the word "perceived" to take into account that intergroup relations may involve comparatively little face-to-face interaction between groups. In such cases, interested parties *within* or outside of either group may present a picture of the relationships between the groups that reflects their own special interests more than the actual state of affairs. This possibility is particularly prevalent in a world in which mass communication is so widespread and rapid.)

The relationships between groups are limited by the respective interests and goals of the groups. The norms for treatment of the other group, as well as the traits attributed to them may be favorable, unfavorable, or both—depending upon these intergroup relationships. If the interests and goals of the groups are harmonious or complementary, the "they" group is pictured in a positive or favorable light. However, if the activities and goals of the groups clash, the characteristics attributed to the out-group are negative and derogatory. In either event, the stereotyped conceptions and beliefs justify the in-group's position in the intergroup interaction. They become a part of the group's culture, constituting their particular brand of ethnocentrism.

Henceforth, intergroup interaction and the behavior of members of the respective groups proceeds from two sets of premises which may, we repeat, be mutually harmonious or almost diametrically opposed. Proceeding from its own premises, each group draws logical conclusions about appropriate behavior and treatment toward the others. Much of the apparent "irrationality" in intergroup behavior is, thus, a product of logical deduction by members of respective groups from diametrically opposed premises. So frequent is this phenomenon that some psychologists, including Charles Osgood (1962), give it the special label "psycho-logic."

Now we consider cases in which one more-powerful group has goals that diametrically oppose or interfere with the goals of another that is less powerful. Specifically, one group takes the position that its members should dominate the interests of other people or that the other people should be working in their interests. If this would-be supremacist has the power to compel or force its position, we have a case of dominance-subordination.

Norms
of Social Distance

When dominance is achieved, at least for a period of time, the dominant group's treatment of the subordinates and their norms regulating intergroup interaction define social distances among the respective groups. The sociologist Robert E. Park coined the term "social distance" to express the observation that the kinds of situations in which contact occurs between a dominant group and subordinates vary in their degree of intimacy: for example, from kinship by marriage—residence in the same neighborhood—work in the same occupation—to no contact at all.

Emory Bogardus, the University of Southern California sociologist, developed a method for studying the social distances among groups in the United States. This method will be summarized in Chapter 16. Here it is sufficient to note that it permits the construction of a scale of social distance at which any group desires to keep others with whom it has functional relations. For example, on the basis of the responses of members of a dominant group, various other groups can be ranked from those who are entirely acceptable in kinship and close personal relations down to those who are entirely unacceptable for contacts except those in which the dominant group is in a superior position (and the subordinate is regarded as in his "proper" place), or to those who are entirely unacceptable for any form of contact ("I would bar them from my country").

When the responses by members of one group toward others are highly similar, we may say that the rank order of social distances maintained from other groups represents a scale of social distances that are *norms* for that group. In the United States, social scientists checked the established scales of social distance for a period of twenty years in which relationships among its various ethnic and nationality groups remained fairly stable (1926 to 1946). The findings showed consensus and similarities for various regions of the country sufficiently great to conclude that a scale of invidious distinctions among groups in this country was as much a social norm as the celebration of Thanksgiving Day.

Table 12.1 illustrates the stability of social distances in the United States at that time by comparing the rank orders of various ethnic and national groups in 1926 and 1946 (Bogardus, 1947). Both lists are based on stratified samples of white adults (18–35 years old) with at least a high school education, which over-represented well-educated persons in skilled or professional occupations. Shifts in the rank of certain groups doubtless reflect the intervening World War II (e.g., for the Chinese and Japanese). However, the most striking feature of the lists is their remarkable correspondence.

During this same period, school children, college students, and adults in the United States who lived in such different regions as Florida, New York, Illinois, and the state of Washington revealed very similar social distance scales (Guilford, 1931; Hartley, 1946; Meltzer, 1939; Zeligs and Hendrickson, 1933–1934 a and b). Even members of groups low on the scale of the dominant group made strikingly similar ratings (Hartley, 1946). Typically, subordinate group members ranked their own group near the top of the scale, indicating greatest intimacy, but the ranks of other groups resembled those made by the dominant group.

There were, of course, some regional variations in social distance maintained for various specific groups. There were also individual variations. A small minority preferred no association with any but their own group. Another tiny minority was willing to accept members of all groups to close relationship. The latter were the only ones who rejected the norms of social distance then prevailing and who could, therefore, be called "unprejudiced" (see the definition above).

It is interesting that most studies of prejudice by psychologists and sociologists during these years consisted of comparisons between samples of subjects with "low" or "high" degrees of prejudice. In some studies persons with low or high degrees of prejudice toward one group (e.g., Jews and Negroes) exhibited unmistakable prejudice toward another. Studies on the so-called dynamics of prejudice and "authoritarian personality" flourished. Many criticisms of the methodology and theory were leveled (e.g., Christie, 1954). However, the major weakness of the flourishing research was its focus on group prejudice as a characteristic of the individual (Faris, 1961). Of course, it is individuals who exhibit prejudice. But their prejudice is a product of past and current exposure to a society in which, both on the local and national levels, discriminatory treatment of various groups was permitted and even encouraged (Horowitz, 1937).

The significant questions about the etiology of the attitudes of prejudice toward other groups on the part of an individual are the following:

A. Does he belong to a group that maintains norms of invidious comparison and social distance toward others?

B. If so, whence came those norms?

The significance of these questions can be readily seen in events since 1956, when

Table 12.1.   Social Distance in the United States in 1926 and 1946

Groups	Rank 1926	Groups	Rank 1946
English	1	Amer. (nat. white)	1
Amer. (nat. white)	2	Canadians	2
Canadians	3	English	3
Scotch	4	Irish	4
Irish	5	Scotch	5
French	6	French	6
Germans	7	Norwegians	7
Swedes	8	Hollanders	8
Hollanders	9	Swedes	9
Norwegians	10	Danes	10
Danes	11	Germans	11
Spanish	12	Finns	12
Finns	13	Czechs	13
Russians	14	Russians	14
Italians	15	Poles	15
Portuguese	16	Spanish	16
Poles	17	Romanians	17
Romanians	18	Bulgarians	18
Armenians	19	Italians	19
Czechs	20	Armenians	20
Indians (Amer.)	21	Greeks	21
Jews	22	Portuguese	22
Bulgarians	23	Jews	23
Greeks	24	Indians (Amer.)	24
Syrians	25	Chinese	25
Mexican Amer.	—	Mexican Amer.	26
Mexicans	27	Syrians	27
Japanese Amer.	—	Filipinos	28
Japanese	29	Mexicans	29
Filipinos	30	Turks	30
Negroes	31	Japanese Amer.	31
Turks	32	Koreans	32
Chinese	33	Mulattoes	33
Mulattoes	34	Indians (East)	34
Koreans	35	Negroes	35
Indians (East)	36	Japanese	36

Source: From E. S. Bogardus, 1947, Changes in racial distances.
Internat. J. Opin. & Attit. Res., 1:58.

the second edition of this text appeared. It is doubtful that the individual frustrations, repressions, or anxieties of individual white Americans have declined appreciably since that date. However, their views on discriminatory treatments, especially of American Negroes, have begun to change.

Figure 12.1 presents data from surveys of stratified, representative nationwide samples in the United States, conducted in 1942, 1956, and 1963 (Hyman and Sheatsley, 1964). In 1954, the Supreme Court ruled against school segregation with the historic statement: "Separate educational facilities are inherently unequal." In 1957, the first

Civil Rights Act since Reconstruction after the Civil War was passed. In 1964, a second and stronger Civil Rights Act was passed. Between 1954 and 1964, conflict, demonstrations, violence, and police action were frequent as civil rights groups struggled to extend the areas of opportunity afforded Negro citizens.

The questions asked in the surveys were similar to those used in studies of social distance.

Do you think that white and Negro students should go to the same schools or to separate schools?

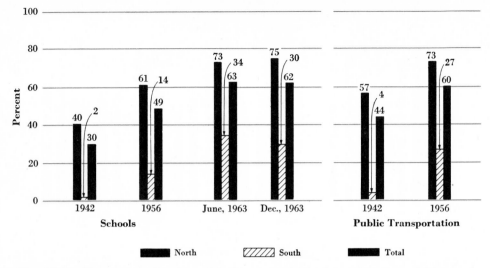

Fig. 12.1. Changes over time in social distances maintained by whites toward Negroes in schools, public transportation, and residence. Results from nationwide surveys in 1942, 1956, June 1963, and December, 1963. (From H. H. Hyman and P. B. Sheatsley, 1964. Attitudes toward desegregation. Copyright © 1964 by Scientific American, Inc. All rights reserved.)

Bars represent percents of nationwide sample (Total) and of samples in North and South agreeing with desegregation of schools, public transportation, and residential neighborhoods. (Samples were all white adults.) The undecided category amounted to about 4 percent on each issue. Two other surveys in 1956 and 1963 (not shown) support the reliability of these findings. The assassination of the President had apparently no effect on the trend of opinion about desegregation between June and December, 1963.

Generally speaking, do you think there should be separate sections for Negroes on street cars and buses?
If a Negro with the same income and education as you moved into your block, would it make any difference to you?

Several results are evident in Fig. 12.1.
1. The trend favoring desegregation of schools is unmistakable—even in the South, where it has met strong resistance and even violence.
2. The breakdown of social distance norms for the use of public transportation, which were in fact not maintained in Northern cities for many years earlier, is striking—especially in the South, where they had been maintained.
3. In the area of greatest intimacy sampled, namely housing, the *rate* of change was greater in the South than in the North where "whites maintain a social distance from Negroes, although allowing them the legal right to use the same public facilities. . . . This social pattern has contributed to the existence of *de facto* school segregation in the North, even though the

great majority of white Northerners are now opposed to school segregation in principle" (Hyman and Sheatsley, 1964, p. 5).
4. Additional results show that in the area of greatest intimacy, namely marriage, the social distance was greatest, 53 percent of Northern whites and 80 percent of Southern whites favoring "laws against marriage between Negroes and whites."

SOCIAL DISTANCE NORMS IN FORMATION AND CHANGE

The perspective gained by studying the background events and context of specific intergroup behavior was easily seen in the experiments reported in the last chapter. The great social distance between Eagles and Rattlers and their mutual hostility cannot be understood apart from the short but eventful history of their intergroup relations. Similarly, an analysis of intergroup attitude and behavior involving members of different ethnic, nationality, religious, political, and economic groups requires an understanding of their eventful and frequently very long

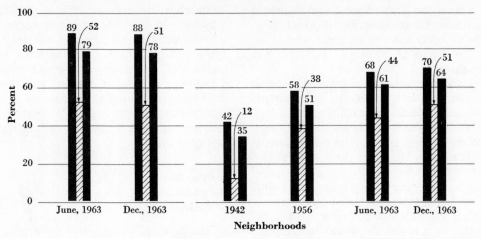

Fig. 12.1. (*Continued*)

histories of interaction as well as their contemporary stance toward one another.

In surveying the history of intergroup relations of various kinds, several generalizations become possible (Sherif and Sherif, 1953; Shafer, 1955).

1. Social distance between different groups, even those differing greatly in cultural values, technological level, and language does *not* necessarily mean conflict between them or hostile views of one another. Lindgren (1938) documented the history of contacts between the Tungus, an illiterate group of nomads in Western Manchuria, and a group of farmers descended from seventeenth century Cossacks, who maintained social distance without any record of conflict. Their economic activities supplemented one another and the more highly developed Cossacks made no attempt to dominate the Tungus, being content to trade with them. Similarly, there are many recorded cases of social distance without hostility between American Indians and the European explorers and settlers, to whom the indigenous peoples were certainly a cultural curiosity (McNickle, 1937). While some Indian groups, such as the Fox, had already developed warlike and aggressive ways of dealing with other groups at the time of European contact, others were not aggressive and hostile, including the Ute and the Blackfoot, who later became hostile.

2. While conflict need not always imply an attempt by one group to dominate the other, the attempted or actual domination by one group over another group, its means of livelihood, or its very lives, invariably leads to great social distance from the subordinated group accompanied by the elaboration of an unfavorable image of them, and prejudice toward them. The history of European conquest and colonialism and the history of the settlement and expansion by Europeans on the American continents are replete with evidence of such developments.

3. The criteria employed by a dominant group for defining which groups are kept at great social distance and invidiously compared to their own group vary enormously and may not have direct or obvious correlation with the original causes of conflict. The original causes of conflict are manifold but typically include either rivalry and exploitation or appropriation in the economic sphere of life. Thus, the stratification of visibly different peoples according to their ethnic or "racial" origins employs "racial" or cultural criteria; there are also social distances according to occupation (e.g., management-union) and religion (Shibutani and Kwan, 1965).

4. The criteria employed by a dominant group and its images of out-groups acquire distinctiveness in its cultural repertoire and become, therefore, a part of "social reality" for members in succeeding generations, regardless of the original conflicts that underlie such selection. Thus, despite the fact that the original causes of social distance between American whites and Negroes included the economic subjugation of the

Negro from the time of their enslavement, the criterion for social distance (race) continued to apply even to Negroes who rose from the depths of poverty to middle-class occupations and prominence.

In Brazil, whose early Portuguese settlers were predominantly male, the criterion of "race" was not as salient in establishing social distance with the native Indians, with whom many intermarried. The development of a plantation economy and the subsequent importation of African slaves produced a society with sharp class lines, with great social distance between the classes, to which the criterion of "race" was subordinate. As a result, there was less prejudice based on skin color than in the United States, which had similar minority groups (Freyre, 1950; Williams, 1949), despite the fact that the upper class was predominantly lighter in color than the lower class (Pierson, 1942).

Hawaii, now a state in the Union, prides itself on its greater ethnic tolerance than the mainland. Following intermarriage among white traders and its native population during early contacts, Hawaii's successive importations of labor for the plantations after about 1850 came from all over the world, including China and, later, Japan. The Japanese, whose government shrewdly insisted that each shipment of laborers include women, became one of the largest minorities. For most of the other dozen or so groups, intermarriage became the rule (Adams, 1937). At the top of the social structure, the dominant white groups maintained considerable social distance, and at least until recent years, light complexion was an aid in obtaining high status. In the 1930s the ranking of the various groups by the dominant whites was similar to that in the United States, except that orientals were ranked higher. A sample of Japanese gave similar rankings except that they ranked their own group first and indicated greater preference for fellow Orientals (Masuoka, 1936).

A particularly interesting series of studies on social distance has been conducted in Lebanon (Dodd, 1935; Prothro and Melikian, 1952; Diab, 1963 a and b). A country of diverse religions and national backgrounds, Lebanon was long ruled by the Turks, who are still the nationality regarded with least

preference, according to Diab. Otherwise, however, in 1935 the greatest social distances were found between different religious groups. Fifteen years later, the greatest social distances were found between nationality groups, a change that Prothro and Melikian attributed to the rise of Arab nationalism in the interim. Christian and Moslem subjects ranked the various nationalities similarly.

**Varying Criteria
for Social Distance
in Different Cultures**

The criteria for determining social distance are not necessarily identical with the causes of social distance. Furthermore, the criteria do differ from culture to culture and from one historical period to another. Therefore, it should be possible to compare the social distances in different cultures according to the relative weight or salience of various criteria. In other words, when a person sizes-up others in order to decide how intimate he is willing to become, which criteria will be more important to him— race, nationality, religion, or occupation?

Triandis and his coworkers have made a number of crosscultural studies of this problem (Triandis and Triandis, 1965). Adapting the Bogardus technique for assessing social distances, they found scale values for the statements listed in Table 12.2 for several cultural groups. Table 12.2 gives such scale values for samples of American students (University of Illinois) and Greek students. With the first statement (would marry) defining zero social distance and the last statement (murder) defining the greatest social distance (100), the relative size of the scale values indicate the degree of social distance described in the respective situation. For example, the American sample regarded a family friend as more distant, socially, than the Greek sample, for whom a family friend implies greater intimacy than accepting a person as a chum in one's club.

By presenting several criteria (such as race, occupation, and nationality) in all possible combinations, the investigators determined which criteria were the more important to a particular sample of subjects. For example, the subject would be asked to indicate in turn whether he would

Table 12.2. Scale Values of Statements Used in Two Cultures

Statement	American Scale Value	Greek Scale Value
I would marry this person	0.00	0.00
I would accept this person as an intimate friend	11.1	13.5
I would accept this person as a close kin by marriage	21.5	28.5
I would accept this person as a roommate	29.5	—
I would accept this person as a member of my intimate social group (in Greek, *parea*)	—	31.1
I would accept this person as a personal chum in my club	31.1	—
I would accept this person as my family's friend	40.9	24.0
I would accept this person as a neighbor	38.7	—
I am going to invite this person to dinner	—	33.3
I would live in the same apartment house with this person	49.4	—
I would rent a room from this person	57.5	42.8
I would be willing to participate in the lynching of this person (in Greece: I would kill this person if I had the chance)	100.0	100.0

Source: From H. C. Triandis and L. M. Triandis, "Some Studies of Social Distance," in I. Steiner and M. Fishbein, eds. *Current Studies in Social Psychology.* New York: Holt, Rinehart and Winston, 1965, pp. 207–216.

do the things listed in Table 12.2 with an individual who was a Negro physician, a white physician, a Negro unskilled laborer, a white unskilled laborer, and so on.

Suppose that a subject says that she would accept a Negro physician as a neighbor (scale value 38.7) but would not accept him in any of the situations listed above that statement in Table 12.2. However, the same subject says that she would marry a white physician (scale value 0). In contrast, she accepts a white unskilled laborer as close kin by marriage (scale value 21.5) but endorses a statement indicating a desire for no contact with the Negro unskilled laborer (scale value 68.7; not shown). Clearly, this person paid some attention to occupation, but, regardless of occupation, exhibited greater social distance according to race.

Through statistical analysis, relative weights can be assigned to several different characteristics, indicating their importance to the subjects. For example, Fig. 12.2 presents a comparison of the relative weights of race, occupation, religion, and nationality for an American and a Greek sample. The stimuli actually presented are listed along the baseline of the figure. The weights were derived through analysis of responses to all possible combinations of the characteristics (e.g., Negro, bank manager, same religion, French; white, bank manager, same religion, French; Negro coal miner, same reli-gion, French; white coal miner, same religion, French; and so on).

It is clear in Fig. 12.2 that the American sample responded to the hypothetical stimulus persons primarily on the basis of race, while the Greek sample was more sensitive to the person's religion. Occupation and nationality were comparatively unimportant for both samples, *relative* to these more salient anchoring criteria.

Through similar comparisons with samples of German and Japanese subjects, Triandis and Triandis (1965) report that American samples gave a much greater weight to race than other samples. The German subjects responded more in terms of occupation and religion than Americans did, while Japanese gave greater weight to occupation and less to race than Americans. The specific characteristics used in the various studies were not identical. Therefore, it is not possible to compare Japanese with Greek or German samples. However, in each study an American sample responded to identical items. The result is that only the American college students responded primarily in terms of race. They consistently used occupation and religion less than the comparison samples taken abroad.

Triandis and Triandis were also interested in individual differences within their student samples. By using a variety of other

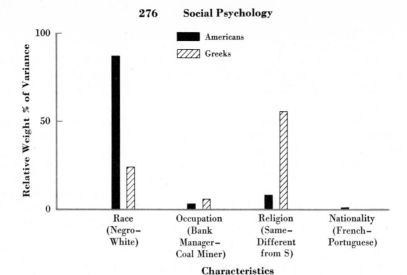

Fig. 12.2. Relative weights of various characteristics affecting social distance for American and Greek university students. (Based on data by H. Triandis and Leigh Minturn Triandis, 1965. "Some Studies of Social Distance," pp. 207–217 in I. D. Steiner and M. Fishbein, eds., *Current Studies in Social Psychology*. New York: Holt, Rinehart and Winston.)

The weights represent the percentage of variance attributable to race (Negro-white), occupation (bank manager-coal miner), religion (same-different), and nationality (French-Portuguese). As in other studies by Triandis and Triandis, American students differentiate preponderantly according to race, while Greek students were more selective according to religion. Changes in the pairs of stimulus characteristics would produce different results.

attitude statements (e.g., "In my opinion patriotism and loyalty are the first requirements of a good citizen"), they found that individuals within all of the samples who agreed strongly with items that conformed to existing social institutions and conservative political viewpoints also tended to exhibit the greatest social distance. This finding would be expected if a scale of invidious comparisons among groups were established in the society.

**Group Stereotypes Arise
to Justify Prevailing
Social Distance Scales**

In the experimental analysis of in-group and intergroup relations, unfavorable views of the out-group were a product of continued conflict between the groups. Recognition of this sequence is important, for it has implications for practical efforts at reduction of conflict. Several important writers have treated group prejudice and unfavorable stereotypes as *causes* of conflict between groups. In the day-to-day dealings of

group with group, including those that occur during sincere attempts to reach common ground, prejudiced viewpoints and blanket conceptions of the out-group certainly may be the most common source of immediate misunderstandings and interpersonal friction. However, most efforts to ease these difficulties by attempting to change the stereotypes alone have not been rewarding.

The term *stereotype* entered social science from the writings of the political commentator Walter Lippmann who wrote in his book *Public Opinion* (1922) of the "pictures in the head" that filter the news, affect what one notices, and how one views it. Because he was particularly interested in exposing many such images as false, the word stereotype was sometimes used to denote any false idea or image of others. Of course, some labels, adjectives, and beliefs attributed to out-groups are demonstrably false. However, these are not the only false labels shared by men.

The distinguishing mark of group stereotypes, as defined in this chapter, is not their truth or falseness. The images of a people that are widely shared by members of another group and endure over a period of time are invariably formulated from the point of view of the in-group's interests and goals as parties to the intergroup relationship. This is the distinguishing mark of intergroup attitude and belief. Initially, the images of the out-group are appropriate to the in-group's position *vis-à-vis* the out-group or the position that they want to achieve.

Stereotyped labels and adjectives for one's own group are almost invariably more favorable than those for an out-group that is rival or oppressor. The historian Shafer (1955) concluded that a part of the development of modern nations and nationalistic movements was the development of shared conceptions about one's own people and a vocabulary to describe them. One's own kind are seen as "kind," "civilized," "progressive." One's representatives in historic events are "heroes" or martyrs. The opponent is harsh, cruel, and backward, and his representatives are zealots. The same deeds are described with different vocabulary, depending upon whether they were executed by the in-group or the out-group.

Buchanan and Cantril (1953) compared the adjectives used by most persons in representative cross sections in nine European and American countries to describe their own nationalities and found them almost entirely favorable. When the German psychologist Hofstätter (1957) correlated the responses in each country with those in each of the others, he found very high correspondence between the images people hold of their own countries.

Social Organization,
Social Distance,
and Group Stereotypes

When intergroup relations are characterized by domination and subordination, the dominant groups control the major facets of living. They control the opportunities and the level of achievements available to others. Social distances among the various groups tend to follow the ordering established by the dominant group. The images of people on the social distance scale flow downward from the powerful and mighty to the subordinated. It is not unusual for subordinate groups to be hostile and prejudiced against the very same groups as their masters. Their images of themselves reflect some of the unfavorable evaluation placed upon them by others, amounting at times almost to self-hatred.

The Indian leader Nehru (1941) wrote about the Indian intellectuals of the late nineteenth century, whose histories "were written entirely from the British imperial viewpoint, and laid stress on our numerous failings in the past and present, and the virtues and high destiny of the British." As with many an oppressed people, the Indian intellectuals for a time accepted this viewpoint, finding comfort in their own conclusion that at least they were superior spiritually.

Only a few decades ago, Negro college students in the United States sometimes accepted the deprecatory images of their own groups as well as the stereotyped descriptions of other groups on the social distance scale (Meenes, 1943). A similar phenomenon was reported by G. Jahoda (1961) in the African Gold Coast before independence, where native school children frequently described natives in the same derogatory terms used by children of European colonialists and used admiring terms for the latter.

Such ironic facts as these tell us another important fact about the nature of group stereotypes. They are not merely false, irrational "pictures in the head." They reflect the arrangements of domination and subordination that prevail or that once prevailed from the viewpoint of the most powerful groups. As Franklin Frazier (1957) pointed out, the Negro did not have to be brainwashed or indoctrinated that he was socially "inferior." The fact was evident in all walks of life in Negro poverty and through the absence of Negroes from positions of power and prestige (and by the presence of whites in those positions).

The promulgation of superiority-inferiority images in a society is merely one means used by a dominant group to maintain its position. Even when it officially seeks to remove the social distances among various groups and to promote harmony among them, it faces the hard fact that these reflect actual inequalities and physical distances. From its dominance, it has created the Black Ghettoes (Clark, 1965) that shame mighty cities and the barren farmhouses whose residents have been replaced in the labor market by machines.

The Elaboration of Group Stereotypes into Superiority Doctrines

Dominant groups throughout history have elaborated their favorable views of themselves and their unfavorable views of those they succeeded in dominating or desire to dominate. Notions of group superiority have been developed into elaborate doctrines about the influence of geography, climate, the stars, and the choices of the gods. In the name of such superiority doctrines, men have fought, killed, and been killed.

Race doctrines have been the most pervasive, the most powerful and effective of the group superiority doctrines in modern history. They were effective because, unlike superiority doctrines based on religious faith, geography or social class, they propose differences that inhere in the biological makeup of the individual. Ideally, therefore, race doctrines picture a world in which "superior" races rule forever and "inferior" races remain forever subordinate. The popularity of racist doctrines coincided with two major developments in human history: the early development of the biological sciences and the rampant growth of European colonialism. The growth of biological science provided an intellectual backdrop to be misused by proponents of conquest and domination.

As Ruth Benedict wrote: "The first lesson of history in this respect is that when any group in power wishes to persecute or expropriate another group it uses as justification reasons which are familiar and easily acceptable at the time" (Benedict, 1942, p. 41). The wisdom of her observation can be seen in the tragic consequences of full-blown racism in a Nazi Germany bent on world conquest. Since World War II, the racist justification, while still virulent in certain parts of Africa and in the American South, has fallen into disfavor in knowledgeable circles. A would-be supremacist today is more likely to couch his justification for his acts in terms of his superior ideology, technological development, civilization, or even freedom.

A textbook in social psychology is not the most appropriate place for an explanation of the concept of race from a biological point of view. Nevertheless, as the doctrine of racial superiority is by no means dead, it is important to note that it contains not one shred of scientific basis according to international bodies of biologists, geneticists, and anthropologists (Montagu, 1951). A statement issued by one such meeting in 1950 clarified the nature of the concept for non-biologists, noting that "race" refers to statistical categories based on external physical characteristics. The statement emphasized that genetically speaking, there are no "pure races." Attempts to classify peoples have produced several different classifications, none of which is without inconsistencies. In any event, none of these classifications includes cultural traits or achievements and none includes mental or psychological characteristics.

Conversely, the psychological literature includes a considerable body of data showing that there are group differences in behavior, but *not* that the origin of such differences is biological or racial (Anastasi and Foley, 1949). There are still a few psychologists who interpret differences on psychological test scores by Negroes and whites as indicative of inherent differences in biological makeup. Yet, there is not a single study demonstrating that differences in test performance are necessarily associated with biological differences. On the contrary, there are many studies showing even greater differences associated with environmental differences. The recourse to a racist explanation of group differences violates the available evidence, and is to be viewed as a political move, not as being scientific.

THE CHANGING NATURE OF GROUP STEREOTYPES WITH CHANGED INTERGROUP RELATIONS

By analyzing newspapers, literature, songs, and cartoons, Goldstein (1948) showed that even within the prevailing doctrine of racism, the image of the American Negro changed significantly during the last century.

The image of the happy Negro slave grew after about 1820. The growth of the care-free, happy creature coincided with the growth of abolitionism in the North and more than two-hundred documented slave uprisings in the South (cf. Rose, 1948), a timing that seems paradoxical except from the viewpoint of slave-owners' interests. With the freeing of the slaves after the Civil War, the hitherto gentle and content Negro was pictured as a "brute," endowed with uncontrollable animal instincts endanger-ing, especially, white women. Still later, with the beginning of migration to the cities, came the comic figure who attempted a crude imitation of "white folks" ways and possessions. Certainly this is a strange se-quence of images if one were not familiar with the historical events that preceded and accompanied them.

Commenting on drastic changes in the image of Chinese immigrants to California during an even shorter period, Klineberg (1950) concluded that the only acceptable explanation for the changes was that it be-came "advantageous for the whites to eliminate the Chinese from economic com-petition," whereas their services had pre-viously been sorely needed.

In South Africa, the image of the native population as inherently inferior to the white man and his civilization—so inferior that it requires the full force of the white government with its apartheid policy to pre-vent contact—began to develop as the Europeans expanded to appropriate land and resources and to require labor (Mac-Crone, 1937). Earlier the native was viewed as a "heathen" to be uplifted.

At the beginning of the nineteenth cen-tury, the Javanese (present-day Indone-sians) were described by the Dutch as "fierce, warlike and violent,"; but after the Dutch colonialists crushed resistance, an officially endorsed image of the Javanese described them as calm, gentle, pliable, and meek (Wertheim, 1956). Less than fifty years later, the Indonesians demonstrated to the Dutch, by founding their own nation, that they were not pliable and meek.

Of course, the data used as evidence of group stereotypes in these historical studies are chiefly from public documents—pronouncements by public officials and the press. There might be a great difference between the images presented in the public media of communication and the images held by the public itself. A survey in Canada compared the opinions of a sample of the "general public" with the opinions of se-lected political leaders, in order to check which sample possessed the more stereo-typed definition of the "enemies" of the country (Paul and Laulicht, 1963). The gen-eral public was in much greater agreement than the sample of political leaders on the nature of the enemy and on the necessity of risking nuclear war. The findings suggest, therefore, that the mass media of communi-cation play a primary role in the develop-ment and maintenance of group stereo-types.

The stereotypes held by Americans of various ethnic and national groups were studied by Katz and Braly (1932), who pre-sented a list of adjectives to Princeton Uni-versity students, asking them to indicate which were typical of the various groups. They found considerable agreement on the adjectives selected for many groups, the favorableness or unfavorableness of the cluster chosen varying with the group's po-sition on the social distance scale. Inter-estingly enough, greater agreement on the stereotype was found for groups with which the subjects were more familiar (e.g., Negroes and Jews) than for groups with whom they had very little experience (e.g., Turks). This finding was supported by more recent studies in the Near East by Diab (1963 a and b), who showed that the lowest agreement in assigning adjectives to na-tional groups was for the more distant and unfamiliar groups (e.g., Chinese). Those groups with whom the Lebanese had had significant intergroup relations (e.g., Turks and Jews) received the most clear-cut images.

In the United States, there is evidence that college students are somewhat more sophisticated about assigning stereotypes to groups than they were when Katz and Braly made their study. A repetition of the study by Gilbert in 1950 found that the con-tent of the stereotypes among Princeton students was not changed greatly, but that a substantial minority of subjects declined to perform the task on the grounds that they had no basis for making the judgments of other groups.

One notable change in intergroup stereotypes in recent years is the rejection of the traditionally unfavorable image of their own group by growing and more vocal numbers of Negro Americans. In order to understand the rapidly changing scene of Negro-white relations in the United States today, it is necessary to go far beyond the social-psychological problem of individual attitude and behavior and beyond the sociological problem of social distance. The increased migration of southern Negroes northward after World War I, the experiences of Negro soldiers in two World Wars, and the expanding American economy all played an important part in weakening the social distance patterns established after the Civil War and in producing groups of Negro citizens who were discontent to accommodate to the dominant white power structure (Frazier, 1957).

These changes in the Negro communities were reflected in a study of community leaders in the South by Killian and Grigg (Killian, 1962; Killian and Grigg, 1964). Whereas the pattern of Negro leadership had been one of accommodation to the white community for many years, they found that the established leaders had been replaced by younger and more militant men. These changed patterns of leadership signalled both the rejection of second-class citizenship by large segments of the Negro population and the growth of groups formed to protest it. An interview study of Negro youth by Jones (1965) revealed that, on their part, discrimination and derogation were no longer acceptable. However, as so often happens in times of rapid change, the views expressed by different Negro youth varied considerably—all the way from the simple desire to be successful in terms of the dominant white society through determination to change it, and to the rejection of white society and identification with African nationalism.

After World War II, the United States found itself a giant world power in a world in which the majority of the population have colored complexion, and where rising nationalisms were struggling to free themselves of Western colonialism. To gain or to retain a favorable image in such a world, the most powerful segments of society came to realize that official changes in the most blatantly discriminatory arrangements in the society had to be made. From desegregation of the military services through the most recent civil rights legislation, the steps toward desegregation that have been most effective have proceeded from the most powerful segments of official society, with or without the assent of the populace in communities most directly affected. The continuing pressure from groups of activists increased the speed of these decisions—as we shall see in Chapters 23 and 24, in which the rise of social movements is discussed.

The relative speed of these steps—which appear "deliberate" to many members of the white community and "hasty" to others, but painfully slow to most Negroes—and their effectiveness have put to rest an old cliché that "stateways cannot change folkways." In fact, they suggest that folkways might never change if stateways do not. On the other hand, in early bursts of enthusiasm, some writers went so far as to suggest that the results of desegregation procedures showed that prejudiced attitudes and negative stereotypes were of no consequence at all in the changing patterns of intergroup relations. Subsequent events have shown that this is not the case and have encouraged more adequate analysis of the problems of intergroup attitude and behavior during times of change (U.S. National Commission [Kerner] Report, 1968).

Intergroup Behavior During Changing Intergroup Relationships

Earlier in this chapter, it was strongly stated that social distance, prejudice, and group stereotypes are products—not initial causes—of intergroup conflicts. Otto Klineberg (1950, 1964) performed a great service to social psychology by amassing evidence from a wide variety of sources that support this conclusion. However, he pointed out correctly that once social distance, prejudice, and stereotypes are established, they do affect the course of encounters between individuals who possess them. Indeed, the alternatives that a person considers, the way he weighs the evidence, the choices he makes, and his very manner toward members of other groups are affected by his images of them. If he is a person of great power, his views may affect the course of relationships between groups in an irrevocable way.

The impact of negative attitudes and stereotyped views in intergroup dealings has been shown in events of major consequence. For example, the Stanford political scientist Robert North and his associates (1962) have analyzed historical and public documents to obtain data on the way national leaders size up and evaluate the "hard facts" of military and economic capabilities of adversaries, as well as their future intentions. In an analysis of the sequence of events leading up to World War I, for example, they showed that such judgments and the policy decisions to which they led were influenced by the "soft facts" of preconceptions about the adversary—attitudes and images shared by many others in their own country.

In the study of Negro-white relations in the United States, the view that intergroup attitudes and stereotypes make very little difference in how a person behaves in a concrete situation was sometimes conveyed. This view was justified on the basis of studies in which it was found that some people (especially businessmen) *said* their attitude was one thing and then behaved in a way not compatible with that attitude. For example, as mentioned earlier in this book, a bartender said that he would not serve Negroes and then proceeded to serve a Negro graduate assistant in the company of whites.

However, the frame of reference for analyzing intergroup behavior, like any other behavior, always consists of both internal and situational factors. Particularly in times of changing patterns and norms for conduct, it is completely inadequate to analyze intergroup behavior without considering both. Donald T. Campbell (1963) made an incisive analysis of these so-called discrepancies between attitude and behavior from this dual viewpoint. More recently, the sociologist Robin Williams (1964) made the issues quite specific through analysis of large amounts of data obtained in a Cornell University project studying intergroup attitude and behavior in both northern and southern

communities during the years before the 1954 Supreme Court decision. Here is his conclusion:

> Situational variations in the responses of the same person seem to be great enough to raise important problems for general behavior theory. One such problem, for example, is whether we can get better predictions from a certain amount of information about the situation or from a certain amount of information about the individual's attitudes or about his past behavior in other concrete situations. There is no simple answer or set of answers to this problem. Different individuals vary in responsiveness or resistance to differences in situations. Different types of situations exert more or less pressure upon personality-determined dispositions to act. The kind of information required for prediction varies with the permutations of individual and situational variables, from instance to instance (p. 312).

Williams provides rich case material showing that, in some instances, the individual's attitude both as a prejudiced white and a businessman concerned about keeping his clientele, were directly evident in discriminatory and hostile behavior. In other instances, the situation was sufficiently ambiguous—in terms of expectations that the individual had of the "ordinary run" of intergroup contacts—so that purely situational factors, such as a customer's words or interpersonal pleading, were decisive in the outcome. The data show that:

> An initial generalized attitude before it actually issues in appropriate social action may be turned in the direction of any of a range of possible behaviors depending upon time, place, persons, and other values and beliefs. A generalized attitude of social distance of a white person toward Negroes may be reshaped by many mediating and countervailing perspectives before it enters into a concrete policy judgment concerning local school desegregation (p. 366).

In short, there is no issue of whether group prejudice and stereotypes are sole determinants of intergroup behavior or whether the individual acts solely according to the structure of the situation. The issue is rather the interaction among these and other determinants, an issue that becomes particularly striking in times of change. Regardless of how the individual acts, the existence of prejudice is an important psychological fact the reverberations of which can be seen in his assessment of his own conduct.

INTERGROUP CONTACTS
AND THE HEAVY HAND
OF THE PAST

As long as there are discriminatory arrangements and social distances among groups, the contacts and communications between them are limited in quantity and to situations acceptable in terms of social distance norms. The obvious remedy would seem to be to increase communication and contact among members of the respective groups. The remedy, however, is not as simple as it sounds. Of course, communication and contact are the prerequisites for changed relationships. However, the *conditions* in which contact occurs, even though the participants may have all of the good will and best intentions, turn out to be critical.

Interactions
Between Groups
in Conflict

In the experimental analysis, we saw that sheer contact between hostile groups, even in otherwise rewarding situations, serves only as an occasion for renewed exchange of insults. Even when two parties to conflict enter into negotiations or conferences aimed at resolution with sincere good will, their ingrained images of one another places such a heavy hand on the proceedings that failure is frequent. From the in-group perspective, the tendency is then to answer the question "Who is to blame?" with the unequivocal conviction that it is the other side.

Blake, Shepard, and Mouton (1964) report a prolonged session between union and management representatives in which each side participated solely to try to agree on a typical picture of their usual attitudes and modes of dealing with each other, with no technical or substantive issues being considered. The union and management in this case had a history of highly conflicting relationships. The agreement to participate was one evidence of an interest in changing this state of affairs. Yet time after time, representatives of both sides antagonized one another by the way they framed questions and responded to the other's statements.

Here are some excerpts of management representatives' remarks just after leaving the union:

"I told you! Anything he [the business agent] said, the others would back up. Those guys don't even know what is fact and what is fiction." . . . "How could they be so wrong?" . . . "I think they really know. . . . It fits everything they do. They always use this tactic. We're always the 'scheming' ones and *they* are the 'innocent' ones. The business agent has been to the International's school. They taught him all the tricks" (p. 180).

Among the union representatives, the following remarks were made:

"How can they honestly think that we are a clique running our organization?" "The whole problem . . . is that they are still living in the 19th century. They can't understand that unions are here to stay. They have no concept of the ideology of unions" (p. 181).

In international relationships, such blame-casting can become a strategy for evading negotiations. Within a society, it is common to hear blame cast upon other groups or institutions, in order to evade responsibility for the difficulty ("outside agitators," "the rascals in Washington," and so on).

Lacking some outside authority whose rulings are binding to both sides, contact to negotiate settlement of differences typically produces a vicious circle of recrimination and blame-casting. It becomes a means of continued conflict, even though each side may have entered with good will.

Contact
with Near-Equal Status
and Social Approval

In discussing the effects of intergroup contacts upon attitude and behavior, the crucial questions are: What kind of contact? Contact in what capacity? Contact in what kinds of situations?

Contacts between groups under prevailing superiority-inferiority arrangements do not encourage changes in attitudes and behavior; rather, they encourage the continuation and entrenchment of dominance-subordinate relationships (Williams, 1964).

On the other hand, surveys done in the military service and in a variety of employment situations in which desegregation was accomplished by legal or official regulation tend to show that interaction in such situations is associated with more favorable attitude and treatment of out-group members in the specific situations where contact occurs (Starr et al., 1965; Saenger, 1953). In recalling the social distance technique, it is easy enough to understand why this might be so. A person can accept another in one situation more close than previously, but still reject association in the more intimate situations involving residence, contact among children, or personal social life.

In contacts made primarily through work situations, the Cornell studies (Williams, 1964) found a persistent correlation between the amount of contact with members of an out-group and favorable attitudes toward them. Such correlational studies are always difficult to interpret, for one cannot be sure whether persons already disposed to be friendly enter into more frequent interaction, given the opportunity, or whether interaction itself breeds more friendly attitudes. However, the correlations are sufficiently frequent and high to lead Williams to conclude that "persons who are relatively unprejudiced are most likely to have ethnic contacts" and that "persons who interact across ethnic lines are likely to be relatively unprejudiced and to form ethnic friendships" (p. 201).

Williams also emphasizes the importance of the situation in determining whether interaction will occur. Studies of government-financed interracial housing units, while subject to the same difficulties of interpretation about who interacts across ethnic lines, nevertheless provide rather clear evidence on the importance of the situation. For example, dwelling in a housing project that also houses Negroes, but in separate buildings, has little if any effect on prevailing attitudes. Attitude change in desegregated buildings may be either positive or negative, depending in part upon whether opportunities for interaction are available (Deutsch and Collins, 1951). Given the opportunity for interaction, positive changes tend to occur more frequently among persons "who have relatively intimate contacts with Negroes and perceive these contacts as socially approved, and as a result change in their attitudes" (Wilner et al., 1952, p. 69).

The great importance of authoritative social approval for frequent interaction across ethnic lines was revealed in a study of an interracial camp by Yarrow, Campbell, and Yarrow (1965). During two-week camp sessions, they compared the behavior and friendship choices of white and Negro children, aged 8 to 13, from low-income families with Southern or border-state backgrounds. During the first three camp sessions, the camps were racially segregated. During the last two sessions they were integrated. Despite the lack of experience in desegregated situations, the children adapted to the integrated camp readily. The authors point to the single most important factor responsible for the smooth transition in these words: "The consistent expectation of equality, as conveyed by a racially integrated adult culture (counselors), enforced by the leader in his control techniques, and expressed in his behavior toward the children, were of overwhelming importance in setting the tone of the situation" (p. 669).

Contact Under Conditions of Interdependence

In extending the experimental analysis to attempts to reduce intergroup hostility and prejudice in actual life, it is important to recall the criteria for superordinate goals (pp. 265 f.). The fundamental criterion is that superordinate goals presume conditions of interdependence between groups in some area of compelling importance to all groups in the intergroup system. If two groups are irrevocably committed to conflicting objectives, there is little point in discussing conditions that are conducive to reducing the conflict. They will continue to cast blame for the state of things on each other, and to attempt strategies or force to attain their own objectives at the other's expense unless some more powerful body prevents it.

In short, there are very real conflicts of vital interest that preclude the emergence of superordinate goals. However, in a modern world torn by strife, it is becoming more and more urgent that social scientists of all descriptions analyze conditions and trends that effectively foster man's peaceable and productive pursuit of life. In this section, therefore, the concept of superordinate goals will be illustrated from three areas: labor-management problems, desegregation, and political life.

Industrial Organizations. As genuine conflicts of interest are very real in community and national life, the question of the nature and relevance of superordinate goals in industrial settings is particularly interesting. A case in point was reported in Lawrence *et al.* (1961, pp. 452–472) involving departments with fairly equal power, each with legitimate but rival claims for bringing a new product into manufacture for their company. The industrial engineers regarded the design as "ours," to the chagrin of the development engineers. The industrial engineers became convinced that the development engineers were out to block production of the product. The production manager was simply puzzled, commenting that everyone was mad and touchy.

Plans for production broke down so badly that top management began to consider withdrawing the product. This common threat brought the two engineering groups together for the first time in cooperative efforts to "save" the product. Production of the article represented a superordinate goal that both sides desired strongly, and which required their cooperative efforts and subordination of rival claims over a period of time. Afterward, persons on each side reported that during these joint experiences they each began to appreciate, for the first time, the problems faced by their erstwhile rivals.

Such cases differ from the usual conflict involving management and labor groups in industry. The early history of labor-management relations in this country is a chronicle of repeated collective clashes between workers determined to alleviate and improve their conditions and owners or managers adamantly resisting or crushing these efforts. Indeed, the origins of union and management groups as organized entities lie in such encounters. It is no accident that the rise of hostile attitudes and negative stereotypes in union-management history resembles that in the intergroup experiments, for we were well aware of the events when the studies were designed.

Currently, however, labor-management relations in this country have become more institutionalized through regulation toward certain "core objectives" supported by both sides, albeit for different reasons. These characteristics, as Dubin (1962) has shown, are the earmarks of an intergroup system, stabilized in some degree for the time. When one side or another focuses on incompatible aims and takes an all-or-nothing stand, the sequence of threat of force and actual force can only lead to open conflict or forced settlement. Within the *modus vivendi* reached, Dubin asserts, the specific purposes of labor and management limit the alternatives that leaders on either side can consider for resolving conflicts. The intergroup system as it exists requires that leadership on both sides take into account the limitations placed on each side by its own organization, if open splits are to be avoided.

The Civil Rights Issue. The most visible area of intergroup conflicts within the United States, especially during the past decade, has been the struggle for civil rights by Negro citizens. More recently the struggle has broadened into movements aimed at social and economic opportunity for all underprivileged citizens, including the disproportionate share that are Negroes (Chapter 23).

The extent of segregation and lack of opportunity in American life were revealed to Americans and the rest of the world by the turn of events, roughly after 1954, belying the prior quietude that had persisted despite the sporadic lynchings and mob violence. Both the outraged cries of avowed segregationists and the puzzled surprise of avowed moderates over the "new Negro" revealed lack of insight into the Negro condition and the poverty of communication between white and Negro citizens. The lost status of erstwhile Negro leaders, who had risen to leadership positions through accommodating to the local citadels of white power, revealed the peculiar combination of force and submission to force required by prevailing arrangements (Killian, 1962).

Protests, initiated by middle-class students and spreading throughout the country, were made in the nonviolent terms formulated by Gandhi, who had faced the overwhelming power of the British in India.

As with Gandhi's efforts, nonviolent resistance brought retaliation, adamant resistance, and counterforce from those who possessed power or were unafraid of the sources of power. Here the similarities end.

In this country, both the duly constituted federal government and the sympathies of many white citizens were on the side of the demonstrators. The demonstrators, in turn, pressed toward "our rightful" places within the American system of life—changed though it might be by their inclusion. Both national and local levels were aware that local protests would have an impact on other parts of the country and on the international scene.

For such reasons, unlike the Indian movement that had to endure half a century of oppression and postponement, the civil rights demonstrations with the more limited aims exemplified in sit-ins and boycotts to end segregation of public facilities began to produce results before the eyes of the participants. The results were not always or even usually exactly what had been requested. Yet there seems to be no doubt that demonstrations and campaigns, with their ensuing experiences of imprisonment and violence for the protesters, were an essential condition for any change to occur in the foreseeable future.

In this discussion, our interest lies in the question of how the changes came about, once the protests were made. Jones and Long (1965) completed an analysis of desegregation decisions in ten of the largest cities in the southern United States, varying in size from 80,000 to 1,000,000, with only two having fewer than 100,000 inhabitants. The changes in these cities, they found, did not "just happen." They followed a pattern of crisis, with some form of open conflict, the resolution of which was the result of settlements worked out by people who urgently recognized the need for steps "that would prove creative rather than destructive in their communities" (p. 3).

The *impetus* for change, they concluded, must give . . . full and due credit to the young direct actionists. What changes have come in the South have been determined in the courts and in the streets, usually due to both the establishment of legal prerogative *and* direct mass action. *How* these changes came about has been the result of negotiation. However, few of the young direct

actionists have participated in the implementation of the changes their demands have won (p. 15).

Jones and Long found that desegregation of public facilities had not been undertaken voluntarily by public officials in any of the cities. In the instances in which voluntary efforts were claimed, the threat of protests had been clear and present. In fact, they comment that "municipal authorities needed the appearance of being forced to act to prevent application of counter forces by segregationists" (p. 13). In most cities, the negotiations were conducted without benefit of official presence, although many of the committees were established by the city governments.

Jones and Long studied the negotiators in the ten cities, their background, the circumstances of negotiation, and reactions to the outcomes. They found that, with local variations, negotiators in all cities were persons who undertook the task and could pursue hitherto unconventional alternatives because, *for different reasons,* they perceived objectives superordinate to the immediate claims of the demonstrators and to the counterclaims of most white persons in the community, including many of their own friends and associates.

The characteristics of the *negotiators* are particularly interesting. They were persons "respected on their own side of the color line and . . . across the line" (p. 59), although not primarily for direct involvement for or against desegregation. In the case of Negro members, this meant that the most active and prestigious leaders of action organizations were not included—a fact that brought criticism from demonstration leaders, but not condemnation of the Negro negotiators. None of the latter was accused of betraying his people.

The typical negotiator was over forty years old, a college graduate following a profession (other than the ministry) or in business, born in an upper Southern or border state, had lived in the city in which negotiations occurred for ten or more years, and had participated in a large number of community and professional organizations, including interracial religious organizations. Some 40 percent of the white negotiators had lived outside the South at some time.

The limitations placed upon negotiators

by virtue of their membership in their communities are shown most clearly by the frequent insistence that their names and affiliations not be revealed publicly even after negotiations were completed. For somewhat different reasons, negotiators in several cities secured cooperation from the mass media not to make public announcements of planned settlements until after desegregation steps actually were put into effect. This policy was designed to prevent opposing segregationists from arriving on the scene before desegregation was accomplished.

The goals that brought and kept the negotiators working were, as noted, diverse. They included "personal philosophy, religious faith, business policy, and political expediency" (p. 60). In each city, however, the overriding consideration to negotiators was to avert the crisis or threat of crisis to their city, regarded as certain if inaction were the course. Thus, the common focus was "what is good" for the community. Their perspectives on what was good for the community had, in many cases, been shaped by participation as professionals and businessmen in mass production and distribution activities of the larger economy with the "personnel and customer relations that these imply: uniformity and interchangeability."

The authors suggest that the changes that occurred in the ten cities, although many were of a "token" nature compared with the ultimate objectives of action groups, are nevertheless significant. They provide a setting more conducive to further social change. They demonstrate both the limitations of public leadership and the possibilities of negotiation backed by community power and conducted by respected representatives who are sufficiently free of alignments to seek new and creative alternatives to old issues.

As applied to the problems of ethnic relations in the United States, Robin Williams (1964) concluded as follows:

Finally, we believe that the total body of evidence we have reviewed overwhelmingly supports the view that cooperation and solidarity among persons who differ in ethnic membership is fostered by any arrangements that produce joint action toward shared objectives (pp. 389–390).

In Chapter 23, the movement of Negro citizens in the 1960s is discussed. In part, the movement arose from the sheer lack of opportunities in the United States for joint action toward shared objectives by the masses of Negro and white citizens.

Political Life. The somewhat grim picture of intergroup relations both *within* many countries of the world today and *between* nations of the world should not blind us to the task of specifying further and further the conditions essential for establishing solutions to intergroup conflicts that are genuine solutions and that, at the same time, avoid the wasteful destruction of human life and the resources of the planet. Consequently, it may stimulate further research and inquiry to propose several problems that need investigation (Sherif, 1966).

The first is that modern life is increasing the mutual dependence of group upon group in ways that are fundamentally incompatible with the unbridled exercise of unilateral power in the direction desired by the most powerful alone. Human beings have become increasingly interdependent in their ways of making a living and in the very maintenance of life. This proposition is, of course, not social-psychological. Its evaluation requires the efforts of economists, political scientists, and other social scientists.

If it is true, then a second proposition is warranted: The areas in which superordinate goals can arise are widening, not decreasing. However, superordinate goals do not spring up by themselves to command attention with no human effort. Especially in a world increasingly dependent upon mass forms of communication, the efforts of many people are required to emphasize the superordinate goals that do exist.

Third, successive waves of superordinate goals that involve widening circles of human beings will have the ultimate consequence of changing and widening the self-identity of the human beings involved, such that their conceptions of morality and, hence, their sense of *conscience,* will not stop at the bounds of in-group membership.

These propositions find support in the histories of many nations, particularly those constituted from previously independent states or localities. The trend can be illustrated in the history of the United States, whose bounds and regulations are experienced as indivisible with the dictates of personal conscience by many of its citizens. Yet, this was not always the case, as Dr. Maurice H. Merrill, Research Professor of Law (University of Oklahoma), reminds us in a summary of legal developments preceding the Civil Rights Act of 1964.

The union first achieved by the thirteen colonies after their common struggle against Britain, it will be recalled, was the loose Articles of Confederation between "free and independent states." In those times, Merrill notes, *when an American referred to his "country," he meant his state.* The several states treated one another very much like separate countries, levying tariffs, imposing embargoes, and sometimes disregarding the treaty obligations entered into by the nation.

The formation of a new and stronger union was impelled by "realized interdependence" in certain important spheres: dealings with foreign powers and defense against the threat of war, commerce, and the promise of settlement in the vast westward lands.

Meanwhile, ties continued to be somewhat loose. Many people did not realize the change in legal theory brought about by the adoption of a Constitution that was to be the supreme law of the land. First one area and then another threatened secession when national policies seemed adverse to its interest. . . . Eventually, the concept of fundamental state sovereignty went down to defeat when the Civil War was fought to retain the South in the Union against its will (Sherif, 1966, p. 160).

The expansion westward and growth of commercial life after the Civil War gradually but irrevocably expanded the spheres in which federal laws were passed to command observance and loyalty above strictly local and state concerns. The Interstate Commerce Act of 1887 initiated control over transportation rates and practices. It was successively extended to regulate the transport of "articles or persons," local laws or practices adversely affecting interstate commerce, state-owned enterprises engaged in interstate or foreign exchange, labor relations in plants supplied by and serving the international market (1937), and conditions of production (1941).

The growth of federal union has gradually expanded in specific spheres of activity that became issues, especially as new conditions brought increased dependence of ways of life in one state upon those in the others. Rules emerging from early controversies over federal powers are now largely taken for granted. For example, the federal government's right to make treaties is undisputed by any state. In the recent dispute over the Mexico–United States border near El Paso, arising from the changed course of the Rio Grande, the citizens of the State of Texas had the greatest personal stake in the outcome. Yet, direct negotiations between Texas and the Mexican government would have brought indignant outcries up and down the country. Federal rules for dealing with foreign powers are so binding for the vast majority of citizens as to be personal conscience.

But this is not true in all spheres, as the recent civil rights struggles in both northern cities and southern states have shown. In this sphere, the conscience of many individuals has abided with the "sanctified institutions" of narrower circles of a "closed society," rather than the prescriptions of the constitutional union (Silver, 1964).

The genuine outrage of those resisting changes toward securing equal opportunity for Negro or other citizens reveals the extent to which the moral myths of discriminatory practices, rooted in local institutions, take precedence in their conscience and sense of loyalty.

The case of the United States is not unique. It is presented here to illustrate the fact that personal identity and conscience of the person are intimately related to intergroup problems. If he is a good and loyal member of a group that puts its own interests above those of any other, to the point of riding roughshod over others, the dictates of his conscience will justify that position self righteously. However, there is nothing in human nature that prevents the development of consciences with enlarged scope, applying to treatments of other groups and their members as well as one's own.

All successful solutions to intergroup problems involve a positive base: the cooperative activity of peoples gripped by realization of a common lot. The invariable product, over time, is a movement toward organization with binding rules of conduct in dealing with one another while doing something about the common problem. Such binding yardsticks for conduct arise in the spheres of life that have concerned them jointly. Always, time is required for them to become binding for all units or all peoples.

It should not be pretended that these things occur without affecting the in-groups in question. Intergroup process, for good or ill, does affect the groups involved. Only occasionally can the emerging organizational forms of an intergroup system be in the image of those prevailing within the respective groups. It follows that the rise of new, more inclusive standards and organizational forms requires the subordination of contradictory designs, practices, and standards prevailing within the groups *in spheres pertaining to their intergroup relationship.* Groups have always had and always will have private spheres of activity and interest that can be managed only by the parties directly involved, and that are, therefore, strictly "internal" matters.

The broadening of human bonds is the prerequisite for morality in dealing with peoples outside the narrow in-group bounds, for creation of a widening sense of "we-ness," and for individual conscience in keeping with an intergroup system free of tension and violence.

The trend is toward larger and larger dependence between peoples and toward the formation of organizations encompassing them. Historical evidence and empirical data of social science support this trend, even though they also show great human "wear and tear," suffering, and reverses for intervals of time.

The great question is whether the trend toward interdependence will be permitted to culminate in the standards of conduct required from all—despite stubborn, last-ditch opposition by islands of resistance—or whether the trend will collapse in the worldwide holocaust of a thermonuclear showdown.

PART IV

Self, Attitudes,
and Reference Groups

13

Introduction to Part IV

The chapters in this Part focus more closely on the lasting attachments, aversions, commitments, stands, and identifications that the individual has developed in the course of his interactions. It is in terms of such attachments, stands, commitments, and identifications that the person carries on the business of living as he encounters other persons, groups, and objects. It is within these terms that he reveals an individuality that characterizes his experience and behavior from situation to situation over periods of time. These elements are component parts of the distinctly human psychological formation that will be referred to as the *self system.*

In a sense, the whole of social psychology is concerned with the relatedness of the person to his surroundings—as stressed throughout this book, beginning with the definition of social psychology. Propositions, principles, and their corollaries governing this relatedness were presented in Part II. They will be pre-eminently effective in formulating a scientific concept of the self system, its components, and involvement of the self in various roles and capacities (ego-involvement). As will be specified in the chapters to follow, the principles presented in Part II and the corollaries derived from them served to guide the conceptualization of self, attitudes, and reference groups. The principles that proved particularly helpful included those pertaining to psychological selectivity, the part-whole relationship, the tendency toward psychological patterning, the relative weights of anchors (internal and external) the relativity of the comparison process (judgment), and man's conceptual level of functioning (Chapters 3 and 4).

In this Part, we shall make explicit much that had to remain implicit in the chapters of Part III dealing with man's interaction in his in-group and intergroup relations. The lasting commitments, attachments, and aversions that are parts of the person's self system are not self-generated. They are psychological products that emerge as a consequence of his interactions with others within a sociocultural setting the properties of which also affect the interaction process. The process of interaction in interpersonal, group, and intergroup relations had to be made explicit first (Part III) to establish a concrete base for the emergence of the person's identifications, commitments, attachments, and aversions, which we now bring to the focus in Part IV. These psychological states do not simply unfold as a natural part of maturation; they are products of the interaction process.

The distinctly human formation—the self system—has preoccupied philosophers, novelists, and dramatists, as well as social scientists and psychologists. Perhaps it is still in the works of dramatists and novelists that we find the most insightful descriptions of the self system as the person lives through episode after episode—whether the particular episode is in tune or at odds with his claims, expectations, or aspirations that reign supreme in his feeling and striving at the time.

Admittedly, the self system is a problem within the domain of motivation. Until recent times, scientific formulations on motivation consisted largely of reports on this or that particular motive or drive (e.g., hunger, sex, aggression, dominance, and achievement) without due consideration of its particular place in the general scheme of the person's motivational pattern. Consequently, relationships among specific motives or drives were sorely neglected. Because of this neglect, what was reported in the name of the psychology of motivation was, on the whole, a series of fragmentary accounts of this or that drive, isolated from others. Such accounts could not assess the place of the particular motive within the person's motivational pattern regnant in interaction situations; hence, they had little or no predictive value for the goal-directed sequence of his behavior.

For some time, therefore, social psychologists have been groping to formulate a theory of the self system that captures its components in conceptualization and measurement without reducing them to unrelated fragments. Unlike the artist, the scientist's task includes the obligation to achieve this feat in a way that is communicable and verifiable (Chapter 1). The chapters that follow are based on representative investigations in this direction. Some of the authors wrote of *self,* while others used the term *ego.* We shall use the terms *self* and *ego* interchangeably, for reasons spelled out in Chapter 17. What is meant by self system or ego will be specified below in both general and operational terms.

SELF SYSTEM

The concept of self system and its less-inclusive, associated concepts are probably among the most integrative explanatory tools in all psychology. For one thing, such concepts are opening avenues that promise to lead to rounded explanations for problems of the consistency and inconsistency of the person's behavior from day to day. The problem of the person's consistency-inconsistency over time has forged to the foreground in current social psychology as a serious issue because of the contradictory demands and appeals that the flux of modern life imposes upon man. In view of this flux, the issue of personal consistency is more than an abstract academic issue.

The continuity of personal identity (a phrase equivalent to self system) underlies whatever consistency a person manages to maintain. It consists of what the person feels intimately that he is in so many respects. For example, it consists of the male (or female) that he is and aspires to be, with all the qualities, emotional tones and strivings that go with being, aspiring to become, or becoming that male (or female). It consists of what the person intimately feels that he is as a friend, as a sweetheart, and as a person who can be relied upon within the family and within other groups dear to him (whatever they may be—fraternal, religious, or political). Being any one of these things that the person cherishes carries deep emotional overtones.

The components of the self system include the person's feeling that tomorrow he will still be the things that he cherishes today. When these things are disrupted or lost, or when he violates them by his actions or even in his own thoughts, the person feels that something precious is lost, disrupted, or violated in his very self. The self system, hence the person's experience of his self-identity, is composed of one's own feeling from day to day that he is the *same person* in these cherished respects. Even though they are not immutable, and even though they are subject to change under changing circumstances and new constellations of human relationships, these unit parts of the self system are not made anew day-in or day-out. They are lasting over time. They resist change except under conditions and pressures toward change that will be specified in Chapters 21–24. These component parts of the self system are the lasting attachments, commitments, values, and identifications of the person, which topics are the focus of the chapters to follow.

Behaviorally, the consistency of the person is inferred from the consistency of his words and deeds in relevant situations and in transactions with other people in expected roles over a span of time. Thus, the consistency of the person can be specified in terms of the continuity of his lasting attachments, aversions, values, and identifications over time. However, this general statement of operational means for studying the self system should be qualified. The person's words and deeds from which his "inner self" is inferred are seldom, if ever, his words and reactions to direct questions or test forms in contrived situations, such as in the laboratory or in an interview forced on him. It is in natural situations, when the individual is not "on guard" as he is in such contrived situations, that his expressions, words, and deeds reflect what he really is and what makes him tick in a consistent way. This generalization, qualifying the operational means for studying the self system, is an application of the principle of the unity of experience and behavior (Chapter 3, Proposition 1).

The application of the principle that ex-perience and behavior constitute a unity, we repeat, requires that study situations, procedures introduced therein, and research techniques do not impose new factors arousing ego concerns and apprehensions (see Chapters 5 and 6). With this methodological consideration in mind, we shall rely as much as possible on research strategies that have utilized indirect and unobtrusive methods for studying the self system and its components.

The usefulness of the concept of self system goes beyond the motivational issues traditionally recognized as self or ego issues, such as concerns over social ties, acceptance, self-esteem, achievement, prestige, or identification. Its usefulness is not restricted to handling topics related to attitude and attitude change, even though effective use will be made of the concept in the chapters on these topics. An account of the self system is crucial in giving coherence to the psychology of human motivation in general.

Ordinarily, human beings do not satisfy their hunger, thirst, or sexual appetites in just any way. They satisfy, postpone, or deny them in terms defined by the self system. This is why the channels and the means of satisfying even the biological needs vary so greatly from culture to culture and from time to time. In this sense, one can justifiably say that satisfaction of biological urges is accompanied also by gratification of the self. Thus, eating becomes an adventure in finding the place, the dish, and the companionship that satisfy oneself and impress one's friends. Efforts in satisfying sexual urges become a challenging sport and conquest. Any comfortable bed will not do for sleeping. Especially to a young lady, it is a matter of considerable concern that the bed is located in a respectable and, if possible, a prestigeful place in the eyes of her friends. In other words (with allowance made for cases in which biological urges of hunger, thirst, or sex reach their thresholds of intensity through deprivation), striving and satisfaction of specific drives involves, at the same time, striving and satisfaction of the person's ego.

We have been discussing the self system in terms of the problem of the consistency of behavior. As we shall see in Chapter 18, the analysis of the self system is also proving useful in explaining certain types of inconsistencies in outlook and behavior that have been topics of controversy in contemporary social psychology. An examination of such inconsistencies will tell us something important about the nature of the self system. A well-known example of such inconsistency occurred during the 1960 United States presidential elections. John F. Kennedy, the Democratic candidate, was Catholic. Richard Nixon, the Republican candidate, was Protestant. In the Protestant "bible belt," a good many ardent Democrats who had voted the straight Democratic ticket all of their lives, and who voted straight down the line for other Democratic candidates in the 1960 election, were inconsistent in their vote for President. They voted for the Republican candidate. Their religious affiliation as Protestants of a particular brand was stronger than their political-party identification. Many other cases of inconsistency in behavior can be explained if we keep in mind the following generalization about the self system:

An individual's commitments, attachments, and identifications can be ranked in terms of their relative importance in his self system. For one person, his politics may be a life-or-death matter; for another, it is his religion; for the third, his business; for still another, his occupation or sex role. The higher the priority of an issue in the self system, the greater the person's consistency in that respect—even at the expense of others lower in his scheme of priorities. His attitudes in other respects move him to a lesser extent, according to their relative rank or priority in his personal hierarchy. In other words, the person is more one thing than another, and he is other things in gradations. He feels and acts more consistently in terms of what he is "more" as a person.

These considerations, which will be expanded in Chapter 17, bring us closer to a characterization and analysis of the self system into its unit parts. The self system is not a unitary structure, cut from whole cloth at a single period of time. Nor is it self-generated, appearing fullblown as an immutable structure—even though the unit parts are interrelated. Nor does the formation of the self system follow as though by the unfolding of a preordained blueprint,

independent of sociocultural influences. From infancy on, the self system acquires as many unit parts as there are objects, things, events, persons, groups, and values that the individual encounters to establish subject-object relationships. Many ties, aversions, and role expectations that emerge and become stabilized in the process of the person's encounters with the referents (things, people, values) of these subject-object relationships make up the component parts of the self system.

The subject here refers to what develops as "my," "me," "I" relative to objects, including events and people within the person's psychological reach. The unit parts of the self system are subject-object relationships that delineate the person himself, define his lasting ties and attachments as well as his aversions, set him *for* and *against* their referents, and define his commitments. We shall refer to these unit parts as *attitudes*. Because the particular attitudes that we have chosen to illustrate the point are those that delineate the person's self-identity from other objects and that define his relatedness to particular objects in positive or negative ways, these will be referred to as *ego-attitudes*. The ego-attitudes are interrelated as parts of the same system. Because they are interrelated, the incompatibility and contradiction among component units become the source of inner conflicts, with all of their wear-and-tear on the person and other unfortunate psychological consequences.

Attitudes:
Components
of the Self System

Attitudes, then, refer to the set of subject-object relationships that the individual builds up in repeated encounters with objects, persons, groups, social values, and institutions and through interaction episodes focused on such objects. The subject, we repeat, is the person himself; the objects are what he encounters, whether as concrete objects or as they may be conceptualized in interaction with others. In short, attitudes define positive and negative relatedness of the individual to everything with motivational relevance to him. They set him for or against things. Happenings in line with his positive attachments and identifications (which are special cases of attitudes) arouse gratification. Happenings at odds with expectations or desires that are aroused by his attitudes cause dismay or frustration, as the case may be.

Thus attitudes, especially those that are unit parts of the self system, are affectively-emotionally charged and give heightened directionality to psychological activity in experience and behavior. Hence, attitudes, when aroused, have all the earmarks of a motive state. Therefore, when we speak of ego attitudes, we are talking about sociogenic motives, social "drives," or other terms used in the literature in discussing social motivation. Other more temporary psychological states that orient and direct behavior should be designated by labels other than attitude.

Now we are ready to pull together the essentials into a characterization of attitude. Attitude refers to subject-object relationships that the individual forms in his encounters with motivationally relevant objects (persons, groups, events, etc.) that set the individual for or against them in some degree in a lasting way. Operationally, an attitude is inferred from the person's consistent, characteristic, and selective modes of behavior toward the objects in question. An operational definition in terms of such modes of behavior will be given in Chapter 15.

The consistent, characteristic, and selective modes of behavior determined by an attitude are evaluative and emotionally charged in various degrees. They are not only cognitive in nature. The evaluative character of the behavior means that objects relevant to attitudes are treated by the person as acceptable-objectionable, agreeable-disagreeable, or good-bad in varying degrees. In other words, the person classifies the domain of relevant objects as positive or negative in some degree.

The unit parts of the self system, then, are attitudes (ego-attitudes)—that is, those attitudes that delineate the person from other individuals and objects and that define his particular positive and negative relatedness to them in the form of stabilized ties, attachments, and aversions. In order to emphasize that the self of the person is not a unitary structure cut from one piece, we

prefer to refer to it as the *self system*. One can speak of a system when it has interrelated functional parts. Having specified what the unit parts are, we can, for convenience, use simply the term self (ego) to refer to the system.

Combining the essentials we have presented here, we can now define the self system:

Self is a developmental formation or subsystem in the psychological makeup of the individual that consists, at any given time, of interrelated attitudes that the individual has acquired (in relation to his own body and its parts, to his capacities, to objects, persons, family, groups, status and prestige symbols, social values, goals, and institutions) which define and regulate his relatedness to these objects in concrete situations and activities.

DEF!

Ego-Involvement

The person is seldom, if ever, neutral toward his surroundings. He is related to motivationally relevant objects, persons, events, groups, and prevailing social values and objects with strong ties or aversions, as well as definite commitments and identifications. He forms and stabilizes an attitude for every single one of these relationships and each generates its particular affectively charged expectations, anticipations, and personal concerns—whether the individual is consciously aware of them or not. Because they are the source of his personal concerns and the gauges regulating his success and failure experiences (regardless of whether he is conscious of the fact), such directive attitudes are referred to as "ego attitudes."

When any one or a combination of his ego-attitudes is situationally aroused, owing to relevance in the particular stimulus situation, the person's behavior acquires unswerving directionality. This unswerving directionality mobilizes the individual to be more exclusively selective in that respect—at times almost blotting-out other things that, under ordinary circumstances, he would perceive, evaluate, and attend to. Thus aroused, his behavior becomes more consistent with his lasting claims and commitments. He then feels and behaves in terms of the characteristic image of himself.

What is referred to as involvement of self or ego simply refers to psychological functioning with a high degree of directionality, because of the arousal of an ego attitude by relevant stimuli in the situation. The following definition sums up the essentials.

Ego-involvement refers to the arousal of an ego attitude (or combinations thereof), which is triggered by a stimulus situation relevant to it. Ego-involving psychological activity brought through the arousal of a situationally relevant attitude of the person generates modes of behavior that are more consistent, more selective, and more characteristic of the person in that respect.

Degree of Ego-Involvement

The definition of self (ego), the analysis of self into its unit parts (ego attitudes), and the definition of ego-involvement lead directly to operational tools for objective measurement of the degree to which an individual is ego-involved in a particular stimulus situation. We will reach the formulation of such measurement for degree of involvement at a particular point in time through two steps.

1. The first step is based upon the fact that ego attitudes can be ranked in terms of their relative importance (priority) in the self system. Various ego attitudes are involved in psychological functioning with differing relative weights. (One person, for example, puts his religion above his politics; for another, his family is supreme; a third puts business profit above his religion, family, *or* politics; and so on). The closer the person's attitude to those that reign supreme in his scheme of things, the more characteristic, consistent, and selective his behavior is when he is involved through the arousal of his attitude in that respect.

2. The second step pertains to the fact that attitudes, including ego attitudes, cannot be adequately represented as a single position, stand, or point. (Most traditional measurement techniques represent the person's attitude as an average, cumulative score or scale value, as we shall see in Chapter 16.) On the contrary, the positive and negative relatedness of the person to relevant objects encompass classifications of objects ranging from those he completely accepts to those that are totally obnoxious

to him. These structural properties of attitudes will be presented in Chapter 16. Here it is sufficient to note them in order to develop the logic for objective measurement of the degree of ego-involvement.

The higher the rank (priority) of an ego attitude in the self system, the more "choosy" the person becomes and the more exclusive he is about embracing relevant objects or committing himself in this respect. He tolerates very few or no alternatives that deviate from what he puts on the pedestal in that respect. (This is the case with an infatuated lover, who feels that no woman other than his sweetheart will do.) At the same time that he becomes exclusive in his acceptances, he categorically rejects other alternatives, with little or no tolerance for suspending judgment; he thus commits himself positively or negatively with no tolerance for shadings between wholesale acceptance and wholesale rejection. He is cocksure of his choice and of his categorical rejection of other alternatives. An extreme illustration of the point is the almost pathological case of a Hitler or Mussolini, possessed by fanatical obsessions and committed to the proposition: "Those who are not for us are against us." The general phenomenon, however, is not pathological. It occurs whenever a person elevates an ego attitude to the pinnacle of his self system.

Variations in the range of what a person accepts and rejects according to the relative priority of the object domain in his self system can be multiplied from observations in the worlds of political ideology, religion, and economics. Such systematic variations provide the basis for operations measuring the degree of ego-involvement and, hence, the structure of an ego attitude. In Chapter 16, the structure of an attitude on a given issue between pro and anti extremes will be analyzed into three segments:

1. *Latitude of acceptance:* That segment that includes the own position of the person on the issue, plus other positions he will tolerate around his own position.

2. *Latitude of rejection:* That segment that includes the position on the issue most objectionable (obnoxious) to the person, plus other positions also objectionable to him.

3. *Latitude of noncommitment:* That

Partioning of an attitude

range on which the individual expresses neither acceptance nor rejection—for reasons of his own.

In a series of studies (Chapter 16), the relative magnitudes of the latitudes of acceptance, rejection, and noncommitment for individuals taking monopolistic and intense stands on various issues have been compared with those who are less involved, less partisan, and even neutral. The results of various studies on social and interpersonal issues have established that the latitude of acceptance for intensely ego-involved individuals are significantly smaller than their latitudes of rejection; they suspend judgment very little, with the result that their latitudes of noncommitment approach zero. In contrast, a person with less involvement on the same issue has latitudes of acceptance and rejection that are more nearly equal in magnitude, as well as extremely large latitudes of noncommitment.

On the basis of these findings, the following *operational measure* for degree of the person's ego-involvement is formulated:

The greater the degree of ego-involvement on an issue (or identification with a group or ideology), the greater the size of the latitude of rejection relative to his latitude of acceptance and his latitude of noncommitment. In extreme cases, the latitude of noncommitment is zero and the latitude of acceptance consists of but *one* object or position.

The less the degree of ego-involvement, that is, the less committed he is on an issue, the greater the size of the latitude of noncommitment and the more nearly equal the sizes of the latitudes of acceptance and rejection.

These operational measures are proving to have high predictive value for the person's behavior in situations involving the self in varying degrees.

Self and Conceptual Functioning

The attitudes that the human person forms are not exclusively to the objects within the narrow range of his immediate physical and sensory grasp. In any culture, man extends his relatedness beyond the range of his sensory equipment at a given moment. This extended relatedness, in space and time, is attested, for example, by his attitudes formed relative to a life hereafter (heaven or hell), the preparations that lead to the hereafter, and his myths about both his own origins and the origins of the universe.

The human child is handed-down verdicts and stereotypes by people other than those he contacts directly—about "foreigners," "white men," "Negroes," and distant peoples like Congolese and Vietnamese on whom the child has never set eyes. Little girls and little boys are provided with prescriptions as to the qualities and actions that a female or male should exhibit long before they actually experience what being male and female implies.

In short, the minds of the new generation are made up for them through value judgments and formulas about the world that are inculcated by the older generation before there is opportunity for the youngsters to come into contact with the referents of the vast majority of attitudes formed. Thus many attitudes are formed *deductively*, on the basis of untested premises handed-down to the child. This mode of attitude formation is in contrast to the usual procedure in psychological experiments on learning or concept attainment, in which the subject builds up a consistent response *inductively* on the basis of repeated encounters with the actual properties of the stimulus domain.

Deductive formation of attitudes is a general case in the socialization process, which makes an American into an American; a Chinese, Chinese; a Turk, Turkish—with the prevailing values of his culture. Therefore, it becomes essential to examine man's conceptual level of functioning and the human language that is its institutionalized vehicle (Chapter 14) before discussing attitudes and self in greater detail.

As the next chapter will show, conceptual functioning through the vehicle of language and attitude formation are not unrelated psychological phenomena. The essentials of man's conceptual functioning were discussed in Chapter 4. Having an attitude amounts to categorizing a domain of objects into favorable-unfavorable, acceptable-unacceptable, valued-obnoxious classifications. The individual discriminates among the objects and, at the same time, evaluates them by placing them into such value categories. We noted briefly the partitioning of an attitude into latitudes of acceptance, rejection, and noncommitment. Within these partitions, the person makes further subdivisions or categorizations. *These differentiations into categories imply a comparison process and the comparison process is a topic in the psychology of judgment.* The individual compares objects and places them into categories that he has formed for evaluating the domain in question. It is on the basis of such considerations that generalizations derived from the psychology of judgment (which amounts to a psychology of categorization) have proved effective in the study of attitudes and problems of attitude change. (See pp. 334–345 and 482–491.)

Role
of

Language It may not be too far off the mark to say that language (any language) consists of a scheme for slicing nature and its happenings into groupings (categories) according to their functional significance in the economy and culture of the group that devised it. Human relationships in terms of kinship, organizational differentiation in a university or a factory, and status relations can be expressed in terms of the vocabulary of categories. For example, a social system based on some scheme of kinship criteria invariably has a correspondingly more elaborate vocabulary for kinship relationships. Study of the psychology of conceptual functioning relative to the categorizations achieved in a language provides solid grounds for the psychological processes underlying the formation of attitudes and the self system.

DEF.

Reference Groups

Reference groups are those groups to which the individual relates himself as a member or aspires to relate himself psychologically.

We postponed to this Part fuller treatment of the reference group concept and its wide applications to various concrete problems. As the above definition indicates a person's reference group may or may not be the group in which he actually interacts in face-to-face situations. It may or may not be a group in which he is a formally regis-

tered member. Thus the person's reference group may be geographically or socially remote from him. In some cases, he may not have actual interpersonal relations with the members of his reference group. Clearly, reference group phenomena are possible only because man functions on the conceptual level and can anchor his self system through conceptual means. The chapters on attitudes and self will be more meaningful if the following generalizations about reference groups are kept in mind:

1. The relatedness of the person to a reference group that is not a group to which the individual actually belongs is achieved conceptually. (This achievement will become clearer as we study the next chapter and will, in turn, clarify the discussion of attitude and self.)

2. Reference groups and associated concepts (reference persons or idols, reference sets) are defined psychologically, in contrast to the sociological definition of the group itself (Part III). In other words, the reference group concept is defined from the point of view of the individual's selection of relatedness to others. Therefore, it is necessary to gain familiarity with the formation and functioning of self in order fully to grasp the uses of the reference group concept.

3. Applications of the reference group concept are flourishing in countries such as the United States, where there are multiple groups of various denominations (in social, political, religious, economic, professional, and other classifications), and hence where many alternatives for individual choice are available. The heterogeneity afforded by societies with some vertical or social class mobility, widespread geographic mobility, and proliferating informal organizations among the population offers numerous alternatives for identification. Similarly, countries with an accelerated rate of social change, as exemplified in many new nations today, present reference group problems for individuals plagued with conflicts between tribal, regional, and national loyalties. Accelerated social change, even in modernized countries, breeds conflicts between the younger and older generations that are aptly conceptualized psychologically in terms of reference groups and their values or norms.

The significance of the reference group concept in such complex and changing conditions is that it permits specification of the sources of the individual's major attitudes and the prediction of his ego-involvements in various concrete situations. The reference group concept has been indispensable in the modern works dealing with the problem of attitude change. Chapters 18 and 19 are devoted to discussion and application of the reference group concept.

14

Man
and His Words

Major Topics of the Chapter

Experiments on concept formation and
  neglected problems
Creating concepts: a study on naming
Its counterparts in social interaction

CONCEPTUAL FUNCTIONING
IS BASIC
IN MAN'S PSYCHOLOGY

Language is as much a part of the human environment as the air we breathe. We are immersed in a linguistic community from the moment of birth. We take it so much for granted that, unwittingly, we lay the foundation for our ethnocentrisms. The language becomes a part of what Donald Campbell calls the "phenomenal absolute"—social experience so immediate and real that it is not questioned. We firmly believe that languages are merely different ways of coding the _same_ experiences, and that everything conveyed in another language can be translated into our own if the translator is sufficiently skilled.

Our formal contact with language is typically in courses on the grammar and vocabulary of our own language or those of another language that we undertake for practical reasons. It is no small wonder that conceptual functioning and linguistic behavior are sometimes viewed as peripheral problems for social psychology—boring at best. It is not surprising that some psychological theorists have regarded linguistic behavior as a troublesome addition to the repertory of man, to be tackled someday when the "basic" principles applicable to all species are mastered. Yet, the dynamics of human behavior necessarily include principles of conceptual functioning, and it is by no means clear that "basic" principles of human behavior can ignore them.

Conceptual functioning, the attainment of language, and the use and creation of language are not merely intellectual or cognitive affairs—even though they are fundamental in human reasoning and intellect. They are highly motivated, affective and emotional as well as cognitive. They are not _merely_ additions to the behavioral repertory at the human level.

In this chapter, we consider man and his words in preparation for the analysis of social motivation, which is treated through the topics of attitude, ego-involvement, and reference groups (Chapters 15–19). The properties of human language will be discussed briefly, for these are properties that the individual faces in interaction situations. Language—any language—has definite patterns and organizational principles, which are studied in their own right by linguists—who usually study modal practices in a language or the range of acceptable linguistic practices (Dinneen, 1967). If we are ever to understand how a child achieves the tremendous feat of learning to speak a sentence in his native tongue, it is essential that we recognize the patterned (structured) character of what he is learning (Chomsky, 1959). Linguistic data are analyzed in terms of patterns.

In recent years, a number of researchers have conducted systematic studies analyzing the structure of children's early speech, as well as their use of conventional language forms and correlated changes in perceptual, motor, and volitional activities. Our brief review of this literature will be continued in Chapter 17, wherein the socialization process is discussed in terms of the developing self (ego) system.

We shall consider experimental findings on the categorization process and the use of linguistic categories as the person perceives ongoing events, assesses them, and deals with them. Assimilation and contrast effects related to categorization will be discussed. Later, in Chapters 15, 16, and 21, we shall see that the anchoring effects of categories are basic to the understanding of attitude and attitude change.

Finally, this present chapter will consider the processes in which linguistic concepts originate. Man not only learns language and uses it; he is also its creator in concert with his fellows engaged in mutually significant activities. He initiates and participates in standardizing and in changing language concepts. No social-psychological account of man and his words is adequate without emphasis on these facts, although they may be poorly explored at present.

LINGUISTIC SYMBOLISM
IS DISTINCTLY HUMAN

Man is notably self-centered in appraising his own powers and intellect. Darwin's evolutionary theory forced reappraisal of this tendency and fostered scientific study of behavior. Within the evolutionary study of behavior, schools of thought developed, the most notable concerning the issue of continuity-discontinuity in evolutionary process. As is the case with most polar opposites, this issue is prone to arouse active proponents to the selective choice of facts.

One version of the continuity proponents was summarized by a psychologist whose work has been primarily comparative, M. E. Bitterman (1965):

A century ago, as Charles Darwin developed his theory of evolution, he denied not only the physical uniqueness of man but also the intellectual uniqueness. In doing so he used the only evidence available to him: episodes described by naturalists, hunters, pet-owners and zookeepers. It was not until the start of the 20th century that the study of animal intelligence was brought from the realm of the anecdote into the laboratory by Edward L. Thorndike. . . . Thorndike's experiments led him to deny the existence of intellectual uniqueness anywhere in the evolutionary hierarchy of animals. It was he who set forth the theory that differences from species to species are only differences of degree, and that the evolution of intelligence involves only the improvement of old processes and the development of more neural elements (p. 99).

Much of the comparative study of behavior in different species proceeded on the tacit assumption that evolutionary changes involve chiefly differences in degree or complexity of the *same* biological processes. For example, one of the classic experimental models for comparing the symbolic capacities of various species was the delayed-reaction experiment, in which the measure of delayed reaction is a matter of degree (time). The basic procedure was to present a goal object to the animal, then to conceal it, requiring the animal to delay his attempt to locate and obtain the reward. As the measure is one of degree (time of delay for successful choice), it is not surprising that the findings show differences in degree as one moves up the phylogenetic scale from rats to man.

This finding, however, does not provide evidence that *only* a difference in degree is involved in the delay. It is possible to set up experiments to demonstrate *qualitative* differences in behavior as well as differences in degree. T. C. Schneirla (1966), for example, examined the kinds of errors made by ants and rats in learning to run a maze. There were differences in this respect that are not reflected when time or number of trials for learning is the measure selected for comparison. Bitterman (1965) reported qualitative differences in the performance of fish, turtles, pigeons, rats, and monkeys, showing that whether such differences are detected depends upon the problem presented to the animal and the extent to which it involves visual processes or spatial orientation.

The delayed-reaction experiment, while designed to study differences in degree, does reveal qualitative differences as well. Summarizing the findings on chimpanzees, Yerkes and Nissen (1939) noted that when spatial or position cues were eliminated, delayed response became very difficult or impossible for most animals; only the brightest succeeded in achieving delay beyond a few seconds. Yerkes who was one of the eminent investigators of primate behavior in the United States, concluded that the chimpanzee's difficulty in delaying response under these circumstances was traceable to the chimpanzee's lack of a "symbol or representative process" comparable to human conceptualization. In short, he lacks the "holding" operation that permits a person to retain the location over periods of days and weeks ("The reward is under the green box").

Similarly, in the Yerkes laboratory, qualitative differences were found in chimpanzees' response to symbolic objects.

Chimpanzees were trained to use tokens to obtain food from a vending machine (Wolfe, 1935). Very much like little children, they came to be fond of the tokens themselves. The tokens were even effective as incentives for learning new tasks (Cowles, 1937). However, once the experimenter rigged the vending machine so that the tokens no longer brought food, the tokens quickly lost all value for the chimpanzees. Yerkes (1943) recognized that there were similarities in the chimps' treatment of the tokens and the reactions of young children. However, he explicitly cautioned against considering the token behavior of the animals as equivalent or even as a "primary functional basis" for the linguistic processes of humans.

More recently, Lenneberg (1967) reviewed evidence from biology, genetics, comparative neurology, and animal behavior studies in the light of the continuity-discontinuity controversy in evolution. He concluded that discontinuity as well as continuity is indicated by the evidence and is compatible with modern theories in developmental biology (p. 228). Human cognitive processes have "biological pecularities" that distinguish them from other species and make language possible (p. 374).

In short, the processes underlying man's attainment of language, his use of language, and the consequences of language in his behavior are not identical with the processes underlying the symbolic behavior of subhuman species. The processes specific to man permit the development of systems for token exchange, in contrast to temporary use of tokens with immediate exchange value. Although diamonds may be a girl's best friend, human beings value, save, hoard, and exchange symbols that are not useful in obtaining immediate satisfaction of physiological needs (e.g., scraps of paper, shells, rocks, old books, souvenirs). They develop systems of exchange (such as shells, silver, and scraps of paper) the value and use of which must be understood in terms of long range and far-flung schemes for power, prestige, and glory—which are distinctly human concepts. In fact, man's attainment of a conceptual level of functioning permits the development of motives that are not derived from biogenic needs, either directly or secondarily. Man's sociogenic motives—his attitudes and ego-involvements—arise during development as he attains a conceptual level of functioning and interacts with persons in his environment.

Perceptual and Conceptual Symbols

The distinction between the perceptually symbolic and conceptually symbolic is not identical to that between nonverbal and verbal behavior. In fact, oral utterance is not essential to human conceptual process, although it is very important in its normal development. It is possible to train some animals to utter sound patterns in specific perceptual situations even though they do not attain a conceptual level of functioning. Some birds are quite adept in this respect.

Two psychologists, the Hayeses (1951), succeeded in training baby chimpanzees to utter three sounds that resembled the words they had attempted to condition to specific stimulus situations ("cup"). (The sound movies of the performance indicate that the resemblance to human words is slight. The chimpanzee was required to perform motor acts that are difficult for a chimpanzee.) More recently, a great deal of publicity was given to the dolphin and porpoise that were conditioned to utter certain sounds: As the animals use sounds in their natural habitats, it is not surprising that the dolphin could be trained to use them with the animal trainer as well. Such an outcome in no way suggests that the dolphin has a "language" in the human sense.

For nine months the Kellogs raised their own son and an infant chimpanzee together (1933). The chimpanzee, Gua, developed more rapidly and surpassed the boy in many respects—for example, in learning to cooperate, to obey adults, to open doors, in toilet training, eating with a spoon, and responding to human commands. Before Donald was two years old, he was beginning to speak and surpass Gua in other respects with ease. The Kellogs did not attempt to condition "verbal behavior" in Gua, but even if they had, the end result would not have differed. Donald began to develop into a socialized human individual and Gua could have become nothing other than a well-trained chimpanzee.

Sapir (1921) pointed out long ago that man's organs of speech are not entirely distinctive in the animal kingdom and, in any event, have other functions as well as speech. In point of fact, blind and deaf individuals can form concepts and function conceptually by using their hands instead of their mouth, tongue, teeth, and vocal cords.

The difficulty of treating conceptual functioning solely in terms of verbal behavior is illustrated in the following report summarized from an Associated Press dispatch (1965) about communication involving concepts, but not the usual organs of speech:

On Turkey's mountainous Black Sea Coast, the 500 inhabitants of Kusköy have developed a code of whistles that carry long distances through the pine-covered forests which muffle the human voice. "The high-pitched sounds carry news of births and deaths, arrivals and departures, love affairs and all the latest gossip. . . . the people of Kusköy can argue or even make love with it." The residents learn to whistle as children and "have developed huge cheek muscles practicing the art, often before they learned to talk." The manner of whistling is also unique: "The whistler curls his tongue around his teeth so that the air is forced through his lips. There is no pucker as in most whistling. To amplify the sound, the palm is cupped around the mouth and the 'words' come out with a terrific blast."

Man's *capacity* to function on a conceptual level is related to the evolutionary development of his nervous system more than to the particular medium that he employs (verbal behavior, whistling, hand movements, electronic signals). As we await new developments in exploration of the brain, we can make inferences from behavior about man's differences from his biological relatives. However, we should not limit our data to verbal behavior alone. Certainly, we should also have to include a repertory of gestures and facial expressions. Unlike the gestures and facial expressions of other animals, many of man's muscular expressions are *conceptually* symbolic. Thus the repertory for expressing emotions and for signaling differs from one culture to another (Klineberg, 1954, gives many fascinating examples).

The behaviors from which we infer conceptual functioning include the way that man uses tools. Man is not the only species to use tools. He is the only species that creates new tools progressively, conceptualizes the relationship between the tools themselves, and accumulates tools and passes them to future generations (White, 1942). He is the only species to develop *language systems,* in the particular sense that an organized system of symbols is standardized, mutually shared and interchanged with or without face-to-face contact, employed both conventionally and flexibly in communication, and transmitted to the young. Man is the only species to transmit social forms, art forms, institutions, and modes of living from one generation to the next and to change these forms voluntarily. These behaviors are quite as tangible as verbal behavior.

Is Man's Capacity to Function Conceptually Innate?

Modern research on the development of behavior has forced a reappraisal on the meanings of *heredity* and *environment* throughout the phylogenetic scale. The upshot of this reappraisal is that any behavior, including behaviors specific to a given species, is always a *product* of the particular organism's development in a particular environment. Thus, behavior formerly viewed as "instinctive" for a species can be entirely absent if an animal is raised in atypical conditions (for example, isolated from other members of the species); it can also vary considerably according to the particular conditions of development, and is profoundly affected by the conditions typical in the organism's natural habitat (see, for example, Schneirla, 1956).

The British researcher M. M. Lewis (1963) starts his book *Language, Thought and Personality in Infancy and Childhood* with the sentence: "A child is born a speaker and born into a world of speakers" (p. 13). The linguist Noam Chomsky (1965) proposed that the fact that children learn any language at all implies that there are "linguistic universals"—properties common to all human languages within which their actual diversity occurs—and that the child has "tacit knowledge" of these universals before he can learn a specific language. Similarly, Lenneberg (1967) writes of a "biological propensity" for language. None of these writers, however, is suggesting that there is anything biologically determined about the particular language spoken or that individual differences are to be explained through exclusive reference to biological factors.

Lewis continues to specify what he means by saying that the human child is a "born speaker": "he has innate capacities, the roots of his linguistic growth . . . that from birth he vocalises and responds to sounds" (p. 13). However, he was careful to specify: "The linguistic growth of a child in his social environment moves forward as the continued convergence and interaction of two groups of factors—those that spring from within the child himself and those that impinge upon him from the community around him" (p. 13). From a variety of sources, we know that the attainment of a conceptual level of functioning depends upon the *combination* of at least the following conditions:

1. Maturation of the nervous system. The human nervous system is not mature at birth and its growth continues well into the childhood years. Interruption of normal maturation by injury or disease also can retard or prevent the acquisition of language.

2. Interaction with other persons who communicate through language and respond to verbal communication.

In short, given a human nervous system without abnormality, the attainment of language and conceptual functioning is contingent upon interaction with members of a linguistic community.

DEVELOPMENT WITHOUT LINGUISTIC INTERACTION

A definitive test of the importance of social interaction as a condition for attaining a conceptual level could be made easily enough if human beings did not value their children: Simply care for a child without responding to his vocalizations or speaking to him. Because such an experiment is repugnant, the evidence available is from "natural events." The best documented case of development without linguistic interaction from birth was reported by the sociologist Kingsley Davis (1947).

Isabelle was six-and-a-half when she was discovered with her mother in a darkened room, where both had been confined during most of the time since her birth. Her mother was a deaf mute, and the confinement was a parental reaction to the fact that she gave birth to Isabelle out of wedlock. To the clinical psychologists and doctors who examined her, Isabelle seemed more like an infant, or an animal, than a six-year-old. She did not speak, making only croaking sounds; she was fearful; she reacted in many ways like a deaf child. Despite this unfavorable picture, a program of speech training was undertaken. It took the persistent therapist a week of sustained effort simply to get Isabelle to respond vocally.

However, the rate of Isabelle's progress thereafter was astounding: She started to form sentences in slightly over two months. After eleven months she could identify printed words and simple sentences. In two years, she was talking and had a vocabulary of almost 2000 words, an achievement that typically takes six years when begun at birth. By eight-and-a-half, Isabelle's performance on "intelligence" tests was normal for her age, and her behavior was not obviously different from ordinary children of her age. She had completed elementary school by the age of fourteen and behaved like a "normal" child.

Isabelle's case provides the clearest evidence that the acquisition of language, the conceptual level of functioning, and the development of a personality that we call "human" are heavily dependent upon growing up in continued interaction with speaking persons. Supporting evidence comes from study of deaf children, who are typically retarded both in speech and conceptual development by the age of two, unless compensatory training is attempted before that age (Lewis, 1963).

Recently, some researchers into the linguistic retardation of children in poverty-stricken environments have drawn a parallel, suggesting that the difficulties of life reduce child-adult interaction and that the language heard by the child is limited in both grammar and range of vocabulary (e.g., Deutsch, 1963). They also recognize that the range of objects and experiences in underprivileged environments differs from that in affluent surroundings.

PROPERTIES OF LANGUAGE

Linguists are social scientists who study languages as organized systems. Accordingly, we turn to linguistics for an understanding of the patterns that the person confronts in ongoing social situations. There are several ready sources for a more detailed understanding of linguistic analysis and the psychological problems associated with it (e.g., Brown, 1965; Dinneen, 1967; Lenneberg, 1967—especially Appendix A by N. Chomsky; Chomsky and Halle, 1968).

What does a child learn when he acquires a language? What is a human language? Any human language consists of an *arbitrary* and *conventional* system of symbols (sounds and signs) that are meaningful to its users. It is *arbitrary* in the special sense that there is no necessary connection between the particular symbols employed and the events to which they refer. It is *conventional* in the sense that both the systematization and the symbols are mutually intelligible to the users—that is, they are standardized within the group. This conventionality is essential to the problem of meaning (semantics). If every person employed his own unique symbols or organized them in his own way, their meaning would be entirely his own. Linguistic meanings are not an individual affair, although there is a range of individual differences within any language group. The range is particularly broad for more abstract concepts (e.g., democracy, freedom, liberty, and liberating).

What properties are universal to language? First, every language has a systematic set of sounds (or written symbols) that it uses, excluding other possible sounds. The smallest unit of analysis used by linguists in study of this *phonological* system is the phoneme, which corresponds very roughly to the vowel, consonant, or consonant combinations.

Because the phoneme is a useful unit of analysis, particularly in transcribing unwritten languages, it has been considered by some linguists as a "basic element" for analysis. However, it is basic only for certain types of analysis. The morpheme, which is a combination of phonemes commonly used in constructing words of the language, may be more useful at times. (For example, *cat, cat*nip, and *cat*nap all contain

the same morpheme, which could be broken down into phonemes.) Finally, every language possesses more complex units—words (a lexical set).

The second universal system in any language is a system for arranging words—a grammatical or *syntactical* system. The order of arrangement is sequential (linear in time or space) but differs greatly from one language to another. For example, the sequential structure of a declarative sentence differs in English (subject-verb-object), German (subject, object, verb), and Turkish (object, verb, suffix indicating subject).

Third, every language has a *semantic system*—relationships between its lexical and syntactical system and referents in the real world, even though language is arbitrary and conventional. While men do play with words and meanings, a language without semantic properties and principles would wither away, if it did not lead to mass chaos first. Linguists are prone to emphasize this point but to neglect semantic analysis. The semantic problem is highly complex and semantic analysis cannot be accomplished without reference to "extralinguistic" factors (e.g., sociological, historical, and psychological, Dinneen, 1969).

Fourth (and this is a rather minor consideration for many linguists), every language has a stylistic system—including patterns of intonation, for example. The stylistic component is not entirely identical with its phonological, lexical, syntactical, and semantic systems. Matters of style are not, perhaps, of great importance for linguistic analysis, but they do have reality as social stimuli. The authors recently heard an 18-month-old-boy who uttered only one or two conventional words, but gave a completely accurate rendition of English intonational patterns for statements, questions, and exclamations over his toy telephone in his own phonemic gibberish.

Each of these analytic subsystems of a language has "its proper units and rules of permissible combination and order" (Dinneen, 1967). The rules set limits for what is acceptable or possible in the language in the sense that their violation results in an "un-French" sound (e.g., *w*), or an "un-English" pattern of sounds (e.g., *gst* as an initial consonant in English) or word (e.g., *enoughing*), or sentence (e.g., "Went boy the paper home tired"), or style (e.g., in English try speaking each sentence throughout a conversation with equal stress on every syllable or with regularly rising or falling pitch in each sentence).

In analyzing the properties of grammatical systems, Chomsky (1965) has emphasized that syntactical systems (grammar) do more than set limits for the "possible" sentence structure, as one might analyze it through a tree diagram. He noted that grammars also provide rules (of which the speaker need not be aware) for generating new sentences and combining them. For example, English provides rules for combining two sentences with conjunctions. "The scene of the movie *and* of the play was in Chicago" is such a combination. However, consider these two sentences: "The scene of the movie was in Chicago." "The scene that I wrote was in Chicago." Combined by the same rule they result in a "nonsentence" in English: "The scene of the movie and that I wrote was in Chicago." Chomsky suggests that when a child learns a language, he is learning not only sounds, words, and sentences, but rules for generating new sentences as well.

This view contrasts with the older view that what children learn is sounds, then words and their referents, and finally proper sentences.

Chomsky (1965) has noted the interdependence of the syntactic and semantic aspects in rules for generating sentences. All of the following sentences are grammatically permissible in English, but note that the different orders are not semantically permissible or meaningful:

even for technical linguistic analysis. The individual encounters language as a series of unitary events patterned in both the immediate context and over time. The growing child is not exposed to all of a language or its rules at once. In fact, most adults probably do not speak to a young child exactly as they do to adults. However, the child's exposures reflect the existing language system, not a sequence of discrete stimuli in random order. With the properties of language in mind, let us examine the typical trends in children's acquisition of language.

ENTERING A LINGUISTIC COMMUNITY

The human child cries at birth and begins to vocalize soon thereafter. In a scant three or four years, he is speaking in sentences, using the major constructions of the language community in which he has developed. This accomplishment, in turn, marks a period of more rapid socialization. It is also the age at which the classic conditioning principles begin to require modification (Razran, 1935; Luria, 1961).

Infant babbling consists of a wide variety of sounds, some more frequent than others, that extend far beyond the range of phonemes used in most languages. (The number of phonemes employed in languages that have been studied range from as few as 20 to about 85, with English using about 45). Although part of this babbling is "expressive," in the sense that it occurs when the child is uncomfortable or content, much of it has no obvious referent. It is activity comparable to the infant's

The boy may frighten sincerity.	Sincerity may frighten the boy.
Sincerity may admire the boy.	The boy may admire sincerity.
John amazed the injustice of the decision.	The injustice of the decision amazed John.

In other words, the semantic consideration is not merely a matter of the meanings of discrete words or their correspondence to particular referents. It is intimately linked with the ordering of words. These examples suggest that transformational rules of sentences involve both order and semantic considerations.

The sound-word-grammar-meaning systems are closely related to one another,

waving his hands, kicking his feet, or turning over. Even congenitally deaf children babble. Unless those who care for the child respond to this vocal activity and the child, in turn, can hear others vocalize, babbling does not change into speech and, without special training, it eventually declines (Lenneberg, 1967, Chapter 4).

What do adults (or older children) do in response to the infant's babbling? Many respond with nonsense sounds while others talk, but the response is a human voice *selectively* using sounds acceptable in the language rather than imitating all of the varied sounds the baby produces. As Lewis (1936) pointed out, every culture has its store of "nursery words"—culturally standardized syllables that normally occur during infant babbling (such as "mama," "papa," and "dada," in English).

The infant responds to the human voice early. The voice is linked with all manner of comfort that he knows. By the time he is sitting upright and beginning to crawl or wriggle about, he recognizes those who care for him and responds affectionately to them. The social bond, in turn, is the medium for exchange and for the earliest stabilization of a "word." The "first word" is frequently more a product of the adults' efforts in this exchange than the child's, and it is often a "nursery" form that adults seize as evidence that the child talks. Children are welcomed to the linguistic community and sometimes pushed into it.

By this time (around the end of the first year or during the early months of the second, on the average), the child has made tremendous advances in sensorimotor development. Usually he can move about on his own, look in all directions from an upright perspective, and touch and explore actively. (The range of individual differences in standing, walking, and speaking is large. Some children move about well before they utter "words" while others form little sentences before they walk. There is, however, a general correlation between motor development and speech suggesting that both are promoted by an underlying maturational process [Lenneberg, 1967, Chapter 6]).

What are these "first words" and how are they attained? They are stabilized slowly and are added at first one or two at a time. Their occurrence resembles that of other motor acts that the child learns to make, to the delight of adults. Adult response reinforces the act (for example, waving bye-bye to daddy, clapping hands, or kissing mama). The course of this learning may follow the fairly simple laws of conditional responses, in the classical Pavlovian model and in the Skinnerian model of instrumental conditioning. It is coupled with a great deal of trial-and-error learning. In short, almost any or all of the "reinforcement" theories of learning can handle the acquisition of the *earliest* words if the response of another human being is viewed as the reinforcing agent.

At this early period of development, the baby's activity is closely tied to the ups-and-downs of his physiological needs, states of comfort-discomfort, and the prominent features or changes of his environment (including other persons). However, even during this period, a change occurs in his acquisition and use of "words." Evidence of these changes is provided by the numerous studies on the growth of "vocabulary" or, more properly, the number of *different* words used by children from about one year of age onward.

The "Naming Stage"

Figure 14.1 presents the *average* number of different words used by a sample of middle-class children in the United States from age six months to 42 months (Smith, 1926). As this was a selected sample, the averages at a particular age need not be representative of children in other cultures or classes, nor need the slope of the curve be identical for other samples. However, all available evidence points to remarkable similarity in the phenomenon of language acquisition across cultures (Lenneberg, 1967). Although averages mask individual differences, the effect of such masking in developmental curves is typically to produce a more linear trend.

As Fig. 14.1 shows, the rate of word acquisition is very slow and nearly linear until about one-and-a-half years (18 months), when it accelerates markedly and continuously during the period presented. The subsequent trend is more gradual and at no other time do we find such a striking change of rate.

What the figure tells us is supported by other behavioral evidence: The gradual acquisition of words during the early months of the second year of life is replaced by an active effort by the *child* to learn the "names of things." The phenomenon is sufficiently common to have been called the "naming stage" (e.g., McCarthy, 1954). The child begins to ask for the names of objects, in his own fashion. For example,

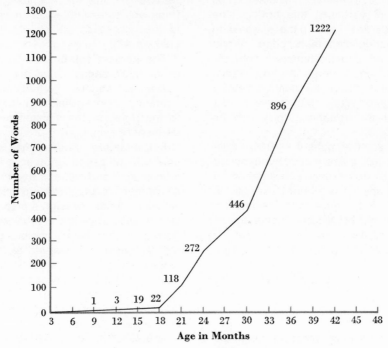

Fig. 14.1. Vocabulary increase from 8 months to 42 months. Note the sharp increase in size of vocabulary beginning at about 18 months of age. (Based on data in M. E. Smith, 1926. An investigation of the development of the sentence and the extent of vocabulary in young children. *University of Iowa Studies in Child Welfare,* **3,** No. 5, Table 8, p. 54.)

Lewis (1936) reported that his son's queries consisted of pointing and saying "eh-eh-eh," the vocalization ceasing when a name was supplied. Other children say "dis?" and "dat?" with rising intonation, while some have acquired a "what" word to serve as the pivot of their queries.

Along with the "naming" phenomenon, still further changes occur in the child's behavior after the advent of the first "words":

1. Verbal activity and words in particular have become *instrumental* for the child. He uses words to communicate wants and to *secure* objects and actions by others. Words are no longer *merely* accompaniments to physical action or specific responses to specific situations (such as saying "bye-bye" when daddy leaves the house but in no other situation). Of course, speaking continues as an accompaniment to much physical action, both in play situations or when the child attempts difficult operations, as Piaget (1928, 1930) observed in his discussion of "egocentric" speech.

Vigotsky (1939) suggested, however, that much of this "egocentric" speech serves an instrumental function other than communication, namely, to order and orient the child's activity. Vigotsky further proposed that this instrumental function does not disappear later (when the child stops speaking aloud as an accompaniment to action), but is "internalized"—functioning as "inner speech." Such silent verbalization continues in adulthood, especially when a difficult problem is faced. ("Let's see, if we put this thing-a-mabob into that whatsit, maybe this motor will start.")

2. The naming phenomenon shows that, roughly between 18 to 36 months, the child has the notion of one basic syntactical structure—the question—even though he may not form definite sentences. Some children form grammatically correct questions ("Whas dis?") at this age, and many use simple declarative sentences as well.

3. The persistent effort to discover words, as opposed to acquiring the object itself, implies an important generalization:

that *objects have names.* Of course the child does not verbalize this notion. The evidence does not warrant the suggestion that the generalization is reached in one piece. The child requests names for objects he commonly encounters, that he wants, that are novel. In short, the naming activity is *selective* and closely tied to the child's interests and the situations in which he finds himself.

Possibly, as Carmichael (1948) concluded years ago, these facts of vocabulary growth require some new coordination in the brain. In any event, theories in neurophysiology have to square with the undeniable fact that the behavioral events occur. (See Lenneberg, 1967, for other neurophysiological correlates.)

Early Words:
Anchoring Effects
and Development

Linguists sometimes describe language as a "system of contrasts" (Dinneen, 1967), by which they mean that words and language structure provide categories that anchor the person's discrimination of the objects and events proceeding in life around him. Research evidence supports this description, if we add that language is also a system for *assimilating* new experience into existing categorizations.

Assimilation and contrast relative to conceptual anchors occur when the child begins to use words instrumentally. Lewis (1963) treats the phenomena as the "expansion and contraction of meaning." In psychology, the terms "generalization and differentiation" are frequently used in a similar sense. We are using the terms assimilation-contrast in order to link the findings to the psychology of judgment. Greater similarity is experienced among objects included in a category (assimilation), and their differences from objects excluded from the label are accentuated (contrast).

As Lewis noted, the ordinary notion of vocabulary growth is that the child acquires a word as he would buy a ticket, adding each to his collection. "But a child's progress towards the mastery of the mother tongue is not, in the early stages at least, this kind of addition. It is, rather, a continued process of modification of the patterns of his linguistic behavior. These patterns are schemata which have developed in the course of the child's experiences" (1963, p. 48).

The earliest words are not words in the usual adult sense. They are attached securely to concrete situations. The first tendency is to assimilate new experiences to the label, to the amusement and bewilderment of adults.

For example, despite the fact that the child recognizes his mother, it is very common around two years of age for him to call *all* women "mama," as did one child with whom we leafed through a magazine. Cindy, at two years, called everyone who helped or waited on her "mama," including her 3-year-old brother and 5-year-old sister. Sue said "joos" when seeing or requesting anything liquid (including a swimming pool). David imitated the name of the family cat (Cheemaw) as "see-see" and applied the label to cats, dogs, birds, and frogs.

The Chamberlains (1904) reported that their child imitated "moon" by saying "mooi" when looking at the moon, subsequently using the word for cakes, round marks on the window, writing on the window, writing on paper, round marks on books, tooling on book covers, faces, postmarks, and the letter O. Guillaume's son learned to say "ato" (*marteau*) for hammer and soon applied the word to the following assortment: buttonhook, hand mirror, comb, handbag, saucepan, hairpin, wooden spade, keys, gun, box, belt, purse, ruler, puttees, basin, safety pin, candlestick, coffee mill, plate, and spoon (1927).

Some of the items included in these elastic generalizations seem to have very little in common at first sight. However, closer inspection reveals principles of order: Assimilation occurs when there is stimulus similarity (liquid or roundness), similarity in function or use (mamas; *ato* as things adults use), and similarity through difference (contrast) from an existing classification (e.g., "all of those cute living things that are not like humans").

While imitation of adult sounds is very important at this period, it is by no means strict or mechanical. On the one hand, the child neither perceives nor produces conventional phonemes accurately—and, on the other, his selectivity is often tuned

**Table 14.1.   Longitudinal Account of Expansion and Contraction of
Meaning for Lewis' Child**

Age of Child	Cat	Cow	Horse	Large Dog	Small Dog	Toy Dog
1; 9,11	– – →tee				– – →tee	
1;10,18		– →tee				
1;11,1						goggie ← –
1;11,2					goggie ← –	
1;11,24			– →tee*–┐→			
1;11,25			– → hosh			
1;11,26			tee*			
1;11,27	pushie					
2; 0,10				– – – → hosh*		
2; 0,20		→ moo-ka		biggie-goggie ←		
	pushie	moo-ka	hosh	biggie-goggie	goggie	goggie

→ First use of a word.
* Adult corrects child.
— Word no longer used.

Source: From M. M. Lewis, *Language, Thought, and Personality in Infancy and Childhood,*
New York: Basic Books (1963), p. 51.

differently from that of adults: While seated in her high chair for a meal, Sue put her hand on the wall where a small decal pictured a Dutch windmill, vocalizing insistently and questioningly. Her busy mother preparing her food said: "Yes. That's pretty. It's a Dutch windmill." Sue responded "dick-a-de-dah," repeating it several times although the mother did not reply. For several weeks, Sue used the same label for the decal, and for any pictures hung on the wall, in books, or on billboards.

Conventional use of words does not arise only through imitation and assimilation. At the same time, the child is differentiating among objects and events, acquiring appropriate labels through his own queries and active adult correctives. Table 14.1 presents a detailed record over a period of about 3 months reflecting these joint processes in the use of several labels by Lewis' son (1963, p. 51). The dash lines indicate assimi-lation of new objects, starting with "tee," which was first the child's rendition of the name of the pet cat (Timmy). Solid lines denote the first use of a new label, and asterisks denote the occasions on which an adult corrected the child by giving the proper word (for example, in the fourth column by saying "horse" when the child said "tee."). The father's correction in the fifth column, when the boy called a St. Bernard "hosh" was simply "dog," but the awed boy quickly contrasted this to "goggie" by calling it "biggie-goggie."

This table, cold and static as it is, reflects an ongoing process to which both child and adult contribute. Our daughter Ann first used "gink" for anything to drink. When her mother designated milk as different, Ann promptly said "mink." At a later date, the milk was colored pink for a party. Ann greeted it with the exclamation "pink mink!" To suggest that learning language is explained by calling it "imitation" is misleading.

Grasping and Using Linguistic Rules

The "naming" phenomena show us that while the child is beginning to utter "words," the single utterance serves different functions. ("Joos" as uttered by the child in different situations with varying expression and intonation functions as: I want joos. I don't want joos. Do you want joos? Hurray, joos! Get me joos!, etc.) However, in a remarkably short time, the child is combining words in novel ways that reflect but do not mimic sentence structure in the language he hears. For example, at 27 months of age, Joan, whose early enunciation of English phonemes was faulty, came to her mother's bedside and asked for her bottle, which she called "bobbie." Told that it was in the refrigerator, she disappeared, but returned shortly to say "no me dee me bobbie me mommie" (translated: I don't see my bottle, mommy).

During the past decade or so, a number of psychologists have embarked on systematic study of the structure of children's earliest word combinations, which begin about the same time as the "naming" phenomenon (cf. Smith and Miller, 1966). Brown (1965), M. D. S. Braine (1963), and Weir (1962) are among those who have recorded and systematically analyzed such combinations from their early appearance until the child's sentence structures approximate the conventional. Such analysis is relatively easier in the early months of verbalization as the child does not vocalize so frequently and tends to repeat his verbalizations. Then, as Braine remarked (1967), "the floodgates open" and the child's productions become both more numerous and varied.

By intensive study of each child's speech with the effort to see if any "rules" for composing phrases are evident, these investigators have reached the following interesting conclusions:

1. Although imitation of adult sounds is certainly involved in children's verbalizations, only a small portion of their utterances are imitational or can be explained as rote learning (word by word). Joan's sentence above is one example that is not imitative of English spoken by adults, although it reflects English structure. Roger Brown (1965, p. 298) lists several earlier and simpler instances: "You naughty are," "A this truck," "Why it can't turn off?" and "Put a gas in."

2. From the earliest word combinations, there is clear indication that the words are not randomly arranged but are ordered with some consistency by a particular child. The most general characteristic of such order appears to be the pivotal construction (Brown, 1965; Braine, 1967): The child acquires a small repertory of verbal anchors that determine the order of other words combined with the pivot. For example, some of the common pivots are *all* (all broke, all gone, etc.); *more* (more car, cereal, joos); *there* or, with French children, ça, la, il y a (there kitty, ball, mama, etc.); *on there,* as well as *in there* and *down there* (hot on there; car on there, etc.)

3. As "the floodgates open" during the "naming" stage, there is marked elaboration and gradually increasing length of combinations. These constructions are typically formed by combining phrases previously used with new phrases (e.g., all messy on stove). Such phrase combinations are the earliest "sentences" and their analysis reveals structure. Brown (1965) has analyzed the progress of the child's earliest phrase constructions toward sentences. He found that there was progressive *differentiation* in the formation of phrases. For example, a child that began combining words by using a modifier (nice) plus noun (kitty, mommy, etc.) began to differentiate between modifiers (my mommy, a coat, that knee, etc.) and to distinguish among different kinds of nouns (proper, mass nouns, etc.). At the same time, however, he found "an integrative process at work" (p. 301). At first standing alone, the phrase began to appear as subject as well as object of longer constructions (see nice kitty; nice kitty there). In short, the child's earliest word combinations reveal "a grammar" of his own, more or less characteristic of children starting to speak. Progressive differentiation and integration of the initially simple structures occur as he is developing sentence structure. He does not string sounds together randomly; he learns to

order words properly by serial acquisition and addition of the separate constituents (e.g., noun, verb, modifiers) and does not simply memorize and repeat adults' sentences.

Perception and Use of Conventional Rules of Grammar

Do children perceive linguistic patterns in the speech about them? Do they react to the patterns studied by linguists? Some of the most convincing evidence comes from the work of Brown and his students. Brown (1965) correctly noted that one way to detect response to language structure was to note regularities in the child's usage that lead him to commit errors. For example, English has rules for forming the plural, past tense, the possessive, and adjectival comparison; these rules cover most cases, but have important exceptions. In children observed from about a year-and-a-half to three, Brown found evidence that the rules were perceived in the fact that the children used them even when they were not appropriate (for example, bringed, gooses, feets).

Berko (1958) prepared a set of pictures especially prepared to see whether preschool and elementary school children had perceived the major rules in English for forming words. For example, one picture showed a man swinging something around his head. The children were told: "This is a man who knows how to gling. He glings every day. Today he glings. Yesterday he ————." The children, even four year olds, typically said "he glinged," using the regular rule for past tense. More sophisticated adults face a dilemma here: Did he gling, glang, or glung?

In another experiment by Brown (1957), pictures were designed to test whether preschool children (ages 3–5 years) perceived the differences between verbs, nouns as categories for objects, and nouns as categories for a mass or quantity of something (e.g., milk, dirt, and dough). In English, object nouns are preceded by a definite article (the, a, an) while mass nouns are used without an article or with a quantitative qualifier (more, some, etc.). Brown prepared three sets of pictures, each composed of four pictures. One set, for exam-

ple, showed a pair of hands performing a kneading-like motion in a mass of red confetti-like material that was piled to overflowing into a round low container. Subsequent pictures reproduced either the mass, the container, or the action (including the mass).

Each child was shown the first picture of a set. One of three nonsense words was introduced to the child (miss, sib, and latt) and, for different children, each of these was used as either a verb, object, or mass noun. For example, a child was asked "Do you know what it means to sib?" (Some children said "yes"!) "In this picture you can see sibbing. Now show me another picture of sibbing." The child was shown the other three pictures. If he correctly perceived the verb form, he would choose the action. A child who was presented sib as an object noun was asked "Do you know what a sib is?" and was expected to choose the picture of the container. The child who received sib as a mass noun was asked "Have you ever seen any sib?" and was expected to choose the picture of the red confetti-like stuff.

Brown found that on the whole the children did perceive the part of speech and correctly identify the appropriate picture. When the word was introduced as a verb, 10 of the 16 children picked the picture of action. When the word was an object noun, 11 of 16 selected the picture of an object. When the word was a mass noun, 12 of 16 selected the picture of substance. Four of the 15 responses that were not as anticipated were failures to answer because the child was distracted from the task at the time. Brown presents additional evidence that the children perceived the aspect of the picture designated by the language form: The experimenter "showed the picture of confetti-kneading and said, 'There is some latt in this picture.' Whereupon his subject said: 'The latt is spilling.' And it was" (p. 5).

The grammatical structure of the experimenter's initial statement and question established a framework or schema for the child's selectivity. He typically focused on the designated aspects of the picture, to the neglect of other aspects. Although the word was new (sib., latt), the concept of object or mass or action conveyed through grammatical construction anchored his perception of the pictures. What was not sib or latt became background.

TRENDS
IN CONCEPTUAL DEVELOPMENT

It would be misleading to suggest that learning to speak suddenly projects the child to the adult level of mentality, or that he uses the childhood years merely to add *information* to his meager repertory. The human being reaches physical maturity slowly, and conceptual functioning is not detached from his physical development.

Research tracing trends in conceptual functioning has proceeded along two major lines, one somewhat more typical in the United States before World War II and one more typical in Europe. In the United States earlier investigators were more likely to study children's *language* in terms of output, vocabulary, parts of speech, and other characteristics that are readily quantified (see McCarthy, 1954). In Europe, several outstanding investigators were more interested in the progression of the child's reasoning and understanding of the social and physical realities about him. The towering figures of the European movement were Henri Wallon (e.g., 1933, 1946) in France, Jean Piaget in Switzerland, and L. S. Vigotsky in the Soviet Union. Meanwhile, British investigators such as Lewis (1936) and Watts (1944) were pursuing empirical studies of children's speech development. The concrete findings from these diverse lines of study are remarkably harmonious. The controversies over the *age* at which trends occur, sparked particularly by American investigators' attempting to replicate Piaget's studies, are largely irrelevant to the problem of whether trends occur.

By adolescence the normal child is capable of conceptual functioning on a par with an adult, although his biological maturation may not be entirely complete (Inhelder and Piaget, 1958; Vigotsky, 1962; Ausubel, 1962).

In early childhood, the general shift is away from the perceptually symbolic toward the conceptually symbolic. The trend is revealed in several ways: Studies of vocabulary show that nouns (and noun phrases) are typically the first and largest class of words used—in short, *names* for objects and events. Their use is closely attached to the object or event itself, and in this sense, is very concrete. Conversely, the young child cannot detach the name from the object. Vigotsky (1939, p. 36) found that when he persuaded a child to change the name of, say, a dog to "cow," the child proceeded to talk about the object (dog) as though it were a cow—having horns, giving milk, and so on.

Piaget's "stages" of intellectual growth (Inhelder and Piaget, 1958, 1964) proceed from the sensorimotor state to a "preoperational stage" in which the properties of objects (how much or how heavy they are, for example) are not abstracted from their perceptual appearance. Thus the same amount of milk poured from a low wide glass to a tall narrow glass is "more milk" as far as the child is concerned because it rises higher in the taller glass. Before the child can reason abstractly about such matters (Piaget's stage of formal operations), he typically has to engage in the concrete operations of holding, touching, seeing, transferring, and manipulating objects himself. Inhelder and Piaget's stages of mental growth propose a progression from the preconceptual sensorimotor to the preoperational stage, followed by a concretely operational stage as the precedent for formal logical reasoning on a conceptual level, whether objects are present or not.

It is during these stages, Vigotsky (1939) wrote, that "The meaning of words develops" (p. 30). By studying the ways that children group a variety of common objects or forms presented to them, Vigotsky (1962) noted a progression that typically began with the child "heaping" objects together on the basis of his own experiences with them (hence different children produce very different "heaps"). Soon the child forms complexes by chaining various attributes in turn. For example, the child might begin by putting together things that move by a motor, but include a stove (because it also is a "machine") and then add a "mother" to cook on the stove.

In recent research (Olver and Hornsby, 1966), young children (6 years) grouped objects more frequently than older children according to perceptible properties (e.g.,

"A banana is yellow and a peach is red and yellow."). Their groupings were more often simply pairs (61 percent). Many of both pairs and large groupings were complexes of the sort Vigotsky observed. (For example, a child grouped a rabbit and carrots together saying "The bunny ate the carrots."). As Fig. 14.2 shows, the majority of the groupings formed by children of 6 years were "superordinate" groupings, classifying items in terms of a formal category ("all food").

The trend from simple perceptual grouping toward more abstract categories is paralleled in the findings on vocabulary growth. A child's early words are characteristically labels for objects or persons with motivational significance (McCarthy, 1954) and are closely tied to his own motor and perceptual experiences. Thus nearly 90 percent of the words used by a blind child reflected nonvisual experience before an operation restoring sight, after which names for visual objects were quickly added (Bean, 1932). The rate of vocabulary growth is related to the scope and variety in a child's environment, being slower in restricted environments and increasing rapidly with travel or other new experiences (McCarthy, 1954).

Words describing the properties of concrete objects (adjectives and adverbs) increase in number with age as the stock of names grows (Carroll, 1939). Discrimination of abstract properties (e.g., color or size) is attained slowly, as reflected in the age level at which such tasks are regarded as "normal" on standardized mental tests. For example, on the Stanford-Binet, discrimination of size is standardized at about the 4-year-old level and discrimination of color and weight at about the 5-year-old level. An abstract property such as "metal" is not conceptualized accurately until the child has reached a "mental age" of about 11 years (Watts, 1944). Similarly, accurate understanding of geographical and political entities such as states or countries is a long, slow process (Piaget and Weil, 1951).

Verbs used by the young child refer to immediate situations in which the child finds himself (Adams, 1938; Lewis, 1937). When he begins to refer to past and future, he ordinarily refers to the very near past and immediate future. One of our children

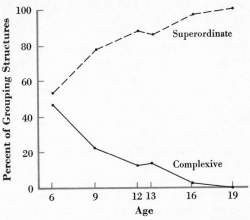

Fig. 14.2. Percentages of children of different ages who categorize stimuli according to superordinate (abstract) classification and by complexive (chaining) principles. (From R. R. Olver and J. P. Hornsby. "On Equivalence," in J. S. Bruner, ed., *Studies on Cognitive Growth.* New York: Wiley, 1966, pp. 68–85.)

used "yesterday" for all time past and "next day" for any possible future date. Precise reference to past and future depends on acquiring a stock of verbal guideposts attached to recurring events and, ultimately, to concepts of number and time.

In short, the trend in vocabulary growth in conceptualization, and thought is from the concrete, readily perceptible toward the more abstract—abstract in terms of events referred to and in operations performed. At the same time, the limits of verbal categories become more sharply defined and their meaning richer.

Conceptual Development and Socialization

Once the child gains some instrumental mastery of language, the process of learning about the world is telescoped. His reception and use of language permit an alternative to learning inductively by repeated experience and inference based on such experience. Much learning now occurs on a deductive basis. By learning a name for a class of objects or events, the child can learn about them verbally often with very little first-hand experience with events themselves. Many concepts of objects, persons, and relationships in the social world are formed much more through the verbal dictums of adults than through actual contact with specific stimulus characteristics.

Even though young children in the United States may have little or no contact with Negroes, Hindus, or Turks, they do acquire concepts of these groups that are at the same time value judgments about them and their characteristics. Well before television, American children who had never seen an American Indian learned clear-cut conceptions of Indians through books and the radio.

By acquiring concepts about objects, people, and places, the child is also forming attitudes relating himself to the world. In a later chapter we shall define attitudes in terms of the individual's categories relating himself positively or negatively to varied aspects of the world. When the child can refer to himself by name or with "me" or "I" (around the end of the second year for most American children), he has an anchorage permitting more accurate distinctions between what he is, who other people are, and others' relationship to him. "You" in the general sense is ordinarily used after self is designated. Most American children do not use the more social "we" until about the third year of life. The attainment of these distinctions along with attitudes toward self and others is a slow gradual process of great psychological significance. We deal with this process in Chapter 17 in discussing the formation of self or ego. The process is inconceivable without language and conceptual functioning, which permit the self-concept to be elaborated beyond a simple body image.

CATEGORIZATION
IN PERCEPTION
AND JUDGMENT

A linguistic concept defines a set to which specific objects (events) belong or do not belong. There is considerable evidence that linguistic categories and relationships affect perceiving, learning, discriminating, and remembering. We shall present representative evidence in this section. It is also important to emphasize how vast the areas of ignorance are and how easily one can fall into the trap of concluding either that

language is of minor importance in human psychology or that it is all-important.

Many years ago, the anthropologist Edward Sapir (1929) summed up the problem as follows:

Human beings do not live in the objective world alone, nor alone in the world of social activity as ordinarily understood, but are very much at the mercy of the particular language which has become the medium of expression for their society. It is quite an illusion to imagine that one adjusts to reality essentially without the use of language and that language is merely an incidental means of solving specific problems of communication or reflection. The fact of the matter is that the "real" world is to a large extent unconsciously built up on the language habits of the group. . . . We see and hear and otherwise experience very largely as we do because the language habits of our community predispose certain choices of interpretation.

Later, another anthropologist, Whorf (1940), illustrated the problem through comparisons of American Indian and Indo-European languages. Figures 14.3–14.5 illustrate the kind of comparisons used by Whorf and other anthropologists. Several anthropologists had noted the very different ways in which various cultural groups designated colors. For example, Margaret Mead (1933) reported that a language spoken in Oceania categorized colors so differently "that [the people] saw yellow, olive-green, blue-green, gray and lavender as variations of one color" (p. 638). Figure 14.6 gives a more recent example of different color classifications for the same wave lengths of light. It compares conventional English color names with those used in Bassa (spoken in Liberia) and Shona (spoken in Rhodesia). Whorf went considerably beyond Mead's inference that the different colors were *seen* differently to suggest that linguistic differences in vocabulary and grammar implied different experience and mentality. All of these writers used linguistic examples—not studies of perception or judgment. What happens when responses are compared to colors for which persons do or do not have different names?

There is as yet no convincing evidence that perceiving colors is entirely dependent upon having names for them. In other

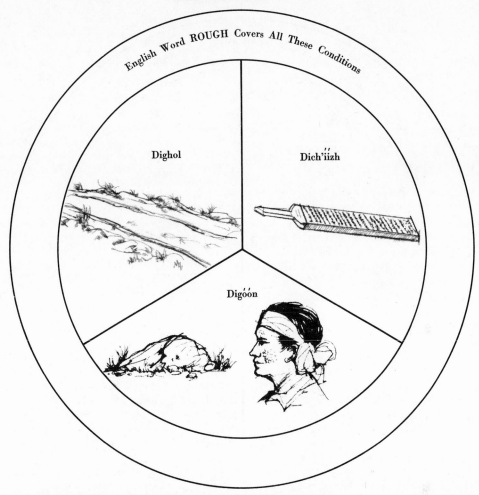

Fig. 14.3. Navaho language distinguishes between these three kinds of roughness, while English does not. (Based on Kluckhohn and Leighton, 1946.)

words, given good eyesight, and excepting cases of color-blindness, the evidence does not justify the notion that people who use different names for hues also *see* them differently. The question is complex because color perception depends on so many conditions other than simply categorization (e.g., background, luminance, the series of colors in which a given color appears).

However, Brown and his students (Brown, 1958, 1965) have shown that categorization does affect behavior relative to colors. Taking agreement on the label for a color as a measure of its "codability," they showed that the subjects reacted more quickly and with less confusion to colors with high codability than to those with low codability.

It is not that individuals cannot discriminate between colors for which they have no name or which are named alike; it is simply that people ordinarily are not faced with the problem of doing so, have no ready verbal categories to deal with the matter, and seldom make the effort to discriminate.

In reviewing studies of the perception of spoken phonemes, Brown (1965) suggested that "learning to speak one's native tongue causes a sharpening of sensory acuity at boundaries between phonemes relative to the acuity within phonemes" (p. 265). Illustrative evidence is presented in Fig. 14.7, which shows the percentage of identifications by one experimental subject to ordered series of sound frequency bands (Haskins). The physical stimulus (sound)

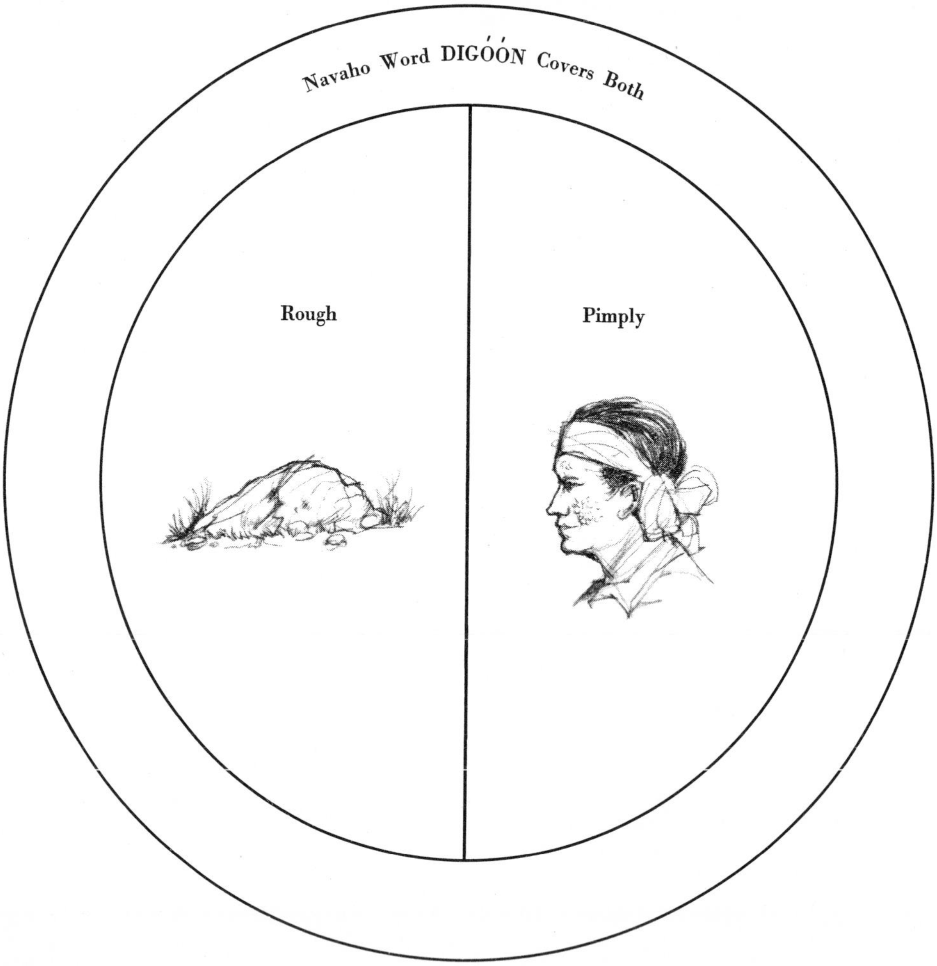

Fig. 14.4. Navaho has one word for these conditions, which are usually referred to in English by two different terms. (Based on Kluckhohn and Leighton, 1946.)

could be ordered through use of the spectograph, which records the patterns visually. The stimulus values along the baseline differed in steps of 120 cycles per second. The sounds range from a pattern perceived by English speakers as (b), through (d) to (g). The method for securing judgments was not categorization but a discrimination method. The figure shows that the subject does make use of categories. (The subject merely had to select one out of two sounds to match a standard sound.) Note that stimuli numbered 1, 2, and 3 were responded to as though they were alike, as were Stimuli 5, 6, 7, and 8. On the other hand, Stimulus 4 was differentiated from 3 and 5 as being different. As Brown concluded: "A cultural system, a language,

breaks an acoustical continuum into phoneme categories" (p. 264).

The consequences of categorization such as shown in Fig. 14.7 are typical of categorization in general. Greater similarity is perceived *within* the bounds of the category, while the differences between stimuli are sharpened—even exagerrated. A good many years ago, McGranahan surveyed the research literature on the effects of language in perceiving and reached the same conclusion: "The effect of language on perception appears to be to make those features of the objective world that are represented by linguistic forms stand out in greater articulation, to give greater individuality to the object or event so represented, to cause similarities to be seen in things

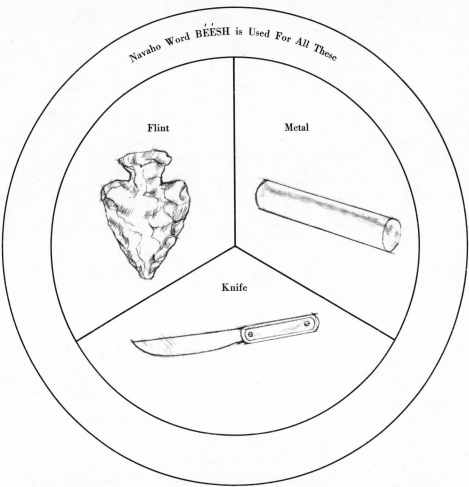

Navaho Word BÉÉSH is Used For All These

Flint

Metal

Knife

Fig. 14.5. Navaho refers to these three with one word, while English requires three different words. Flint was replaced by metal in Navaho culture after European contact. (Based on Kluckhohn and Leighton, 1946.)

similarly represented, and in general to influence perception in the direction of speech forms" (1936, p. 202).

The shapes of the response distributions produced by categorization do not resemble the typical curves for stimulus generalization in a conditioning experiment in which, for example, the percentages of response decline gradually as the stimulus differs more and more from the conditioned stimulus. They are more nearly flat, dropping sharply when the boundaries of the category are reached.

An interesting example was reported by Secord (Secord, Bevan, and Katz, 1956; Secord, 1959) in judgment of photographs varying systematically from marked Negroid

to marked Caucasian physical characteristics. The subjects judged the series of photographs both with respect to "negroidness" and with respect to personal attributes. The subjects were differentiated as being "low" or "high" in prejudice against Negroes. Secord's question was whether the unfavorable personal qualities attributed to Negroes in the traditional stereotype decline as a function of the physical appearance of the person, or whether categorization of a face as Negro also arouses the stereotyped qualities associated with the category, regardless of appearance? As Fig. 14.8 shows, the latter was the case.

The first seven or eight pictures were identified as Negro by most subjects and

English

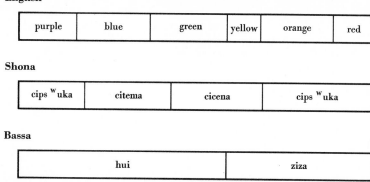

Fig. 14.6. How the color spectrum is mapped in three different languages. (From Roger Brown, *Social Psychology*, p. 316. Reprinted with permission of The Macmillan Company. Copyright © 1965 by The Free Press, a Division of The Macmillan Company.

uniformly assigned the stereotyped traits. There is no significant decline as the pictures become increasingly Caucasoid. Both those low and high in prejudice assigned the stereotype traits to photographs they *identified* as Negro, regardless of the extent of Caucasian features—the tendency being greater for the more prejudiced persons. Interestingly enough, a minority of the subjects identified the most Caucasian of the pictures (at the right) as Negro and their judgments of them were as stereotyped as their responses to the average Negro photograph.

Harvey, Hunt, and Schroder (1961) summarized the conditions in which concepts produce such affect-laden assessments:

The less compelling or the more ambiguous the stimulus variables, the greater the influence of the motivational state in the cognitive outcome. . . . The condition under which motives are maximally influential, then, is high stimulus ambiguity and high motivational arousal. Conversely, motivational influence in concept functioning is minimal and stimulus determinants are maximal under conditions of high stimulus structure and low motive arousal (pp. 15–16).

When there is a wide margin for variations in responding to a stimulus situations, linguistic concepts exert the greatest categorical effect—whether in the direction of enhancing accuracy or of distortion. Bartlett (1932) found this in studies on remembering, by using the method of serial reproduction. Bartlett presented pictures of simple forms as well as more complex drawings to a subject, then later asked him to repro-

duce it. His reproduction was given to a second subject, who later recalled it, and so on. Bartlett found a pronounced tendency for these successive reproductions to progress toward conventional forms. For example, through the course of ten reproductions, an extremely abstract and primitive drawing labeled "Portrait d'Homme" became a conventionalized representation of a human face.

However, certain variations in Bartlett's results are instructive. First, he found that some simple, well-structured forms did not change in subsequent reproductions. For example, a simple drawing И was called "N" but consistently reproduced correctly (backwards). In the more complex drawings, naming had a much greater effect. Figure 14.9 shows one fairly simple stimulus picture (left) and reproductions by three subjects, two of whom labeled it a "picture frame" and the third "two carpenter's squares placed together." Only the latter reproduced the figure correctly. Similarly, a complex line-drawing that was reproduced erroneously by most subjects was named a "mathematical function" by a mathematics student, who produced a correct reproduction.

The role of categorization in a complex figure is illustrated in Fig. 14.10. After successive reproductions it was presented to a subject in the form labeled A in Fig. 14.10. The subject reported that he said to himself "A heart at the top, then a curve and a straight post down to a little foot at the bottom. Between these two a letter W, and half

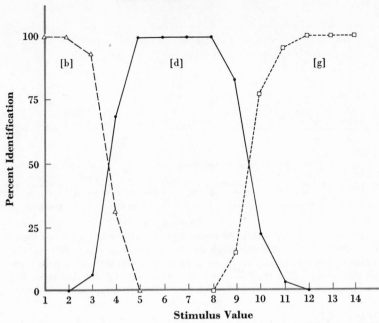

Fig. 14.7. Categorization occurring in identification of phonemes [b], [d], and [g]. Physical differences between sound stimuli were constant (120 cycles per second), but correct identification breaks sharply at Stimulus 4 and 10, indicating categorization as well as discrimination. (These data from one subject in the Haskins Laboratory were reported by Roger Brown, *Social Psychology*, p. 264. Reprinted with permission of The Macmillan Company. Copyright © 1965 by The Free Press, a Division of The Macmillan Company.)

a heart half-way up on the left-hand side" (p. 183). The subject's reproduction is labeled B in Fig. 14.10, and it may be seen that it reflects the names he gave to the various parts.

Carmichael, Hogan, and Walter (1932) made a systematic study of the extent to which recall was influenced by the names given simple forms. The subjects were presented a set of twelve simple line-drawings. Different subjects were given different names for the same drawing. For example, the first drawing in Fig. 14.11 was presented to some subjects as a bottle and to others as a stirrup. The drawings represent some of the more striking examples of changes in the direction of the label. The overall results of the study show that more than the names affected recall of the drawings. As they were clear-cut drawings, most of the reproductions were fairly accurate. However, the reproductions that the investigators classified as involving *pronounced* changes were predominantly in the direction of the names. An average of 74 percent of the pronounced

changes were in the direction of one list of names and 73 percent in the direction of the other list.

Much greater change in the direction of names was obtained by Zangwill (1938), who used ambiguous ink-blots of the kind labeled Critical Figure in Fig. 14.12. A control group was told that the pictures resembled either animals or mountains. Both they and the experimental group were shown first one then another series of five blots. The Critical Figure was in both series; however, experimental subjects were told that the first series represented animals and the second was suggestive of mountains. Ninety percent of the control subjects recognized the fact that the same blot appeared in both series while only about a third of the experimental subjects had noticed its appearance twice. Figure 14.12 shows the reproductions made by six subjects who were not aware that the "critical figure" appeared twice. Their reproductions are clearly influenced by the categories assigned to the lists.

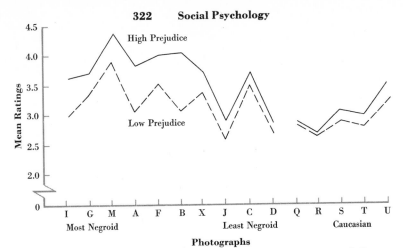

Fig. 14.8. Average ratings of photographs varying in Negroid and Caucasian characteristics by judges high and low in prejudice. Note that categorization by race produces a nearly equal rating regardless of physical character of photographs. The resulting curve is quite unlike a stimulus generalization gradient. (Adapted from P. F. Secord, 1959. Stereotyping and favorableness in the perception of Negro faces. *J. abnorm. soc. Psychol.*, **59**, 309–315. Copyright 1959 by the American Psychological Association, and reproduced by permission.)

Categorical Scales and Anchors in Sequential Tasks

In actual life, most consequential action and psychological processing proceeds over time sequentially, usually with some kind of order to events. Categorization plays an important part in the performance of sequential tasks by human beings.

For example, Cook and Harris (1937) showed that when human subjects are instructed about the sequence of stimuli in a conditioning experiment (for example, a green light followed by shock), the strength of the conditioned galvanic skin reflex bore no consistent relationship to the number of trials. The conditioned response could appear in full strength after one trial; similarly, it could be extinguished by telling the subject that the shock would no longer follow.

Learning to execute a hand maze occurs over time as the subject gradually eliminates the blind alleys and follows the correct route. The following table is based on findings by Warden (1924), who compared the average number of trials required to learn a maze by subjects who used words to categorize and order the sequence, those who relied on visual imagery, and those who relied more heavily on motor performance (e.g., getting the "feel" of it).

	Mean No. of Trials
Words	32.2
Visual imagery	67.9
Motor performance	123.9

The following table is based on an investigation by Pyles (1932) of children ages 2–7 years who were presented with three different sets of papier-mâché forms: a set of five "nonsense shapes" that were not named; a set of five nonsense shapes with nonsense names; and a set of five familiar animals. In each set, one shape always contained a toy. It was the child's task to find this form. The criterion for learning was four successive trials in which the target figure was chosen correctly. The table gives the average number of trials required for success.

	Mean No. of Trials
Animal shapes, names known	5
Nonsense shapes, named	37
Nonsense shapes, unnamed	69

Pyles observed that some children spontaneously gave names to the unnamed nonsense shapes. The 13 children who did so required significantly fewer trials than the 69 reported as average in the table. Of course, such spontaneous verbalization need not always facilitate the learning pro-

Stimulus Figure   **Name Assigned to by Subjects**

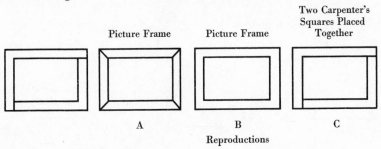

Fig. 14.9. Effects of names on immediate recall of a simple drawing (After Bartlett, 1932).

cess in the direction of efficiency or correctness. There is some evidence that older normal children perform less efficiently on very simple tasks than mentally retarded children do, precisely because they set up hunches about the task, the experimenter's intent, and/or the solutions—all of which are too sophisticated for the correct performance of the simple-minded task at hand.

We have already seen that very young children do not size-up things in a way identical to adults and that the capacity to do so involves a process of growth and learning. Sizing up and appraising events are among man's most frequent activities —their objects of judgment ranging from size, weight, and color to the state of the weather, the behavior of the younger generation, the prices currently charged in stores, the length of skirts, and political events.

In experiments on judgment, the subject is typically presented with a set or series of stimulus items, passing judgment on each in turn. If the particular series is unfamiliar to him, as it typically is, it takes time for him to judge the individual stimuli accurately. He does by learning to fit to the particular stimuli presented him category names (light-heavy; 50–500 grams) or a series of numbers provided by the experimenter. As noted in Chapter 4, the research literature shows that the subject is, thereby, establishing a *reference scale* which he uses in sizing-up particular stimuli, placing each in one of several categories.

By the time adolescents or adults come to serve as subjects in an experiment, they have already formed fairly firm reference scales composed of fairly clear-cut categories, each applying to given subsets of stimuli in some important matters. Suppose now that we let the individual decide what categories he will use and how to use them in assessing stimuli that are significant to him? Will he reveal his established refer-

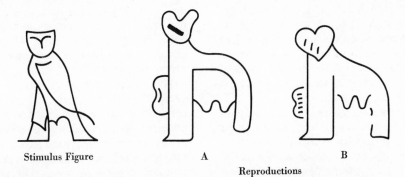

Stimulus Figure   A   B

Reproductions

Fig. 14.10. Remembering and reproduction of a complex form influenced by the names the subject assigned to separate parts (After Bartlett, 1932).

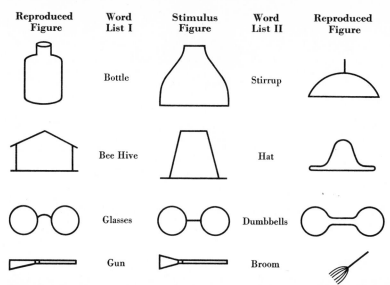

Reproduced Figure	Word List I	Stimulus Figure	Word List II	Reproduced Figure

Bottle · Stirrup

Bee Hive · Hat

Glasses · Dumbbells

Gun · Broom

Fig. 14.11. Most pronounced examples of the effect of different names on reproductions of the same stimulus figures (After Carmichael, Hogan, and Walter, 1932. Published in *J. exp. Psychol.*, American Psychological Association.)

ence scale in the way he categorizes the material? This was the problem of an experiment by Sherif (1961, 1963). Having conducted research among white and Navaho Indian adolescents in the southwestern United States, she knew that money was about equally important to both groups, but that the children differed in their conceptions of how much to spend for various items.

As a control, the subjects in both cultural groups first sorted a series of numbers, being told simply to put the smallest numbers at their left and the larger ones at their right, using as many or as few categories as seemed necessary. Figure 14.13 shows how the subjects performed this task. There were no significant differences between the performance of white and Indian subjects. On the average, subjects used four or five categories and seemed to do their best to distribute their judgments equally among them, while attending to the divisions of the decimal system (10, 20, 30, etc.).

The subjects also sorted the same series of numbers to which dollar signs were affixed. They were told to sort them as they would price tags on a rack of winter coats. Figure 14.14 gives the results for white and Indian subjects.

The "short series" (ranging from $5–54) fell well within the acceptable range for white subjects. None of them found any of the prices "prohibitive" when they labeled their piles after sorting them. However, for the Indian subjects, on the average, anything above $40 was prohibitive. The subjects used somewhat fewer categories in sorting the price tags than in sorting the neutral numbers and, somewhat surprisingly, did not double the number of categories they used when the range was doubled from $5–54 to $5–104. Instead, typically, they simply added one category to take care of the monetary values that they considered prohibitive. One general effect of the longer range was to reduce differentiation within the acceptable range of prices and to lead to acceptance of higher values (assimilation). On the other hand, there was marked piling up of values in the objectionable category (contrast). As Fig. 14.14 shows, the contrast effect was particularly pronounced for Indian subjects.

Results This methodology is called the "own categories" procedure, which has been used more extensively in the study of social attitudes. It reveals the anchoring effects of the individual's reference scale through assimilation and contrast effects in judgments of specific stimulus items. The study shows that people do have categorical reference scales which they rely on when it comes to sizing up specific events.

Critical Figure

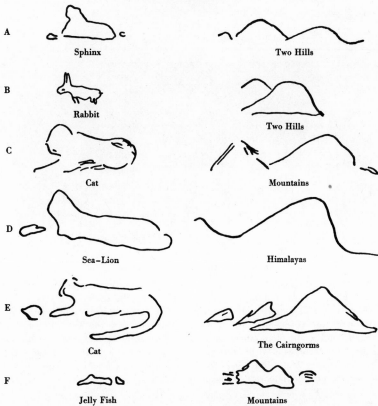

A   Sphinx   Two Hills

B   Rabbit

Two Hills

C   Cat   Mountains

D   Sea–Lion   Himalayas

E   Cat   The Cairngorms

F   Jelly Fish   Mountains

Fig. 14.12. Reproductions of ambiguous figures when named as animals (*left*) and mountains (*right*). (From O. L. Zangwill, 1938. A study of the significance of attitude in recognition. *Brit. J. Psychol.*, **28**, 15.)

HUMAN GROUPS AND THEIR WORDS

The varying linguistic classifications for the environment in different historical periods and societies show us that concepts of a language are not based simply on objective similarities and differences among stimuli to which they refer. However, this does not mean that language concepts are merely arbitrary classifications determined by sheer accident or the perverse whims of individuals.

Words do not drop from the blue. The concepts of a language are social products. They arise and are standardized by people interacting in the vital matters of living, satisfying their needs, dealing with their environments, understanding the world they live in, and controlling or changing various of that world's aspects.

Studies of different societies have shown that the vocabulary of a group, hence its classification of things, tends to reflect the practical activities of the group in its vital pursuits (Hocart, 1912; Malinowski, 1930). This is most evident in rather small and relatively isolated human societies. In larger, more complex societies, words are spread from group to group within the society and are borrowed from other languages. Another complicating circumstance is that, once standardized, words tend to persist even though they are no longer applicable to conditions and activities of group living. However, this persistence has limits. Outworn and inappropriate concepts disappear in time. New concepts are

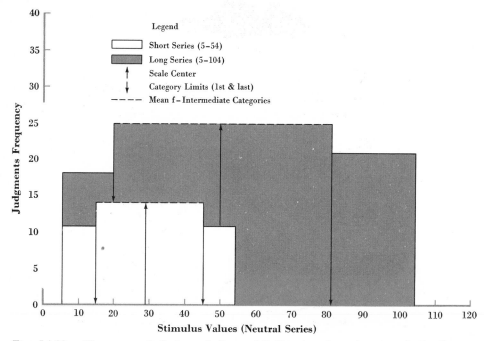

Fig. 14.13. "Own categories" of non-Indian and Indian Americans for neutral stimuli were similar, whether for a short or long series of stimuli. (Results of the two samples combined.) Navaho Indians and non-Indians sorted two series of numbers into piles, using any number of categories with any frequency they wished. Most used four or five categories, regardless of series length, and grouped numbers as nearly as possible in terms of the decimal system. As the number of categories used by different subjects varied, only the first and last categories are strictly comparable. The middle bars for both series represent the average number placed in the number of intermediate categories used by the subject. (Based on data in C. Sherif, 1961.)

formed when people face new and significant circumstances.

A group in Central Asia had names for each kind of horse they used, depending on its color and markings, but no word to refer to horses in general. At one time it was concluded that such specificity indicated that the "primitive mind" was more concrete and could not generalize. As Hocart (1912) pointed out, such differences are not indicative of the inferior generalizing capacities of people, but of differences in the vital activities carried on by groups in certain definite environments. Concepts arise and are standardized to deal with such differences.

The Masai of East Africa were a group of people whose chief occupation was raising cattle. The Masai had at least seventeen terms for cattle. A cow with one calf, a cow with two calves, and a sterile cow were all referred to with separate words. Each of the cattle was given a name of its own (Merker, 1904).

The Ifugao of the Philippines lived in valleys surrounded by mountains which for centuries isolated them effectively from the outside world. Their chief crop was rice, which was grown on irrigated terraces. In the Ifugao language, which is one of the Malay group, rice in various stages of planting, growth, and harvesting was given 20 different names (Barton, 1930).

Hocart related that in the Solomon Islands one of the staples was a nut. Two nuts so alike in appearance that they seemed identical except for size were given different names: *vino* and *ngari*. These names signified an important distinction. The two nuts, similar in appearance and both vital in the living of the islanders, had different seasons, were gathered differently, and were cracked and preserved differently. In fact, in terms of the activities which the

White Ss

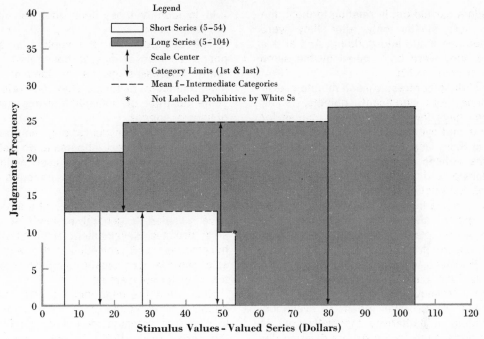

Fig. 14.14. Own categories of non-Indian and Indian Americans for valued stimuli differed markedly, both for a short and long series of stimuli. Compared with similar results sorting neutral stimuli (combined in Fig. 14.13), Indians and non-Indians categorizing the same numbers designated as dollar values for the prices of apparel used different categories and with different frequency. These differential results reflect prevailing scales for purchases.

a. (*above*) Note that non-Indian subjects used a very small category as the last in their short series. Unlike Indian subjects (**b**) the white subjects did not label the last category as "prohibitive" for clothing.

b. (*below*) The increase of items in the last category for both series represents a contrast effect relative to the Indian subjects' acceptable latitude for clothing expenditures. A similar effect occurred for non-Indian subjects (**a**) only when the long series was presented for values exceeding $80.

Indian Ss

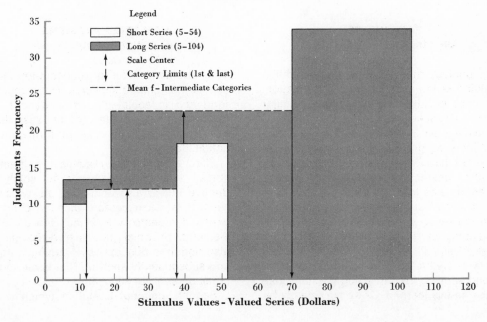

islanders carried out in relation to them, the nuts were similar only after they were roasted and made into pudding. And at this stage, they were both called by the same name (Hocart, 1912).

In striking contrast to such minute classifications for significant objects, some groups have few or very vague names for objects and events that are not very important in their lives. Malinowski observed that groups whose activities center around gardening and raising animals had many names for single species of plants and animals designating various stages in their development and utilization. On the other hand, a tree, plant, or bird with no value to the group for food, clothing, or decoration was dismissed with some phrase like, "Oh, that is just 'bush,'" or "merely a flying animal" (Malinowski, 1930).

Groups whose chief means of livelihood is hunting or gathering, especially against great odds, such as the Arunta of Australia or the Siriono of Bolivia, have standardized names for almost all of the neighboring flora and fauna (Holmberg, 1946; Spencer and Gillen, 1927).

Such findings point to the conclusion that different linguistic classifications found in various societies *are not simply arbitrary ways of "slicing" experience and objective reality. Concepts are related to the interactions of peoples engaged in differing activities in definite environments.*

EXPERIMENTS
ON CONCEPT FORMATION

In psychology there is a research tradition identified as the study of concept formation. The experiments have used very similar methods (Vinacke, 1951).

Typically, an individual is shown a series of objects or drawings. Certain stimuli in the series have elements, patterns, objects, or other characteristics in common. The subject may be told that he is taking part in a memory experiment and be required to learn nonsense syllables as names for the stimulus series. Then he is shown a second series of stimuli having something in common with the first, and is asked to name the second series correctly, using the nonsense names he has learned. Or he may simply be told to identify those items that belong to the same class.

The concepts that the subject is supposed to discover may be concepts he already possesses—names of familiar objects, numbers, or forms. They may refer to some abstract or unfamiliar arrangements of lines or shapes.

Usually the individual's only source of motivation is any desire he has to do well in the task. Some studies have used children as subjects and have given concrete rewards, such as candy.

The findings from such lines of approach have revealed, in general, a slow trial-and-error process, development of hunches or hypotheses, and sometimes the sudden solutions that are usually taken as indicative of insightful learning.

Hull noted the importance of "set" produced by calling the individual's attention to elements common to various stimuli in the series (Hull, 1920). Heidbreder's findings in a series of experiments indicate the crucial significance of the perceptual situation. The greatest ease in concept formation was found in relation to concrete objects, as contrasted to more abstract relationships (Heidbreder, 1945). In addition, various situational factors, such as the order of presentation of the stimulus series and the inclusion of negative as well as positive instances in the stimulus series, have been studied.

NEGLECTED PROBLEMS
IN CONCEPT FORMATION

The traditional line of concept-formation studies has limited implications for concept formation in social life. Its limitations are imposed by the neglect of at least three problems typical of concept formation in actual life.

First, after a child reaches the "naming stage," concept formation is not solely inductive but is also deductive. As we have seen, it is not necessary that the child be exposed repeatedly to stimuli the common elements of which he must discover. He also acquires concepts by learning a name and subsequently applying that name to objects, persons, or situations.

Second, concept formation typically occurs in relation to objects or situations with some motivational or functional significance to the individual. A striking illustration is provided by children who develop categories and names which are peculiar to them, based on distinctions whose meaning lies in their own activities. For example, Watts (1944) reported that a 16-month-old boy called all portable objects with handles *yo-yos; yo-yos* with lids were called *go-gos.*

Third, concept formation in real life is typically not a strictly individual affair, but occurs during social interaction. Young children sometimes standardize unique labels in interaction. Jespersen (1923) reported that 5½-year-old twin boys who were frequently left to shift for themselves developed a whole set of words to communicate with each other, even though they sounded like "gibberish" to adults. Such unique standardizations by twins are sufficiently common to be noted in standard texts on "speech defects" (Berry and Eisenson, 1945; Van Riper, 1947). In one family the twins used a word *tedaden* to mean "climb upon." *Ding-a-ding* was used by the same children to mean "trade" or "you give me what you have and I'll give you what I have."

A Study on Standardization of Names

With these problems of concept formation in actual life in mind, the authors carried out a study in 1948 on the formation and standardization of names by young children who had some instrumental use of language (Sherif and Sherif, 1949).

The following hypotheses were suggested:

1. If an individual attempts to deal with an unnamed object with motivational value in a situation requiring communication to attain the object, he will name it and will use this name consistently in referring to it.

2. When individuals interact around an unnamed object with motivational value to all of them and which can be attained only through communicating, the object will be named and this name will become standardized for each individual.

3. Names stabilized by individuals and in

group interaction will be used instrumentally in communication with others.

Preschool children were shown toys for which they had no names. The situation was arranged so that the children could not point to the object or get it themselves. In order to get a toy, it was necessary to request it from the experimenter. No particular kind of verbal response was required. The children were given the toy in response to any request which differentiated the object from others also available.

Twenty-two children took part individually with the experimenter. Twenty-seven other children took part in groups of two or three. The children were from poorer economic groups. Thus, it was possible to present highly attractive toys which they had not seen before and for which they had no conventional names. Most children were kindergarten age (about 5 years); a few in the individual sessions had attended the first grade in elementary school.

A label or name was considered standardized (1) when it had been used by the child at least three times successively without the intervention of other verbal responses in relation to the object and (2) when the child responded to the researcher's use of the name accurately. Each child participated in four sessions on different days. In the last session, every subject was alone with the experimenter in order that his acceptance of the label could be checked through his response to the adult's use of it.

Results of Individual Sessions. In the individual sessions, four unnamed toys were presented. Twenty of the 22 subjects standardized a total of 44 labels for the toys. Eighteen of these labels were names—one word used for a toy for which they had no name at the outset. Nine of the labels were brief descriptive phrases—a "one" or "thing" designation plus an adjective (e.g., "wire one" or "red thing"). Seventeen were descriptive phrases of three to five words (e.g., "all red one" or "one that winds up"). One of the findings was that longer phrases of more than four or five words were simply not standardized.

Results of Interaction Sessions. Responses were observed to one toy which was unnamed and proved to be conducive to cooperative activities among kinder-

Table 14.2.   Standardization of Names in Group Interaction

Group	Standardized Response (Name)	Time of Standardization (Minutes)[a]	No. Times Name Used by Each S	Subject First Using Name	Correctives		
					From	To	No.
1	"Big green thing"	67	B—6 N—3	B	B	N	3
2	"Big green thing"	64	E—8 C—3 F—3	E	E E	C F	1 1
3	"Derrick"	20	G—7 J—3 M—3	G	G	J	1
4	"Steps"	5	D—5 R—4 P—4	D			0
5	"Erector"	30	G—7 R—4	G	G	R	3
6	"Tractor"	10	A—6 L—11	A	A L	L A	6 3
7	"Steamshovel"	20	M—5 V—3 A—2[b]	M	M	V	1

[a] Time of standardization was reckoned from the first use of the label to the exclusion of all designations for the unnamed object other than the name adopted by the group. Time from exposure of the stimulus object to the first use of the name ultimately standardized ranged from 1 to 5 minutes.

[b] Subject A in Group 7 was present only for Sessions 1, 2 ,and 4.

garten children. The toy was a model bucket-loader built of green metal with a black conveyor belt. It stood about 16 inches high. The toy could be loaded with sand and moved, and the sand could be caught in a receptacle and carried away. Sand and auxiliary toys were provided to make this cooperative activity possible. Representative data are summarized in Table 14.2.

On the basis of the data at the right in the table pertaining to the subject who first used the particular label standardized and the corrrectives made by the children in standardizing the term, the following description is typical of the process:

One child, typically the one who most frequently initiated activity in the play situation, gave a name to the unnamed toy in his efforts to co-ordinate group play around it. The name for the object was useful to him in assuming a directive role in play activities. Therefore, when the other children used different words and phrases to refer to

the toy, he tended to correct them verbally. For example, if one said "that big, big thing," he would respond "you mean ————," giving the label he had used. Eventually other children responded and sometimes corrected others. When a name was thus standardized, it was used consistently in play activities and in every case responded to accurately when later used by the experimenter outside of the group setting.

It should be noted that Groups 1 and 2 each standardized the same label. This occurred because Subjects B (Group 1) and E (Group 2) communicated about the toy outside of the experimental situation before Group 2 participated in the experiment.

The names standardized in each group had a categorizing effect such that members of different groups (except Groups 1 and 2) could not communicate about the toy. During the third session a member of Group 7 said: "J—— in Group 3 said yesterday you didn't have no steamshovel in here when they came in to play. Didn't you?" Group 3, of which J—— was a member, called the toy a "derrick."

Thus, the group sessions demonstrated the tendency for interacting individuals to *standardize* names for novel and desired objects in order to deal with these objects and *communicate* with each other about them.

Concept Formation in Actual Life

The proposal that concept formation typically occurs during interaction in response to new objects or situations with motivational significance is not new or startling. The study summarized in the last section was essentially an attempt to duplicate happenings of real life within a more restricted research setting.

Gangs of youngsters in large cities invariably standardize terms and phrases which refer to more or less unique situations and relationships they deal with. In prisons, at least a portion of the prison argot originates in the prison situation. A large share of these words pertain to prominent aspects of the prison life—notably, relations between prisoners and prison officials, and sexual activities (Clemmer, 1940).

Lewis concluded that the development of "special languages" within the framework of a larger society is a phenomenon found throughout the history of language. "Whenever men are organized into groups for the purposes of specific action, they tend to develop a language foreign in some measure to the language of the larger society in which they move" (Lewis, 1948, p. 48).

In time of war, thousands of people are faced with new objects and new problems and situations of great significance to them. Many new names and terms are standardized in group interaction and spread through the armed services. Such new terms have been noted in both the American (Elkin, 1946) and the British armed services (Hunt and Pringle, 1943). In the British services, 240 entirely new words were reported during the early period of World War II, and in addition hundreds of existing words were put to new uses. New editions of standard dictionaries reveal the constant additions being made to vocabulary with the introduction of new cultural elements and changed situations.

The formation of concepts, like children's learning to communicate through language, is a social process in which the motivations of the participants, interaction among them, and the functional uses of the linguistic response are essential. Thus, concepts are both cognitive and motivational in their very origins. In the next chapter, we shall see that this generalization is basic to understanding the formation of attitudes.

15

Attitudes

Major Topics of the Chapter

Importance of attitude concept in social psychology

Six criteria distinguishing attitudes from other motives

Attitudes as cognitive-motivational-behavioral systems

Definition of attitude for research

Scales for assessing attitudes: theoretical problems and issues

Attitudes as anchors in judgment

Psychosocial scales and individual attitudes

Disguised or unobtrusive methods of measurement: psychological basis and properties of stimulus situations

Projective techniques

Error choice technique

Attitudes revealed in judgments of fact and truth

Measuring attitude as the individual's own categories: the Own Categories Procedure

ATTITUDE:
A FOCAL CONCEPT
IN RESEARCH

In this second half of the twentieth century, people are more keenly aware than ever before of the differing beliefs, assumptions, values, and ways of life upheld by various human groups. Man's mastery of his physical environment has created a new world, foreshortening time and space in exchanging words, goods, people, and missiles. People differing drastically in outlook and aspiration find themselves in contact— whether they like it or not and whether for good or ill. At the same time, man's changing environment and society strain his traditional assumptions and viewpoints, demanding new modes of adaptation. All of these developments have brought the problems of attitude and attitude change out of the textbooks and into the negotiating hall, the legislature, the marketplace, the schoolroom, the neighborhood, and the living room.

Attitude problems have long been recognized as central in social psychology in accounting for socialization and individual social behavior. W. I. Thomas, the sociologist, selected attitude as *the* central concept for a viable social psychology. Contemporary social psychologists devote approximately one-quarter to a third of their texts and probably a larger proportion of their research to problems of attitude and attitude change. A disproportionate share of their activities has been devoted to the measurement of this or that specific social attitude, to refinements of existing measurement techniques, and to experimental studies of attitude change. We say "disproportionate share" because the fundamental problems of attitude and attitude change are still far from settled.

Fundamental problems in the psychology of attitudes include the following: What are the properties of an attitude? From what modes of observed behaviors can an attitude be inferred? What kind of research procedures are required to secure valid indicators of attitude? What is the appropriate yardstick for comparing an individual's attitude toward a given object with that of other individuals?

In order to measure anything, we have to know something about the properties of what we are measuring. It would be considered foolish to try to measure a person's height with a pair of scales. The tools of research have to be chosen for their appropriateness to the phenomena in question. A sieve is not an appropriate tool for catching a whale. In order to secure valid indicators of anything, we have to decide what kind of evidence is admissible. Few people would be willing to accept a fisherman's report on his own skill at fishing. They want to see the fish he caught.

Such issues are basic to problems of attitude change. How can we accurately analyze and predict change of something if we are not able to characterize it in the first place?

In this chapter, we shall characterize an attitude. This characterization is based on extensive surveys of the research literature (Sherif and Cantril, 1947; Sherif, 1948; Sherif and Sherif, 1956; Sherif and Hovland, 1961; Sherif, Sherif, and Nebergall, 1965). It is conducive to an operational definition of attitude that squares with its properties.

THE PLACE OF ATTITUDE
IN SOCIAL PSYCHOLOGY

Without a doubt, the accumulated literature on attitudes in socialization, attitudes as factors in psychological activity, attitude measurement, and attempts at attitude change through communication or other social process is more extensive than on any other single topic in social psychology. This is as it should be. The products of social interaction are revealed, psychologically, as sets of attitudes formed by the individual. Socialization of the human child consists in large degree of the individual's internalization or learning of the values, norms, roles, and way of life in his family and that part of society in which his family lives.

We were dealing with attitudes in Chapter 6 when we discussed the research subject's compliant response to a research situation representing "science" to him. Reciprocal and shared attitudes were involved when we traced the process of group formation in Chapter 7, and the stabilization of roles and statuses in Chapter 8. The development of social norms that are binding to individual members implies, on the psychological side, the formation of attitudes by individual members regulating their behavior within the latitude of acceptable behavior and justifying sanctions for deviation (Chapters 9 and 10). The demarcation of an in-group, its glorification by members, and the rise of friendly or hostile norms for treating out-groups with stereotyped conceptions justifying the treatments imply the formation of a set of attitudes regarding one's own group and a set of attitudes regarding the other groups which fall within the latitude prescribed as proper and commendable by the norm—as long as a person is concerned with being a good and loyal member in these respects (Chapters 11 and 12). We have already seen examples, in discussing each of these topics, of how the attitudes of individuals affect their appraisals, their perception, and their judgment and behavior in relevant situations—both experimental and natural.

Following a period of quiescence immediately after World War II, a resurgence in the study of attitudes brought huge quantities of research literature. Fortunately, there are now available a number of summaries and critical evaluations of theory, techniques and findings (e.g., McGuire, 1968; Edwards, 1957a; Berelson and Janowitz, 1966; Shaw and Wright, 1967; Sherif, Sherif, and Nebergall, 1965; Sherif and Sherif, 1967; Fishbein, 1967; Halloran, 1967). The following discussion is based on the literature to date, particularly that articulated with attitudes as constituents of the person's self (see the Introduction to Part IV and Chapter 17). There is a growing body of research oriented in this direction, which will go a long way toward tying together research on attitudes and that traditionally labeled "personality" research (e.g., Bieri *et al.*, 1966).

CRITERIA DISTINGUISHING ATTITUDES FROM OTHER INTERNAL FACTORS

Attitudes are inferred from *characteristic, consistent, and selective modes of behavior directed toward or against relevant objects, persons, and events.* However, not all such modes of behavior indicate an attitude. For example, any normal newborn child, when hungry and presented with the breast, will consistently turn his head and begin to suckle. There is no need of a concept such as attitude to explain such behavior. However, when an adult craves lobster, or an orthodox Mohammedan or orthodox Jew becomes nauseous upon learning that he unwittingly ate pork, an attitude is indicated.

Definite criteria are needed to differentiate attitudes from temporary sets or expectations, dispositions, and organic states or motives, unless the concept is to become a catchall for explaining any and all nonrandom modes of behavior. The following criteria will serve to make this distinction:

1. *Attitudes are not innate.* Attitudes belong to the domain of human motivation the initial appearance of which depends upon learning. They are acquired during the individual's life history and are not carried genetically by the organism or in any kind of inherited substratum or unconscious.

2. *Attitudes are not temporary states of the organism but more or less enduring once they are formed.* Because attitudes are formed, they are not immutable. However, once formed they are not subject to change from moment to moment with the ups and downs of homeostatic regulation of the body or with every change in stimulus conditions.

3. *Attitudes stabilize a relationship between the person and objects.* Thus every attitude is a subject-object relationship. Attitudes are not formed in thin air, nor are they self-generated. They are formed or learned in relation to identifiable referents, whether these factors are persons, objects, groups, values, institutions, social issues, or ideologies. It is primarily the subject-object relationship that makes the study of attitudes central in social psychology. Stabilized person-object relationships are the lasting products of interaction between individual and environment. The scientific study of attitudes is not possible unless the *objects* in the subject-object relationship can be specified. A very important source from which attitudes are derived is the set of values or norms prevailing in the person's groups, social class, institutions, and his culture.

4. *The subject-object relationship has*

motivational-affective properties. When a person forms an attitude, he is no longer neutral toward the domain of objects in question. He is *for* some things and *against* others. Many attitudes are formed in highly significant social interactions and are directed toward objects with social significance in the lives of the participants. These attitudes, and others not always so heavily laden with social value, acquire emotional overtones and *directive* properties as parts of the developing self system, which itself becomes a highly charged anchor for experience and behavior. Therefore, the linkage between self and environment is seldom neutral.

5. *Attitude formation involves the formation of categories encompassing a small or large number of specific items.* The referent of an attitude constitutes a set of objects that may range from one to a large number of objects. In actuality, formation of a positive or negative stand toward one object typically implies differential attachment to others in the same domain. For example, a strong attraction to one person involves a *comparison* with other persons who are similar and different, whether the person is conscious of the fact or not. Therefore, attitude formation involves the stabilization of a set of categories varying from two to many. Psychologically, the number of referents subsumed by the attitude does not differentiate the functioning of attitudes. The negative attitude by members of one adolescent group toward a rival group produces judgments that the six or eight members of the rival group are "treacherous." Similarly, the verdict of the adult generation that "X nation is aggressive" produces attitudes in the younger generation such that they see any X member out of millions in X country as "aggressive." In short, attitude formation involves concept formation (Chapter 14), a process that need not be conscious or deliberate. The categories thus formed are used to differentiate among objects in a domain and to define the person's positive or negative relation to its various subsets.

6. *Principles applicable to attitude formation in general are applicable to the formation of social attitudes.* Attitudes directed toward social objects, values, social issues, groups, and institutions are "social" attitudes. The individual forms other attitudes, some of which may be highly idiosyncratic (for example, an inordinate fondness for evergreens as compared with other trees; an exaggerated preference for the hours just after sunrise as compared with the rest of the day). However, the psychology of attitude formation and functioning applies equally to social and more idiosyncratic subject-object relationships. Typically, the frame of reference for analyzing *social* attitudes includes social interaction processes. The objects are social stimuli (material and nonmaterial). The person forms attitudes relating himself to others in interpersonal relations, group relations, and intergroup relations; to his household furnishings and possessions (e.g., his car); cultural and class values, ethnic affiliations, and so on.

Many of the subject-object relationships traditionally considered as "personality" variables—such as masculinity-femininity, self-esteem as student or worker or mother, aggressiveness-shyness—are social attitudes to the extent that they involve normative standards or interpersonal and group comparisons (cf. Bieri *et al.,* 1966). There is, therefore, no sharp separation between social or personal attitudes, and no basis for altogether different theory and conceptualization of attitudes and such personality variables. The historical cleavage between "social" and "personality" psychologists, fortunately, is fading.

Implications for Cognitive vs. Motivational vs. Behavioral Approaches

Within academic psychology in recent years, there have been sharp divisions between theoretical approaches that are labeled "cognitive," "behavioral," and "motivational or dynamic." It is obvious that the criterion for attitudes stating that attitude formation involves concept formation (Criterion 5) requires a cognitive approach. However, Criterion 4 means that the cognitive approach must be motivational as well. Finally, the theory of attitudes must be behavioral because the only possible data from which an attitude can be inferred are observable behaviors, verbal or nonverbal. Attitudes are necessarily cognitive-motivational-behavioral. Any sharp separation of these criteria in theory or research practice is bound to be arbitrary and to distort the nature of attitudes.

Similarly, a number of researchers prefer to distinguish among the "cognitive," "affective," and "behavioral" *components* of attitudes. Individuals differ in the beliefs or ideas that lead them to take a positive or negative stand toward an object. Different individuals are committed toward the object in varying degrees. Likewise, and related to the foregoing observations, the probability that attitude will be revealed in overt action varies from individual to individual and situation to situation. Nevertheless, in any specific task or situation that arouses an attitude, the cognitive-motivational-behavioral are not insulated components. The best evidence available indicates that a particular individual's beliefs, emotional feelings, and behavior toward the attitude object are highly correlated (McGuire, 1968a) and that this consistency is greater to the extent that the person is highly ego-involved (Sherif *et al.*, 1965).

In actual research practice, treatment of the cognitive, motivational, and behavioral as "components" typically amounts to comparing samples of the person's behavior in *different* tasks or in situations at different points in time. As the frame of reference for experience and behavior *always* involves both internal and external factors, we can *learn* learn more about the person's attitude by comparing his behavior in a wide variety of relevant situations over time (Cook and Selltiz, 1964). The factors in the various social situations will invariably produce some "inconsistencies" in behavior because a single attitude under study is not the only determinant operating across all situations. The criteria for attitudes lead to a definition of attitude that can be translated into research operations for attitude assessment.

OPERATIONAL DEFINITION
OF ATTITUDE

Definitions of attitude in the literature have certain features in common. One of these is that attitudes are acquired or learned. Another is that attitudes are in-ferred from characteristic, consistent, and selective behavior over a time span (Thomas and Znaniecki, 1918; Allport, 1935; Murphy, Murphy, and Newcomb, 1937; Sherif and Cantril, 1947; Sherif, 1948; Campbell, 1950, 1963; Hovland, Janis and Kelley, 1953; Smith, Bruner, and White, 1956).

Attitudes are inferred from verbal or nonverbal behavior, preferably both. However, as LaPiere (1934) pointed out years ago, it is naive in the extreme to equate a single verbal response to a pointblank question ("Will you accept Chinese as guests in your establishment?") with the person's attitude as revealed in a variety of situations relevant to the attitude over time. This point was raised in Chapter 3 when the proposition on the unity of experience and behavior was discussed. Most situations arouse not one but a *complex* of attitudes, including the person's views of the person asking the question or administering procedures in a research situation. Adequate assessment of attitude cannot be made if one ignores the stimulus situation in which the individual's attitude is aroused (see also Chapter 6).

The individual's behavior in situations related to his attitude becomes *characteristic, consistent,* and *selective* if he sizes up ("defines") the various situations using characteristic standards that are particularly salient to him. A comparison process (judgment) underlies the behavior from which an attitude is inferred (Sherif, 1948; Sherif and Hovland, 1953). The individual places objects or events within the domain of his attitude, he discriminates and compares them by using categories he has formed for dealing with that domain of objects, and these categories are, at the same time, *evaluative* in nature. (It is as though he were expressing "I like and desire this one," or "This is my kind," while avoiding other alternatives or rejecting them as objectionable, disgusting, or "definitely not my kind.")

Accordingly, attitude can be defined in a way that leads to definite research operations in assessing attitudes.

DEF. **An attitude is the individual's set of categories for evaluating a domain of social stimuli (objects, persons, values, groups, ideas, etc.)**

which he has established as he learns about that domain (in interaction with other persons, as a general rule) and which relate him to subsets within the domain with varying degrees of positive or negative affect (motivation-emotion).

Many of the person's social attitudes are derived from dictums, formulas, and examples within the family, church, school, mass media of communication, etc. Typically, interaction with significant others is the setting for attitude formation.

It follows from the definition that attitudes can be inferred from what a person selects from the stimulus field out of so many stimuli objectively available, and how he evaluates them. Having an attitude becomes a matter of degree, rather than an all-or-none affair. To the extent that a person consistently selects items relevant to the attitude and consistently locates them within categories acceptable or objectionable to him, we may say that his attitude on the issue at hand is stabilized. Change of attitude is inferred from changes in these modes of behavior.

WHAT KIND OF A SCALE FOR ATTITUDE MEASUREMENT?

In order to measure anything, there has to be some standard basis for comparing specific objects. The ease, reliability, and validity with which we now measure many physical dimensions are products of centuries-long attempts to find adequate units and tools for measurement and further efforts to reach agreement on standards. It is not surprising, therefore, that in the comparatively recent endeavor to measure social attitudes, there is as yet no consensus on the appropriate scales to use.

Early psychologists interested in man's sensory capacities soon discovered that without the aid of standard measuring tools (e.g., ruler, weighing scales, vertical rod, etc.) man's judgments of physical dimensions were subject to systematic errors. The psychophysical scale for judgment does not correspond precisely to the physical scale, but it can be assessed in terms of standard physical scales (such as length, weight, light frequencies, etc.).

What, then, was to be the standard or scale against which a person's attitude would be assessed? Some attitudes, it is true, are directed toward social objects with physical dimensions or objective ranks that provide a basis for measurement. For example, the attitudes of a jet pilot and a peasant who travels by donkey about a "comfortable and safe speed" can be assessed relative to the common dimension of speed. Attitudes toward weight, height, or skin color can be assessed relative to standard units for weight or height, or a graded series of hues.

In social life, however, man has strong attitudes for which no physical measures are feasible; for example, whether sexual abstinence before marriage is desirable and, if not, what kind of heterosexual activity is appropriate; whether organized religion contributes to the benefit or detriment of society; whether the programs and candidates of various political parties are equipped to benefit the people and precisely in what respects; and whether a person's behavior is "masculine" or "feminine." As long as different groups of people uphold different positions on these and other significant issues in human relations, we may speak quite properly of a "scale" in such matters, but it is not a physical or psychophysical scale. It is a *psychosocial scale.*

A psychosocial scale is based upon consensus or agreement about the positions it includes at a given time and in a given setting. Some psychophysical scales have been based on consensus, too. At some point, however, they can be checked against physical events. For example, the American Indians whose calendars were calculated inaccurately soon found that the planting season fell at the wrong time for planting, and they added or subtracted a few days to adjust for it. In contrast, the value of money (which can be counted) is a product of lengthy and complex decisions; its value rests, ultimately, upon agreement among those who exchange the money.

Psychosocial scales refer to social facts and to schemes of categorization based on them through consensus. Their referents are the regularities in social life: groups that uphold different stands, values, or norms with their patterns of acceptability and rejection; status and role relations; social institutions, ideologies; technology and its products. Unless there are regularities in the pattern of social life, there cannot be social science, much less a scientific study of social attitudes.

Psychosocial scales consist of categories defining consensus on what is acceptable and in what degree, and what is objectionable and in what degree, within a given group or for the various groups composing society. Such scales do differ from culture to culture and from society to society. They do change during different periods of history. The present decade in the United States has seen a decided shift in the psychosocial scale regarding the social position of the country's Negro citizens, owing to the growth of social movements and vocal groups that have taken positions much more extreme than previously in the direction of equal and independent action by Negroes. A hundred years ago, the possibility of a federal graduated income tax in the United States was extremely objectionable to the great majority and was supported only by a rew radical groups and "crackpots." Currently, various positions are taken about raising or lowering the tax and about which groups should benefit; but very few citizens seriously advocate abolishing the income tax.

Here we are making explicit what almost every theoretical model has assumed (either explicitly or implicitly) in the construction of scales or "tests" of attitude. This assumption is revealed in the selection of items for assessing attitudes by the traditional methods. For example, one of the early attempts to measure attitudes was Bogardus' Social Distance Scale. Its items consist of a series of situations that can be ordered according to the intimacy of social contact between members of different groups (e.g., white and Negro). The validity of the test depends, in the first instance, on some consensus in a society about what constitutes intimate contact and with whom. As we mentioned earlier, Triandis and Triandis (1965) found that in Greece a "family friend" was regarded as more intimate contact than a "member of your social club," an order that is reversed in the United States (see pp. 274–276).

By far the most ambitious and sophisticated model for constructing a scale for assessment of attitudes was that developed by Thurstone (Thurstone and Chave, 1929). Actually, the model is put to research use more frequently by experimentalists studying judgments of nonsocial stimuli, such as color, or studying social judgment itself than in the assessment of attitudes (Torgerson, 1958). Test results from standardized Thurstone scales are often used as the basis for proclaiming the "validity" of another technique that an investigator has developed as less time consuming and easier. More accurately, a high correlation between the two indicates that individuals respond in similar ways to the two tests (Shaw and Wright, 1967).

The appeal of the Thurstone model and the fact that advances in the model have been almost entirely technical are readily understandable. Thurstone attacked the problem of constructing a scale of positions on a social issue (such as attitude toward the church, social position of Negroes, etc.) as a direct analogue with a scale for measuring a physical dimension. He aimed at an attitude scale that could serve as the yardstick for measuring individuals' attitudes, with equal units analogous to inches or centimeters. In the case of social dimensions, however, it was the judgments themselves that were to provide the basis for the scale.

Years earlier, the psychologist Wells (see Murphy, Murphy, and Newcomb, 1937, pp. 712–714) had noted that judgments of some social stimuli were remarkably uniform and suggested that low variability in the judgments of individuals over successive trials or among members of a group could be considered an objective "quantitative criterion" for the existence of social value. Proceeding from the same idea, Thurstone developed ways of treating the variability of judgments statistically, with the assumption that individual differences represented "error" which is distributed randomly in the form of the normal curve. The resulting scale was to have some of the important properties of physical scales, notably equal units ("equal-appearing intervals").

The steps in constructing a Thurstone-type scale are as follows:

1. Collect from printed and oral state-

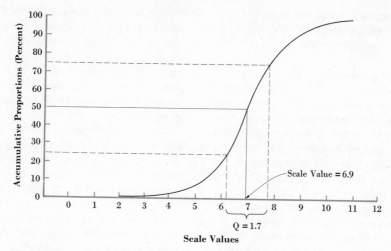

Fig. 15.1. Accumulative proportions (ogive) curve for judgments of Statement 51 in the construction of Thurstone's scale for the measurement of attitude toward the Church. The scale value of the statement and Q of the distribution are indicated graphically. (Adapted from L. L. Thurstone and E. J. Chave, *The Measurement of Attitude.* Chicago: University of Chicago Press, 1929, p. 38, Fig. 3.)

ments on an issue a large number ranging from one extreme to the other. (Note that the investigator's knowledge of his culture is assumed or a systematic content analysis of positions is necessary.)

2. Present this pool of statements (100–200) to judges, instructing them to sort the statements into 11 piles (categories) ranging from those most unfavorable to the object (e.g., Negroes) to those most favorable to the object, making the number of statements in the piles as nearly equal as possible. (Alternatively, the statements may be presented two at a time, the subject being asked to pick the one most favorable in each pair. However, this paired-comparison procedure is so time-consuming and laborious for the judge when there are more than ten or so statements that it has, in fact, seldom been used in constructing attitude scales.)

3. For each statement calculate the category number (from 1 to 11) that represents the median of the judgments (i.e., divides the judgment distribution into halves). This is the "scale value" for that statement. Similarly calculate the 25th and 75th percentile, using half the distance between them as a measure of variability (Q). Figure 15.1 illustrates this procedure.

The final scale is constructed by select-

ing items which (1) have scale values about equally spaced between 1 and 11; (2) have small Q values; and (3) are clearly relevant to taking a *pro* or *anti* position on the topic.

The validity of this procedure for constructing a scale with equal intervals rested on Thurstone's assumption that individuals could make social judgments unaffected by their own attitudes on the issue. "If a scale is to be regarded as valid, the scale values of the statements should not be affected by the opinions of the people who help to construct it" (Thurstone and Chave, 1929, p. 92).

Several investigators checked this assumption on different issues and concluded that an individual's attitude did not affect the scale values of statements to any significant extent (e.g., Hinckley, 1932; Ferguson, 1935; Pintner and Forlano, 1937). This conclusion amounts to saying that an individual's attitude does not anchor his judgments unless one specifically asks him to indicate his personal acceptances-rejections on a topic. As this assumption is critical both in Thurstone-type scales and others that instruct the individual to make judgments of the "distance" between attitude objects independent of his own endorsements or rejections (e.g., Coombs, 1952), we shall assess its validity.

INDIVIDUALS OWN POSITION
AS AN ANCHOR
IN JUDGMENT

Consider for a moment the process of judging something about which the person has a strong preference or commitment, pertaining to his self-concept (e.g., his height, weight, attractiveness, or skin color). How does an individual appraise himself in such respects? A number of experiments have been conducted, with the following findings:

1. The extreme representatives of such attributes serve as objective anchors for judgment such that a person who is extremely tall seldom considers himself average in height, nor a skinny girl herself plump, nor a very dark-skinned person himself light.

2. Within bounds set by the extremes, a person *assimilates* his own place *toward* that most valued and desired in his group or society (a value that does differ in different cultures). In other words, in judging his own position, the individual errs in the direction of the socially defined ideal (Marks, 1943; Hinckley and Rethingshafer, 1951; Jourard and Secord, 1955; Fillenbaum, 1961).

What happens, then, when the individual judges another person on the same attribute? The classic study by Marks (1943) on judgments of skin color by Negroes is illustrative. C. S. Johnson, the sociologist, had observed that *at the time* Negro youth preferred light-brown skin color. He noted, for example, that students tended to displace the actual skin color of popular school principals toward the light-brown and that of unpopular principals in the opposite direction. Marks' subjects were Negro students. By means of a matching technique, he obtained independent measures of objective skin color. Then the students rated each other on six characteristics, using an eight-point scale. The characteristics included "very attractive-very unattractive" and "very dark-very light."

Marks found that the student's own skin color served as an anchor for judging others'. Persons lighter than the rater were judged "light" and those darker than the rater were placed on the "dark" side. In addition, the students gave others whom they considered attractive the same benefit

that they gave themselves: they rated them closer to the desired light brown. The skin colors of those considered unattractive were not displaced toward this ideal. These tendencies occurred within the intermediate range of shadings between very light (which was not desirable) and very dark (also not desirable).

Marks' results are, in part, a function of a social norm prevailing among Negroes at the time, which reflected their position in a dominant white society—a norm which can be expected to change as that position changes. In the present context, these results illustrate the general finding in many studies of social perception and judgment that the person's own position relative to a valued object does affect his experience and behavior within limits established by objective (stimulus) factors.

Why, then, should not a person's stand on a social issue affect his placement of verbal statements about that issue? This was the question asked in a series of experiments using 114 statements originally used by Hinckley (1932) in developing a Thurstone scale on the social position of Negroes in the United States. Hinckley had found very high correlations between the scale values for two groups of white subjects with differing attitudes toward Negroes and between whites and a Negro sample ($r = .98$; $r = .93$). He followed a procedure suggested by Thurstone and Chave (1929), namely, that of discarding the judgments of anyone who placed 30 or more statements in any one category, on the assumption that such subjects were "careless." Hinckley observed that this criterion for "careless" subjects eliminated "certain of the white subjects" and many of the Negro subjects.

On the hunch that the criterion for "carelessness" had eliminated the subjects who were most strongly committed (ego-involved) on the Negro issue, Sherif and Hovland (Hovland and Sherif, 1952; Sherif and Hovland, 1953) replicated the Hinckley study, taking great pains to secure highly involved Negro students (the first admitted to a previously white university) and active white participants in the desegregation movement, as well as Negroes at a segregated university, unselected white students, and consistently anti-Negro students. Each

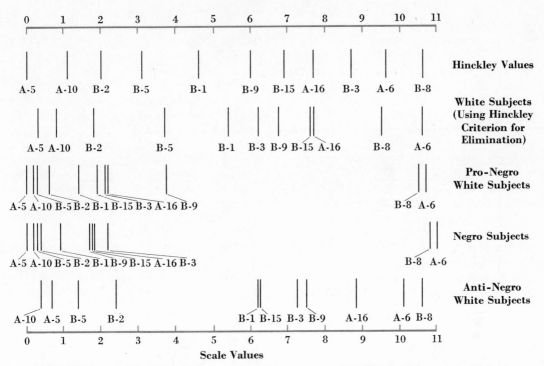

Fig. 15.2. Scale values of selected statements on the status of the Negro in the United States, based on judgments of persons with varying attitudes and involvement on the issue. Top bar locates scale values as determined by Hinckley. Below are scale values for white subjects—using Hinckley criterion for careless judges. Next are scale values for strongly pro-Negro white subjects, followed by those for Negro subjects and anti-Negro white subjects without elimination. (From M. Sherif and C. I. Hovland, *Social Judgment.* New Haven: Yale University Press, 1961, p. 109, Fig. 9.)

of these students sorted the 114 statements prepared by Hinckley. The item pool contained pro-Negro and anti-Negro statements with a large number of intermediate items having high Q values (large variability).

Figure 15.2 shows the scale values (median categorization) for eleven items obtained by Hinckley and for the various subject groups in the replication. The scale values for white subjects after eliminating those who placed 30 or more items in one pile were similar to those obtained by Hinckley (r = .96). However, the highly involved students gave very different judgments, especially of the intermediate items.

It was not surprising that the systematic variations were found in the items *intermediate* to the extremes. Edwards (1946) had already noted that, compared with extreme statements, intermediate statements were particularly likely to have large Q values.

Figure 15.3 shows how the subjects dis-

tributed their judgments into the 11 categories imposed by instructions. It may be seen that the highly involved subjects produced bimodal distributions of the statements into categories because they neglected intermediate categories, shifting "intermediate" statements toward the extremes—especially the extreme that they found particularly objectionable.

Sherif and Hovland reported in some detail on the difficulty they had in finding college students who were overtly anti-Negro and willing to serve as subjects in their experiments. The findings in their study were more clearcut for *pro* Negro subjects than for *anti* Negro subjects (see Fig. 15.3). Some investigators suggested that the systematic shifts in judgment are peculiar to persons who *favor* or *support* an attitude object and that persons *against* it would not exhibit the same tendency. Therefore, an experiment by Vaughan (1961) is particularly interesting.

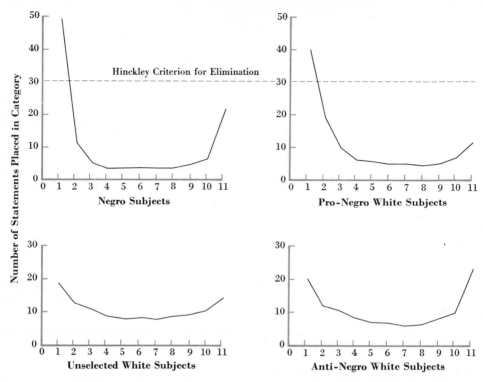

Fig. 15.3. Frequency of statements placed in 11 categories imposed by Thurstone procedures by various subject samples. Note that the Hinckley criterion for eliminating subjects would not have affected unselected white subjects or anti-Negro white subjects, but would have eliminated most Negro and pro-Negro white subjects. The U-shaped distributions of the latter occurred through displacement of intermediate statements relative to the subject's stand (assimilation-contrast effects). (From M. Sherif and C. I. Hovland, *Social Judgment.* New Haven: Yale University Press, 1961, p. 107, Fig. 8.)

Vaughan (1961) constructed sixty items on the position of Americans of Mexican origin near the Texas-Mexican border. Her subjects were (1) intensely anti-Latin residents of South Texas selected on the basis of their overt avoidance of contacts with "Latins" and verbal deprecation of them; (2) South Texas residents who were not overtly anti-Latin; (3) unselected college students in South Texas; and (4) unselected college students in north Texas where there were few Americans of Mexican origin (hence, subjects presumed to be uninvolved in the issue). Figure 15.4 shows the distributions of judgments into eleven imposed categories.

The distribution for intensely anti-Latin subjects is almost a mirror image of that found for Negro and pro-Negro whites in the previous study (Fig. 15.3). Again, the intermediate categories were neglected and the extreme *opposed* to the subjects' own

positions (a favorable extreme in this case) was disproportionately crowded. Other subjects distributed their judgments fairly evenly into the 11 categories.

Subsequent experiments done with comparable methods and comparable items to be sorted have supported the following generalizations about the social judgments of persons with differing attitudes toward the objects of judgment:

1. Almost everyone places strongly worded, unequivocal statements of extreme positions into the extreme categories—consistently and with low variability (Sherif and Hovland, 1961; Zavalloni and Cook, 1965).

2. The placement of items intermediate to the clear-cut extremes differs for highly ego-involved persons and less involved or noncommitted persons.

3. The distributions of judgments by a highly involved person are bimodal, the concentrations of judgments into categories

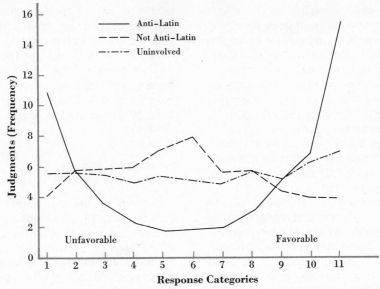

Fig. 15.4. Frequency of judgments in 11 categories imposed by Thurstone instructions for judging statements about Spanish-speaking Americans (Latins). Note that persons who were not anti-Latin and those uninvolved with Latins distributed their judgments fairly evenly into the 11 categories. Anti-Latin subjects, on the other hand, piled-up statements at the end favorable to Latins, a reverse shift to that found for pro-Negro subjects judging statements on the status of Negroes (Fig. 15.3). (Adapted from K. Vaughan, 1961, unpublished study.)

with which he strongly agrees and disagrees occurring at the expense of categories intermediate to them.

4. The bimodality of distributions is achieved by systematic variations in judgment of intermediate items that are equivocal, vague, or open to alternative interpretation (La Fave et al., 1963; Zimbardo, 1960). (Zimbardo gave the following example used in a study of *pro* and *anti* attitudes toward science: "Anyone who has ever known a scientist knows why science is in the state it is today.")

5. The *direction* of the systematic shifts depend on the discrepancy between the statement and the person's own position on the issue, which serves as a major anchor in categorizing such statements. Statements near the individual's own position are assimilated toward it (Manis, 1960). If his stand is extreme, he rates neighboring items as more extreme than someone not involved in the issue (Zavalloni and Cook, 1965; Upshaw, 1962, Webb and Chueh, 1962). On the other hand, statements differing considerably from the person's own stand are contrasted to his stand, seen as

more discrepant, and bunched into categories that are highly objectionable to him (Webb and Chueh, 1962; Upshaw, 1962; Zavalloni and Cook, 1965).

In other words, the person's own stand serves as an anchor for his judgments if he is highly ego-involved in the object of judgment, resulting in what Webb called "bidirectional displacement" that can be explained in terms of the similarities and differences of the items to the individual's stand. The assimilation and contrast effects result from the process of comparison relative to a specified anchor; they are not opposed "mechanisms."

What do these experimental findings imply about the construction of psychosocial scales and about attitude measurement?

1. Individuals committed to opposing attitudes do differ in their judgment of items in the relevant domain. Therefore, the assumption that scale values for an "equal interval" scale can be obtained without regard to the attitudes of judges is not warranted. While this conclusion does not invalidate the Thurstone model for construct-

ing a scale within a limited, more or less homogeneous population, it does invalidate its use for comparing individuals belonging to groups with strikingly different viewpoints and norms. At best, the procedure yields *rank orders* of statements (not an interval scale) that may be comparable across a variety of groups (as high correlations of rank orders suggest).

2. The construction of a psychosocial scale should order the objects or positions on the social issue, but should also include representation of categorization of those positions according to the norms of the groups upholding each differentiated position. For example, groups of white liberals in the United States may very well differentiate between "equal job opportunity" and "equal education" for Negroes. However, some Negro citizens place both items within a category denoting "social equality" and do not rank one above the other. In other words, the range of positions that members of a given group accept and the range of positions that they categorically reject are important properties of psychosocial scales.

PSYCHOSOCIAL SCALES
AND INDIVIDUAL ATTITUDES

The need for interdisciplinary study is nowhere more evident than in the study of attitudes. By historical accident, studies of group processes and studies of attitude and attitude change proceeded simultaneously without integration of theory and findings. Yet, the study of groups provides the objective basis for assessing individual attitudes. As noted in Chapter 9 on social norms, every group prescribes a latitude for acceptable behavior and a latitude of objectionable behavior in matters of consequence to the group. As long as members are loyal, their *attitudes* fall within the bounds prescribed by the norm. Knowledge of the norm prevailing within a group and knowledge of the norms of various groups pertaining to the same object provide a basis for assessing individual attitudes.

The psychologist F. H. Allport (1934) called attention many years ago to the fact that social attitudes in a group are not distributed normally, a function typical of individual differences in other respects (e.g.,

height or weight). Social attitudes are distributed more nearly in a J shape. Figure 15.5 illustrates the theoretical comparison between a normal and J-shaped curve. The J curve shows that the majority of members have similar attitudes, while the number of individuals deviating from the modal attitude *decreases* as the degree of deviation *increases.*

Group Norms, Attitudes,
and Reference Groups

Knowledge of the norms in various groups provides an objective baseline for assessing individual attitudes. However, the assessment of a norm, which is a group property, is not identical to measurement of attitude, which is a psychological concept. For example, as suggested earlier, we might very well establish the existence of a norm for regular church attendance in a small congregation by keeping records of attendance, noting when the membership committee calls on infrequent attenders to urge them into the fold, and observing when nonattendance leads to derogating, ignoring, or excluding the deviant. However, the problem of attitude assessment remains. The attenders may include, for example, a nonbeliever who attends for the sake of his business, and a small boy who attends because his parents force him. Similarly the nonattenders may include believers who do not attend because of illness or because the particular church is not their religious reference group.

Most studies of attitudes specify certain background characteristics of the samples studied in terms of ethnic, socioeconomic, sex, age, religious, or regional classifications. Within such broad classifications, different groups uphold different stands, with the result that the distribution of attitudes within a given classification may reveal considerable variation. Figure 15.6 gives such distributions for college students, separated according to their major religious classifications, on the question of the existence and nature of the deity (Katz and Allport, 1931).

Note that the distribution for Catholics closely resembles a J-shape curve, but that the distributions for Jews and "no-church" are more nearly flat. These distributions of attitudes would be more meaningful if they were analyzed in terms of the reference groups of the individual respondents who happened to be included in the samples (see p. 418). For example, the Protestant respondents could be specified as Church of God, Baptist, Presbyterian, Unitarian, and so forth. Similarly, the Jewish respondents could be specified as members of orthodox and other congregations, and perhaps, as nonmembers. The distribution of attitudes for individuals classified as "no church" might be clarified the most if their reference groups (including political, social, and intellectual groups) were specified. If this were done, we would predict a J curve for each reference group, with the peak of the J curve falling on the focal value for that group.

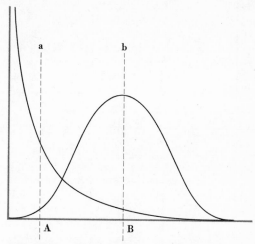

Fig. 15.5. J-shaped curve compared with normal distribution. The dashed lines a and b represent the medians of the distributions. The J-curve is typical of conforming behavior and social attitudes. (Reprinted from *Psychology at Work*, edited by Paul S. Achilles, by permission of McGraw-Hill Book Company, Inc. Copyright 1932, McGraw-Hill Book Company, Inc.)

THE MEASUREMENT OF ATTITUDES

In Chapter 6, the "social psychology of the research situation" was discussed. The implication was that the investigator, the procedures, and research instruments may be such important factors in the social (research) situation that the individual responds to them as much or more than he does to the stimulus material that the investigator hoped to make focal. The same considerations become important in the assessment of the individual's attitude. It is now well established that research subjects respond differently when they think, for example, that they are being given an information test than when they are aware that the instrument is designed to study their attitude. Merely administering the same attitude test form twice, with some communication or other research procedure "in between," alerts subjects to the fact that attitude change is being studied—with decided effects on their behavior.

The extensive work by Allen Edwards and his associates (1957b, 1961, 1962) confirms what individuals do when they are confronted with a direct attempt to investigate their attitudes about themselves (as used in self-report "personality" questionnaires) or attitudes toward social objects and issues. These investigators have shown that under such circumstances individuals endorse items that they also rate as "socially

desirable." What the individual rates as "socially desirable" is, of course, socially desirable under the conditions of the test. The subject is aware of the appraising eye of the investigator. In other words, for all but a few subjects who decide to be "sincere," the findings on personality inventories and direct attitude tests represent individual views of the social norms (psychosocial scales) defining how persons *should* act, not how they themselves *do* or *would* act.

These findings bear on the *validity* of attitude assessment techniques, that is, their accuracy in assessing the person's attitude as it functions in actual-life situations related to his attitude. If any measurement technique is worth using, it has to demonstrate its utility in predicting behavior.

Of course, there are some situations and some attitudes that *can* be investigated validly by techniques that confront the individual with direct inquiry about his views. The national presidential election in the United States is an important example. Probably very few people would hesitate to state their personal choice between the Democratic or Republican candidates just before an election, either of whom may be supported publicly without fear of loss of

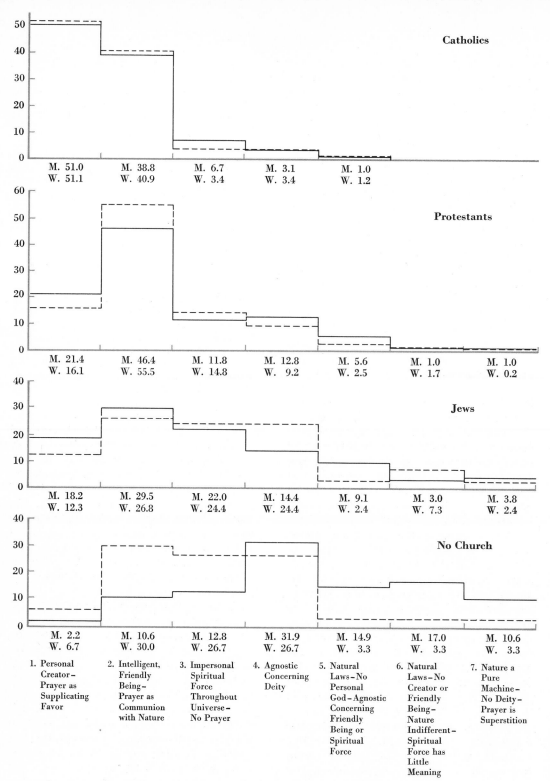

Fig. 15.6. Distributions of percentages of 1,219 students (Syracuse University, College of Liberal Arts) endorsing each of seven statements on the question of the existence and nature of a deity. Seven opinions (see abscissa) elicited a distribution from Catholics that approaches the J-curve most closely. Most divergent distribution is "No Church" subjects. Men's curves, solid lines; women's broken lines. From D. Katz and F. H. Allport, *Students' Attitudes.* Syracuse: The Craftsman Press, 1931.)

status, reprisal, or legal action. It goes without saying that all elections everywhere at all times are *not* public matters in this sense. Every person has views on certain matters that he would not reveal without taking into account to whom he was speaking and how the information would be used.

Unobtrusive or Disguised Methods of Attitude Measurement

One obvious way to circumvent the production of artifacts in attitude measurement is to assess the individual's attitude *indirectly,* that is, to infer his attitude from behavior in a task that he does not see as an attempt to probe his attitude. Such tests can be understood in terms of the principle on the relative weights of internal factors when the stimulus situation or task allows response alternatives (i.e., lacks structure in some degree; Proposition 9).

For example, in studying the development of attitudes toward Negroes by Southern white children, Hartley and Hartley (Horowitz and Horowitz, 1938) presented the children with complex pictures, each for about two or three seconds, then "tested" their perception and memory by asking questions, some of which were deliberately misleading. In one picture, the question "Who is cleaning the grounds?" produced the answer of "Negro" in about 70 percent of the cases. Similarly, answers to a question, "What is the colored man in the corner doing?" (there was no such figure) reflected the development with age of the view that Negroes should be in menial positions. The literature up to 1950 on the use of indirect techniques for attitude assessment was reviewed by Campbell (1950). The following are examples of *indirect* tests of attitude.

"Projective" Techniques

By far the most popular of the indirect measurement techniques in attitude assessment has been Murray's Thematic Apperception Test (TAT) or some adaptation of it (Tomkins, 1947). For example, the popular line of research on "achievement motivation" by McClelland and his associates (1953; Atkinson, 1958; McClelland, 1965) has relied heavily on this technique, with the conception that achievement is a

"need" located within the person that will be revealed when he is asked to describe what is happening in a picture (a task allowing many response alternatives; see pp. 62–66).

Proshansky (1943) used the TAT to study pro- and antilabor attitudes. He inserted into the series of pictures several directly relevant to labor issues with the hypothesis that "extreme groups, i.e., those inclining toward strongly pro-labor or anti-labor attitudes, would reveal their social orientation through their manner of reporting upon pictures of social conflict situations" (p. 393). Proshansky projected each picture for 5 seconds, then asked the subjects to write a description of each, allowing 2½ minutes for each description. The subjects also filled-in a direct questionnaire on their attitudes. Their descriptions of the labor pictures were rated by three judges, whose ratings were reliably in agreement. Their ratings correlated positively with the subjects' scores on the direct attitude test.

The following description by a subject was rated as *pro*-labor, and probably most judges would agree with this rating. "Home of a man on relief—shabby—dresses poorly. Scene is probably in a shack down South. Also, might be the home of some unemployed laborer. Horrible housing conditions. Why don't the government provide for these people? The ordinary worker is always forgotten and allowed to rot" (p. 394).

The next description by another subject was rated *anti*labor; again, a rating that would probably be highly reliable with more judges. "Picture of one room, very messy, stove in the center, woman on the left, man standing next to stove, couple of children near them. This is a room of what we call 'poor people.' They seem to be messy, sloppy people, who seem to enjoy dwelling in their own trash" (p. 394).

These two descriptions illustrate the finding that such projective techniques for attitude assessment (including responses to pictures, sentence completion tasks, doll play, etc.) can reveal the person's attitude quite clearly, particularly if the person's attitude or bias is very strong. However, this and other such projective techniques have a serious disadvantage: All responses are not so clear-cut as those presented above.

There are all kinds of variations between these extremes. Reliance on judges to code and rate the responses entails the same difficulty that appears in constructing psychosocial scales on the basis of judgments: judges have their own biases and these are likely to affect the ratings of precisely those responses for which their services are needed most. The descriptions falling between the obvious extremes are most subject to displacement according to the person's own attitude.

The remedy for this coding problem in projective tests lies in using stimulus material and securing reactions that can be scored directly by anyone who can count. The next-described indirect technique is one of the successful attempts in this direction.

Judgments
of Fact and Truth
Revealing Attitudes

The research literature contains many positive correlations between the amount and kind of information that individuals have on some issue and their attitudes on the issue (cf. Campbell, 1950; McGuire, 1968a). Needless to say, these correlations pertain to those kinds of "facts" and those kinds of "truth" that are open to interpretation. Without entering the philosophical questions on the nature of truth or the evidence needed to establish fact, let us merely note that there are many areas in which "information" and "fact" are sources of controversy, that is, where there are alternatives that various groups support as equally feasible.

For example, in studying anti-Latin attitudes, Vaughan (1961) reported that many of the anti-Latin subjects who were told simply to categorize statements objectively according to how *pro* or *anti* Latin they were objected strongly that many of the pro-Latin statements were *not true*. They had all kinds of "facts" from personal experience and first-hand reports to support their objections. Another example is the bewilderment of many dentists and enlightened citizens in the United States at the failure of referendums to permit the fluoridation of local water supplies as a measure against tooth decay. Backed by scientific research

on the beneficial effects and safety of the measure, the profluoridation campaigns fell on deaf ears of people who distrusted both doctors and the local power structure, but who had "facts" provided by sources they *did* trust on the bad effects of tampering with nature and regarding past medical errors.

Hammond (1948) took advantage of the "indeterminancy" of certain facts and the obscurity of others to construct a test of attitude that was disguised as an information test. In his error-choice technique, subjects were presented items with two alternative answers, the subject being asked to pick the "correct" alternative. Some items pertained to facts that few people were likely to know accurately (for example: "Average weekly wage of the war worker in 1945 was (a) \$37 (b) \$57"). Others were "indeterminable" because no agreement prevailed on the matter (for example: "Russia's removal of heavy industry from Austria was (a) legal (b) illegal"). In order to disguise the test as an information test, the error-choice items were embedded within an equal number of items with a factually correct answer. These factual items were made easy so that most subjects could choose the correct alternative.

Hammond administered the information tests concerning labor and concerning Russia to a group of businessmen and a group of men employed in a labor union. The measure of attitude on each issue was simply the number of (erroneous) alternatives chosen that were biased favoring or against labor, and for or against Russia. Hammond found that the businessmen and the labor union employees did choose erroneous alternatives in line with their attitudes, to the extent that there was "a positive systematic error for one group as against a negative systematic error for the other."

To check the value of such an indirect test of attitude, Hammond conducted a second experiment in which one group received the tests marked "Info-form" while a second group received the same tests marked "Att-Info-Form." That small designation "Att" was sufficient to alert many subjects that their attitudes were under investigation. On the labor test, a third of them chose alternatives consistently differ-

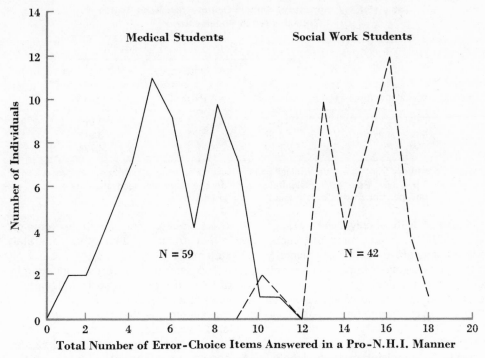

Fig. 15.7. Frequency of errors in pro-national health insurance direction by two samples. Of 18 error choice items, which present person with errors in two directions, medical students consistently err less in "pro" direction than do social work students (*dashed line*). (From A. J. Kubany, 1953. A validation study of the error-choice technique using attitudes on national health insurance. *Educat. and Psychol. Measurem.*, **13**, 157–163.)

ent from those subjects whose forms were marked "Info." The effect of the "Att" label on the test about Russia was still more marked. Thus the effort to measure attitudes indirectly was justified.

The error-choice technique has not been used as much as its initial success warrants, possibly because it is difficult to construct items with the assurance that subjects will not have definitive information. Still, it is well worth greater use in research than it has received. For example, Fig. 15.7 shows the distribution of errors by medical students and social work students on the matter of a proposed national health insurance. Kubany (1953) knew that, in general, medical students and doctors were opposed to such insurance while social workers, in general, supported such proposals. He checked this general assumption after administering an error-choice information test by asking a direct question as to whether the subject favored or opposed some form of national health insurance. He eliminated the four social work students

and the 10 medical students whose replies were not in the direction typical for their sample. The responses of the remaining 101 subjects to 18 error-choice items revealed that the average number of errors in the *pro* direction was 14.64 for social workers and only 5.93 for medical students. As Fig. 15.7 shows, the overall distribution of errors for the two samples overlap very little.

Judgments of Truth by Partisans in Collective Controversy

Another experiment taking advantage of the "indeterminacy" of many social facts and the lack of agreement between various social groups on the rules of admissible evidence was conducted in Oklahoma just before the last of five referendums in 50 years on the repeal of prohibition for the sale of alcoholic beverages (Sherif and Jackman, 1966). Openly "dry" groups (e.g., the Women's Christian Temperance Union, United Drys, and certain religious sects)

Table 15.1.   Judgments of Truth in Controversy: Mean Degree of Truth Judged in Statements[a]

Statements	Person's Stand on Issue		
	Dry (N = 89)	Moderately Wet (N = 150)	Wet (N = 66)
Dry	4.31	8.57	8.97[b]
Moderately dry	1.56	2.94	3.91[b]
Wet	8.87	5.51	4.77[b]

[a] "Very true" = 0; "Very false" = 11

[b] p < .001. See text for significance of comparisons between students and partisans (wets-drys pooled).

were compared with openly "wet" groups (such as the United Oklahomans for Repeal) and with an unselected sample of university students who were moderately wet in their attitudes toward drinking.

Each subject was asked to rate a series of statements according to how true or false each was. The judgments were made for each statement by checking an unmarked linear scale 11 centimeters long, labeled "very true" at one end (0) and "very false" at the other (11). Some of the statements were selected from the campaign statements of dry groups, some from those of wet groups, and some were moderately dry statements which mildly indicated the possible dangers of drunkenness. The following are examples of the three types of statements:

Dry: "Drinking greatly increases the crime rate." "Most fatal accidents are the result of drunken driving."
Wet: "One can be truly religious and still take a drink." "Drinking has led very few women into prostitution."
Moderately dry: "Many automobile accidents occur because of drunken driving." "Some crimes are committed under the influence of alcohol."

Table 15.1 presents the average (mean) judgments of truth for these three kinds of statements by the dry, wet, and moderately wet (student) samples.

The differences in judgment of truth by the three groups of subjects were significant for each type of statement. Comparisons among groups for each type revealed that the means for wet and dry samples differ significantly in each case. Note that the wets rated the moderately dry statements significantly less true than drys did.

The students differ from the extreme groups in their ratings of all but the moderately dry statements.

The importance of the "indeterminacy" of truth in producing such systematic variations in judgment was revealed in ratings of two statements that were included as "truisms" which both sides would accept or reject almost unanimously. ("Sometimes people do things while drunk which they are sorry for afterwards"; "A few drinks before the game helps a basketball player perform better.") Without exception every sample rated these statements very near the appropriate end of the scale, with variabilities significantly smaller than those for other statements.

The data were also analyzed according to the percentage of statements from one's own side and from the opposition that were judged extremely true, extremely false, or intermediate (within the middle 3 centimeters of the scale). (The source was not labeled.) As predicted, approximately 75 percent of the ratings by wets of dry statements and by drys of wet statements were "false." However, each side rated only about 55 percent of the statements actually emanating from its own side as true, judging about 22 percent as false. The uniformity of these differences in judgment of the statements on one's own side and one's opponents for the two groups reflects a general finding about individuals who are highly ego-involved in their own stand:

Rather than blanket acceptance of all positions "sympathetic" to one's own position, the highly involved person becomes more "choosy" about accepting support (his threshold for acceptance is raised).

On the other hand, his threshold for rejection is lowered, so that he lumps together almost all of his opponent's statements as extremely false.

For this reason, judgments of the truth of statements the factual basis of which is controversial reveal the person's attitude when his judgments of his own side are compared with his judgments of the opposition. His ratings of statements made by his own side are less extreme (true) than those of the opposite camps (extremely false). This rating method permits systematic variations in between the extremes.

Measuring Attitude as the Individual's Own Categories

In Chapter 14, a study using the "Own Categories Procedure" for comparing neutral and evaluative categorizations was summarized (pp. 323–325). The stimulus objects to be categorized were unequivocal, but the number of categories to be used and the distribution of items into the categories were left entirely to the person. The study showed that the number and the width of categories varied systematically according to the range of objects that were acceptable and objectionable to the person. The individual is more choosy, slices the object domain more finely, and distributes his judgments evenly when he is dealing within the range that he accepts.

The Own Categories Procedure for indirect assessment of the person's attitude developed from studies in social judgment on the effects of internal and external anchors in producing systematic displacements in categorization (Sherif and Hovland, 1961). Such research had shown that when a stimulus that differs greatly from the objects being judged is used as a standard for comparison (anchor), the judgments of the objects shift systematically *away* from the anchor value (contrast effect). Conversely, an anchor stimulus near the value of the objects being judged produces systematic shifts in the opposite direction, *toward* the anchor (assimilation effect). Such systematic shifts in social judgment were reported earlier in this chapter in presenting the work on scaling of statements on

the Negro issue (pp. 340–342). In that work, the systematic shifts of intermediate items were interpreted as assimilation and contrast effects relative to the person's own position on the topic.

The Own Categories Procedure is indirect in that the person is not asked about his attitude toward the objects but is instructed to sort the objects into any number of piles he chooses, so that the objects in each pile "belong together" and the piles represent gradations of favorableness-unfavorableness toward the object. (In short, the task is presented as an "objective" task in judgment.)

The Own Categories Procedure allows assimilation-contrast effects to be manifested freely by using a large number of ambiguous or equivocal statements, and having the individual decide on the number of categories to use and how he will distribute judgments into them. Unlike other "card sort" techniques for the study of attitudes and self-concept, great pains are taken *not* to suggest a given number of categories and *not* to suggest that any particular distribution of items into the categories is preferred.

The Own Categories Procedure yields two related numerical measures of the person's attitude and relative involvement in the issue:

1. *Number of categories used:* The more highly involved the person, the fewer the categories he uses to categorize a range of items from one extreme to the other.
2. *Category widths of designated categories:* The person with some involvement in the object domain distributes his judgments bimodally, the largest mode indicating objectionable items and the smaller the most acceptable items.

In addition, the investigator can analyze the items contained in the various categories used by the person in terms of the content clusters. The basis for inferring the person's attitude from the objective indicators will be made explicit through illustrative research.

Own Categories on Status of Negroes. In the research on the scaling of statements about the status of Negroes, Sherif and Hovland (1953) had some subjects catego-

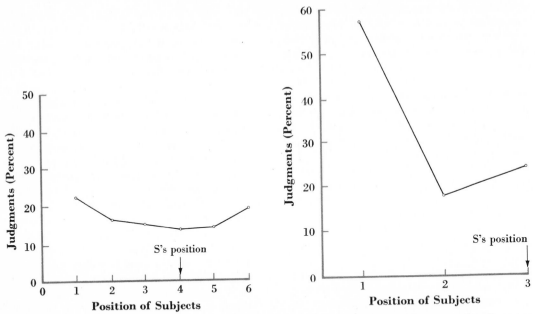

Fig. 15.8. a. (*left*) Distribution of percentages of judgments on the Negro question by less involved individuals using the own categories method. (Adapted from Sherif and Hovland, 1953). Subjects using six categories with own categories procedures. On the baseline, Category 1 is most unfavorable to Negroes while 6 is most favorable. These less-involved white subjects found Category 4 most acceptable on the average. **b.** (*right*) Distribution of percentages of judgments on the Negro question by highly involved pro-Negro subjects (Category 3 most acceptable). (Adapted from Sherif and Hovland, 1953.) Subjects using 3 categories. Note bimodality using the own categories procedure, even more accentuated than the bimodality for highly involved, pro-Negro subjects using the imposed 11 categories of Fig. 15.3.

rize the same statements twice, about two weeks apart, once using the standard Thurstone procedures that imposed the use of 11 categories (imposed categories) and once using the Own Categories Procedure. The order of these two procedures was counterbalanced for half of each subject group, so that the results could not be explained as an order effect.

Figure 15.8 presents the distribution of judgments on this controversial issue into own categories by *pro*-Negro subjects and by *moderately "pro"* subjects in the experiment. The less involved moderate subjects used, on the average, about five categories with the Own Categories Procedure and, as the figure shows, distributed their judgments about as equally as they had using imposed categories. Highly involved pro-Negro subjects, on the other hand, used fewer categories than the less-involved moderates. Their tendency to distribute judgments bimodally was greatly accentuated as a result. In fact, the most militant

Negro subjects used, on the average, fewer than four categories—placing 65 of the 114 statements in a single category highly objectionable to them and 27 in a category acceptable to them. Unselected white students placed 43 of the 114 statements in objectionable categories and 38 in categories that they later indicated were acceptable to them.

Vaughan (1961) reported similar findings in her study of *anti*-Latin and uninvolved subjects in Texas (pp. 342 f.). The same subjects who distributed their judgments into 11 imposed categories (Fig. 15.4) also categorized the statements by using the Own Categories Procedure. More than 85 percent of the *anti*-Latins used three or fewer categories, while almost 92 percent of the uninvolved subjects used 4 or more categories. The range was 2–5 categories for anti-Latins and 2–11 for uninvolved subjects, but only 8 percent of the uninvolved subjects used 3 categories or fewer.

Number of Categories as One Index of

Involvement. In the experiment on the own categories of Navaho and white high-school students reported in Chapter 14, each subject sorted four sets of material: (1) the neutral series of numbers, (2) the same numbers with dollar signs affixed, (3) brief descriptions of teenage behavior, and (4) the names of various ethnic and national groups. By means of a paired comparison procedure, the three sets of socially valued items (2–4 above) were ranked in terms of their personal importance to the students. With the neutral series as least involving, Sherif found significant differences between the number of categories used, the trend being toward the use of fewer categories for more-involving items than for less-involving and neutral items.

Similar results were reported by Glixman (1965), who used different subjects (college students) and three different sets of materials. Each person sorted a set of familiar objects (paperclip, chalk, etc.), a set of statements on a social issue, and a set of descriptive statements about themselves. As in the Sherif study, there was a low (about .35) significant correlation between the number of categories used by the same individuals for the three sets of items. More categories were used in sorting the familiar objects than the self descriptions, despite the fact that there were more self descriptions than objects to be sorted. Glixman concluded that these differences, as well as the highly skewed distribution of the self descriptions, indicated that the findings could not be accounted for by a "response style" of the person without regard to item content and his attitude toward that content.

Reich and Sherif (1963) compared the categorizations of mature women (35–50 years) with median education exceeding four years of university study. One group was composed of active members of the League of Women Voters, which had dedicated its major effort that year to study of the problem of legislative reapportionment. A sample of school teachers, matched as closely as possible for age and education, was known to be favorable to reapportionment but relatively uninvolved in the issue, as indicated by expressions of opinion and lack of any overt acts. Reich and Sherif had both samples categorize sixty statements.

Half of the statements had been judged in pretests with great variability and the remainder were equally divided between extremely *pro* and extremely *anti* statements. Although the League members were certainly better informed on the issue and might be expected to differentiate among the statements more finely, 74 percent of them used four or fewer categories, while only 26 percent of the teachers used such a small number of categories.

Width of Acceptable and Objectionable Categories. After completing the "objective" task of sorting items according to their *pro* and *con* position about the subjects, subjects in the Own Categories Procedure can be asked to label the categories that are acceptable to them and objectionable to them. (Note that this request does not force them to label all categories.) In the Sherif-Hovland study (Fig. 15.8), highly involved pro-Negro subjects rejected more statements than they accepted. Similarly, La Fave and Sherif (1968) found that 87 percent of Negro subjects placed more items for desegregation into categories they labeled as *favoring segregation* than in those favoring desegregation. Among a fraternity sample from which the investigators hoped to obtain pro-segregation sentiments, 59 percent of the sample judged more statements as *favoring desegregation* than segregation. By comparison, more than half of the unselected white students placed equal numbers of items into favorable and unfavorable categories.

This general tendency of highly committed persons to see things in black-and-white terms, and to see more black than white, has been observed in many walks of life. Politicians sometimes say that people may not be sure what they want, but they are very sure about what they are against. The novelist Robert Penn Warren (1956) commented on the tendency when he toured his native South after the 1954 Supreme Court decision desegregating the public schools and gave several examples: "I ask my question of the eminent Negro scholar. His reply is immediate: 'It's not so much what the Negro wants as what he doesn't want. . . . He is denied human dignity' " (p. 41).

The well-informed, mature, and well-educated women in Reich and Sherif's study who belonged to the League of Women Voters were also very clear about what they were against. Using three or four categories, these women placed over half of the sixty statements into unfavorable categories which they found extremely objectionable, whereas the less-involved teachers placed about the same number of statements into their categories favorable and unfavorable to reapportionment.

The strength of the attitude, or the person's involvement in the issue, is the key to the broad categories for objectionable statements. Koslin, Waring, and Pargament (1965) had Peace Corps volunteers categorize series of statements on five issues that the subjects also ranked according to how much time they spent talking about the topic. The amount of time spent served as an index of relative ego-involvement in these issues. The investigators examined the width of acceptable and objectionable categories for each issue, and found that from the least-involving issue (housing in India) to the most-involving issue (segregation in the United States), the width of acceptable categories decreased and the width of objectionable categories increased, being greater than the latitude of acceptance on the segregation issue.

The Critical Factor in Systematic Shifts: Intermediate Items. Sherif and Hovland (1961) proposed that assimilation-contrast effects occur primarily through systematic displacements of the objects intermediate to the extremes. This hypothesis was tested with the Own Categories Procedure by La Fave and Sherif (1968) in their study of the desegregation issue mentioned previously. Tracing down the items responsible for the bimodal distributions of most Negro subjects and the majority of members of a fraternity reputed to be anti-Negro, they found that the items shifted in opposite directions by these two subject samples were 13 of their 25 statements with high variability (Q values). The Negro subjects accumulated such statements in categories unfavorable to desegregation. The fraternity members accumulated the statements in categories favoring desegregation.

Selltiz, Edrich, and Cook (1965) have proposed the categorization of statements about a group as an indicator of attitudes toward that group by using a fixed number of categories imposed by instructions. Imposed categories yield "neater" data, in the sense that everyone uses the same number of categories. However, these "neater" data are obtained at the expense of eliminating variance in the number of categories used, which is a significant aspect of judgment in actual encounters with the object of attitude.

The Own Categories Technique has also been shown to be a *reliable* procedure. Koslin (1966) prepared two sets composed of different statements on motives for joining the Peace Corps. The two sets were matched in terms of standard scores for the statements derived from paired-comparison judgments. By having Peace Corps volunteers sort both sets of statements at different times, Koslin showed that reliability of placement is very high ($r = .95$).

The Own Categories Procedure is an indirect test of attitude because the person is not instructed to reveal his attitude and he is not aware that the measures (number of categories and distribution) reveal anything about him as a person. Because the task of sorting or grouping objects is very simple and is found in almost every known culture, the technique is suitable for cross-cultural research and for a nonconfrontive method in locating areas of personal concern in personality study. The specific content (objects) to be sorted can be adapted to the particular culture in which it is used; however, the logic of the method can be invariant because it is based on general principles of human judgment.

16

Methods
in Attitude Measurement

Major Topics of the Chapter

Requirements for valid and reliable attitude measurement

Needed concepts in attitude research: latitudes of acceptance, rejection, and noncommitment

Method of ordered alternatives

Extremity of position, structure of attitude, and involvement

The "undecided" and moderates are not homogeneous in outlook

Degree of ego-involvement measured by relative sizes of latitudes of acceptance, rejection, and noncommitment

Direct techniques for attitude assessment: advantages and limitations

Thurstone scales

Likert technique
Bogardus social distance scale
Cumulative scale (Guttman)
Semantic differential (Osgood)
Public opinion survey methods
Cross-national research: self-anchored
   scales (Cantril)
Overview of attitudes

ATTITUDE MEASUREMENT

This chapter continues the previous chapter's discussion of kinds of research procedures and the kind of concepts required by the properties of attitudes. The concepts of latitude of acceptance, latitude of rejection, and latitude of noncommitment are based on the findings (summarized in the last chapter) on the person's own categories in assessing relevant objects. They will be used in future chapters on self, reference groups, and attitude change.

The needed concepts for valid attitude measurement lead us to the problem of the importance of an attitude for the person. The variations in latitudes of acceptance, rejection, and noncommitment with varying degrees of ego-involvement are basic to the discussions of ego-involvement and attitude change here and in Chapter 21.

The remainder of this chapter summarizes the major direct techniques for attitude assessment. The circumstances in which each may be preferable are indicated, as well as the limitations of each. Despite the critical view taken in this chapter concerning the validity of direct techniques, it should be strongly emphasized that the procedures described are to be preferred to the casual improvisation of questionnaires or check lists (Shaw and Wright, 1967). Direct techniques are dependable when the investigator can establish that the social setting and the research situation itself are conducive to the manifestation of the attitude under study, not to its deflection or concealment.

Requirements for Valid and Reliable Attitude Assessment

Every beginning student in psychology or sociology is taught that the desirable characteristics of measurement techniques are (1) reliability (from one situation to another or one point of time to another) and (2) validity. What are the requirements in attitude research for measures that will be reliable and valid? The following are minimum requirements:

1. Ways and means to ensure that the individual responds in terms of his <u>attitude</u> toward the object, rather than to factors peculiar to the research situation (including what he thinks the investigator expects of him) that lead to "socially desirable" responses. This concern with validity led us to focus attention on indirect methods for attitude assessment.

2. Indicators of the range of positions toward the object that the individual categorizes as acceptable or objectionable in some degree. For purposes of predicting the individual's behavior, it is not sufficient to know simply the rank of his most acceptable position relative to others or the rank of his average response relative to others. As he encounters stimulus situations that support or challenge his attitude in varying degrees, it is crucial that we have an estimate of the ranges of his tolerance and his rejections if we are to predict his behavior. The individual's attitude is a set of categories, not a point affair.

3. Indicators of how committed or personally involved the individual is relative to

the attitude objects. If valid predictions are to be made, we must have some estimate of the salience of the attitude for the person. In the flow of natural social situations, an individual is likely to overlook trivial matters and attend to matters of some personal importance. The issue of the person's relative involvement in an attitude object is related both to valid prediction and reliable measurement.

These requirements for valid and reliable attitude measurement point to concepts needed in attitude research.

NEEDED CONCEPTS IN ATTITUDE RESEARCH

Conventional techniques for attitude measurement aimed at securing a single score, average response, or number to express the individual's attitude. The single numerical expression or rank of the person's attitude is, of course, a great convenience for statistical manipulation. However, as Sherif (1960) pointed out, the person's attitude is indicated most inadequately by a single score if we want to predict his reactions in relevant situations. Individuals who accept the same position on an issue do differ in the range of their tolerance, and they do differ in what they reject. Accordingly, the following concepts were developed to specify the structure of an attitude. These concepts follow directly from the definition (p. 336) and the findings on the Own Categories Procedure.

1. *Latitude of acceptance:* If a person voluntarily states his view on a topic, he usually gives the position most acceptable to him. The latitude of acceptance is simply this most-acceptable position plus other positions the individual also finds acceptable.

2. *Latitude of rejection:* The position most objectionable to the individual, the thing he most detests in a particular domain, plus other positions also objectionable to him define the latitude of rejection.

3. *Latitude of noncommitment:* While accepting some and rejecting others, the individual may prefer to remain noncommittal in regard to certain positions. Ordinarily, in public opinion surveys, there are a sizable

number of "don't know," "neutral," "undecided," "no opinion," or "no comment" responses. Most attitude tests, on the other hand, instruct the individual to respond to every item presented to him. If the individual is not forced to respond, but is required only to indicate his most acceptable and most objectionable positions, he often refrains from responding to all items. The positions that he does not evaluate as either acceptable or objectionable under these circumstances constitute his latitude of noncommitment.

These concepts are based on the findings of research about the individual's own categorization of attitude-relevant material. What we have referred to as category width may now be expressed in terms of latitudes (ranges) encompassing all of the individual's acceptable, objectionable, and non-committed categories. The latitudes are short-cut expressions for the evaluative differentiation among the individual's own categories.

Let us consider how these concepts help in the study of attitudes through reviewing further research that has utilized these concepts.

Systematic Variations According to Extremity of Position

The size (magnitude) of the latitudes of acceptance, rejection, and noncommitment vary systematically according to the position the person upholds. This generalization has been established in studies of the 1956 and 1960 United States Presidential elections (Sherif and Hovland, 1961; Sherif, Sherif, and Nebergall, 1965); the prohibition issue (Hovland, Harvey, and Sherif, 1957); a farm policy issue (Whittaker, 1965); labor-management issues (Elbing, 1962); the Arab Unity issue (Diab, 1967); and a senatorial campaign (Beck and Nebergall, 1967).

The findings will be illustrated by a study of the 1960 Presidential elections in which data were obtained from more than 1500 persons in two sessions about a week apart and just prior to the election (Sherif, Sherif, and Nebergall, 1965). The procedure used in obtaining the data is called the *method of ordered alternatives*. The individual is asked to indicate his acceptances and rejections. However, the task is partially indirect because the instructions do not reveal to him that the investigator is interested in the relative sizes of his latitudes of acceptance, rejection, and noncommitment.

Statements are formulated through a content analysis of positions actually upheld by different groups on the issue. A convenient and limited number (9 or 11) are chosen that represent the entire range of the psychosocial scale and can be ordered (ranked) reliably from one extreme to the other. No assumptions are made about the equality of intervals between the available alternatives. The subject is asked first to indicate the one statement that is most acceptable to him (his own position), then he is asked to check any other statements that may be acceptable. Third, he is asked to select the one statement most objectionable to him, and, finally, any other statements that may be objectionable. Note that he is not forced to respond successively to every statement. The positions that are neither accepted nor rejected constitute the latitude of noncommitment, a measure that is closely related to the person's degree of involvement in the issue.

The following were the statements presented to the subjects in the 1960 presidential election study:

A.   The election of the Republican presidential and vice-presidential candidates in November is absolutely essential from all angles in the country's interests.

B.   On the whole the interests of the country will be served best by the election of the Republican candidates for president and vice-president in the coming election.

C.   It seems that the country's interests would be better served if the presidential and vice-presidential candidates of the Republican party are elected this November.

D.   Although it is hard to decide, it is probable that the country's interests may be better served if the Republican presidential and vice-presidential candidates are elected in November.

E.   From the point of view of the country's interests, it is hard to decide whether it is preferable to vote for presidential and vice-presidential candidates of the Republican party or the Democratic party in November.

F.   Although it is hard to decide, it is probable that the country's interests may be better served if the Democratic presidential and vice-presidential candidates are elected in November.

G.   It seems that the country's interests would be better served if the presidential and vice-presidential candidates of the Democratic party are elected this November.

H.   On the whole the interests of the country will be served best if the presidential and vice-presidential candidates of the Democratic party are elected this November.

I.   The election of the Democratic presidential and vice-presidential candidates in November is absolutely essential from all angles in the country's interests.

Fig. 16.1 summarizes the relative sizes (number of positions) included in the latitudes of acceptance, rejection, and noncommitment by persons choosing each of these alternatives on the 1960 presidential election as most acceptable. The findings are entirely comparable to those obtained in the 1956 election (Sherif and Hovland, 1961). The figure shows the average (mean) number of positions included in each of the three latitudes by persons endorsing a given position (represented on the abscissa) as most acceptable to them. The person's own position (endorsed as most acceptable) is shown on the baseline from A (most extreme Republican) to I (most extreme Democratic). The ordinate represents the mean number of statements that were accepted (solid dots), rejected (x), and the mean frequency of noncommitment (white circles). Above any position, the means add to nine. The relative sizes of the latitudes of acceptance, rejection, and noncommitment refer to how the subject divided his responses to these nine statements.

The findings in Fig. 16.1, which are confirmed by other research cited above, support the following generalizations about the structure of attitudes according to extremity of position:

1. The size of the latitude of rejection increases with the extremity of the person's own position, such that on bipolar issues the function is curvilinear.

2. The size of the latitude of noncommitment is also inversely related to extremity of position and approaches zero for persons with the most extreme positions.

3. The latitude of rejection is disproportionately greater relative to the size of the latitude of acceptance, and the latitude of noncommitment is smaller as the person's own position becomes extreme.

Note that in the figure, the size of the latitude of acceptance is almost the same across all of the own positions. Other research has shown that the latitude of acceptance does vary for strongly committed individuals and less-involved persons (e.g., Whittaker, 1965; La Fave and Sherif, 1968; Reich and Sherif, 1963; Bieri *et al,* 1966; Atkins *et al.,* 1967). However, on the average, the size of the latitude of acceptance does not vary systematically merely according to extremity of position.

Uniformities and Individual Differences in Latitudes for Persons Adopting the Same Own Position. Figure 16.2 presents nine graphs (A–I) constructed separately for persons upholding each of the nine positions on the 1960 election issue. Each graph is based on data by subjects choosing a different statement as most acceptable to them. Thus each graph elaborates the means shown at a given position on the baseline of Fig. 16.1. The graphs show the percentage of the subjects with differing own positions who accepted, rejected, or remained noncommittal to the other eight positions on the issue.

Several generalizations are possible on the basis of these findings:

1. If one compares the distributions by persons adopting a pro-Republican position (A or B) with those adopting the comparable position on the Democratic side (I or H), the Republican and Democratic graphs form almost a mirror image. The shapes of the curves are the same for Republicans and Democrats, but reversed.

2. There is individual variation in latitudes of acceptance, rejection, and noncommitment for subjects upholding each position. In these particular data, analysis of variance showed that variabilities were similar for subjects upholding all positions except E, the middle position, for which individual differences were significantly greater (*see below*).

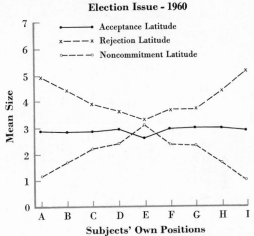

Election Issue - 1960

•——• Acceptance Latitude
×----× Rejection Latitude
○----○ Noncommitment Latitude

Mean Size / Subjects' Own Positions (A B C D E F G H I)

Fig. 16.1. Average size of latitudes of acceptance, rejection, and noncommitment (*ordinate*) for persons upholding different positions as most acceptable (baseline) from A (most extreme Republican) to I (most extreme Democratic). Means of statements accepted, rejected, or not evaluated ("noncommitment") out of nine statements, when instructions required only selection of one statement as most acceptable and one statement as most objectionable.

Extremity of Position and Relative Degree of Ego-Involvement. Earlier research on attitudes showed that, in general, self-ratings on how intensely an attitude was held increased as the extremity of the position increased (Cantril, 1946). As "intensity" may be interpreted as personal importance or ego-involvement, the generalization that persons upholding extreme positions are more committed than those upholding moderate positions is well established in the literature. From the findings on latitudes of acceptance, rejection, and noncommitment, we may therefore infer that the sizes of the person's latitudes of rejection and noncommitment relative to his latitude of acceptance are indicative of the degree of his involvement in the issue at hand.

The size of the latitude of rejection was used in the study of the 1960 election issue

Fig. 16.2 A–I. (*on the following five pages*) Frequency distributions (percent of subjects) for acceptance, rejection, and noncommitment of 9 statements on the outcome of 1960 presidential elections from A (most extreme Republican) to I (most extreme Democratic) on baseline. Each graph represents the distribution of responses for subjects who accepted the same position as "most acceptable" to them. Note that the distributions for subjects finding A most acceptable and those finding I most acceptable form almost a mirror image, as do those for subjects at B and H, C and G, D and F. Persons who found E as most acceptable were undecided.

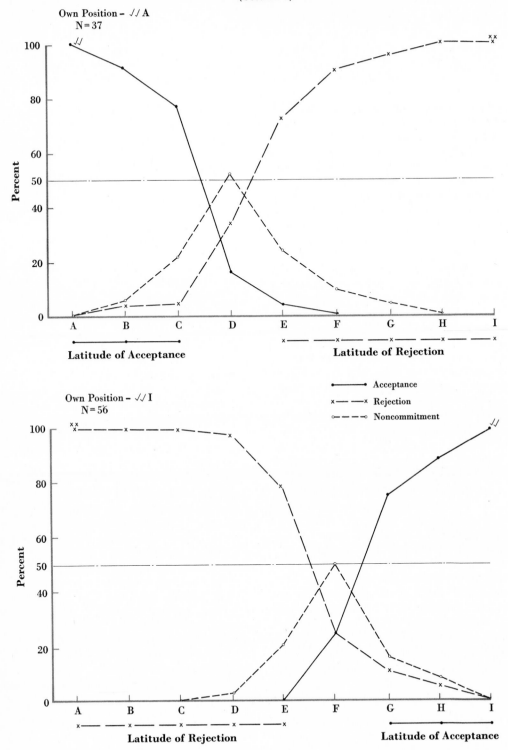

Election Issue - 1960
(Session 1)

Election Issue - 1960
(Session 1)

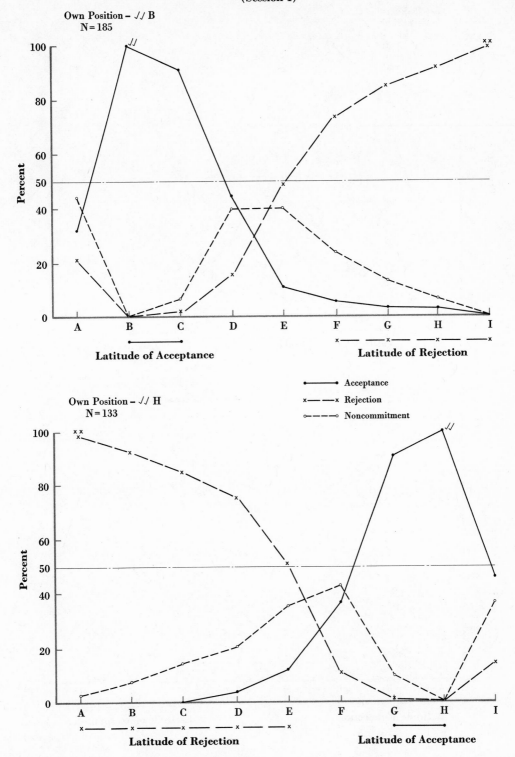

Own Position – ✓✓ B
N = 185

Own Position – ✓✓ H
N = 133

● ——— ● Acceptance
× — — × Rejection
○ ─ ─ ─ ○ Noncommitment

Latitude of Acceptance

Latitude of Rejection

Latitude of Rejection

Latitude of Acceptance

Percent

361

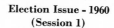

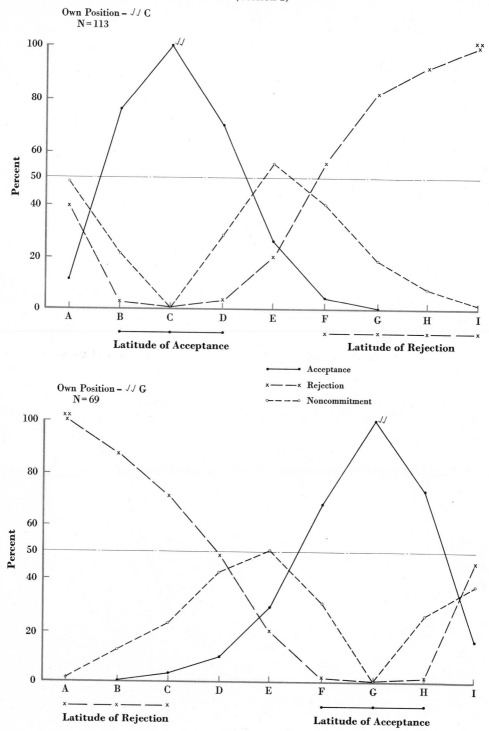

Election Issue - 1960
(Session 1)

Own Position – ⟋⟋ C
N = 113

Latitude of Acceptance   Latitude of Rejection

•——• Acceptance
×——× Rejection
∘———∘ Noncommitment

Own Position – ⟋⟋ G
N = 69

Latitude of Rejection   Latitude of Acceptance

Election Issue - 1960
(Session 1)

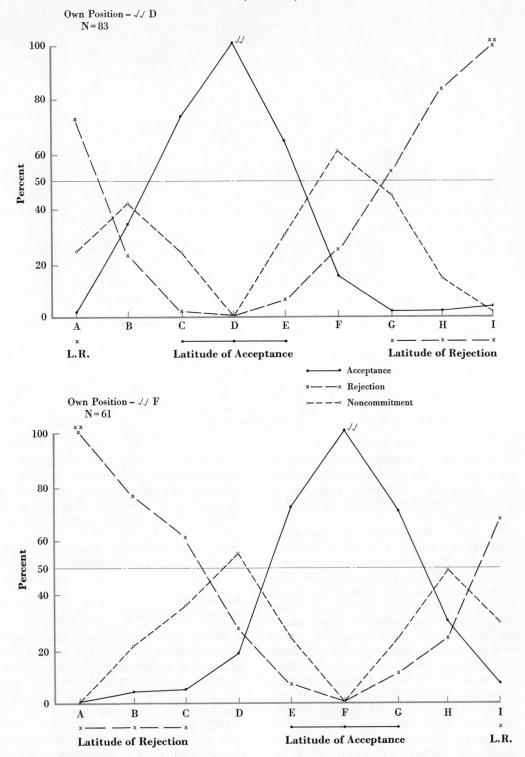

363

Election Issue - 1960
(Session 1)

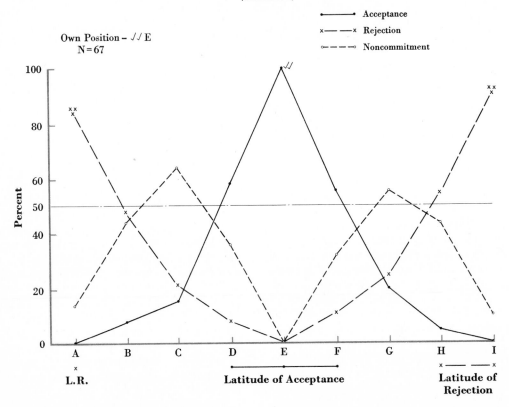

as an indicator of degree of involvement in the outcome of the election to make predictions about the individual's judgment of communications on the election, as we shall see in Chapter 17.

The size of the latitude of noncommitment has also proved useful as an indicator of ego-involvement. In one study, students were interviewed to find what issues concerned them, then they ranked the issues according to personal importance. Their latitudes of noncommitment were much smaller on the most important issue (grades) than the less important (political) issues (Sherif, Sherif, and Nebergall, 1965). In a thesis written at the Pensylvania State University, Tittler (1967) showed that the latitude of noncommitment was significantly smaller for topics ranked as personally important by students than for uninvolving issues and, further, that experimental attempts to change the attitudes in question were significantly more successful for those issues on which the latitude of noncommitment was large.

Thus the relative sizes of the latitudes of noncommitment and rejection serve as an indicator of degree of ego-involvement regardless of the person's most acceptable position. Those taking extreme positions are not necessarily highly involved and those with moderate positions may be highly involved, as this indicator reveals.

**Involvement
and the "Undecided"**

In the 1960 election issue, the persons choosing E (middle position) as their most acceptable statement turned out, upon inspection, to be quite *heterogeneous* as to the sizes of their latitudes of acceptance, rejection, and noncommitment (see Fig. 16.2E). Seventeen percent of them chose only the E position as acceptable and rejected almost all of the other positions. About one-third were "leaners," adopting E as most acceptable, but accepting one other position, either toward the Republican or Democratic side. Altogether, 40 percent

Table 16.1. Latitudes of Acceptance, Rejection, and Noncommitment for Politically Active and Inactive "Neutrals" Compared with All "Neutrals" in 1960 (Southwest)

Mean Size	Politically Active, 1966	Politically Inert, 1966	All Neutrals (Southwest), 1960
Latitude of:			
Acceptance	1.7	2.4	2.5
Rejection	6.4	2.6[a]	3.0
Noncommitment	.9	4.0	3.5
N	91	59	48

[a] $p < .001.$

of these E subjects rejected four or more positions—a latitude of rejection more typical at the extreme positions.

In a study of attitudes on Arab Unity in Lebanon, Diab (1967) reported that many of his noncommited E subjects were strongly against Arab Unity, rejecting almost all pro-Unity statements and showing patterns of reading (newspapers and periodicals) that resembled the extreme anti-Arab Unity subjects.

It would appear, then, that regardless of own position, the size of the latitude of rejection indicates the person's degree of ego-involvement. Support for this hypothesis was found in the study by Beck and Nebergall (1967) of the 1966 election for United States Senator in Texas. The Republican incumbent was known for his conservative views, but the Democratic nominee proved to be even more conservative. The liberal wing of the Democratic party bolted the nominating convention and refused to support the Democratic candidate. Beck and Nebergall administered statements similar to those on p. 358 (substituting the senator's office and the names of the two candidates) to members of politically active

groups as well as to captive classroom samples who were, by and large, politically inactive. In both samples they found large numbers who chose the E position as most acceptable (approximately one-third of the Democrats attending political meetings). Calling these two samples the "politically active" and the "politically inert," respectively, the investigators compared the sizes of the latitudes with those obtained in the same region during the 1960 presidential election for persons adopting E as their own position. The results are shown in Table 16.1.

The same Texas samples yielded a number of active Democrats who had resolved their dilemma by opting for mild support of either the Republican or Democratic candidate, that is, upholding moderate positions equivalent to D or F on p. 358. Table 16.2 shows that the latitudes of rejection of these moderate supporters differed significantly from those of the politically inactive students who chose the same position as most acceptable.

The importance of these findings for attitude study is that they demonstrate that the extremity or polarity of attitudes is not iden-

Table 16.2. Latitudes of Rejection for Politically Active and Politically Inert Who Upheld Moderate Positions Supporting a Candidate (1966, Texas)

	Politically Active		Politically Inactive		
	Mean	N	Mean	N	p
Moderate Republican (D)	4.2	53	2.9	49	$< .001$
Moderate Democratic (F)	3.5	21	2.7	42	$< .05$

tical with strength of commitment or ego-involvement. An individual can be highly involved in a moderate or noncommittal stance. The practical importance of this point is related to the problems of how the individual will react to communication and of his susceptibility to attitude change (Chapter 21).

For example, the measure of personal importance (intensity) in one test of attitudes, the Semantic Differential (p. 375), is extremity of the subject's ratings (polarity). Recent study of this technique (Weksel and Hennis, 1965) has also shown that extremity of ratings cannot be equated with the intensity with which a person upholds his attitude.

These findings have such important implications in the study of attitudes that we shall consider some issues they raise as preparation for the chapter on self system and ego-involvements.

Extremity, Ego-Involvement, and Personality

There is a widespread assumption in much of the psychological literature that extreme stands and extreme judgments are signs of pathology. It is possible that the assumption stems from an ethnocentric view of "normality" imposed by cultural norms that make "liberal moderation" socially desirable. In Fig. 16.2B and H, it may be noted that the Democrats and Republicans who chose B and H positions (next to the most extreme positions) did not, on the average, accept the most extreme positions (A and I). Most of these subjects were active members of their respective organizations. They were publicly committed to their respective candidates and active in their cause. However, the most extreme statements (A and I) seemed a little too "far out" or "crackpot" for the majority to accept.

The cultural influence is found by comparing these results to those by Diab (1967) in Lebanon on the issue of Arab Unity. Contrary to the findings on the United States election, he noted that *pro* and *anti*-Arab Unity subjects who chose the next-to-the-extreme position as most acceptable also accepted the most extreme statements on their side. In the Middle East setting, the issue is socially and politically of major importance in the daily lives and activities of the students.

An alternative view to the pathology explanation for persons who give extremely negative or positive ratings is that the individual who is strongly committed on one or on several attitudes will be more likely to give extreme judgments than a person uninvolved in the same issues. Tajfel and Wilkes (1963) reported that when subjects were allowed to mention personal characteristics they regarded as important in sizing up a person, they were likely to give extreme ratings on those they mentioned first. Similarly, a recent review of literature on whether extremity or polarity of judgments is a sign of heightened involvement or a sign of pathology (O'Donovan, 1965, p. 365) concluded that "studies in which the subject has the opportunity to provide his own personally meaningful dimensions" or to select dimensions more significant to him personally support the hypothesis that extremity is associated with personal significance (involvement). On the other hand, if the investigator sets out to show a relationship between pathological tendencies and extremity in ratings (judgment), he is likely to be successful if "rating dimensions are imposed upon the subject."

The variable of personal significance or ego-involvement can be investigated systematically in attitude research (cf. Sherif *et al.*, 1965; Rokeach, 1968). At the same time, research that relates the attitude under study to the individual's other attitudes and to his ideology will increase accurate prediction of behavior in a variety of situations.

For example, Rokeach (1960) has developed items within the context of the United States to assess individual differences in "belief systems" which are conducive to flexibility and an analytic approach to events as opposed to inflexible and non-analytical reactions. The "open-minded" person is better able than the "closed-minded" person to detach the content of a communication from its source and to evaluate each separately (Powell, 1962). Within the United States and within the range of attitudes in a university student population, the Rokeach dogmatism scale is correlated significantly with the size of the latitude of rejection on social issues (Powell, 1966).

The correlations are not large, but it is possible that further research combining measures of relative ego-involvement and of general belief systems may be more conducive to accurate prediction of reactions to relevant persons and communications.

DIRECT TECHNIQUES
FOR ATTITUDE ASSESSMENT

A technique for attitude assessment may be called "direct" if the individual is subjected to a request to indicate his attitude on a topic. Descriptions of direct techniques for attitude assessment may appear to the reader either as a cookbook of tested recipes or as a wastebasket for unimportant trivia. The orientation of this chapter is intended to avoid both appearances.

Direct techniques for attitude assessment have been and probably will continue to be the most widely used. They are useful when there is good reason to believe that the population being studied (1) has attitudes toward the object of interest and (2) freely expresses their attitudes in word and deed to anyone who may inquire. If there are constraints in the society, in one's group, or in the test situation against revealing one's attitude to an investigator, each of the direct techniques for assessment will be misleading. If the investigator does not trouble to determine whether his study sample has attitudes on the issue in question, he may obtain a quantity of irrelevant opinions.

For example, Kornhauser and Sheatsley (1961) report several illustrations of public opinion surveys in which the vast majority simply had no attitudes—even though most of them freely passed judgment on the matter. In one study, 70 percent of a nationwide sample passed judgment on a nonexistent piece of legislation. Kornhauser and Sheatsley reported:

An opinion-poll question asking about who is to blame for a list of specific strikes found that from one-half to four-fifths of the respondents did not know enough about these strikes to express an opinion. In similar questions that did not directly ask whether people had the information, almost all the respondents expressed opinions regardless of their probable lack of information (1961, p. 555).

Such data may reflect the respondents' attitudes toward strikes in general or toward labor-management problems in general; but the problems of data interpretation are formidable without further information. The respondents may simply have tried to present a good face to the interviewers.

Students and aspiring researchers are particularly apt to have spotted a problem for investigation that requires an attitude assessment technique. Therefore, an introduction to available techniques should include the pitfalls and inadequacies as well as the "recipes." The following cautions are intended to aid in evaluation of attitude research and the decisions made in undertaking new investigations.

1. In actual research practice, the development of standardized and tested instruments for attitude assessment constitutes a tiny fraction of attitude research. In surveying the literature for attitudes scales with "at least minimal reliability and validity," Shaw and Wright (1967) emphasize this point and its "unfortunate consequences." They noted: "Far too often the researcher is not sufficiently careful in selecting the tools used to test his hypotheses" (p. ix). They cautioned (1) that research into the same attitudes may not be comparable when performed by investigators using different assessment techniques, and (2) that the quality of the measuring instruments is often poor. Particularly in the flourishing literature on attitude change, one frequently finds that the researcher simply states "a scale was used" to assess this or that attitude and its change. The scale may simply be a series of questions or self-rating scales or a checklist that he improvised as suitable for an attitude that it proved convenient for him to study. Shaw and Wright present a collection of direct attitude assessment techniques on a variety of topics for which standardization of items and reliability measures were available.

2. Shaw and Wright specifically caution that the reliability and validity of the direct attitude tests found in the literature "does not warrant [their] application . . . as measures of individual attitude"; they recommend their application only for research purposes and group comparisons. This caution is particularly sound both because of the hazards of direct tests them-

selves and because most direct tests bear little theoretical relation to the concept of *individual* attitude.

3. Generalizations from research using direct techniques are limited by (1) the technique used and (2) the samples on which they were standardized and to which they are applied. As with any other psychological tests, the use of direct tests is limited to samples comparable to the standardization sample. For example, there is no reason to expect that a test on attitudes toward war, standardized on a student population in the 1930s, is directly applicable to a student population in the 1970s— much less to nonstudent populations in the 1960s. On the other hand, sampling is not the sole problem. The now-sophisticated sampling techniques in survey research secure samples representative of the entire population. The use of adequate sampling techniques does not by itself insure valid findings. The findings of surveys must also be evaluated in terms of the techniques used. Research that employs a sophisticated sampling procedure but crude techniques for securing data can be as misleading as that applying sophisticated techniques standardized on one small sample for assessing the attitudes of a very different sample.

With these cautions, the following methods for constructing direct assessment techniques are presented.

Thurstone Scales

As noted in Chapter 15, Thurstone developed an elaborate model for constructing attitude tests. The fundamentals of the technique for scaling statements were summarized on pp. 338–339. The emphasis in that context was upon the effect of judges' attitudes upon the scale values of items. Such effects were found in Thurstone's method of equal-appearing intervals, in which the subject sorts statements into 11 categories.

Through statistical manipulation of judgments obtained from sortings into 11 categories (a manipulation called "method of successive intervals"), differences between scale values of Negroes and whites can be reduced. The data-gathering procedures, as described by Edwards (1957, p. 123), are

identical to the method of equal-appearing intervals. The statistical manipulation of the data depends upon the assumption that the "cumulative proportion distributions are normal for each statement when they are projected on the unknown psychological continuum" (p. 124). This is a very big assumption. The statistical manipulation involves, in Edwards' words, the "stretching" or pulling of the scale values obtained directly from the judgment distributions.

The method of successive intervals is justified as follows: Imagine that you have a rubber ruler of unknown units, some of which are smaller than others (for example, at each end). You stretch the ruler until the units appear equal, then proceed to measure objects with the now uniform units. Note, however, that in attitude scaling, the original units were derived from judgments by persons who have attitudes toward the objects of judgment. What you are doing by stretching the judgment scale is, in effect, stretching the person's categories so that they conform to your idea of what a scale should be. In fact, psychosocial scales may, as we have seen, include categories with widely differing widths. In actual life, people do not stretch their acceptances and rejections merely to conform to the objects judged.

The assumption involved in the method of successive intervals is that the investigators know the psychological dimension that they deal with and the domain of the function, which is hardly justified because these are the very things that they are attempting to measure through scaling attitude items.

Systematic displacements according to the judge's attitudes can be reduced by forcing the judges to compare each statement with each of the remaining statements (paired comparisons). For example, Kelley, Hovland, Schwartz, and Abelson (1955) chose 20 of the 114 statements on the Negro issue collected by Hinckley to test the hypothesis that the displacements in scale values found with the equal-appearing intervals method were caused by the failure of pro-Negro judges and Negro judges to discriminate among the statements. The scale values for these 20 statements covered the entire range of values. When each was paired in all possible combinations with the others, 190 pairs of statements re-

Hs

sulted. Negro and unselected white students in the same region of the country sampled by Sherif and Hovland compared the pairs, choosing the most favorable statement in each pair.

The findings showed that with the paired-comparisons technique there was high correspondence between the scale values of the statements for Negro and white subjects. This means, of course, that the bunching of items into extreme categories by pro-Negro subjects with the equal-appearing intervals technique was not caused by any lack of ability on the subjects' part to discriminate among the verbal statements. Even when choice between two items was forced, however, the scale values of four items were different for the two samples. (For example, the statement "Negroes must undergo many years of civilization before they may be said to reach the social level of the whites" was judged significantly more favorable to Negroes by white subjects than by Negro subjects.)

Coombs' study (1967) of the scale values derived from paired-comparison judgments on the seriousness of various crimes showed quite clearly that scale values do differ according to attitudes even by the method of paired comparisons. He replicated Thurstone's 1927 scaling study of the judged seriousness of crimes, with the results shown in Fig. 16.3.

Coombs interpreted the results as showing that (1) attitudes toward crime among college students were more homogeneous 40 years ago; (2) attitudes toward various kinds of crimes (offenses against the person, and property and sex offenses) have changed in the United States; and (3) there is "no valid way" to equate two points on the 1927 scale with two points on the 1966 scale (p. 90). In other words, Coombs has shown that attitude *does* affect scale values derived from paired-comparison judgments and that the intervals between values derived from different populations are noncommensurate.

atts

Because adjustments by the method of paired comparisons can make the scale values obtained through the Thurstone technique more comparable for subjects with different attitudes, some authors have treated the problem of whether Thurstone scales are "true interval scales" as a prob-

lem in "method." The case is not an abstract issue of method apart from empirical findings on the nature of psychosocial scales. The analogy suggested by those who consign the problem to matters of method may make the point clear.

By using the method of paired comparisons, it is suggested, the individual is in a position that he has to compare each stick with other sticks in making his judgment. Certainly it is important that by forcing the subject to compare just two statements, he can discriminate between them. However, psychologically, it is equally important that when he is *not forced* by an investigator to make such comparisons, he does not make a distinction between them. This important psychological fact reflects the psychosocial scales prevailing in his group. His own categories subsume various positions without distinction unless circumstances force him to make a choice.

In actual practice, these issues are more important in the psychology of social judgment than in the construction and use of a Thurstone scale. Thurstone's notion that a score of, say, 6.5 on a scale toward religion was equivalent to a score of 6.5 on a scale toward war has long since been abandoned (McNemar, 1946).

What the test constructor actually does in constructing a Thurstone attitude test is to select items with scale values spaced about equally apart and with very low Q values after having performed an item analysis to eliminate statements that do not differentiate between groups with known *pro* and *anti* stands.

For illustrative purposes only, 11 statements chosen from 32 actually used in a study of attitude toward war (Peterson and Thurstone, 1933) are presented below. These statements were used in a study of attitude change. The scale value of each statement is given on the left. In this case, 0.0 is the most anti-war end and 11.0 is the most pro-war end. In actual administration of the test, of course, the scale values do not appear on the form, and the statements are presented in mixed order to avoid a directional set. It will be noted that scale values from statement to statement are rather evenly graduated.

(0.2)   There is no conceivable justification for war.

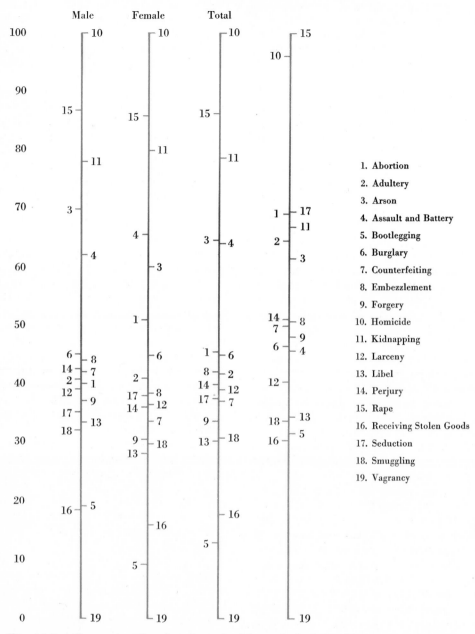

Fig. 16.3. Changes in scale values determined by method of paired comparisons on serious-ness of 19 offenses from 1927 (Thurstone) to 1966 (presented separately for males, females, and total sample of university students). Note the general downward shift in judged serious-ness and the changed values of numerous crimes. (Adapted from C. H. Coombs, Thurstone's measurement of social values revisited forty years later. *J. pers. soc. Psychol.*, **6**, 88. Copyright 1967 by the American Psychological Association, and reproduced by permission.)

(1.4) War is a futile struggle resulting in self destruction.	(4.5) We want no more war if it can be avoided without dishonor.
(2.4) War is an unnecessary waste of human life.	(5.5) It is hard to decide whether wars do more harm than good.
(3.2) The benefits of war are not worth its misery and suffering.	(6.6) There are some arguments in favor of war.

(7.5)   Under some conditions, war is necessary to maintain justice.

(8.5)   War is a satisfactory way to solve international difficulties.

(9.8)   War stimulates men to their noblest efforts.

(10.8) The highest duty of man is to fight for the power and glory of his nation.

Preceding these statements are the instructions, which include "Put a check mark if you agree with the statement." The stand (attitude) of the individual on the issue is taken to be the average of all the scale values for the statements with which he agrees.

The controversy over whether the intervals between Thurstone scale values are equal or not is rather unimportant in the actual use of test results. It would be difficult to find a researcher who would contend that the person who receives a score of, say, 4.0 has an attitude that differs by five equal intervals from a person whose score is 9.0. One reason is that his score could be obtained by agreeing only with the statement with a scale value of 4.0 or by agreeing with the statements with scale values of 3, 4, and 5—which is not at all an improbable event. The primary value of the Thurstone method is that it provides a rational means for selecting items on an attitude test. Scores, especially at the extremes, are useful in ranking individual attitudes relative to a known distribution of scores or to each other.

Generalized Thurstone Scales. Remmers (1934) used the Thurstone method to develop a number of "generalized scales" for assessing attitudes toward specific objects. The judges do not sort statements about a specific class of objects (e.g., Negroes, war, or religion) but about a general class (any group, any social practice, any institution). The following are statements on a scale developed by Grice (1934) and shortened by Remmers (1960) to assess attitudes toward any group that the investigator may choose. These scales have proved useful; however, it may be readily seen that all items may not be equally appropriate for use with all groups or by all samples. The reader can see this by reading the statements several times, each time keeping a different group in mind (e.g., the John Birch Society, Episcopalians, white Americans, Negro Americans, atheists, etc.). In short,

there may be decided context effects, depending upon the group presented for evaluation.

Scale Values

10.2   Can be depended upon as being honest.

9.5   Are far above my own group.

9.2   Some of our best citizens are descendants from this group.

8.9   Deserve much consideration from the rest of the world.

8.5   Command the respect of any group.

8.1   Are quick to apprehend.

7.7   Are a God-fearing group.

6.8   Have an air of dignity about them.

6.0   Are highly emotional.

5.8   Take exceptional pride in themselves.

4.6   Are superstitious.

3.6   Are self-indulgent.

3.1   Do not impress me favorably.

2.5   I am not in sympathy with these people.

2.2   Would likely prove disloyal to our government.

1.6   Belong to a low social level.

1.0   Are mentally defective.

Again, the subject is asked to indicate which statements he agrees with and his score is the median scale value of the items he endorses.

Likert Technique for Measuring Attitudes

As part of a larger investigation on social attitudes undertaken by Gardner Murphy in 1929, Likert (1932) developed a technique for measuring attitudes which has been widely used for studying many issues—including quite broad topics such as "internationalism," "morale," "conservatism," and "progressivism." The following are 4 items of the 18 statements included in the "Negro Scale," in Likert's original study:

No Negro should be deprived of the franchise except for reasons which would also disfranchise a white man.

Strongly Approve	Approve	Undecided	Disapprove	Strongly Disapprove
(5)	(4)	(3)	(2)	(1)

Negro homes should be segregated from those of white people.

Strongly Approve	Approve	Undecided	Disapprove	Strongly Disapprove
(1)	(2)	(3)	(4)	(5)

If the same preparation is required, the Negro teacher should receive the same salary as the white.

Strongly Ap-prove	Ap-prove	Un-decided	Dis-approve	Strongly Dis-approve
(5)	(4)	(3)	(2)	(1)

All Negroes belong in one class and should be treated in about the same way.

Strongly Ap-prove	Ap-prove	Un-decided	Dis-approve	Strongly Dis-approve
(1)	(2)	(3)	(4)	(5)

The subject is asked to choose one alternative (e.g., from "Strongly Approve" to "Strongly Disapprove" above) for each statement. Thus, each item in the test is a rating device designed to reveal both the direction of the individual's stand on the issue and the intensity with which he holds it. The number in parentheses below each alternative is the score value for that choice. On this scale the higher value indicates a *pro* stand and the low value indicates an *anti* stand. These score values are assigned by the investigator.

An overall test score is obtained by finding the sum of the numerical scores for the alternatives an individual checks on the various items. This overall individual score can be interpreted only in relation to the distribution of scores made by other persons. In other words, as is the case with the scores for a good many achievement and educational tests, the scores made by subjects who have actually taken the test are the basis for evaluating an individual's score.

A high score on a Likert-type test is taken as indicative of a stand toward one extreme on an issue and a low score as a stand toward the opposite extreme. For example, suppose that the "Negro Scale" had 10 items such as those above. The highest possible total score would be 50 and would be obtained by a person who chose categories with the score value of 5 for all statements. This would represent the most *pro* stand on the test. The lowest possible score for 10 items would be 10 (*anti* stand). Scores in the middle range can be obtained either by checking the "undecided" category fairly consistently or by checking some statements in the pro and some in the anti

direction for the issue in question. Such scores are more difficult to interpret.

The statements included on such tests are chosen from a large number collected from other tests, current periodicals, and books, or are formulated on the basis of empirical observation of different viewpoints on the issue in question. Items are selected to be clear-cut and unambiguous statements on the issue which represent definite favorable or unfavorable stands. An equal number of pro and con statements is included. Statements for any one scale should pertain to only a single issue, but should not include statements on which all persons in a population will agree or disagree. All items are statements pertaining to desirable or undesirable behavior or courses of action, and are not statements of fact.

Final statements are selected after the preliminary test has been administered to a large number of subjects. The results of this preliminary testing are analyzed to cull out items that do not differentiate between subjects who have high and low total scores on the test and are not highly correlated with total test scores. In practice it is possible to present such tests on several issues at the same time by mixing the items from the various tests and then scoring them separately.

Cumulative Scales
for Attitude Assessment

The property "cumulative" in a scale for attitude assessment is an analogy with physical scales of measurement. For example, a foot ruler marked in inches is cumulative in the sense that any given length, say 5 inches, includes all smaller lengths (1, 2, 3, and 4 inches). The first social scale with this property was developed by Bogardus for the assessment of the social distance which members of a group preferred to maintain between themselves and members of another group.

Although the choice of items on Bogardus' scale are frequently justified as "logical," Bogardus (a sociologist) chose the particular items on the basis of his knowledge of the society in which he worked. There is nothing inherently logical in the fact that admitting persons "to my street as neighbors" is more intimate than "to citizenship in my country." In fact, one can well imagine circumstances in which the former would be less intimate (e.g., on Park Avenue in New York City) than the latter—for example, if the decision to admit as citizens would increase daily contact with the group in question. The items on the Bogardus scale have exhibited the cumulative property because they do represent more or less stable degrees of intimacy in American society during their years of use.

First, Bogardus (1924–1925) found that individuals could rank various national and ethnic groups in terms of the friendliness or antipathy they felt toward them, and that their statements concerning these preferences expressed highly generalized attitudes rather than specific affection or antipathy stemming from concrete experiences with specific individuals. Then he devised a list of statements representing varying degrees of social intimacy or distance and asked subjects to mark those classifications to which they would willingly admit members of a given group. These statements were:

1. To close kinship by marriage.
2. To my club as personal chums.
3. To my street as neighbors.
4. To employment in my occupation.
5. To citizenship in my country.
6. As visitors only to my country.
7. Would exclude from my country.

These categories were listed across the top of the test form. Down one side, the names of 39 national and ethnic groups were listed. The subject's task was to mark the statement(s) he considered appropriate for each group.

The ratings made for a particular group (e.g., Chinese) by the individuals studied can be averaged, then these averages for all groups can be ranked according to their magnitude. The smaller the average rating, the less the social distance maintained and the higher that group is ranked on the social distance scale. Social scientists have used the social distance test to check the rank position of various groups on the social distance scale for years. Results obtained by these means were summarized in Chapter 12.

Or, the individual's ratings for all groups

on his form can be averaged. In this way, a score indicating the general level of social distance that the individual wishes to maintain is derived. For example, Hartley (1946) found that some individuals kept all groups but their own at great social distance, while other individuals generally expressed willingness for more intimate contacts.

Use of the Bogardus test is limited to attitudes toward groups. The development of "scale analysis" that aimed at cumulative scales for other attitude objects was not developed for another two decades after Bogardus' work.

Scale Analysis or Scalogram Method

During World War II a research project of monumental scope was undertaken to assess soldiers' opinions in the United States armed forces (Stouffer et al., 1950). It was necessary to devise techniques to find out a good many things about large numbers of men in short order. Some of the problems pertained to the men's attitudes, such as the enlisted man's views of officers. The research projects concentrated on the use of a small number of items. One of the developments in this large project was conducted by Guttman and his associates (Chapters 1–9, Stouffer et al., 1950; Guttman, 1947).

The Guttman procedures are not procedures for selecting attitude items. In fact, so intuitive was the selection in the original descriptions of scalogram analysis that Edwards and his associates (Edwards, 1957) developed an elaborate procedure combining Thurstone scaling (equal-appearing intervals) and pretests of the item pool by using Likert scoring as a rational basis for selecting items. Scalogram analysis typically results in the elimination of all but a narrow range of items, for reasons that will become clear (cf. Festinger, 1947; McNemar, 1946).

If a set of items is "scalable" according to the Guttman model, the pattern of agreements and disagreements with the items will have the following characteristics:

(1) *Reproducibility:* A scale is reproducible if, from each person's rank relative to others on the test, it is possible to reproduce his responses to each item.

(2) *Random departure from reproducibility:* Errors made in reproducing the responses of each individual must be randomly—not systematically—distributed.

Suppose that we ask subjects to check whether they become nervous or anxious in each of the following situations:

1. Trying on clothing in a store.
2. Trying to introduce a friend whose name you have suddenly forgotten.
3. Speaking before a large group.

If this set of items meets the reproducibility criterion, the distribution of responses for persons making scores of 0, 1, 2, or 3 will be as follows:

Person's Score	Response to Item					
	Yes			No		
	1	2	3	1	2	3
3	x	x	x			
2		x	x	x		
1			x	x	x	
0				x	x	x

In other words, a person with the score (rank) of 3 will respond "yes" to each question; a person with the score of 2 will respond "yes" to items 2 and 3 and "no" to item 1; and so on. In a study by Barth (in Hayes, 1964), the above items were included in a total of seven. When administered to several samples, the coefficient of reproducibility was over .90 (1.00 is perfect).

If the set of items is reproducible, users of this model say that the scale is "unidimensional." A word of caution is needed. All that the term "unidimensional" means is that the responses satisfy the reproducibility criterion. It does not mean that the items or the attitudes involve only one social or psychological dimension (variable). For example, in the statements above, one's attitudes toward shopping are very complex—involving one's tastes compared with the prices, the store, etc. These elements in turn bear little obvious relation to attitudes toward appearing before a large group. Yet, the statements are "unidimensional" as defined by the Guttman model: answers differentiate among persons according to their attitudes toward interpersonal and public situations.

In practice, of course, it is exceedingly difficult to meet the reproducibility criterion perfectly. Consequently the decision whether to use the scale as a cumulative scale becomes a question for decision on a probability basis (cf. Riley, 1963). An unfortunate consequence of the effort to meet the criterion of reproducibility is that most Guttman scales turn out to contain few items, encompassing a narrow range of alternative positions. In some research (e.g., Hayes, 1964) this narrow range of possible scores is increased by adding a Likert-type set of alternatives for intensity (strongly agree, agree-disagree, strongly disagree).

The Guttman method of cumulative scaling has been a principle technique used by sociologists for a good many years (e.g., Riley, 1963). It has the advantage of an orderly procedure for ranking individuals in a study population. However, there is no guarantee that the scoring procedures developed on one study sample will be applicable to another sample (cf. Selltiz *et al.,* 1961, pp. 376–377) or that the scoring of items is independent of the context of other items (Hayes, 1964). Hayes found that the context of judgment does affect the rank of items in the Guttman technique. These context effects not only produce differences in the reproducibility of the responses but also affect the score that particular individuals obtain on the test.

By far the most serious limitation of Guttman scaling, however, is that psychosocial scales are not always cumulative (as physical scales are). Sherif and Hovland (1961) called attention to this fact in their study of attitudes toward the 1956 presidential election. Note in Fig. 16.2, p. 360, that Republicans adopting the most extreme Republican position (A) or Democrats adopting the most extreme Democratic position (I) do *not,* on the average, accept statements expressing mild support for their own side (statements D and F, respectively). Similarly, the ardent supporter of desegregation will *not* accept a statement that "Desegregation should proceed at a reasonable pace." This apparently pro-desegregation statement smacks of tokenism in his mind and he rejects it. A "moderate" proponent of desegregation, on the other hand, finds the statement most acceptable.

By eliminating such portions of the psychosocial scale that do not "scale" according to the model, the Guttman technique is not equipped to deal with some of the important phenomena of attitudes: For example, what is "moderation" at a given time? Why do extreme and moderate groups on the same side of a controversial issue clash so frequently? The cumulative scale model and its refinement by subsequent investigators is at its best when used for the study of attitudes toward social dimensions with cumulative properties—for example, social distance or role and status expectations in large organizations.

Semantic Differential

Another widely used technique in attitude research in recent years is the "Semantic Differential" developed by Osgood, Suci, and Tannebaum (1957). The instrument is a series of rating scales, typically with seven points from which the subject chooses one for each scale. Osgood's interest in the technique is related to his studies on "meaning"; however, the method has been frequently applied to the study of attitudes.

The individual is presented with a concept or a set of concepts (e.g., "Negro," "God," "Democrat"). In turn, he rates each concept on a series of seven-point scales whose extremes are labeled with adjectives, for example:

Good : : : : : : Bad

In attitude research, these adjectives are typically evaluative (fair-unfair, clean-dirty, good-bad, valuable-worthless, etc.). Through factor analysis, the investigators found that other bipolar adjectives yielded ratings that were not perfectly correlated with ratings on such evaluative pairs. For example, some bipolar adjectives pertain to the "power" or "potency" of the object (strong-weak, large-small, heavy-light), while another set seems to pertain to the active-passive polarity (active-passive, hot-cold, fast-slow).

Although the latter polarities are seldom used in the study of social attitudes, Diab (1967) has emphasized the utility of the "power" dimension in the study of social attitudes, particularly as they pertain to

groups, institutions, or social movements. For example, he found decided differences between the reactions of Lebanese students with pro- and anti-Arab Unity attitudes that could be traced to the view of the pro-Unity subjects that the Unity movement was powerful and active, whereas the anti-Arab Unity subjects perceived it as weaker.

When the individual has rated a concept on a set of bipolar scales, his attitude is inferred from (1) the direction (good-bad) and the (2) polarity of his ratings (from -3 to $+3$). It is assumed that the more extreme his rating, the more intensely he holds an attitude in the indicated direction. Thus, he can obtain a score on any one scale from -3 through 0 to $+3$. His total score is the total or average of his ratings. The score is a positive number, a negative number or zero.

The Semantic Differential is easy to assemble and to score. Its disadvantages lie in certain assumptions that make interpretation difficult. Available evidence indicates that the bipolar adjectives suitable for one attitude object (concept) may not mean the same thing when applied to another object. (For example, clean-dirty may apply to a given group but have an entirely different meaning when applied to gardening.) The assumption that intensity of attitude is equivalent to extremity of rating has recently been challenged (Weksel and Hennis, 1965). Further, the interpretation of zero ratings is not at all clear. The arbitrary assignment of numbers from -3 to $+3$ does not guarantee that the scale is composed of equal units that can be added or averaged. (To illustrate, a person whose score is $-.5$ may have an attitude more similar to a person with a score of $+.5$, which is one unit away, than to a person with a score of -1.5, which is also one unit away.)

If the investigator wants to investigate the beliefs and specific stereotypes that a person classifies as acceptable or objectionable, it is difficult to secure the needed data from the Semantic Differential. If, on the other hand, he is interested mainly in the overall evaluative aspect, the technique is very useful. As with any rating scale, the Semantic Differential has the advantage of yielding finer gradations than techniques that require simply "agree" or "disagree" answers.

"Public Opinion"
Surveys

The survey of "public opinion" is so thoroughly a part of the modern scene in the United States that comparatively few analysts question reports published in the newspaper. Some outsiders, including some psychologists, equate survey research with "field research" and survey findings with the sociological method. The comments on survey research here are confined to those surveys that study attitudes. In thus limiting the discussion, there is no intent to suggest that attitude surveys are the best use for survey methods.

The political scientist V. O. Key (1960) made a good case for the expansion of research designs in the most popular of survey topics, namely, political attitudes pertinent to voting. Key observed that cross-sectional surveys of attitudes at given points in time would gain political relevance if the research design related them more closely to the ongoing political process (including the governmental machinery and institutions, the choice of candidates by the political parties, etc.). If anything, the literature is now flooded with survey data on this or that attitude as expressed to interviewers, with little attempt to relate the findings to either sociological or social-psychological problems of importance.

The survey technique is, in the first instance, a set of methods for obtaining representative sampling of a population. Second, it depends upon the use of interviews and/or questionnaire forms that directly confront the individual with the request to express his attitude. Interpretation of survey results, therefore, is beset with the same difficulties that plague any direct techniques for attitude assessment. The vast majority of techniques used in public opinion surveys were borrowed from those developed in small-scale research.

There is innovative research into attitude problems within the context of public opinion and market research (e.g., Krugman, 1966). However, an introduction such as this necessarily concentrates on characterizing the bulk of the activity.

The greatest reliance can be placed on surveys conducted just prior to national elections—for the simple reason that any organization attempting such surveys, whether commercial or noncommercial, marshalls all of its machinery toward the best effort possible. Public elections are still the most clear-cut test for the validity of survey research. In 1948 most of the survey organizations made erroneous predictions that Truman would be defeated for President. Since then, the major organizations have taken the most strenuous steps to avoid another such humiliation. At their best, surveys of attitudes toward the candidates, parties, and the issues can reveal more than any other method about the demographic, socioeconomic, political, and ideological factors associated with the choice of candidates. The outstanding example is *The American Voter* (Campbell, Converse, Miller, and Stokes, 1960), an analysis of data obtained on the 1952 and 1956 presidential elections. The chief limitation of this research was no fault of the researchers—namely, that the same presidential candidates ran in both elections and that one of them (General Eisenhower) was a popular war hero.

When we concentrate on the pitfalls of survey data, therefore, we refer especially to the flood of survey results that *cannot* be checked against actual events and that do not have the benefit of mobilized resources and efforts. We are in complete agreement with Doob's early caution (1948) that the validity of such surveys should be viewed with "extreme skepticism" (p. 150).

The following represent cautions for the student or researcher who hopes to use published survey data:

1. *Interviewer bias:* Assuming an adequate representative sample, there is a built-in source of bias in survey research in the hiring and utilization of interviewers. It has long been known that substantially different results are obtained when Negro interviewers and white interviewers question Negro respondents, and presumably the reverse is also the case. Interviewers identifiable as Jewish obtain different results than non-Jewish interviewers when questioning non-Jews. Middle-class and working-class interviewers produce different results for working-class samples (Cantril, 1944; Doob, 1948, Chapter 2; Parten, 1950, Chapter 6). These sources of bias will not "go away" and will continue until survey re-

search systematically considers the question of who is appropriate to interview whom, as well as the context of the interview.

2. *Question bias:* In view of the difficulties of inferring an attitude from more sophisticated direct techniques, the use of the single question in survey research is simply not justified (cf. McNemar, 1946). Buchanan and Cantril (1953) illustrated this convincingly by comparing the responses in several Western European countries and the United States in 1948 to the following two questions: "Do you believe that it will be possible for all countries to live together at peace with each other?" and "Do you think there will be another big war within the next ten years?" In the United States, 49 percent of a nationwide sample answered "yes," that peace was possible. To the second, 57 percent replied "yes," that they thought there would be another war within ten years. Clearly, one's optimism or pessimism about the possibility of war depends to some extent on how the question was asked.

One remedy to the single question is the use of items that permit the individual to select alternative responses. For example, a majority of responses approving a particular policy (such as war in Vietnam) quickly evaporates when alternatives are provided for other policies. The classic example of the importance of choosing alternatives pertains to social-class identification. Polls in the United States asked for class identification with the alternatives upper, middle, or lower. The result was that the vast majority of respondents identified themselves as middle class. The following distributions of responses were obtained by adding to these three the alternative "working class" (Form A) and to the other (Form B) "laboring class" (Cantril and Buchanan, 1953, p. 115):

	Form A (%)	Form B (%)
Upper	3	4
Middle	38	53
Lower	3	4
Working (A)	52	—
Laboring (B)	—	35
Don't Know	4	4

The type of question most conducive to free expression of an attitude is the open-ended question or series of questions. (For example: "I'd like to ask you what you think are the good and bad points about the two parties. Is there anything in particular that you like about the Democratic party? Is there anything in particular that you don't like about the Democratic party? Is there anything in particular that you like about the Republican party? Is there anything in particular that you don't like about the Republican party?" Campbell *et al.*, 1960, p. 224).

Answers to such questions require coding. For example, the following is a response reported by Campbell *et al.* (1960) to the foregoing questions. The response was to be coded in terms of its "level of conceptualization" of the election issues.

(*Like about Democrats?*) Well, I like their liberalness over the years. They certainly have passed beneficial legislation like social security and unemployment insurance, which the average man needs today.

(*Dislike about the Democrats?*) The Communists linked to Roosevelt and Truman. Corruption. Tax scandals. I don't like any of those things.

(*Like about Republicans?*) I also like the conservative element in the Republican party. (*Anything else?*) No.

(*Dislike about Republicans?*) No, not at present.

The responses were coded into four broad categories representing different levels of conceptualization: A, ideology; B, group benefits; C, nature of the times; and D, no issue content. In which broad category would you place the above response?[1] If you feel some hesitancy in coding these answers, you will be sharing an experience of practically any researcher who has had to code such responses. One may succeed in getting reliable coding by carefully instructing two or more raters; but one can never be sure that other raters with strong convictions of their own would not have come out with different *codes* and different *distributions of responses* into them.

[1] The response was presented as an example of a subdivision of A (ideology), which the investigators called "near-ideology." There is no intent to criticize the coding in this particular research, but merely to illustrate the complexity of the decisions that coding involves.

Cross-National Comparisons
in Survey Research

Cross-national comparisons bring to light a problem that is present but is sometimes obscured in surveys conducted within a single country: The items, questions, or alternatives to be checked do not always have the same meaning to respondents in different societies or in different social classes or groups within the same society. Nor can it be assumed that the standards used by members of different cultures in making comparisons or passing judgments (opinions) are comparable.

For example, suppose that you want to compare the optimism or pessimism of people in different countries about themselves and their countries. Such attitudes are always relative to how one sees the existing state of things and the actual conditions that exist. A cross-national survey directed by Cantril (1965) tackled this problem by the use of a "self-anchored scale."

Cantril (1963) used self-anchored scales in the context of an interview on personal worries, fears, hopes, and aspirations; the international situation; and concerns over the national situation in 13 countries. Figure 16.4 illustrates the "self-anchoring scale" used in most of these countries. (Among certain illiterate groups, a sketch showing climbers moving up a hill was used.) The subject was asked to let the top of the ladder represent the "best possible life." Then he was asked where he personally stood now, where he stood five years ago, and where he expected to stand five years from now. The same technique was used to obtain self-anchored judgments of the person's country in the past, present, and future. Figures 16.5A–H are illustrative of the findings, most of them obtained around 1960. Proper evaluation of the results requires the kind of specification given by the investigators about the samples studied (e.g., socioeconomic level, education, etc.) and the background of sociopolitical events. The absolute values on the ladders are not, of course, comparable from country to country. What can be compared is the *relative* discrepancies between views of past, present, and future. For example, compare the ratings in Cuba and the Dominican Republic with those in the United States and in India.

Cantril also compared the degree of correspondence (correlation) between ratings for personal and national prospects, with the interesting finding that the two correspond more closely in developing nations with strong national movements than in a developed country like the United States. Within the United States, Cantril found differences between white and Negro samples that reflected the Negro respondents' more negative views of their past and present and somewhat less optimistic view for the future. The self-anchoring scale technique is particularly appropriate for investigating attitudes (toward self, group, and institutions—as well as nations) that involve expectations and aspirations for the future. For example, it could be adapted to project expectations over periods of time (one year . . . ten years). It is one of the few innovations in method for attitude assessment that has been successfully used within the context of survey research in recent years.

OVERVIEW ON ATTITUDES

Attitudes are inferred from characteristic, consistent, and selective modes of behavior. In Chapter 15, social attitude was distinguished from other internal factors conducive to such modes of behavior in terms of six definite criteria. As the behavior from which attitudes are inferred invariably implies a comparison (judgment) process, attitude was defined operationally in terms of the individual's own categories for both classifying and evaluating objects in the relevant stimulus domain.

Because much research on attitude measurement has proceeded without due consideration of the kind of scales and the kind of research procedures that are required by the actualities of attitudes, the first chapter on attitudes focused on those measurement approaches that observe some or all of the minimum essentials for valid as well as reliable measurement. These minimum essentials were as follows:

1. Assessment without arousing concerns in the research situation that lead to "so-

cially desirable" responses. (This consideration led us to focus on indirect assessment techniques in Chapter 15.)

2. Indicators of the structure of the person's attitude beyond its overall rank relative to the attitudes of other individuals as "for" or "against" an object. (This consideration led to the concepts of latitudes of acceptance, rejection, and noncommitment, as well as to research related to these concepts.)

3. Indicators of the relative importance (degree of ego-involvement) of the attitude for the person. (This consideration led to the introduction of operational indicators for degree of involvement, the behavioral consequences of which will be discussed in later chapters.)

It remains for future chapters to show that assessment techniques meeting these minimum requisites result in greater predictability from attitude measures to the person's behavior in relevant situations. Research pertinent to this question is presented in Chapter 17 on the self and in Chapter 21 on attitude change.

Some points mentioned in these present two chapters deserve further emphasis. If psychosocial scales are the proper standards for assessing attitudes, then attitude research will have to be integrated much more with research on the properties of groups and institutions, especially their normative property. If behavior is a product of interacting factors (internal and external), it follows that attitude measurement made solely by one method or in one situation will be improved by the use of multiple indicators in a variety of situations. Finally, if the social situation for research affects behavior, it follows that great attention should be focused upon the appropriate techniques and situations for studying various attitudes. The major conventional techniques now in use confront the individual directly with the task of expressing his attitude, usually verbally. The validity hinges, therefore, on determining that neither the social context nor the research situation deflects the individual from open expression of his true attitude and toward "socially desirable" or evasive responses. Major direct methods of attitude assessment were described and discussed in the latter part of this chapter.

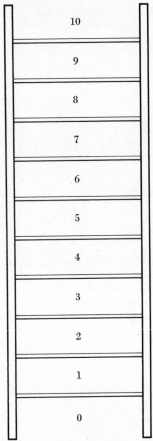

Fig. 16.4. Stimulus for self-anchored scales. Subject is asked to consider top of the ladder as best possible life for him and the bottom the worst possible. Then he locates his position, at present, where he was 5 years ago and where he will be 5 years from now. (After H. Cantril, A Study of Aspirations. Copyright © 1963 by Scientific American, Inc. All rights reserved.)

The pattern of an attitude is not properly represented as a single point, average, or score. An attitude is more adequately represented as a range with a modal point within it (latitude of acceptance), the measurement of which is clarified by assessing it in conjunction with its associated latitudes of rejection and noncommitment. In fact, research has shown that these associated measures (latitudes of rejection and noncommitment) are more discriminating than taking the latitude of acceptance as a single measure. The use of the three latitudes in relation to one another provides a more adequate measure of the person's attitude or commitment. They enable the investigator to make more precise predic-

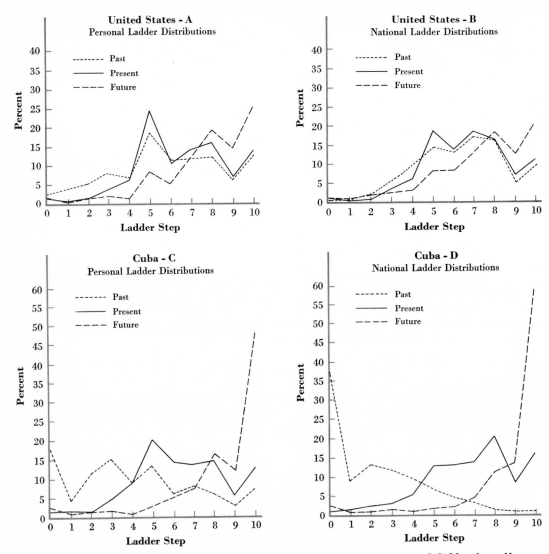

Fig. 16.5. Comparison of frequency distribution of locations on personal ladder for self and for one's country by samples from four different countries. (Adapted from H. Cantril, *The Pattern of Human Concerns*, New Brunswick, New Jersey: Rutgers University Press. Figure IV 1 & 2, p. 40; Fig. VII, 1 & 2, p. 128–129; Figure V, 5 and 6, p. 88; and Figure VII, 3 and 4, pp. 135–136.)

A-B. As a whole, ratings by United States sample reveal more optimism for future personally (**A**) than for one's country (**B**). **C-D** In contrast to United States sample, Cuban

tions about the person's degree of susceptibility to change when he is exposed to communication or other social appeals for change. At the same time, the analysis of the person's latitudes of acceptance, rejection and noncommitment provides an effective tool for evaluating the significance of the "undecided" response, with unmistakable pointers on the direction of the person's leanings on one or the other side of the fence, that is the direction of his susceptibility to change. The topic of attitude change is discussed in Chapter 21, where it is placed in its proper context, namely the general problem of social change of which attitude change is an integral part.

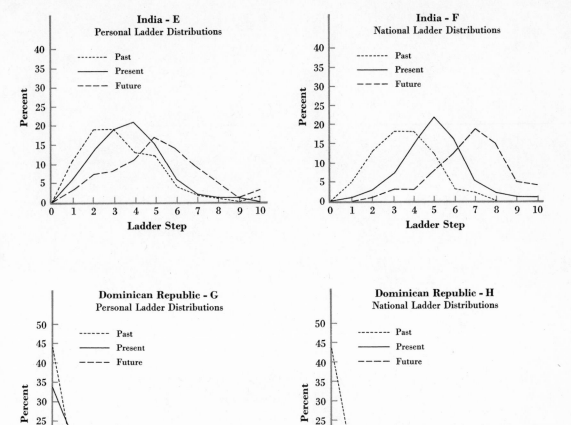

sample saw a bad past being replaced by a hopeful future—both personally and especially for one's country (**D**). **E-F** Indian sample quite consistently saw steady progress from past, present, to future. Optimism for future of one's country (**F**) was greater than for one's personal future (**E**), but, in general, ratings were higher for the country. **G-H** Both past and present look grim in this distribution of responses in the Dominican Republic. Despite this discouraging picture, a sturdy minority sees their personal future as somewhat brighter and has hopes for the future of their country (**H**).

17

The Self
and Its Involvements

Major Topics of the Chapter

Self-concept brings coherence to study of
   human motives
Integrative function of the self (ego)
Defining concepts
Relation of self and attitudes
Making ego-involvement operational in
   terms of degrees of consistency and selectivity in behavior
Making the degree of ego-involvement operational in terms of the relative sizes of
   acceptance, rejection, and noncommitment latitudes
Experimental verification
Ego-involvement and consistency of behavior
Consistency in setting goals for performance

SELF CONCEPT BRINGS COHERENCE TO THE STUDY OF HUMAN MOTIVES

As we have stressed, social psychology is in large part the study of the individual's relatedness to other persons, peoples, and cultural objects. Therefore, it needs conceptual tools to handle the various facets and functional workings of this relatedness. The concept of self or ego is a major concept that can serve as an effective theoretical tool in pulling a vast quantity of descriptive facts into coherence.

As long as man's motivation, interpersonal relations, group relations, prejudice, and other attitudes were treated as though each were an entirely separate topic, social psychology could not make substantial headway. The concept of self or ego—that uniquely *human* formation developing in the individual's life history—contributes a great deal of coherence to the treatment of these topics.

We will start this chapter by expanding the discussion on the integrative function of the self that was initiated in the Introduction to Part IV, in which the chapters deal with conceptual functioning, attitudes, and reference groups as well. Then the definition of self will be discussed. The conception of self will be elaborated through verified findings along the following lines:

1. Experimental findings that have been verified time and again during the last quarter of a century.
2. Longitudinal studies and experimental comparisons through the course of human development on the appearance of the self system in infancy and its formation and change from childhood through adolescence to old age.
3. Cross-cultural comparisons of ego concerns in different societies, which help us to avoid an ethnocentric account of self and, at the same time, permit a definition that is not culture-bound.
4. Experimental and empirical findings on uncertainty, anxiety, and breakdowns of the self system—which further confirm the definition and the accounts of the formation and functioning of the self.

The concept of self is needed for a rounded explanation of human motivation, including the operation of specific bodily needs (such as hunger, sex, etc.) as well as the person's ambitions and setting of consistent, long-range goals with regard to his social and occupational attainments, his ego concerns in interpersonal relations, and the directions that he takes in group relations.

It will help the reader to add a terminological clarification to these opening remarks. The terms *self, self system,* and *ego* will be used interchangeably. The reason is that the distinctions made between concepts of self and ego by various authors have led to great confusion in the literature, which is reviewed elsewhere (Sherif, 1968). It might be preferable to use an altogether different label for what we shall define as the self system or ego, but the coining of new labels can also impede the continuity of research findings. In fact, we shall retain the term *ego-involvements* to refer to involvement of the self system because most experiments during the last three decades were labeled as ego-involvement experiments. Finally, the reader should be cautioned that self or ego as used in this chapter includes the "super-ego" of Freudian-oriented therapists. A good many sociologists and social psychologists, as well as therapists (e.g., Sullivan, 1947) have used self or ego in this way. In recent years, developmental accounts and experiments on moral development have made it untenable to separate sharply between the growth of "conscience" and other aspects of the self system.

INTEGRATIVE FUNCTION
OF THE SELF

Over long years, piecemeal and fragmentary accounts of human motivation and personality proved to be sterile. Such accounts could not make valid predictions of what the person will actually do as he lives his life and interacts with other people In the face of this failure of accounts that neatly compartmentalized human motives, the need for integrative formulations that have bearing on actualities dawned on all concerned—both within academia and among people concerned with maintaining the integrity of their personal identity in a world of flux and conflict. As a consequence, certain expressions became the order of the day in discussions of motivation and personality, such as the "whole person," "personality dynamics," and "heuristic concepts."

Self or ego is among the terms that came to the foreground during this upsurge of seeking integrative concepts and formulations. Let us first mention some of the questions to which the concept of self or ego is contributing a measure of coherence, with corresponding gains in predictive value:

Hierarchy of Ego-Concerns. Is a person who is, say, honest or considerate in one situation also honest or considerate in general as well? Or are such personal characteristics specific to specific situations? In more general form, are personality characteristics specific or general traits of the person? This question is one aspect of the problem of the *consistency* of the person.

In brief, the problem of the person's consistency in this or that respect cannot be handled in the abstract. To answer such questions as those above, we have to *know at least what are the directive components in the person's self system and the relative rank of the personal characteristic in question* (for example, being honest or considerate or argumentative). The problem is, at the outset, the problem of determining the *hierarchy of importance* attached to various components in the self. This is not all. We also have to know the *properties of the situations* in which the person transacts. Personal qualities or traits built in the course of the person's life history do not function in a vacuum.

Barring out-of-the-ordinary situations, research findings warrant the following generalization about this question: A personal quality (e.g., honesty or tenacity) is general to the extent that it has high priority (importance) in the person's self system. The quality or characteristic will change from situation to situation to the extent that it does not have high priority in the person's self system. Personal consistency from situation to situation will be lacking in those qualities that are not focal in the person's ego concerns or that are altogether unrelated to them.

Other Human Motives Are Attended-To With Associated Ego-Concerns. Why do people go out of their way, even to the point of deprivation, to satisfy their sexual urges and needs for food or sleep in definite ways when the cycle of bodily homeostasis requires more expedient and immediate means of meeting these needs? Why will a person endure sleeplessness and wear and tear for days on end, for example, to seek a high political office? Such cases drive home the lesson that specific bodily needs and motives do not function in insulated compartments. They have to be studied as they are related to the functioning of other motives. Specifically, there are ego-concerns associated with each specific need (in terms of which satisfaction is regulated). *This means that the associated ego-concerns have to be taken care of at the same time that the person tends to the gratification of his more specific needs.*

Person's Consistency-Inconsistency in Reacting to Communication. Why does the person easily change his mind *on some particular issues* when he is exposed to messages or pressures advocating some point of view or the purchase of some wares when, *on other matters,* he remains deaf and dumb to appeals, sales talk, or attempts to persuade him? Why is it that this same person will, on certain matters, react more negatively than usual to communication— even to the point of making active effort to eliminate such "obnoxious" appeals and their source? On the surface, these three modes of reaction to external appeals by the same person are contradictory. Isn't the person being inconsistent to react so differently to communication? Or is he being consistent in some respect? Do these modes of reaction have anything to do with the target of the appeals, namely whether the targets are beliefs and commitments high in his ego system? These are illustrative cases within the *consistency-inconsistency problem* that has belatedly become a focal research issue for scholars in the area of attitude change (cf. Abelson, Aronson, McGuire, Newcomb, Rosenberg, and Tannenbaum, 1968).

Research into the problem of consistency-inconsistency is providing the needed corrective to the practice of drawing sweeping conclusions about attitude change in general on the basis of findings applicable only to specific situations in which the person's ego-concerns are not strongly involved. Studies of attitude change through exposure to communication that is discrepant from the individual's attitude have been said to be contradictory. It is argued by some authors that one set of findings sup-

ports one theory and another set another theory, or that none of the competing theories are supported (cf. Halloran, 1967). When we take the trouble to evaluate the research findings at closer range, we find that they do fall into a sensible pattern, as we shall see in Chapter 21. The findings fall into a pattern that is conceptually coherent when we evaluate these studies reporting change, no change, or boomerang effects in terms of the relative importance (rank) of the attitudes in the self system that are triggered by the communication or appeal in question. When the relative rank (priority) of the particular attitude that is the target of communication is assessed, predictions are made as to whether the person will change toward the position advocated in communication, whether he will resist change, and even whether he will become more strongly entrenched in his original views (Chapter 21).

More recently, we have seen a healthy trend to bring into the picture the importance of the *kind* of ego-involvement in accounting for whether the individual changes. It is the hallmark of any human person to maintain the consistency of those ties, commitments, values, and identifications that he cherishes. The stability of his self-identity consists of maintaining them from day to day. When he is subjected to appeals and communications aiming to disrupt his established ties, commitments, and identifications, his very experience of personal stability is disrupted. Such disruption arouses tension. It is conducive to putting his self-identity out of balance. Against such onslaughts, the person strives to maintain and restore his stability proportional to the importance of the commitments and ties that were the target of the communication.

However, restoring stability in any form or *at any price* will not do. He has to restore stability in terms of the level claimed by his lasting commitments and lasting values. In other words, what is involved is not automatic leveling (such as the water level in a hydraulic system). The individual does not reduce the tension he experiences or restore stability on any terms without regard to the consequences. *He attempts to restore stability at the level of his ego demands,* including those required by his self-identity and the expectations of others who are near and dear. Otherwise, the result is greater disequilibrium and more staggering imbalance than that produced by discrepant and inimical pressures from outside.

DEFINING CONCEPTS

Now that we have become acquainted with problems of conceptual functioning (Chapter 14) and attitudes and attitude measurement (Chapters 15 and 16), the definition of self will be more meaningful. For convenience, the definition given in the Introduction to Part IV is repeated here.

Self **is a developmental formation or subsystem in the psychological makeup of the individual that consists, at any given time, of interrelated attitudes that the individual has acquired (in relation to his own body and its parts, to his capacities, to objects, persons, family, groups, status and prestige symbols, social values, goals, and institutions) which define and regulate his relatedness to these objects in concrete situations and activities.**

This definition of *self* or *ego* is conducive to empirical analysis and experimental testing in terms of various related dimensions. It avoids reification of ego or self, which easily ends (as Ausubel put it) with "homuncular" entities that "control" the individual (1952). By identifying the component parts of the self system as attitudes, the definition links the study of attitude formation and change with the larger problem of personal consistency-inconsistency in behavior. Furthermore, as we shall see, the definition is conducive to operational means for specifying what is meant by ego-functioning and ego-involvements.

Before proceeding to operational terms for studying self and its involvements, the definition will be elaborated briefly as follows:

1. By approaching the study of the self system in terms of general principles applicable to the study of attitudes, the known facts about cultural differences in ego concerns can be handled without improvising a new psychology for each culture. As attitudes constitute subject-object relationships, it follows that the objects will vary from one culture to the next. However, these cross-cultural differences can be handled through general psychological principles about attitude formation and functioning.

2. When one analyzes empirical and experimental studies of self or ego, one finds that various ego problems are always studied in terms of the person's attitudes, expectations, and aspirations toward given objects, persons, and events (past, present, or future). The definition of ego or self makes this explicit and leads to analysis of self in various dimensions (ego-attitudes) and their interrelationships. The methods and techniques for studying self are, therefore, linked to the study of attitudes, which technically is more developed.

3. The self system and its involvements in ongoing psychological activity are not coextensive with the psychological makeup and functioning of the human person. This cautionary statement is needed because of the tendency to equate the problems of self with all problems of psychology. Self or ego is a *subsystem* in the psychological makeup, as the Gestalt psychologists Koffka (1935), Köhler (1929), and Lewin (1935) also stressed. Involvement of the self (ego-involvement) occurs when component attitudes are aroused owing to their relevance in given situations or activities. They participate within the frame of reference at the time as internal factors. The criteria differentiating ego-attitudes from other internal factors are the same as those applying to attitudes in general.

4. The subsystem designed as self is a developmental formation. It is not present at birth. Once formed it is not immutable throughout life. Self develops as one's body and its parts are differentiated from the environment and as attitudes are formed defining modes of relatedness to various objects (including one's own body), persons, groups, and values in the sociocultural setting. Throughout life, as the individual acquires new social ties, new roles, and changed status, because of his accomplishments or his age, the self system does change and must change if he is to behave consistently in terms of his altered relationships and responsibilities.

5. The self system is not a unitary structure, either in its formation or in its arousal.

The constituent parts (ego-attitudes) are functionally related as parts in a system. However, it is quite misleading to think that "functional relationships" and "integration" mean the same thing. There may be conflicts among the component parts of the self precisely because they are interrelated. In various roles and capacities, the individual does acquire attitudes that, *when aroused simultaneously,* are not harmonious and cannot be integrated. The modern professional woman caught in a situation that requires her to act in the same breath as a professional person and as a mother or sweetheart experiences severe conflict. The "marginal man" who is pulled asunder by ties to two antagonistic reference groups is another example of such conflict.

Making Ego-Involvement Operational

Involvement of the self simply means, therefore, the arousal of any one of the self's components—each of which signifies a specific subject-object relationship. (Again, "subject" refers to the person as he perceives himself in a particular set of relationships, and "object" may be other persons, a group, a social value, or any valued object, and it may be his own body, his abilities, and his claims.) As a person's enduring relationship in any respect is stabilized as an attitude, ego-involvement refers to the arousal of an attitude of the person that defines, delimits, and regulates his characteristic modes of behavior to the stimulus that triggers his behavior. We refer to such attitudes as ego-attitudes.

Ego-involvement refers to the arousal of a situationally relevant ego-attitude, whose participation in ongoing psychological activity generates modes of behavior that are more consistent, more selective, and more characteristic of the person in that respect.

This definition of ego-involvement lends itself to research operations that distinguish the *degrees* of consistency and *degrees* of selectivity of the behaviors elicited.

When one examines experimental and empirical findings over the last quarter of a century, one finds an amazing degree of convergence in the results. The converging finding is that when research procedures arouse an ego-attitude on an issue or in performance of a task, reactions become more consistent and more characteristic of the individual. This consistency and selectivity means that the person ego-involved in a particular situation is less responsive to other external stimuli or stimulus dimensions that are irrelevant to his attitude. On the other hand, a noninvolved person attends to other stimulus aspects of the situation and is distracted by them. Experimental findings to this effect will be presented in the next section (pp. 388–401).

Making the Degree of Ego-Involvement Operational

The definitions of self and its involvement in some respect provides a rationale for demonstrating the presence or absence of ego-involvement. The definitions provide the needed rationale for specifying the degree of involvement of the person under specified conditions: The higher the priority (rank) of an ego-attitude of the self system that is triggered by the situation, the more consistent and the more selective he is. Thus degree of involvement can be inferred from degrees of selectivity and consistency of behavior of different individuals in the same situation or of the same individual in different situations.

In order to move toward the precision required to express degrees of involvement, we should first be able to express the ego-attitude in question (e.g., attachment, aversion, identification, etc.) in quantitative terms. As we saw in Chapter 16, it is not sufficient to express the person's attitude as a point or an average of his responses. An attitude involves a pattern of acceptance, rejection, and noncommitment. Thus, assessment of degree of ego-involvement requires that we be able to operationalize the structure of the attitude dimensionally.

The concepts of latitude of acceptance, latitude of rejection, and latitude of non-commitment (pp. 357 ff.) are derived from the study of social judgment. The language of social judgment, or categorization, is conducive to dimensional analysis of an attitude. In fact, these concepts and findings derived through their use in actual research permit an operational definition of degree of ego-involvement.

Operationally, the degree of a person's ego-involvement in ongoing psychological activity is inferred from the relative magnitudes of his latitudes of acceptance, rejection, and noncommitment in categorizing the relevant stimulus domain: The greater the size of the latitude of rejection relative to the latitude of acceptance and the latitude of noncommitment, the greater is the person's ego-involvement in that stimulus domain.

We have already presented the measurement procedures of these concepts (pp. 358 ff.).

EXPERIMENTAL VERIFICATION

In this section, we shall review illustrative experiments from the research literature on ego-involvements. The experiments demonstrate (1) heightened *consistency* in behavior when the person is ego-involved, (2) *selectivity* as a function of ego-involvement, and (3) *systematic variations* in judgment as a function of the kind and degree of ego-involvement.

In selecting illustrative experiments, we have preferred those not relying entirely on self-reports. Of course, a person's report about himself is behavior and may be the only data available in some circumstances. However, there is an unfortunate tendency in both professional and popular literature to equate self-reports with the person's subjective self-concept, even though verbal reports are not infallible indicators of experience (cf. Smith, 1968). The extensive research literature on self-reports as data for study of the self system was analyzed critically by Wylie (1961). The concept of self as defined above is not merely "phenomenal self;" it is inferred from behavior—verbal and nonverbal.

How does an experimenter study ego-involvement? Two general procedures have been used, with variations by different investigators. One way is to select research subjects with a known stand or commitment—for example, persons who actively participate in some cause or who publicly declare their commitment. Then, one presents a task, an activity, or a stimulus ob-ject that is relevant to that commitment or stand, without any special instructions referring to the person's ego-attitude. (A special case of this general procedure is to present a task related to one's sex role, occupation, or ethnic classification.)

Another general procedure is to vary ego-involvement of subjects through instructions in the research situation itself. For example, if the subjects are students, they may be instructed that their performance in a task reveals something about them as a person, or that the results will become a part of their school records. In such procedures, the researcher's success in arousing an ego-attitude depends upon his knowledge of the subject (his important roles) and the values prevalent in his reference groups. We cannot measure ego-involvement *directly,* nor can we measure the psychological tension a person may experience when he is confronted by an incompatible situation. Such qualities are inferred from behavior relative to a given stimulus condition. Therefore, experimental manipulation of ego-involvement depends upon the accuracy with which the researcher can, on the basis of his own sociocultural experiences and observations, create conditions that trigger relevant ego-attitudes in the experimental situation (cf. Sherif, Sherif, and Nebergall, 1965, pp. 68–70; Bem, 1967, p. 198).

Ego-Involvement and Consistency of Behavior

It follows from Proposition 3 that behavior at a given time is a joint product of stimulus situations and internal factors and that the person's behavior will vary in different stimulus situations. Why is it, then, that we observe an individual performing a variety of different tasks and interacting in various specific situations in fairly characteristic fashion and with directionality that we consider "typical" of that person? Why can we predict that Person A will cheat on an examination, if given the chance, and that Person B will not? Why does Person Y consistently shoot for an A in every course, while Person Z feels content with C's, even though he could make A's?

In the earlier research literature, there were studies that seemed to show that behavior characterized as honest, reliable, or generous occurred only in specific situations, hence was situationally determined. Other studies suggested generality in the person's actions in these respects from one situation to the next. In reviewing the conflicting results, G. W. Allport (1943) concluded that a person is consistent from one situation to others if he is ego-involved in the situation, but that his consistency is less if the trait, the task, or the situation itself is unimportant to him. If he is not ego-involved, his behavior is affected *more* by the particular properties of the stimulus situation at hand.

Klein and Schoenfeld (1941) studied a person's *confidence* in his own performance in several tasks, and their findings illustrate Allport's point. The tasks were neutral paper-and-pencil tests of the sort that might (but do not) appear on an intelligence test. In one experimental condition, university students were told that the tasks were designed to assess their intelligence and that the results would be sent to the personnel office of the university. In a control condition, students performed the same tasks as research subjects without special instructions. All students rated their confidence in their own performance on each task. The main findings were as follows:

1. The confidence ratings for the different tasks were significantly correlated when subjects were ego-involved. In other words, if a subject was highly confident of his performance on one task, he tended to be highly confident on the others; low confidence on one task tended to accompany low confidence on others.

2. Confidence ratings differed from one task to the next according to task difficulty when the tasks were presented simply as research exercises.

In short, ego-involvement increased the generality of the person's confidence with the result that his ratings were more consistent from one task to the next.

Consistency in Setting Goals for Performance. William James noted many years ago that one's experience of success or failure was always relative to the level he set for himself in that respect. Using this concept of "ego level," Kurt Lewin and his associates initiated a series of experiments on estimates of future performance or level of aspiration. Among the early findings were that individuals tend to be fairly consistent in estimating their own performance, changing their estimates much less frequently than one might expect if the estimates were based solely on the ups-and-downs of performance. The characteristic reaction to repeated "failure" was to lower the aspiration level, while the characteristic reaction to success was to shoot even higher.

Holt (1945) showed that the characteristic "rigidity" in estimating one's own future performance, as well as the characteristic shifts, were a function of the person's involvement in his performance of the tasks. By selecting tasks that differed in their personal relevance to the subjects, Holt found that personal consistency was characteristic in the ego-involving tasks, but not in those that were less involving. In the more neutral tasks, estimates of future performance were "more specific, more peripheral and responsive to outer environmental forces"—in short, to the task itself and to one's actual performance in it.

Consistency in Estimating Performance by Oneself and Significant Others. The relative "rigidity" of estimates for one's own future performance, in comparison with the "tracking" of past performance by another person, led some investigators to suggest that self-judgments and judgments of others were very different phenomena (cf. McGehee, 1940). However, self-judgments do follow general principles of judgment if we regard the person's "ego level" as one example of a potent anchor for his judgments. As the person's own body, attributes, and performance are not the only "objects" related to the self system, it seems reasonable that one's attitudes toward significant others might also become anchors for judging such people's performance. If this is true, judgments of significant others should resemble judgments of one's self in certain important respects.

An experiment comparing the person's estimates of his own future performance and his estimates of performance by another person with whom he is ego-involved was conducted by C. Sherif (1947). The subjects were parent-child and husband-wife pairs. Each pair participated together in dart throwing, a task that was presented as a test of eye-hand coordination. After a few practice trials by one member of the pair, the thrower began to announce his estimate of his own performance before each trial. The second member simply watched and wrote down estimates of his partner's performance before each trial. After 25 trials, this second member became the performer, estimating his own performance, while his partner now became the "judge." Thus, each subject made 25 estimates of his own performance and 25 of his partner's performance.

In this situation, there were no significant differences in the judgments about one's own performance and those of one's partner (one's parent, child, or spouse). In both cases, individuals tended to maintain a level for their estimates above actual performance and to shift upward and downward only with pronounced success and with marked decrements in performance. In other words, behavior was as *consistent* relative to the significant other as it was towards oneself. Other actions indicated that the subjects were equally or even more involved when their partner was performing —more visibly tense and more obviously delighted with success. ("Don't tighten up!" "You're taking it too casually, dear." "Get that yellow! Get it for Daddy!" "Hurray!") While no subject excused himself for performing poorly, some partners "explained" failures by the other. (One husband said that his wife had not felt well all day.)

Proceeding from these findings, Harvey and Sherif (1951) reasoned that estimates of future performance might reveal the degree and direction of a person's involvement with others. Although absolute level of estimates depends upon the actual performance observed, the *difference* between actual past performance and estimates of future performance should reveal something about the affective tie with the person judged. Accordingly, the investigators selected four kinds of subject pairs in a replication of the earlier study: (1) college students who were in love, (2) high-school students who were "going steady," (3) high-school students who were friends, and (4) high-school students who had either recently had a fight or were known to be competing for the attention of the same boy or girl. Thus, the pairs

ranged from (1) intensely and positively attached through (3) more moderate positive attachment to (4) overt rivalry and dislike. The findings were as follows:

1. Again, consistency in estimating future performance of a loved person was comparable to that in estimating one's own.
2. The *degree* of consistency in judgment varied with the intensity of the positive tie, being greater for lovers than for mere friends.
3. Estimates of performance by a person with whom one's own involvement is negative (against) differed from those of one's own performance in the direction of devaluing the other person.

Theoretically, the significant conclusion is that self-evaluation and self-estimates are governed by general psychological principles, when it is recognized that ego-attitudes are involved as potent anchors in the judgment process. The extent to which consistency will reflect the ego-attitude (positive or negative) that is triggered in the situation is a function both of the degree of the person's involvement and of the properties of the situation, a consideration to which we now turn.

Consistency in Ego-Involving Tasks as a Function of Stimulus Structure. In earlier chapters, experiments were presented showing that estimates of future performance and judgments of actual performances by fellow members of a group revealed the participants' reciprocal expectations associated with differing status in the group (Chapter 8, pp. 164 ff.). Similarly, the Rattlers and Eagles revealed their identifications as group members and their common hatred of the detested rivals through their estimates of performance by members of the two groups in the bean-toss task (Chapter 11). Now, it is clear that these consistent variations in judgment are, psychologically, special cases of the effects of ego-involvement in judgment (*see above*). What needs to be emphasized again is that in all of these experiments, the behavioral consistency occurred in situations lacking objective structure in some important respect. The experimental outcomes were predicted on the basis of Propositions 3, 6, and 11.

The importance of numerous *alternatives* for judgment in order that the behavior reflect the person's involvement was shown by Feather (1967). Feather compared estimates of future performance in a task that could be varied in the degree of ambiguity about one's performance. He also administered projective tests (adaptations of the TAT) that indicate (1) motivation to achieve and (2) excessive anxiety.

The task required the person to pull a string which, by means of a pulley arrangement, lifted a cone that supported a steel ball on its apex. The challenge was to raise the cone as high as possible without knocking off the balanced ball. The height to which the cone was raised was visibly marked by a centigrade scale (0–100). However, unknown to the subject, the ball was held in place by an electromagnet which the experimenter could deactivate at will by silently pressing a concealed foot pedal. Thus, the subject's performance could be completely programmed by the experimenter throughout 11 trials.

In one condition of the experiment, the sequence of performance was programmed to show steady improvement from an initial score of 30 to 70, as shown in the solid dark line in Fig. 17.1. In another condition, the sequence of scores was highly irregular and fluctuating—as shown in the solid dark line in Fig. 17.2. A third condition (not shown) was intermediate with respect to the ambiguity of performance from one trial to the next.

The main findings in Feather's experiment were as follows:

As Fig. 17.1 shows, the estimates of future performance ("What you are actually going to get?") in the least variable condition tracked the sequence of actual scores closely, although the estimates were consistently higher than performance.

In the most variable condition (Fig. 17.2), estimates of future performance bore little relation to actual performance, being both high and consistent throughout. Other comparisons showed that the estimates by these subjects resembled those in the typical level of aspiration experiment much more closely than did estimates in the least variable condition.

Finally, correlations between the scores on the projective tests for achievement mo-

tive and anxiety were significant only in the most variable condition of the experiment, being zero order in the least variable condition. In other words, the consistency that a subject displayed in the most variable condition reflected in part his attitudes toward challenging tasks. The low but significant correlations showed that those with high achievement motives tended to change their estimates less, in general, and to be less responsive to temporary success. High anxiety scores, on the other hand, were associated with the tendency to raise estimates after success, to lower them after failure, and to keep the level of estimates closer to actual performance.

In short, Feather's experiment shows once more that the effects of internal factors (in this case, the involvement of ego-attitudes in the judgment process) are revealed when the stimulus situation permits numerous alternatives in psychological patterning (pp. 62 ff.).

Judgments in Unstructured Situations as Indicators of Interpersonal Attitudes

Utilizing the autokinetic situation, Sherif (1937) demonstrated that behavior in an unstructured situation can reveal a person's attitude toward another person. As a part of an experiment on the experimental formation of consistent modes of behavior as a function of social influence, he asked Professor Robert Woodworth's graduate assistant in psychology at Columbia University to cooperate with him in an experimental session in which the naive subject was a girl psychology student who thought highly of the assistant. The following is a verbatim report by the cooperating subject:

Miss X and I [Assistant in Psychology, Columbia University] were subjects for Dr. Sherif. I was well acquainted with the experiment but Miss X knew nothing whatsoever about it. Since she was a close friend of mine, and I carried some prestige with her, Dr. Sherif suggested that it would be interesting to see if we could predetermine her judgments. It was agreed beforehand that I was to give no judgments until she had set her own standard. After a few stimulations it was quite clear that her judgments were going to vary around five inches. At the next appropriate stimulation, I made a judgment of twelve inches.

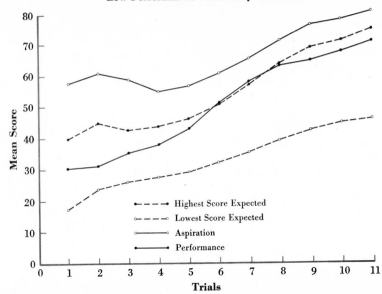

Fig. 17.1. When variability in performance is small, aspirations follow performance level closely (From N. T. Feather, Level of aspiration and performance variability. *J. pers. soc. Psychol.* **6,** Fig. 3, p. 41. Copyright 1967 by the American Psychological Association, and reproduced by permission.). Note that when performance (*solid line, black dots*) rises regularly and steadily, the person's estimates of the lowest and highest scores expected, as well as aspirations (*top*), follow the performance curve.

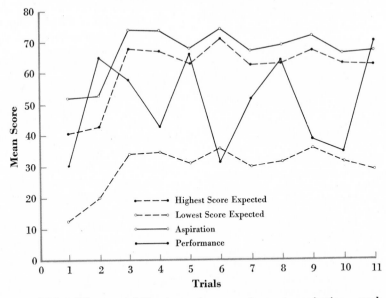

Fig. 17.2. When variability in performance is great, aspirations reach a level which is maintained with less variation following ups and downs in performance (From N. T. Feather, Level of aspiration and performance variability. *J. pers. soc. Psychol.* **6,** Fig. 1, p. 40. Copyright 1967 by the American Psychological Association, and reproduced by permission.). Note the erratic performance curve (*solid line, black dots*). Despite its gyrations, the lowest and highest score expected and aspirations (*top*) maintain a fairly even keel.

Miss X's next judgment was eight inches. I varied my judgments around twelve inches and she did the same. Then I changed my judgment to three inches, suggesting to Dr. Sherif that he had changed it. She gradually came down to my standard, but not without some apparent resistance. When it was clear that she had accepted this new standard, Dr. Sherif suggested that I make no more judgments lest I might influence hers. He then informed her on a subsequent stimulation that she was underestimating the distance which the point moved. Immediately her judgments were made larger and she established a new standard. However, she was a little uneasy with it all, and before the experiment had progressed much farther whispered to me, "Get me out of here."

When we were again in my office, I told her that the point had not moved at all during the experiment. She seemed quite disturbed about it, and was very much embarrassed to know that we had been deceiving her. Noting her perturbation, I turned the conversation to other matters. However, several times during our conversation she came back to the subject saying, "I don't like that man" (referring to Dr. Sherif) and similar statements indicating her displeasure with the experience. It was not until some weeks later when she was again in my office that I discovered the full extent of her aversion. I asked her to serve as a subject for me in an experiment and immediately she exclaimed, "Not down in *that* room," pointing to Dr. Sherif's experimental room.

Zeaman (1946) extended this demonstration by using two cooperating subjects, one of whom was regarded affectionately and one of whom was regarded antagonistically by the young man who was naive about the purpose of the experiment. Zeaman described these relationships as follows:

One male graduate student of the Anthropology Department at Columbia was used as subject. He was cooperative, and intelligent, but entirely naive about the experimental procedure and apparatus, and about the autokinetic effect. The relationship between the observer and the two experimenters was primarily that of very close friendship although after a period of sharing an apartment for one year, different modes of behavior had set in on the part of the subject with respect to the male and female experimenter. It is . . . this difference in relationship that forms the independent variable in this experiment. The relationship between the subject and the female experimenter was a noncompetitive, pleasantly affectional relationship. . . . Between the subject and the male experimenter, on the other hand, there existed a relationship characterized by mutual striving for ascendancy, aggression . . .

and a consequent tendency to deprecate the judgments of the other person. Over a period of many months, these relationships had proved relatively invariable.

The experiment proceeded by the naive subject giving 35 judgments alone, then 35 with the female plant, who deliberately made judgments near the average given by the subject in the alone session and then lowered her judgments considerably (see Fig. 17.3). After a brief rest, the subject gave judgments alone again. Then the male plant began giving judgments slightly above those of the subject, increasing them throughout the session. Finally, the subject gave judgments alone again.

Figure 17.3 gives the means for each five successive judgments by the naive person and the two plants. The average of the judgments in the first alone session was 5.9 inches. The female plant's judgments averaged 1.9 inches and the average by the subject during the same session was 3.4 inches. When subsequently alone again, the subject's judgments averaged 2.4 inches. The effect of the male plant's judgments (mean at 5.9 inches) was to produce a shift away from them (mean of 1.57 inches).

In short, when the stimulus situation being judged lacks objective structure, the person is responsive to the spoken judgments of another person and the cognitive process is affected by his motivational attachment to or rejection of that other person. It is particularly in situations lacking objective structure that cognitive processes (judgment, in this case) are influenced by motivational factors that are situationally aroused.

Sampson and Insko (1962) performed an experiment in which subjects were led to like or dislike a partner before making judgments of autokinetic movement. Judgments of autokinetic movement resembled those of the liked partner and diverged from those of a disliked partner. Thus, the Sherif and Zeaman findings were confirmed through the use of a larger number of subjects.

**Psychological Selectivity
as a Function
of Ego-Involvement**

When there are many things to see, many things to hear, many things to learn and to

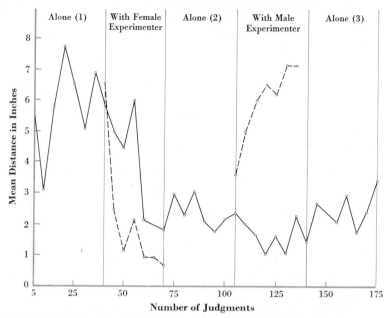

Fig. 17.3. The effects of positive and negative personal involvements on judgment. The means of each five successive judgments of extent of auto-kinetic movement are indicated by the solid line. The two experimenters' "planted" judgments are shown by the broken lines. The five situations are specified at the top. (Courtesy of D. Zeaman.)

remember, what of all these things does the person select? In Chapter 3, psychological selectivity was discussed in some detail. In this section, we are concerned specifically with ego-attitudes as factors in selectivity.

The composer Beethoven was known for his intense selectivity when composing. Even before he became deaf, he sometimes was "deaf and blind" both to what went on around him and to his own actions. While in the throes of composition, he was undressing one day before an open window. The loud shouts of laughter from some children in the street below caught his attention, but he was completely unaware that his own actions were the cause of their merriment. A musician who played under the great conductor Toscanini reported that the maestro focused his attention so exclusively on the orchestra's sounds that he could detect even one false note from a single instrument. However, he was completely oblivious to the fact that he himself habitually sang loudly as he conducted. Once in Salzburg, during a tense dress rehearsal, Toscanini suddenly halted the orchestra: "Silence," he roared. "Who is singing

here?" No one answered, so the rehearsal continued with Toscanini's warning that whoever it was should shut-up (unsigned, 1947). Such intense involvement of self in a creative activity produces a selectivity so exclusive that one's own ordinary actions go unnoticed or, when suddenly forced into awareness, pass unrecognized as belonging to one's self.

Ego-Involvement in Selective Learning and Remembering. In a series of experiments directed by Gardner Murphy, first at Columbia and then at the City College of New York, the role of ego-attitudes in the selective learning and recall of relevant pictures and verbal material was demonstrated quite conclusively. Experiments by Seeleman (1940), Clark (1940), Levine and Murphy (1943), and Postman and Murphy (1943) showed that how quickly material was learned and how well it was remembered were related to the person's ego-attitudes toward the materials. Most of these studies indicated that what was learned most quickly and retained best was what was consistent or congruent with the person's own identifications. For example, verbal material congenial to a pro-Communist position or an anti-Communist position was learned more quickly and retained better by persons sympathizing with each position (Levine and Murphy, 1943). However, the selection of supportive material was not the universal case, even in these early studies. Postman and Murphy (1943), for example, investigated recall for pairs of words which varied in their compatibility or incompatibility with either pro-Allied or pro-Axis sympathies of the eighth-graders who served as subjects during World War II. (For example, German-kindly was one such pair.) The students also rated each pair on a five-point scale indicating how strongly they agreed or disagreed with each pair. The tendency to recall pairs compatible with the person's own attitude was much smaller than the tendency to recall pairs that were rated extremely on the five-point scale, whether the rating was "strongly agree" or "strongly disagree." In other words, the intensity of agreement or disagreement determined selectivity of recall more than sheer compatibility with the person's attitude.

Kamano and Drew (1961) compared the retention of a short personality description by subjects who were instructed that the paragraph was an evaluation by a clinical psychologist of their own performance on a personality inventory with retention by subjects who were simply instructed to listen closely to the description because they would be asked to report on it later. The personally-involved subjects were matched with the control subjects on the basis of their previous performance in remembering a neutral passage. The result was that ego-involvement resulted in recall of significantly more of the personality description, whether the subject was asked to reproduce the passage immediately or with a two-day delay. (In immediate recall the ego-involved subjects remembered almost a third of the material while the control subjects recalled only slightly more than one-fifth.)

What kind of material was remembered best, that which was enhancing to the person or that critical and unfavorable to him? Figure 17.4 compares the ego-involved subjects with the control subjects in terms of immediate and delayed recall for items

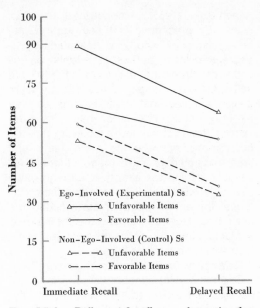

Fig. 17.4. Differential effects of ego-involvement on immediate and delayed recall. Recall by ego-involved subjects (*solid lines*) was consistently superior, notably for the unfavorable items. (Adapted from data of Kamano and Drew, 1961.)

that were judged by independent raters as favorable or unfavorable. The passage was designed so that there were equal numbers of each. As these figures indicate, there was a significant tendency for the ego-involved students to recall unfavorable descriptions of themselves.

In the experiment just summarized, there was no attempt to assess whether the unfavorable descriptions were more extreme in their unfavorableness than the favorable items were favorable. Therefore, it is not possible to conclude that under any and all circumstances persons will recall unfavorable descriptions of themselves better than favorable. Note also that both control and experimental subjects in the experiment knew that they would be called upon to recall the passages. The instrumental functions of selectivity are closely related to the person's ego-attitudes and, in turn, affect whether retention for incompatible material will be superior or inferior.

If the person is highly involved in a task and wants to present himself well, or is strongly committed to a view and eager to promote it, selectivity for unfavorable material is certainly functional. Jones and

Aneshansel (1965) demonstrated this fact neatly by presenting anti-segregation material to students who were classified as pro-segregationist or anti-segregationist on the basis of direct attitude tests. Half of the students were simply instructed to learn eleven anti-segregation arguments as well as they could. The other half was forewarned that they would be asked to provide counter-arguments to the same items, and then instructed to learn them. Students for whom the task was simply a learning exercise differed in recall in terms of their attitudes: the anti-segregationists recalled the items best. However, among the forewarned subjects, the pro-segregationist students learned the statements better.

Selectivity in Successive Reproductions.

The method of successive reproductions developed by Bartlett has bearing on the transmission of rumors. Allport and Postman (1947) applied the method to the study of rumor transmission by brief exposures of pictured material to a subject who described the picture to another, who passed the report on to the third, and so on. These investigators found marked distortions in the successive reports reflecting the attitudes of subjects. Similarly, Wood and Johnson (1944) found that successive reproductions of verbal material designed to be equally weighted with pro- and anti-Negro statements ended up as either pro-Negro or anti-Negro passages, depending on the attitudes of the individuals transmitting the information. These systematic distortions are not surprising in view of the fact that the recall of the brief exposure of a picture and the reproduction of complex verbal material are both tasks permitting many alternatives, hence a determining role for the person's attitudes.

A less frequent topic of study is the accurate transmission of rumors (regardless of whether the rumor itself is true). Higham's study (1951) bears on this problem because he compared the accuracy of transmission from the persons originally exposed to information (a "story") when it was relayed successively through seven other people. Fig. 17.5 gives the results of his experiment in terms of the percentages of details correctly retained from four different stories. The "ego-involved story" was certainly important to the students who

served as subjects, for it dealt with a conversation between a professor and his Senior Lecturer about the nature of an examination that the students were to take in three weeks. As the figure shows, this story or rumor survived transmission with much less distortion than less-involving stories, one of which was initially recalled equally well ("egg story"). Again, the instrumental functions of selectivity in learning, in communication and in retention are demonstrated.

**Selectivity
in Appraising Two Sides
to the Question**

In the study of attitudes toward the 1960 presidential election in the United States reported in Chapter 16, Sherif *et al.* (1965) used a natural communication situation to study selectivity of partisans on each side who varied in their commitment to the Republican or Democratic candidates. The two candidates engaged in a series of four television debates, each participating for an equal length of time. The subjects were asked to use a linear rating scale to indicate "Who had the edge in the debate?". One end of the rating scale was labeled as the Republican candidate and the other end was labeled as the Democratic candidate. Figure 17.6 presents the average ratings made by persons who adopted each of nine positions (A to I on the baseline) as most acceptable in expressing their attitude toward the election, with A indicating the most partisan Republicans and I the most partisan Democrats. As the figure clearly shows, subjects consistently rated the superior performance in line with their stands on the election issue, even though the debates witnessed were the same debates by the same candidates. The Republicans and Democrats apparently were highly selective in *what* they attended to and recalled about the two candidate's performance.

These ratings differ considerably from the preponderant assessments of the professional critics who concentrated on the tired appearance of the Republican candidate, especially in the first debate. The Republican candidate himself subsequently reported that he was tired and had been recently ill, but that apart from his appear-

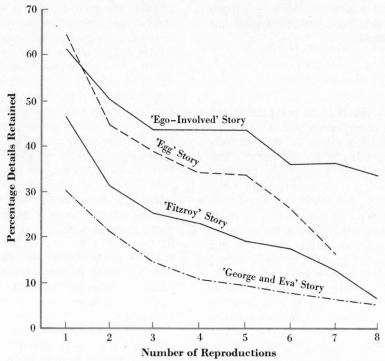

Fig. 17.5. Percentage of correct recall of stories varying in ego-involvement over 8 successive reproductions. (From T. M. Higham, 1951. The experimental study of the transmission of rumour. *Brit. J. Psychol.* [general section], **42**, 42–55.)

ance he felt that his arguments successfully countered those of his opponent (Nixon, 1964). Apparently his ardent supporters agreed.

In a study done after the election of the Democratic candidate, the debates were shown to pro-Republicans and pro-Democrats with remarkably similar results to those in Fig. 17.6 (Rosnow, 1965). The one difference was that Republicans tended to regard the Republican candidate's performance less favorably, a fact that might re-

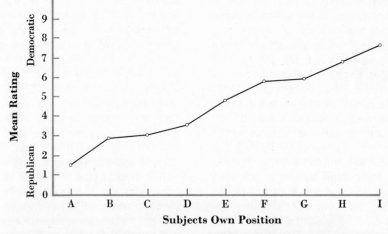

Fig. 17.6. Mean rating by persons upholding different positions on the 1960 presidential candidates as to which candidate had the edge in the television debates. (Adapted from Sherif, Sherif, and Nebergall, 1965.)

flect both the critical opinions of experts and the fact that the Democratic candidate was then President.

Selecting What to Perceive

In studying response to mass communications on a controversial social issue, the first and crucial question is "Who actually receives and attends to the communication?" Students of the effects of mass communication (e.g., Klapper, 1960, 1967) base their answers chiefly on survey research and reply that the majority tends to select communication that is congenial to their already-existing attitudes. While this broad generalization is doubtless true on a broad scale, it is inadequate in the analysis of specific situations and circumstances. For example, it is true that a Communist speaker in a capitalist country attracts few anti-Communist listeners except those eager to refute him, while the same selectivity in attending to pro-capitalist messages doubtless is found in Communist countries. Nevertheless, individuals taking opposing positions on social issues, particularly within the same country, are not totally in ignorance of the opposition stand. Someplace along the line, someone listens selectively to opposition arguments, regardless of whether the communication affects his own attitude.

Fortunately, the problem of whether an individual exposes himself to information and what kind he selects has become a topic for experimental inquiry. The findings to date indicate that selectivity in receiving a communication is related to the person's ego-attitudes, as indicated, for example, in the preferential choice of communications related to them (e.g., Freedman, 1965; Sears and Freedman, 1965) or in the effort which is expended to obtain static-free reception of communications presented to them (Brock and Balloun, 1967). (In the latter case, college students pressed buttons to clear static more frequently for talks on the military draft or denial of a link between smoking and lung cancer than they did for a talk about educational films.)

Furthermore, as the studies of selective learning and recall have shown, research on selective exposure has found that whether the person seeks supportive or incompatible information depends upon (a) whether it is novel to him or presented as a rehash of arguments he already knows (in which case he is more interested in the opposition); (b) whether he is offered information (by mail) for his own private consumption (in which case he is more likely to prefer novel, discrepant information) or for use in a discussion or debate; (c) and how strongly or intensely he is committed to his own attitude (Sears, 1965; Clarke and James, 1967). In addition, while it is very difficult to demonstrate *avoidance* of discrepant information in an experimental situation, there is some evidence (Brock and Balloun, 1967) that individuals expend less effort to receive discrepant information; and from actual life we shall have to account for observed cases of "switching off," "tuning out," and running away from such communication.

The problem of ego-involvement as related to selectivity will be discussed later in Chapter 21 on attitude change and communication.

Measuring Degree of Ego-Involvement

In several contexts, the intensity of an attitude or its importance in the individual's scheme of personal priorities has been emphasized as an important consideration in determining how he will react to relevant stimuli. Now we ask "How can we assess the rank of an attitude in the individual's self system?". If we can determine degree of ego-involvement, do persons with similar stands toward an object but different degrees of involvement behave differently when the attitude is situationally aroused?

It is possible for individuals to rank various values, activities, and issues in terms of their importance to them. However, a difficulty appears when one attempts to assess the meaning of such rankings. The first rank for one individual may not be at all equivalent in importance to a rank of one for another individual. This danger is particularly evident when what the individual ranks is chosen by an investigator, who may completely miss the things that really concern the person. For example, college students can rank social and political issues accord-

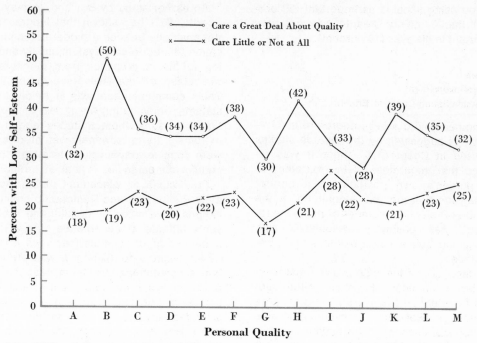

Fig. 17.7. Self esteem is lowered more frequently by deficiencies that we care a great deal about than by deficiencies in qualities that are trivial to us. (Based on data in Rosenberg, 1967, p. 33.)

Legend for personal qualities enumerated on baseline: (A) Good student; (B) likeable; (C) dependable and reliable; (D) intelligent, good mind; (E) clear thinking, clever; (F) easy to get along with; (G) realistic, able to face facts; (H) honest, law-abiding; (I) good sense, sound judgment; (J) kind and considerate; (K) get along well; (L) well-liked by many different people; (M) moral and ethical.

ing to how much they are concerned with them; however, by using other procedures, one finds that most of them are more concerned about grades, heterosexual and social relationships, and other more immediate matters (Sherif *et al.,* 1965).

Rosenberg (1965) was able to show the importance of the rank (priority) of personal qualities in the individual's image of a desirable person in a study of 5000 high-school students from different social classes in New York State. The students rated 44 personal qualities according to how much they themselves valued these qualities in people. Then they rated themselves according to whether they considered that they possessed each quality "very" much, "fairly" much, little, or not at all. In addition, Rosenberg devised a Guttman-type scale of self-esteem (p. 373), in which a high score indicated high self-esteem and a low score was associated with depression, feelings of inferiority, and psy-

chosomatic complaints. Selecting the 16 qualities that were rated as most highly valued by the overall high-school sample, Rosenberg (1967) inquired whether feeling that one was lacking in these respects would be associated with low self-esteem in general.

From the 5000 students, he selected those who indicated that they themselves possessed the quality little or not at all. Would these students by and large have low self-esteem in general? The answer was that it depended on how important each quality was to the individual. If he regarded himself as poor on the quality and also cared a great deal about the quality, he was more likely to be quite low in general self-esteem than if he did not care much about the quality in question. Figure 17.7 shows Rosenberg's results for the 16 most valued qualities. For example, if a person rated himself low in being likeable, he was more likely to have low self-esteem if he also regarded being likeable as important (50 percent) than if being likeable was not very important in his eyes (19 percent).

Degree
of Ego-Involvement
and Assimilation-Contrast Effects

Another way to assess degree of involvement was suggested by the attitude studies reported in Chapter 16. There it was reported that, regardless of the extremity of the person's own position on a controversial social issue, the magnitude of the latitude of rejection (number of positions rejected) was positively associated with strong and active participation in relevant activities.

In the study of the 1960 presidential election issue, the most actively committed subjects rejected, on the average, five or more positions out of nine. Consequently, this number was chosen as the cutting point to divide the subject sample (over 1500 in all) as highly ego-involved (reject 5 or more positions) and as less involved (reject four or fewer positions) on the election issue. (Another sign that degree of involvement and extremity of position are not perfectly correlated was that a sufficient number of persons upholding each of the nine positions from extreme Republican to extreme Democratic fell into these two categories.)

One part of the experiment was the presentation of tape-recorded communications about the election to individuals with varying attitudes on the issue. After hearing a communication the person was asked to rate what position the talk represented with regard to the election. He marked his judgment on a 9-centimeter scale marked only at one end as "extremely Republican" and the other as "extremely Democratic." The two communications of particular interest here were (1) a mildly pro-Republican communication designed to represent position D and (2) a mildly pro-Democratic communication designed to represent position F. Each was a cautiously worded statement of the issues in the campaign. At the end, the speaker indicated that the decision was difficult, but it was probable that the country's interests might be better served if the Republican (or Democratic) candidate were elected. (See statements D and F, p. 358.)

An earlier study by Hovland, Harvey, and Sherif (1957) had shown that judgments of the positions of such a moderate communication tended to vary systematically according to the *discrepancy* from the person's own stand on the issue (see Figure 17.8). Their communication was a mildly "wet" statement advocating the repeal of prohibition to persons whose attitudes ranged from extremely dry to extremely wet, all of whom were considerably involved in a state referendum campaign for repeal of prohibition.

Predictions on placement of the moderately Republican and Democratic communications were made by considering the person's latitude of acceptance as the major anchor in his judgments (see *Own Position as an Anchor,* pp. 340 ff.). It was predicted that a communication falling near the limit of the person's latitude of acceptance (the closest position he accepted) would be *assimilated toward* his own position on the issue. However, a communication discrepant from his latitude of acceptance would be contrasted—that is, seen as *more* discrepant from his own position than it was. Further, it was predicted that these tendencies would differ for less involved and for highly involved persons.

Figures 17.9 and 17.10 give the results for judgment of the mildly Republican communication. Figure 17.9 gives the average placements (*ordinate*) by highly involved persons; Fig. 17.10 gives that for less-involved persons. The triangles represent means for persons who chose an extreme position as most acceptable and the circles represent means for persons who chose a more moderate position as most acceptable. These symbols are located above the baseline to show which position in the latitude of acceptance was *closest* to the communication.

As predicted, persons who accepted mildly Republican positions judged the communication as *more* Republican than persons who accepted mildly Democratic positions, while extreme Democrats placed the communication as more Republican than extreme Republicans, who displaced it away from their own stand. The differences were statistically significant. Figure 17.10 indicates a similar but less marked trend for less involved subjects.

Figures 17.11 and 17.12 show comparable

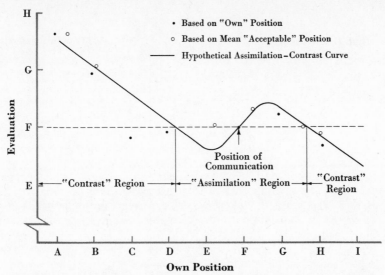

Fig. 17.8. Average placement of the position advocated in a moderate communication by persons holding different positions on the prohibition issue.

The communication advocated a moderately wet position (at F on the baseline). Note that Drys judged the communication as very wet, while Wets placed it near the neutral position (contrast). Persons with moderate views on the issue tended to assimilate the communication toward their own position (After Hovland, Harvey, and Sherif, 1957).

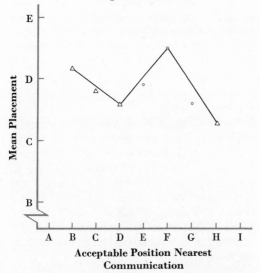

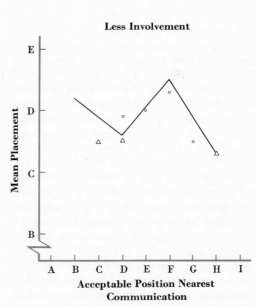

Fig. 17.9. Judged location of a mildly Republican communication (at D on ordinate) by highly involved Republicans (A–D) and Democrats (F–I) on baseline. Subject's position on graph indicates (1) position he accepted *nearest* D and (2) whether the single position most acceptable to him was extreme (*triangle*) or moderate (*circle*). Judgment higher on Figure represents less-Republican location; lower position indicates judgment as more Republican. Note that subjects accepting positions near communication assimilated its position to their own stand, while those whose attitude was remote from the communication (near A or I) contrast it to their own stand. (Adapted from Sherif, Sherif, and Nebergall, 1965, p. 157.)

Fig. 17.10. Judged location (*triangle*, extreme; *circle*, moderate) of a mildly Republican communication (at D on ordinate) by persons less involved in the election, as indicated by a small latitude of rejection. Compared with the graph of highly involved persons (Fig. 17.9), assimilation-contrast effects are less clear, although Democrats at H-I exhibit marked contrast effect. (Adapted from Sherif, Sherif, and Nebergall, 1965, p. 157.)

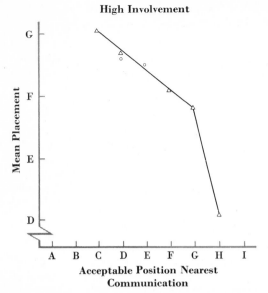

High Involvement

Fig. 17.11. Judged location (*triangle*, extreme; *circle*, moderate) of mildly Democratic communication (at F on ordinate) by highly involved Republicans (*left*) and Democrats (F–H). Contrast effects predominate with Republicans judging the communication as more Democratic and extreme Democrats (H) judging the communication as pro-Republican (at D). (Adapted from Sherif, Sherif, and Nebergall, 1965, p. 160.)

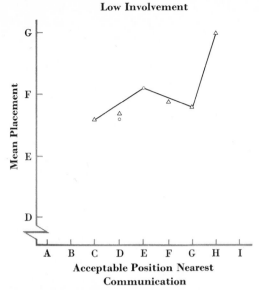

Low Involvement

Fig. 17.12. Judged location (*triangle*, extreme; *circle*, moderate) of mildly Democratic communication (at F on ordinate) by less involved Republicans (*left*) and Democrats (F–H). Unlike the highly involved subjects in Fig. 17.11, these subjects tend to assimilate the communication—particularly the more extreme Democratic subjects (at H), who judge the communication as a fairly strong statement of the Democratic position. (Adapted from Sherif, Sherif, and Nebergall, 1965, p. 160.)

findings on placements of the mildly Democratic communication. The comparatively fewer moderate Republicans and moderate Democrats who heard this speech made a test of the assimilation effects difficult. What does appear in these Figures is that in judging the mildly Democratic communication, extreme Republicans and extreme Democrats who were highly involved exhibited marked contrast effects (Fig. 17.11), each displacing the communication away from their own stand. Less-involved persons with extreme stands (Fig. 17.12), however, exhibited an equally marked assimilation effect—placing the communication nearer their own stands.

The findings on placement of the moderate communications in the 1960 election study provide support for the phenomena of assimilation-contrast as a function of the discrepancy between a person's stand and the position of communication; but they also show that the extent to which assimilation or contrast occurs is critically affected

by the degree of the person's ego-involvement in his stand.

These findings on placement of communication by persons varying both in position and degree of involvement will be referred to again in Chapter 21, when problems of communication and attitude change are considered. After all, the person's evaluation of the communication is an important event that affects his appraisal of it and whether it will influence him positively or negatively.

DEVELOPMENT OF SELF
IN THE HUMAN PERSON

A glance at a sequence of major events in human development will clarify the self and its functioning. The account in this section is based on extensive findings, chiefly in Europe and America. As we shall see, differences in the specific ages marking the general sequence, as well as difference in what is included in and excluded from the self are to be expected in varying socio-economic and cultural contexts.

Self is not innate, nor does it spring into being fullblown. How do we know? This generalization is one of the most extensively documented in all psychology. Since the nineteenth century, observations of infant and child behavior (cf. Sherif and Cantril, 1947) and, more recently, experimental evidence show that differentiation of behavior into consistent modes of response to the body and to external objects is lacking at birth and in the early months of life. Observed consistency of behavior in infancy consists of quiescence and momentary directionality attributable to bodily states or intense stimulation.

Although the infant's body is the center of gratification and distress from birth, psychologically it is differentiated from other bodies and other objects only gradually. It is a matter of months, even years, before the body and its parts, along with the experiences of touch, pain, muscular strain, and organic sensation, are differentiated accurately as a whole from the surroundings (Murphy, 1947, p. 481). Observing the gradualness with which the body is differentiated and its parts localized, one early observer (Preyer, 1890) reported that when he asked his year-and-a-half old son to give him his foot while dressing, the boy tugged at his own foot, trying to hand it over as he just had a shoe. Very young children notably lack the ability to point to the locus of discomfort, particularly if the pain is internal (an earache or visceral pain).

The elemental differentiation of the body as an object in a world of other objects emerges gradually as the child interacts with the surroundings. To be sure "self stimulation" plays a part. The baby begins to explore and to manipulate parts of his own body, with "double sensations" from his hands and the locus of exploration. He learns that it is not the same thing to pound a wooden bed and to pound his own head. As he begins to move, he encounters pleasant touches as well as resistances of and even collisions with objects.

However, as the eminent French psychologist Henri Wallon (1947) pointed out, the human child is so immediately dependent upon others at birth that his earliest interaction with the environment consists of relatedness to other persons, long before he can act upon or be acted upon by physical objects. The child's part in interaction with other persons is indeed primitive and elemental during the early months of life; but very early he begins to respond to feeding schedules (Marquis, 1941), to touch, and to the sight of a human face. His early smiles, vocalizations, and accommodations to human treatment quickly become an interaction process with adults. His role in the process expands with sensorimotor development and especially with the instrumental functions of speech.

Thus, although the growth and decline of the physical body are closely related to formation and change of self throughout the life cycle, there is no factual basis for the notion that the human self system just "grows up naturally" or develops solely through biological maturation. The self develops through interaction with others—as emphasized by William James (1890), James Mark Baldwin (1895), George Herbert Mead (1913), and Charles Cooley (1902), as well as by modern theorists (Piaget, 1932; Ausubel, 1952). In fact, the differentiation of self from others is so intertwined that Baldwin, basing his conclusion on observations of his own children, stated "the ego and alter . . . are thus born together" (Baldwin, 1895, p. 338).

The earliest behavioral manifestations of self-awareness are consistent differentiations of the body and its parts from other people and objects. The development of this "bodily self" does not occur immediately in one piece, but gradually in successive concrete experiences and concrete situations, to which its manifestations are closely tied. Thus, the earliest stage of self-formation is frequently called a "perceptual stage" (Wallon, 1933; Piaget, 1932; Murphy, 1947). More than any other events, the child's acquisition of language and its instrumental and then conceptual functions transforms the concrete differentiations between body and other objects and elaborates them into a *conceptual* system (see Chapter 14).

Thus Murphy (1947) traced the sequence in self-formation from a perceptual stage into an attributive stage (the body self is elaborated with labels of boy or girl and adjectives—pretty, good, bad, etc.) and finally more and more into a categorical system. The categorical nature of the self system is evidenced, for example, when a person is asked to respond to the question, "Who am I?" (Bugental and Zelen, 1949–50; Kuhn and MacPartland, 1954). Following one's name, the most frequent responses are in terms of social classifications (a man, a Baptist, an American, a Southerner, a white man, a businessman, a father, etc.). The more strictly personal classifications follow and even these reflect their categorical nature—"Oh, I'm just a big fat slob."

The differentiation and growth of the self system as a conceptual system can also be studied in terms of its end products— namely, the content and relationships among beliefs that the person maintains about himself and others. Rokeach (1960) has approached this problem through the "dogmatism" variable—how "closed" or "open" the person is in evaluating information. Harvey, Hunt, and Schroder (1961) focused on the abstractness-concreteness of the person's beliefs and attitudes. Harvey (1967) has shown that the conceptual content (or ideology) and the organization of beliefs in the concreteness-abstractness dimension interact in complex ways that produce quite different reactions to a variety of experimental situations by individuals varying in ideology and the "literalness" of their beliefs.

The crucial role of language development is shown most clearly in American studies by comparison of the ages at which children, *on the average,* manifest and are expected to show consistent modes of response in certain respects. Although the research is widely scattered and conducted by many different authors, the astounding generalization is that the period when the child becomes able to speak in the sentence form of his language and the instrumental use of language in communicating has been mastered is also the time when his *social* behavior starts to become consistent. His typical play activities become social. From the earlier forms of solitary and "parallel" (side-by-side) play, he now engages in "role play" ("You be the mother and I'll be the father") and in genuinely cooperative play (Beaver, 1932; Berne, 1930; Parten, 1932, 1933; Salusky, 1930; Green, 1933). From the sheerly social interchange that took on the verbal forms of competitive behavior without being consistently competitive ("I won"; "So did I"; "We all won"), he begins to compete consistently in activities with agemates (Hirota, 1951; Greenberg, 1932; Leuba, 1933). From impassive spectator or amused onlooker at the distress of another, he now begins to manifest consistent *sympathy* at the distress of another (Lois B. Murphy, 1937)—a form of behavior that develops when the child can "put himself in another person's shoes." From lack of responsibility for his own actions ("It isn't my fault; my hand did it"), he not only attempts independent acts but also assumes responsibility for them. From simple perceptual differentiation among peoples whose skin color differs from his own, he begins to exhibit responses revealing consistent and invidious comparisons prevailing in his social milieu—hence the first consistent signs of color prejudice (Clark and Clark, 1947; Horowitz, 1939; Goodman, 1952; Morland, 1966).

When the child designates self and others through verbal means (his name, "I," "me," "you," and, last of all, "we"), he begins to classify himself relative to others and others relative to self—endowing each with favorable or unfavorable attributes. Such classifications reflect the values and norms prevailing in his social surroundings as well as the more specific evaluations placed on his own characteristics by significant others. In the process, even the perceptual body image is transformed. Thus the boundaries, the properties, and the parts of the body are viewed so differently by individuals according to their sex, age, culture, and bodily health that Fisher and Cleveland (1958) concluded that the most accurate concept of the bodily self is that of "a representation of attitudes and expectancy systems" related to the body and the views of other people toward one's self.

Thus, the profoundly affective and motivational character of the self system—although grounded in bodily experiences of satisfaction and discomfort that permit its segregation as an object in a world of objects—is transformed through conceptual elaboration into a body image. In this process, the reactions and treatments of others, reflecting psychosocial scales for evaluating the human body and its abilities, share disproportionately in the product. The self-as-others-see-me or what Cooley (1902) called the "looking glass self" is not a mirror image of the person's body. The child (or an adult who has never seen a mirror) does not immediately recognize his reproduction in a mirror. As Darwin demonstrated many years ago, he first treats that mirror image as another person. Young children, and brighter chimpanzees, look behind the mirror to see more of that person. But only the human comes to recognize the image as himself and, ultimately, to view it with favor or disfavor as his perception is shaped by the social image derived from the reactions and treatments of other people (his "looking glass self").

The Shift from External Control to Self-Control of Social Behavior

How does behavior become liberated from the domination of physical states and immediate stimulation in infancy? How does self-regulation of behavior become possible? Again, certain landmarks stand out in the converging findings from developmental psychology.

Of course, the persons who care for the child (family or otherwise) play the earliest role, and their significance cannot be doubted. However, the role of the family and, in particular, the "child rearing practices" of parents, have been emphasized so one-sidedly in research that other trees in the forest of influences have been obscured. The parents' ideology and treatments of the child do make a difference in the development of responsibility for self and in treatments of others (e.g., aggressively, friendly, etc.; cf. Sears, Maccoby, and Levin, 1957). But child-rearing practices alone are only part of the picture and certainly cannot receive full credit or blame for differences in the socialization of children in different socioeconomic classes. For one thing, the "fashionable" and accepted ways of treating children in a higher class in one generation are apt to become "fashionable" in a lower-class setting within a decade or so (e.g., Bronfenbrenner, 1965). Nor can we be at all sure that the particular aspects of child rearing that investigators single out for study—for example, "permissiveness" vs. "authoritarian," "punitiveness," etc.—are in fact the most important aspects of child-parent relations (cf. Sears, 1960; Sewell, 1963; Eleanor Maccoby, 1965).

Nor is the adult role in self-development adequately represented simply by adult *treatment* of the child, as if the child were an inanimate object whose behavior was simply *shaped* as Rousseau would have shaped Emile. From the earliest months, adults and children interact—even though adults are the more powerful parties. Research has neglected this point, as noted by Dubin and Dubin (1965, p. 809) in reviewing research on children's social perception: "Only a handful of studies have focused attention on children's perceptions of parental behavior or on children's feelings about and reactions to parents' childbearing methods."

The implicit assumption that "what the parent does shapes the child's development" is being questioned as an oversimplification from several points of view. For example, John Campbell (1967) has emphasized the importance of the child's perception and evaluation of parental behavior about health and illness. He has found that a child's report that he has been scolded by his mother for endangering his health is more closely associated with his reactions to illness than whether the mother says she scolds him to take care of himself. (Children who recall being scolded are more likely to accept responsibility for being ill *and* to worry about being ill.)

Linked to the child-care situation and the portion of the social world that it occupies, accounts of self-development are focusing more and more upon the role of other adults, of mass media of communication, and on the company of agemates and other children—as indeed they should in a complex and rapidly changing world. Recent studies have shown that young children not only perceive the superior power of their parents but can also differentiate among other adults in terms of their power role (e.g., Bandura and Walters, 1963). In selecting "models" for their own behavior, therefore, children do not choose randomly or from sheer desire for what an adult possesses that the child does not. Their models are likely to be people with power to influence what happens.

However, neither coercive power of adults nor their loving care (whether within or outside the family) can receive full credit for self-regulation of behavior.

In a series of research, Piaget (1932) demonstrated the important role of interaction with agemates and other children. Piaget was interested in the development of moral behavior—that is, the adherence to moral rules defining what is acceptable, proper, and desirable behavior (see the definition of social norms on p. 141). He observed that very little children follow rules established by adults, but easily lapse from them when the adult is absent. He called this early period of following rules sheerly through the rewards for adherence and punishment for lapses as the stage of *heteronomy*—that is, control from outside by other people.

autonomy By questioning children about what was right in different situations and observing their activity in following the rules of simple games, Piaget concluded that the interaction among agemates was the primary setting in which the child could begin to see others as equals (instead of power figures) and to "take the role" of another person— hence to understand that adherence to rules involves give-and-take among people. Only in this way, concluded Piaget, can the child cease to see rules as something absolute handed down by authority and, instead, participate voluntarily in activities following rules autonomously in a reciprocal give-and-take with others (stage of *autonomy*). Through interaction with equals or near equals, the child comes to the understanding that rules can be changed when all parties agree and abide by the new rules.

The child's association with siblings as well as playmates may be the setting for the kind of learning that Piaget emphasized. His research brought the problem of moral development into articulation with accumulated findings on children's play activities. Furthermore, it served to correct the older view that moral development, as one aspect of socialization, represented the simple *reproduction* of adult values. Piaget used the terms "internalization" and "incorporation," but he did not mean thereby that the child simply swallowed adult values whole. Instead, he referred to the development of autonomy in regulating behavior relative to social rules.

The more recent studies of moral development by Kohlberg (1963) and others confirm the broad trend noted by Piaget from external control to self-regulation of social behavior according to social rules. However, by focusing on more-complex issues of morality, Kohlberg has shown that the shift from heteronomy to autonomous regulation of behavior is not accomplished all at once and that the social situation is invariably an important determinant on the interpretation of moral rules. His finding that older children come to regard social rules as their own personal standards, rather than as imposed by society, is well supported in other research on self formation. For example, Horowitz and Horowitz (1937) found many years ago that color prejudice was first justified by young children in terms of parental reactions and punishments but that older children regarded their views of minority groups as their *own personal view*, developed independently.

Self as a System
Continually Linked
with Object Relations

Gof

Despite the subjective experience that a person has, or his continuity from day to day, the maintenance of self-stability is closely related to continuity in the situations encountered by the person. The sociologist Erving Goffman (1959) emphasized this fact by calling the self in situation after situation a "collaborative manufacture" in which the expectations and treatments of other people continue to be at least as important as the conceptual relationships the person has already established. Even the perception of one's own body is profoundly affected by its relationship to the physical environment and by the relationship between its parts and proportions and social definitions (Wapner et al., 1965; especially papers by Wapner and Werner, Witkin, and Fisher and Cleveland).

The continuing link between self and environment in maintaining stability on the one hand, or producing instability and change, is a topic covered later in this chapter in the discussion of ego tensions and insecurity. During the life span, societies expect and demand changes of the person during adolescence, maturity, and old age which, coupled with bodily changes, produce temporary instabilities in the self system and, ordinarily, changes in its components.

THE SELF SYSTEM IN DIFFERENT SOCIOCULTURAL SETTNGS

The comparison of self-other attitudes in different cultures produces such contrasts that a theory is immediately contradicted if it proposes an inevitable blueprint for personality development. What is important and desirable for persons in one cultural setting may be entirely lacking in another. The relative importance of the "same" object (e.g., old persons, mothers, a social value) differs profoundly from one culture to the next. The challenge of cross-cultural comparison is to formulate generalizations that are not ethnocentric reflections of one's own culture but are applicable in accounting for the cultural variations. The undeniable fact of cultural variations is not caused by the operation of different psychological principles but rather is the product of the same psychological principles under varying conditions of social systems and cultures within them.

Especially in the 1930s and 1940s, many investigators became concerned with the empirical relationships between culture and human development. This "culture and personality" movement included diverse theoretical orientations, both about culture and about personality development (cf. Sargent and Smith, 1949). More recently, there has been some disillusionment about the fruitfulness of the "culture-personality" approach (cf. Lindesmith and Strauss, 1950; Sherif, 1963; Holtzman, 1965). Some of its shortcomings will illustrate reasons for this disenchantment:

1. Despite the aim of relating culture to the socialization process, the focus of interest was on a few specific cultural practices, often with little attention to others related to them. In particular, many studies focused exclusively on child-rearing practices and on those particular variables (e.g., weaning, toilet training, and punishment of the child) that Freudian psychoanalysis emphasized.

2. Investigators frequently gave too little attention to the status, class, and group classifications of respondents within the culture studied. Representative sampling of the population was perhaps too much to ask of research in societies in which population statistics were inadequate. However, the location of samples within the social system of the culture was essential for establishing empirical links between socialization and cultural environment. The problem was frequently ignored or glossed over. The result was particularly acute in studies of more complex societies and "national character," wherein generalizations based on the upper class or another single status group were sometimes completely inappropriate when extended to the entire culture.

3. On the psychological side, measurement techniques were used, often uncritically, simply because they were available and fashionable in Western societies. The "projective techniques" became particular victims of such grab-bag utilization. In reviewing 150 studies in 75 societies using projective techniques, Kaplan (1961) concluded that the generalizations warranted by the results were sparse indeed. As Holtzman (1965) remarked, "considering the present state of development of psychological techniques for personality assessment in our own culture, it is premature to expect much to be gained from the application of these techniques" in other cultures, especially nonliterate societies (p. 68).

What a Person Considers as Himself. Awareness of oneself as a person is not identical for all times, for all cultures, for man and woman, or for dominant- and minority-group members in the same culture. The continuing core of identity associated with one's personal name, as McDougall observed, often becomes "a handle by aid of which he gets hold of himself as a striver, a desirer, a refuser." A change in name, therefore, is not contemplated lightly. Traditionally, the woman in most Western societies changes her last name upon marriage, although many modern women with professional identity are reluctant to do so or retain their maiden names. Radcliffe-Brown (1922) reported that the Andamanese girl gets a new name at the time of first menstruation. This "flower name" (p. 119) marks her personal transition to adulthood. In one of the Melanesian groups, the act of marriage marks a turn in personal identity, according to Rivers (1924, p. 347), when "both man and woman change their names and assume a common name."

What the man or woman desires to be as a person reflects cultural definitions for the sex role. For example, a man in the United States today is expected to be a tangible "success" as a provider and as a wielder of influence and prestige measured in material possessions and public acclaim. Malinowski (1922) noted in contrast that the Trobriand Islander "wants, if he is a *man,* to achieve social distinction as a good gardener and a good worker in general" (p. 62). In Mexico according to Diaz-Guerrero (1965), to be a *man* in a family is to be unquestioned authority and to be a woman is to be pure and reconciled to obedience. The concept of masculinity, in turn, is glorified into a blend of sexual potency and disregard for female authority, expressed as *machismo,* which is evident in the attitudes and behavior of Mexican adolescent boys even in the United States (Sherif and Sherif, 1964).

The cultural definitions of masculinity-femininity are also shown in research findings in the United States that the physical differences in strength, size, etc., that do differentiate the sexes correlate negligibly with the degree of masculinity-femininity as culturally defined (Seward, 1946). The cultural character of sex roles is strikingly revealed in historical comparison of women's role, which has changed more rapidly than men's. Two hundred years ago, even fifty years ago, a man would have felt disgraced

to depend on his wife to support him, even through college. The ideal woman was "solitarie and withdrawne," one who could "boast of silence" and would "talke to few" (Stern, 1939, p. 203). Today, many a college graduate has a wife to thank for support of his education, and few expect their wives to be withdrawn or quiet.

Still, the customs of older patterns for the sex roles linger and are ingrained in the self systems of modern youth. Consider the question of who proposes marriage. Most college students would agree that the proposal is up to the man; a girl can scarcely imagine making the suggestion. However, this is not at all biologically determined. Among the Eddystone Islanders, Rivers (1926) reported that "the initiative in proposing marriage seems often to come from the women. If a girl takes a fancy to a man, she will carry off his basket and run with it to the bush. . . . Carrying off the basket is a definite sign of preference and, if the man is willing, he will begin negotiating with the parents of the girl" (p. 80).

Who a Person Considers Close to Himself. Certainly, the first persons with whom an individual becomes personally involved are usually within his own family. Family ties frequently continue throughout his lifetime, despite the great mobility and fragmentation that modern life brings to family life. Yet just whom he feels close to and whom he does not and how he regards these others and himself relative to them are matters that vary with particular kinship systems. In Mexico and other Spanish cultures, the person believes and feels that mother deserves the highest respect and devotion, even if concrete experiences between mother and offspring do not warrant it (Diaz-Guerrero, 1965). In other societies, both the range of persons who are considered "kin" and one's relationships to the various persons differ radically from those accepted in modern Western societies. In fact, Radcliffe-Brown (1941) noted that the narrowed scope of kinship ties in modern Great Britain would seem very "primitive" to the member of a society whose kinship system prescribes relationships with a much more extended and elaborate complex of kinfolk. In surveying the kinship systems of the world, he remarked: "If you will take time to study two or three hundred kinship systems from all parts of the world, you will be impressed, I think, by the great diversity they exhibit" (p. 17).

Nothing could be more naive, however, than to suppose that psychological "closeness" follows biological relationships, for the kinship system may include criteria about age, religious beliefs, and group membership as well as consanguinity. Malinowski reported that in one society tracing descent through the mother's line, the mother's brother had a relationship with her children much more like that of the Western "father" role, while the biological father had a relationship more like an "uncle" or "cousin." Davis and Warner (1937) concluded as follows: "Every concrete system of sociologically related kin diverges from the biological distances, sometimes moderately and sometimes radically" (p. 296).

Beyond such differences, however, the very importance of kinship relatedness and relatedness to other people varies tremendously. In some societies in which kinship relations are the most important human relationships, "a native may be at a complete loss how to treat a stranger who falls outside of the established rubrics" of kinship (Lowie, 1925, p. 8). In Mexico, family identity and solidarity are much greater than in the United States (Holtzman, 1965). Thus, the person sees his achievement as achievement by and through the family, whereas achievement in the United States is seen as residing in the person's own ability and initiative.

What is Related to a Person Varies in Range and Importance. Those consistent modes of behavior toward others called "competitive" and "cooperative" are presumed to be universal. Yet the objects of competition and the partners in cooperative relationships vary enormously in different cultures. Furthermore, the prevalence of one mode or the other in a society and which mode is considered more desirable, or even "normal," are culturally regulated. In a series of studies by Margaret Mead and her associates (1937), an attempt was made to characterize the modal behaviors in several cultures. In some (the Manus, Kwakiutl, and Ifugao) competitive behavior in interpersonal relations was modal. However, in other societies, cooperative behavior, in

varying situations and degrees, was more typical—for example, among the Samoans, Bathonga, Maori, and several American Indian groups (e.g., Zuni, Iroquois, and Dakota). In fact, among the Zuni Indians, "in the economic as well as the ceremonial field the aggressive, competitive, non-cooperative individual is regarded as the aberrant type" (Goldman, 1937). Thus, the range of persons and of activities in which competition or cooperative behavior is valued depends upon the cultural setting, despite individual differences in all cultures.

The varying significance of cultural elements, of social institutions, and of values and objects in different cultures is leading many psychologists to question the wisdom of attempting generalizations about personality development without first defining the reference scales prevailing in a culture (e.g., Holtzman, 1965; Diaz-Guerrero, 1965). They may study behaviors that are "called the same things" in different cultures, only to find that the significance and consequences are very different.

For example, Peck and Diaz-Guerrero (see Diaz-Guerrero, 1965) studied the concept of "respect" in Mexico, on the Mexican–U.S. border, and in the United States. Respectful behavior and personal feelings of respect were found in all locations, but their objects differed enormously, reflecting differences in ego-attitudes. For example, respect in the United States was accorded to individual achievement, individual merit, youth, middle-class people, and other objects reflecting socioeconomic criteria. In Mexico, respect was accorded women, old age, childhood, poor people, and beggars as well as rich people. Similarly studies in Mexico and the United States among college students indicate that interpersonal friendship ties were much more ego-involving for Mexican than for United States students. Disturbance of such relationships upset the Mexican considerably more than his United States counterpart.

The differing cultural significance of personal ties and social objects is not an abstract phenomenon. It is reflected in the specific perceptions and judgments of persons, in what concerns them, and what disturbs them personally. For example, in the earlier-mentioned study of Navaho In-

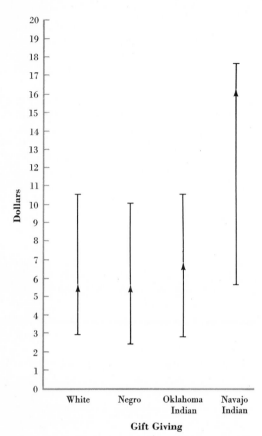

Fig. 17.13. Reference scales for cost of a gift for a loved one in four populations. Horizontal bars represent median judgments of the minimum and maximum expenditures for this purpose. The arrows represent median expenditures that would bring pride to the giver. (From Sherif and Sherif, p. 97, in S. B. Sells, ed., *Stimulus Determinants of Behavior*. New York: Ronald Press, 1963.)

dian and Oklahoma youth, Sherif and Sherif (1963) included questions about the amount of money that one would spend on a gift for a loved one, securing a range of judgments from the least one would spend to the most one could spend as well as the amount for a gift which one could feel glad to give. The Oklahoma youngsters gave highly similar answers, their judgments varying only slightly between 5 and 10 dollars for a gift that they could feel proud of. As Fig. 17.13 shows, the Navaho youngsters, who were economically much more deprived, felt the need to expend a much larger amount in order to maintain self-respect. This result is somewhat surprising when one considers the further finding that in expenditures for

clothing and leisure, as well as conceptions of material success, the less-advantaged Navaho youngsters consistently undershot the Oklahomans. However, the finding is not at all surprising in view of a well-documented tradition of gift giving among the Indians, in which *what* one gives and the *relationship* between the person and the giver are intimately felt as an expression of oneself.

BREAKDOWNS
IN THE SELF SYSTEM

The self or ego, then, is a developmental product consisting of interrelated attitudes that define the value of one's own body and its parts, and objects, tasks, persons, and groups in one's scheme of living. These ego-attitudes constitute the individual's particular mode of relatedness to specific situations in various capacities or roles. The individual's unique consistency from day to day and from situation to situation is dependent upon the continuity of these stabilized modes of relatedness (ego-attitudes). When they are disrupted, either through internal states or through loss of external referents, the organizing balance of his behavior is seriously disturbed. Behavior then becomes more variable, more floundering.

Functioning on a conceptual level, the human individual lives in both present and future, making his adjustments to the present in terms of goals set for years to come. When the level of functioning is lowered, the individual becomes more distractable, more stimulus-bound, and more subject to the ups and downs of his momentary whims. Such behavior by an adult is referred to as regression to a more childlike or a more primitive level. Such *ego-breakdowns* may be produced by the effects of alcohol, by serious brain injury, through the onslaughts of great passion in conflict with ego-attitudes high in the person's scheme of life, or by great disillusionment. A few illustrations will make the implications of ego breakdowns more concrete.

The conscientious objectors in the semi-starvation study during World War II ceased to care about appearing like gentlemen (pp. 68–70). They licked their plates in the presence of others. A few broke their pledge and stole food. Similarly, starving mothers in several countries of postwar Europe not only engaged in prostitution but sent their own children on the streets to solicit food. When the organism's balance is subject to the powerful onslaughts of physiological demands, sociogenic motives (ego-attitudes) tend to succumb. To be sure, there are unusual individuals who can uphold their ego values to the bitter end. But such heroic people are few.

During the depression years of the early 1930s, suicides increased not only among unemployed people but also among people who had lost title to their business or enough of their wealth so that their only prospect was to live in a manner that they had long considered beneath their level. The psychological effects of prolonged unemployment include breakdowns of some ego-attitudes, and a narrowing or even collapse of the ego. If unemployment is prolonged, the unemployed person may come to feel that he is useless and superfluous. Eisenberg and Lazarsfeld (1938) found that "the last stage of unemployment consists of a general narrowing of wants and needs. Yet there is a limit beyond which this narrowing cannot go; otherwise, a collapse occurs" (p. 378).

Brain injury and surgical procedures in which various portions of the frontal lobes are removed or connecting fibers are severed have consequences that clarify the formation of the self system as well as its breakdown. Goldstein and others presented cases in which brain damage produced regression to a more concrete level of reactions: the person became more easily distracted by external stimuli and his behavior was less consistent. According to Goldstein and Scheerer (1941), the abstract attitude is at the "basis for the *conscious* and *volitional* modes of behavior." Among such modes of behavior are the following: "To account for acts to oneself; to verbalize the account. . . ."; "To hold in mind simultaneously various aspects. . . ."; "To plan ahead ideationally; to assume an attitude towards 'mere possible' and to think and perform symbolically" (p. 4). On the other hand, the "concrete attitude" is characterized as follows: "We surrender to experiences of an unreflected character; we are confined to the immediate apprehension of the given thing or situation in its particular uniqueness" (p. 2).

PERSONAL STABILITY IS STABILITY OF SELF-ANCHORAGES

In specific contexts, we have stressed the motivational character of the ego or self. This motivational character is crucial in defining whatever integration the person achieves and whatever upsets of integration he undergoes, whether momentary or lasting.

As we have seen, the differentiation of one's own body from surrounding objects is the outcome of varied experiences which are heavily charged with affective qualities. In time, the body itself becomes a central anchorage in experiencing other things. Achieving psychological relatedness to the environment implies that one's self becomes part of an ordered time and space. There is satisfaction in this orderliness. When it is disrupted, we feel lost in both a physical and a psychological sense. Because of all the affectively charged experiences which culminate in a differentiated bodily self, the body inevitably becomes an object of value. Herein may lie the basis of self-love, which is often treated under the title of "narcissism." What is true of our attitudes toward our body and its parts is true also of other ego-attitudes. The referents of ego-attitudes are objects of value for the person. As established modes of relatedness, these attitudes function as *anchorages* for experience in relevant situations, lending to behavior a sustained directionality.

The importance of ego-attitudes in sustaining directionality and consistency in behavior becomes strikingly evident when the stability of relevant ego components is disrupted for some reason. The consequences of such disruption help us to understand the nature of the self system as well as the motivational character of ego-attitudes.

Loss of Stable Anchorages Arouses Ego-Tensions

It is helpful at this point to recall the general functional scheme presented in terms of twelve principles (Chapters 3 and 4). Perceiving, judging, appraising, and behaving take place within a frame of reference. Even in rather simple activities, ambiguity or unstructuredness of the stimulus field delays judgment time and renders ongoing activity rather tense and difficult. Even at a simple level, this is not a pleasant experience. The ego is no exception in regard to the tendency toward stability and the discomfiture of facing indeterminacy. Once it is formed, with all its diverse relatedness to objects, persons, and groups with varying affective ties, the ego tends to be anchored safely in its many roles and capacities. When these ties to the social environment are disrupted, we experience insecurity. In fact, the feeling of personal security consists mainly of stability in our relatedness to others and to events in various roles and capacities.

It is not a coincidence that when we face confusion and disorder in our social ties or feel "left out," our main concern becomes to *belong*—and to belong at any cost. The experiences of being left out or being marginal in situations that touch our self-concerns are painful. They may lead to unfortunate consequences. Belongingness in personal and group situations becomes a major goal of our strivings.

One telling piece of evidence about the sources of personal security comes from developmental findings on the experience of anxiety (as distinguished from simple fear). Human anxiety appears only after the bodily self has formed with some stability. In the psychiatrist Harry Stack Sullivan's words: "With the appearance of the self system or the self-dynamism, the child picks up a new piece of equipment which we technically call anxiety. Of the very unpleasant experiences which the infant can have we may say that there are generically two, pain and fear. Now comes the third, 'anxiety' " (1947, p. 9).

When the stability of ego-attitudes is disrupted, the consequence is *ego-tension*—the degree and consequences of which vary from case to case. The degree of ego-tension is proportional to the importance of the disrupted ego-attitude(s) in the self system. The higher the rank of the ego-attitude disrupted, the greater the ego-tension. The

hurt aroused is reflected in feelings of disillusionment, insecurity, feelings of loss in self-esteem, and (in more extreme cases) the shattering of the experience of self-identity.

We use *ego-tension* here as a generic term to refer to painful, unpleasant experiences such as anxiety, insecurity, personal inadequacy, aloneness, and shame, which can be accounted for only with reference to the ego system. When ego-tension is caused by failure or potential failure threatening our sense of adequacy or our sense of self-esteem, or by blockage of our goals, the appropriate designation may be *anxiety*. When the ego-tension arises from disruption of the stability in our relatedness or belongingness to the physical or social surroundings (when it is a consequence of blows to our status strivings), a more appropriate term may be *insecurity*. When ego-tension owes to physical or psychological isolation from individuals or groups we are identified with (viz., reference groups), the appropriate term may be *aloneness*. When ego-tension is aroused by a serious discrepancy between our actions and the level of our ego-values, the resulting product may be referred to as *shame*. In those cases in which the deviation is related to our few most central, fundamental ego-values, the resulting ego-tension may be termed the experience of *guilt* (Sherif and Harvey, 1952).

Ego-tensions also arise through *conflicts* between different attitudes. For example, ego-tensions result when we are caught in a situation which demands that we function simultaneously in contradictory roles. As we shall see in the next chapter, tensions of this kind are frequent in "casually patterned" societies with contradictory values existing side by side. They have been treated extensively by sociologists, psychologists, and novelists who are seriously concerned with the plight of modern man.

In the present social scene of flux, when conflicting ideologies and solutions are competing to win the hearts of man to their camp, ego-tensions are aroused also when the person is subjected to unwelcome propaganda and indoctrination counter to the values and commitments of his self system. As with any kind of ego-tension, here, too, the result is the disruption in the stability of the self system. Such disruption is hard to take. The person reacts—with every means at his disposal—to regain the stability. But restoring stability at any price or along any channels expedient at the time will not do. For the person, restoring stability or balance in his identity is, as a rule, restoring it at the level and along the channels required by ego-attitudes disrupted through such discrepant and obnoxious propaganda. Restoring psychological stability is not like the leveling of the water when the dam is broken. This timely topic of the effects of propaganda aimed at changing the individual's attitudes will be discussed in Chapter 21, after the discussion of reference groups in the next chapters.

An Experimental Demonstration of Insecurity

Proceeding on the basis of the theoretical formulation summarized in this chapter, Sherif and Harvey (1952) produced situational insecurity experimentally by eliminating external anchorages in the situation surrounding the subjects. The general hypothesis of the experiment was that the performance of a task under conditions that lacked stable external anchorages would result in increased variability in behavior, such as the floundering frequently observed when ego ties are disrupted.

The problem was to produce situational insecurity through elimination of spatial anchorages, thus affecting the stability of some of the earliest ego relationships, namely, spatial anchoring of the self. Variability of behavior was tapped through simple judgments, with the assumption that even complicated motivational states are reflected in such reactions when the stimulus situation lacks objective structure (see Chapter 4).

The autokinetic situation was utilized (see pp. 202 f.). Through preliminary trials, three conditions representing three degrees of situational uncertainty were standardized. Under Condition A, the subjects were taken to their seats in an ordinary experimental room the proportions of which they glimpsed briefly. Then 50 judgments of ex-

tent of autokinetic movement were obtained from each subject. Under Conditions B and C, judgments were obtained after the subjects had performed the rather difficult task of locating their seats in a large hall in pitch-black darkness. In Condition C, all possible anchorages were eliminated. In fact, obstacles were introduced that hindered the subject's smooth orientation. (See Fig. 17.14 for the experimental setup in condition C.) He had to proceed from the door, mount and descend stairs, and continue at an angle to his seat entirely on the basis of verbal instructions. The experimenter did not even speak to him after he entered the room. These procedures were so effective in eliminating anchorages under Condition C that some individuals became thoroughly disoriented. They thought they were moving West while they were actually moving East. Their verbal reactions revealed this disorientation and uncertainty: "Felt helpless and ill at ease—was very puzzled"; "Completely confused. Lost as heck." Condition B was intermediary between A and C in availability of anchorages for orientation before the autokinetic sessions started.

Sixty students took part in the experiment. Under all three experimental conditions, each subject took part first in an individual session and later in a group session with another subject. There were 10 pairs of subjects under each of the three experimental conditions.

In line with the hypotheses, the results revealed that:

1. The more uncertain the situation, the greater the range within which judgmental reactions were scattered, that is, the greater the variability of behavior (see Fig. 17.15).
2. The more uncertain the situation, the greater the magnitude of the norm or standard around which judgments were distributed (that is, autokinetic movement was greater).
3. The more uncertain the situation, the greater the individual differences in the ranges and norm established alone.
4. The more uncertain the situation, the greater the tendency to converge toward the judgments of another person in the social situation.

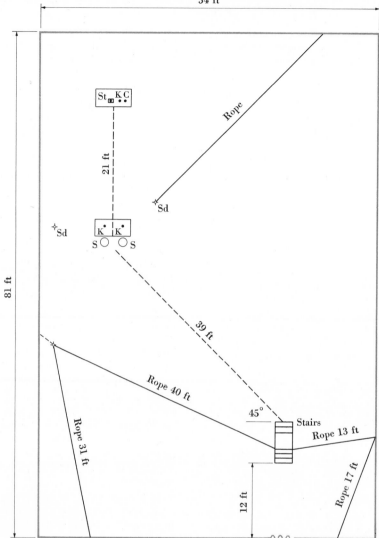

Fig. 17.14. Disposition of the experimental condition depriving subjects of most anchorages in the study of insecurity. (Adapted from M. Sherif and O. J. Harvey, 1952. A study of ego functioning: Elimination of stable anchorages in individual and group situations. *Sociometry,* **15,** 272–305.)

Measuring Personal Insecurity Through Variability of Reactions

In the experiment just reported, it was established that judgments and other reactions under experimentally created conditions of situational uncertainty become markedly more variable. It was reasonable to predict that persons who were already persistently insecure and floundering in search of stable ties in actual life would exhibit more variable reactions to an unstructured situation than would more "typical" or "normal" persons.

The hypothesis was, therefore, that individuals whose behavior and test performance revealed that they are rather characteristically anxious and insecure would give judgments of autokinetic movement that differed significantly in variability from the judgments of subjects from a "normal" population.

The hypothesis was tested in an experiment carried out by Virgil T. Hill (1952).

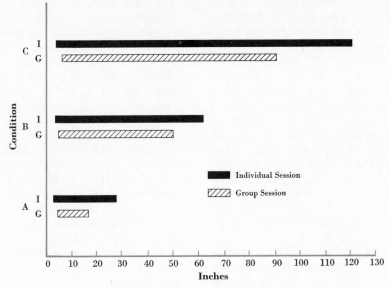

Fig. 17.15. Spread of individual judgment ranges under Conditions A, B, and C in individual and social situations. Condition A provided the most and C the fewest anchorages. (Adapted from M. Sherif and O. J. Harvey, 1952. A study in ego functioning: Elimination of stable anchorages in individual and group situations. *Sociometry*, **15**, 272–305.)

There were nine experimental subjects who were referred to a clinic of pupil guidance because of their insecurity, emotional instability, and other disordered personality manifestations. The control subjects were nine individuals of about the same age, judged to be normal. Ninety-eight judgments of extent of autokinetic movement were obtained from each subject in two alone sessions.

The results showed strikingly greater variability in the judgments of the "insecure" subjects than in those of the "normal" subjects. The smallest variability shown by the insecure subjects was far greater than the largest shown by the control subjects. In other words, the results gave two different and distinct distributions of behavioral variability. The quantitative results gained further support from the more uneasy and protesting behavior manifested by the insecure subjects in the autokinetic situation.

**Implications
for Insecurity
on a Wider Scale**

Heightened variability in behavior following the disruption of accustomed environ-

mental anchors is not confined to experimental situations or to persons enduring persistent anxiety. A mature and ordinarily "collected" person may engage in unusual or even bizarre behavior when suddenly plunged into total darkness, exposed to an earthquake, or simply placed in unfamiliar surroundings.

For example, a botany professor looking for specimens in a rugged timber area one morning suddenly realized that he was in unfamiliar terrain with no idea of how to retrace his steps. Although he knew the rules about fire building and its possible dangers, by afternon he was sufficiently disturbed to start a signal fire and allow it to get out of control. Fleeing the fire in panic, he stumbled onto a road only a short distance from the "impenetrable forest" where he had felt so lost. The fire burned five acres of timber (*New York Times,* August 9, 1952, p. 11).

The implications of insecurity on the part of many people are twofold: they may engage in behavior that is highly unusual for them and they are much more susceptible to guideposts and dictums from other people. It may be objected that the examples given of these tendencies all involved the elimination of stable anchorages in the environment, when the person was alone or on his own to deal with the situation. However, there is evidence that insecurity produced by other self-concerns when the person is with other people has similar consequences.

Walters, Marshall, and Shooter (1960) compared the effects of the experimenter's influence on judgments of autokinetic movement after subjects had either been socially isolated, or had taken certain tests, or had taken the tests in a situation designed to arouse their anxiety about their abilities. Regardless of whether they had been isolated, subjects who had taken the tests in anxiety-arousing situations were influenced significantly more by the experimenter than were other subjects (whether isolated or not). This experiment indicates that the experience of insecurity or anxiety is sufficient to increase susceptibility to social influence. Further, the comparison of isolated and nonisolated subjects suggests that certain of the unusual forms of behavior observed in other experiments on "sensory deprivation" (e.g., Scott *et al.,* 1959)

may have been the product of ego-tensions aroused by loss of stable anchors when the subject was placed in the experimental environment designed to deprive him of sensory inputs. While prolonged reduction of visual, auditory, and tactual stimuli doubtless requires a period of adaptation for "normal" sensory functioning, some of the unusual modes of behavior reported from the sensory-deprivation studies reflect the person's ego-tensions in such an unusual situation. (Another indication comes from the comparison of experimental subjects when they do or do not have a "panic button" to obtain release from the situation.)

Thus there is experimental evidence to support observations that when ego ties are disrupted on a wide scale, people may engage in forms of behavior highly unusual and atypical and are, at the same time, prone to be influenced by others who offer clear-cut guides for action, including demagogues. Further implications of widespread insecurity are discussed in Chapters 23 and 24 on collective interaction and the rise of social movements.

18

Reference Groups:
Anchor Groups
for the Person's Ego-Involvements

Major Topics of the Chapter

Reference group as anchor group: unequivocal definition of concept

Psychological and sociological bases of the
concept

Dissatisfaction with prevailing social arrangements: alienation

Breakdown or conflict of stable social
anchors

Normlessness

Search for new alternatives: rise of social
groups and movements

Availability of multiple reference groups

Psychological basis: man's conceptual level
of functioning

Applications of reference group concept

A note on the concept in view of ambiguous
usages

REFERENCE GROUPS
AS ANCHORS
FOR THE PERSON'S RELATEDNESS

No man is an island. As documented in the last chapter, the person's ties and his commitments and identifications that give goal-directedness to his aspirations and other ego concerns are psychological products related to other people in one way or another. Certain persons and groups have special salience in the derivation and functioning of these ego-attitudes. The last chapter defined the self system and ego-attitudes, giving examples of their involvement in various psychological activities. In this chapter, we are concerned with persons and groups that have special salience for the person. They have been assigned a special designation: *reference groups* and the associated concepts of *reference person* (*reference idol*) and *reference set*.

Reference groups are those groups to which the individual relates himself as a member or aspires to relate himself psychologically.

The concept of reference groups is used to designate the source from which the person derives his goals and standards for erecting his aspirations and gauging his performance. Thus reference groups define aspirations that regulate the person's feel-ings of success and failure in related activities.

This particular definition of the reference group concept has been widely adopted since its formulation in the first edition of this book in 1948. The concept was formulated on the basis of generalizations verified in experiments on the effects of major anchors in the processes of judgment and perception. Just as a salient stimulus anchors the pattern of comparisons among stimuli in laboratory studies, so the person's reference group and its values serve an anchoring function in his evaluations in social relations. It will be recalled that anchors (reference points) were defined as weighty factors in shaping experience and behavior (pp. 72–80).

The following are examples of definitions from the social-psychological literature in line with that just presented:

Any group with which an individual identifies himself such that he tends to use the group as a standard for self evaluation and as a source of his personal values and goals. The reference groups of the individual may include both membership groups and groups to which he aspires to belong (Krech, Crutchfield, and Ballachey, 1962, p. 102).

A reference group is thus any group with which a person psychologically identifies himself or in relation to which he thinks of himself (Lindesmith and Strauss, 1956, p. 241).

Note that the concept of reference group is a social-psychological concept and is defined in terms of the *person's* relatedness either as an actual or aspiring member of a group. It is, therefore, clearly distinguishable from the definition of group (p. 131), which is sociological (that is, refers to the pattern of interaction among individuals). There are cases in which a person may be a registered member or physically present in a group day in and day out, but is doing everything in his power to identify with and belong to another group whose members may not even know of his existence.

A reference group may be a nonmembership group for the person as well as a membership group (cf. Merton, 1956, pp. 236 ff.; pp. 288–297). Merton and Kitt (Rossi) analyzed a mass of unrelated attitude data from the studies of the *American Soldier* during World War II, and showed how the concept of reference group as membership or nonmembership group brought coherence to a variety of specific findings.

The definition of *reference person* takes note of the fact that the source of the person's values and aspirations in some respects may be a loved or idolized person instead of a group. *Reference set* is appropriately used when the person's attitudes and goals are anchored in a category of people that are not, properly speaking, a group. Whether the anchorage is a group, a person, or a social category (e.g., women, a social class, an ethnic stratum) is, of course, very important in actual research. If the anchorage is a group, one would start by studying the group in question to learn its organization and values before one determined how the person viewed that group, where he stands relative to it, and so on.

PSYCHOLOGICAL AND SOCIOLOGICAL BASES OF THE CONCEPT

At first consideration, the reader who identifies himself with groups of which he is actually a part (his family, his friends, his church, fraternity, school, or political group) may find it hair-splitting to differentiate membership and nonmembership reference groups. But there are individuals who see the grass greener in groups other than their own—in many cases with objective justification for their desire. There are alienated individuals who find their lot within their own group unrewarding or unbearable for one reason or another and who do aspire to move toward what they see as greener pastures. Such persons long to change their membership and do shift their identification to other groups that hold promise of better life.

In the modern world, there are a good many persons in complex societies with a high rate of geographical mobility who are caught by the circumstances of location, economics, or politics, and find themselves at school or at work with people at great odds with their strong preference, had they any choice in the matter.

In societies changing at an accelerated pace, and in societies under colonial subjugation or oppressive authority, yearnings to change prevailing social and political affiliations increasingly become the order of the day (Chapter 24). Of course, yearning for change in identification is not sufficient, for there must be avenues of change and an awakening to the state of existing social arrangements. If the walls are impregnable, if there are no alternatives available, the strongest yearnings will not produce change in actual membership.

These are illustrations of individuals for whom the groups to which they relate themselves inwardly or aspire to belong are not their actual membership groups. In brief, then, reference groups may be one's actual membership groups. They are one and the same, as a rule, in stable and homogeneous strata of society in relatively normal and prosperous periods. But there are periods, as in the present social scene, when old and new values are in conflict, as well as the loyalties each requires. There are social settings in which the *haves* and *have nots* in material comforts, in prestige, and in opportunity and available privileges are strikingly discrepant and even worlds apart. When such conditions prevail and it dawns on many individuals that they can change their lot, the state of their identifications can be best characterized in terms of the reference group concept.

With the above illustrations as orientation, we can proceed to sociological and psychological bases that have made the reference group concept a useful conceptual tool for handling various social-psychological topics. The first two are basically sociological, with psychological consequences, while the third is psychological.

Dissatisfaction with Prevailing Conformities and Social Arrangements: Alienation

The problem of *alienation* has been one of the persistent problems in sociology for a century, beginning with the analysis by Marx (cf. Coser and Rosenberg, 1964, pp. 519–525). Marx analyzed the wage earner's alienation from the products of his labor and his powerlessness in the scheme of things, as well as other forms of estrangement in social relations. In recent years, the concept has come to the foreground in the work of an increasing number of social scientists in a variety of contexts (Fromm, 1955; Merton, 1946; Seeman, 1959). There have been efforts to specify the various meanings attached to the concept of alienation (e.g., Seeman, 1959). There have also been attempts to classify reactions to alienation into different "types" (Parsons, Bales, and Shils, 1953). A number of sociologists have attempted to measure alienation, typically through a set or sets of questions that are believed to include typical reactions to alienation (Nettler, 1957; Neal and Rettig, 1967).

In all its usages, there is a common denominator to the concept of alienation. Alienation refers to the psychological state of dissatisfaction with and estrangement from the prevailing social arrangements in which the individual lives and the norms or values that regulate these arrangements. This state is a reaction to prevailing social conditions.

For example, the different meanings of alienation as used in the sociological literature include *powerlessness, meaninglessness, normlessness, isolation,* and *self estrangement* (Seeman, 1959). Such terms express dissatisfaction with or breaking off from the prevailing state of things, as a result of imbalance, inequity, or undue burdens placed on the individual by social arrangements and dysfunctional, obsolete norms or practices. Because the exact conditions that give rise to such dissatisfaction are as varied as the social conditions faced by various individuals in a society, the attempt to catalogue the varieties of alienation or reactions to alienation in a classificatory scheme is bound to be a thankless task. It will always be easy to find another variety.

For example, to the meanings listed above, we might add "self-hatred" toward one's own group that is found among some members of minority groups (e.g., some Negroes or Jews; Lewin, 1948). The common thread in the analysis of self-hatred by various authors is that the individual finds his membership in a minority group a handicap for attaining opportunities and privileges enjoyed by the dominant group. He cannot become a member of the dominant group and sees his own group as the block to his aspirations. Self-hatred is but one more case of alienation and one could easily find others not ordinarily included in lists such as that given above.

A more fruitful approach to the problem of alienation may be to relate the person's dissatisfaction to the specific social conditions that produced it and then to follow its consequences over time. Having dislodged himself psychologically from erstwhile ties with his actual membership group and allegiance to its role system and norms, the alienated person *then* lacks stable anchors and stable guides to action. As was concluded at the end of the last chapter (pp. 411 ff.), this is a condition conducive to being "up in the air," restless and confused. It is conducive to wide fluctuations in behavior, some of which may deviate from the bounds of acceptable behavior. This is the state of "normlessness" referred to above. If a sufficient number of individuals are in the same predicament, there is a state of *anomie* as described so forcefully by the sociologist Durkheim (1951) and as further analyzed by Merton (1956). In other words, the state of normlessness is a product of alienation and follows it in the sequence of time.

But, as we have seen, being torn from stable anchors or becoming detached from them is psychologically painful. The state of normlessness is not comfortable, even though it may involve indulgence at the moment in hitherto forbidden activities. In the long term, stability of the person's self-identity and its continuity from day to day consist in no small part of his stable and continuing social ties and adherence to norms that he cherishes. Disruption or shattering of such ego components can produce insecurity and anxiety. Thus a state of normlessness cannot be endured indefinitely.

One of the most acute motivational-emotional tensions for a person to endure is the loss of stable ties to others and the lack of any values that can give some sort of integration to his feelings about himself. To lack a sense of belongingness, to feel isolated from people around one, to see little or nothing left to hang on to, arouses strivings to restore one's ties or to re-establish new bearings, to find new values or idols to uphold. Underlying these strivings is the tendency, even in very simple situations and activities, toward psychological patterning (Proposition 6). The self system is no exception to this tendency. If new self-identity with others is not actualized, if the person must continue to flounder about in search of it despite his resort to all kinds of measures (realistic or unrealistic) and can see nothing but a dead end to further effort, the last resort may be suicide, as conceptualized by Durkheim (1951).

But, in the majority of cases, human beings do not succumb to such desperate measures as suicide. They strive instead in more viable ways to reach a new stabilization for their lost identity and fortunes. These viable ways are various, and their variety depends on the particular social conditions that prevail around the person, the sociocultural background of the conditions, and the *avenues available* on the current scene. If these factors are such that the person sees others afflicted with the same feelings of alienation, he is likely to gravitate toward them. There is truth in the old saying that "misery loves company."

Therefore, the state of normlessness or anomie is seldom the end of the road. If the alienated are sufficiently numerous, and if they can interact, exchange gripes, and formulate their protest, what was initially normlessness may be the basis for the rise of a social movement, as we shall see in Chapter 24. If, on the other hand, avenues

for open protest and action are barred by brute force of existing order, alienated people in the same boat are more likely to interact toward retreat from the conditions that provoke their agony. Revivalist orgies or new religious movements (such as that of Father Divine during the Great Depression of the 1930s) are examples.

The search and the drift toward new groups as well as the formation of groups by alienated persons also occur in less dramatic circumstances. When societies are changing rapidly or are in a state of flux, substantial portions of the younger generation become alienated from the values of the older generation. When social conditions permit, young people gravitate toward one another to form their own reference groups, at least during their transition to adulthood. One product of the sequence from alienation toward new belongingness is what is referred to as "youth culture" or "youth subculture," as manifested in distinctive lingo, in style, and in form of expression as well as in distinctive action and protests.

In brief: especially in modern times, the conditions of living have produced alienation for large numbers of people, a state that is often associated with discrepancies between membership groups and reference groups.

Availability
of Multiple Reference Groups

In extremely simple societies or in societies with virtually no social mobility, the reference group concept adds very little to an analysis based on the effects of membership in groups. No matter how large the number of alienated individuals and no matter how great the degree of alienation, strivings toward change from one's membership classification are unlikely to find fruition as long as social mobility is barred because of rigid group or class lines. For example, in the eighteenth and early nineteenth century in the United States, there were more formidable barriers to aspirations by American Negroes toward the white upper class (Frazier, 1957). The reality of such barriers is evident in the fact that until the mid-twentieth century, the majority of Negro leaders expressing the hopes of their people, and most who maintained their leadership, were leaders who accommodated to white power, in contrast to the militant leaders on the contemporary scene (Killian, 1962; Killian and Grigg, 1964).

Thus the existence of alternatives or multiple groups is a prerequisite sociological basis for most phenomena with which the reference group concept deals. Social mobility or its possibility across groups and classes (i.e., horizontal and vertical mobility) produces problems in reference group identifications (cf. Hartley, 1951; Lipset and Bendix, 1959; Merton, 1956; Williams, 1960).

In highly differentiated and complex modern societies, people face another kind of reference group problem. Even those who are not alienated from their "primary groups" (such as the family) have not one but many reference groups. In his multiple reference groups and reference sets, the person has varied roles. For example, the person is father (or mother) in the family; he is also a church member contributing to charity and serving on committees; he is a member of a Chamber of Commerce promoting business in the community or of a labor union, as the case may be; he is a member of a profession or a trade; he is a citizen of a state and country with obligations to serve it in various capacities. These different reference groups (which are also membership groups) form a matrix defining the person's roles in various situations and capacities.

While the person's roles in his multiple groups need not necessarily conflict, the fact remains that in modern societies undergoing change (particularly those that are in the sociologist Robert Lynd's apt phrase, "casually patterned") or that maintain the old along with the new, the individual's roles in multiple groups and the values of these groups may be incompatible.

If multiple memberships are compatible, the person's role in one is congruent with his other roles in others, and the values from his various groups are mutually supportive. But if they are incompatible, the individual either has to keep his roles and associated attitudes in separate compartments as he moves from situation to situation, or he will be exposed to contradictory and conflicting situations.

Almost everyone faces a situation now

and then when contradictory roles and values from two different reference groups are called upon in the same situation. One illustration is the plight of the modern woman who simultaneously relates herself to her family as mother, her work as a professional person, her women friends, and various community groups. Shifting gears rapidly as she moves from the home, to work, and to community and social gatherings, she may keep these roles separate much of the time. However, sooner or later, she is likely to face a stiuation in which two or more are aroused simultaneously and are incompatible. Then, she may well find herself torn between being a good mother and a professional person, or between being accepted by her women friends and pursuing her other activities.

Obviously, the problem of multiple reference groups poses the problem of the relative importance of various groups for the person and is, therefore, pertinent to the earlier discussion (Chapter 17) about consistency-inconsistency of social behavior. We frequently find inconsistency in behavior relative to problems of desegregation which is greatly clarified by reference group analysis.

The person may tolerate desegregation within the fold of one reference group while also identifying with another reference group that has supremacy premises. Thus his behavior can be inconsistent as he moves from the orbit of one reference group to the orbit of another.

In short, the existence of multiple groups and, particularly, of social mobility produces a need for the reference group concept in handling discrepancies between membership and reference groups and in locating the sources of the person's values as manifested by his actions in various situations.

Psychological Basis: Man's Conceptual Level of Functioning

Psychologically, the reference group concept is based on man's capacity to relate himself to persons and groups that are not immediately present in his environment or that may even be distant geographically and in time (past or future). Very young children form identifications with their face-to-face groups early (e.g., family and playmates), but considerable development of conceptual thought is required before they respond to groups and institutions that are not face-to-face. Below the human level, the concept of reference groups is simply unnecessary, as the well-known investigator of animal behavior J. P. Scott (1953) has emphasized. The animals' social relations are confined to perceptual interaction.

Through conceptual thought, a man can relate himself to persons whom he has never seen and to groups that do not know of his existence. We take this capacity so much for granted that many times it is simply assumed in analysis of man's group relations. Yet, its importance is evident when we find a person located physically from day to day among people and yet behaving quite differently from them in important respects. If he has adopted a different reference group, he has also adopted attitudes and goals more appropriate to the way of life in that group than in his own. The sociologist Merton (1956) called this phenomenon "anticipatory socialization." When anticipating or desiring membership in another group, the person selectively develops skills, attitudes, and modes of behavior appropriate to such membership.

APPLICATIONS OF REFERENCE GROUP CONCEPT

After World War II in the late 1940s, the concept of reference group as defined here became a tool for unifying a number of problems that had previously been considered separate. We have seen that the concept specifies more precisely the etiology of behaviors that, by any standard, are inconsistent—for example, why the same person practices desegregation in one setting and then participates in segregationist actions when his identification as a member of the "superior race" is aroused. Here, we shall exemplify certain problems that were considered special topics prior to reference group analysis. The reference group concept provided a tool that could be used efficiently in dealing with these diverse problems.

A Note on the Reference Group Concept.

If reference group analysis is to be unambiguous, the concept cannot mean all things to all people. Unfortunately, the concept has sometimes been used as a blanket term to explain anything and everything, and some serious researchers have tolerated its use in two entirely different senses.

In part of the literature, the reference group concept is used to refer to a group to which the person relates himself psychologically as a member or to which he aspires to be a member, in line with the definition here. In another part of the literature, this definition is used along with another definition of reference group as any group that is involved in making a comparison. In the first instance, it is said that the reference group serves a "normative function." In the second, it is said that the reference group serves a "comparison function."

There is no denying that when an individual judges or evaluates any object (whether it is a weight, a line, or a social object), he compares it with others that he has experienced or that are presented to him in the laboratory (Sherif, 1936; Volkmann, 1951; Helson, 1959). Such a comparison object certainly has an influence on the behavioral outcome. All judgments are relational affairs, as we have seen. A person cannot render a judgment unless he compares two or more objects—whether he is conscious of it or not. Therefore, there is no need to give a special name to the comparison object. As Kelley (1952, 1965) remarked in discussing the confusion in use of the term reference group, "Comparison groups are, after all, only one of many kinds of comparison points within referential frameworks."

When the person consistently uses one object as the standard for comparing others (regardless of whether he is aware of it), it makes sense to conceptualize what that standard is, particularly if it is a real group or a real category of people. The person's reference group(s) or sets designate such anchors. Such a concept lends predictability to the analysis: If a particular group is a major anchor for the individual's comparisons, his judgments and evaluations, his comparisons of relevant stimuli, and his experiences of success or failure become more consistent and hence predictable in terms of his reference group.

Reference group analysis stems directly from the frame of reference formulation, as explicitly stated by Hyman (1942), who first used the term. As we have seen, the frame of reference formulation posits that the character of experience (hence, behavior) is patterned by major anchors operative at the time (pp. 72–80). The effectiveness of reference group analysis is contingent upon unequivocal designation of such major anchors for psychological activity.

The proper use of the concept reference group is to designate groups that consistently anchor the person's experience and behavior in relevant situations. Any other group serving as a comparison point for his judgments or evaluations can be referred to as a *comparison* group. The use of a central concept such as reference group in two different senses contributes only to confusion and ambiguity about the referents (Sampson, 1961).

While the reference group concept is relatively recent, the social phenomena and behaviors handled through the use of the concept are not new. They were described by social scientists before there was such a concept and were analyzed with various kindred concepts that overlap the denotation of reference group (cf. Merton, 1956, pp. 275–280). For example, the sociologist Charles H. Cooley (1909) differentiated among the groups with which the person associated by singling out "primary groups"—groups "that are fundamental in forming the social nature and ideals of the individual." Certain aspects of reference group phenomena were vividly described through individuals caught in the throes of upward mobility and exhibiting adaptive or maladaptive moves to be in the shoes of the upper-class set. Veblen's *The Theory of the Leisure Class* (1899) and Molière's *Le Bourgeois Gentilhomme* provide examples. Such accounts are particularly relevant in showing that the person's reference group is not merely a passing standard for comparison, but an ever-present anchor for him in his expenditures, in acquiring possessions, in regulating his manners and tastes, in acquiring "culture," and in his strivings.

One of the most influential theories of criminal behavior has been Edwin H. Sutherland's theory of "differential association" (1947) and its subsequent specifica-

tion as *differential identification* with persons and groups that endorse criminal behavior (Glazer, 1956). As Robert Clark (1965) has observed, the differential association theory of criminal behavior and the acceptance of associated values is "a special case . . . of reference group theory." Again, note that although the criminal doubtless compares himself with noncriminal groups, including law-enforcement officers, his reference groups and persons who endorse criminal values provide consistent anchors for his reactions, including comparisons with those noncriminal persons.

**Caught Between Two
Reference Groups:
Marginality**

Both sociological and psychological literature have presented cases of marginality, a term that derives its meaning from the individual's location on the margin between two related groups (Stonequist, 1937; Lewin, 1948). The most frequent examples of marginality involved persons from a minority ethnic, religious, or color group who are attracted by the values and rewards of the dominant group but are unable either to gain acceptance in the dominant group or to break completely from their minority identification. As a result, they are "betwixt and between." By conceiving of this situation as a special case for reference group analysis, the marginal person's inner conflicts and insecurity are readily understandable. He cannot ignore either reference group, yet the incompatibility and conflict of their values and demands upon him places him repeatedly in situations in which he is pushed one way and pulled another—a process all the more painful because his ties are shaky with both sides.

The advantage of taking marginality as a special case for reference group analysis is that similar phenomena are found in large organizations in which the person's role is not "marginal" in any functional sense. For example, the *foreman* in industry certainly is not marginal in the organization but he faces problems similar to the "marginal man." He ordinarily rises from the ranks of workers, but his role is viewed both by workers and by management as management's representative. (Management calls him the "grass roots level of management" while workers call him the "boss." Roethlisberger, 1945; Whyte and Gardner, 1945). However, he is not at the level of higher management and cannot disclaim his worker background. As a result, the foreman repeatedly faces the conundrum of "either getting the worker's cooperation and being 'disloyal' to management or of incurring the resentment and overt opposition of his subordinates" (Roethlisberger, 1945, p. 290). The foreman feels himself betwixt and between the workers and management. In the words of one foreman: "It's a hell of a situation because I get on edge and blow my top and say things that I really didn't mean to say" (Whyte and Gardner, 1945, p. 20).

The noncommissioned officer in military organization is another role that can be analyzed in terms of conflicting reference groups. In the American Soldier studies of World War II, Stouffer and his associates (1949) reported that the "noncom finds himself in conflict situations involving official responsibility to his officers on one hand and unofficial obligations to the other enlisted men on the other hand."

The conflicting expectations and demands of different reference groups are similarly found in other large organizations —for example, in educational institutions. Educational administrators in public schools or universities occupy roles that involve cross-pressures from different reference groups, particularly if they have themselves been faculty members. Their positions are complicated by the fact that they must perceive the norms and goals of both faculty and higher administrative bodies accurately and make decisions in cases of their conflict.

Getzels (1963) has presented evidence that school superintendents do not always perceive the expectations of their school boards accurately. Furthermore, Gross, Mason, and McEachern (1958) report considerable conflict between the expectations of teachers and of school board members. For example, most teachers and superintendents expect the superintendent to defend teachers against community attacks when they express controversial views and to advance their salaries, while refraining from prying into their personal lives. Most

board members in this study expected the reverse. On the other hand, most superintendents expected the board to appoint teachers only on their recommendations and to leave administrative problems to them, while board members felt that administrative problems were also their concern and did not feel bound by superintendents' recommendations for teachers.

An analysis of marginality and of roles in formal organizations in terms of the individual's multiple reference groups brings a variety of specific problems into conceptual coherence, as we shall see later in this chapter when we consider problems of decision-making and choice.

Discrepancies of Status in Different Reference Groups: Status Equilibration

When the individual relates himself to multiple groups, he often faces the problem that his status is quite different in two groups. In analyzing the relationships between different status positions, the sociologist Benoit-Smullyan suggested that "there is a real tendency for the different types of status to reach a common level" (1944, p. 160). In a country such as the United States, in which financial status and its symbols are very important, examples of this tendency often involve money. For example, a millionaire whose financial status is very high teams up with a public relations expert to win respect also as a public servant or patron of the arts, or he endows a foundation or library in order to improve his status among those who prize education.

In a study with college students, Fenchel, Monderer, and Hartley (1951) determined status and upward status strivings in five significant reference groups. They found that there was a tendency toward equilibration, as revealed in significantly greater strivings for status relative to groups in which the person had lower standing. "The results indicate a definite tendency for the status ratings to approach a common high anchorage level within the individual's status structure, as defined by his different reference groups" (p. 477).

In short, *there is a tendency to strive toward consistency in one's position rela-*

tive to different reference groups. As long as active moves hold promise of bringing discrepant statuses into line, the individual has the possibility of reconciling the contradictions he experiences from discrepant statuses. However, when, for example, he has a higher-than-average educational level and meets irremediable obstacles in attaining a commensurately high occupational level, the result may be insufferable for the person. Tuckman and Kleiner (1962) found that an index of the discrepancy between a person's relative status educationally and occupationally predicted the incidence of schizophrenia better than measures of social class (e.g., occupation or place of residence). Great discrepancies were associated with a higher rate of incidence both for whites and Negroes (for whom the general rate was higher and who suffer status discrepancies in other respects as well).

Other Applications. One of the most fruitful applications of reference group analysis in recent years has been in the study of attitude change (Chapters 19, 21). In the remainder of this chapter, experiments will be summarized showing how the person erects aspirations using his reference group as anchor and how the level of his reference group relative to others affects his own performance. Then reference group analysis will be applied to certain problems of decision making or choice. In all of these areas of application, including attitude change, one advantage of the reference group concept is that it unifies numerous problems that are apparently separate. The person's attitudes, aspirations, and goals related to his reference groups are manifold, not discrete. Therefore, significant changes in his reference group affect not just one, but a complex of his behaviors. His use of the perspective of his reference group in a variety of relevant situations means that his reactions to a host of different stimuli are anchored by that perspective. For example, the study of what people considered funny remained a matter largely for conjecture until the topic was related to reference groups (La Fave, 1961). La Fave found that one's sense of humor was aroused much more by jokes that ridiculed persons with a religion different than one's own. Priest (1966) showed the generality of reference group analysis by study-

ing humor aroused by jokes about Goldwater and Johnson on the day of the 1964 presidential election among college students supporting each candidate. Johnson supporters enjoyed jokes about Goldwater, and Goldwater supporters enjoyed jokes about Johnson.

THE LABORATORY ANALYSIS OF REFERENCE GROUP PROCESS

The Chapman-Volkmann Experiment

Previously, we have had occasion to refer to studies on estimates of future performance or level of aspiration (pp. 389 ff.). The experimental literature on this topic includes a number of studies in which the person is presented a fictitious level of performance attributed to some group. By considering the person's reference group as the main anchor, the effects of experimentally introduced comparisons upon the aspiration level are readily predictable.

An early study along these lines was conducted by Chapman and Volkmann (1939), who regarded the conditions affecting the setting of an aspiration level "as a special case of the effect upon a judgment of the frame of reference within which it is executed" (p. 225). College students were presented a test of literary information with 50 multiple-choice items. As they had never taken the test before, they had few objective criteria on which to base estimates of their performance. As Fig. 18.1 shows, the control group (no special instructions) set their performance estimates at about 26.9 on the average, showing that the task was seen as difficult. One experimental group was told prior to their estimates that the average score obtained by a sample of laborers (WPA workers) was 37.2. The second experimental group was told that a sample of literary critics obtained a score of 37.2. As the figure indicates, the subjects whose *comparison group* was lower than their *reference sets* (college students) gave higher estimates, while those whose comparison group was higher gave lower estimates. *Although no mention was made of college students, this reference set was spontaneously used as the major anchor by the*

[margin handwritten note:] Purpose of following experiments

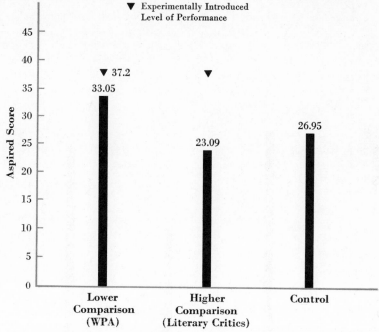

Fig. 18.1. Average aspired score on literary test according to comparison introduced in experiment. (Based on data from Chapman and Volkmann, 1939.) Control represents average level for reference set (college students). Subjects comparing themselves with WPA workers raised their aspirations; those compared with literary critics lowered aspirations.

subjects who appraised its level as higher in literary knowledge than that of WPA workers and lower than that of literary critics. Note that the aspiration levels did not vary around 37.2, the fictitious level, but around 26.9—indicating that the task difficulty for college students was an important factor in this social situation. A further indication of the correctness of this analysis is that on a second task which subjects had performed before and, therefore, knew their own level, *the comparison standards from other groups had no effect.*

A series of studies substantiated Chapman and Volkmann's findings using different reference groups and different comparisons (cf. Lewin *et at.,* 1944). Hansche and Gilchrist (1956) became interested in why the *comparison standards* did not exert a greater effect than they did. None of the subject samples had estimated their performance as high as the fictitious score (see Fig. 18.1). Accordingly, they varied the level of the comparison score, as well as the comparison group and the difficulty of the task. The task was a test of general knowl-

edge of psychology with a maximum score of 100. Comparison groups were high-school students, college sophomores, and first-year graduate students. (Since the subjects were students in introductory psychology, most of them were presumably around the sophomore level.)

Figure 18.2 shows that the results were similar to the overall findings of Chapman and Volkmann: aspiration level was lower relative to graduate students and higher relative to high-school students than when one's reference set coincided with the comparison standard (college sophomores).

Figure 18.3 shows, however, that the absolute level of the comparison standard made a difference. On the average, subjects exceeded the lowest standard used (54.4), approximated the middle standard (69.4), and fell far short of the highest standard (84.4). On the basis of the subjects' past experience, a grade of 84 seemed too high for such a test. Estimates also varied with item difficulty (67.2 for the easiest and 62.9 for the most difficult). For all orders of difficulty, the subjects' estimates corresponded

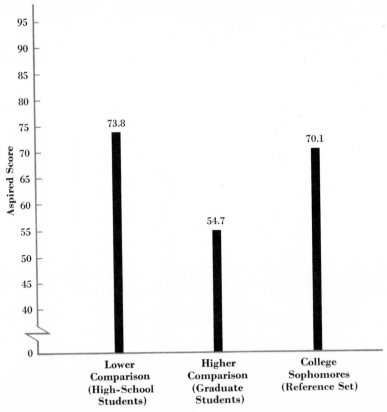

Fig. 18.2. Replication of Chapman-Volkmann experiment using college sophomores compared with high-school students and graduate students. (Based on data in Hansche and Gilchrist, 1956).

most nearly with the comparison standards when they were identified as scores by college sophomores (their reference groups).

We Try Harder
for Our Reference Groups

If one's reference group is the anchor in appraising his potential performance to that of other groups—thereby also the standard for his feelings of success or failure—it is not surprising that the effort a person is willing to expend is also affected by his reference group's level. In several experiments, a close relationship has been found between the person's persistence or willingness to endure discomfort, on the one hand, and his reference group, on the other.

Lambert, Libman, and Poser (1960) compared the pain tolerance of women students (a) without special instructions (control) and (b) when their identification as members of a religious group became relevant to

the amount of pain they would tolerate. The measure was a pressure reading taken from a pressure cuff with sharp projections inside. Figure 18.4 summarizes their results. Control subjects typically tolerated less pain at a second session than on the first trial. In one experimental condition, subjects were told that their own reference group (Christian or Jewish) tolerated *less* pain than a comparison group (Jewish or Christian). In another experimental condition, subjects were told that their reference group tolerated more pain than the comparison. The challenge that one's reference group was inferior produced significant increases in pain tolerance, as the graph shows. Jewish and Christian subjects reacted differently to the information that their own group tolerated *more* pain than the other: Jewish subjects increased their pain tolerance slightly, but the Christian subjects widened the gap even more—as though they had received a pat on the back.

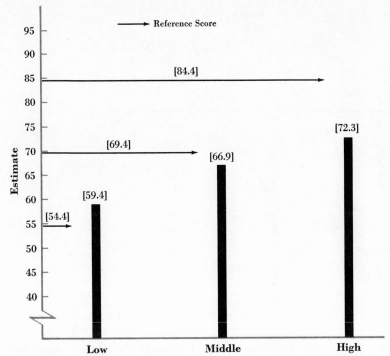

Fig. 18.3. Level of comparison score introduced in experiment (indicated by arrows) affects aspirations as well as level of comparison set relative to reference set. The findings in this experiment indicate that subjects in the Chapman-Volkmann study (see Fig. 18.1) were presented with comparison scores that appeared unreasonably high. (Based on data in Hansche and Gilchrist, 1956).

Interestingly enough, when Christian subjects were referred to as "Protestants" (which the subjects were), the instructions produced no significant effect, suggesting to the authors that "Christian" was a more salient reference set for these Protestant subjects.

In a refinement of the research design, Buss and Portnoy (1967) had college students at the University of Pittsburgh rank-order a number of possible reference sets in terms of their importance and how strongly committed the students were to them. From the results, they chose three reference sets of varying significance for the subjects (American, male-female, and the University of Pittsburgh, in that order). As comparison sets, they arbitrarily chose "strong" comparisons (Russian and Penn State) and "weak" comparisons (Canada and Carnegie Tech), with the opposite sex serving as the only possible comparison for sex identification.

Figure 18.5 gives the results for these conditions in terms of the *increase* in electric shock that subjects tolerated. (Control subjects endured less shock.) As the Figure shows, the degree of pain tolerance was a direct function of the rank of the reference group when the comparison group was "strong." The "weak" comparison groups produced a small but significant increase. The authors correctly explain these results in terms of the relative weight of the reference set as a contrast effect produced by the divergent comparisons: "Presumably, the more distinct . . . the comparison group, the greater is the individual's feeling of being a member of the reference group, that is, the more salient is group identification" (p. 108). In addition, one may note that at the time of the study, the relation between each of the reference sets and strong comparisons was one of competitor or rival (American-Russian, male-female, Pittsburgh-Penn State). As with the Rattlers and Eagles (p. 253), the person's reaction might be "We'll show those so and so's." This extra

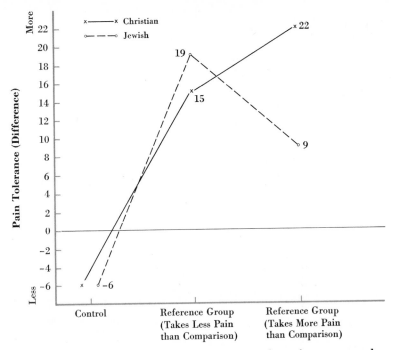

Fig. 18.4. Tolerance to shock with instructions that reference group has less tolerance and more tolerance for pain than comparison group. When reference group becomes salient, more shock is tolerated, but differentially by Christian and Jewish subjects. (Based on data from Lambert, Libman, and Poser, 1960.)

effort is indicated by the graph, proportional to the importance of the reference set in the person's scheme.

The importance of determining what the individual's reference group or set consists of may be illustrated further in a study by Lefcourt and Ladwig (1965). Noting that considerable laboratory research suggests that American Negroes in biracial situations often show compliant, noncompetitive and low achievement orientation, these investigators reasoned that Negro subjects might be more achievement oriented and more persistent in biracial competition if the task related to an important reference group in which they had experienced some achievement already. Accordingly, they compared persistence in a task by Negro inmates of a correctional institution who belonged to a jazz club with other inmates, who had never joined a music group and a sample who had joined the jazz club and dropped-out after a few meetings. The control subjects (nonjoiners) simply performed the task as a test. The experimental subjects were told that they had been chosen because of their interest in jazz and were interviewed about their interests and tastes. In the second session they were also told that the task related to the skills of a jazz musician. Actually the task was a "pick up sticks" game played against a white "plant" who had memorized the combinations of sticks necessary to win every time. The question was, then, in the face of continuous failure, would identification as a member of the jazz club or as a person interested in jazz affect the subjects' persistence in the game? The subject could stop playing any time with less loss (in packages of cigarettes) than by continuing to lose. A total of 15 games was allowed.

Figure 18.6 gives the results in terms of the average number of games played by control subjects, those interested in jazz, and those with a jazz reference group. Those who had become identified as active performers with the jazz club persisted significantly longer than either of the other samples.

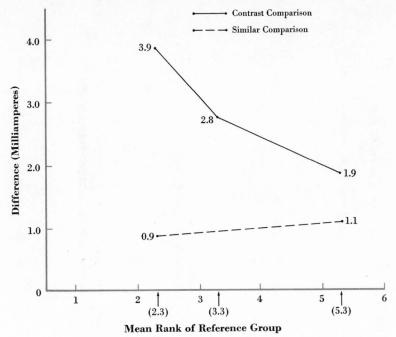

Fig. 18.5. Differences in shock tolerated when reference groups of different rank (*baseline*) are made salient and compared with similar (*dashed line*) and contrasting comparison groups (*solid line*). (Based on data in Buss and Portnoy, 1967.)

Decision-Making and Relative Importance of Various Reference Groups

Ordinarily the person's roles in different reference groups are kept in separate compartments because the situations related to them and the acitivities they require do not overlap in space or time. However, the person is sometimes placed in situations in which he must choose and reach decisions that, in effect, mean a choice of one reference group over another. The dilemma is reflected, for example, in the following words written by the first Negro American to serve in an executive capacity on the White House staff: "These are difficult hours for me as I try to carry out my responsibilities to the President and not appear completely disloyal to my race in the eyes of my friends" (Morrow, 1963, p. 248).

When events force the person to make a decision, we have an excellent opportunity to determine the relative importance of his reference groups or sets. Individuals facing the same dilemma do make different decisions. At least some differences in choice reflect the fact that reference groups differ in importance. For example, when the parochial schools were desegregated in New Orleans, Louisiana, in 1962, several prominent Catholics faced a choice between being excommunicated and adhering to their active opposition to desegregation. One legislator conferred with the Archbishop after being threatened with excommunication. Afterward he announced that he still opposed desegregation, but would abide by the laws of the country and the decisions of the church (*Southern School News,* 1962). Three other persons continued their opposition and were excommunicated. Each was active in organizations aimed at blocking segregation. The relatively greater importance of their prosegregation groups is revealed in the following words of one of them, who fell to her knees before the Archbishop during a Holy Week pilgrimage: "I ask your blessing, but I am not apologizing. Look up to heaven and admit that you know it's God's law to segregate. Don't listen to Satan, listen to God" (*Newsweek,* 1962; *Time,* 1962).

DeFleur and Westie (1958) arranged a research situation that required white students to make decisions on whether they

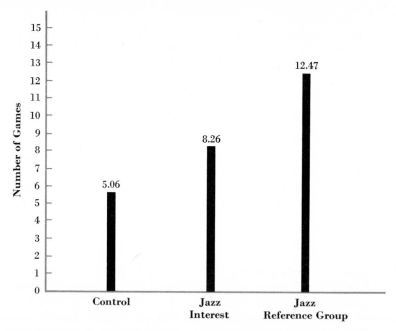

Fig. 18.6. Persistence in difficult activity as a function of strength of reference group ties: Negro subjects who participated in jazz group compared with subjects with interest and little interest in jazz. (Based on data in Lefcourt and Ladwig, 1965.)

would be photographed in social situations with a Negro of the opposite sex, and on what use could be made of the photograph. They devised a "photograph release form" that permitted the student to decide not to be photographed or to permit the photograph's use in situations ranging from laboratory research, the classroom, or the student newspaper to a nationwide publicity campaign. Half of the students had previously revealed high prejudice and half low prejudice on a direct attitude test; however, about 30 percent of the students made decisions contradictory to their stated attitudes. (More than 60 percent of these were students whose scores indicated little prejudice but who preferred not to have their photograph distributed.) In follow-up interviews, they found that these inconsistent students had made their choices with definite reference groups in mind, chiefly their friends: "Whatever the direction of this [choice], however, it was a peer-directed decision for the majority, with the subjects making significant use of their beliefs concerning possible approval or disapproval of

reference groups as guides for behavior" (p. 673).

Critical Decisions Reveal the Reference Group That Counts Most. Catastrophe and crisis in a community often force immediate choice between loyalties that are ordinarily not conflicting—for example, between being a devoted father and a fireman, or between being a good pastor of the flock and a man of God. In studying disasters caused by tornadoes and explosions, Killian (1952) found that the most frequent dilemma faced was whether to stay on one's job, to assist in relief and rescue work, or to search for one's family. The great majority interviewed had rushed to find their families, the notable exceptions being officials who knew that their families were out of town or otherwise safe.

Upon inquiring why complete chaos did not result from the prevalent choice of family over other reference groups, Killian found that many of these "family first" people had also engaged in rescue work in the process of reaching their families. Other types of conflict reported by Killian included the decision whether to do one's job, even though it meant leaving fearful and suffering friends or neighbors, and decisions involving conflict between loyalties to the community and to one's company or union.

The person's decisions in such conflict situations are particularly revealing, for they provide an index to his personal hierarchy of reference group ties, of which the person may not be aware until the time of decision. The result may be surprising both to the observer and to the person himself.

Campbell and Pettigrew (1959) studied the puzzling behavior of clergymen during the violent crisis accompanying the initial attempt to desegregate the public schools in Little Rock, Arkansas, which included the use of federal troops. Thirteen of the 42 ministers faced no problem in this situation because their own interpretation of the Bible, their church, and the congregations all supported segregation. Another five segregationist ministers were opposed to violence and offered prayers for community tranquility without being confronted by a difficult choice. Of the remaining two dozen, only eight decided to voice the message of peace, justice, and equality to their congregations and the community. (Most of them were young men with small churches, and several later transferred out of Little Rock.) The remainder of the ministers whose gospel was not favorable to discrimination simply kept quiet and refrained from referring to the crisis.

How can the decision *not to act* be explained, particularly when such inaction violated basic tenets of the persons' faith? Campbell and Pettigrew found that in each case the quiet ones faced a dilemma between beliefs as a minister of God, their leadership roles in their immediate congregations, and their roles as administrators within their larger church organizations. On the average, they estimated that 75 percent of their congregations opposed desegregation. Their church superiors did not actively discourage their taking a stand, but generally assessed their performance on the basis of administrative criteria (keeping and enlarging their congregation, improvements on the building, etc.). So powerful were their ties with congregation and church or-

ganization, in comparison with the church's message, that these inactive ministers actually came in time to feel "courageous" because they failed to speak out or dared to offer a sermon on "brotherly love" without reference to the ongoing crisis.

Predicting the Person's Hierarchy of Ego-Involvements from His Major Reference Groups

One advantage of knowing the relative importance of the person's reference groups for him is that the hierarchy of important values in the person's major reference groups is likely to be reflected in his ego-attitudes. In other words, the person's major reference group provides a basis for predicting what will be more and less ego-involving for him. This problem was explored by Russell and Sherif (1966) in a study of foreign students attending a university in the United States.

As the number of foreign students coming to the United States increased to more than 100,000 by 1966, there has been a great deal of research into their problems. This research indicates that the problems faced by the visiting students vary a great deal—depending upon Americans' views of their country, differences in cultures and customs, and their particular location in the United States. Almost all research also indicated different reactions by individuals from the same country. For this reason, it was decided to see whether priorities of problems important to students were related to their reference groups. Students were chosen from two quite different cultural and geographical areas, the Middle East and South America. Through a combination of informal interviews and rating schedules, problems were selected that these students regarded as very important to them personally, to the United States, and to their home countries. From these important problems, six were selected for their importance in each context (personal, U.S., and home country) and judged by the students using a paired-comparison procedure.

The nationality reference of the students was ascertained through their ratings of

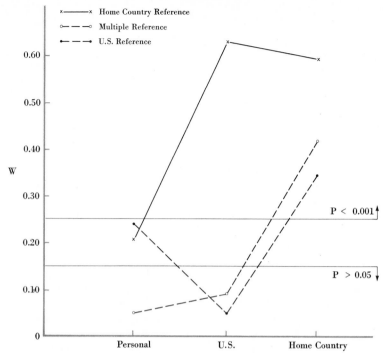

Fig. 18.7. Degree of agreement (W) on ranking various issues by foreign students in the United States with differing reference sets for nationality. (Based on data in Russell and Sherif, 1966.)

various countries as to how desirable-undesirable they were for working and for permanent residence. Only about a third of the students were unequivocally committed to their home country, while the remainder were either identified with the United States or had multiple reference groups (equal preference for several countries, usually including Western European countries). (The exact proportions differed for the two nationalities sampled.) In addition, through observation and interviews, it was possible to locate seven informal reference groups among these same students, consisting of from four to fifteen members. Their members regularly ate together and interacted in other ways. About one-third of the students had no informal reference groups of this kind.

Was the student's national reference group useful in predicting how he would order the issues according to their importance? Figure 18.7 shows that it was. The statistic plotted there is a measure of agreement among individuals with the same nationality reference (home country, U.S., or multiple) in their rank-ordering of the

same problems (Kendall's W or the coefficient of concordance). The closer W comes to 1.00, the nearer perfect is their agreement. The Figure shows that agreement was greatest among foreign students who were clearly identified with their home country, particularly when ranking problems in regard to the United States and their home country. The greatest variation among persons was found in ordering personal problems (e.g., grades, money, friends, etc.).

When the reference group analysis was refined further by comparing agreement among members of informal student groups and agreement among students who did not have such membership, even higher degrees of agreement were found than among students who simply had the same national reference (Fig. 18.8). The important finding here is that students who interacted regularly with one another agreed significantly and to much higher degrees than students without such informal reference groups on the relative importance of problems, even though all made their ratings individually and apart from their reference group. (The sizes of W in Fig. 18.8 for the informal

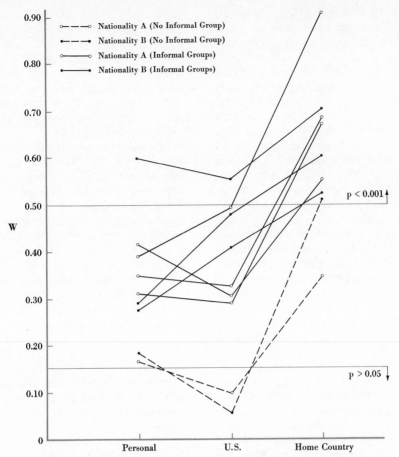

Fig. 18.8. Comparison of degree of agreement (W) on ranking various issues by students of two nationalities in the United States according to whether they did (*solid lines*) or did not (*dashed line*) participate in informal groups with fellow students. (Based on data in Russell and Sherif, 1966.)

groups are much larger than those in Fig. 18.7, and all are statistically significant despite the fact that the informal groups were very small.)

How did the foreign students compare with United States students matched according to sex, age, and college major? They were most similar in ranking personal problems, except that they were less concerned about grades and more concerned about financial problems. But with regard to the problems in the United States and their home countries, the foreign students differed considerably from their United States counterparts. For example, the matched United States students rated the problem of integration of minority groups low in this set of very important problems, while foreign students typically saw it as much more im-

portant. In addition, United States students de-emphasized problems of their country's role in world affairs, which foreign students regarded as primary in importance.

INTERPLAY OF REFERENCE GROUP AND NOMINAL MEMBERSHIP IN A GROUP

In the discussion of social norms in Chapter 9, the phenomenon of "rate setting" in industry with the piece-work incentive system was explored. Briefly, it was noted there that some workers deviate from the production norm set informally by the workers—their familiar appellation being "rate busters"—which the student will find meaningful in terms of the "curve busters" in examinations. In surveying the literature on the topic, W. F. Whyte (1955) estimated that about 10 percent of workers in factories using a bonus incentive system are rate busters.

M. Dalton (in Whyte, 1955) studied the backgrounds and the in-factory and outside-factory activities of rate busters and discovered that, from all angles, the rate buster had different reference groups than workers who conform, by and large, to the norm. The rate busters were typically from "farms or . . . urban lower-middle class families—both types . . . being strongholds of the belief in economic individualism" (p. 42). Inside and outside the plant, he was either a "lonewolf" or a person with strong aspirations for upward mobility who "cuts himself off from others on the same level and seeks association with those of superior status" (p. 42). He was less responsive to fellow workers in the plant, even in such simple activities as making contributions for gifts and activities (despite the fact that he had more money). In contrast, the conforming workers were typically from urban, working-class backgrounds, interacted more with fellow workers, and contributed more in informal associations with them.

It would be a mistake, however, to conclude that rate busters are untouched by their daily membership and interaction with other workers. To be called a derogatory name, to be "binged," to be derided, and even to be given the cold shoulder are not experiences that most people can ignore.

Attitudes as a Function of Membership and Reference Groups. To his important field study at Bennington College, carried out during the depression years in the late 1930s, Newcomb (1943, 1948) applied reference group analysis to attitude change as students progressed from the freshman through senior year. He focused on political attitudes. He also found that membership in the college community had effects on persons who did not come to identify with the community and who did not change their attitudes in line with the prevailing "liberal" norms. The Bennington study began during the first year that there was a senior class in the new college, which is situated in a geographically isolated and relatively self-sufficient location. On the whole, both the administration and faculty of the new insti-

tution upheld liberal stands on sociopolitical issues in the "depression-torn America and . . . war threatened world" of the 1930s. Most of the students, however, came from "urban, economically privileged families whose social attitudes were conservative." Because of the college's size and aims, it permitted unusually close faculty-student interaction.

Newcomb administered a Likert-type test of attitudes (pp. 371–372) on nine social issues each year for a four-year period to members of the four classes. He found that for the great majority of the students, the liberal college community became a major reference group for their political views, despite their conservative backgrounds. On six of the nine social issues, there was a significant change toward the liberal direction from the freshman to senior years. Furthermore, prestige and leadership were acquired by the girls who kept pace with the liberal atmosphere. However, the college experience was not devoted entirely to politics. It was not surprising, therefore, that some students did not change their political attitudes at all and a few openly resisted the prevailing norms for political belief.

In analyzing the deviant cases (deviant in terms of political norms), Newcomb found that most of the cases could be explained through the reference groups of the subjects: Some girls became involved in intimate informal groups that did not concern themselves with politics; many maintained strong ties with family or boyfriends outside of the community and did not feel themselves identified with Bennington. However, many of these girls with small closed reference groups or outside anchorages did reveal effects of being a member of the larger community. Some indicated feelings of conflict ("Family against faculty has been my struggle here.") Some became defensive about their views of their own family and their intellectual level, in effect contrasting the liberal political norms at Bennington with their own and thereby committing themselves more firmly to conservative views.

Any analysis of data from field studies can be somewhat misleading if it identifies what actually occurred with a theoretical explanation of what happened, without regard to the background of the events. For example, it is entirely possible that the adoption of a new reference group diverging sharply in values from the person's former reference groups has actually been preceded by alienation from the erstwhile anchor and keen awareness of the differences between it and the potential reference group (e.g., a college community). In fact, Ruth Hartley (1960) found such alienation and awareness of difference were more typical of college students (men in this case) who adopted their college as a main anchor.

Therefore, an experiment in the field by Siegel and Siegel (1957, 1965) is particularly revealing about the effects of membership and reference groups. The clarifying circumstance was that students were *randomly* assigned to live in dormitories that (1) coincided with their reference groups; (2) were merely a membership group for a year, while the students' aspiration resided elsewhere; or (3) became the reference group through belonging as a member. This random assignment permits us to assume that the effects of membership and reference groups were not merely the result of predisposing factors. The measure of effects of membership and reference groups was score on the California E-F scale, a questionnaire form that is probably best interpreted as assessing the person's willingness to reveal unquestioned acceptance of conventional, lower-middle-class values. The usual trend in studies of scores on the E-F scale during student days in a university is a decline in such acceptance.

One of the neat aspects of the study was that taking the test and being assigned to a dormitory were completely unrelated in the eyes of subjects—in fact, dormitory assignment was a chance event. Nevertheless, the finding was that being assigned to a dormitory of one's choice or remaining in a dormitory not chosen both had measurable effects on the students' attitudes.

The most prestigious dormitories for women were located along "fraternity row" and hence were called "row houses." From the women who at the end of the freshman year turned in their preference to live in a row house, the investigators studied the following samples:

(a) Women who did gain assignment to a row house and wanted to stay there at the end of the sophomore year (reference group and membership group the same).

(b) Women who did not gain entrance to a row house as sophomores but who indicated preference for a row house again at the end of the sophomore year (membership and reference groups discrepant).

(c) Women who did not gain entrance to a row house and indicated at the end of the sophomore year that they wanted to remain in a nonrow house (mere membership group became reference group).

The E-F test results for all row girls showed that they had the most conservative attitudes. Thus the effects of a nonrow house were revealed by a greater change toward less conservatism. What Siegel and Siegel found was that students whose reference group and membership group coincided during the sophomore year (a, above) maintained the most conservative attitudes. Girls who still desired to be in a row house showed the effects of being a member of a nonrow community by being less conservative (b, above). Finally, the greatest change toward lower E-F scores was found among those girls who changed their reference group from a row house to their membership group (c, above). Thus it can be concluded that while the person's reference group and its change are needed to predict attitudes, it is also necessary to know his membership group, which does have an impact on attitude as well as daily behavior.

Final Conclusion

This conclusion is particularly important as we consider the impact of social class or cultural background on the individual. To say that the person identifies with a different group or a higher class is not to say that he is completely unaffected by his actual membership, as we shall see in comparing the conceptions, attitudes, and aspirations of persons from different social classes.

19

Adolescent Reference Groups and the Social Context of Ambition

Major Topics of the Chapter

Re-formation of the self system during adolescence

Shift from parental to agemate reference group

Socioeconomic and cultural setting

Socioeconomic rank and ambitions for upward mobility

Social context of ambition (by Ralph H. Turner)

Self, reference groups, and the social context

Individual in his group in its setting: research program in three facets

Contradictions in the social context

Adolescents in their reference groups within different sociocultural environments

YOUTH IN HIS GROUP
IN HIS SETTING

In this chapter, we shall discuss adolescent reference groups—that is, groups of youth's own choosing under conditions of modern life. The concepts of attitude, self, and reference groups that were introduced earlier in this Part are particularly useful in analyzing certain aspects of the transition to adulthood. The problem of analyzing how the person's attitudes and self-concept are shaped requires specification of the gamut of influences affecting him, instead of merely studying one influence at a time.

In recent years, a great deal of research in the United States has focused on the problems of youthful behavior, misbehavior, and goals for the future. This research has shown that socioeconomic background, the cultural and physical settings in which youth interact, and youths' relationships with one another all affect adolescent attitudes and behavior. However, there are few one-to-one relationships between any one of these sets of factors and behavior. Rather, they interact in complex fashion, as we shall see in research by the sociologist Ralph Turner on the social context of ambition.

The study of behavior within the pattern of interpersonal relations with significant others and within the specific context of socioeconomic and cultural environments will be illustrated through a research program on adolescent reference groups initiated by the authors in 1958. (See also Chapter 8). This program represents the scope and design of research that are required to accommodate the gamut of influences shaping attitude and behavior.

RE-FORMATION
OF THE SELF SYSTEM
DURING ADOLESCENCE

The changing body of the adolescent compels changes in his self-concept. Even if others take no note, the altering appearance of the body and its unaccustomed sensations tell him that he is changing. However, others do take note. His family, teachers, and friends expect new things of him, and the compelling images of the mass media depict a different way of feeling and acting for his age group. He is expected to be more responsible and less dependent upon adults, at least in the conduct of routine activities and self-care. He or she is expected to start acting more "adult"—to dress, stand, and walk in ways befitting the approach of adulthood. If the adolescent is to meet these expectations, he has to re-define relevant ego-attitudes. If he did not, despite manly or womanly figure and voice, he would retain the dependency on adult control, and the short-term consistency and physical freedom that are typical in childhood but atypical in adulthood. In short, the fundamental psychological problem of adolescence is the general and important problem of forming and re-forming ego-attitudes (cf. Sherif and Cantril, 1947; Ausubel, 1954; Horrocks, 1963).

In modern societies, however, the steps and procedures for attaining adulthood are by no means clear. For several years, the youth faces a period of being someone who is primarily defined by what he is not: neither child nor adult, neither dependent nor independent. Socially and economically, he is betwixt and between for the period. Adults are not clear about the exact timing of steps and responsibilities he is to assume. At times, when life has changed rapidly from the period when adults were adolescents, the guidelines that adults offer are so different from the paths open to the youth that the "rules" appear unacceptable to him. Finally, adult treatments are not consistent from time to time. The young person is treated as an adult in one respect, but subject to the restrictions and sheltered world of childhood in others.

Thus the adolescent period in modern industrial societies is conducive to a dilemma for the individual, to the extent that it is a prolonged transition lacking clear or satisfactory procedures for gaining adult status. The experience of being "in between," of facing contradictory expectations from one time to the next, and of treading the narrow path between being "too childish" or acting "beyond your age" and "reckless" are not pleasant.

What do individuals do when they face uncertainty and conflict about such central problems? As we have seen (Chapter 17), they typically search actively for stable guideposts, for some certainty, and for some way out of the conflict. Adolescents can and do turn to the adult world for such guides. However, a rift between the generations is built into modern life and is markedly accentuated by arrangements in school, community, and work that segregate the ages. The perspective of adulthood is different even when the adults in question are sympathetic. The urgency experienced by the adolescent is countered by counsel to plan, wait, and work. Thus, even sympathetic adults are classified as "nice for a grownup"—though overt conflict between the generations (which is common enough) may be lacking.

Modern industrialized societies provide many conditions conducive to alienating adolescents from the adult world that nurtured them in childhood. Another attempt to resolve the predicament of adolescence is to seek relief in fantasy, day dreams, and a retreat to private worlds. Such reactions were so typical half a century ago that the diary and mystic experiences provided a rich source of data to the student of adolescence in this country. This "solution" is less frequent in the United States today. Even youth who "tune out" of adult society are more likely to do so in the company of others.

Today, the social schemes for school, community, and leisure encourage the alternative that is most typical: The adolescent discovers that there are others in the same boat—namely, others near his age. Thus social interaction among adolescents becomes more intense, more frequent, and more significant than in childhood. Adolescents in the United States are encouraged in moving toward agemates by the emphasis on social activities, by parents and other adults who want them to be "in," by school programs, and by the varied mass communications that deliberately feed on appeals to youth. The actual movement toward agemates is also symptomatic of a general shift away from the strong ties of dependence upon adults. For the time being, at least, the guides that the adolescent follows, the standards that count, the opinions that are salient in deciding whether *I* am "normal," "average," "superior," or "inferior" are those within the domain of adolescents.

"My Pop vs. Your Pop" Becomes "My Friend vs. My Pop"

The shift in reference groups from family to agemates was studied experimentally by Prado (1958), who compared judgments by children and by adolescents on the competence of their fathers and their best friends in a simple task. Prado selected 25 boys between eight and eleven years old and 25 boys between fourteen and seventeen years old. In order to minimize the possibility of getting boys who had unusually poor relationships with their fathers, he chose only boys who consistently selected their fathers as their most valued and trusted parent. He singled-out the boy's best agemate friend from sociometric data obtained at school.

Each boy came to the laboratory with his father and his best friend to perform the simple task of throwing a dart at a target. The task was so arranged that the exact score could not be ascertained by the subjects. As his father and then his friend threw the darts, each boy judged the performances by using scores from 0 to 24. The children and the adolescents were about equally accurate in their judgments, with an average error of 4.5 in judging their father's performance and about 3.5 for their friends' performance. By comparing the difference between errors in judging fathers and errors in judging best friends, we have an index of the comparative tendency to overestimate or underestimate performance by father and best friend.

Figure 19.1 illustrates Prado's findings. A positive difference in this graph means that the error in judging the father's performance was greater than that in judging the friend's, and in a positive direction. A negative difference means that the father's performance was underestimated compared with that of the friend, even when actual performance levels were taken into account. The Figure shows that children tended to _overestimate their father's performance_ while adolescents _under_estimated their father's performance compared with that of a friend. Prado also reported that, although boys at both age levels were equally consistent in choosing their best friends on several sociometric questions, the adolescents reported that they engaged together in a significantly greater number of activities than the younger boys. His experiment illustrates the shift of reference set from adults to agemates during adolescence.

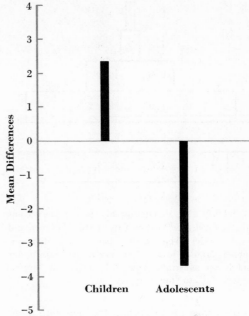

Fig. 19.1. Overestimation by children and underestimation by adolescents of parent's performance as compared with that of best friend's. (Based on data in Prado, 1958.)

SOCIOECONOMIC
AND CULTURAL SETTING

In the gamut of influences that contributes to the formation and re-formation of self-identity during adolescence, the socio-economic and cultural milieu requires consideration at the outset. Social stratification, social class, and culture are concepts in any attempt to define the social stimulus situations in which the individual develops. It is very well known, for example, that the adolescent experience is quite different in other cultures. Within a single society attitudes and ambitions vary systematically according to the social class of one's origin. The social psychologist who attempts research that utilizes the concepts of culture and social class faces a severe problem, however. As John Campbell (1967) aptly remarked, the concepts are "boxcars" that carry a great deal of freight; but in research on individual attitude and behavior, it becomes necessary to specify what is in the boxcars.

One approach to specifying social class was that identified with the work of Lloyd Warner and his associates (1941). These investigators studied relatively small communities and specified the social class of residents through their evaluations of each other (e.g., "she does not belong" or "they belong to our club," p. 90). As Fig. 19.2 shows, most of this research indicates that

the majority of the population is situated in a lower class, with the proportions decreasing markedly as one moves upward. In his study of Elmstown's youth, Hollingshead (1949) coupled this approach with measures of occupation, housing, and education and concluded that the particular social stratum into which one was born in a small midwestern community affected attitudes, aspirations, and opportunities from an early age. The Lynds' studies of _Middletown_ and _Middletown in Transition_ (1937) spelled-out in detail what it meant for both adults and youth to live as a member of the "business" or "working" class in a small midwestern city in the decades after World War I.

In order to specify social environments as lower, middle, or upper class for social-psychological research, some indicators of class are needed. In the United States, the choice of indicators is complicated by two conditions, which can be illustrated briefly:

1. _Discrepancy Between Membership Class and Reference Class._ Being situated in a particular stratum of society does not mean that the person will necessarily identify himself as a member of that stratum. Public opinion polls indicated that, given the choice between lower-, middle-, and

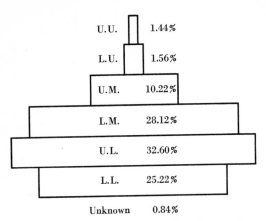

U.U.	1.44%
L.U.	1.56%
U.M.	10.22%
L.M.	28.12%
U.L.	32.60%
L.L.	25.22%
Unknown	0.84%

Fig. 19.2. Representation of class demarcations and hierarchy in Yankee City. (After Warner and Lunt, 1941.) The three major class divisions (upper, middle, lower) were partitioned into upper and lower substrata. Thus U.U. refers to "upper-upper," L.U. to "lower-upper," etc.

upper-class membership, the overwhelming majority of Americans considered themselves middle class. Centers (1949) studied the problem of discrepancies between occupational classification and class identification in a nationwide survey of adult white males. The respondent could choose from the following class identifications: middle class, lower class, working class, or upper class. Each also selected from the following criteria what he usually thought of as indicating a person's class: who his family is, money, education, or beliefs and outlook. Finally, each responded to six questions designed to assess political conservatism-radicalism.

Centers found that more than half of the respondents thought that a person's attitudes and beliefs were the best indicator of his social class. A third mentioned education and only about one-fifth referred to money or family. Despite this prevailing belief that ideas were the earmark of social class, there was a relationship between occupation and the choice of class reference. For example, about 75 percent of those in business, management, professional, or white-collar occupations identified themselves as "middle class," while 79 percent of those occupied in manual labor called themselves "working class."

What about those who identified themselves with a class that did not include their type of occupation? By classifying the an-

swers to the political questions as "conservative," "radical," or "indeterminate," Centers showed that a person was more likely to have political attitudes resembling those of his reference class, even when it differed from his membership. In his words: *"If people's class identificatioms are the same, their attitudes tend to be similar even though their objective occupational positions are different"* (p. 308, italics in original).

Centers' findings show that it is important to know what a person's reference class is. However, if we wish to study upward mobility, for example, we also need some way to determine the social-class environment of the person at the time—independent of his verbal report on his reference set. This is one reason why sociologists typically use such criteria as occupation, source and amount of income, and educational level as measures of social class.

2. *Complexity of Social Stratification in a Multicultural and Racially Segregated Society.* In a highly complex society stratified according to ethnic membership as well as socioeconomic criteria and containing both urban-rural and regional economic disparities, a single criterion for social class is bound to be inadequate to specify differences in the sociocultural environment. For example, occupational descriptions group together persons with different incomes which are related to important differences in the social environment. Educational attainment, which by itself has only limited utility as an index of social class, may be much more important as an indicator of the person's milieu when he belongs to an ethnic or racial minority that meets systematic discrimination in entering certain occupations and in income.

For such reasons, in modern industrialized and urbanized societies, an index of social class should include at least indicators of income, educational level, occupation and, when relevant, membership in racially segregated groups. In later sections, specific examples of class indicators will be included in reports of social-psychological studies of youth. In actual research practice, it becomes virtually impossible to obtain reliable indication of income, so that other correlated measures are more commonly used.

Families and Individuals by Income Levels: 1959

Fig. 19.3.   Graphic presentation of proportions of families and individuals with yearly income at different levels, 1959. (From U.S. Bureau of the Census, *How Our Income Is Divided,* Graphic Pamphlet No. 2, 1963.)

Because they are elsewhere notably lacking in social-psychological research and indicate clearly the existence of differential environments, illustrative data on income in the United States are shown in Figs. 19.3 and 19.4. The income pyramid in Fig. 19.3 is not complete because it groups the top of the pyramid into the top 5 percent of the population with incomes of $15,000 or over (smallest figure). The top 1 percent of the population (about half a million families) received more than $25,000 a year. At the apex, about 28,000 persons divided 1 percent of the total national income in 1959.

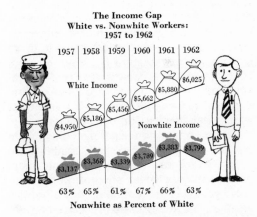

Fig. 19.4.   The income gap for white and nonwhite workers in the United States, 1957 to 1962; while income increases, the gap grows. (From U.S. Bureau of the Census. *Current Population Reports —Consumer Income,* Series P-60, annual issues.)

SOCIOECONIMIC RANK
AND AMBITIONS
FOR UPWARD MOBILITY

In a series of studies the sociologist Ralph H. Turner has studied problems of upward mobility, particularly through the medium of educational achievement. In his book *The Social Context of Ambition,* Turner (1964) reported research on high-school seniors in Los Angeles attending schools that served residential areas differing in socioeconomic rank. Professor Turner's summary of his findings on upward ambitions, written for inclusion in this book, is presented in the next section.

In selecting high schools for study, Turner used Census Tract statistics to determine socioeconomic rank, which was calculated with a formula developed by Shevky and Bell (1955) for comparing social areas in a city. In this case, socioeconomic rank (low, middle, or high) is relative to all Census Tracts in Los Angeles. Specifically, it is computed from the percentages of the population in each tract that (1) engage in manual labor and (2) have 8 or fewer years of education. Having selected 10 schools, Turner then secured information from the students themselves about the family bread-winner's (a) occupation, (b) education, and (c) independent-employee status as the basis for a "background index" for each student.

As have several other investigators, Turner found that the average level of ambition, as well as the percentage of students with ambitions for high occupations and education beyond high school, varied significantly with the socioeconomic rank of the school. For example, 54 percent of the boys in the high-rank school wanted to become professionals, as compared with 20 percent in low-rank schools. Seventy-one percent of the boys in high-rank schools wanted to complete 4 or more years of college as compared with only 21 percent in the low-rank schools. However, compared with their family attainments in these respects, ambitious youth were found in every school: youth who were shooting well beyond their fathers' occupational and educational attainments. It is well to keep in mind this relative basis for singling-out ambitious youth when reading Turner's summary.

Future orientation and ambition were typical of the high-school students in Turner's research. He focuses his summary on several hypotheses about upwardly mobile youth. For example, he inquires whether the values of self-reliance and deferring gratification are associated with ambition and, if so, whether they merely reflect background training or also involve anticipatory socialization. Taking note of the importance of agemate associations during adolescence, he relates ambition to sociometric choice of friends in the classroom. If persons with either high or low socioeconomic background chose others from their own backgrounds exclusively, upward mobility or anticipatory socialization would be very difficult for those from a low

background. While such "cleavage" in classrooms does exist in about half the classrooms, it is not, Turner concludes, sufficiently general to prohibit association across class lines. However, as reported in the next section, he found that the relationships between upward ambition and adolescent reference sets were by no means simple: they probably differ according to the general socioeconomic level of students in a school.

The Social Context of Ambition
Ralph H. Turner
University of California at Los Angeles

The individual who elevates himself in adulthood to a socioeconomic level above that of his parents and his early neighborhood is called _upwardly mobile._ Commonly accepted sociological theories of social stratification predict that the upwardly mobile person encounters somewhat distinctive experiences en route to his destination, with probable consequences in personality formation. One prevalent hypothesis holds that he often becomes a _marginal man_, intensely involved in two incompatible worlds of social values and interpersonal ties, thus unable to choose consistently between these worlds. The class subculture of his childhood has trained him to value types of behavior and achievement that are not rewarded at the higher level to which he is moving, and has not trained him to value those which are rewarded. The aim of the investigation was to determine whether the situation in the senior year of high school was conducive to marginality, and to search for differences in the situations of ambitous young people at various socioeconomic levels.

A questionnaire was devised to secure four types of information. Questions were asked about the student's own occupational, educational, and monetary ambitions, and about the socioeconomic level of his parents. Comparison between these two sets of information serves to identify the upwardly mobile students.

The major portion of the questionnaire consisted of paired value statements, each requiring the students to make a positive choice. The items were devised on the basis of previous research and theory on social stratification, so as to reflect values that are believed to be class-related, or to be indicative of youth culture. Finally, three simple sociometric queries were employed to establish interpersonal ratings.

The questionnaires were administered to nearly all of the seniors in ten high schools, chosen as socioeconomically representative of the Los Angeles metropolitan area. Most of the questionnaires were administered in individual class-rooms by the investigator or his trained assist-ants. A total of 2793 boys and girls completed the questionnaire. It is important to remember that this investigation does not include the many students who have dropped out of high school before the senior year.

The findings were consistent with those of many prior studies in the United States in show-ing that occupational and educational ambitions are high, and that expecting to be upwardly mobile is the rule rather than the exception. Students from high and low socioeconomic back-grounds were not radically different in their value choices, indicating the absence of sharply differ-entiated class subcultures in the senior year of high school. Students' values were, however, somewhat more extensively differentiated accord-ing to their level of ambition. Indeed the hypoth-eses drawn from community studies of class subculture were supported better when students were grouped according to their ambitions than when they were classified by family background.

For example, the traditional "middle-class" value of *self-reliance* (as contrasted with mutual aid) distinguishes both men and women of high ambition, but is not distinctive to students from high backgrounds. A positive value placed on *deferring gratification* marks ambitious men but is unrelated to background. Hence there is some basis for concluding that the social order in high school is so geared to the future that a class sys-tem comes into operation on the basis of socio-economic destination, rather than exclusively of background. Occupational and educational goals are still considerably shaped by social origin, as indicated by correlations between background and ambition measures. But the blurring of lines between value subcultures and their reorienta-tion toward the future, as embodied in aspi-rations, may obviate marginality for those who can establish themselves in the future-oriented school society, at least temporarily. To a con-siderable degree, the socioeconomic transition is facilitated by *anticipatory socialization*—learning in advance those values and attitudes that will be needed in a future life stage.

However, not only values but social ties are also involved in the mobile person's transition. The upwardly mobile person is likely to be a marginal man *if* members of different social strata look upon each other with suspicion and hos-tility, viewing the person who tries to move up as a traitor. If, on the contrary, the dominant at-titude is respect for higher strata, the friends and relatives of the upwardly mobile person can themselves gain prestige through identifying with his successes. Under the latter circumstance, the mobile person will have support from his earlier associates and will not be confronted with

Table 19.1. Analysis of Sociometric Choices in Each Classroom

Socioeconomic Background (or Ambition) of Persons Choosing:	Socioeconomic Background (or Ambition) of Persons Chosen:	
	High (frequency)	Low (frequency)
High	HH	HL
Low	LH	LL
	Total 1	Total 2

Preference for high background = Total 1 > Total 2.
Index of cleavage in classroom = (fHH) (fLL) − (fHL) (fLH).
(See Table 19.2 for results of these two analyses in 89 classrooms.)

the necessity of repudiating old friends as he rises.

The following sociometric question was used to observe which pattern of social ties prevails in the senior year of high school. "Suppose you wanted to pick some people to be your *close friends*—people you would enjoy doing things with and would like to have as close friends for a long time. What *three* people who are *in this classroom right now* would you pick?" For each of the 89 classroom groups in which the ques-tionnaire was administered, a simple fourfold table was prepared (see Table 19.1). Subjects were placed into high and low socioeconomic background according to the medians for their respective schools, with the characteristics of choosers on one axis and of the chosen on the other axis. In each classroom a simple count tells us whether more votes are received by the highs than the lows. Table 19.2 (left column) shows that students from high socioeconomic backgrounds are preferred in the majority of classrooms.

A general preference for persons from high backgrounds can be more of an obstacle than a help to mobility if there is *cleavage* along socio-economic lines. If lows prefer lows and highs prefer highs, the mobile person has difficulty gaining acceptance as he rises. In order to identify cleavage, we substract the product of the frequencies in the high-low and low-high cells from the product of frequencies in the high-high and low-low cells (see Table 19.1). If the differ-ence is positive, students are attracted to others of like socioeconomic background. If the differ-ence is negative, then "opposites attract." An

Table 19.2. Preference and Cleavage by Background and Ambition

Type of Pattern	No. of Classrooms	
	Background Index	Ambition Index
Preference		
Highs Preferred	51	63
Lows Preferred	29	17
Equal Preference	9	9
Total	89	89
Cleavage		
Positive Cleavage	44	62
Negative Cleavage	44	26
No Cleavage	1	1
Total	89	89

exactly equal number of classrooms showing positive and negative balances (Table 19.2, left column, bottom) suggests that there is no general pattern of cleavage according to socioeconomic origin. The obstacle exists, but it is not universal.

A second set of tabulations, employing high and low *ambition* rather than background, rounds out the analysis. Table 19.2 (upper right column) shows that the preference for persons with high ambitions is more prevalent than the preference for persons from high backgrounds (left column). Indeed, the latter might simply be explained on the basis of the correlation between background and ambition. But the striking contrast is found in the marked tendency toward *cleavage* according to ambition (lower right column). Whereas there is no universal tendency for students of like backgrounds to prefer one another, there is a widespread tendency for students to select others with ambitions similar to their own.

This evidence on social ties of ambitious students reinforces the main conclusion from the findings regarding values. *By the senior year of high school, students are more concerned with the future than with the past.* Consequently, for those students who have not dropped out of school earlier, stratification according to destination tends to complicate the stratification according to origin. The transition is therefore made easier for the upwardly mobile person: He is relatively shielded from influences conducive to marginality as long as he remains within the special world of the school. On the other hand, once identified as having low ambition, the student may be trapped by his

social ties with other less ambitious students and upward revision of his aspirations impeded.

The data in the Tables treat all schools together, using the average (median) background in each school as the cutting point for dividing the *lows* from the *highs*. There is danger, therefore, in concluding from these findings that informal social organizations invariably smooth the path of the upwardly mobile student. The problems of ambition, opportunity, and social ascent may well be different in those schools in which there is a heavy concentration of students from low socioeconomic backgrounds—hence, where the general level of ambition is lower. A separate examinaton of the three lowest schools suggests that they are somewhat different.

The level of ambition is lower in the three lowest schools; but it is even lower than would be predicted from the socioeconomic backgrounds of indivdual families. Similarly, I.Q. is lower than expected on this basis. One possibility, widely suggested in the literature, is that high ambition is disparaged in such poor neighborhoods. This common view is not supported by the data, which show just as great a preference for ambitious students in the low schools as in the other schools. There is also a preference in the lowest schools for those students who, in answer to another question, are singled-out as especially good students. The explanation for the lower-than-expected ambition and I.Q. in the lowest schools must lie elsewhere than in direct community pressures against vocational and academic aspiration.

A composite picture for an adequate explanation can be drawn from several separate items of data. For simplicity, we shall refer only to white "Anglo" men. First, the relationships between ambition and both background and I.Q. are substantially less in the socioeconomically low schools. Furthermore, in these schools, there is no general preference for students from higher backgrounds. These findings might suggest a "classless" society in these schools; however, the low relationship between I.Q. and ambition suggests another interpretation. It is more likely that ambition is more fortuitous in these schools and that the general social structure is amorphous in this respect. The latter interpretation is reinforced by the data for values.

A composite *class value index* was computed on the basis of the nine most important items. The index was correlated with background level and ambition level. The relationships between the class value index and levels of background and ambition are both significant in the two high-level schools and in the five middle-level schools. Neither correlation is significant in the three lowest schools (Table 19.3, left columns). The socio-

**Table 19.3.   Correlation of Class Values
and Manipulative Individualism
with Background and Ambition (by Neighborhood, for Men)**

| | Coefficient of Correlation—Pearson r | | | |
| | Class Value Index | | Manipulative Individualism | |
Neighborhood	Background	Ambition	Background	Ambition
High-level schools	.12	.18	.14	.16
Middle-level schools	.17	.32	.17	.22
Low-level schools	.07	.04	.22	.01

metric data from the low schools indicate that ambitious students do tend to name students from higher backgrounds than their own as preferred friends according to the reference group hypothesis for upward mobility. But the low-school students whose backgrounds are relatively higher may not have middle-class values, and may not be, therefore, available as models for the upwardly mobile students. Under these circumstances, anticipatory socialization to middle-class values by the ambitious student would not take place.

One distinctive value pattern appears among four value items that incorporate a theme of manipulating other persons. Together they reflect the traditional enterpreneural freedom from collective controls and individual manipulation applied unilaterally in order to control others. Thus, positive choices of these items can be called manipulative individualism. As indicated in Table 19.3 (right columns), an index based on these four items tends to be high for men from high backgrounds in all schools. It is also associated with high ambition in the middle and high schools. However, the index is completely unrelated to high ambition in the low schools.

The failure of upwardly mobile men from poorer neighborhoods to adopt the manipulative value may well place them at a disadvantage if they actually try to move up. The subculture into which their success carries them would appear harsh and unattractive to them. Why do upwardly mobile students in low neighborhoods fail to adopt the one value complex that is clearly manifested in the students from higher backgrounds whom they appear to accept as a reference group? Perhaps there is no general neighborhood expectation that the upwardly mobiles should be like them. Or perhaps a generally neg-

ative attitude toward manipulativeness prevails in the neighborhood. In support of the latter interpretation, the sociometric data show less correlation between choices of students for their social prominence and choices for friendship in the low neighborhoods than elsewhere. In other words, in the low schools, there is less liklihood that the socially prominent student will also be chosen as friends.

The peculiarity of social organization among boys in the lower neighborhoods may be summarized as a pattern of future orientation without anticipatory socialization to manipulative individualism. Ambition and academic success are valued, but the distinctive values appropriate to the destination of the highly ambitious are not incorporated along the way. The prevalence of mobility orientation throughout most of the schools mitigates the circumstances otherwise conducive to marginality for the upwardly mobile. However, the ambitious boy who attends a high school that is peopled overwhelmingly by students from low socioeconomic backgrounds does not share in this protection and may well become the marginal man if he persists in his efforts to rise according to the American dream.

SELF, REFERENCE GROUPS, AND THE SOCIAL CONTEXT

Projections to the future are an important aspect of the self system, particularly during adolescence when adulthood is in the near future. As Turner's research suggests, the sets of factors shaping such attitudes, aspirations, and expectations for the future must be sought at all levels of the social context: the ideology of the larger society that promotes upward ambition through both its public institutions (schools) and mass media, the family and neighborhood backgrounds, and the social systems among youth.

The importance of the social system within the school which awards status for certain values and not others cannot be ignored easily by the adolescent, tuned as he or she is to the agemate reference set. In studies of Midwestern schools, Coleman (1961) found that the "leading crowds" were more likely to prize athletic success for boys and popularity for girls than academic orientations (being a good student). Nevertheless, Wilson (1959) found that a lower-class boy is more likely to be upwardly mobile in his educational aspirations if he attends a school populated chiefly by students with higher socioeconomic background than if he attends a school populated chiefly by other lower class students. The importance of agemate influence at this age level cannot be ruled out even when family strivings are conducive to upward mobility, for boys from such families are also more likely to choose other upwardly mobile boys as friends when they have the chance (Haller and Butterworth, 1960; Bell, 1963).

**Contradictions
in the Social Context**

The complexity of the determinants of the self-image can be understood by comparing the model for adulthood that is conveyed to youth by official sources and the specific social contexts in which particular youth actually move. In modern societies with efficient means of mass communication and public educational institutions, youths learn what values and goals are prized in society. However, acceptance of the goals does not always mean that daily actions are appropriate for realizing them.

For example, in New Zealand, Ausubel (1965) studied the attitudes and ambitions of both Maori and European youth in urban and rural settings. Finding considerable difference according to rural or urban residence, he selected samples in the country and in the city, matching each Maori with a

European in the same school class and ability group and whose father's occupation fell into the same category. On a battery of tests designed to secure aspirations, attitudes toward achievement, and personal characteristics supportive of achievement, he found important urban-rural differences but few differences in these respects between the matched Maori and European youth either in the country or city. This lack of difference was surprising because, in fact, the Maori youth tend to drop out of school much more frequently at 15 years of age and few Maoris have actually pursued the skilled trades and professions to which the subjects said they aspired.

By observations of Maori life and interviews, Ausubel found that the social context of the Maori student outside of school militated against their realization of goals fashioned on the European image. Maori parents, already familiar with European discrimination but fairly uncommunicative about it to their children, put few pressures on their children for achievement and offered little encouragement. Maori culture put a high value on relationships with peers, which required considerable time and effort in interpersonal relations that did not reward individualistic achievement but rather accomplishment within the peer group. Thus there was a considerable discrepancy between societal values and the possibility of translating them into action in the Maori's actual social context. Remarkably similar findings were obtained in studying lower-class Spanish-speaking youth in the southwestern United States (Sherif and Sherif, 1964).

The question arises whether membership in peer groups during adolescence inevitably interferes with attainment of socially desirable ambitions. At times, the literature on "youth subcultures" in the United States seems to see such influence as almost inevitably negative. However, cases are found, as we shall see, wherein the adolescent reference group functions to support socially desirable ends as well. Hechinger (1967) observed that peer-group influences were strongly stressed in the United States in educational practice but regarded as "independent 'sub-cultures' governed by standards of their own making," while educational practice in the Soviet Union places a similar stress on the peer group as a vehicle for securing commitment to "adult standards, mores and morals." Thus apparently the effects of peer influence are not independent of the larger social system in which they are manifest.

Bronfenbrenner's report (1967) on a comparative study of sixth graders in the two countries suggests that the different significance of peer group influence starts much earlier than adolescence. Their reactions were compared in a series of situations designed to test readiness to cheat on a test, deny responsibility for property damage, and other actions ordinarily viewed as morally reprehensible by adults in both countries.

The results indicate that American children were far more ready to take part in such actions. The effect of the peer group (friends in school) was quite different in the two societies. When told that their friends would know of their actions, American children were even more willing to engage in misconduct. Soviet youngsters showed just the opposite tendency. In their case, the peer group operated to support the values of adult society (p. 62).

ADOLESCENTS
IN THEIR REFERENCE GROUPS
WITHIN DIFFERENT
SOCIOCULTURAL ENVIRONMENTS

In a research program initiated in 1958, Sherif and Sherif (1964, 1965, 1967) developed a design and procedures to study intensively the behaviors of adolescents as they interacted in informal groups of their own choosing. Because leisure time outside of school gives the American youth the opportunity to select his own companions and activities, such groups were chosen as most likely to be reference groups for individual members—more likely than groups organized according to blueprints and programs of adults. As described in Chapter 8, the groups were selected on the basis of observed frequency and regularity of their association and were studied without alerting members that they were the objects of research interest.

Small informal groups are not closed systems. Therefore, the research design explicitly included data collection on the sociocultural settings. These sociocultural data were used to specify the frame of reference within which group interaction and individual behavior occurred. In order to show differences in behavior within groups according to the sociocultural setting, it was necessary to select groups with different socioeconomic class (low, middle, and high) and subcultural backgrounds (e.g., Spanish-speaking, Negro, white). In capsule form, the following summarizes the research design:

I. *Intensive study of interaction* among members on the spot during regular observation periods for six months to a year, in order to specify the group structure and norms within which individual behavior occurred.

a. Case history materials on the individual members and the origins of their group were collected at the conclusion of the observation, in order to specify individual life histories. This step was the final one in order that the anonymity of research procedures be preserved during observation (see *Study Cycle,* below).

II. *Specification of the urban areas and neighborhoods* where the group members met and engaged in activities together, including the Shevky-Bell Social Area Analysis for ranking the areas according to socioeconomic rank, family-urban status, and segregation (*see below*), as well as mapping of facilities.

III. *Surveys of the values and goals* prevailing among adolescents who attended high school in each of the areas studied, in order to have a yardstick for assessing the attitudes and aspirations of the members of small groups studied. The Self Radius and Goals Schedules developed for this purpose were administered to representative samples of students. The distributions and modal tendencies in their responses were used to (a) define norms prevailing among the adolescents who were the reference set for particular individuals studied in their groups and (b) to ascertain how typical or atypical a particular small group was in its particular setting.

The Study Cycle
in Observation

The observation and rating methods used in this research were summarized in Chapter 8. Here the sequence of steps will be summarized briefly. The purpose of all the steps and their sequence was to secure valid and reliable data on group interaction as it actually occurred, without disrupting the flow of interaction and without alerting the individual members that they were being observed. These procedures have been followed successfully for several dozen groups in large cities in the southwest and eastern sections of the United States. The entire study cycle for each group required from six months to a year.

First an observer was chosen on the basis of his training and his "fit" into the area he would study (which might be lower, middle, or upper class, and with varying ethnic composition). His first job was to master the instructions and methods of observation (Sherif and Sherif, 1964, Appendix, pp. 331–360). Then he went regularly to the study area to single-out a group for observation—entirely on the basis of the observed frequency and regularity of association among a minimum of five or six boys (for example, on street corners, in recreation areas, soda fountains, pool halls, and other hangouts).

Meanwhile, the observer had developed a reasonable pretext for being in the area which would permit him to establish a relationship with the group. This development of a role in the area was crucial for two reasons: First, the observer himself is observed from the moment he begins to frequent an area. Second, it is essential that he be categorized as a harmless or neutral person without any authority in the area, and not as a researcher or investigator.

When and if the observer succeeded in establishing contact with the cluster that he had singled-out, he proceeded according to a definite sequence of instructions to study it intensively. The study cycle started with a written report on each observation period, focusing on the interaction patterns among the boys. The observer made ratings after each observation period of the relative *effective initiative* exhibited by each boy during their activities and patterns of defer-

ence to one another. (See Chapter 8 for a definition of effective initiative.) Later in the study cycle, an independent observer was introduced to cross-check the observer's ratings, and sociometric choices were secured informally from each individual, as reflections of the members' views from inside the group.

Next, the observer focused on group products peculiar to the group, by reporting on recurrences of activities, labels and nicknames, jokes, jargon, common practices and preferences, and, especially, reactions to deviation. Finally, observation centered on the strength of group ties or solidarity. At this stage of the study, it was usually possible to introduce special test situations to check solidarity, in addition to observations. For example, in one group the observer had developed sufficient rapport with the group so that he could arrange an important group event to coincide with the time that one member had a date with an attractive girl. In this instance, the boy went with the group, after considerable hesitancy on his part and concerted urging from other members.

Such tests, as well as sociometric choices, were not introduced until there was clear evidence of observer rapport with the group. As indicators of degree of rapport, it was necessary to develop objective evidence. For example, rapport was assessed in terms of the observer's success in finding where the group congregated when it was not in plain public view, their toleration of the observer in these more private places, and the degree of intimacy of the activities they would discuss or engage in freely when he was present.

Specifying the Sociocultural
and Ecological Characteristics
of the Area

The Shevky-Bell Social Area Analysis was used to designate the ecological characteristics of each urban area. This analysis was based on the finding that the large number of separate measures contained in Census Tract statistics tend to be intercorrelated and can, therefore, be reduced to three (or more) basic factors. Since certain measures are better measures of these three factors

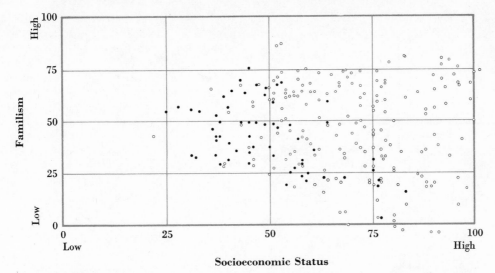

Fig. 19.5. Distribution of census tracts in social areas of San Francisco Bay Region, 1950, used in a study by Bell. The familism index (*vertical*) is the same as the urbanization index. Dark dots indicate areas with a predominance of population low on the social distance scale; open dots, high. Dots located outside of the coordinates occurred because standardization formula was based on social area analysis of Los Angeles some years earlier. (Adapted from Wendell Bell, 1965.)

than others, only a few of them are actually used in computing each of three indexes as follows (Bell, 1965):

Index of Socioeconomic Status	Index of Urbanization or Family Status	Index of Ethnicity or Segregation
Rent Education Occupation	Fertility ratio Women not in the labor force Single-family detached dwellings	Race Nativity Spanish surnames

Shevky and Bell standardized scores on each of these three indicators according to the range present in Los Angeles in 1940. This standardization makes it possible to compare the rank of areas in different cities, even though the basic yardstick (Los Angeles, 1940) was arbitrarily chosen. For example, Figure 19.5 gives the distribution of census tracts in the San Francisco Bay region in 1950 according to socioeconomic status (baseline) and family or urbanization status (ordinate), with white dots indicating that the population was predominantly *not* low in ethnic status and dark dots indicat-

ing considerable segregation of ethnic groups with low status. It may be noted that compared with Los Angeles in 1940, the San Francisco Bay Area was composed of largely middle- and upper-rank areas in socioeconomic status (some even exceeding 100 as standardized in Los Angeles) and that there was considerable variation in the style of family life. (Those areas high on the vertical axis were characterized by apartment dwellings, a lower birth rate, and more women working.)

Findings: Variations in Goals and Settings

Despite the rather sharply graded socioeconomic and ethnic stratification in the United States, there were marked similarities among the youth in different urban social areas. Although differing in appearance, specific styles of dress, and sometimes speaking different languages, the adolescents all bore the unmistakable stamp of the larger culture with its stress on individual success in private and material respects. The ingredients of individual success desired by nearly 100 percent of every sample of high-school students included au-

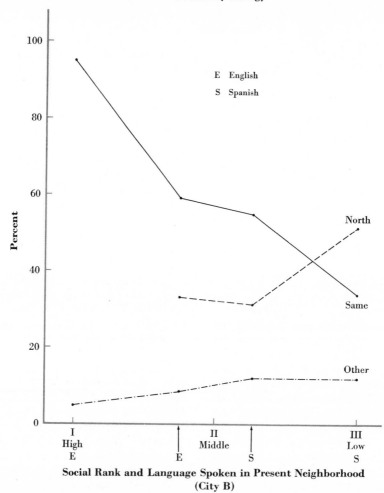

Fig. 19.6. Contentment and discontent with own neighborhood expressed by adolescents living in areas of different social rank. Proportions of high-school youth living in areas of high, middle, and low socioeconomic rank (left to right on baseline) who desire to move to another area (north or other) and to remain in the same neighborhood. The location of the area with high rank (left) is north. (From Sherif and Sherif, 1964.)

tomobiles, attractive clothing, spending money, at least a couple of hours a day "to do what I want to do," and comfortable homes. Figure 19.6 shows the responses of students in social areas of low, middle, and high socioeconomic rank in one city who filled the blank in this sentence: "If I had my way, I'd like to live in a neighborhood in the————part of the city." It shows the percentages responding with the same location where they currently lived, the "north side" of the city (which was undeniably the most comfortable), or some other location. As the Figure shows, the desire to stay in the same location decreased

regularly from the high- to the low-rank neighborhood, while the desire increased to move north (where the high-rank sample lived).

Because students in a high school are likely to give questionnaire responses that they consider "socially desirable," it is interesting to note that what is socially desirable differs in some respects according to socioeconomic rank of the area. As Turner's study would lead us to expect, the level of goals for future occupation, education, and income differed systematically from one area to the next. However, it was found that what was conceived of as "suc-

Table 19.4. Discrepancy Between Own Desired Occupation and Father's Occupation: City A

	Rank of Area		
Occupational Rank	High %	Middle %	Low %
1. Highest professional top managerial	−.8	+2.5	+3.0
2. Professional, business, technical	−12.5	+20.3	+12.1
3. Lower professional, small business	+11.6	+10.6	+17.0
4. Sales and clerical	+10.1	+8.6	+9.7
5. Skilled	−7.6	−25.6	−4.9
6. Semiskilled	−.8	−10.3	−22.6
7. Unskilled	0.0	−6.1	−14.3
% differing from rank of father's occupation	21.7	42.0	41.8

cess" in these respects also differed. For example, Fig. 19.7 shows the average (median) responses to a series of items concerning how much weekly income was needed to "just get along," to be comfortable, and desirable personally within 10 years. Clearly, the radius within which one sets his future aspirations differs from the high- to the low-rank areas. Psychologically, his reference set establishes bounds for the radius of the self in these respects.

Nevertheless, relative to their fathers' attainments and to their own conceptions of success, aspirations for upward mobility were common in middle- and lower-rank areas. Table 19.4 shows that approximately 40 percent of the youth in low- and middle-rank areas of one city aspired to occupational levels higher than their fathers'. This upward shift was largely at the expense of desiring manual labor with gains in the upper occupational categories.

Similarly, in response to inquiry about the amount of education "necessary for a person who wants to do the things I want to do" and the amount personally desired, the aspirations of students in low, middle, and high areas differed systematically (see Fig. 19.8).

Greater Heterogeneity in Middle- and Lower-Rank Areas

The data in Fig. 19.8 serve as a point of departure for another important finding:

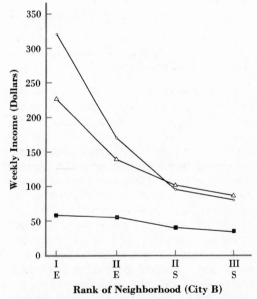

Fig. 19.7. Reference scales for evaluating weekly income in areas of different social rank. Median estimates in high (I), middle (II), and low (III) areas as to the minimum income for subsistence (squares), for comfort (circles), and personal goals for future (triangles). E indicates English speaking; S, Spanish speaking. (From Sherif and Sherif, 1964.)

The values and goals that prevail among adolescents in lower- and middle-class neighborhoods are more heterogeneous than those in upper-rank areas. Figure 19.9 consists of the same data on educational

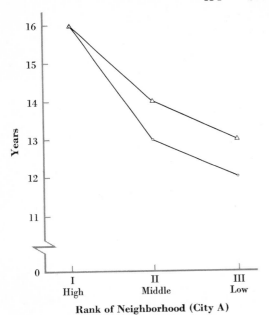

Fig. 19.8. Median years of schooling considered "necessary" (circles) and personally desired (triangles) by high-school students in areas of different social rank. Median estimates defining an "educated person" coincide with those considered "necessary." (From Sherif and Sherif, 1964.)

goals as shown in Fig. 19.8, but they are presented as a frequency distribution of the responses (number of years desired) for the low, middle, and upper samples. The responses of youth in the upper-rank school were most homogeneous, about 85 percent desiring four or more years of education beyond high school. While the typical response in the lower-class area is for a high-school education, a sizable minority aimed at college. Certainly there is little hint here of the supposed derogation of school that once was believed typical of the lower class. Similarly, the distribution in the middle-rank area reveals considerable heterogeneity, even a bimodality.

In this and several respects, the findings showed that youth in upper-rank areas were most like-minded. Coupled with the fact that youth in such areas are also more frequently and extensively involved in formally organized activities in school and community, this finding suggests that we might also expect to find less variety in the impact of agemate reference groups in high-rank areas. The intensive study of natural groups in lower and middle areas supported the conclusion that the impact of the group

varied tremendously in terms of whether it supported or went contrary to the values prevailing in and promoted by the high schools.

THE IMPACT OF THE ADOLESCENT REFERENCE GROUP

NB #1, 2, 3

The observational procedures described briefly in this chapter confirmed the following predictions about the natural groups and their impact upon member behavior.

1. Associations among adolescents that recur regularly over time are patterned affairs: they are groups in the sense defined in Chapter 7. Although their organization is informal and is subject to change, these groups are sufficiently stable that their status and role structures can be reliably assessed.

2. Such groups do generate norms of their own that are binding for members in varying degrees. These norms may or may not promote conformity to values and goal strivings approved by society. Whether they do cannot be predicted solely on the basis of the class and ethnic rank of the members, but is a complex product of the group's interaction in its particular environment and its relationships with other adolescents and adults.

3. Such groups are reference groups for individual members and do serve to provide standards for the individual in evaluating his own behavior and that of others. To the extent that the adolescent reference group becomes the major anchor for the individual (at the time), he can and does violate norms for behavior upheld by family, school, and adult authorities without feelings of guilt or shame—at least as long as such violation is known only to fellow members. (In other words, the member's conscience is tied to the group to this extent and under these circumstances.)

TRANSMISSION OF NORMS THROUGH GENERATIONS

During the research on natural groups, it was possible in one fairly stable lower-class neighborhood to trace the norms of one group through three generations of adoles-

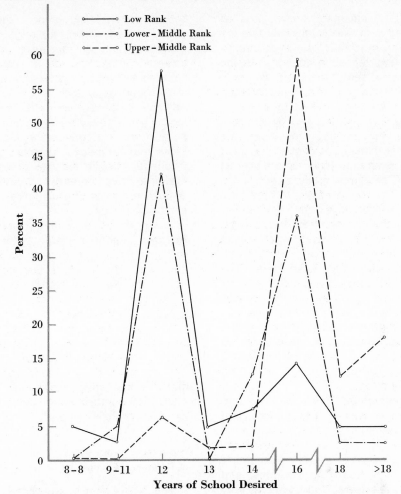

Fig. 19.9. Bimodality of distribution of personal goals for education in areas of different socioeconomic rank. Note that the goals in the highest rank area (single dashed line) are most homogeneous. Distributions in lower-middle and low-rank areas are bimodal. (Based on Sherif and Sherif data.)

cents. Early in the project, a group called "Los Apaches" was observed by Eduardo Villarreal. Subsequently, he returned to the neighborhood to carry through the study cycle with young adults in the same neighborhood who were just somewhat older than the boys (mostly in their twenties) and former members. When this study cycle was complete, he returned to Los Apaches, whose membership had changed in the interim.

The neighborhood itself had changed very little in this time, but several things had changed about the city itself:

A. The city was more prosperous—thus the families had more money and some had cars.

B. The "anglicization" of the city through the schools and mass media had continued.

Accordingly, two questions were asked:

A. What norms of the Apaches had survived three generations of membership?
B. Were any changes that had occurred related to social change in the city?

First generation: The observer found that the group had acquired its name during an escapade with the police when one of the young adults still in the neighborhood (dubbed "El Apache") had been its leader. The group had existed prior to that time. In this generation, the members had all quit school in the elementary grades and as adults worked at unskilled jobs with two exceptions (auto mechanic and shoe repairman). They had very little contact with the next two generations of members except in the parental home of one member of each generation. (This was verified by observations over several months and by a picnic arranged by the observer for older and younger generations.) The former leader of the second generation (now almost twenty) and other older youths made moves to be accepted by the young adults, but the third generation (thirteen to eighteen years old) kept a respectful distance from their elders. Members of the first generation refused to help the younger ones during a conflict with a traditional rival—the Lakesiders. The young adults said that the present generation was not so tough as they were, and has more money, but that Los Apaches and Lakesiders will "always" be rivals. They also said that the police are not so tough as they used to be, but maintained an implacable dislike for the police, as did the younger generations.

Second generation: This was the group first observed, consisting of twelve boys and occasional hangers-on (See Sherif and Sherif, 1964). Most of its members were known to police and detention-home officials for stealing, carrying weapons, and fighting the Lakesiders. The boys had very little money, engaged in frequent theft, regular beer drinking, and occasional glue sniffing. They seldom if ever had the use of a car (except the observer's). They spent long periods of time together. After three years, however, the members were no longer affiliated with Los Apaches, some had jobs, and some (including the former leader) were thinking of getting married.

Third generation: As the second generation moved away from Los Apaches, a former lieutenant who was considerably younger took over the leadership position. Several new members were added at high-status levels as well as a number of younger boys with lower status. The observer detected very little change in what the group did or its norms after nearly three years and the changed membership. Occasionally, the members stole (always in twos or threes), but they did have more spending money to buy beer and occasionally had the use of a

relative's car. They placed a much higher value on education, although none had progressed beyond the ninth grade. Beer, solvent-sniffing, and the use of marijuana were part of group get-togethers, but (as in the second generation) beer was the only universally consumed refreshment of its kind. Their slang was identical to that of the second and first generation (Spanish), but these younger members spoke English more frequently. Unlike the two preceding generations, they preferred to sing current popular songs in English rather than Mexican popular music.

In short, as a miniature culture, Los Apaches endured with minor changes through three generations of adolescent members. The changes that occurred reflected the impact of broader social change in the city. Like most adolescent reference groups, Los Apaches ceased to affect its members as they grew into their twenties and "settled down" as adult members of the community. However, those ex-members who stayed in the neighborhood still associated—considering themselves now too adult for the antics of the "kids," but still as members of the same set.

Implications from Study of Reference Groups

The research on adolescent reference sets and groups has emphasized the gamut of influences that interact in shaping the adolescent's attitudes and behavior. As a transition period between childhood and adulthood, adolescence requires the person to form and re-form many significant attitudes in the self system at a time when whatever psychological stability he has achieved in childhood is shaken—by a changing body and, especially in industrialized urban societies, by pervasive ambiguities and uncertainties of the adolescent status. Combined with the gap between adult and youthful generations, these conditions produce the intense motivations toward affiliation with peers that are conducive to a proliferation of adolescent groups.

However, what occurs during interaction *within* adolescent reference groups, their organizations and norms, and their impact on the individual are products of the larger social system and its dominant ideology, of the position and character of the particular sociocultural milieu within that society, and of the small group's relationship to its particular milieu—as well as the more immediate motivations and skills of the group members. This chapter may serve, then, as a caution against oversimplified explanations of attitude and behavior.

Nevertheless, research findings indicate the great importance of membership in an adolescent reference group, whether its effects are socially desirable or undesirable. To the extent that the group is, for the time, stable and solidary (cohesive), its role and status relations and its norms become anchors for the individual during specific behavior episodes. This conclusion, coupled with the undeniable impact of the sociocultural setting upon the group, is essential in understanding the actions of youth in periods of crisis and rapid social change—so characteristic of this century. It is particularly pertinent to the analysis of collective interaction episodes and social movements involving youth, who like other persons involved, may face great risks and perform deeds of both heroic and degrading character when gripped by their identifications within the circles of interaction therein encompassed. As collective interaction and social movements constitute significant aspects of social and psychological change, they will be discussed in Part V, which deals explicitly with problems of change.

PART V

Man as Agent and Target of Social Change:

Process, Products, Change

20

Introduction to Part V

When we look at any social system in any country, we note certain regularity, stability, and persistence in its adherents' way of life or ideology, in basic beliefs, in values or norms, in the ways its people conduct their business among themselves and relative to outsiders. When we look at the same country at another period sufficiently separated in time, we note changes in various of these aspects of social life. The changes in some respects may be a matter of degree or frequency, while others are more substantial.

Changes in degree or frequency are referred to as evolutionary changes. For example, in the United States, the federal government's power to levy taxes was constitutionally established. Yet, a hundred years ago, a federal income tax was considered a proposal espoused by only a few nonconformist crackpots, as mentioned earlier in this book. The federal income tax gained acceptance gradually and is generally accepted today. The change in the place of women is another example. The change from that of housewife with responsibility for household and handicraft tasks and with the virtues of submissive restraint to that of women in professions, business, or politics or to the wife putting her husband through school is another illustration of an important evolutionary change, if viewed within sufficient time perspective.

On the other hand, the changes may be more drastic—so great in degree or kind that the course of living itself has changed. Changes that are not only a matter of degree or frequency but also a matter of the very course of events are referred to as

461

revolutionary changes, particularly if they occur within a fairly short time period. The changes produced by the American revolution, the French revolution, the Russian revolution, and, more recently, the Chinese revolution are examples. Other examples of revolutionary change have been initiated in Africa and Asia where erstwhile tribes, castes, or kingdoms under colonial power now strive to transform their social arrangements. We shall return to the topic of revolutionary changes and the social movements that produce them in Chapter 24.

A great many drastic changes that have transformed man's relations to man across countries as well as within countries were brought about by the unprecedented technological developments in modern times, especially during the lifetime of people born in the twentieth century. Such changes have increased the interdependence of people within nations and across nations in various spheres of life, altered their transactions, and transformed their notions of space, time, and, in fact, their notions of the world we live in. We shall return to the impact of technological changes upon man's attitudes, his relations to others, and his habits of doing things in Chapter 22.

In social psychology, our primary concern is man himself as an *agent* and as a *target* of social changes, whether such changes occur through social movements, or through breakthroughs in technology, or through the impact of communication from the mass media (radio, television, newspapers, etc.), or through participation in person-to-person or group interactions. Man is not a passive agent in any of these changes. If they are to be durable, all social changes have to involve changes in man himself—in his outlook, commitments, identifications, and attitudes, hence the very yardsticks that he uses for evaluating and coping with events.

There have been controversies among social scientists and essayists as to whether man is ever-conforming by nature (stability) or nonconforming and thus a seeker of new ways of doing things (change). The question is irrelevant and the controversy, put in these terms, is sterile. As noted in various contexts in previous chapters, it is in man's nature to strive toward establishing stability in his ties with others in personal and group relations, and to establish some orderliness in the run of his daily life through adherence to regularities, routines, and regulation by norms or values that he cherishes (see Proposition 6 and Chapters 11 and 17). It is also in man's nature to change the regularities, values, or norms that define his role when the prevailing stability becomes the source of restlessness, uncertainty, deprivation, or frustration. Thus stability and change are complementary hallmarks of man's nature.

As we have seen, the stability of the person's self-identity as he perceives and feels it requires stability in his interpersonal and group relationships with others and the world around him (in terms of familiar objects, time tables, routines, and institutions). This experience of self-identity is not a self-generated product and is not wholly self-sustaining.

Yet, achievement of some measure of stability within the person through orderly ties and role relations with the world around him and normative regularities is not a static condition that stays put, undisturbed for good. When his beliefs, commitments, identifications, or his role in established social arrangements become agents of his inner conflicts (instead of inner harmony), when they become tools for his degradation, when they become restrictive channels conducive only to his deprivation, and when they become determinants of severe frustrations, then he is in search again for new avenues or alternatives. He is on the move to discover a new identity. Thus the tendency toward change is inherent in the very process of achieving a new stability.

But the search for new avenues and alternatives for self-identity is not accomplished overnight. Repudiation of habitual restraints and channels of well-ingrained beliefs and attitudes is not an easy matter, something to be accomplished in one stroke. The feat is accomplished only through a great deal of psychological simmering, doubt, wear and tear, and interaction with others in the same boat. It requires that the person at least glimpse new alternatives with supportive promptings during interaction with others who had the good fortune to develop an enlarged perspective through intellectual awakening and through identification with people sharing a predicament in common. This requirement implies, of course, leadership.

In other words, the individual's moves to find and to adopt new alternatives do not occur in a vaccuum. Always, and everywhere, they are channeled within a range of the alternatives formulated by previous dissenters and by the resistance to change from representatives of the status quo. As a rule, there is an Establishment with power superior to the discontented innovator. The Establishment closes ranks when confronted by threats to its central interests, as any group does when threatened (see Chapters 12 and 24). It uses its superior power to block, quell, or destroy the impertinent or "dangerous." Even reformers advocating evolutionary change to bring actualities in line with the Establishment's own declarations meet this power, as the Civil Rights movement in the United States shows. On far less consequential issues, in which change threatens only what is seen as respectability, the reactions of established and powerful groups to reform may well exceed the bounds of what seems reasonable to men on the move, just as their moves appear outrageous to respectability. However, the resistance of group to group is not the only brake on change.

Many observers have noted the persistence of values, beliefs, and norms that have outlived their function and have become a source of maladjustment relative to actualities. Social scientists use the term _cultural lag_ to refer to this state of affairs, which is widely prevalent in the contemporary world. Simply stated, cultural lag is a lag in time in the change of values and other normative standards long after they have become a source of maladjustment in man's adaptation to the actualities of prevailing conditions.

Cultural Lag
and the Social Psychology
of Change

The cultural lag has important implications for social-psychological study of change. Despite man's dissatisfactions and alienation, relinquishing the commitments,

beliefs, and identifications (in short, ego-attitudes) that he has come to cherish is not like shedding a wornout coat. It is more nearly like giving up something long held close and dear as a part of oneself. This is one reason why it is so difficult for individuals and for groups to change their attachments to beliefs about their way of life, their family, their religion, or their politics, even when they are in a quandary about their value.

As we have seen before, norms prevailing in social, religious, political, and ethical spheres are products expressing predominantly the prevailing social arrangements of the "Establishment." They are not like the "givens" in the physical world, in the sense of similarities and differences in a physical stimulus continuum (such as size, length, or weight of objects). Normative behavior expresses value judgments more than discriminations among physical attributes, the correctness or incorrectness of which can be more easily ascertained by external checks on physical reality. The external checks on value judgments ultimately consist of the consensus among people. Therefore, we have referred to categories embodying value judgments as _psychosocial_ scales (pp. 79–80). It will be recalled that psychosocial scales and their change can be assessed with appropriate methods. In assessing the stability or change of psychosocial scales, the end points and the various categories within them have to be assessed in terms of what is most acceptable, what is most objectionable, and varying degrees thereof within given groups. The individual's attitudes and their change are properly assessed relative to psychosocial scales. We shall return to the problems of such change in Chapter 21.

Although more resistant to change, even after outliving their possible usefulness in regulating social relationships, psychosocial scales of values, beliefs and commitments are not immutable. Psychosocial scales are products of interaction in various spheres of living (kinship, religion, politics, or business) and are, therefore, subject to change under specifiable conditions. The conditions optimal for their change are conditions of great uncertainty, ambiguity, or crisis, as represented by a general depression like that in the United States in the 1930s or by conditions of dislocation, hunger, and confusion produced by war. Such conditions that render people more suggestible are conductive to the change of established norms, for such conditions lack objective structure in varying degrees and pertain to matters of high motivational concern. In such conditions, the individual is most open to guidelines offered or promoted by others, either in the form of proposals made during interaction in reference groups or from the mass media of communication.

Compared with the greater resistance to change of psychosocial scales, psychophysical scales adapt much more readily to change. One of the generalizations well established by anthropologists, sociologists, and other social scientists is that attitudes in regard to technological innovations (such as cars, radio, television, and jet planes) change more quickly than related attitudes concerning the family, religion, politics, and ideology. Innovation and change in technology provide readily available and objective checks on the appropriateness of prevailing habits and attitudes most directly related to adoption of the innovation. It does not take much to convince a peasant in an industrially underdeveloped region that a truck or jeep is a superior means of transport to his donkey. A few trips are enough to establish the fact and achieve change of attitude in this regard. Similarly, it requires not too many cases to demonstrate that quinine or its derivatives are more effective in controlling malaria than wearing charms to ward off the agents of sickness.

Technological devices and systems, with their immediately perceivable utility and convenience, produce changes in standards and conceptions established for the activity at hand that are accepted with relatively greater ease than changes involving religious, political, and ideological spheres. The social-psychological explanation of this differential rate of attitude change lies in the availability of readily obtainable external checks on prevailing habits and attitudes directly related to technology. Thus technological devices and the comparisons they involve belong to the domain of psychophysical scales, wherein ready adaptation to change is the general rule.

Conditions Conducive to Attitude Change

The foregoing account of social change in psychosocial and psychophysical scales provides realistic leads as to the determinants of attitude change. By and large, people do not change their attitudes, beliefs, and values merely to adapt to a temporary or trivial change in their environment. There must be a motivational base before changing one's attitude in a particular sphere of living becomes a feasible alternative for the person. In the domain of psychosocial scales, conditions producing widely shared uncertainty, deprivation, and frustration produce such a motivational base. They provoke a search for new alternatives in value orientation and in redefining the self-identity. They provoke a search for external social checks from others sharing the same predicament and who will risk a new alternative. Hence such conditions generate changes of norms within groups and the adoption of new reference groups by individuals. Whether in interaction with like-minded fellows or from the prestigeful mass media, communication advocating the choice of a particular alternative over others becomes more effective under such conditions. Such are the considerations that led us to include the chapter on attitude change in this book within the context of Part V, devoted to social change. As noted in Chapter 21, this is not the first time that the problems of attitude change have been considered.

The usual practice in the experimental study of attitude change has been, on the whole, to present a brief communication or exposure to some other brief procedure discrepant from the person's opinion and comparing opinion before and afterward as indicated by some convenient questionnaire or rating form. In such before-after designs, experimental subjects exposed to the communication (perhaps 15 minutes in duration) may be compared with control subjects who were not exposed to it. As noted in Chapter 21, the results of such research have been contradictory and inconclusive; this is not surprising. Only recently has the degree of the person's involvement in the issue of the communication been considered systematically.

Unless we are content merely to study the individual's willingness to adopt one brand of toothpaste in preference to others or his adaptiveness to clues in the experimental situation about guesses he is asked to make, the study of attitude change either in laboratory or the field has to incorporate the variables that make attitude change an important problem in social life. Such variables necessarily include the person's commitment to his attitude and the social conditions both within and outside of the laboratory that provoke susceptibility to change. It is one thing to try to change a person's guess or an opinion given off the top of his head. It is quite another thing to change his commitment to a stand on an issue related to his sex role, his family, his religion, or his politics, as the case may be.

Experimental methods in the study of attitudes and their change can become powerful research tools when they are applied to analysis of the actualities of attitude formation and change through incorporation of major variables, such as those mentioned here as conditions for change. Experimentation and appropriate assessment procedures can be utilized in studying the important problem of attitude formation when no attitude exists. Finally, even short-range events in the laboratory can be employed to study the important problem of how individuals perceive, judge, and evaluate communications or other attempts designed to change their attitudes. These and related problems of attitude change are discussed in Chapter 21.

21

Attitude Change Through Communication in Interaction Situations

Major Topics of the Chapter

Frequency of change in the laboratory and field research

Expected and unexpected effects of communication

What is attitude change?

Individual as target of change in interaction process

Norms emerging as decisions during interaction are binding

Changes in reference groups alter a host of related attitudes

Attitude formation and change in reference groups

Implication of reference groups for models of attitude change

Equilibrium models

Social judgment-involvement formulation

ATTITUDE CHANGE
AND INTERACTION PROCESS

The title of this Part, "Man as Agent and Target of Social Change," indicates the focus of this chapter. The formation of attitudes and their change will be viewed within a framework of interacting influences from within the person and from his surroundings, in which he himself is an active participant. On the one hand, neither his motivations nor cognitive processes associated with attitude change are independent of the social conditions around him. On the other hand, attitude formation and change cannot be viewed as a one-way process, in which the individual is merely a target, reacting to environmental forces. Particularly in times of crisis or rapid social change, the person's heightened sensitivity, his choices within the widened range of environmental alternatives, and his active participation with others in the same boat identify him as an agent of the existing stability or of change.

While among the most popular topics in social psychology, attitudes and their change are also among the most complex of its problems. *We are dealing here with no less a problem than the acquisition and change of consistent and characteristic modes of behavior toward motivationally and socially significant objects, persons, groups, and institutions.* It follows that a rounded social psychology of attitude formation and change will, eventually, incorporate principles from such now scattered topics as human perception and learning,

conceptual functioning and judgment, as well as motivation, social influence, interaction processes, and their enduring products.

Fortunately, the background and history of attempts to study attitudes and their change are readily available (e.g., Fishbein, 1967; Jahoda and Warren, 1966; Halloran, 1967; Klapper, 1960; McGuire, 1968; Schramm, 1963; Sherif and Sherif, 1967). Therefore, the aim of this chapter is to steer a path through the voluminous research literature and welter of rival theories that will permit perspective on the variables that have to be included in an adequate approach to problems of attitude change.

McGuire (1969) compared the situation of the theorist on attitude change to a person lost in a forest and who can emerge into more open territory only if he chooses a certain direction and keeps going on the same path to avoid traveling in circles. Pursuing his analogy we start with a brief review of some dead-ends, in order to narrow the choice of alternative routes.

APPARENT CONTRADICTIONS
IN RESEARCH FINDINGS

By and large, the contradictory research reports on attitude change in the United States reflect a long-term preoccupation with separate, specific, and immediate problems confronting social agencies that try to cope with attitude problems (cf. Bauer, 1964; Klapper, 1960; Schramm, 1963). Such problems include salesmanship and promotion in the mass media, propaganda and persuasion in political and international affairs, indoctrination and training in the military service, and the diverse problems of education and "re-education" on social relations within schools and training programs.

As a result of long-term preoccupation with social agency problems, the predominant research model was some variation on a formula derived from classical rhetoric: "Who says what, how, to whom and with what effect?" This formula amounts to the assumption that the media and tools of influence available to formal agencies of social control are, in fact, the major causes of attitude formation and change, thereby focusing research upon a one-way flow of communication from source to target.

The contradictory state of research findings on the effects of the mass media of communication collected since the late 1930s, is one fruit of the model. In particular, the survey and field (panel method) studies conducted under the aegis of Lazarsfeld and his associates alerted the sponsors to the difficulty of pinpointing the "effects" of the most powerful agents directing change attempts to the public. A study of the 1940 presidential elections, *The Peoples' Choice* (Lazarsfeld, Berelson, and Gaudet, 1948), indicated that very few voters changed their original party of choice during the campaign and that those who did referred to their family, friends, and other interpersonal ties more frequently than to the mass media (at the time, radio and newspapers). Information campaigns, combining the power of the mass media with information, yielded such meager "effects" that a still-popular article was entitled "Some Reasons Why Information Campaigns Fail" (Hyman and Sheatsley, 1947).

McGuire (1969) summarized the state of affairs as it concerns mass media research:

A tremendous amount of applied research has been carried out to test the effectiveness of the mass media by those who work in marketing, advertising, and political behavior areas. . . . The outcome has been quite embarrassing for proponents of the mass media usage, since there is little evidence of attitude change, much less change in gross behavior such as buying or voting. . . . Indeed, some of the results make

it appear that mass media campaigns may even have the reverse of the intended persuasive impact. . . . Since communication campaigns designed to change attitudes . . . via the mass media represent an investment of perhaps $20,000,000,000 per year in the United States alone (which probably places it as our third largest investment of national resources, in a distant but respectable third place behind expenditures to support the military establishment and to conduct formal education) those who are directly or indirectly engaged in this enterprise are loath to accept these negative findings at face value.

In the following two sections, we consider some major confusions in the research literature that reveal the inadequacy of a model of one-way flow of communication. Broadly labeled under the titles "Frequency of Change" and "Unexpected Effects of Communications," these discussions will orient us toward the *conditions* of research responsible for the apparent contradictions in the findings. In this early period of scientific study on this most complicated of topics, we are on much firmer grounds if we examine what findings have accumulated, the conditions in which data were collected, and see whether any coherent pattern emerges.

Frequency of Change in Field and Laboratory Research

In apparent contradiction to the typical failure of short-term field studies to demonstrate attitude change associated with communication from the mass media, laboratory studies frequently reveal change by substantial proportions of their captive targets (Hovland, 1959; Klapper, 1960). In some studies, the proportion of persons changing their response to opinion statements after a communication has run as high as 50 to 75 percent. Table 21.1 gives illustrative data from a study by Hovland and Weiss (1951) on the effect of the source of communication. The percentages listed in the table are *differences* between the percent of research subjects who changed their initial opinion *toward* the position presented in communication and the percent who changed *away* from the position of the communication. Such *net changes* represent a sort of profit-and-loss statement in assessing the effects

**Table 21.1. Net Changes of Opinion
in Direction of Communication
for Sources Classified as High or Low Credibility[a]**

Topic	High Credibility Sources		Low Credibility Sources	
	N	%	N	%
Antihistamines	31	22.6	30	13.3
Atomic Submarines	25	36.0	36	0.0
Steel Shortage	35	22.9	26	−3.8
Future of Movies	31	12.9	30	16.7
Mean		23.0		6.6
Difference		16.4		
p		< .01		

[a] Net changes = positive changes *minus* negative changes.

of a communication, thus an underestimation of the total change that occurred.

The credibility or trustworthiness of the source was determined in this study on the basis of the subjects' prior ratings of a long list of possible sources. The data show that the trustworthiness of the source in the subjects' eyes makes a substantial difference in the net change toward the same communications, to the point that net change was reduced to zero or in the direction away from the communication on two topics when the source was not credible.

The mean net change for the high credibility source (23 percent) would certainly be substantial enough to delight, for example, an advertiser or a political candidate. In comparison, Bauer (1964) called attention to the fact that "commercial promotions convert only a very small percentage of people to action," adding that such small percentages may also be worthwhile to the sponsors: "No one cigarette now commands more than 14% of the cigarette market, but an increase of 1% is worth $60,-000,000 in sales. This means influencing possibly .5% of all adults, and 1% of cigarette smokers" (p. 322).

The apparent contradiction between the frequent change in laboratory studies, on the one hand, and the much smaller changes in short-term field studies, on the other, can be resolved through attention to certain factors not central in the one-way communication model:

1. Field studies are typically undertaken on issues of considerable motivational ap-peal—that is, on more ego-involving issues than those studied in the laboratory. Note the topics listed in Table 21.1 from the study on communication source. In 1949 when these data were collected, it is unlikely that the sale of antihistamines, the feasibility of building an atomic submarine, responsibility for the then-current steel shortage, or the future of movie theaters represented matters of great concern to the subjects. A careful survey of both field and laboratory studies reveals that there are striking variations in frequency of change according to the issues studied. In short, degree of ego-involvement is a variable of great importance for the frequency or amount of change, whether in the laboratory or in the field.

2. Most (though not all) field studies investigate responses to communication to which the subject is exposed by his own choice, or by happening to be on the spot at the time. In contrast, most laboratory studies use captive audiences who are aware that their reactions to communications presented to them and, possibly, that their own attitudes on the topic are of research interest. The laboratory setting and captive audience simply shortcuts the usual sequence of exposure to communication by eliminating the question of *selective choice* and *selective attention.* We shall consider the effects of selective exposure in a later section.

3. The "Who says what, how, to whom and with what effect" model is a one-way model appropriate only for short-term, immediate effects because time allows all

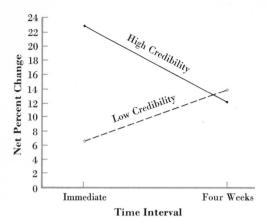

Fig. 21.1. Changes in the extent of agreement with position advocated by sources of differing credibility (high or low) immediately after exposure and four weeks later. (From C. I. Hovland and W. Weiss, 1951. The influence of source credibility on communication effectiveness. *Public Opin. Quart.* **15,** 635–650.)

sorts of other factors, including other communications on the topic, to intervene. Comparatively few laboratory studies have followed-up their subjects over periods of time. Figure 21.1 presents longitudinal data (averaged over the four topics) for subjects in the Hovland-Weiss study already referred to in Table 21.1. After a month, the net change for subjects exposed to a highly trustworthy source decreased markedly and that for subjects exposed to a source of low credibility increased enough to erase immediate differences attributable to the source. (Hovland attributed the slight net increase for the low credibility condition to forgetting the source.)

On the other hand, field studies that have traced attitudes over periods of rapid social change have found sizable and significant attitude changes. Figure 21.2 traces the increase in percentage of white Americans who believe Negroes to be as intelligent and educable as whites (Hyman and Sheatsley, 1964). This figure shows that field research does find attitude changes even on highly involving matters when it is conducted over a sufficient period of time during which important social changes are occurring. In this case the changes included return to civilian life after World War II, urban and northward migration of Negroes, changes in governmental and legal

policies, and a period of affluence which offered advantages to segments of the Negro population as well as the white population.

In short, the apparent contradiction in findings between field and laboratory research are not merely a matter of methods. They are to be resolved in terms of factors that cannot be readily subsumed in a model of one-way communication flow.

**Expected
and Unexpected Effects
of Communication**

Both laboratory studies and field research frequently find that the same communicator presenting the same message produces no attitude change among some individuals, change toward the advocated position among others, and change away from the advocated position for still others. In fact, the unexpected, negative change was sufficiently frequent that *net change* was introduced as a measure to take it into account.

When the net change measure is negative (as in the right column of Table 21.1 for the steel issue), it means that more people changed away from the communication than toward the position it advocated. Zero net change can mean that exactly the same proportions changed toward and away from a communication, cancelling each other. Finally, "no change," which indicates some consistency and the likelihood of a fairly stable attitude on the topic at hand, is seldom considered an important issue in attitude change studies.

One reason for the confusing and sometimes unexpected outcomes of attitude change studies, both in field and laboratory, was that until the last two decades very little attention was paid to the following questions:

1. Does the person have an attitude toward the issue in question to start with, and if so, how stable and entrenched is it?

2. Relative to the person's stand (if he has one), how discrepant is the position advocated in the communication?

As Klapper (1960) aptly remarked in reviewing experimental literature on attitude

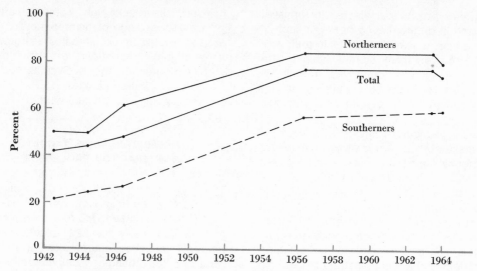

Fig. 21.2. Long-term changes in percentage of white adults stating the belief that Negroes are as intelligent and educable as whites. Note that the greatest change occurred between 1946 and 1956. (From H. H. Hyman and P. B. Sheatsley. Attitudes toward desegregation. Copyright © 1964 by Scientific American, Inc. All rights reserved.)

change, a great many laboratory studies present little or no evidence that subjects have an attitude on the issue at hand. Their findings are, therefore, best viewed as studies of incipient attitude formation. When so viewed, much laboratory research can be interpreted in harmony with findings from survey research on the effects of mass media in shaping viewpoints and attitudes on unfamiliar and uninvolving issues, where their impact is undeniable. In order to deal with the second question above, we need to reconsider what it is that is studied in attitude change research.

WHAT IS CHANGED
WHEN AN ATTITUDE CHANGES?

As defined in Chapter 15, when we refer to the person's attitudes, we are not talking about momentary or transitory affairs. We are talking about psychological factors responsible for the individual's characteristic and consistent modes of reacting for or against a class of objects and subsets within that class. Being cognitive-motivational and behavioral systems, attitudes include more or less lasting assumptions about the world, premises and regular expectations about the way the world operates and people within it, beliefs and perspectives about one's own kind and

other people, and sentiments and convictions about what is right and wrong and to be desired and to be scorned. Clearly these are vital matters for the individual. Some of his attitudes define what he includes within the radius of his self-concept and what he excludes. They define what family relatives, what nonrelatives, what groups, what schools, what political party, what religion, what ideology are *his* and what are *not*.

The foregoing description of attitudes implies that the behavior from which an attitude is inferred always involves a comparison, a choice or a decision among alternatives. That is why the psychology of judgment is relevant to attitudes and their change. That is why the person's categorizations of a stimulus domain into acceptable, objectionable, and noncommittal latitudes serve as an operational definition of his attitude (Chapter 16). Similarly, changes in these categorizations may be taken as indicators of attitude change, provided that some consistency in the person's categorizations has been demonstrated in the first place.

Despite the consensus in defining attitude in terms of consistent, characteristic modes of behavior, few studies of attitude change have included indication of consistency or characteristic response. Most standardized attitude tests (Chapter 16) give some indication of consistency through their use of many items previously selected in terms of relevance in differentiating between subject samples with known differences in their attitudes. However, many studies labeled attitude studies have employed responses (agree-disagree, ratings, or choice among multiple alternatives) to one or a very few items.

Some investigators have, in fact, called their research "opinion change." While this is perfectly legitimate, it does not warrant extending such findings uncritically to a theory of attitude change. An opinion is simply a verbal statement or a judgement. It may or may not indicate an attitude, which can be inferred only if some consistent and characteristic modes of behavior (including verbal opinions) are demonstrated.

When a person is called upon to render an opinion or judgments on attitude items, he can be fairly objective about it as long as the object of judgment does not bear on his own attitude, as we have seen (pp. 340 ff.). However, when his attitude is involved, the judgment process is no longer neutral. To the extent that the situation or the object of judgment involves ego-attitudes high in the individual's personal scheme, the position(s) that he upholds affect the very way that he sizes-up a situation—hence the way he evaluates the situation, the communication, and its source.

In Chapter 17 on ego-involvements, we have seen that a person's ego-attitude can serve as an anchor in his judgments of relevant stimuli, producing assimilation-contrast effects according to the discrepancies between his own position and positions presented to him in the words or deeds of others. This is why both *degree of ego-involvement* and the *discrepancy* between the person's stand and the position advocated by another person are crucial variables in understanding the apparently contradictory findings of no change, change *toward,* and change *away* from the same communication in the same social situation.

In recent studies of the "discrepancy issue," apparently contradictory results have also been reported by different investigators. As we shall see, these apparent contradictions are readily understandable in terms of the conditions of particular experiments. These conditions include:

1. *How* discrepant the communications were (the range of discrepancy)
2. The degree of stimulus structure-ambiguity (gradations of structure)
3. The degree of ego-involvement in the person's initial position
4. The source of communication.

THE INDIVIDUAL AS TARGET IN INTERACTION PROCESSES

The one-way flow model for attitude change was modified by Lazarsfeld and his associates (1948) into a *two-step* flow on the basis of their findings in the 1940 elections that personal influence emerged as a greater "source" for changing voting preference than the mass media. Subsequent research by Merton (1949), Bereleson, Lazarsfeld, and McPhee (1954), Katz and Lazarsfeld (1955) and others (Coleman *et al.,* 1959, 1966; Rogers, 1962) dealt with such diverse topics as voting decisions, magazine preferences, fashion preferences, marketing, and innovations (especially the use of new drugs by physicians).

In all of the problems studied, there were some individuals who were more *interested* in the topic at hand, who exposed themselves and were exposed more to communication on the topic, who were socially active with respect to the topic (whether politics or fashions), and who were regarded by others as being competent in that respect (Katz, 1965). Such "opinion leaders" were not, however, universally to be found within the prestigeful, the glamorous, the politically powerful, or the elite in a community or profession. Considering various topics across the board, the opinion leaders were scattered throughout the population.

On careful examination, however, the "opinion leaders" tapped through questioning individuals in a survey turn out to be differentiated from others in exactly the ways that high-status persons are differentiated from those with lower status within a group, whether informally or formally organized. Within the radius defining a reference set (e.g., profession, sex, color) or reference group (my friends, my church, my family, my kind in the community), those who turn-up in the surveys as "opinion leaders" are distinguished in the following ways (Katz, 1965, p. 205):

1. They "personify" certain values (they adhere more closely to the norms of the particular set or group).
2. They are regarded as "competent" (through experience and/or past communications, their initiative has proved trustworthy and effective).
3. They are "strategically located." (They interact with greater frequency within the set or group and, at least in certain cases, serve as a major linkage with other groups.)

Here, then, is where a simple modification of the one-way flow of communication breaks down: All of the descriptions of "opinion leaders" imply interpersonal "networks" (Katz and Lazarsfeld, 1955) within groups, institutions, and the broad stratifications in society. For sociological research on the dissemination of mass media messages, this fact poses severe methodological problems as long as the interview or questionnaire method is the sole means of data collection. No amount of "snowballing" or complete community surveys getting people to talk about themselves and other people can adequately uncover all of the significant reference sets and groups in a complex and highly differentiated society unless coupled with a "return to the study of group life" (Wilensky, 1966, p. 318).

For social-psychological research on attitude change, the implications for both laboratory and field are evident: The one-way flow model of influence does not embody the typical case in modern life. Exposure to communication does not take place in an antiseptic environment, wherein pure dosages in specific quantities of source characteristics or message characteristics and channel characteristics (how) can be administered to any normal adult. *Even in the laboratory* (not to speak of the classroom or neighborhood), the very properties of the source (his trustworthiness, competence, expertise, and credibility) depend upon his relationship to the reference sets or reference groups in which the person participates, or his standing therein. These facts are reflected in research in which interaction processes and group membership

have been explicitly considered as sources (independent variables) of attitude formation and change.

Norms Emerging as Decisions During Interaction Are Binding

The inadequacy of a one-way flow model for attitude change was shown by Kurt Lewin and his associates in a series of experiments initiated during World War II (Lewin, 1947, 1965). Lewin's avowed purpose in conducting the studies was to contrast the situation in which the person is viewed as a passive target for communication directed *at* him (by lecture) and that in which he becomes an active participant in interaction focused on the communication.

The first experiment was conducted during World War II with the objective of changing food habits to include meats not ordinarily included in the diet of American families, such as sweetbreads, beef hearts, and kidneys. The subjects were organized groups of Red Cross volunteers (13–17 per group). Three groups of volunteers heard a lecture exhorting the audience to use the meats, linking their use with the war effort (there was a meat shortage) and providing information on their preparation, as well as their health value and economy. Mimeographed sheets containing instructions for preparation and recipes were distributed.

Another three groups of volunteers were presented the topic by Alex Bavelas, who linked the problem of using these cuts of meat both to health and the war effort and asked the women to discuss "whether housewives could be induced to participate in a program of change." During these discussions, the women themselves brought up problems that had been dealt with in the lecture, such as their family's distaste for the cuts, the odor during cooking, and so forth. Essentially the same information was provided to them and the same mimeographed sheets were distributed. At the end of the period, it was requested that a decision be made about trying out the cuts, indicated by a show of hands.

Both for lecture and discussion, only 45 minutes were available for the procedures.

Some time later, all of the women were asked whether they had included the food items in their meals. Only 3 percent of those who heard the lectures had tried any of the food items, as compared with 32 percent of the women in discussion groups. The difference is impressive especially when one considers that most of the housewives had reacted initially with such distaste to the idea that one might have equated their reactions with deep-seated aversions (Lewin, 1965).

Interpretations of the preliminary studies on meats were varied, since the differences between the lecture and the discussion sessions were more than mere form. For example, the discussion was conducted by a trained group worker who was not the lecturer. Radke checked out the possibility that personality differences of the researchers might have produced the results by having one person, who was not a trained lecturer or group worker, serve as both lecturer and discussion leader. Again, the subjects were housewives—this time not members of formally organized groups but women who lived in the same neighborhood or who visited the nutrition service of a community center. Within the samples of each session (six to nine women), Lewin reported that "a good proportion . . . knew each other." The issue at hand was the increased use of milk, either in fresh or evaporated form. Figure 21.3 shows the percentages of these women who reported increased consumption of fresh milk and evaporated milk following a lecture or a discussion in which they were presented with the problem of "what housewives might do" and eventually asked for a decision. Two features are particularly interesting: First, again the discussion was clearly more effective than the lecture, even for evaporated milk for which (presumably) information was somewhat more novel at that time. Second, far from decreasing, the percentage of change was maintained from two to four weeks.

Noting that in these experiments only those who made a "group decision" had been told that their behavior would be checked on later, Levine and Butler (1953) compared lecture and discussion with a control sample (no communication) in an industrial plant. The subjects were super- visors who rated the work of men under their supervision. The men were paid at three different hourly rates, and supervisors typically over-rated the men in higher-paying positions. The problem was to correct this bias. The lecture and control samples did not eliminate the bias in their ratings. The ratings of men who participated in the discussion showed marked improvement, although they had received the same information about correcting errors as given in the lecture and none had been forewarned of a checkup.

The findings of the "group decision" studies were interpreted by some practitioners as showing a manipulative technique—namely, the "discussion method"— to change attitude in the direction desired by the discussion leader. Others correctly pointed out that a great deal more went on than sheer discussion, which in any event can turn into endless wrangling in the absence of some common focus or goal. For example, the subjects were asked to reach a decision and to indicate their decision *publicly.* Positive decisions apparently were the rule. What was it in the social situations created by Lewin and his associates that lead to greater attitude change than one-way lectures?

An attempt to specify the conditions of interaction was made by Pelz (1965) in a study of volunteering as subjects for psychological research by students in introductory psychology at the University of Michigan. Using a total of 473 subjects, Pelz compared volunteering after class discussion and lectures on the *pros* and *cons* of serving as a research subject with a control condition in which the volunteering opportunity was simply stated without *pro* or *con* arguments. For each of these three conditions, in turn, some classes were dismissed without being asked to indicate a decision, others wrote anonymous statements indicating their willingness, still others raised their hands and, finally, some classes were asked both to show their hands and give their names. Several days afterward, all subjects received a letter inviting them to report during a limited time period to register as prospective subjects. The percentage of students who actually signed up was the measure of effectiveness.

We may note, first of all, that there is no

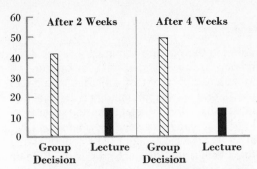
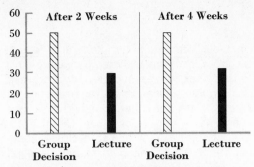

Fig. 21.3. Percentage of mothers reporting increased use of fresh milk (left) and evaporated milk (right) 2 weeks and 4 weeks after participating in group decision or hearing lecture. (From K. Lewin, Group decision and social change, p. 430 (Figure 3), in H. Proshansky and B. Seidenberg, eds., *Basic Studies in Social Psychology*. Copyright © 1965 by Holt, Rinehart and Winston, Inc. Reproduced by permission of Holt, Rinehart and Winston, Inc.)

indication of *attitude change* in the Pelz experiment. Those who did schedule their activities so that they actually signed up may have been those who were already interested in serving as subjects. However, we can legitimately ask whether any of the factors Pelz studied or some combination of them could have been responsible for "group decision" effects.

In brief, Pelz found no significant differences in volunteering attributable simply to discussion or to the lecture. Similarly, there were no significant differences according to whether students wrote anonymous statements, showed their hands, or gave their names. Whether a decision was asked for in class or not had no significant effect; however, coming to a decision *not* to volunteer was a significant event. Of the 85 subjects who had been asked to reach a decision and reported later that they had decided *not* to volunteer, not one showed up.

There were differences between the classes asked to reach a decision in the proportions who decided to volunteer, but apparently these differences (from 41 to 75 percent) bore no clear relationship to the experimental conditions. Pelz divided the classes who were asked to reach a decision into those with high and low consensus to volunteer (above or below the average) and compared their rate of actually signing up with the rate for all students who were not asked to volunteer. She found that 34 percent of the students from classes in which decisions were requested and in which consensus to volunteer was high did sign up, while only 15 percent signed up when no decision was requested.

Pelz concluded, therefore, that *reaching a decision in a situation in which high consensus on the decision was perceived* was the essential combination to heighten the rate of volunteering.

Interaction Within Different Cultural Settings. The upshot of the group decision studies is that decisions reached when the individual has the opportunity to test his views against those of others in his reference set (e.g., other housewives, supervisors, students, etc.) are more binding for the individual. Personal involvement in reaching a decision that others also support produces an effect that survives the exigencies of subsequent situations.

However, it should not be thought that the *form* of the interaction or the *sources* of communication that are most effective are invariant across social systems and cultures. An investigator in India, attempting to use the so-called discussion technique in order to promote changes in caste attitudes found that democratically programmed discussion was less effective than a lecture with emotional appeals. He wrote:

India

Contrary to our original expectation and hypothesis, these young boys do not seem to be in a position to exploit fully the discussion technique, in bettering their social relationships. Does it indicate that our boys have got to get used to democratic ways of discussion and at present prefer to be told what are the right attitudes rather than to be allowed to talk them out? (Ram and Murphy, 1952, pp. 114–115).

**Changes
in Reference Groups Alter
Many Related Attitudes**

In the normal course of a human life during more or less stable times, changes in reference sets and reference groups occur gradually during maturation and aging, therefore involving attitude changes relative to one's sex role, occupation, and age set. Such attitude change is regarded as so natural in the particular society that no one considers it remarkable (see Chapter 19; Neugarten *et al.,* 1965). Yet, a close examination of such changes reveals several enlightening findings.

The formal social agencies of social control (e.g., family, mass media, government, and educational system) emit dictums regarding what changes are required and how to accomplish them, but the degree of conformity or deviation exhibited by individuals reflect their relationships with peers and the presence or absence of supportive interactions with them. When the formal agencies of social control attempt attitude change in directions contrary to those congenial within the person's reference set or group, they face formidable obstacles.

When changes in reference sets and groups occur, attitude change is not singular, but plural: A host of related attitudes change in the process. The most dramatic illustrations of changed reference groups are conversions, which as a rule are the climax in a long period of inner conflict, uncertainty, and search—in contrast to the rather smooth and quick switches from say, being a Methodist to being a Baptist, or a Democrat's voting for a Republican because the leader is more attractive, the atmosphere more pleasant, or the association more prestigeful.

For example, a young man known to the authors was converted from Roman Catholicism to the Church of the Nazarene, a wide shift in the Christian spectrum. Once the decision was made a host of attitudes changed rapidly in line with the new reference group: Nazarenes should not smoke or drink; he stopped. Nazarenes have certain obligations to their church differing from those of a Catholic: he started. At every step of the way, his increasingly intense interaction with fellow Nazarenes was the context of change.

Newcomb's study of attitude change at Bennington College, which has already been reviewed (Chapter 18), points to a similar conclusion. Those students who adopted the college community as their reference group changed not just one or two attitudes, but a set of attitudes related to the liberal norms promulgated by the faculty. Those who thereby departed most from the conservative views of their families were also those who sought and found stable roles within the informal groups of students and, particularly, status in the student body at large. In follow-ups of the girls, Newcomb (1950) reported that the extent of change and the persistence of political attitudes were related to the length of residence in the community (p. 206). Subsequent followups indicate that prolonged effects are related to whether the girls' careers as wives, mothers, and professional or community members provided the opportunity to interact with others of like mind (Newcomb *et al.,* 1967).

An Experimental Model of Attitude Formation and Change in Reference Groups

The sociological and anthropological literature on small groups, social movements, and acculturation is filled with case studies of attitude change over time in a group context. Experiments on attitude formation and change in the context of group relations by Sherif and his associates were presented in Chapter 11. Although these experiments are not ordinarily labeled attitude studies, they were originally conceived as a model for attitude formation and change. The measures used (dependent variables) were attitude measures (direct or indirect, see pp. 243–261).

The conditions of the experiments contain the key to their import for attitude change: Each phase or stage involved experimental manipulation of the *conditions* whereby the individuals and then the groups could or could not attain highly compelling goals with strong motivational appeal. Many of the problem situations and goals arranged by the researchers were compelling because of attitudes already formed by the subjects as members of middle-class families in a society prizing outdoor activities, adventure, excitement, and competition for boys of this age.

In this context, let us review briefly the major conditions and findings on attitude formation and change from the group experiments:

1. Unacquainted individuals highly motivated toward camping experiences interact in campwide activities. They start to form interpersonal attitudes of preference as they cluster in twos or threes in terms of existing similarities in attitudes (interests, etc.).

2. Experimental conditions divide the clusters, presenting two sets of individuals with a series of goals highly desired by all (camping out, eating when hungry, etc.) that can be achieved only by pulling together with others during prolonged and intense interaction. The results were:

(A) Shifts in attitudes away from erstwhile preferred companions toward preference for others within one's newly formed group (pp. 231–232).

(B) Definite attitudes toward the various members of one's own group, as defined by preferential categorization of the members from most effective and most preferred to least effective and least preferred (pp. 238–240).

(C) Definite attitudes about proper ways of behaving, doing things, places to go, and things to do, as well as favorable attitudes toward one's own group (pp. 233–239).

3. Experimental conditions present highly compelling goals (competition, winning victory, and prizes) that can be attained only by one group at the expense of the other. The results were:

(A) Shifts in attitudes toward others within the group when the contributions of the various members to the group activity changed owing to intergroup competition and conflict (p. 252).

(B) Shifts in attitudes toward what was the proper way to do things and what to do, as a result of the increasing importance of intergroup conflict (pp. 243–252).

(C) Formation of attitudes toward the out-group that were hostile and stereotyped as well as elaboration of glorifying attitudes toward the in-group (p. 243).

4. Experimental conditions present highly compelling goals that can be attained only when both groups pull together (superordinate goals). The results were:

(A) Gradual decrease in negative stereotypes and hostile attitudes toward the out-group (pp. 261–262).

(B) Formation of friendly attitudes toward the out-group and at least some of its members (pp. 256 f.).

(C) Decrease in glorifying attitudes toward the in-group, even though the evaluation of the in-group remained favorable (pp. 262 ff.).

(D) Changes in attitude toward various activities that had been deemed right, proper, and even enjoyable (e.g., harassing the out-group, shoving to be first in line, engaging in "garbage wars") (p. 256).

This series of experiments shows, then, that attitudes form during interaction as reference groups take shape and function in problem situations permitting numerous possible modes of reaching highly appealing goals. Similarly, when the problems faced by group members change, particularly when the nature of goals prescribe a definite range of alternatives (intergroup competition or cooperation, as the case may be), interaction processes toward those goals effect changes in individual attitudes as well. Having had a part in shaping the mode of behaviors adopted to meet the problem situations at hand, the individual member experiences the assumptions and perspectives formed in his group as his own personal feelings and convictions.

Henceforth, as the individual participates in situation after situation, he is ego-involved in terms of his attitudes, the origins of which lie in his group membership. Henceforth, he is not amenable to persuasion by a communicator or a message that is not acceptable to his own group. In the experiments, a favorable word about the detested rivals fell on deaf ears. By definition, words originating in the out-group were suspect. In the Blake and Mouton (1962, 1964) studies with training groups of adults, an "impartial" judge did not prove to be an unimpeachable source for conflicting groups. When his verdict went against the in-group, it was derided and the erstwhile "fair and impartial" source was discredited as biased.

Implications
for Theory and Research
on Attitude Change

In brief, experiments on attitude formation and change in the context of interaction—particularly interaction within and between groups—do not contradict the findings of survey research that grew from the hypothesis of a "two-step" flow of communication. On the contrary, they specify further the origins and the effects of interaction processes that can only be pointed to and speculated about on the basis of interview (survey) data.

Joseph T. Klapper (1967) described the change that has occurred in the theoretical model for mass communications research, primarily on the basis of empirical findings. As experimentalists on attitude change have been tardy in recognizing the important revisions that have been made, Klapper's words should be seriously read and digested.

With rare exceptions, mass communication research up to the late 1950's was designed on the implicit or explicit assumption that the communication was a pure stimulus, like the serum in a hypodermic syringe, which, when injected would either produce a response or would fail to do so. This simple S-R model was of course duly modified into an S-O-R model, with the audience member as the organism. Although this was a step in the right direction, it can hardly be said that it provided any dramatic breakthroughs. Not until the late 1950's and early 1960's did this model give real ground to the current model (p. 299). . . . In brief, this approach no longer conceives the phenomenon under study as a unidirectional affair with one independent variable [communication]. Instead the mass communication situation is viewed as an interactive life experience, in which the audience member and his social milieu affect the nature of the communication that he is exposed to and mediate its effects upon him. The process is regarded as multidirectional, and the independent variables are recognized as numerous (p. 300).

The "mediating factors" that Klapper identified are fundamentally psychological —namely, *selectivity.* He cited evidence (1960, 1967) that mass media communications are subject to selective exposure, selective retention, and selective perception or, as he prefers, *interpretation.* With reference to the studies of "opinion leaders"

and "personal influence," he located the roots of the predispositions producing these selective processes in the interaction processes of organized social life.

On the basis of research, largely in the United States, Klapper is convinced that the net effect of mass communication via these mediating processes is reinforcement of prevailing attitudes within the diverse segments of society. By reinforcement he means more than mere maintenance of attitudes; rather, he means they are buttressed and enhanced. The exceptions, he concludes, occur when the mediating processes are themselves in a state of flux and change, or when they are absent—for example, when a topic is presented in mass media about which groups have no norms and opinion leaders take no stand. Klapper emphasized that the latter case—namely, the creation of opinions when none exist— is of greater than mere academic interest. The most powerful effect of mass media may lie in crystallizing views about events and people outside of one's own class, country, or immediate experience.

Despite complex research situations and designs, experimental research of the last decade has, for the most part, been designed in what Klapper called the "hypodermic model" (the "one-way flow" model). Noting that the first "handbook" of *experimental* social psychology (Murphy, Murphy, and Newcomb, 1937) emphasized the group and cultural context of attitude formation and change, E. L. Hartley (1967) commented as follows:

Despite these guidelines, researchers continue to study attitudes and attitude change without regard to reference groups. Almost all aspects of an experimental situation are described except for the nature of the social group which *is* the experiment: the local norms and expectancies for the subject role and the relationship between the experimenter and the subject (p. 102).

For example, comparatively recently, experiments were performed on the effects of the before-after measurement of attitudes such as is made in the most common design of attitude change studies. As one might suspect, it does make a difference whether subjects become aware that an experimental attempt is being made to change their attitudes (Kerrick and McMillan, 1961;

Sherman, 1967). For this reason, some researchers prefer to use matched experimental and control samples, assessing the effects of a communication by comparing their responses afterward. On the other hand, a study by Fendrich (1967) indicates that sheer responsiveness to the research situation itself and hunches about the researcher's intentions are much less important when subjects are asked to commit themselves for or against specific actions (such as participating in controversial discussions or joining an organization). He correctly notes that much attitude research, confined to the laboratory, has a "play-like" character (cf. Weick, 1967). When it is linked to extra-research actions, the research situation becomes more predictive of actual behavior.

By far the most popular models of what Klapper referred to as the S-O-R type have been some variant of a much larger class of psychological theorizing referred to variously as "consistency," "balance," "consonance," or "equilibrium" theories (cf. Feldman, 1967; McGuire, 1968, 1969). As reviews of such theoretical attempts are readily available, we will consider here only two equilibrium models directly relevant to attitude change.

Equilibrium Models

The fundamental assumption of the "consistency" theories is that there is a basic psychological tendency toward equilibrium, paralleling the dynamic *equilibrium* in the flow of liquids and gases or the homeostatic processes whereby variations in such crucial physiological processes as regulation of body temperature, oxygen intake, and blood pressure levels are maintained within comparatively narrow limits.

The psychological *phenomena* to which the equilibrium theories refer have been documented by psychologists since William James: Events, situations, or communications that are at great odds with the person's cherished values, commitments, beliefs or understanding of the world are psychologically disturbing. The balance or consistency theories proceed to definite predictions about the effects of psychological tensions thus engendered and the individual's reactions to them.

The *congruence* model developed by Osgood, Suci, and Tannenbaum (1957) was closely tied to the measurement technique described in Chapter 16 as the "semantic differential." It is concerned with the individual's reactions when his evaluations of a concept (object of attitude), a message and a source, as assessed by the semantic differential, are disparate. For example, suppose that a person evaluated a Republican candidate at a position of +3 on the semantic differential, the concept of "open housing" for Negroes at −1, and listened to a message from the candidate mildly favoring open housing (+1). According to the congruence model, the tendency is for the person to fit the message into his prevailing "frame of reference" (referring only to internal factors) by changing his evaluations. The most polarized (most extreme rating on the semantic differential) will always exert the greatest effect, according to the model.

In the case given, the person might do one of three things: shift his evaluation of open housing toward the source, lower his evaluation of the source, or change his evaluation of the position of the message (a possibility not systematically considered in the congruence model). Giving more weight to the source than the attitude object (through an "assertion constant"), the theory would predict in the above case that the person would evaluate open housing more favorably. Another correction was added to the theory to accommodate cases in which both source and concept are equally polarized—for example, if the spokesman rated at +3 made a positive assertion about a concept at −3. In such an event, the tendency toward congruence is said to break down owing to the "incredulity" of the situation. Although this addition does not follow from the arithmetic or logic of the model, it is harmonious with the general assumption that change in evaluating attitude objects is inversely proportional to the polarity of the "interacting elements."

Unfortunately, there is nothing in the congruence model to connect the communication situation to the person's reference sets or groups or the communicator to social process. The variables are operationally defined in terms of the person's ratings on the semantic differential. It is necessary, for example, to add at least the qualification that the source be "relevant" to the concept. There is little reason to suspect that a big league baseball player's approval of an alliance (+3) with a slightly unfriendly country (−2) would have any effect whatsoever on evaluations of the country.

Another equilibrium model, called *cognitive dissonance* by Festinger (1957, 1963, 1964), is a tension-reduction model in which dissonance is conceived as an unpleasant drive state. No measurement methods are associated with the model. Festinger stated simply that when two or more "cognitive elements" are relevant to one another and dissonant, there will be a pressure to reduce that dissonance, the pressure being proportional to (1) the "importance" of the elements and (2) the proportion of cognitive elements that are dissonant. No precise definition was given as to what constitutes a "cognitive element" (cf. Festinger, 1964).

In research practice, a belief, opinion, or attitude have all been identified as "elements," and more recently the person's perception of his own behavior has been taken as an element. <u>Dissonance</u> is defined by Festinger in a strictly logical sense: "Two elements are in a dissonant relation if, considering these two alone, the obverse of one element would follow from the other" (1957, p. 13). Importance is defined only in the commonsense idea of "important to the person." More recently, a number of researchers have begun to use the term involvement or ego-involvement in referring to importance (Brock and Becker, 1965; Walster and Festinger, 1962; Zajonc and Burnstein, 1965).

The person's efforts to reduce dissonance increase with the amount of dissonance created. As applied to opinions or attitudes, Festinger stated that these efforts could include any one of the following alternatives to reduce dissonance (the choice of one or another depending on what was possible in the situation and on individual differences in preferred mode of dissonance reduction): (1) change his own opinion or behavior; (2) attempt to change the communicator; (3) seeking social support for his own opinion; or (4) derogating or otherwise discrediting the comunicator. If a communication arouses dissonance, the model predicts that attitude change would increase proportional to the discrepancy of the communication and importance of the issue to the person—unless the person, for some reason, substitutes one of the other alternative ways to reduce the dissonance.

**Comment
and Orientation**

The two most important equilibrium models pertinent to attitude change appear to be logical and simple. The research stimulated by the models briefly summarized above has been, quite literally, enormous. After a decade, agonizing reappraisals were undertaken which were extensive and intensive (cf. Abelson *et al.,* 1968; Feldman, 1967; Chapanis and Chapanis, 1964; Feather, 1967; Jordan, 1964; McGuire, 1968, 1969; Sherif and Sherif, 1967). Some lessons of these reappraisals are relevant to the issue at hand—namely, the adequacy of an equilibrium theory.

The behaviors of participants in this, as in other more important controversies, illustrate the flaw in an equilibrium model for attitude change that adheres strictly to analogy with either a physical (e.g., hydraulic) system or physiological needs (drive reduction). The psychological tendency toward stability proceeds over time on particular terms that can be defined as (1) the priority of values in the person's self system, which is closely related to (2) the relative significance of his reference groups with their respective scales of values, and (3) the concrete interaction situation in which he goes about the business of living, earning a living, and maintaining a self-identity. These terms have not been included in the models systematically. If one attempts to do so, the models are no longer simple and the logic is undermined at the level of basic assumptions.

Experimental research on attitude change which is basic research should shift its focus from detailing the *effects* of psychic tension that the researcher has managed to create to a more careful analysis of neglected questions such as the following: What issues or objects or persons are capable of arousing ego tension (inconsistency, incongruity, dissonance, etc.) for people and in what social context? How discrepant or different does a stimulus object have to be to arouse ego tension under these circumstances? How do the properties of objective problems (their familiarity, degree of structure, etc.) affect the arousal of ego tension and efforts to do something about the problem?

The social judgment-involvement formulation (Sherif, Sherif, and Nebergall, 1965) was developed to tackle such problems as those mentioned above. Starting with principles concerning how people size-up the stimulus world (judgment), it proceeded to link the judgment process to the sociology of groups through the concepts of attitude, self system, and their derivative—ego-involvement. This procedure led to several new methods for measuring attitude and attitude change (Chapters 14–16).

The social judgment-involvement formulation was developed with the intention of providing a solid research basis from psychology for a theory of man as both agent and target of change in interaction processes. In previous chapters (Chapters 15–17), the research basis was specified. Accordingly, the remainder of this chapter consists of a summary of what has been learned through the social judgment-involvement approach to attitude change.

SUSCEPTIBILITY
TO CHANGE AND SELECTIVITY

When a researcher gets a person into the laboratory or classroom or interview situation, he has already achieved a major triumph. Quite unlike many situations in life, he can usually assume that the person has consented to be present, to perform tasks, or to talk on some subject and to pay some attention to what goes on in the situation. Ordinarily, he will perform tasks requested of him and respond to stimulus arrangements or to questions that the investigator has prepared.

The laboratory, the classroom, and the formal indoctrination session omit, therefore, the first and crucial phase of most communication situations: Anyone who communicates (whether in a group, a meeting, a family, or on mass media) must secure a listener and hold him for the duration of his message.

Studies of readership, listening, and viewing by American audiences have, quite consistently, revealed significant selectivity in exposure to mass media presenting a partisan point of view (Klapper, 1960, 1967). For example, a "telethon" broadcast (extended program) sponsored by Republicans on election eve was designed to convert Democratic voters but was viewed by two Republicans to every Democrat (Schramm and Carter, 1959). A campaign to win supporters of the United Nations in the United States was heeded, almost entirely, by persons who were already both well disposed and well informed about the United Nations (Star and Hughes, 1950).

In a check on the readership preferences of students in Lebanon, Diab (1965, 1967) found that those who were against Arab unity, as well as others who professed to be moderates or undecided, showed a decided preference for anti-Arab unity literature—a selective bias more pronounced than that of the pro-Arab unity students. However, his subjects were not exclusive readers of material supporting their own sides. In a continually changing situation, such as that in the contemporary Middle East, the person who seeks or selects only information that presents his own point of view is a person who buries his head in the sand, and may be completely buried by events from one side or the other.

In Chapter 3, some important findings about psychological selectivity were reviewed. There we found that the person's attitudes and other motives toward the source and the stimulus situation affect what he attends to and what he heeds. In Chapter 17, several experiments were referred to that failed to support a simple hypothesis of the avoidance of dissonant and selective preference for congenial information (cf. Rhine, 1967). In fact, the proportions of persons seeking out any information at all on topics presented in field experiments is surprisingly low (Lowin, 1967; Clarke and James, 1967). However, we would be poor social psychologists indeed if we laid all the effects of mass communication, whether toward maintenance or change of attitude, to selectivity as a function of the person's attitude.

The properties of the external situation also affect selectivity—for example, the prominence of events (in various dimensions), repetition, degree of structure, novelty, and the competition of simultaneous events or activities.

On the basis of other research findings, we can pinpoint at least two sets of factors that affect psychological selectivity through the production of differential susceptibility to change. One pertains to the stability-instability of reference group ties and/or prolonged conflicts endured among values of the person's various roles. The second pertains to the degrees of structure-unstructure in the external stimulus situation or problem.

Instability of Reference Group Ties. In Chapters 17 and 18 on self and on reference groups, we noted that prolonged instability or conflict either in the person's role relationships or between the values of his various reference groups (sets) produced personal insecurity, uncertainty, or anxiety. In such a state, the person's selectivity is not bound by the normative prescriptions of his reference groups. He is restless, dissatisfied, and searching. Under such circumstances, the individual is highly susceptible to proposals that would seem to solve his dilemma. In fact, he is aroused to search for them.

Jerome D. Frank (1963), psychiatrist and social psychologist, has credited such motivational states with producing great susceptibility to the therapist's words and reactions when a person decides to seek actively the help of a psychiatrist or psychotherapist. Studies of the effects of propaganda broadcasts (Klapper, 1967) conducted by the United States government suggest that neither the clever design of communication nor specific selectivity for American propaganda was primarily responsible for defections to the United States. In all of these studies, the findings reveal personal crises of varying intensity, lack of stability in reference group ties, and susceptibility to new alternatives, even before the propaganda was received.

Tajfel (1969) has noted the importance of stimulus structure in promoting susceptibility to social influence, correctly stating that neither the lack of structure nor the highly structured situation violated by contradictory social influence is typical in real life. In fact, if one studies social change over periods of time, one may conclude that the search for the "typical instance" is futile,

because what is typical in one decade can be readily found atypical in the next. What is needed is intensified study of *gradations of stimulus structure* in relation to gradations in the stability of internal factors.

In times of catastrophe or of dramatically rapid social change, the individual is likely both to search selectively and to be extraordinarily susceptible to alternatives to which he might, in more stable times, be quite unreceptive. Thus his selectivity and his susceptibility to change are a joint function of the stability of his attitudes at the time and the degree of structure in the world that he faces.

Research Indicating Differential Susceptibility to Change

Whatever its precipitating circumstances, differential susceptibility to seek out and to change in the direction of communication has been demonstrated. Public opinion pollsters have long since learned that, as a rule, a large proportion of respondents answering "Don't know" or "No opinion" in interviews about an issue means that the ground is fertile for events and propaganda focused on that issue (Marks, 1949; Hyman and Sheatsley, 1965).

Conversely, it is well established that the degree of the person's ego-involvement in his stand is inversely related to the probability of his changing his attitude, contrary to the prediction of the dissonance model about personal importance. Size of the latitude of noncommitment proves to be an index of susceptibility to change. It will be recalled that a large latitude of noncommitment is typical of persons who are less ego-involved in their stand.

Table 21.2 gives the percentages of change in the most acceptable positions on the 1960 presidential election by 956 persons whose latitudes of acceptance, rejection, and noncommitment were assessed twice, about a week apart, just prior to the election. It will be recalled from Chapter 16 (p. 359) that the persons taking moderate stands on the election issue had significantly larger latitudes of noncommitment than those taking extreme positions. The incidence of change among those taking moderate positions, in turn, was approxi-

Table 21.2.   Changes in Most Acceptable Position
on 1960 Election

Most Acceptable Position (Session 1)	Northwest N	Northwest Change (%)	Southwest N	Southwest Change (%)
Extreme Republican (A–B)	171	28.1	119	27.7
Moderate Republican (C–D)	167	48.5	106	61.3
Noncommittal (E)	47	40.5	36	38.9
Moderate Democrat (F–G)	86	49.9	46	50.0
Extreme Democrat (H–I)	134	22.4	44	22.7

mately twice as frequent as for those taking extreme positions (ranging from 48.5 percent for moderate Republicans in the Northwest to 61 percent for moderate Republicans in the Southwest). Very few of these changes in own position involved switching parties (about 2 percent in the Northwest and 10 percent in the Southwest region). As the election reached its climax, the majority of shifts (57–59 percent) were shifts toward a more extreme partisan stand.

Further evidence of the relationship between the latitude of noncommitment and the propensity to change is provided in a study by Elbing (1962). The issue in this case was the so-called right-to-work issue, a proposal that would prohibit the union shop in industry. Elbing's experimental variable was a role-playing experience, in which the subjects argued either for or against their own position. Before the role playing experience, he assessed the latitudes of acceptance-rejection-noncommitment of the subjects, finding the same trend of increasing noncommitment from extreme to moderate stands as that in the 1960 election study. However, the average size of the latitude of noncommitment was much larger in Elbing's study than for the election issue. The latitude of noncommitment was approximately two positions out of nine for subjects finding the extremes most acceptable and increased to nearly four positions for subjects adopting moderate stands.

Table 21.3 gives the percentage of subjects who adopted extreme and moderate positions on the right-to-work issue and who did *not* change their positions following the role-playing experience or who changed to more or less extreme positions. Note that almost 75 percent of the subjects with moderate stands changed in one direction or the other, while only about 54 per-

cent of those with extreme stands changed. In particular, note that the frequency of change was much greater, on the whole, than in the election study.

Certainly, it could be argued that in both studies, the comparison is between moderate and extreme subjects, and that the latter can only change by becoming less extreme. Therefore, an experiment by Tittler (1967) assessing latitudes of noncommitment and change for the same individuals on different issues is particularly interesting.

Using college students as subjects, Tittler conducted interviews and then had several samples rank issues in terms of their relative personal importance to them. On the basis of these pretests he chose two issues that were consistently ranked high by both male and female students—namely, the relative importance of potential income level in selecting an occupation and the importance of developing the ability to understand and get along with other people. In contrast to these two ego-involving topics, he selected two from an earlier study by Janis and Field (1959) in which a high incidence of attitude change had been reported, especially among girls. He felt safe in assuming that these two topics would be uninvolving for college students. One issue concerned the historical role of General von Hindenburg (a World War I German general) and the other concerned the probable success on television of a (fictitious) new comedian ("Jack O'Keefe"). The latitudes of acceptance, rejection, and noncommitment were assessed for each subject on each of the four issues.

Very few students adopted extreme positions as most acceptable on any of the four issues. Tittler designed communications on each issue to be read by the subjects at a second session. One message on each

Table 21.3. Incidence of Attitude Change Among Extreme and Moderate Subjects After Role-playing Session[a]

| | Individual's Initial Stand | |
	Extreme (%)[b]	Moderate (%)[c]
No Change	46.1	25.2
Change: More Extreme Stand	27.7	33.3
Change: Less Extreme Stand	26.2	41.4

[a] Data compiled from Elbing (1962) on most acceptable positions for the right-to-work issue.
[b] N = 65.
[c] N = 111.

issue represented the third position and one the seventh position in a series of nine statements prepared for the method of ordered alternatives. Each subject received a communication on a given issue that was somewhat divergent from his most acceptable position and in the opposite direction (pro or con). As a check on the test-retest procedure, an equal number of subjects read communications that had nothing at all to do with the four issues (irrelevant communications).

Initially, the latitudes of noncommitment of subjects on the two ego-involving issues were significantly smaller than their latitudes of noncommitment on the uninvolving issues, On the average, female students were more noncommittal than males, although these differences were not so large as those according to issues. Table 21.4 shows the incidence of changes in the latitude of acceptance on all of the four issues for male and female subjects. Significantly greater percentages of change were found for both males and females who read the four relevant communications than for those who read the four irrelevant issues. Further, the same individuals changed more on the less ego-involving issues than on the more ego-involving issues (for which their latitudes of noncommitment were significantly smaller). As the greater frequency of noncommitment among female students would lead one to expect, there was a tendency for the females to change more frequently than males, although this trend was not statistically significant. In assessing the frequency of the changes in Table 21.4, it should be noted that very nearly one-third of the comparison samples who were presented irrelevant communications made

Table 21.4. Mean Percentages of Change[a] on Issues According to Size of Latitude of Noncommitment

	Less Noncommitment (%)	More Noncommitment (%)
Males (N = 66)	52.3	75.8
Females (N = 59)	55.9	80.6

[a] The percentages of change in this table are not comparable with those in Tables 21.2 and 21.3. The changes in this table represent any change in the latitude of acceptance in the direction of the communication from Session 1 to Session 2.

changes in their latitudes of acceptance at the second session.

The level of noncommitment is related to susceptibility to change.

CATEGORIZATION AND EVALUATION OF COMMUNICATIONS AND THEIR SOURCE

In Chapter 17, the concept of ego-involvement and degrees thereof was introduced. Data were presented showing that assimilation-contrast effects in categorization of a communication occurred according to the degree of ego-involvement in the issue and the relative discrepancy of the communication from the latitude of acceptance. When the communication fell within the person's latitude of acceptance or latitude of noncommitment, it was categorized as closer to the person's stand (assimilated). The closer the communication to his latitude of rejection and the further within the range of positions he rejects, the greater was the tendency to exaggerate the discrepancy (contrast effect).

Several studies have shown that favorable evaluations of a communication as fair, factual, and unbiased are most frequent for communications that are within the latitude of acceptance and that the opposite evaluations (unfair, propagandistic, biased) increase as communication falls within the latitude of rejection. Larimer (1966) showed that favorable evaluations on the issue of French-Canadian and Commonwealth unity were highest when the communication was within the latitude of acceptance and were significantly higher when the communication was within the latitude of noncommitment than when it fell within the rejected latitude.

Figure 21.4 was prepared from data of Diab (1967), combining findings from a study by Hovland, Harvey, and Sherif (1957) on the prohibition issue in Oklahoma with his own findings on the Arab-unity issue in Lebanon. In both studies, the communication was located as nearly as possible at F (baseline), which was a mildly pro-repeal position in that prohibition study and a mild anti-Arab unity position in Diab's research. Both curves show that favorable reactions to the moderate (F) communication increased as the distance between the person's own stand and the position advocated in communication decreased. However, there are differences. The 1957 prohibition study received, in general, less favorable reaction from those on the same side of the fence (F–I) and, furthermore, favorable reactions declined at the extreme positions on that side.

In both studies, persons opting the extreme positions showed marked contrast effects in categorizing the communication, even more so in the Arab unity study. In short, anti-Arab unity subjects were categorizing statements such as "unity may possibly do more harm than good" as *favorable* to Arab unity while, at the same time, evaluating them as fair, realistic, good, and honest. Diab's examination of this difference shows the importance of linking the concept of ego-involvements to the subjects' *reference groups* and the concrete interactions with groups opposed to their positions.

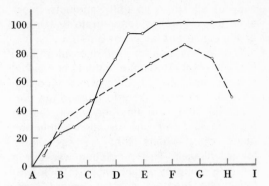

Fig. 21.4. Comparison of percentages of favorable evaluation of a mildly unfavorable communication (F on baseline) by subjects upholding various positions on Arab unity (solid line) and by subjects upholding various positions on repeal of prohibition (dashed line). The data on prohibition were reported by Hovland, Harvey, and Sherif (Assimilation and contrast effects in reactions to communication and attitude change, *J. abnorm. soc. Psychol.*, **55**, 244–252. Copyright 1957 by The American Psychological Association, and reproduced by permission.) while those on Arab unity were reported by Diab (1967). In both studies, data were collected using the method of ordered alternatives and ratings of the communication assessed its fairness, credibility, etc. (Adapted from Diab, in Sherif and Sherif, 1967.)

According to Diab, the extremely anti-Arab unity subjects were sharply segmented among themselves into groups favoring Lebanese nationalism, Syrian nationalism, or both, and were in agreement only in their "overwhelming hostility to their 'common enemy' Arab nationalism" (p. 150). As assessed through the method of ordered alternatives and the semantic differential, these same subjects were highly noncommittal about the probability that Arab unity might be achieved again (following a short-lived union in 1958) and exhibited considerable uncertainty about the potency of the movement (pp. 151, 154). Thus, according to Diab, even a statement categorized as mildly pro-Arab unity (actually at F) could be pleasing to such individuals—something pleasant to hear at a time (early 1963) when negotiations were going on for the formation of a new United Arab Republic, because it at least cast doubt on the advisability of the proceedings. This same set of information, suggests Diab, accounts for the pronounced tendency of all anti-Arab unity subjects (moderate to extreme) to concentrate their readership in sources known as anti-unity.

The implications for prediction of attitude change are that communications somewhat different from the person's own position on an issue are most likely to change the person when they are not only evaluated as pleasing and fair but are also within the range of positions that he assimilates toward himself. This prediction was borne out in a study by Atkins *et al.* (1967), who found the greatest change toward communications when the communication fell within the latitude of acceptance. Communications falling outside of the latitude of acceptance produced little effect, chiefly negative (see also Bieri, 1967). Accordingly, the social judgment-involvement formulation assesses the probability of change toward a communication or away from communication in terms of the factors that affect this *range of assimilation.*

At least four factors affect the range of assimilation and will be considered in discussing attitude change:

1. Degree of the person's involvement in his own position.
2. Degree and kind of ego-involvement with the source of communication.
3. Degree of structure in the stimulus situation.
4. The relative discrepancy of an object (e.g., communication) from the individual's own position.

DEGREE OF EGO-INVOLVEMENT AND ATTITUDE CHANGE

The general prediction of the social judgment-involvement approach about attitude change is that, if the person is susceptible to change at all, communications advocating positions within his latitudes of acceptance or noncommitment will produce the greatest change, while communications advocating positions within his latitude of rejection will either produce no change or, if they are sufficiently discrepant, will result in change away from the communication. Figure 21.5 is a diagram of this general expectation.

As the person highly ego-involved in his own position will have a very small or no latitude of noncommitment, he is unlikely to

change in the direction of a communication. On the other hand, a person who is relatively uninvolved in his own position will exhibit increasing attitude change over a wider range of positions, because he has wide latitudes of acceptance and noncommitment.

However, the individual seldom responds merely to the content of a communication. There is considerable evidence that his evaluation of the *source* may be equally important or even more important than the object or the message (Asch, 1940; Lowin, 1967; Osgood *et al.,* 1957). However, one man's king is a knave to the next man. Therefore, it is necessary to conceive of the source in terms of its relationship to the person's reference group(s) or set(s). It would be possible to determine the person's latitudes of acceptance, noncommitment, and rejection for various sources. If this were done, we would find that—depending on the person and the issue—potential sources would be categorized according to the following: (1) whether they were within the person's own group, in a friendly group, or an antagonistic group; and (2) their standing in these various sets with respect to the content of the communication.

In general, a source with high status in the person's reference scheme can produce attitude change over a much wider range of positions than a person with moderate or low status. However, the member of an antagonistic group will be ineffective in producing change—or successful, if you will, in producing change away from the position he advocates.

Because efforts to change attitudes do not occur in a vacuum, the *degree of structure* in the stimulus situation also has to be considered. Lack of stimulus structure, as we shall see, is conducive to change over a much wider range of positions. Experiments that use unstructured stimulus situations may seem quite remote from attitude change as we have defined it. However, there is a conceptual parallel with periods of rapid social change, catastrophe, and crisis: The lack of structure arouses uncertainty and feelings of insecurity at the very time when possible alternatives are suddenly increased. This combination of circumstances is conducive to attitude change by others who offer what appears to be a reliable assessment of the situation, as we

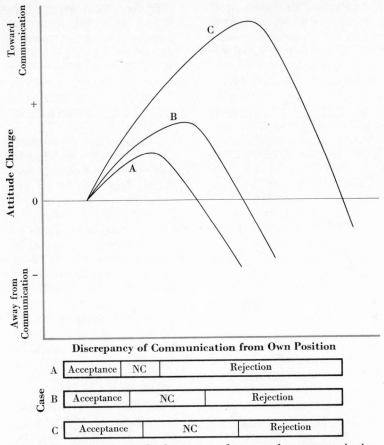

Fig. 21.5. Expected attitude change toward or away from communications advocating positions of varying discrepancies from the positions accepted by persons with varying latitudes of acceptance, noncommitment and rejection (cases A, B, C). The social judgment-involvement formulation predicts attitude change as a curvilinear function of communication discrepancy from the latitude of acceptance and degree of involvement. Increased change occurs as the communication departs from the acceptable latitude into the noncommitment range (NC). The inflection point is the latitude of rejection: communications falling in the latitude of rejection have progressively smaller effects, eventually crossing the zero line and resulting in change *away* from the position advocated (boomerang effect).

shall see in Chapter 24 on social movements.

The sky is not the limit in the extent to which low involvement, a highly valued source, or lack of stimulus structure can extend the assimilation range and produce increasing attitude change with increasingly discrepant communications. Depending upon these factors, there is a point beyond the person's own position where he will cease to be influenced and, instead, will contrast the advocated stand with his own.

The sharp categorization of a source and his message as totally different from one's own stand and one's own reference groups can be accompanied by a shift in one's own stand away from the outlandish views of the outsider. In fact, change away from the position intended is sufficiently frequent in the literature that it must be considered at least as important a phenomenon to explain as change toward the intended position.

**Discrepancy
Between Attitude
and Communication**

It has been said that research findings concerning the size of the discrepancy between the person's stand and that advocated in a communication for maximum attitude change are contradictory or controversial. Indeed they are unless we consider the factors outlined above that affect the assimilation range. When we do, the findings fall into a meaningful pattern. As the range is closely related to problems of change involving, on the one hand, highly structured technological innovations, and, on the other, periods of social crisis, we shall first consider the degree of structure in the stimulus situation.

Discrepancy and Degree of Stimulus Structure. A number of studies of social influence that varied the discrepancy between a person's initial judgments (opinions) and the judgments spoken by a plant or confederate found increasing change with increasing discrepancy (Fisher and Lubin, 1958; Whittaker, 1967). Therefore, the conclusion was widely circulated that advocating great change was more effective than advocating smaller degrees of change. The stimulus situations were not made central in the analysis of the results.

Whittaker (1963) had subjects make 40 judgments of the extent of autokinetic movement, enough that each stabilized a range and mode of judgment. In a second session, each subject served with a plant who made judgments in accordance with a prearranged scheme. For some subjects, the plant centered his judgments around a median 1 inch higher than the subject's largest judgment in the same session, distributing them within a range identical to that used by the subject so that his judgments did not seem to be erratic. In other conditions, the plant distributed his judgments about a median and within a range much further away from those made by the subject in Session 1. In the most extreme discrepancy, he started making judgments ranging upward from a value twelve times the subject's largest judgment in Session 1.

Figure 21.6 shows the results of the study in terms of the difference between the subject's judgments in Session 1 and Session 2 (change score).

Compared with the control condition (no discrepancy), the greatest change occurred when the plant's judgments overlapped those of the subject (Condition B), thereafter declining with increasingly discrepant judgments by the plant. In a later study,

Whittaker (1964) added a condition between A and B in this illustration—namely, the plant set his lowest judgment 1 inch above that of the subject. The result was an average change of 1.67 inches upward. In other words, he found increasing change with increasing discrepancy up to a point, but beyond that the decline in change that was predicted.

Degree of Ego-Involvement in Own Position. Paralleling the studies using more or less neutral and unstructured stimulus situations, Freedman (1964) presented a concept-formation task to subjects who were presented with a number of geometric forms representing a concept and asked to decide what the correct concept was. Some subjects were told that their first response indicated intelligence and perceptiveness, while others were not thus involved in their first response. Subsequently, the experimenter presented additional examples of the concepts that deviated in various ways from the initial concepts. Discrepancy was defined in terms of the number of differences (e.g., size, position, location, etc.) between the first and second set of figures. Then the subject was asked for a final description of the concept. Figure 21.7 shows Freedman's results for what he called low and high involvement in his experiment.

If Freedman had included discrepancies greater than the largest, it would be expected that even in the low-involvement condition, the limit of influence would have been reached. Whittaker (1965) found this to be the case in replicating an earlier study by Hovland and Pritzker (1957) that used verbal material. The issues in the Hovland-Pritzker study were not highly involving ones (for example, Washington was a greater president than Lincoln; a cure for cancer will be discovered within five years). College students indicated their opinions on a series of such issues by checking a scale from "agree strongly" to "disagree strongly" for each statement. They also indicated a group whose opinion they would respect most on each issue.

Later, the same questionnaires were returned to the students to be filled in again, this time with a position marked for each issue and attributed to a group that they had indicated as authoritative on the matter at hand. These fictitious check marks differed systematically from those that the subject had made initially; however, the maximum discrepancy was only three positions away. Hovland and Pritzker found greater change with greater discrepancy within this range.

Whittaker repeated the study with several important changes: First, he added some issues that he suspected would be more involving for students (e.g., "There should be curfews for male students"). Second, he attributed all fictitious check marks to other college students. Third, he increased the range of discrepancy from three to eight steps. Figure 21.8 shows the median change obtained over twelve issues with the varying degrees of discrepancy from subjects' initial checkings.

In more naturalistic studies of political issues, no change or frequent change *away* from a position advocated in highly discrepant communications has been found, with maximum change toward the communication at moderate discrepancies (Hovland, Harvey, and Sherif, 1957; Sherif and Hovland, 1961; Whittaker, 1964, 1965). Several studies have presented unfavorable information to a person about himself. Whether the person was susceptible to change would depend upon the degree of his involvement in the characteristic criticized. Eagley (1967) found that students were significantly less influenced by unfavorable information about themselves than when the same information was given about another person. Johnson (1966) showed that when change does occur, it is a function of the degree of discrepancy from the person's own evaluation, declining markedly at the extreme discrepancies.

One of the most convincing studies of the effects of ego-involvement in the person's own stand was performed by Norman Miller (1963). The issue was fluoridation of the water supply, a problem that was probably not highly involving to most high-school students. By subject selection and research procedures, however, Miller was able to *vary* degree of ego-involvement convincingly. He selected students at the upper and lower 25 percent (opposite extremes) from a sample of 800 high-school students. From four to ten months later, the students' stands were checked in an informal inter-

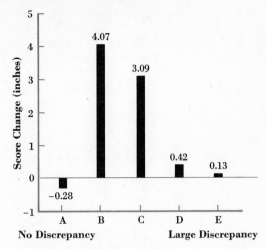

Fig. 21.6. Mean change in judgments of autokinetic movement as a function of the discrepancy between the person's judgment scale and the planted judgments of a confederate. (Adapted from Whittaker, in Sherif and Sherif, 1967.)

view not related to the questionnaire. He then selected subjects who were consistent in giving extreme responses.

In the experiment, all students took part in a procedure designed to enhance their involvement with the fluoridation issue or in an issue irrelevant to the controversy. This procedure involved a talk on the importance of the issue to students and of their opinions on the topic, a statement supporting

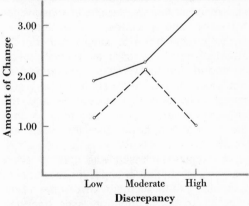

Fig. 21.7. Mean change in concept choice from initial to final response as a function of low involvement (solid line) or high involvement (dashed line) and amount of discrepancy in communication (baseline). (After Freedman, Involvement, discrepancy and change, *J. abnorm. soc. Psychol.*, **69**, 290–295. Copyright 1964 by The American Psychological Association, and reproduced by permission.)

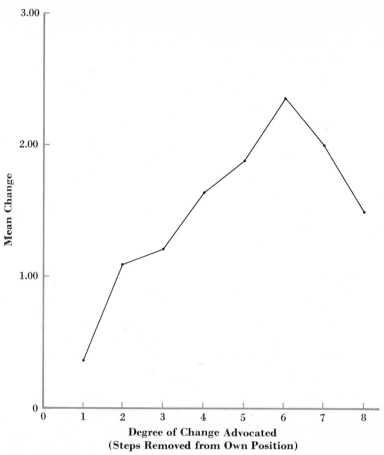

Fig. 21.8. Mean change score according to discrepancy of advocated change relative to person's initial opinions. (Based on data in Whittaker, 1967.)

the particular student's stand, a written statement by the student giving reasons for his stand, and a pledge to distribute materials on the issue to family and friends. Then all students heard a communication on fluoridation highly discrepant from their own point of view and ostensibly part of a taped interview with a lawyer. Finally, the attitude measurement was repeated on both the fluoridation issue and the irrelevant issues.

The significant result was that on every measure of attitude change, those students who had gone through the "involvement procedure" on the fluoridation issue changed *less* than those who went through the same procedures on irrelevant issues.

A great variety of research on specific aspects of the communication situation also reveals the importance of ego-involvement as a variable producing resistance to change. McGuire and his associates (1962, 1969) conducted systematic studies of the

stability of "cultural truisms," such as the value of cleanliness and health care. When such truisms are attacked, people seldom abandon them—but the strength of their belief can be weakened fairly easily. By providing the person with arguments that support the practice in question, some resistance to such attack is found. However, even greater stability of the cultural truisms occurs when the person is also provided with arguments to refute possible attacks.

Thus far, the effects could be explained in terms of the person's genuine lack of information to support a belief that he has taken for granted. However, McGuire also found that the same resistance to attack occurs when the subject is provided arguments to refute attacks that differ from the attacks he actually hears in a subsequent communication. In other words, the experience of hearing *any* counterargument to attack on a belief taken for granted produces sufficient involvement that the individual is better able to generate his own arguments against different attacks.

The question arises whether the concept of "importance" in the dissonance model and ego-involvement mean the same things and have the same effects. This question was examined in a naturalistically designed experiment by Rand (1967), conducted on a university campus, and which involved newspaper articles planted in the student paper on athletics, religion, fraternities, and war. Measures of both importance and ego-involvement were included. In general, the study confirmed the lack of conceptual distinction between importance and ego-involvement and supported the social judgment-involvement approach in showing that greater importance or ego-involvement leads to greater resistance to change.

Source and Discrepancy. The effectiveness of different sources in changing attitudes is not independent of the degree of stimulus structure or the degree of involvement in the person's own position. The literature on source effectiveness is unanimous in showing greater effectiveness for a source who is evaluated by the subjects as prestigeful, reliable, and trustworthy than a source who is not so regarded or is a member of an antagonistic group. In fact, the in-group and out-group delineation appears to be a particularly potent determination of source effectiveness, One study found that the same news stories, purportedly taken from the *New York Times* and representing exchanges between Americans and British spokesmen, produced a shift toward nationalism or internationalism depending on which position was taken by the American. The British spokesman did not have such an impact on these American readers (Adams, 1960). When a source is not designated or when the source is forgotten, there is a tendency for persons to attribute statements that they accept to a friendly source and objectionable statements to an unfriendly source (Sherif and Jackman, 1966; Sherif, Sherif, and Nebergall, 1965; Klapper, 1967).

Unfortunately, the available studies have not varied source and ego-involvement in the issue as well as discrepancy. With the use of relatively uninvolving issues, two studies have shown that a source with relatively low prestige on the issue at hand produced increasing change from small to moderate discrepancies and decreasing change with larger discrepancies. While the cognitive dissonance approach would predict marked increases in derogation of the communicator to occur as an alternative substitute for attitude change, the data in these studies do not show significant increases as attitude change drops off (Aronson *et al.*, 1963; Bochner and Insko, 1966). However, Bochner and Insko did find increased negative evaluations of the communication itself with increasing discrepancies, both for low and high prestige sources.

The involvement of subjects in the issues was low in both studies. Aronson *et al.* studied ratings of the alliterative value of poetry, and Bochner and Insko presented communications on the number of hours of sleep needed to college students. The high-prestige communicator was more effective in both studies. The most discrepant communication resulted in no significant increase in opinion change in the Aronson *et al.* study, and decreased change in the Bochner-Insko study.

The needed research varying ego-involvement with both the issue and the source as well as the discrepancy of communication remains for future exploration. Meanwhile, recent research clearly shows that "credibility" is not an attribute of the communicator, but a judgment by the recipient that is a function of his reference group ties (Rodgers, 1968).

CONCLUSION

This chapter has given an account of the struggles to develop adequate research models to account for the stability and change of attitudes toward or away from an advocated position. Its most important emphasis has been on the inadequacy of a one-way flow model of the communication process, insisting that attitude change and maintenance in real life occur relative to the context of social interaction and the person's reference groups. The person's susceptibility to change as well as his selective choice and his evaluations of information (or propaganda) can only be understood relative to the context of his reference groups and the stability of his ties with them. Attitude formation and change in experiments on group formation and intergroup relations, attitude change in interaction situations as compared with one-way communication, and attitude change with changes in reference groups were used to cite the importance of the social context in defining the person's ego-involvements and his responsiveness to varying sources of communication.

The attempt to specify psychological processes that maintain attitudes or predispose the person to change was illustrated through models that assume a tendency toward psychological equilibrium and through the social judgment-involvement formulation. The concepts of latitudes of acceptance, rejection, and noncommitment were used to define the conditions in which psychological tension aroused by discrepant information will lead to attitude maintenance, or change toward or change away from the source. Through the use of principles from the psychology of judgment, the probability of attitude change and the amount of change are predicted in terms of the discrepancy of communication as defined relative to the person's latitudes of acceptance, rejection, and noncommitment.

Variations in degree of ego-involvement, in the structure of the situation, and in the source were shown to affect the range within which increasingly discrepant communications produce greater change in the direction advocated—providing that the person is susceptible to change at all. Within the bounds of the latitude of rejection, increasingly discrepant communications produce no change and even change in a direction opposite to that intended.

Both field and laboratory research on attitude change will gain as the procedural designs vary such factors as those mentioned above, relative to interaction processes wherein people are faced with genuine problems related to their attitudes. The next chapter, dealing with the highly structured situations created by technological change, and the following chapter on social movements, will indicate that the most significant attitude changes occur under conditions in which the person's choice is not merely whether to accept or reject, or agree or disagree with a communication, but also involve his participation in the vital problems of existence with other people.

22

Attitude Change Through Technological Change

Major Topics of the Chapter

Attitude change problem relative to psycho-social and psychophysical scales

Vital motivational relevance of psychophysical scales created by technology

The place of technology in attitude change in various cultures of the world

Interacting effects of material and nonmaterial culture

"Hard facts" vs. "soft facts"

Automation: its effects on people caught in the process—their jobs, dignity, seniority, labor-management, other human relations

Technological change and the "cultural lag"

Ogburn on "cultural lag"

Technology as structured, compelling stimulus situations

NEGLECTED PROBLEM IN SOCIAL PSYCHOLOGY: TECHNOLOGICAL AND ATTITUDE CHANGE

The research on attitude change in the last chapter concerned attitudes the objects of which are other people, groups, political issues, institutions, and ideologies. The assessment of such attitudes and their change must be made relative to *psychosocial* scales—whose categories reflect primarily *consensus* within a group or the positions taken by different groups with respect to what is acceptable and objectionable in a particular domain (see pp. 79–80).

In this chapter, we are concerned with attitudes and attitude change whose referents are parts of man's material culture—namely, the technological means by which he pursues the urgent problems of getting and making a living, travels from place to place, communicates with his fellows, produces and exchanges vital necessities and luxuries, takes care of vital bodily functions, spends his leisure, and conducts relationships with other groups with the aim of friendly commerce or subjugation or annihilation. As parts of material culture, the referents of such attitudes form *psychophysical* scales (see pp. 76 ff.). Unlike those formed in the psychophysical laboratory, however, these psychophysical scales are seldom composed of categories lacking in motivational relevance. On the contrary, they are decidedly relevant to man's motivation.

Despite the great emphasis in psychology on defining the stimulus situation, social psychology has sorely neglected study of the effects of social stimuli the properties of which are readily defined in physical units—namely, the technological world in which individuals interact and conduct some of their most significant transactions. Much of the social-psychological literature in the United States, for example, takes the technological aspects of the environment and the consequences of them wholly for granted, just as the fish is the last to discover the importance of water. In fact, it is only within comparatively recent years that psychologists have become seriously concerned about defining the technical and geophysical as well as the cultural environment (e.g., Sells, 1963) with its ecological and spatial characteristics (cf. Barker and Wright, 1954; Sherif and Sherif, 1964).

Yet, without such definitions of the social stimulus conditions, the picture of man which emerges from research findings is that of a disembodied spirit whose concerns and actions are dominated by interpersonal relations, problems of conformity-deviation, and value conflicts. They picture a man apparently not affected by his immersion in a technological world of enormous cities and mechanized farms, of automobiles and super-highways, jet aircraft and rockets, gigantic dams supplying recreational facilities and power, television, flush toilets, several million bath tubs, and automated factories and offices. Yet, still only a small fraction of the world's population lives in such a world. In this chapter, we shall have a glimpse of the significance of the level and kind of technological environment for several fundamental problems in psychology and social psychology.

THE PLACE OF TECHNOLOGY
IN STUDYING ATTITUDE CHANGE

Social psychology lags behind other social sciences in explicit concern with technological aspects of the social environment. Especially since World War II the social sciences have been forcibly confronted with problems of cross-cultural contacts, the plight of modern cities, the threat and the hope of nuclear energy, the decline of empires accompanied by the rise of new nations, as well as new forms of economic domination and of modern warfare—all of which directly involve massive technological changes that continue unchecked.

Yet, it was not many decades ago that American anthropology, for example, was so preoccupied with "patterns of culture" in distant societies that studies of acculturation or "culture contact" were rare. (In the 1930s, the American Anthropological Association took a vote at its annual meeting on whether acculturation studies were to be included in anthropological journals; Beals, 1953).

According to Beals (1953), the growth of "culture contact" studies coincided in Great Britain with colonial unrest that stimulated an interest in colonial administration. In the United States, Melville Herskovits emphasized the importance of acculturation studies (culture change); and Linton (1940) brought together historical accounts of *Acculturation in Seven American Indian Tribes.* However, as recently as 1953 (Beals, p. 635), the overwhelming majority of studies on acculturation focused on "culture-personality" problems, in which configurations of cultural values were correlated with personality patterns, often on a highly conjectural level (see pp. 407–408). The relative stability of values and institutions in traditional societies was sufficiently impressive that few anthropologists were struck by the fact that technological changes were, nonetheless, altering attitudes, social behavior, and institutions.

By the end of World War II, the ever-increasing trend toward interrelationship and interdependence among technologically developed and "underdeveloped" countries was reflected in the social sciences. The eminent British anthropologist Malinowski (1945) emphasized the departure from the study of "closed" cultural systems in the following words:

> The anthropologist is becoming increasingly aware that the study of culture change must become one of his main tasks in field work and theory. The figment of the "uncontaminated" Native has to be dropped from research in field and study. The cogent reason for this is that the "uncontaminated" Native does not exist anywhere. The man of science has to study what is, and not what might have been. . . .
> The anthropologist could also usefully reflect on the fact that evolution and diffusion are processes not so different as they appear at first sight. Culture change in Africa does not differ profoundly from that which is at present transforming the rural and backward countries of Europe from peasant communities, living by indigenous age-long economic systems, by folklore and kinship organization, into a new type closely akin to the proletariat found in the industrial districts of the United States, England, or France (1945, pp. 2–3).

The importance of culture contact and, in particular, the impact of technology is not, however, merely a recent phenomenon. Perhaps the impact of technology in earlier times may best be seen in the literature on warfare on the North American continent by the Plains Indians, whose vigorous and at times *violent* reaction to conquest in the last century was often viewed as a cultural "war complex." Secoy (1953) showed the impact of technology (the domesticated horse and the gun) upon the culture of the Plains Indians from the seventeenth to the nineteenth centuries and concluded that it was much more decisive than pre-existing "culture patterns" in producing the war complex. The following is his conclusion:

> It is evident, then, that the military technique pattern of any one culture was largely formed in response to external influences from other cultures in the spheres of war and trade. The strength of these external influences is illustrated in this study by the speed with which all cultures that came in contact with a superior military technique pattern adopted that pattern, unless clearly prevented from doing so by temporary insurmountable, external political or trade barriers. The existence of a linkage between the military technique pattern of a given culture and those other aspects of the culture, such as religion, which formed self-contained systems within the culture is unquestioned. But the strength of that linkage, in terms of its influence on the form of the military technique pattern of

culture, appears minimal when viewed in relation to the strength of the influences coming from outside cultures (p. 95).

The changes produced by such technological impact are reflected in the interpersonal relations and attitudes of persons involved. This becomes evident in ethnological studies examining single Indian groups or tribes more intensively. Lewis' historical study of the effects of white contact on Blackfoot culture, for example, traces the effects of the introduction of the horse, gun, and fur trade upon the warfare of these Plains Indians (1942). Pre-horse warfare among the Blackfoot involved concerted action of the tribe motivated chiefly by the desire to defend and expand tribal hunting grounds or by vengeance. Lewis finds no historical evidence of a static, unchanging "war complex." Rather, with the coming of horse, gun, and especially the fur trade, warfare became a more deadly business characterized by smaller raiding parties which utilized stealth and secrecy to secure the horses and guns which became so vital to their pursuit of the fur trade and for social status and prestige.

Among the Southern Ute of Colorado, the coming of the horse facilitated the development of "band" organization, in contrast to the pre-horse family hunting groups. Opler (1940) who reported on this change, refers to Julian Seward's conclusion that for this area "the western limit of the horse also was the western limit of true bands" (p. 154).

Among the Ute, warfare in pre-horse times was "mere localized defense of one's kin." But with the development of the band organization, war became a means of enriching the entire band. "The mobility afforded the Ute band by the introduction of the horse led to a type of warfare motivated socially by a desire to loot." With this *Why?* change, the qualifications for leadership changed as well. A man had to prove his worth as a daring scout and a wise organizer. The most popular camp leaders became those "who called out most often that tonight they danced and tomorrow they raided" (p. 164).

Today, with major countries sending emissaries, technicians, and field workers around the world, it is evident that "technical development" represents a major problem area for culture change. New nations as well as old desire technological innovation (even as they may be unsure or uncommitted with respect to the cultural and ideological values of those who possess the means for them to achieve it).

INTERACTING EFFECTS OF MATERIAL AND NONMATERIAL CULTURE

Let us remind ourselves of other social stimulus situations the effects of which we have studied in earlier chapters. Material culture or technology is not an isolated or discrete aspect of the social situation. It is part of the stimulus situation for persons who are members of groups, larger social organizations, institutions, and societies, each with role and status systems and values or norms.

Technological innovation or change, in turn, confronts an individual who already has ego-attitudes that are directly or indirectly relevant to the product and its use. Thus, his reactions to technological change are influenced significantly (and, at times, profoundly) by his own attitudes, as well as by active pressures from significant others who are motivated to maintain the existing order of things or to shape his reactions in significant ways. For example, in the United States, there was considerable resistance for a time to automobiles—not only from manufacturers of horse-drawn vehicles but also from many persons who had no "vested interest" in other modes of transportation. Anthropologists (e.g., Foster, 1962) report many instances of resistance to technological devices and procedures that would seem to promote only convenience and health. Such resistance is often directly the result of ingrained values, customs, and attitudes.

To repeat, the effects of technology upon individuals are always "confounded" effects. They always involve the interaction of persons in groups with particular organizations, norms, and existing technology. Quincy Wright (1949) was among those to make this point quite forcibly in relation to technological change and its impact on societies: "The effect of a particular technological invention or importation upon a particular social order depends upon the way in which it is utilized, and that utilization is in large measure influenced by the values and the culture of the social order" (p. 177).

"Hard Facts" vs. "Soft Facts"

The statements in the preceding paragraphs are pertinent to larger controversies about social change. Some social scientists, as well as policy-makers and military strategists, tend to draw a sharp line between what they call the "hard facts" and the "soft facts." By the former, they typically mean material culture, including economic productivity and potentialities, technology, and military might. By the latter, they typically mean cultural and ideological sys- *soft* tems, social organization and psychological *facts* states—including human motives.

From the viewpoint of traditional philosophical controversies, it is perhaps ironic that in the United States, where materialism is officially rejected as a basis for political ideology, social scientists in recent years have repeatedly called to public attention of policy-makers and the military the importance of "soft facts" (e.g., North, 1962). Many social scientists have felt the need to caution policy-makers that too much reliance was being placed on elaborate calculations of "hard facts."

This controversy over "soft" vs. "hard" facts sometimes acquires ideological overtones. In particular, an emphasis on the "hard facts" by social scientists (as contrasted with practical politicians or military men) is sometimes condemned as crude materialism, or some other one-sided, mechanistic view of society and history. Without denying that there have been one-sided and crude views, it is worth noting that social scientists who have actually studied culture change, including technological change, become fully aware of the need for both "hard facts" and what is called "soft facts" and, especially, the need to examine the consequences of their interaction. This recognition was also explicit in the writing of dialectical materialists in the last century who, along with their ideological and political descendants, are most frequently accused of economic determinism by contemporary social scientists. For example, Engels answered the charge in the following frequently quoted passage:

> According to the materialist conception of history, the determining element in history is *ultimately* the production and reproduction in real life. . . . If therefore somebody twists this into the statement that the economic element is the *only* determinng one, he transforms it into a meaningless, abstract and absurd phrase. The economic situation is the basis, but the various elements of the superstructure—political forms of the class struggle and its consequences, constitutions established by the victorious class after a successful battle, etc., forms of law, and even the reflexes of all these actual struggles in the brains of the combatants: political, legal, philosophical theories, religious ideas and their further development into the systems of dogma— also exercise their influence upon the course of historic struggles and in many cases preponderate in determining their *form*. There is an interaction of all these elements. . . . Otherwise, the applicaton of the theory to any period of history one chose would be easier than the solution of a simple equation of the first degree (quoted in Guest, 1963, p.53).

In social psychology it is important to emphasize the interacting effects of material and nonmaterial culture and to "clear the air" of ideological bias. Then we may proceed to an approach for studying the effects of technology through the application of appropriate psychological principles. In actual day-to-day living, such factors as organizational channels through which people regulate their lives or adherence to norms which people feel are binding are stubborn enough in their consequences that they cannot be pushed aside under the devaluative label "soft facts."

AUTOMATION: A REPRESENTATIVE ILLUSTRATION

Automation is not, of course, a completely new concept in highly industrialized countries. Under the label of "mechanization," powered machinery in the United States had already made the draft horse and horse-collar manufacture obsolete, largely eliminated the need for vast numbers of farm laborers (including cotton pickers on Southern plantations), and transformed transportation when the term came into use. Similarly, mechanization in industry had eliminated jobs by the score, altering the status especially of highly skilled craftsmen who were once the best-paid and most prestigious of industrial workers (cf. Sayles, 1952). However, especially in mining, manufacturing enterprise, and the bookkeeping functions of business, *automation* achieved after World War II presented potentialities that are still unrealized and immediately perceivable situations with far-reaching consequences for both business planners and working men directly affected.

What the new automation amounted to was the elimination of human labor for the various detailed steps of production or manufacture, considering labor in its usual sense of expenditure of physical or mental energy, and the substitution of machines that both programmed and performed the sequence of steps in production. Of course, men designed, programmed, and repaired the machines. However, for ordinary workers in an oil refinery, in an automobile plant, or in a payroll and bookkeeping department, what automation meant was that their jobs were replaced by machines.

The men and women who remained in such automated plants were "scanners" who could spot dysfunction in the machinery, and button-pushers who could transfer the process from one phase to the next. We will not here elaborate on the fact that automation either in industry, factory, or office creates the need for new personnel—designers of machinery, programmers, and especially repairmen. While there will be for some time a paucity of such highly skilled workers in the United States, the increased utilization of automated factories and offices will set a definite limit on the number of individuals who can be gainfully employed in such highly technical occupations.

The present chapter cannot consider all of the ramifications of automation much less the realistic possibility of cybernetic systems completely controlling production. In the present context, the significant points about automation are twofold:

1. Once the decision is made and the transfer to automation complete, literally thousands of individuals are suddenly con-fronted with a highly compelling and well-structured situation: their job is to be taken over by a machine.

2. The event immediately affects conceptions and attitudes related to years of personal striving and achievement, including notions of the dignity of work, the *seniority* of position (for which organized labor groups fought for well over half a century), masculine values of independence and protectiveness of family, and worth as a human being. Automation in the mines and factories immediately confronts skilled workers with the twin dilemma of telling their families, "Well, you're now looking at an unemployed husband," and the knowledge that their skills are obsolete (*Life,* 1963).

Figure 22.2 contrasts an automobile assembly line before and after automation. Although labor unions in some industries have protested and struck to prevent automation, the apparent inevitability of continuing automation has led some unions to initiate joint planning with industries for relocation and retraining members, an almost unprecedented shift in intergroup relations (*Life,* 1963, pp. 79 ff.; Diebold, 1959).

Work in an automated plant, in turn, confronts the worker with very different tasks and social relations (Faunce, 1958, 1960). On the one hand, 68 percent of the workers in an automated automobile factory expressed satisfaction with the decreased handling of materials and physical labor while, on the other, indicated dissatisfaction that they no longer had any control over the rate or quality of the products. "[I don't like] the lack of feeling responsible for your work. The feeling that you're turning out more work but knowing it's *not yours really* and not as good as you could make it if you had control of the machine like before." "On my old job, I controlled the machine. On my present job, the *machine controls me*" (Faunce, 1960, p. 374).

While 80 percent of the workers reported that on their old jobs they were able to talk with fellow workers frequently, "many of the workers are virtually isolated socially on automated production lines" (1958, p. 404). Under these social conditions and machine control, the development of informal groups

Fig. 22.1. Mechanization can eliminate both back-breaking work and jobs for entire communities. **a.** (*above*) Cotton picking by hand was once a major occupation in the southern section of the United States. (Watson from Monkmeyer.) **b.** (*right*) One man and a mechanical cotton picker eliminate the field hands. (International Harvester Company.)

and worker regulation of the rate of work as reported in Chapter 8 becomes well nigh impossible. "The workers in this plant were able to identify a certain number of people with whom they worked, but the work group thus identified was defined almost exclusively in terms of spatial proximity or similarity of function" (1958, p. 407).

On the other hand, the foreman job involves much more frequent contacts with the individual worker. This situation led a large proportion of the workers to report dissatisfaction with the foreman, despite the fact that the foremen in the automated plant had also been foremen at the old factory. "It was better on the old job. Nobody breathing down your neck. Over here it's altogether different, just push, push, push all the time." "They never say hello . . . treat you like a machine. They used to be friendly. Now they seem to be under a strain" (Faunce, 1958, p. 405).

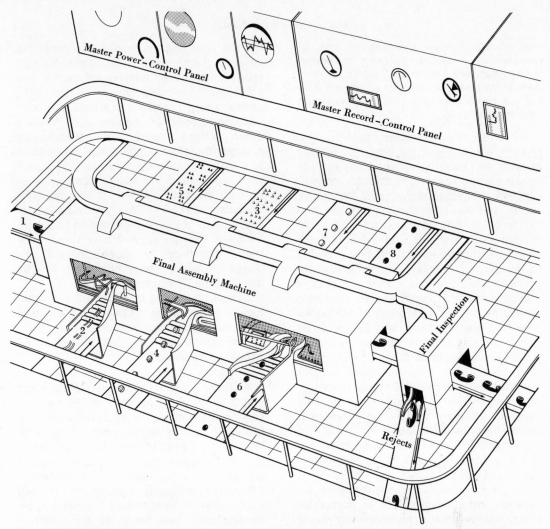

Fig. 22.2. Automation: the point of no return. **a.** (*opposite page*) An assembly line before and after automation (Ford Archives, Henry Ford Museum, Dearborn, Michigan; Ford Motor Company.) **b.** (*above*) Central control of operations not only eliminates occupations but changes the human problems of those who work in automated factories (see text).

TECHNOLOGICAL CHANGE AND THE CULTURAL LAG

Perhaps the most incisive formulation of the impact of technological innovation and its unforeseen social consequences was the work of the sociologist W. F. Ogburn (1964). Ogburn first published his "hypothesis of cultural lag" in 1922. His general definition of the hypothesis was as follows: "A cultural lag occurs when one of two parts of culture which are correlated changes before or in greater degree than the other part does, thereby causing less adjustment between the two parts than existed previously" (1964, p. 86). The following is one of his documented examples—namely, the problem of law concerning responsibility in the case of industrial accidents:

In this case, the independent variable was technology; the machinery of which, before the factory system, had been simple tools, such as those on early farms, to which the common law of accidents was very well suited. But after the coming of the factories in the United States, around 1870, accidents continued to be dealt with by the old common law and with much maladjustment, for where workers suffered loss of life or an injury to a limb, there was little compensation and long delay in paying for these disasters to the indvidual or his family. It was not until around 1910 that employers' liabilty and workman's compensation were adopted in this country. So that there was a lag of about thirty or forty years when the maladjustment could be measured by inadequate provision for several hundred thousand injuries and deaths to which there would have been a better adjustment if we had had laws of employers' liability or workmen's compensation (p. 90).

Numerous other examples could be cited of such lags between the actual conditions of living and working produced by technological change (especially through industrialization and urbanization) and the norms, values, and institutions coming down from earlier times. For example, working in industrial establishments and living in large cities are incompatible with many of the norms defining family obligations and responsibilities that survived from earlier days when the extended family was an economic as well as a living unit. Many of the norms governing the behavior and the roles of women became anachronisms when women started to work outside of the home in technical occupations. Or, at a much simpler level, the surviving norms about courtship, adult supervision of youth, and chastity were put to severe test by the widespread availability of the automobile.

Although Ogburn was sometimes accused, in his own words, of "a technological interpretation of history," he did not confine the hypothesis to technological innovation and survival values or norms. He noted, however, that in modern times nearly all of the cases with which he documented the hypothesis did prove to involve "a scientific discovery or mechanical invention," a fact that traced to the "almost universal observation" that in our time "technology and science are the great prime movers of social change" (pp. 90–91). In fact, he observed that both in sheer number of patents and in their importance, discoveries and inventions have been increasing at "something like an exponential curve," so that "lags accumulate because of the great rapidity and volume of technological change" (p. 92). When they accumulate, a society becomes ridden with *social problems.*

Ogburn noted that wars caused some cultural lags to "crumble" while preserving others and creating new ones. For example, World War II was marked by Negro service in the armed forces and migration to cities, thereby speeding the closure of a gross lag between the status of Negroes and the surviving etiquette of treating slaves. On the other hand, the development and use of the atomic bomb created many new lags with ingrained ways of viewing and treating other nations. Aside from evolutionary change, therefore, Ogburn saw revolutions as a major medium for the crumbling of cultural lags, citing the many "lags having to do with the family and rural life and Confucianism" as well as the bondage of women and of feudal organization that were "toppled" by the revolution in China after World War II (p. 93). Such changes produced by great social upheavals will be discussed in Chapters 23 and 24.

Before continuing to discuss the psychological basis for the lag between the rate of technological change and change in values or institutions, two additional complications should be mentioned:

1. Technological change frequently meets resistance and, as we shall see in the next section, only in part is such resistance attributable to the psychological considerations that we shall discuss. Major emphasis should be given to the role of organized groups and institutions of society which either see no benefit in the change to their way of life or have vested interest in preserving their own ways. As the historian Black (1966) wrote in surveying the "modernization" of societies, "no two elements of a society adapt themselves at the same rate" (p. 27). In particular, no two groups adapt at the same rate to the *significant and rapid* changes produced by modern technology. Therefore, a thorough understanding of technological change must also be a thorough understanding of intergroup relations over time (see Chapter 12).

2. The reasons that institutional and value change frequently lags behind technological change do not lie solely within the nature of the changes themselves or in the characteristic reactions of individuals to such changes. At times, existing institutions and cultures are maintained deliberately by the powers that be, at the very time that those powers are introducing technological change. Numerous examples could be cited from the history of the erstwhile colonial

powers of Europe in Africa and Asia, where the official policy was to deal through and support existing institutions and their leaders in order to maintain stability and docility to authority, while introducing technological changes in the form of factories, mines, etc. (for example, see Eisenstadt, 1966). Nor is this practice unknown in the dealings of more modern governments, where the policy of encouraging *local tribalisms* and other indigenous institutions is, at times, a deliberate means for preventing the rise of institutions and consolidation of new nations more adaptive to contemporary conditions (Wallerstein, 1966).

TECHNOLOGY AS STRUCTURED STIMULUS SITUATIONS

Without oversimplifying, it will be helpful to recall the psychological bases for the frequent observation that *the concrete and immediately perceivable is more readily assimilated than the more abstract, nonmaterial aspects of culture.* Psychologically, the "cultural lag" becomes understandable when we recall that technological devices and methods are well-structured (see pp. 51–56), allowing few alternatives for psychological patterning or adaptive behavior. For example, in the perception of highly structured objects, perception is organized predominantly in terms of the objective properties of the stimulus field.

In discussing the "relativity of judgment" (pp. 74–80), we learned that when individuals repeatedly face or use certain magnitudes, objects with certain proportions, or certain sounds, they form reference scales for judging them that reflect, on the whole, the range, the relationships, and other properties of the stimulus series. Subsequently, when they face these stimuli or others related to them, they react to them in terms of their established reference scale. This means, in short, that even in responding to well-structured stimui, there is a "lag" in adaptation to *change.* However, it is also a fact that adaptation to change of well-structured stimuli is remarkably rapid. For example, Tresselt (1948) had professional weight lifters and watchmakers judge the same series of twelve weights to deter-

mine whether their contrasting experiences outside of the laboratory would be reflected in a laboratory experiment. Both kinds of subjects adapted to the laboratory series, using categories that ordered the stimuli in the same way. However, at first, the weight lifters placed heavier weights than the watchmakers in the categories they considered "medium," thereby revealing their established reference scales based on their frequent hefting of much heavier weights.

In another experiment Tresselt (1947) presented the same series of twelve weights to subjects who had previously had varying amounts of practice in the laboratory with either the four heaviest or the four lightest weights. Analysis of the judgments of "medium" led Tresselt to conclude: "There is a definite effect of different amounts of practice upon the first judgment of stimuli in the expanded stimulus-range. The greater the amount of practice, the more slowly does the scale of judgment shift to its new position" (p. 260).

However, psychophysical scales do adapt to alterations in the stimulus series comparatively quickly (Johnson, 1955; Helson, 1964). In fact, this rapid adjustment has made it possible to develop fairly accurate formulas for predicting judgment of physical dimensions simply on the basis of a knowledge of the stimulus values the person will face and his immediately preceding experience with the stimulus domain in question, all of which affect his "adaptation level" for gauging specific stimuli (Helson, 1964).

According to Proposition 7, perception and judgment of well-structured stimulus situations are less subject to direct attempts at social influence than those for unstructured situations. Although it is relatively easy (given a stimulus series that is difficult to discriminate) to influence a subject's judgments of physical stimuli in the laboratory, it is difficult if not impossible when the stimuli are clearly discriminable. People are not fooled in the presence of clear evidence.

In an experiment in which the structure of stimuli presented for judgment was varied, the Luchinses (1955) concluded unequivocally: "The experimenter's decision was influential in getting subjects to accept or reject any proffered structurization of the line for the ambiguous perceptual stimuli but . . . it was very ineffective in producing any deviations from objectively true judgments when nonambiguous stimuli were employed" (Luchins and Luchins, 1955, p. 297). As Volkmann (1951) emphasized quite impressively, the problem of social consensus in groups is not entirely a question of mutual influence, prestige, or suggestion. Social consensus also occurs for the simple reason that the members all repeatedly face the same range of stimulation that has definite bounds or end points and well-graded intervals between steps.

In an experiment, Tresselt and Volkmann (1942) showed that individuals who had differing prior experiences with stimulus series rapidly came to a *uniform opinion* when they all were presented the same stimulus series.

These findings are pertinent to certain reactions to technology that are sufficiently frequent to be reported again and again in the research literature. For example, relative to the limited range of travel speed in a village where a donkey is the only means of transportation other than walking, a peasant's first trip on a wornout bus at a leisurely rate seems a terrific speed. Or, relative to the reference scale for riches in a peasant village, we can easily understand why a yearly income of $300 can be considered as riches and an occasion for joy.

Recalling the assimilation-contrast effects in psychophysical judgments (pp. 77–80), we can also understand the frequently reported finding that cultural artifacts and symbolisms resembling those already in use are more readily assimilated and even enthusiastically endorsed, particularly if they are obviously more useful. For example, a steel tool easily replaces a wooden one (Foster, 1962).

We are not suggesting that reactions to technology or attitude change accompanying technological change are as simple as the formation and change of psychophysical scales in the laboratory, particularly when the experiment concerns acuity of a specific sensory modality (such as vision, hearing, taste, etc.), as so many orthodox psychophysical experiments have. However, certain of the findings about psychophysical scales are not confined to judgment along a single dimension (Sherif and Hovland, 1961; Johnson, 1955; Helson, 1964; Volkmann, 1951). For example, the effects of established reference scales, the adaptability of psychophysical scales to changes in the range of stimuli, end-anchoring, and assimilation-contrast effects are *general* phenomena in human judgment and evaluation. Their significance becomes, if anything, greater when observed in reactions to technology which, above all, represents man's means to easing the rigors of his life as a biological organism on a planet that is not always gracious in granting the necessities for his survival.

For example, the latitude of acceptance does expand toward technological change when the innovation produces clearly perceivable improvement in life conditions. Many examples could be cited. The following pertains to universal human activities (the birth and care of infants) and illustrates assimilation of technical innovation despite lags in related cultural practices.

As a part of the Smithsonian health research, Charles Erasmus interviewed a number of mothers in a fine new maternity hospital in Quito, Ecuador, which had had immense success after a very short time. The mothers all criticized the hospital for forcing things upon them that conflicted with their beliefs: wrong food, open windows admitting fresh air, daily baths, compulsory fingernail cleaning, and a host of other routine acts which they insisted endangered their and their infants' health. But when Dr. Erasmus asked why they came to the hospital, they replied that they had noticed babies born in the hospital were lots healthier than those born at home—so culture appeared, in this case, to fly out the window as a barrier to acceptance of new medical practices (Foster, 1962, p. 237).

Before going to concrete studies of the effects of technology, a few words are needed concerning the psychophysical scales produced by exposure to material culture. Such psychophysical scales are seldom value-free. Technological devices have significance in vital activities, in human effort and labor, in producing pain or pleasure, and as means to important goals. Therefore, they acquire, at times, intensely personal significance. *The farmer's tractor, the construction worker's bulldozer, the pilot's airplane, or the teenager's automobile become parts of the self.* At times, the person can scarcely conceive of himself without these objects. Similarly, the housewife who is accustomed to a modern house with labor-saving devices feels personally miserable and lost in surroundings that her great-grandmother would have regarded as luxurious.

Tajfel (1957, 1959) conducted psychophysical experiments with lifted weights in which rewards were attached to certain categories and found that, even in the laboratory, value affected the properties of a psychophysical scale. Discrimination of objects near the valued categories became keener. The valued categories were, psychologically, further separated from neighboring categories. When the extreme categories defining the stimulus range were valued, an intensified end-anchoring effect occurred.

The astounding achievements of technology in mastering the physical environment, producing goods, and easing man's age-old burden of backbreaking labor have created a "passion for technology" among many peoples of the world (Barringer, Blanksten, and Mack, 1965). Thus, many technological objects and procedures have acquired an aura of prestige that few "communicators" of persuasion could acquire during a lifetime. Depending upon the strength and value of people's established reference scales and their exposure to this prestigeful aura of modern technology, the range of technological innovations that would be readily assimilated by people should vary. Chiefly because of the prestige of technology, we would predict that the range of assimilation for accepting technological innovation would be much greater than psychophysical experiments with neutral stimuli might lead one to expect.

The prestige of modern technological devices is well recognized by political leaders, as witness the "race to the moon" and the eagerness to be included among the "atomic club" of powers. As the economist de Schweinitz (1964) has documented, technology also becomes a part of the modern nation's "monuments" whose functions are symbolic rather than strictly operational or utilitarian. Thus a small country goes to considerable lengths to acquire two jet aircraft when they urgently need roads and railroads, and when the distances within their country are too short for the efficient use of jet-powered planes.

THE EFFECTS
OF DIFFERENTIAL CONTACTS
WITH MODERN TECHNOLOGY

The Turkish Villages[1]

On the basis of the findings in five Turkish villages with differing contact with modern technology, we may draw the following conclusions concerning the effects of differential contact in producing psychological variations:

1. When individuals in a social organization have little contact with modern technology and the internationally standardized units of distance, space, and time which accompany it, anchorages for the perception of distance, space, and time are standardized. The nature of these anchorages depends largely on: (a) the periodicity of work activities and social-economic activities (e.g., market days); (b) the periodicity of natural events (e.g., sunrise-sunset, or cycles of the moon) and the appearances of compelling features in the surroundings (e.g., a mountain peak); and (c) the human effort involved in accomplishing tasks (e.g., walking, riding) with the means available. The anchorages standardized on these bases lack precision in varying degrees. Perception and other experiences are significantly affected by the particular nature of the anchorages developed and thus may not be comparable along a given dimension (e.g., distances traveled by train cannot be translated into distances walked).

2. As one passes from more isolated to less isolated, from technolgoically less-developed to more-developed villages, international units of distance, space, and time are used roughly in proportion to the degree of the impact of modern technology, and their use becomes correspondingly more precise.

3. A scale of wealth exists for every village. The limits of the scale are set by the

[1] Documentation of the generalizations drawn in this section is reported in Sherif, 1948, Chapter 15, pp. 369–401; Sherif and Sherif, 1956, Chapter 20, pp. 692–701.

financial levels of the rich and the poor in the village. The standards which an individual uses in judging wealth vary according to his own relative position on that scale.

4. The radius of the world in which the individual lives his daily life and to which he can adapt easily widens with the degree of contact with the products and facilities of modern technology, with modern means of transportation.

The Hollow Folk in America

Rather than presenting further material from different culture areas, we will continue with an example from the United States, a country where technology has reached perhaps its highest and most widespread development, but where groups of people were isolated from the impact of modern technology until fairly recent years. One such area in the Blue Ridge Mountains

Fig. 22.3. In countries such as Turkey, as well as others, the old and new existing side by side create problems of adjustment. (Courtesy of Professor M. B. Kiray). a. (*left*) A Volkswagen on a street meant for pedestrians and donkeys. b. (*below*) Truck and donkey, as well as traditional elders and modern children travel the same thoroughfare.

of Virginia, about 100 miles from the nation's capital, was studied for two years by a staff of social scientists and psychologists. The results were reported by Sherman and Henry in their book *Hollow Folk* (1933). Four communities were studied. Starting with the most isolated, these were Colvin Hollow, Needles Hollow, Oakton Hollow, and Rigby Hollow, the least isolated. Briarsville, a small farm and sawmill town in the valley, was similar to other rural towns in different parts of the country.

The authors noted that the differences they found between the four Hollow communities did not seem to relate to differences in quality of land or natural resources. In this respect "all four communities are on an approximately equal plane. Yet because of the use of tools and equipment the output of Rigby yields incomes sufficiently large to maintain a standard of living far in excess of the three neighboring hollows" (p. 187). Thus, in the authors' opinion, it is the degree of impact of modern technology which is at the root of the great differences found.

The Most Isolated Community. Colvin Hollow was a scattered collection of cabins each with about two acres of garden. There was no road or system of communication with the outside world. The little trading done was carried on by one man who made about four trips a week across the almost trailless mountains to the valley. Over a high ridge, about three miles away by a narrow path, was a summer resort where some of the residents worked occasionally at unskilled jobs. The main means of livelihood was gardening, which was carried on with no modern tools. There were "rudiments of a home industry"—basket weaving. No one in the Hollow could read or write.

In many ways this community was more isolated, and the technological level was probably lower, than the most isolated Turkish village (Karlik). Perception of distance was even less precise. Residents did not ordinarily differentiate a quarter-mile from a mile. The usual designation for distances within this range was "over thar a piece." One child differentiated a short and long distance with the phrases "not a far piece over the hill" and "a good piece through the woods."

Expressions of time were also vague. Only three children in the community knew the days of the week. Even children in their teens did not ordinarily know one day from the other. "It is not vital for them to have this information because their way of living does not take into account time or days. All days are practically alike in Colvin Hollow" (p. 135). Three children had heard of Christmas and Thanksgiving but did not know what was done on those days.

People from outside the Hollow were viewed as strangers, with great suspicion. The people knew almost nothing of the outside world, except the town at the foot of the mountains, which they visited occasionally. Because of the nature and limited radius of the Hollow's world, the investigators found that people had few wants other than satisfying the most fundamental motives. The work tempo was observed to be very slow and irregular. As a result, people at the resort who sometimes employed the residents or ordered baskets tended to regard them as "unreliable."

The Less Isolated Communities. Next to Colvin Hollow, the more isolated community was Needles Hollow, which was connected by a trail with a country road leading to the valley. Here farms averaged about five acres apiece and almost every family had a pig and a chicken. A few men were literate. In this Hollow, a scale of riches made its appearance, whereas in Colvin Hollow equal poverty was the rule. This scale was based mainly on land; and the investigators thought it significant that many of the farmers said that they had 20 or 30 acres of land when they actually had less. But in this Hollow the tempo of life was still so different from the outside world that few residents left the community permanently. Even the former schoolteacher, who sold his belongings and moved to a small West Virginia town, found it difficult to adjust to the routine of life imposed by work in a sawmill. When asked why he came back:

" 'Wal,' he drawled, 'it's much better here. I gits up in the mornin' when I wants and I do what I wants. No gettin' up with a whistle and eating with a whistle here' " (p. 196).

The third community, Oakton Hollow, had more organized agriculture. A surplus of apples and corn was traded in the valley.

There was a store and post office, and nearly every home had a mail-order catalogue. Even the women made occasional trips to Briarsville in the valley. Here the scale of riches was clear-cut. Wealth was based on having a surplus of goods and the kind of clothes, house, and other articles which are outward signs of a surplus. The men of Oakton Hollow kept regular work routines when they worked outside the community. The community had lost population to the outside world, and the migrants tended to stay away if they left.

Rigby Hollow, the least isolated of all, was on a country road and was even more similar to other rural towns in different parts of the country. In Briarsville, the valley town with a sawmill and shopping center, regular working hours were maintained by the residents.

This study of the Hollow Folk illustrates the rather profound contrasts in concepts and attitudes found among people with differing degrees of contact with modern technology and the routines of life which accompany them. The investigators of the Hollow Folk observed that these differences were found even in the motives and aspirations of individuals. *In Colvin Hollow, the children hardly seemed to understand what was meant when asked, "What do you want to be when you grow up?"* When it was explained, the usual answer was "I wants to be what I am" (p. 104). They had never come into contact with a diversity of occupations. Likewise, at each level, the desires and tastes of the residents were found to increase in number and variety. The authors concluded: "wants develop only with experience, once elemental desires are attained" (p. 102).

TECHNOLOGICAL CHANGE: SHORT-TERM AND LONG-TERM EFFECTS

In selecting technology as that aspect of material culture most amenable for studying a number of social-psychological problems, it is necessary to distinguish between short-term effects and long-term effects. The long-term effects of technological change produce social changes involving so many aspects of life over successive generations of individuals that they are properly handled by social scientists whose units of analysis deal with aspects of social systems and culture rather than by social psychologists. The sweeping social changes produced by industrialization and urbanization, for example, can scarcely be accounted for in terms of attitude change on the part of so many individuals.

On the other hand, within the span of the human life, attitude change has occurred as a result of technological innovation. One dramatic illustration was reported by Lang (1946) in a study carried out in China in 1935–1937. In studying peasants who were beginning in larger numbers to work in modern industry, she found striking changes in attitudes toward parents and toward other family members that were directly traceable to experiences in industry. Of course, particularly among literate peoples, such attitude change is frequently associated with ideological influences. However, Lang concluded:

The environment is mainly—if not exclusively—responsible for the changes among the peasants and workers. They have heard very little, if anything, of modern ideas; but those who live in industrial cities or in rural districts where innovations have taken place and especially those who work in modern factories have seen their family life and relations changed by industrialization (p. 337).

Her survey showed a great decline in the traditional authority and honor granted fathers, who were treated with less respect and at times neglected by their children after they had started work in modern industry. Girls who worked in factories changed their formerly submissive attitudes toward their parents, asserting their independence and, in a few cases, defying parents by keeping the money earned in the factory for themselves. Wives who worked in factories found themselves with more authority at home and newly accorded respect from husbands. In some cases, the wife who worked actually became head of the family. One wife explained: "I have worked in the factory since I was very young and I know more of the world than my husband, who has never left his native village" (p. 206).

Another example of technological innovation that produced attitude change within a generation was documented by the historian Walter Prescott Webb (1936). As farmers in the United States began the westward expansion after the Civil War, they were confronted by cattlemen determined that no fences would be erected to bar the free movement of cattle on the open range. Equally determined, farmers strung fences and built hedges to protect their crops from grazing herds. Bitter conflict, violence and small wars broke out between the two groups in Texas, Wyoming, and New Mexico "wherever men began to fence and make private what hitherto had been free land and grass" (p. 313).

In the 1870s, barbed wire was developed and manufactured. The cattlemen cut the wires and "fence-cutter wars" broke out. Legislatures passed laws to regulate the actions of both sides, but to little avail. In the end, the cattlemen lost and were reconciled—more through the irresistible production of barbed wire than through laws. The change was reflected in the words of one cowboy who visited a factory producing barbed wire: "When I saw a barbed-wire machine at work manufacturing it and was told that there were thousands of them at the same work, I went home and told the boys they might just as well put up their cutters and quit splitting rails and use barbed wire instead. I was as confident then as I am today that wire would win . . . and that between barbed wire and the railroads the cowboys' days were numbered" (Webb, p. 317).

Long-Term Effects and the Cultural Lag

Many of the social institutions and the values that individuals in modern industrialized countries share and cherish today are, in part, products of social changes accompanying industrial growth and development in the last century (see, for example, Smelser, 1959). Although in the hearts and minds of persons whose self-concepts incorporate such values the present forms of the human family, of government, and of political and social life seem natural and naturally good, the growth of modern technology and its organized forms had a great deal to do with the formation of these con-

Fig. 22.4. What will be the effects of the technological revolution in communications? Despite poverty, the family living in this house in South Texas owns a television set (see aerial) that brings vivid images of the products of modern technology far beyond their grasp.

cepts and will doubtless produce changes in the long run. The maintenance of "old ways" and nostalgia for the past are reflected, psychologically, as efforts to maintain personal stability or, in some cases, to revitalize personal identity. Yet, as Theodorson (1953) pointed out, modern industrialization and urbanization bring certain trends in living that cannot be avoided and cannot be ignored. The concept of "cultural lag" is useful in pinpointing the origins of attitudes that, in any logical terms, are conflicting.

The Indian anthropologist-sociologist M. N. Srinivas (1966) gave several examples from contemporary India, where technological change proceeds while the historically entrenched caste system persists as the major organizational feature of social life. For example, he noted (p. 54) that the schedules of work required in urban life have produced many changes in eating habits and the foods consumed, although tradition still persists that defines permitted and prohibited foods. On the other hand, technology itself can directly affect important attitudes and behaviors about work, while leaving untouched attitudes and beliefs pertaining to less-structured problems. Thus, a man who drove a bulldozer for his living and could repair it saw no incompatibility between his work and his belief in "black magic" which he practiced and demonstrated for others.

In the modern world, cultural lags are accumulating at a rapid rate as a burgeoning technology has made it literally possible for man to close the terrible gaps that separate the "haves" from the "have nots," even as these gaps actually become more and more marked. A lag was brilliantly documented by the sociologists Lipset and Bendix (1959) in comparing the rates of social mobility in a number of societies with beliefs about the likelihood that anyone with ability and determination can better themselves. In the United States, the faith in the Horatio Alger legend and the "success" myth is strong, whereas in certain other societies (e.g., France) class barriers to social mobility are emphasized. They found, however, that actual rates of social mobility are remarkably similar in Western *industrial* societies, regardless of the prevailing mythology.

Perhaps the greatest lags of all lie in those institutional and value complexes related to the conduct of war, at a time when the technology of war on land and in the air has achieved the capability of destroying man himself and rendering much of the planet uninhabitable.

Social science and social psychology should not remain aloof from the problems of attitude formation and change related to technological change and the conflicts arising from cultural lags. Aside from their importance in the modern world, these problems offer in addition a fertile field for the development of research and measurement techniques at the frontiers.

23

Collective Interaction in Emergencies and Social Movements

511

COLLECTIVE INTERACTION
CHARACTERIZED

Human interaction in out-of-the-ordinary
conditions with lasting import for changes
in man's relations and outlook has traditionally been referred to under the rubric of
collective behavior. The same label (collective behavior) has also been applied to collective interaction in the face of temporary
emergency or disaster. We shall retain the
concept collective behavior, but shall differentiate between that instigated by emergencies and that instigated from within—
that is, by a previously existing motivational
base generated by deprivation or by dissatisfaction with things as they are.

In this chapter, our main task will be to
analyze what is meant by collective behavior, finding out what is common to any
human interaction, what is distinctive, and
what lies behind its occurence. We shall
distinguish between those cases instigated
by emergency or disaster, on the one hand,
and those instigated by social dissatisfaction and the social movements they may
produce, on the other. This distinction will
prepare us for an analysis of collective
interaction as it bears on the rise of social
movements.

At the end of this chapter we shall discuss the Negro protest movement in the
United States as illustrative of a social
movement. In the next chapter, we shall
extend the analysis and conceptualization
to social movements with broader scope. As
we shall see, these illustrative cases will
help us to establish that social movements
are vehicles of the most consequential evolutionary or revolutionary changes in man's
relation to man and his attitudes.

INTERACTION
AND COLLECTIVE INTERACTION

As with any other social behavior, collective behavior does not take place in a
vacuum. It takes place first and foremost
during interaction. It takes place in a situation within a larger setting. As we have
insisted throughout, there is much more to
any social situation than what meets the eye
immediately, than who said or did what to
whom, and whether the words or deeds
were kind-unkind, nasty-generous, or con-
structive-vandalistic. Any social situation
has to be described and analyzed within the
framework of four sets of factors. Collective
behavior and collective interaction are not
exempt.

As such factors were presented early in

Is a riot spontaneous?

this book (pp. 107 ff.), let us summarize briefly the four sets that have to be considered in any social situation, including collective behavior situations:

1. The set of factors pertaining to participating individuals (their composition, number, homogeneity-heterogeneity, previous relationships, motives for participating, etc.).
2. The objectives, tasks, or focus of participation.
3. The location, facilities, instrumentalities, and arrangements of the setting.
4. The relationships and the relevance of the above three sets of factors for the particular participants.

When collective behavior is analyzed within its appropriate framework, derived from the above sets of factors, we do not have to invoke altogether new concepts and principles to deal with the phenomena that are typically listed as characteristic of collective behavior. Examples of such phenomena are the *rapport* that permeates the participants, their feelings of unity, and even "we-ness." Many writers have commented upon the accentuated and extreme emotional expression, actions, and movement in collective behavior. Considered in terms of the four sets of factors above, we can see that these reports are all examples of differential effects on experience and behavior. As noted when differential effects were discussed in more detail (Chapter 6), social situations do produce experience and behavior that are not manifested when the same people are by themselves, even though they may experience similar motivational urges in private.

Let us consider such differential effects in collective interaction. What of the *rapport,* which so resembles the feelings of sharing that arise within a group, but which are not, in this case, the products of group interaction? When individuals share motivational urges (e.g., deprivation, frustration, or aspiration) or are suddenly confronted with common threats, their interaction enables them to learn quickly, even immediately, that all are in the same boat. Already emotionally aroused, they say things, hear things, and do things related to that focus that they would not wish or dare to express within the circumscribed grooves of daily life. Thus, the "rapport" that the sociologist Robert E. Park described as characteristic of collective behavior is generated through the interaction of participants aware that all are focused on a common problem or goal. This genesis of rapport is evident when we consider spectators or officers of the law who are not gripped by the same focus: rapport with the participants is lacking.

The rapid manifestation of a feeling of *"we-ness"* or *"psychological unity"* in collective interaction is likewise no accident. The presence of those actively involved in collective behavior is by no means a random event. We learn from historians, for example, that the crowd that stormed the Bastille did not just happen to assemble by chance encounter. Agitation, urgings, and various organized meetings got them to the Bastille as the detested symbol of tyranny (cf. Tilly, 1965).

What of the actions that occur during collective behavior? Despite the contradictory explanations of the actions, the literature contains a surprising consensus in depicting behaviors in *accentuated* modes, whether they involve violence and destruction or self-sacrifice and heroism. They include behavior that does not occur when individuals are alone or within the grooves of their customary lives.

Accentuated modes of behavior and emotionalism are not the exclusive property of collective behavior situations. All interaction situations have *differential effects*—including activities of organized groups, although to a lesser degree when interaction occurs under *ordinary* conditions of everyday life. When interaction occurs among larger numbers of persons simultaneously prompted by stronger motivations within situations of greater fluidity, ambiguity, or even crisis, the differential effects are intensified. In fact, the greater the departure of the situation from the established channels of ordinary events and routine, the greater is the likelihood that collective interaction will arouse emotional and extreme forms of behavior.

Summarizing what has been presented so far, collective behavior is but one instance of *interaction.* The limiting property that differentiates collective behavior from others is not sheer number of people involved. Army drills or commencement exercises involve large numbers—but they hardly fall within the domain of collective behavior in that they usually occur within prescribed channels and programmed sequence, drawn-up and announced beforehand by people in charge. Nor is the differentiating criterion the location—that is, open places or streets vs. rooms and halls. Nor is collective behavior distinguished by the personal traits of individuals participating, their age, sex, or race. What then does differentiate collective behavior—which includes crazes, orgies, revivals, protest rallies, strikes, panics, riots, and insurrection—from other interaction situations?

Differentiating Criterion of Collective Behavior

The differentiating criterion of collective behavior is that it is behavior of participating individuals *interacting under out-of-the-ordinary conditions, outside the daily routine of events in social life prevailing in a social setting.*

The key phrase in this characterization is "out-of-the-ordinary," and it refers to events and circumstances that exceed the expected bounds of regularities, programmed routines, and channels of everyday living. It means that people do not engage in collective behavior every day, even though they do interact with others in work, home, community, union or club. However, out-of-the-ordinary does not refer merely to infrequency of occurrence. Out-of-the-ordinary also refers to events outside the bounds of daily expectations (an earthquake, for example), or outside the latitude of acceptance (behavior that is disapproved, frowned upon, denounced by the public), or outside of the bounds of orderliness and regularity (disruption of transportation movement, etc.).

A Glance at the Problem Area

The problem of collective behavior has been stamped indelibly for decades by the imprint of Gustave Le Bon, as acknowledged, for example, by Gordon Allport (1954) and Robert Merton (1960). Le Bon's most direct impact was through his book *The Crowd* (1895), which was soon trans-

lated into several languages and reprinted widely.

Perhaps, as Robert Merton noted, Le Bon is best viewed as a "problem-finding" author in the history of social psychology. His descriptions of crowd behavior were coupled with keen insight into the problem posed by the extreme forms of behavior and the emergence of *new characteristics* precipitating men into emotions and actions that they would not have engaged in by themselves. In short, he clearly recognized the differential effects of collective interaction situations. For example, consider his account of a "psychological crowd."

> Whoever be the individuals that compose it, however like or unlike be their mode of life, their occupations, their character, or their intelligence, the fact that they have been transformed into a crowd puts them in possession of a sort of collective mind which makes them feel, think and act in a manner quite different from that in which each individual of them would feel, think, and act were he in a state of isolation. . . . In the aggregate which constitutes a crowd, there is no sort of a summing-up of or an average struck between its elements (Le Bon, 1960 edition, p. 27).

A great deal of collective turmoil had taken place in France when Le Bon was around, including the Paris Commune which served as an object lesson for the revolutionary writers and leaders at the time and since then. Along with its insights, Le Bon's account abounds in verdicts as to the credulity, feeble-mindedness, lack of judgment, irrationality, and vandalism of the crowds. As Merton stated in his instructive introduction to a recent edition of *The Crowd:* "Strewn throughout this little book are evidences of Le Bon's curious admixture of ideological images and commitments. He is an apprehensive conservative, worried by the growth of the proletariat with its socialist orientation" (Merton in Le Bon, 1960 edition, p. XXXVII).

The social psychologist Roger Brown (1954) made a similar evaluation:

> Le Bon had an aristocratic bias which inclined him to equate the lower classes (economically and socially) with the mob. "Civilizations as yet have only been created and directed by a small intellectual aristocracy, never by crowds (1903, p. 19)." To Le Bon, the French Revolution was the beginnng of crowd rule (p. 842).

Again:

Le Bon believed that our concious acts are the outcome of an unconcious substratum. This unconcious is atavistic. Le Bon described it as "under the influence of the spinal cord" and as more characteristic of beings belonging to inferior forms of evolution—women, savages and children, for instance (Brown, 1954, p. 844).

Even though he has been criticized, it can be said that a great deal of the literature on collective behavior until recently bore the imprint of Le Bon's treatment (cf. Merton, 1960, pp. VI and VII). As one recognized authority in the problem area stated: "The field is clearly in need of conceptual analysis—an analysis that will establish a basic rationale, lay out the separate areas of important interest, and show their generic relationship" (Blumer, 1957, p. 128).

Ours is a time of rapid change with the rise of new nations, with revolutions, crises, riots, and multifold expressions of unrest and the search for something to hold on to. There is lively interest in the study of social movements and associated collective interaction episodes. One tradition in the literature, as exemplified in the works of Blumer (1946, 1957) and of Turner and Killian's Collective Behavior (1957) stems from Park and Burgess in their Introduction to the Science of Sociology (1921). Associated with the University of Chicago, which was at the time the most influential center for sociology in the United States, Park and Burgess are probably responsible for subsuming the problem area of social movements under the rubric of "collective behavior." For example, in the fifth printing of their book (1928), nearly a hundred pages were devoted to the problem area including the broad topic "mass (social) movements," but all under the label of collective behavior.

Park and Burgess were far too sophisticated as sociologists to take Le Bon's accounts without raising questions, although his influence is evident. For example, they questioned the adequacy of Le Bon's account in the following words: "Neither Le Bon nor any of the other writers upon the subject of mass psychology has succeeded in distinguishing clearly between the organized or 'psychological' crowd, as Le Bon calls it, and other similar types of social

groups" (Park and Burgess, 1928, p. 876). In Turner and Killian's Collective Behavior, Le Bon's sweeping generalizations and verdicts on the irrationality and emotionality of interaction in social movements was subjected to a much-needed critique (e.g., pp. 16–17).

A landmark that moved social psychologists toward more coherent conceptualization of the problem area was the work of the social psychologist Hadley Cantril. In The Invasion from Mars (1940, Torchbook edition 1966) and The Psychology of Social Movements (1941), Cantril moved toward a realistic social psychology of collective interaction by basing the formulation on solid experimental foundations from the study of perception, judgment, and evaluation under structured and unstructured (e.g., crisis) conditions. In this formulation, the individual participant is not considered as one leaf in a passive heap of leaves that is merely swept away in the torrent of the crowd or social movement. The individual participant is seen as an active agent, searching and striving to find something stable and worthy in his eyes to hold on to, to explain events that puzzle him under conditions of uncertainty, frustration, deprivation and external crisis. Cantril balanced description of collective interaction, sometimes dramatic, by giving due weight to the conditions of crisis, uncertainty, and disarray that gave rise to the collective interaction. Thus the episodes of collective behavior could be understood and analyzed in perspective, whether they took place in the warm orgy of "angels" in Father Divine's "heaven," or in the sadistic and brutal cruelties of Nazi storm troopers in Hitler's Reich.

Cantril's analysis did not stop with the account of collective behavior at the moment of occurrence. Cantril was keenly aware of the shortcomings of taking the "fool's paradise" created by social movements as a closed world. He included in the picture the impact of the "macrocosm"—that is, the larger world surrounding the movement. More recently, Cantril's formulation was brought up to date and extended by his student Hans Toch (1965). From the beginning, Toch is careful to differentiate between short-lived, transitory collective behaviors instigated, for example, by a disaster, and collective behaviors instigated by a social movement of long duration with a clear purpose and program (p. 5).

Another landmark in the problem area is the work of the sociologist Rudolf Heberle with his *Social Movements* (1951). Heberle's book—with its focus on the role of political parties, their strategies, power concerns, maneuvers, and manipulations of interaction episodes toward the definite ends they pursue—should serve as a corrective on journalistic descriptions of collective interaction in which the individual is protrayed as helplessly credulous, swept off his feet and engaging only in irrational deeds.

Value-Added Theory. A notable attempt toward systematization of the problem area in a broad framework of sociological theorizing is Neil J. Smelser's book, *Theory of Collective Behavior* (1962). The theory presented is too broad and intricate for us to do justice to it here.

However, we can present here the six determinants constituting Smelser's "value-added" theory. The six determinants below are introduced in the first chapter (pp. 12–18) and then elaborated in later chapters with tabular listings in various contexts. The "value-added" label is an analogy represented by the conversion of iron ore through stages of mining, tempering, shaping, and combining the steel to end up in a completed and painted product—say, a car. The final product (the car) in the analogy is supposed to be the flare-up of collective behavior.

Each stage "adds its value" to the final cast of the finished product. The key element in this example is that earlier stages must combine *according* to a *certain* pattern before the next stage can contribute its particular value to the finished product (pp. 13–14). . . . As the value-added process moves forward, it narrows progressively the range of possibilities of what the final product might become.

The determinants that produce collective behavior are:

1. Structural conduciveness of the setting. For example, urban centers such as Los Angeles or New York, with high degrees of mobility, fluidity, and heterogeneous composition, are conducive to the rise of revivals, sects, and "hippie" manifestations.

2. Structural strain. "Financial panics develop when loss or annihilation threatens the holders of assets." This is the underlying unrest of a collectivity caused by hard times, oppression, etc. We shall refer to this determinant later as the motivational base (pp. 552–557).

3. Growth and spread of a generalized belief. In the race riots, for example, this is represented by the stands of antagonistic parties as to the aggressive intentions and hostile attitudes of the other side.

4. Precipitating factors. These are triggers for flare-ups when other factors have already primed the flare-up. A relatively minor incident, which might be *habitually* taken for granted, may serve as a trigger.

5. "Mobilization of participants for action" by the leadership.

6. The operation of social control. This is really a "counter-determinant" (such as police or legal-power apparatus) working against the occurrence or for control of the flare-up. Obviously this is deterrence power of the establishment which "arches" over all the other determinants (p. 17).

All these determinants and "counter determinants" (social control) are plausible as a pattern. It is helpful in the conceptualization of any collective interaction situation to consider all these determinants in their *patterned* form. Smelser's theory is a sociological *level* conceptualization which provides a framework to study the particular place (e.g., leader, rank and file, agent or target of collective behavior) of particular participants.

The puzzling problem in the theory is the "added-value" analogy exemplified by the conversion of iron ore to finished product (e.g., a car). The "added-value" theory may be a perfectly good theory in economics. The iron ore gains added value from stage to stage of processing. Iron ore is a neutral object. But even in an incipient movement, an emerging belief or platform (not to speak of an ideology which is an integral part of any social movement) is *not* a neutral object. From the very inception, a social movement always rises in opposition to the establishment. Especially a revolutionary movement ("value-oriented" movement in the terminology of Smelser's theory) is from its very inception in enemy territory. Its basic premises (its ideology) might have been formulated decades earlier on any place on earth. Invoking here in defense of the theory the counter-determinant of social control as "arching over" them all, amounts to stretching the iron-ore analogy to the breaking point. The theory can be effectively used and tested without the trapping of "added-value" analogy, which may be a perfectly good theory in conceptualizing the value of manufactured goods.

Differentiating Collective Behaviors Through Their Instigators: Emergency or Social-Movement

Two general classes of instigators provoke departure from customary, habitual modes of interaction. These two classes of instigators must be emphasized, for they have different impact upon the pattern of collective behavior episodes and upon subsequent human relations and attitudes.

1. *Collective behavior instigated by emergencies.* The instigation is an external event, typically sudden and disrupting—such as a wreck, fire, tornado, or other disaster. Typically their duration is limited to the duration of the event itself and, in some cases, to recovery and preventive efforts.

2. *Collective behavior episodes instigated by a social movement.* Collective behaviors instigated by a social movement are only episodes in the movement itself. They are integral parts of the movement, but not the whole of it. They cannot be understood adequately apart from the movement.

Table 23.1 presents a comparison of emergency-instigated and movement-instigated collective behavior. It compares the two in terms of their instigation, timing, staging and action episodes, emergent products, recurrence, interpartisan encounters, and consequences. Through reference to this Table, the ensuing discussions of collective behavior instigated by emergency and collective behavior instigated by social movements will be clarified.

All of these differentiations presented in tabular form point once more to the necessity of studying any interaction episode cross-sectionally within the *situational pat-tern* and longitudinally within the *temporal pattern* of which it is a part. Any instance of collective behavior is also a case of an interaction episode and subject to demonstrated impact of the situational pattern and temporal pattern within which it occurs.

EMERGENCY-INSTIGATED COLLECTIVE BEHAVIOR

Until scientific studies of disasters and other emergencies started in the 1950s with substantial support from the federal government, the bulk of literature on such collective behaviors was journalistic descriptions (cf. Chapman, in Baker and Chapman, 1962, p. 14). Naturally, such descriptions were frequently dramatic, capturing the extreme forms of behavior, emotionalism, panic, heightened suggestibility to the point of credulity, cases of vandalism, and cases of heroism. Similarly, sociologists bearing the imprint of Gustave Le Bon's descriptive analysis and value judgments stressed the theoretical model analyzing collective behavior primarily in terms of the state of the individual and his irrationality. The scientific study of such emergencies pointed instead to the out-of-the-ordinary nature of such emergencies—hence the departure from the routines and normative regulations of daily life, proportional to the scope and suddenness of the emergency.

The emergency situation, as well as its collective nature, did produce differential effects on behavior; however, many examples of panic, fleeing, and heroism turned out to be goal-directed and understandable. For example, Killian (1952, Turner and Killian, 1957) found that apparently irrational behaviors during and after explosions or tornadoes were the accentuated efforts of individuals to reach their families, save their children, or, in a few cases, fulfill their community role as policeman, fireman, etc. One man who saved the audience in a theater from destruction by storm winds through superhuman efforts in keeping the doors closed from outside, said afterward that his only concern at the time was his children, who were among the audience. A policeman, passing by friends and neighbors in

**Table 23.1. Differentiating Properties
of Emergency-Instigated and Social-Movement-Instigated
Collective Behavior in Relevant Dimensions**

	Emergency-Instigated	Movement-Instigated
(1) Instigator	Emergency (disaster, catastrophe, real or perceived danger). Fire, flood, explosion, earthquake, storms, etc.	Simmers; persistent agitation, actively seeks occasions for outburst or flare-ups
(2) Attitudinal-emotional commonality of participants: *motivational base*	Commonality on the particular *focus* for *duration* of emergency. Additional confusion as to the alternatives in course of action with heterogeneous composition. Emergence of orienters of action if collective behavior is not transitory (such as escape from a theatre fire).	Commonality or commitment, attitude, emotion prompted by *bill of gripes* and *platform* of demands and charges. Alternatives to action more specific; direction by the leaders of the movement. Proclamation of protest, assertion of goals in terms of formula or *slogans* of movement. Less likelihood of panic except in face of great danger (machine gunning, brutal suppression, etc.)
(3) Timing	Sudden, time unexpected or not sought.	Movement actively seeks opportune moments for collective action.
(4) Staging	Not staged.	Staged or primed for staging.
(5) Collective behavior	Differential effects in behavior and emotion. Degrees of orderliness-disorderliness, confusion, emotionality, proportional to the size of emergency (disaster, catastrophe), suddenness, presence-absence of forewarning, time interval of forewarning. Occurrence of panic proportional to the combination of above set of factors.	Differential effects in behavior and emotion. Departure from habitual modes of function proportional to scope of changes advocated; reform or revolutionary character; sizing-up of repressive power of "establishment." Policy of violence-nonviolence according to demands of ideology; discipline by movement as movement is stabilized in its bill of gripes, ideology, and strategy. Emergence of new modes of action or alternatives unanticipated by movement. Course of events may go out of hand (*see text).*
(6) Recurrence	Nonrecurrent unless emergency recurs. Apprehension of recurrence.	Collective behaviors are only episodes in the pattern of movement. Subject of minute analysis by partisans and antagonists as to effect, tactics, alternatives, their implications for staging new ones. Building ritual as to heroes, martyrs, defectors (for staging future events).

Table 23.1. *(Continued)*

	Emergency-Instigated	Movement-Instigated
(7) Interpartisan encounters	General public and/or official sympathy, help for victims, participants. Not appreciable interpartisan confrontation except specific in search for culprits or saboteurs if any (e.g., in case of fire, explosion, or power failure).	Sharpening of gap between partisans of movement and establishment (official and public committed to established order). Accentuation of interpartisan stereotypes, name-calling. Further entrenchment of intraparty commitment (especially by die-hards) on both sides.
(8) Consequences —especially in attitude and self-image	Consequences to victims or participants with subsequent personality reverberations if experience stressful and traumatic. Other personal consequences to relatives or friends (loss, care, etc.). Technical changes to prevent recurrence if applicable.	Changes in norms (values) and associated attitudes, self-image in scope and duration proportional to the reform(s) or revolutionary recasting advocated. If movement prevails, transformation of norms and human arrangements with the rise of new order, new respectability and establishment. New formulations and norms becoming basis of new way of life and educational process replacing those discredited.

serious need of help, was actually hurrying to the next town for aid.

Whatever its specific nature, the emergency compels the attention of individuals exposed to it because it is typically sudden in onset, disruptive, frequently threatening or damaging to life, and overrides temporarily the stimuli in one's habitual setting. However, the ingredients of an emergency are not only unusual sensory events with arresting characteristics and impact. They are danger signals or actual catastrophic events requiring quick action or immediate solution for survival (e.g., escape). Thus, emergencies become *focal* in the situation in which they occur, signifying danger (actual or perceived) and possibly catastrophe. To survive, people have to reach a safety zone, to escape and then recover or rehabilitate themselves.

The *focus* of an emergency, therefore, is a pressing, urgent problem situation which has to be attended to or solved without delay by individuals caught in the situation (cf. Toch, 1965). It is small wonder that the motivational character of the situation is urgent and is shared by the individuals. Not only is the common problem shared, but it also demands immediate action. For each

individual, the emergency is "out there" with its grim presence. People caught in the situation do not have to be given a detailed description to know and to feel that they are in the same boat or to feel, in concert, rapport and a sense of "we-ness." The rapport that permeates the participants stems from this motivational base.

The suddenness or unexpectedness of emergency that requires an appropriate escape route or solution through immediate action generates intense emotions. There is nothing astounding about this, of course. The generation of emotions by sudden events is a universal principle of behavior. While emotional arousal may be disruptive, temporarily, it also is essential for goal-directed mobilization of the organism, as was so cogently formulated by Leeper (1948).

Whether emotional arousal and mobilization will be utilized effectively toward adapting to or solving the problem of the emergency, or wither away through maladaptive, conflicting, and futile moves is another matter. As it is sudden and unexpected, the emergency creates a crisis situation fraught with danger, misfortune, and other problems with great motivational impact the solution of which cannot ordinarily be tackled through specific, established alternatives of everyday life. The emergency creates conditions of fluidity in which, suddenly, people must resort to untried alternatives—and (without precautionary measures) they are highly uncertain about them.

At times, the crisis is so great and the uncertainty so pervasive that no clear alternatives are objectively presented. In such a situation, people rely more heavily on the actions and solutions offered by others. Their reliance becomes directed to others in the same boat, not only to leaders. For example, in a disaster, the victims become highly dependent, even submissive, to agents of help, both from formal agencies or informal efforts (Chapman, in Baker and Chapman, 1962).

From the principles about unstructured situations, it can be predicted that under such circumstances, people will tend to become more reliant on others and more suggestible. Crisis situations lack, on the whole, reliable external guidelines to cope with the situation. We have already seen that such situations are highly conducive to greater reliance on social influence from others (Chapters 4, 6, 9, and 17).

What have we learned about *increased suggestibility* in such situations? It is a general principle of human psychological functioning that susceptibility to follow the words and actions of others is greater in situations lacking definite objective guidelines and stable objective anchorages. Crises are such situations. It is universally true that such susceptibility, as is the case with any behavior, is subject to individual variations and, further, to accentuated individual differences. The accentuated individual differences follow from the principle that internal factors (e.g., motives, attitudes, and identifications with significant others) will be revealed more clearly when the stimulus situation is unstructured.

People would not be human if they did not become emotionally aroused in the face of emergency. They would not be human if they did not become more suggestible under crisis than ordinary conditions. They would not be human if they did not react to crisis in ways revealing their more enduring attitudes, identifications, fears, and aspira-

tions. These generalizations apply, in appropriate degrees, whether the individuals are American, French, British, or Chinese, and whether the person is a professor of logic or an artist or a working man or a housewife.

It follows, of course, that collective behavior in the face of a specific emergency depends to a great degree on planning and precautions that have been taken in anticipation of just such an emergency, as well as upon the adequacy and coordination of civil agencies in prompt and effective efforts to deal with it. The recent research into disasters, for example, has largely been undertaken as a basis for developing guides in such respects.

Natural History of a Disaster

In line with earlier work, Dwight Chapman divides the "natural history of a disaster" into seven temporal phases: (1) warning, (2) threat, (3) impact, (4) inventory, (5) rescue, (6) remedy, and (7) recovery (Chapman, in Baker and Chapman, 1962). Our interest here is in interactions of people caught in disaster among themselves and with outsiders (official or informal). In addition, we are interested in the effects of forewarning and the impact of disaster on the amount and the character of differential effects.

Fritz and Marks (1954) found that warning and charting the course of action in advance tended to decrease the likelihood of extreme behaviors, such as panic. However, warning too briefly beforehand to prepare for the emergency was no more helpful, and probably less helpful, than no warning at all. In such situations, the individual is exposed to even greater psychological stress because he is aware of impending disaster and helpless to take steps. The interested reader may consult the detailed analysis by Janis (1962) on stress in response to various kinds and amounts of warning and its psychological consequences.

On the whole, however, the study of people caught in disasters shows that people do not inevitably become disorganized into panic (Chapman, 1962). For a time, during the initial period, they may become "fragmented," subdued, more suggestible, and more dependent than under ordinary condi-

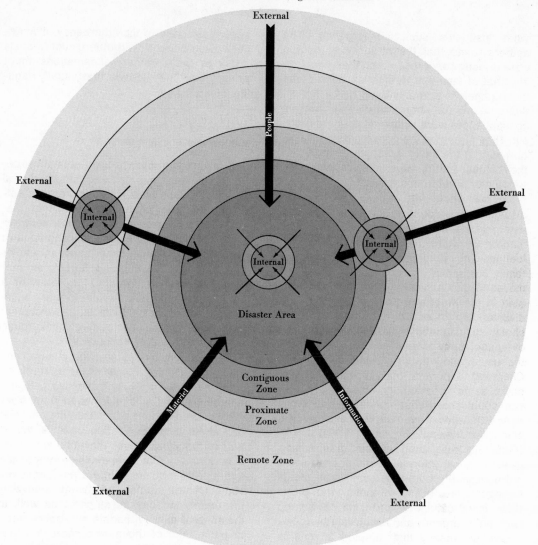

Fig. 23.1. Convergence of people during emergency-instigated disasters and factors conducive to their congregating. (From C. E. Fritz and J. H. Mathewson, *Convergence Behavior in Disasters: A Problem in Social Control*, p. 7, Plate 2. Publication 476, Committee on Disaster Studies, National Academy of Sciences—National Research Council, Washington, D.C., 1957.)

tions. But they soon strive to reach a state of certainty about the uncertainties the disaster has produced and to reach recovery. In this process, both people caught in the emergency and people within a wide radius tend to converge upon the focal areas. The extent of this convergence varies with the enormity of the emergency, but it is frequently so great as to cause traffic jams and crowds that interfere with the effective flow of aid.

In their monograph on *Convergence Behavior in Disasters* (1957), Fritz and Mathewson state:

In every disaster, irrespective of geographical location and size of the stricken community, or the type of disaster, the magnitude of convergence has been great enough to hinder organized rescue and relief operations or otherwise impede the restoration of the orderly processes of life (p. 27).

Thus, collective behavior also occurs after the emergency, at least under conditions of modern life. Fritz and Mathewson present a spatial model of "convergence behavior," as shown in Fig. 23.1.

Of even greater interest, from the social-psychological viewpoint, is the question of what instigates such convergence. The authors found that the majority of people were directly concerned about their own fate and that of family or dear ones; then came those eager to give a helping hand; finally, those people for whom the disaster and its consequences were simply an event of interest. They classified the convergers as (1) returnees, (2) the anxious, (3) the helpers, (4) the curious, and (5) the exploiters who hope for gain or profit from the event.

On the whole, the recent research on disasters casts doubt on the older view that emergencies were the occasion primarily marked by widespread acts of selfishness, looting, and vandalism. On the contrary, family ties, family and community roles, and moves to give a helping hand are accentuated in the reports of people caught in the disaster and of outsiders. After the initial shock and stunned state of aftermath are over, sociability increases, doing away with the usual etiquette of getting acquainted. Chapman reported that "differences of status seem to have been swept away, that you could share your concerns and emotions with almost everybody, that strangers acted like friends" (Chapman, 1962, p. 16). If officially designated leadership is lacking in emergency, informal leadership arises—not necessarily from those with high status in regular life, but from those who prove their resourcefulness and skill in coping with the emergency and its aftermath.

One emergency that affected 30 million Americans in the Eastern region of the United States occurred at 5:28 p.m., Tuesday, November 9, 1965, when sudden failure of the power system blacked out lights and all electric power for people in their homes or caught in city streets or in subways and railroad stations. The emergency was chronicled by two editors of the New York Times in The Night the Lights Went Out (Rosenthal and Gelb, 1965). The accounts include vivid descriptions of differential behaviors of varying degrees and kinds, as various bunches of people were caught by the emergency. In the authors' words, they ranged through "confusion, courage, humor and adventure." For example: "1700 subway passengers rescued from atop Williamsburg Bridge," Inmates of Massachusetts prison go on two hour rampage," "Bachelor asks train conductor to perform marriage ceremony." Figure 23.2 shows

people stranded in the emergency, illustrating how in concert with others such a crisis dissolves their ordinary expectations about privacy and the niceties that usually regulate sleep.

Background Setting and Context of Emergency

Any conceptualization of collective behaviors in emergencies and afterward will be lacking substance if the background setting of the emergency is left out of the picture. By *background setting* we refer to conditions in the society and conditions of even broader significance, such as war or threat of war, widespread unrest, or economic depression. Whether an actual or a perceived emergency will trigger widespread collective behavior is, in substantial part, a function of the general background setting within which it occurs.

An excellent example of the effect of the background upon both perception of an emergency and ensuing collective behavior is provided in Cantril's *Invasion from Mars* (1966). On October 30, 1938, the realistic and effective dramatization of H. G. Wells' *War of the Worlds* over the radio was sufficient to frighten at least a million Americans and plunge thousands into a panic-stricken state. Cantril studied the event, analyzing the underlying causes of panic as well as the state of mind of people who succumbed to panic, and of those who heard the program but critically resisted succumbing. In more stable times, no matter how realistically and colorfully dramatized, a mere play would not have reached the threshold of arousal for the very people who were so fearful and panic-stricken. They would have waited for further announcements, which included the fictional nature of the presentation.

What was the background to their panicky behavior? Since 1929, when the Great Depression started, there had been prolonged years of uncertainty and crisis. At the time of the broadcast, the air was tense with the threat of impending war. As Cantril wrote, we are dealing here with "an episode of human behavior brought about by a pattern of circumstances providing a matrix for high suggestibility." For some people, the fact that it was Halloween time added to the matrix.

Fig. 23.2. The night the lights went out in New York City and much of the Northeast people found themselves in extraordinary situations even when doing ordinary things. (United Press International Photo.)

Within a background of confusion and genuine catastrophe, even an ordinary natural event can produce panic. After the explosion of the atomic bomb in Hiroshima, some of the survivors tried to find refuge in a park; rain began to fall and the raindrops themselves became ominous. Panic spread like wildfire: "The Americans are dropping gasoline. They're going to set fire to us!" (Hersey, 1946, p. 52).

**Background Conditions
and Increased Frequency
of Collective Interaction**

In periods of instability, general apprehension and ubiquitous anxiety brought about by conflict of values or the breakdown of norms, sectors of people who lack clear-cut guidelines to follow and reliable anchors resort to unusual collective extravaganzas. Under these conditions, they seek comfort in the presence of large numbers of other people, usually focused toward some erstwhile symbol of stability. For example, they seek comfort and salvation through participating in mammoth revivals, as pictured in Fig. 23.3. They are particularly susceptible to congregating the minute a public figure appears who may provide evidence that the world is in joint. They are more likely to become prey to the exhortations of demagogues who promise them the

Fig. 23.3. Collective interaction at a revival: A Billy Graham rally in Great Britain. (Carl Mydans—LIFE Magazine © Time, Inc.)

Fig. 23.4. A television idol of youth sits on the window ledge of his New York hotel, ready to drop the comb with which he has just combed his hair (Courtesy of Dr. Christian Probst.)

world and heaven as well if only they will yield and follow.

Adolescents in the modern world are often caught both in the uncertain times and their own psychological conflicts of the betwixt-and-between period (Chapter 19). Floundering in alienation, into which they are thrown from childhood, they do create their own reference idols. In the presence of these idols, their collective actions represent almost classic cases of the descriptions of the rapport, increased suggestibility, and excitement of collective behavior (see Fig. 23.4).

**"Tune In,
Turn On,
Drop Out"**

States of dissatisfaction and alienation from the prevailing social values, conflict of norms, and normlessness invariably lead to search for something to hang onto in concert with others in the same plight. But what is resorted to, what kind of new bonds are established, and what kind of values are adopted need not always be directed toward bringing about changes.

The plight of many disenchanted young people in various Western societies, particularly in the United States, and of many intellectuals today illustrates the point. Many of them seek haven by building castles in the air in closed worlds of their own creation, asking to be "let alone" by the rest of the society which they reject. In Chapter 19, we discussed group formations among adolescents with their particular norm formations and activities for coping with their plight. A concrete phenomenon of escape is the hippie culture of the 1960s—created by a segment of disenchanted youth and young adults, given broad publicity by the mass media, and joined by a small but vocal minority of intellectuals (see Fig. 23.5).

The lack of clear function and responsibility for youth in the social fabric conspires to promote escapist solutions with their distinctive "cultures"—fragmented clusters of small cliques and cults. The solution of the hippies is epitomized in the dictum of the psychologist, Dr. Timothy Leary: "Tune in, turn on, drop out." This formulation is conducive to the haven of "psychedelic" retreat which may be found in bohemias of

Fig. 23.5. (*above*) The disaffection and alienation of some youth lead to retreat from the world. (Burton Wilson.) But other alienated youth join in social movements directed toward changing the state of things that seems to cause their plight. (*below*) Paris, May, 1968— Reporters Associes. (*opposite top*) New York, April, 1968—United Press International Photo. (*opposite bottom*) Berkeley, Calif., Oct., 1967—United Press International Photo.

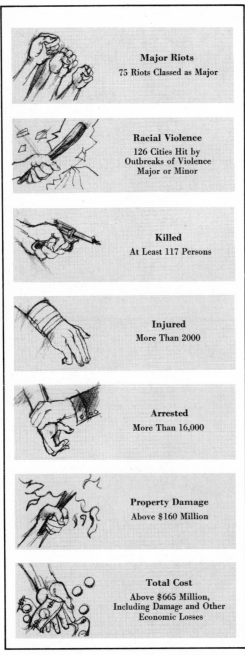

Major Riots
75 Riots Classed as Major

Racial Violence
126 Cities Hit by
Outbreaks of Violence
Major or Minor

Killed
At Least 117 Persons

Injured
More Than 2000

Arrested
More Than 16,000

Property Damage
Above $160 Million

Total Cost
Above $665 Million,
Including Damage and Other
Economic Losses

Fig. 23.6. Riot record for 1967. (Data from *The Philadelphia Inquirer*, Jan. 7, 1968.)

large cities with exotic symbolisms and expressions of other worldliness from past cultures, such as the East Village of New York City and the Haight-Ashbury district of San Francisco in the late 1960s, as well as similar suburban colonies, especially in large metropolitan areas (Brown, 1967).

Because one cannot really escape anything in a large metropolitan area, a growing trend for the young people swept into the hippie culture became that of further retreat to form their own colonies near to nature. "There are at least 20, maybe 30, hippie rural communes studded across the U.S. . . . No one knows the exact number because hippie communes try to avoid the puritanically straight scrutiny of local game wardens, health officials and truancy officers" (Brown, 1967, p. 63).

Disenchanted by the main currents of society, trying to build a microcosm of their own in psychedelic retreat and uninhibited search through raw pleasures, such young people are also prone to participate in collective interaction and various sorts of protests initiated by others. However, participation in political, social, and other collective protests that smack of this world is not a strong orientation with them. In fact, there is some resentment of political involvement by those in their midst. As one hippie put it: "They look like we do and they talk like we do—but they don't think like we do. . . . They live down here—but they're just not hippies" (Brown, 1967, p. 4).

SOCIAL-MOVEMENT-INSTIGATED COLLECTIVE BEHAVIOR: ORIENTATION

A social movement is a formation over time. No matter how urgent, vital, and widespread the *motivational base* on which it arises, the pattern of a social movement does not develop overnight. No matter how widespread the frustration, how intense the deprivation, or how keen the aspirations for a better life, a social movement is a temporal affair. It may take years, even decades for a movement to acquire a structure and a momentum proportional to the scope of its motivational base and to the scope of changes for which it strives.

During the formative phases, the overt actions of a social movement may be crushed time and again by the overwhelming forces of the establishment. For example, in his *Anatomy of Revolution* (1965), Crane Brinton describes "abortive revolutions." In such cases, the visible portion of the movement—that called collective behavior—may diminish or be submerged completely in favor of camouflaged and clandestine activities that require extreme caution, planning, and cold-blooded calculation. Such activities in the pattern of a social movement are almost exact opposites to the character of collective behavior, with its excitement and accentuated modes of expression and action.

Therefore, collective behaviors instigated by social movements constitute only so many *episodes* in the development of the movement. As episodes they are important parts of its activity pattern. However, we miss completely the character and the directionality of collective behavior instigated by a movement if we become transfixed in fascination with descriptions of the behaviors at a point in time: increased suggestibility of participants, lessening of critical judgment, and emotional expressions.

A social movement is a formative affair, proceeding in phases. It does not come into existence full-blown with a coordinated expression of its goals for change, much less with coordinated formulation of its methods and tactics. There are often factions and crises of leadership. The problem of *factionalism,* which is typical in early phases of widespread movements, will concern us later.

HUMAN-RIGHTS PROTEST OF BLACK PEOPLE AS A SOCIAL MOVEMENT

We shall first give a digest of the protest movement; then we will elaborate on it. The nature of the protest movement with the changes in attitude and mood of the black community is not something to be taken lightly. Nor has the change dawned suddenly without prior signals. It has been simmering for decades, especially since the decision of the Supreme Court on May 17, 1954, that struck down the "equal but separate" doctrine in education.

Overt manifestations of Negro discontent, unrest, and exasperation have multiplied in recent years. For example, in 1967 alone, the open outbursts of violent actions reached proportions that shook the foundations of the social order in their impact, as represented in Fig. 23.6.

The transformation in the black commu-nity, exemplified by both violent and non-violent collective action that is organized in some instances but is sporadic and unorganized in others, is not reflected in just this or that episode of action by this or that particular organization included in the movement. The movement is an ongoing and growing pattern of attempts on the part of its active leaders and rank and file to bring about change. Only when the events are conceived as an ongoing, growing social movement can one develop an insight into the nature of this transformation in mood and attitude of the black population in the United States, and the changes advocated. Only through insight into the nature of social movements can one appreciate the potential of this social movement as a creative force, rather than merely a disruptive force.

Nothing is gained by either denouncing such collective actions as pathological or as the doings of a few agitators and troublemakers, or as impulsive outbursts during the summer's heat. Such denunciations lead to punitive, repressive measures by police or federal forces. Such repressive measures will be conducive to greater outbursts in the long run. Outbursts of collective action, especially in the form of riots, are damned in an unqualified way by opponents of the movement, who advocate more stringent repressive measures. However, the afflicted people, and especially those who sympathize with or participate in such actions consider the label of "riot" a fabrication of the mass media of communication and prefer to characterize the collective actions as "frustration reactions."

Only by going to the root causes of such collective actions and considering them as episodes in a social movement that has been simmering for decades can one achieve a proper diagnosis and, eventually, modes of coming to terms with the movement. As many people have pointed out recently, poverty, lack of equal opportunities in work and education, the ghetto existence, miserable housing and living conditions, and the existence of both open and more subtle forms of prejudice and acts of discrimination in all spheres of social life are certainly among these causes.

But here, too, it is no longer sufficient for

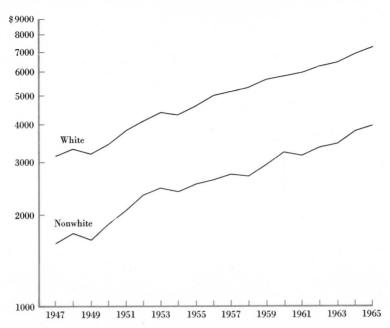

Fig. 23.7. One sign of the motivational base for growing black unrest: The income gap between whites and non-whites does not close despite rising income (*above*). (U.S. Bureau of the Census, *Current Population Reports*, Dec. 28, 1967, Series P-60, No. 53, p. 4) **23.7b.** (*opposite page top*) (Chas. Moore from Black Star) **23.7c.** (*opposite page bottom*) (United Press International Photo.)

a human being in this country—black, white, or yellow—just to have a steady job, a roof over his head and some food to eat. It is not enough to have the bare essentials of education. For human beings—be they white, yellow, or black—do not judge what they are and what they have and what they do in absolute terms, but in relation to others—especially if the others have assumed an air of superiority, with special privileges and claims of dominance, and practiced their dominance by brute force and laws they imposed for decades.

The relative nature of the experience of satisfactions and dissatisfactions can be illustrated easily in the area of income. It is true that income has been rising in this country, including that of the Negro population, and that some segments of the non-white population have enjoyed substantial increases. However, the Negro unemployment rate is still much higher and, more specifically, the pitiful gap between white and non-white income has not closed. The persistence of this gap is illustrated by the distribution of average income for whites

and non-whites between 1947 and 1965, as presented in a diagram (Fig. 23.7) adapted from Herman Miller, an expert at the Census Bureau, who based his figures on the *Current Population Reports* (1967). As this diagram shows, relative to white income, the non-white community is no better off than it was twenty years ago.

Such facts as these, as well as the social-psychological consequences, must be included in any analysis of the emerging angry, defiant mood and attitude of the changing black community. The emerging mood and attitude have reached such a state of exasperation that what they want and rightly claim is no longer just getting any old job, or some education, or even a good position in life handed down by the established power structure of the status quo. Like anyone else, they want the necessities of life, the good things of life, education, and a station in life with full participation—but with control over their own destinies.

The analysis of the roots or causes of protests, demonstrations, riots, and other

violent or nonviolent modes of collective behavior requires that we evaluate the antecedent conditons and the conditions prevailing in the larger scene.

We can gain insight into the workings of many forms of collective flare-ups, including riots, if we view them as part and parcel of a social movement of long duration, rather than discrete events created by a few agitators or as results of particular failings on the part of this or that policy or city during the heat of summer. The particular events associated at the moment with such flare-ups are, in fact, only triggers to action, for which other triggers could easily be substituted. Flare-ups in American cities, for example, are not unique events of the long, hot summers of the 1960s. Way back in 1943, the Detroit race riots, in which whites perpetrated the violence, were triggered by a relatively minor incident on a bridge at Belle Island. But as the sociologists Lee and Humphrey (1943) noted in their book on the Detroit race riot, the outbursts might easily have been triggered at any of a number of places by other incidents during the thick simmering tensions of Detroit instead of on that humid Sunday evening of June 20, 1943.

When seen as parts of a social movement rising from accumulated deprivations, frustrations, and injustices, the causes of collective flare-ups of various sorts acquire quite a different significance than when regarded as so many disorders without rhyme or reason, or as the result of sheer impulsiveness, or psychopathology, or the doings only of a few agitators and trouble-makers.

During February of 1960, the four college freshmen who staged a sit-in at a lunch counter of the Woolworth store in Greensboro, North Carolina, and the tens of thousands who participated in sit-ins the following year were denounced for everything from breeding strife to inciting anarchy (Zinn, 1964). Their nonviolent collective actions, prompted by the denial of their most elementary human rights, were seen as unwarranted disorders, as the doings of outside agitators, and as the impulsiveness of headstrong youth. Yet, according to the evidence, the sit-ins started spontaneously, in the sense that they were initiated by the students themselves, and they were anything but impulsive. After a few experiences, the young people held classes in

school and disciplined themselves in ways to avoid being hurt. For example, here is a sample of the instructions actually used in such a training session: "You may choose to face physical assault without protecting yourself, making plain you do not intend to hit back. . . . To protect the skull, fold the hands over the head . . ." (pp. 19–20) and so on.

**Struggle
for Self-Determination:
Key to Evaluating
Ameliorative Measures**

Now, in the light of the differentiating criteria of a social movement (see Table 23.1) and the brief characterization given above, let us state a few implications for the black movement. Throughout, it is important to emphasize that the current mood and local events are always dependent upon the particular stage of development attained in the movement. For example, measures that might have been satisfactory to the rank and file before the movement takes shape—such as improvement of living and working conditions, exhortations appealing to people's sense of order, or even pouring money in their direction—may be altogether unsatisfactory in their eyes at a later stage, when the movement has gained a sense of confidence, self-identity, and pride in its achievements. Perhaps a few billion dollars toward insuring civil rights and equal opportunity fifty years ago might have gone a long way all by itself. Today, after so many disillusionments and broken hopes, money alone is not seen as any kind of cure-all.

A perspective on the black movement in this country shows very clearly that improvised half-measures and the usual pat formulas for dealing with great problems will not work now. In this connection it is instructive to remember that there is a tendency to see money as the solution of all social problems. This tendency was cogently noted by the Harvard historian Crane Brinton (1965) in writing on great social changes as the American tendency "to emphasize the . . . individualistic economic motive and to minimize such motives as pride, envy, the 'pooled self esteem' of nationalism (and racism) . . ." (p. 270). The ring of truth in Brinton's criticism comes through in the writings of the more militant

Negro leaders today. For example, Carmichael and Hamilton (1967) wrote:

> Our basic premise is that money and jobs are not the final answer to the black man's problems. Without in any sense denying the overwhelming reality of poverty, we must affirm that the basic goal is not "welfare colonialism" . . . but the inclusion of black people at all levels of decision-making. We do not seek to be mere recipients *from* the decision-making process but participants *in* it (p. 183).

The black American is no longer in the mood to wait for the fulfillment of broken promises of equality in employment, housing, education, recreation, and other necessities and good things of life. They have been disillusioned and disenchanted so many times after the abolition of slavery more than a century ago that they are no longer in the mood to tolerate tokenism. Having had bitter experience and humiliating disillusionment with counting on the generosity and largesse of masters and the existing power structure, people in the black social movement now want to achieve *self-determination* of their own lives, full participation in decision-making and in charting their own destiny, and not reliance on the proclaimed good will and intentions of those whose interests need not coincide with theirs (cf. King, 1963).

New Self-Identity

A core aspect of the movement is forging toward a *self-identity* or *self-image* proud of its mass origins and basis in the fields of Mississippi and Alabama as well as northern cities, proud of its African origins and culture, proud of black skin, and proud of its sympathy for other erstwhile downtrodden peoples similarly asserting their self determination. This central core (moving to forge a proud and confident self-identity dedicated to self-determination in charting the course of the well-being and future of black people) has to be kept in mind if one is to understand the social movement or the changes that it advocates.

The current mood of the black movement toward self-determination and forging a self-identity and self-respect is eminently understandable when we take even a quick glance at the historical background. For the masses emancipated from the cruel and archaic institution of slavery, the period of abortive reconstruction in the South turned into the treacherous path of "back to slavery" (DuBois, 1935). The waves of segregationist Jim Crow laws adopted in state after state reflected actual conditions of suppression and exploitation in which black people lived constantly in the shadow of violence and frequently were its witness and victim. In 1896, the United States Supreme Court's "separate but equal education" verdict in the Plessy vs. Ferguson case amounted, of course, to the legitimization of the institution of segregation which was not repealed until May 17, 1954.

Meanwhile, the Negro leaders who were supported by important white figures were those who, like Booker T. Washington, accommodated to the overwhelming power of white dominance with the hope that industrial education, business enterprise, and moral uplift could secure "the cooperation of the whites and . . . the best possible thing for the black man" (Washington, quoted by Walden, 1960, p. 105). This accommodation meant, of course, that the Negroes would be more efficient farm hands and servants. The decline of accommodating leadership, documented by Killian and Grigg (1964) in Southern communities of the 1950s, represented a reaction in the Negro community delayed half a century by the stone wall of racism. Not the least, but the most influential representatives of the power structure let it be known that, for them, a nigger was a nigger, no matter what his accomplishments.

A senator from Mississippi (J. K. Vardaman) stated the white supremacy view very concisely: "I am just as opposed to Booker T. Washington as a voter with all his Anglo-Saxon reinforcements, as I am to the coconut-headed, chocolate-colored, typical little coon, Andy Dotson, who blacks my shoes every morning. Neither is fit to perform the supreme function of citizenship" (quoted by Lomax, 1962, p. 40).

Despite the penetrating analysis made by Negro intellectuals and the determined efforts of Negro educators and white liberals toward education and more nearly equal opportunity for Negro citizens, the historical trends that lifted Negroes from *de facto* slavery were not primarily their doing. As well documented by the sociologist Franklin Frazier, it took two bloody World

Wars and their aftermaths—socioeconomic trends that brought Negroes and whites alike from countryside to swelling cities, and the struggle against Hitler's racism in which Negroes shared only to return home to the homegrown variety wherein the black man was still "last to be hired and first to be fired" (Frazier, 1957).

After World War II, neither whites nor blacks could ignore the blatant inequalities in their own country when colored people were rising all over the world to take their destinies into their own hands as independent nations. Indeed, the spokesmen of the federal government were mindful of America's image in the eyes of the world as the Supreme Court handed down its historic 1954 decision and, subsequently, as the concerted struggle for desegregation began (Killian and Grigg, 1954). Too, Negro Americans were struck by the harsh contrast between the dignity of new nations in Africa and Asia and the degradations suffered daily by Negro Americans. James Baldwin wrote sardonically: "At the rate things are going, all of Africa will be free before we can get a lousy cup of coffee" (quoted by Lomax, 1962, p. 88).

Of course, the land of opportunity had opened doors to some Negroes—educators, intellectuals, artists, performers, athletes, and businessmen. And what had the golden opportunities to success on the basis of individual achievement brought the growing middle class under the circumstances? Franklin Frazier, in his *Black Bourgeoisie* (1957), found a cloudy reflection of white middle-class life, a "world of make believe" in which the Negro middle class was without roots "in either the Negro world with which it refuses to identify, or the White world which refuses to permit the black bourgeoisie to share its life" (p. 24). Like all men thus caught betwixt and between the margins of two worlds, the Negro successful by society's standards was, in Frazier's description, full of "emotional and mental conflicts," and "rejected by the white world"—with resulting "self hatred, since it is attributed to their Negro characteristics" (pp. 25–26). As Frazier stated, the Negro middle class was fast on its way to becoming "NOBODY."

Some months before his assassination, Martin Luther King (1968) strongly endorsed

Frazier's analysis in his address to the 76th annual convention of the American Psychological Association.

F. Franklin Frazier (1957), in his profound work, *Black Bourgeoisie,* laid painfully bare the tendency of the upwardly mobile Negro to separate from his community, divorce himself from responsibility to it, while failing to gain acceptance into the white community. There has been significant improvement from the days Frazier researched, but anyone knowledgeable about Negro life knows its middle class is not yet bearing its weight. Every riot has carried strong overtones of hostility of lower class Negroes toward the affluent Negro and vice versa. No contemporary study of scientific depth has totally studied this problem (p.183).

Literary expressions of the empty self-identity awaiting the Negro who stepped upward or aside from the Negro masses are not lacking. Baldwin wrote that *Nobody Knows My Name,* and Ralph Ellison pictured the transition to the northern metropolis as becoming an *Invisible Man.* More recently, Carmichael and Hamilton (1967) started their discussion of Black Power with the imperative: "We must first redefine ourselves" (p. 34).

Certainly it is no coincidence that rank and file citizens, tired to death of ill treatment on buses on which they constituted 75 percent of the patrons, took the first steps toward action in Montgomery, or that young students were the first to grow impatient and unwilling to wait for access to segregated public facilities. Of course, they had behind them important federal support in the form of legal decisions and rulings gained by the NAACP. But the middle-class Negro leaders, for the most part, had neither the clear self-identity nor the daring to take what seemed then such bold steps.

Crisis in Leadership and the Role of Rank-and-File in Shaping Leaders

The more recent "crisis in leadership" has been analyzed by the Florida State University sociologists Killian and Grigg (1965) as well as by Louis Lomax (1962), and, among others, Stokely Carmichael and Charles Hamilton (1967). This crisis can be understood in part as a crisis in self-identity that American society created for its Negro intellectuals and middle class in making "success" contingent upon standards that divorced them from the Negro masses, on the one hand, while denying full entry into the dominant majority, on the other. The crisis of leadership refers to the difficulties and lack of agreements in formulating a bill of gripes and a platform for change with clear-cut action programs that touch the motivational base affecting the masses who constitute actual and potential adherents of the movement. Desegregation of restaurants and airline terminals, after all, did not benefit the great bulk of the people who could not afford to eat out or fly—even though it removed one more humiliating barrier for middle-class Negroes.

As we shall see, the crisis of leadership in the Negro movement, noted by various authors, is closely related to how well the bill of gripes and the positive platform fulfill the needs aroused in the rank-and-file, as they themselves see them. Thus, in recent years, there has been a trend toward rejecting the Booker T. Washington-type diagnosis and platform of "uplift" for the Negro people as they fulfill lowly (however necessary) functions, and a shift toward documenting the guilt of the white community (Walden, 1960). The resonance aroused by the shift to "whitey" as the source of ills was observed as the Black Muslims came into the public eye, with their platform of religious virtue and separatism and clear denunciation of white racism and colonialist exploitation (Malcolm X, 1964, 1965). Referring wryly to their diagnosis, James Baldwin remarked that other factions "had the faith" but the Muslims had "the facts" (Lomax, 1965, p. 191). At this date, therefore, it is not surprising that the words of Malcolm X and Stokely Carmichael, for example—proclaiming the bill of gripes with the status quo—seem to find more eager receptive ears among the afflicted masses.

From the crisis of leadership we gain valuable clues about the role of leadership in a social movement. Of course, leadership is crucial in the development of a social movement, both in polarizing its program and in coordinating action. Of course, leaders do shape the character and tactics of the movement. However, leadership of a social movement is always and inevitably shaped by the rank-and-file, who share the motivational base both within and outside the movement.

Martin Luther King, Jr. at the time a twenty-seven-year-old Baptist minister, rejected the presidency of the NAACP in Montgomery because he felt he was too new in town—just three weeks before he was chosen to head a mass meeting held to formalize the bus boycott of December 1, 1955 (Lomax, 1962, p. 93). Yet he emerged from the boycott a national and international figure. Later, in 1963, while in a Birmingham jail, he wrote with regret to white religious leaders who had tagged him as an extremist: " . . . I stand in the middle of two opposing forces in the Negro community. One is a force of complacency. . . . The other is one of bitterness and hatred and comes perilously close to advocating violence" (King, 1964, pp. 72–73). He correctly predicted that dismissal of his moderation would lead millions toward the more militant position.

As Louis Lomax, in turn, observed, "the Black Muslims have forced every Negro spokesman in America to assume a position more extreme than that he would have assumed had the Muslims not been among us"—the reason he gives is that once the Muslims stated their case "the Negro spokesman who speaks less of the truth . . . simply cannot get a hearing among his own people" (p. 191).

In brief, a social movement cannot be understood simply as the doings of a few leaders for, in fact, the leaders are continually shaped by the rank-and-file. Of course, the leaders contribute to the rise of a social movement. But the conditions that gave rise to the movement have a great deal to do with the shaping of its leaders. This point has important implications for the constraints placed upon leaders in their negotiations with the opposition. There are limits to which the leaders can commit their own rank-and-file without being deposed from their leadership position.

Sharpening the Self-Identity

As the movement has proceeded more recently, the resolution of the dilemma in self identity has consisted of two aspects, both visibly underway for a number of years:

1. The dissociation from those white standards, institutions, and values that define a black man as inferior and, in some cases, the repudiation of whites themselves as the symbols and cause of the Negro's plight. This disenchantment with or even rejection of white values and institutions that affect the black man was manifested in various ways and in varying degrees throughout the movement. To the Black Muslims, the mental divorce was to be complete, so that Malcolm Little became Malcolm X, symbolizing rejection of the slave name tagged on by white masters. The extreme forms of rejecting everything American and directing the search for self-identity exclusively to non-white symbols, as represented by the Black Muslims, were seen by the Oberlin sociologist Yinger (1965) as "illustrative of the consequences of discrimination," and he advises that "our objective should be, not to suppress such movements, but to change the conditions that produce them" (p. 91).

2. The other aspect of the resolution of the self-identity crisis involved turning toward other nonwhite people and looking elsewhere for values to replace those they rejected in White America. Of course, this aspect involved closing ranks among themselves, but it also involved appreciation of national movements of colored people around the world. The Black Muslims repeatedly emphasized the common lot with other Muslims and other non-whites who, of course, constitute the majority of the world's population (Lincoln, 1961). More recently, Carmichael and Hamilton (1967) stressed that the black American's efforts toward equality must not "be viewed in isolation from similar demands heard around the world" (p. 179). The analysis by the Florida sociologists Killian and Grigg (1964) refers to the appeal of the emerging African nations to the masses of black Americans.

Whatever the white man's evaluation of these events, Negroes find in them a new source of "race pride." But this is not the sort of race pride the white man has so long encouraged the Negro to develop, an illogical sort of pride which would let him still look up to the white man (p. 127).

To some white Americans, including those liberals who have participated in civil-rights organizations, the twin rejection of white values and the positive assertion of blackness is a somewhat disturbing phenomenon, particularly if one has been schooled in the dictum that the color of one's skin does not count, but rather what a person does. Now, to the surprise of a good many white liberals, many Negroes are saying that the color of one's skin *does* count and that they want respect for their identity as black men of African origin and that respect on the basis of individual merit should come, not first, but afterward.

Killian and Grigg (1964) have put the matter in perspective by indicating what integration means to the black community under the present circumstances and what changes are needed to remove the threat to the black man's self-identity:

At the present time, integration as a solution to the race problem demands that the Negro foreswear his identity as a Negro. But for a lasting solution, the meaning of "American" must lose its implicit racial modifier, "white." Even without biological amalgamation, integration requires a sincere acceptance by all Americans that it is just as good to be a black American as to be a white American . . . so that the status advantage of the white man is no longer an advantage, so that an American may acknowledge his Negro ancestry without apologizing for it (p. 108).

Today, in an American society not yet ready to encourage black identity on a genuine par with white identity as American, there is not yet consensus in the black movement on the diagnosis of ills and the steps required to bring needed changes. In fact, it is a social movement ridden with factions and competing leaderships—ranging from the older moderate organizations such as the NAACP and the Urban League through Martin Luther King's Southern Christian Leadership Conference and the Congress on Racial Equality to militant groups including SNCC (Student Nonviolent Coordinating Committee) and separatist groups such as the Black Muslims and the black power militants. In analyzing the crisis of leadership several years ago,

Lomax (1962) noted that "there is a basic disagreement between the Negro masses and some of their leaders" centering both on goals and organizational forms and tactics (p. 90). In his view, there was no doubt that "the Negro masses are angry and restless, tired of prolonged legal battles that end in paper decrees" (p. 165) and "demanding that their leaders come from behind their desks and walk and suffer with them" (p. 167).

Today, it is quite safe to say that the trend for the rank-and-file to push leadership toward action and to affirm their black identity has gained ground since Lomax wrote. The ground swell of sentiment now flows not only from the lowly but also from the most fortunate and advantaged young black people. For example, students at Harvard, Columbia, Cornell, Pennsylvania, and other universities are forming Afro-American groups—asserting their black identity in organizational form as well as symbols (Hechinger, 1967). For example, Fred Hechinger reported in *The New York Times* for October 29, 1967, that the Harvard-Radcliffe Association of African and Afro-American Students was the center for most activities for black students, who declined "token presence" in other undergraduate organizations in preference for the Association's "sense of unity and expression." As for the urban masses, it is likely that they have seen a lesson in the repeated demonstration that collective action seems to be required in order for them to be noticed. With reference to the devastating riots of the summer of 1967, Whitney Young (1968) of the Urban League felt constrained to tell a group of businessmen that for masses of black people it had become better to be "hated than ignored."

**Trend
Toward Coordination
of Movement**

Yet, there are also trends toward coordination of leadership in the black movement. Martin Luther King has spoken of the need for a "summit meeting" of black leaders (Lomax, 1962). The conference on Black Power meeting in Newark in the summer of 1967 was called in the effort to bring the leadership of various organizations to-

gether. *Newsweek* of January 22, 1968, reported that Stokely Carmichael of SNCC had called a coalition meeting in Washington bringing together "Negro leaders of all strategic shadings from the Urban League to . . . SNCC (p. 28). Such varied efforts indicate the tendency for a movement with shared objectives to attempt coordination as time moves on. In fact, it is this coordination that is referred to as Black Power. *"Before a group can enter the open society, it must first close ranks.* By this we mean that group solidarity is necessary before a group can operate effectively from a bargaining position of strength in a pluralistic society" (Carmichael and Hamilton, 1967, p. 44).

It follows that any practical measures directed toward improvement of community and state relations and the conditions of Negro citizens will have to recognize the existence of both new leadership and new alignments within the movement, even if the mood is defiant and the position extreme. In a much-publicized meeting in Detroit on January 30, 1968, concerning jobs and job training, the Reverend Albert Cleague stated on NBC news that the Negroes themselves were not properly represented, despite the presence of Negroes at the conference. And it can be predicted that future attempts to deal solely with what some black organizations call "hand-picked and captive leaders" of the white community who do not represent anyone, and failure to recognize leaders who are securing the ears of the masses, will be exercises in futility.

Of course, no one—white or black—can pretend that meetings with militant leaders asserting their identity and demands for change are as cozy and pleasant as discussions with representatives who are hand-picked for their ability to "see the white man's point of view." However, on the basis of their observations in the South, Killian and Grigg (1964) point out that "paradoxically, this interaction within a conflict relationship seems to produce positive changes in the attitudes of the individuals involved"— in this case white businessmen whom they called "moderate segregationists." Perhaps, they suggest "White Americans may have to learn respect for Negro Americans as opponents before they can accept them as friends and equals" (p. 140).

Racism and Social Distance Are White Problems

The trend toward self-determination and assertion of self-respect as a black man will be increasingly reflected in the black community in the future. However, this trend with the associated notion of black power as a means for developing rank-and-file participation as well as developing weight to secure the changes desired by the movement through political process does not mean that white Americans are to have no part in the process. On the contrary, the success of the movement toward equal opportunity depends, as it always has, on efforts that only white Americans can make toward eliminating their own institution of discrimination and prejudice with all of its cruel and degrading consequences. The existence of the institution of racism and prejudice is in no doubt, as indicated by the evidence presented in Chapter 12. Comparing the social distance scale over a period of twenty years ending after World War II, the American Negro was down right at the bottom, along with Turks and Hindus. There has, of course, been change since these data were collected, especially as many of the younger generation reject the racist doctrines of their parents. Yet, the reaction to voter registration in the South, to school desegration and genuinely open housing in the North, as well as persistent discrimination in employment, leave no doubt that the doctrine of racism and its institutions are still alive today.

As the more militant Negro leaders such as Malcolm X and Stokely Carmichael stated, racism is not a Negro problem but a problem for the white community to solve. Unless racism with its superiority doctrine and attitudes ranking people by race, religion, and national lines are eliminated, prejudice and discrimination are bound to creep into human relations in spite of all the good intentions and policy decisions to bring about friendship and live-and-let-live across race and nationality. Here is what Carmichael says in this regard.

Racism in America is a white problem, not a Negro problem. And we are trying to force white people to move into the white community to deal with that problem. We don't need them from Berkeley in SNCC. We don't need the white college students. Tell the white college students: "Don't come where the action is . . . but start where the action is going to be" (i.e., in the white community) (quoted in Bennett, 1966, p. 30).

The practical implications of this analysis are obvious—namely, that efforts in the United States toward creating opportunities in jobs, job training, education, housing, and recreation will not be sufficient to bring about working intergroup relations freed of hate and distrust with their associated episodes of violence as long as deeply ingrained racist attitudes and conscious or unconscious superiority claims by the dominant white groups still persist.

As long as superiority claims persist in conscious or unconscious forms, they are bound to poison the relations across races, nationalities, and religions. Superiority claims, conscious or unconscious, will prompt new forms of exploitation as long as the white group assigns to itself the race qualities needed for decision-making and sees in other groups—black, white, or yellow—potentialities only for physical labor and skills. On the basis of the brief analysis presented, we recommend that if we mean business we need (1) careful assessment of intergroup attitudes prevailing in the dominant groups in the white community—without noise, fanfare, or publicity, because effective practice can only follow correct diagnosis; and (2) on the basis of such realistic analysis of prevailing intergroup attitudes and claims, initiation of a concerted movement in churches, schools, business circles, and through mass media toward elimination of superiority doctrines and prejudices and the practices they produce. For psychological and social science has proven beyond the shadow of any doubt that there is no scientific or factual evidence whatsoever of any inherent superiority or inferiority of any group over any other.

THE UPHILL COURSE OF SOCIAL MOVEMENT AND ITS LEADERS

Once a social movement gains momentum, along with expressing its bill of gripes, it will not settle down in terms of expedient accommodations or compromises merely because the unrest is fraught with tension or wear and tear for all concerned. It has its stated platform and a bill of demands that are typically considered unreasonable by the establishment. Concessions from the ruling circles that might have been seized some decades earlier are spurned. These facts show better than perhaps any others the obsolescence of the orthodox theories of social systems based on the indiscriminate, uncritical use of the concept of equilibrium or balance.

When a social movement gains momentum, pressures and demands on leadership are great and exacting. Only those leaders thoroughly identified with the pulse of the movement can stand the wear and tear and sacrifice demanded. Those who cannot fade from view or lose their voice. The uphill struggle of the movement with the increasing pressure and demands placed on leadership is well-described by Lewis M. Killian of Florida State Univeristy, one of the most outstanding authorities on social movements and collective behavior, in documenting the reactions of Negro leaders to the outbreaks of violence in major United States cities in 1964–66.

Excerpt from
The Impossible Revolution?[1]
by Lewis M. Killian
University of Connecticut

The established Negro leaders, whether of the old elite or of the newest, most militant generation, had to react to the riots even though they did not desire them. It was their response to the violence of the crowd that brought illegal rioting into the mainstream of the revolution and made it part of the strategy of protest. This response was essentially one of using the riots as a weapon of protest even while deploring them. There was little else that the leaders could do if they were to preserve even a semblance of leadership.

With relationship to the people who composed the crowds, these spokesmen for the Negro's cause were what George Rudé (1964) has called "outside leaders" (p. 247). Deriving his propositions from the relationship of the *sans*

culottes to the Jacobin leaders in the French Revolution, he points out that men who provide the ideological background for the activities of the crowd are seldom drawn from the same social class as their followers. The deliberate and rather self-conscious adoption of overalls as the "uniform" of SNCC reflects the fact that even these militant protest organizations have a class barrier to overcome in order to reach the Negro people. According to Rudé's analysis, the consequence of this sort of separation in the French Revolution was:

> By his position "outside the crowd," the leader was always in danger of losing his control over a protracted period, or of seeing his ideas adapted to purposes other than those he had intended. . . .
> The leaders (and this was particularly the case in a protracted movement like the French Revolution) were at times compelled, in order to maintain their authority, to trim or adapt their policies to meet the wishes of the crowd (pp. 248–249).

Confronted with the riots of 1964 and 1965, the outside leaders of the Negro Revolution theoretically had two choices. One was to condemn the riots and the rioters in unequivocal terms as being without legal or moral justification. Yet this was no choice at all. While a Negro leader might afford to deplore lawbreaking, he could not with impunity or honesty deny the grievances of the rioters. To do so would be to reject the inhabitants of the ghettoes and to align himself with the white resistance. He would be in a position of accepting their definition of the crucial issue as law and order, not justice and equality.

The live option was to interpret the riots in terms of what were perceived as the underlying causes. But faults that could be ascribed to irresponsibility on the part of the rioters themselves were inadmissible as causes. Already the major civil rights organizations were distressed by the implications of the riots for their own position. After Watts, James Farmer commented, "Civil rights organizations have failed. No one had any roots in the ghetto" (*Newsweek,* 1965, p. 19). The ultimate causes had to be sought outside the ghetto—in American society itself. Thus the riots were interpreted as symptoms of brutality, segregated housing, segregated schools, economic exploitation of ghetto residents, tokenism in employment practices, the indifference of white politicians, and the inadequacy of the federal anti-poverty program. The line between explanation and justification was a thin one. As Rudé has suggested, ". . . leaders, far from exercising undisputed control over their followers, might be overruled by them, and in a sense, the role of leader and follower would be reversed!" (p. 249). Martin

Luther King denounced vigorously the mood reflected by "Burn, Baby, Burn," but he embraced the issues that the physical attack on the ghetto symbolized. He moved his base of operations to the city of Chicago, and he announced that his next goal was to "end the slums."

To explain the riots in terms that condemned not the rioters but the society that had created their grievances carried another implication that brought the riots even more definitely within the strategy of the revolution. The implication was that if these grievances were not corrected, and soon, there would be more riots. It is at this point that the magnitude of the Watts riot becomes significant. The amount of destruction that actually occurred and the size of the forces required to end the carnage generated a nightmare in which an entire American city would be destroyed because the fires could not be checked. Once this terrifying specter was glimpsed it could not be forgotten. Massive, violent racial conflict was no longer just a theoretical possibility among the speculations of sociologists. Part of the terror had been a reality. No longer could the urgency of the Negro's demands be discussed without conjuring up the image of another Watts. Within a few days after the rioting in Los Angeles, Charles Evers, the top NAACP leader in Mississippi, warned the citizens of Natchez that if the demonstrations he was leading did not produce results the kind of thing that had happened in Watts might occur in their city (*Los Angeles Times*, 1965, p. 3). He made it clear that he did not advocate such a tactic, but he predicted that frustrated, angry Negroes might use it. A year later Francisco Rodriguez, an NAACP lawyer and one of the forgotten heroes of the early legal battles, warned the citizens of Tampa, Florida, "We stand on the threshold of the same riots that took place in Cleveland, Atlanta and other cities" (*St. Petersburg Times*, 1966, p. 12B). His prophecy was tragically realized when Tampa erupted in violence in the late spring of 1967.

Neither the actuality of Watts nor the dire prophecies of more riots to come were sufficient to forestall the spread of ghetto violence. In the summer of 1966, there were riots in thirty-one cities. The deaths, injuries, and property damage in Newark almost equalled the record of Los Angeles. Later in July, Detroit became a new symbol of the nightmare of the cities. The forty-two deaths in that city exceeded the toll in Los Angeles. As in Watts, most of the victims—all but eight—were Negroes. Detroit achieved another distinction: not only the National Guard but also regulars from the army's strategic reserve were called in to restore order.

The position of responsible Negro leaders in the mid-sixties came to have a striking resemblance to that of moderate white southerners during the previous decade. Neither advocated extralegal violence; both found themselves using the possibility of its occurrence as part of their strategic appeal to the opposition and to the uncommitted public. King reflected the dilemma of these leaders in statements made before a national television audience in September, 1966 (CBS Reports, 1966). First, there was his own rejection of the tactics of violence: "For the Negro to turn from nonviolence would be both impractical and immoral." But then came the note of sympathy and understanding for those who in desperation turn to violence: "A riot is the language of the unheard. . . ." Next came the warning: "We don't have long. The mood of the Negro community is one of urgency. . . ." And, finally, in response to the question, "How long must we expect such outbursts to go on?," the placing of the blame: "White America will determine how long it will be!"

A dozen years before, white attorneys and journalists had pleaded with the NAACP and the United States Supreme Court to relent in their demands for immediacy so as to save the South from a race war. Now Negro leaders were pleading with white America to abandon its posture of gradualism and tokenism in order to save the nation from a race war. Both attested to their condemnation of open, violent conflict, but both disclaimed their power to prevent it. To both, the only answer in this conflict situation was for the other side to surrender.

24

Social Movements: Process, Products, Change

Major Topics of the Chapter

THE CREATIVE
AND THE BEASTLY
IN COLLECTIVE INTERACTION

It is only too easy to become fascinated with the colorful ups-and-downs of man's deeds during collective interaction episodes of a social movement. However, the social psychology of social movements cannot be advanced by succumbing either to horrified indignation or enthralled fascination with such dramatic collective episodes. The social psychologist has to guard against conscious or unconscious praise or damnation in the study of social movements. Otherwise, the social psychology of social movements cannot move beyond the dramatic descriptions and verdicts such as those presented decades ago by Gustave Le Bon (1895) who wrote about the French Revolution as a conservative and "frightened anti-intellectualist" (Brinton, 1965).

A social movement has to be traced through its natural history, for it has a temporal pattern. Thus, its background conditions, the motivations that instigated it, its growth through formative phases and its multifaceted activities become as important to its analysis as collective outbursts (cf. Heberle, 1951). This is not all. The episodes of collective action have to be viewed in the light of the subsequent impact of the movement. The subsequent impact of a social movement (such as the American Revolution) in changing power arrangements and associated attitudes, and in transforming the self-image of its heirs and of others

within its reach, is incomparably more significant than the behaviors and misbehaviors at the time. Unless we view a social movement from its inception through its impact, we shall not appreciate the verified generalization that social movements are the most effective vehicles of change in attitudes, in self-pictures, and in the designs of man.

The far-reaching changes produced by social movements and the collective episodes at the moment they take place are not self-generated. Superficially, many collective episodes, such as the Boston Tea Party, may appear sheerly wasteful and vandalistic when shorn of the pattern in which they take shape. The specific episodes and the changes they advance have their springs in serious human concerns, in the conditions that give rise to those concerns, and in human designs and efforts. Historians and political scientists have devoted volumes to these conditions, events, and their sequence —enough to fill a library. The social psychology of social movements can be extracted from such literature and formulated on that basis.

What can social psychology contribute beyond what is learned from the historian or political scientist about the background and events of social movements? Social psychology can contribute formulations concerning the properties of the interaction process and its products under given stimulus conditions and the relative contribution of internal (motivational, attitudinal) factors under these conditions (Propositions 3 and

11). These and other principles that were utilized previously will prove to be handy in conceptualizing the products and changes brought about by social movements. It is not sufficient to view interaction, especially collective interaction, as a process at a given time, considering its effects only as contemporaneous. As documented in earlier chapters (for example, those on norm formation and role and status differentiation), interaction is conducive to the rise and crystallization of new values or norms, and new status and role arrangements. These, too, are essential parts of a social movement, as we shall see.

DEFINITION OF SOCIAL MOVEMENTS

Representative definitions of social movements intersect (1) in specifying that their aim is social change(s) and (2) in emphasizing the discontent of participants with things as they are. Here are a few definitions of social movements:

The main criterion of a social movement, then, is that it aims to bring about fundamental changes in the social order, especially in the basic institutions of property and labor relationships (Heberle, 1951, p. 6).

The rise of social movements in a society is a symptom of discontent with the existing social order. . . . Genuine social movements . . . aim at changes in the social order (Heberle, 1951, p. 454).

Social movements can be viewed as collective enterprises to establish a new order of life. They have their inception in a condition of unrest, and derive their motive power on the one hand from dissatisfaction with the current form of life, and on the other hand, from wishes and hopes for a new scheme or system of living (Blumer, 1946, p. 199).

A social movement is a collectivity acting with some continuity to promote change or resist a change in the society or group of which it is a part (Turner and Killian, 1957, p. 308).

A social movement occurs when a fairly large number of people band together in order to alter or support some portion of the existing culture or social order (Cameron, 1966, p. 7).

Cantril (1941) and Toch (1965) include and discuss both unrest and change as properties of social movements.

An adequate definition of social movements should include the properties common to the above definitions. It should also be applicable to the examination of a specific movement at any phase of its formation—for example, the human-rights movement among Negroes in the United States which we used to illustrate the formative phases of any movement over time (pp. 529–540). Now we are in a position to offer such a definition.

A social movement consists of a pattern of attempts over time—prompted by a state of common unrest, discontent, or aspiration shared by a large number of individuals—to bring about change in, to establish, to maintain, or to suppress a definite scheme of human relations and values through pronouncements, literature, meetings, and direct collective action (e.g., rallies, boycotts, marches, strikes, insurrection, etc.).

It will be helpful to expand the definition's terms into a framework for the analysis of any specific social movement.

Pattern of Attempts. The pattern of attempts develops in formative phases over time, starting with sporadic interaction, at the initial stage, among people prompted by commonly felt deprivation, frustrations, or rising aspiration. We shall refer to the pattern of motivational components of a social movement as its *motivational base,* instead of trying to enumerate all of the cases of unrest and aspiration that may be found in the literature. As we shall see, the motivational base is the essential condition for the pattern of a movement to take shape over time. However, the motivational base, although *necessary,* is not the *sufficient* condition.

The sufficient condition is that interaction among those afflicted or moved by the motivational base leads to active attempts, in concert with others, to make the common discontent known. *Over time,* such attempts take on a pattern which has to be viewed longitudinally and, at any given time, cross sectionally.

If the number affected by the motivational base is large and spread in various localities over a wide area, the various local attempts and collective actions are uncoordinated initially, and may even work at cross purposes. Owing to different and even conflicting interpretations of the underlying causes of their misfortune, the various localized attempts may appear unpatterned. In spite of the common motivational base, all individuals involved in a social movement do not necessarily constitute a group as we have defined it (pp. 137–142). However, social movements do, typically, spread from a nucleus (one or several) that does constitute a group. At any given time, there may be varying numbers of sympathizers, followers, or temporary adherents.

Over time, the pattern of a movement proceeds in formative phases, regardless of whether it is ultimately successful. The rise of overall organization and leadership is an accomplishment over time, which arises from the need for coordinating local attempts and for a comprehensive formulation of the causes of discontent, and the purpose and the forms of action to achieve relief (ideology). Necessarily, therefore, the pattern of attempts has to be studied *longitudinally,* especially as it acquires leadership and organization. At any point in time during the longitudinal stages of a movement, the *cross-sectional* pattern of the movement may vary in geographical radius, in number of adherents and their concentration, their local organization and the degree of coordination among them.

Motivational Base.   The motivational base of a social movement varies in scope from highly specific gripes to all-inclusive discontent permeating every sphere of social life. By motivational base, we do not refer to any single motive common to the participants, but to the composite patterns that are conducive to their interaction. Examples of a more specific motivational base are the need for an old-age pension, or women's right to vote. Greater scope is represented by widespread dissatisfaction over working conditions (e.g., hours, seniority prerogatives, the right to strike, and collective bargaining) or civil rights in its many aspects (in public facilities, privileges of citizenship, equal opportunity in work and housing, intermarriage, etc.).

The broader the motivational base—that is, the more spheres of living that it encompasses—the more likely it is that the social movement will advocate broad changes in the social system through evolutionary or revolutionary means. Most authors differentiate between evolutionary and revolution-

ary movements. While the motivational base of a movement does not determine what means will be attempted, it is not unrelated to these means. For example, most revolutionary movements have a motivational base of broad scope affecting large numbers of people, which requires change of political power for their solution.

Participants.   The movement is carried out by those who are directly affected by conditions producing the motivational base and by others who throw their lot with them—frequently intellectuals who are not necessarily affected directly by the motivational base. Later, we shall discuss the problem of participation from the viewpoint of the leadership, rank-and-file, and opponents.

Protest, Assertion, and Action.   The broader the scope of the motivational base and its geographic radius, the greater is the need for the rise and crystallization of overall leadership(s) and organization(s). Such coordination is needed for the following tasks:

1. To give precise expression in the form of a bill of gripes (*protest or repudiation of the state of things*) concerning the motivational base for the rank-and-file to use as a springboard and as guidelines to action.
2. To formulate the rationale, direction, and specifics of the changes to be brought about (*positive, assertive aspect*).
3. To chart the tactics, strategies, and other instrumentalities, such as appeals to the public, slogans, agitation, and episodes of direct collective encounters with the opposition (e.g., strikes, rallies, collective resistance, boycotts, demonstrations, marches, or insurrection). This is, of course, the collective *action* aspect.

The analysis of prevailing conditions, the expresson of gripes, the formulation of a rationale and charting the course of action all constitute parts of the ideology or platform of the movement. These provide the *sufficient* step linking the motivational base to solidification of the movement toward a pattern that pulls together the erstwhile sporadic and uncoordinated trials of the early phases. The evolutionary or revolutionary character of the action episodes are not independent of the movement's analysis of the causes of the unrest and the rationale developed.

The particular instrumentalities and lines of action, including the episodes of collective behavior, are necessary parts of the movement which can be understood only by studying them as part of the growing pattern of the movement.

Planning and Action. The pattern of a movement includes both the rank-and-file and leadership(s) who provide formulations in expressing and articulating gripes and its rationale, and in charting the course of action. Thus, leadership of a movement and its acting participants are interdependent parts of the movement. Neither leaders nor rank-and-file can be understood independently of the other. Successful leaders of movements have been the first to recognize this fact—including, for example, leaders of the American Revolution and of the Indian nationalist movement seeking independence from colonial power. The same point was emphasized in noting the increasing militancy of Negro leadership, which reached the point that moderate statements were repudiated. Therefore, it is off the mark to consider a social movement either as a wholly spontaneous achievement of the masses seeking the changes they want (as enthusiasts of social movements would maintain) or as the doings of a tiny circle of "agitators" or "conspirators" (as detractors of successful movements are eager to proclaim, cf. Brinton, 1965).

Reaction and Counter-Movements. A social movement, whether it seeks reforms within the system or aspires to bring about change of the system itself, does not move in a smooth path. It always is countered by opposition from the establishment from the moment the movement starts to take shape with proclamation of its gripes and assertion of the changes proposed. The rise of a movement, therefore, is associated with delineation, sharpening or intensification of interpartisanship between its adherents (including leadership and rank-and-file) as one camp and the established social order or that sector which is affected or threatened by the advocated changes.

To the extent that interpartisanship is intensified, it takes on all of the properties of *intergroup* conflict (Chapters 11 and 12). Defensive or repressive measures are taken in the face of the rising movement and may even acquire the character of a counter-movement, with its own expression of gripes against the excesses of the movement, with entrenchment and intensification of its own camp. In brief, counter-movements develop with platforms, ideology, and action ingredients in reaction to social movements. The French movement, *l'action française,* which developed as a counter-movement to the French Revolution with the aim of restoring the monarchy, is an illustration. The Ku Klux Klan and its variants became very active after the Civil War as a counter-movement during the so-called Reconstruction days in the South and experienced a revival countering the Civil Rights movement of the 1950s. The John Birch Society of the 1950s is an organizational expression of another counter-movement.

Summary Characterization of Social Movement

Pulling together the essentials of the foregoing discussion of the terms, the following summary characterization can be offered:

A social movement is:

1. a formative pattern of attempts that develops in phases over time;
2. initiated through interaction among people prompted by a motivational base (e.g., unrest, frustration, disaffection, insecurity, rising aspirations);
3. carried out by those directly affected and by others who throw their lot with them;
4. developed through *declaration of gripes,* and formulation and proclamation of platform or ideology;
5. for the purpose of bringing about evolutionary or revolutionary changes or transformations (movements or revolutions), or of suppressing change (counter-movements);
6. effected by means of appeals to the public, slogans, symbolisms, agitation, episodes of collective action, and encounters with the opposition (e.g., strikes, rallies, collective resistance, boycotts, demonstrations, marches, riots, insurrection, etc.).

Impact of the Larger Scene

A social movement arises in a social system and within a broader political and social setting of which many of its members (including the leadership) may have only dim awareness and over which the movement has little or no control. Such circumstances include the relative prosperity or hard times, severe depression, stability or instability of the social establishment (governmental or otherwise), the degree of dislocation generated in the establishment by the movement's existence, the availability or absence of ways and means for collective action in the society (including the means of communicating and the possibilities for assembly).

Especially in modern times, the course of a social movement is invariably affected by circumstances outside of a particular country: peace or war; sympathy, encouragement, help from outside, or their lack; and the existence or nonexistence of similar movements elsewhere, with their successes or failures. The impact of such events depends in part on the perceptiveness of those within the movement to similar and antagonistic movements on the larger scene.

Without due attention to such circumstances within and outside of a particular society, the emergence and success of many national movements in Africa and Asia following World War II scarcely makes sense. For that matter, it would be difficult to understand the timing of the French Revolution, which occurred within a decade of the successful American Revolution.

Our account of the black Americans' movement toward civil and human rights (Chapter 23) is incomprehensible without proper emphasis on the United States' position in the world following the destruction of Hitler's racist regime in World War II, the impact of the war itself, and the rise of new nations in Africa and Asia. The rise of the new nations, in turn, cannot be understood without grasping the breakdown of the old colonial system. As late as the 1950s, there were powerful and influential voices saying that there was no will in the colonies to take their destinies into their own hands.

Thus the course of a social movement toward either successful accomplishment of its aims or abortive attempts to achieve them is, to an important extent, affected by circumstances outside the movement. Of course, a great deal depends on the perceptiveness of its leadership in assessing these circumstances as they relate to the movement.

MOVEMENTS THAT CULMINATED AS TURNING POINTS OF SOCIAL CHANGE

Revolutionary movements are particularly fertile grounds for study of changes in attitudes and self-identity of participants because they accentuate both the scope and the rate of changes in values and institutions, which are the hallmark of a social movement. Before proceeding to a more social-psychological account, it will be helpful to gain a concrete notion of the common features in the early phase of three successful revolutionary movements—the American, French, and Russian. The following account by the historian Crane Brinton (1965) also refers briefly to the British revolution of 1640. It will be helpful to keep this account in mind as we proceed to analysis of the phases of social movements.

The First Stages of Three Revolutions:
American, French and Russian[1]
by Crane Brinton

In a sense, you can maintain that the American Revolution really began in 1765 with the Stamp Act; or at any rate that the agitation which culminated in the repeal of that Act was a kind of rehearsal for the great movement of the seventies. The imperial government was determined to do something about the American colonists, and Townshend's mild duties on tea, glass, lead, and a few other articles imported into America were accompanied by an attempt to collect them. The result was a series of clashes with increasingly well-organized groups of Americans. Tarring and feathering of informers, stealing sequestered goods from under the noses of customs officers, jeering at British troops, led up to the more dramatic incidents enshrined in textbooks: the seizure of the *Gaspee* at Providence, the Boston Massacre of 1770, the Boston Tea

[1] From *The Anatomy of Revolution* by Crane Brinton. © 1952 by Prentice-Hall, Inc. Published by Prentice-Hall, Inc., Englewood Cliffs, N.J.

Party, the burning of the *Peggy Stewart* at Annapolis.

The closing of the port of Boston, the dispatch of Gage and his troops to Massachusetts, the Quebec Act itself, were all really measures taken by the imperial government against colonies already in revolt. You may, if you are interested in such matters, discuss at length the question as to just when the American Revolution is to be considered as formally beginning. You may go as late as the first Continental Congress in 1774, or the battles of Lexington and Concord in 1775, or even the most famous Fourth of July in 1776. But the complex group-struggles out of which revolutions actually grow only later turn into formal sources for patriotic ritual.

The French Revolution of 1789 may be said to have been incubating for several decades. Overt and definite resistance to the royal government, as in the parliaments of Charles I and in the American colonial assemblies, is not to be found in France, which was wholly without such representative bodies. The nearest thing to such a body was the *Parlement de Paris,* a kind of supreme court composed of judges who were nobles and held their positions by heredity. It was precisely this *parlement,* followed by the provincial *parlements,* that began in the 1780's an open quarrel with the Crown, which culminated in a dramatic defiance of royal power and the forced exile of the judges. Popular opinion, at least in Paris, was overwhelmingly with the judges, and privileged nobles though they were, they became heroes and martyrs for a day and their "aristocratic revolution" an important step in the revolutionary process.

Approaching bankruptcy had forced the King to call in 1787 an Assembly of Notables, a kind of hastily gathered special commission of prominent persons, from whom Louis XVI in good eighteenth-century style no doubt expected enlightenment. This he certainly obtained, for the Assembly contained many upper-class intellectuals, like Lafayette, who were convinced that France must cease to be a "despotism," must endow itself with an up-to-date constitution of the kind of the states of the American union were making fashionable. The Assembly of Notables was clear that further consultation with the nation was necessary. The Crown finally yielded, brought back into the government the Swiss commoner, Necker, who had a reputation as a financial wizard, and summoned a meeting of the Estates-General for the spring of 1789.

An Estates-General had last met in 1614, and there was some uncertainty as to how one went about electing one. The antiquarians came to the rescue, however, and three hundred representatives of the First Estate, or clergy, three hundred of the Second, or nobility, and six hundred of the Third, or commons, were chosen, practically in time for the first meeting. The double representation of the Third Estate had no precedent in 1614 or earlier. It was, in fact, a revolutionary step, an admission that in some way or another the Third Estate was more important than the others. In the old constitution, however, final decisions—they were merely advisory to the Crown—were made by the orders as units. When the Estates met in May, 1789 the great question was whether to follow the old constitution and vote by orders, or to vote in one great assembly of twelve hundred members in which the doubled Third Estate, plus the "liberals" among the other two orders, would have a clear majority. Louis and his ministers had characteristically permitted this problem to remain vague and unsettled, and only after the Third Estate had insisted on one great assembly did the Crown insist on three separate ones.

The issue out of which the French Revolution formally grew was this simple one of vote by orders or vote by individuals in one assembly. The Third Estate stood pat, and refused to transact any business until the other orders joined it in what was to be called—and the name was a sound piece of propaganda for the revolutionists—the National Assembly. There are certain dramatic moments in a two-months' struggle which was essentially parliamentary. Shut out by a royal blunder from their usual meeting place, the Third Estate on June 20, 1789, met hastily in a large indoor tennis court, and swore not to disperse until they had endowed France with a constitution.

Thanks partly to David's famous painting, which is more symbolic than realistic, this episode is now second only to the taking of the Bastille in the patriotic ritual of the French Republic. At a dramatic session on June 23rd Mirabeau is said to have made his famous reply to a request from the King's Grand Master of Ceremonies that they in turn withdraw: "We are assembled here by the will of the nation, and we will not leave except by force." Shortly afterward the King yielded, though probably not to Mirabeau's rhetoric. By the beginning of July the National Assembly had been duly constituted. The first steps in the French Revolution had been taken.

Those who insist that you must have violence before you can label revolution as begun will date the great French Revolution from July 14, 1789, when a Paris mob, aided by soldiers who had gone over to the popular side, took the gloomy fortress-prison of the Bastille on the eastern edge of the city. Bastille Day is the French republican Fourth of July, a great holy day in one of the best organized of our contemporary nationalist religions. As such it has been surrounded by legends, endowed with a martyrology, safely withdrawn from the unedifying touch of history. To an outsider, the taking of the Bastille seems an involved and confusing process, at least as much the result of the weakness of the royal governor, De Launay, as of the strength of the besiegers. What is important for us is that Paris was in the hands of a mob for three days, and that this mob was clearly shouting against the Court, and shouting for the National Assembly. After the rioting had died down, the National Assembly—or rather, the revolutionary majority in the Assembly—could proceed in the useful assurance that the people were on its side, could feel that it had *carte blanche* to neglect royal protests as it went about its task of remaking France.

The revolution in Russia got under way with great speed. . . . there were plenty of precedents for a Russian uprising, and several generations of Russians had been discussing the inevitable coming of the storm. The first steps which led up to the February Revolution of 1917, however, took even advanced leaders like Kerensky somewhat by surprise. Socialist parties the world over had been used to celebrating March 8th as Women's Day. On that day—February 23rd of the old Russian calendar, whence the name, February Revolution, by which it has gone down in history—crowds of women workers from the factory districts poured into the streets of Petrograd calling for bread. Each day thereafter crowds increased. Orators of the radical groups harangued at street corners. Soldiers from the large wartime garrison mingled with the crowds, seemed indeed to sympathize with them. Even the Cossacks were not hostile to the people, or at any rate, seemed to lack stomach for fighting.

Meanwhile the authorities were consulting, and as piecemeal measures failed to work, they decided on March 11th to repress the trouble in accordance with a fine neat plan already drawn up on paper for just such emergency. But the plan didn't work. The soldiers of the garrison, anxious not to be sent to the front, began to waver. On March 12th the first of the mutinies broke out, and one after another the famous regiments of the Imperial Army poured out of the barracks, but to join, not to shoot on, the crowds. Obscure leaders, sergeants, factory foremen and the like arose and directed their little groups at strategic points. Out of all the confusion and madness which makes the detailed record of events in this week the despair of the historian, one clear fact came out. There was no imperial government left in the capital, no formal government at all. Gradually there emerged the nucleus of the Petrograd Soviet government to come, organized through trade-unions, Socialist groups, and other working-class sources. The Czar and his advisers, too bewildered and incompetent to control the movement, did prevent the legal duma from taking control. Instead, moderates of all sorts got together to form the nucleus of the provisional government to come. In such a chaotic condition, indeed, it would seem that the action of the moderates is a uniformity of revolutions. Their sentiments and training impel them to try and put a stop to disorder, to salvage what they can of established routines.

Socialists and liberals alike were agreed that the Czar must abdicate. Nicholas himself had started from Army headquarters for his palace at Tsarskoe Selo near Petrograd, but was held up at Pskov by the increasing disorders. Here, on March 15th, he decided to abdicate in favor of his brother, the Grand Duke Michael. What centralized power there was in Russia seems to have been in the hands of a committee of the duma, and this committee waited on Michael in person. The Grand Duke refused the crown. Russia was to be a republic. Michael's own decision to refuse seems to have been dictated by personal cowardice. One of the nice problems of history-in-the-conditional centers around the question of what would have happened had this Romanov been a man of courage, decision, and ability. No one can say, but the question reminds us that even in its most sociological moments, history cannot neglect the drama of personality and chance.

With Michael's abdication on March 16, 1917, the Russian Revolution had clearly begun. There were repercussions in the provinces, and in some remote spots the fall of the Romanovs was not known for weeks. But the work of those eight days had destroyed a centralized bureaucratic government at its most vital point—its head and nerve center. Much in Russia was unchanged by the February Revolution, but politically a week had done what it had taken months to do in England, America and France. The Romanovs had gone much more rapidly than the Stuarts, the Hanoverians and the Bourbons.

PATTERN IN THE DEVELOPMENT OF A SOCIAL MOVEMENT: THE SOCIAL-PSYCHOLOGICAL FORMULATION

As the foregoing historical account illustrates, a social movement does not emerge suddenly, full-blown with all of its ingredients. Its pattern takes shape *over time* and its ingredients are crystallized in phases through interaction within the movement and through encounters with its opposition. What happens within the movement (for example, whether factional splits and crises

Fig. 24.1. Night attack on a Tory sheriff. Collective interaction in the American Revolution.

of leadership occur) is dependent to a large extent upon preceding intellectual preparation of the rank and file, upon the acumen and organizational skills of leadership, and upon the scope and intensity of the motivational base. However, what happens within the movement is also affected powerfully by its opposition, which is usually ready to divert the rank and file from their gripes and positive aims, to divide and weaken the leadership and, in some cases, to alter the motivational base through seductive appeals or merciless repression. Similarly, the reactions and positive programs of the opposition or of counter-movements are heavily colored by their appraisals of the current state of affairs within the movement—its bill of gripes, platform, and the scope of its support.

In short, the phases of development in a social movement do not necessarily follow any preordained or inevitable blueprint. Rather, the sequence of the movement, its ups and downs, fortunes and misfortunes are inescapably a product of circumstances and complex interactions within the movement, and between the movement and its specific social context.

On the other hand, in any social movement, there are relationships among its ingredients as it develops and forges into a vehicle of social change—complex as these relationships may be. In the rest of this chapter, we shall give a social-psychologi-

Fig. 24.2. Women in North Carolina supported the Continental Association, declaring a boycott on tea and English-made clothing.

cal account of social movements, considering the ingredients in more detail. We shall introduce this account by considering, briefly, some of the interdependencies among the ingredients.

The *motivational base,* while essential to instigate social action and closely related to the ideological and action phases of a movement, is not a sufficient ingredient, as emphasized earlier. Under conditions to be noted, however, the motivational base becomes an instigator for re-evaluation and recasting the self-picture of people jointly affected by it. When the motivational base instigates disaffection, disengagement, or *alienation* from the existing state of things, the stage has been set for a significant leap toward subsequent phases in the development of a movement.

Disaffection, disengagement, or alienation imply the progressive weakening of ties and norms that bind people to prevailing institutions and social arrangements. However, the psychological process implied by these terms is not quick or simple. Values, norms and ties that have regulated people's personal expectations and self-image are not shed readily, as one might discard a worn-out dirty shirt. More often, the person experiences a period of conflict, torn between what he has been—even though it now seems obsolete and dysfunctional—and new aspirations and images, which initially may not be clear or crystallized.

Fig. 24.3. Patriots pull down the statue of King George in lower Manhattan (July 9, 1776). Tearing down the principle of monarchy and the image of King George "struck at the very foundations of the British Constitution and largely destroyed its sanctity in the eyes of Americans" (Miller, 1943). This collective action, five days after July 4 and on the very evening that General Washington declared that the Declaration of Independence should serve as an incentive to every officer and soldier, symbolized the break with the past. The 4,000 pounds of lead from the statue was turned into musket balls for Washington's army. (Collection of Gilbert Darlington, New York.)

Fig. 24.4. The oath of the Tennis Court (French Revolution). (Musée National de Versailles, Paris.)

Fig. 24.5. Storming of the Bastille, hated symbol of tyranny, by French citizens.

Such states of conflict, of the absence of definite or dependable guidelines, even of *normlessness* in some cases, are not to be endured for long. As we have seen, they are conducive to *searching for new alternatives* that promise ways out of the plight. Among these alternatives, people in active search find others in the same boat and enter into interactions with them.

In the course of interactions, new norms and a new set of reciprocities can emerge that contribute to a new definition of self, hence new and changed attitudes. Whether these interactions—private or collective and public—foreshadow a social movement, however, is now a joint function of two closely related ingredients, one chiefly ideological and one chiefly organizational. As distinct from other collectivities, an emerging social movement converges on a *bill of gripes* expressing its particular diagnosis (or diagnoses) of the cause of the ills. The *platform of positive changes* to be achieved and the *action strategies* to conduct then follow from the diagnosis pro-

claimed in the bill of gripes and in concordance with the platform. These ideological developments are, of course, related to the motivational base, to intellectual preparation by leadership, and the scope of the organizational efforts (local vs. broad). Thus, at every phase in the development of a social movement, its ingredients are interdependent, and they act and react on one another.

**The Motivational Base
of a Social Movement**

Defi The phrase *motivational base* is used in a generic sense. It refers to arousal produced by conditions that affect a large number of people simultaneously or within a specifiable span of time. The motivational base could be mass deprivation of food or in living conditions. It could be the mass frustration of living under oppression or colonial rule, subjugation to injustice, discriminatory practices in work and various phases of social life, or denial of what

Fig. 24.6.   Violent episode from so many heroic and beastly ones during the French Revolution.

people or a class of people feel is their right. All such conditions produce tension or strain and give directionality to the social movement.

The unrest, discontent, the impatience, the defiance that instigate the rise of a revolutionary movement stem, as a rule, from a disjointed state of affairs in the scheme of human arrangements. In the case of the French Revolution, on one side there was the ruling class made up of decaying aristocracy. On the other side there was the rising middle class (bourgeosie) and its al-

lies at the moment of crisis, with heightened *aspirations* characteristic of a class on the rise. This disjointed state of affairs is well formulated by Mathiez, the historian of the French Revolution, in his classic work on the topic: The French Revolution "arose Why ? from the ever-increasing divorce between reality and law, between institutions and men's way of living, between the letter and the spirit" (Mathiez, 1929, p. 1). This disjointed state of affairs is exemplified also by the rise of modern nationalist movements: on the one side an obsolete colonial rule

Fig. 24.7. Background of the Russian Revolution included abortive uprisings and harsh reprisals. Here earlier revolutionaries are massacred by guards (December 14, 1869).

Fig. 24.8. Harsh counter-measures by the Czar's soldiers against striking workers in January, 1905 (above), were followed a week later by mass firing into unarmed marchers in a demonstration, killing a thousand.

that had its heyday in the past; on the other side, the subjugated people on the move, repudiating the humiliation of subjugation and forging ahead toward a new self-identity free of the shackles of the masters. The colonial power cautions its subjects for orderly conduct, for gradual financial and political gains, for rule of moderation and reason. The captive people protest with defiance. Whose rule? Whose reason? Moderation and gradualness in *whose* interest? These are the invariant themes in the works dealing with nationalist movements (e.g., Delf, 1961; Emerson, 1960; Nehru, 1958; Nkrumah, 1961).

The reality of a motivational base is evident in all of the literature on social movements and, particularly, on revolutions. It is important, especially for social psychologists, to distinguish between the motivational base of a social movement and the particular, more ephemeral factors (both situational and motivational) that may spark collective interaction. Stone (1966) has remarked that this distinction is well established in the literature. "Here everyone is agreed in making a sharp distinction between long-run, underlying causes—the preconditions, which create a potentially explosive situation and can be analyzed on a comparative basis—and immediate, incubated factors—the precipitants which trigger the outbreak and which may be nonrecurrent, personal and fortuitous" (p. 164).

The motivational base of a social movement may be highly specific and confined to one segment of the population. The Townsend movement of the 1930s with its platform of old-age pensions was composed largely of older persons, facing economic insecurity, and not knowing how they would make ends meet—despite their appeals to others suffering in the depression (Cantril, 1941).

At the other extreme, the motivational base produced by the years preceding the great revolutions affected a much larger number of people in more sweeping ways. Taine, who was an historian of the French Revolution, wrote a composite account of the motivational base in the eyes of a Frenchman, in the following words:

I am miserable because they take too much from me. They take too much from me because they do not take enough from the privileged classes. Not only do the privileged classes make me pay in their stead but they levy upon me ecclesiastical and feudal dues. When from an income of a hundred francs, I have given fifty-three and more to the tax collector, I still have to give fourteen to my seignor and fourteen more for my tithe and out of the eighteen or nineteen francs I have left, I have yet to satisfy the excise-officer and the salt-tax-farmer. Poor wretch that I am, alone I pay two governments—the one obsolete, local, which is today remote, useless, inconvenient, humiliating, and makes itself felt through its restraints, its injustices, its taxes; the other new, centralized, ubiquitous, which alone takes charge of every service, has enormous needs and pounces upon my weak shoulders with all its enormous weight (quoted by Gottschalk, 1929, p. 39).

Illustrations could be multiplied with even more wretched and extreme plights of men before other revolutions—for example, those in Russia and China. Of course, in the case of revolutions, the motivational base often has much to do with the way or the level at which men try to earn a living. Brinton (1965) concluded on the basis of his study of the English Revolution of the 1640s, the American Revolution of the 1770s, the French Revolution of the 1780s and 1790s, and the Russian Revolution of 1917 that it is "incontestable" that "the years preceding the outbreak of revolution witnessed unusually serious economic or at least financial difficulties of a special kind" (p. 29).

However, it is an error to equate degradation in the extreme and a social movement. An astute observer noted that "revolutions do not occur when the repressed classes are forced down to the depths of misery . . . [but] after the repressed classes . . . have been in the enjoyment of increasing prosperity" (Edwards, 1927, p. 36). Similarly, Davies (1962) proposed that revolutions "are most likely to occur when a prolonged period of objective economic and social development is followed by a short period of sharp reversal" (p. 5).

Such hypotheses about the motivational base, taking note of the fact that the most miserable people are not necessarily those most likely to start a social movement, serve to emphasize a point made earlier: A motivational base is the necessary condition for a social movement, but it is not the *sufficient* condition for the rise of a movement of consequence.

The human individual does not plunge

Fig. 24.9. Twelve years later (1917) a mass demonstration called by Bolsheviks before the Winter Palace. (Sovfoto.)

into defiance or disruption of the social order until a boiling point is reached. The human individual in any culture is so inculcated from childhood on with prescriptions—ties and roles relative to others and to the world around him, as well as a world hereafter—that he does not shed tradition, custom, and authority figures easily, no matter how miserable and degrading they may be. He is brought up to conceive and experience his very identity, his place relative to others and to institutions within a scheme of normative and organizational arrangements. Tearing off or disrupting these norm and role arrangements amounts to disruption of his personal sense of stability and orderliness. To take the fateful step of initiating or participating in a social move-

ment with the purpose of changing these arrangements or some important aspect of them, the ingrained components of his existing self-identity have to be weakened or broken down.

Alienation

Disengagement from and disaffection with the existing norm and role arrangements on the part of an increasing number of individuals is a phase in the growth of a movement that seeks important changes. This process, referred to as *alienation* by social scientists, is becoming an important problem area under the tense, unsettled, and contradictory conditions of the contemporary scene (Seeman, 1964). It has been a focus of study in its various aspects for more than a century—since Marx analyzed the plight of the working man of his day (see Marx in Coser and Rosenberg, 1964).

There have been attempts to classify different kinds of alienation. Because dissatisfaction with things as they are can occur in so many different contexts and settings, it will be a thankless task to try to develop a taxonomy of types of alienation. Perhaps, therefore, the more parsimonious procedure is to analyze the particular context and settings in which people are alienated and use labels appropriate to the context, such as dissatisfaction, disaffection, disengagement, weaning of allegiance, repudiation, and so on, as the case may be.

Relative Deprivation

In analyzing the motivational base and cases of alienation, the concept of relative deprivation is helpful (Merton, 1957, pp. 227–250; Stouffer *et al.*, 1949, pp. 125 ff., 153 ff., 564). This concept expresses in a nutshell the social-psychological principle, noted in various contexts throughout this book, that human evaluation of one's well-being and one's success or failure is not made in absolute terms, but relative to the possessions, privileges, and positions of others. Especially once individuals are alienated from things as they are, the standing of their reference group relative to others may be the crucial anchor in their comparisons (Chapter 18).

Apologists of the status quo in a society are puzzled and even irritated by expressions of dissatisfaction, alienation, and uprisings of people who have something to eat, who are not physically in dire need, who have jobs, and would seem to have a secure place under the sun. The Americans living in the thirteen British colonies were not the most deprived or frustrated people on earth in absolute terms. However, their basis for comparison of their own fortunes was not absolute, but relative to those of Englishmen, for whom taxation without representation was not a practice to be tolerated. In the words of George Mason of Virginia: "We claim nothing but the liberty and privileges of Englishmen, in the same degree, as if we still continued among our brethren in Great Britain" (quoted by the historian Miller, 1943, p. 168).

The concept is equally applicable to analysis of the alienation of many American Negroes, translated into vigorous protest and action after World War II. This analysis was well expressed by Pettigrew (1964).

. . . conventional wisdom dictates that Negro Americans should be more content today than at any previous point in America's history. After all, have Negro gains not been faster in recent decades than any period since Emancipation? Why, then, are many Negroes so unusually restive, so openly angry, so impatient for further gains? Relative, not absolute, deprivation once again provides a social-psychological explanation. The great majority of Negroes in past years dared not cherish high aspirations. While never satisfied with their lot, . . . they had to be content with what crumbs they did receive. But Negro Americans in recent years hunger for much more than crumbs . . . they have tasted significant progress and can fully appreciate what further progress could mean. Indeed, Negro aspirations have risen far more swiftly than Negro advances. Thus, while better off in absolute terms than ever before, Negroes today are relatively more deprived than they were before the last twenty-five years of racial progress (p. 179).

The concept of relative deprivation acquires fuller significance when considered in the light of reference group phenomena *anchors* (Chapters 18 and 19). Both the "haves" and the "have nots" have their own Joneses by which they gauge their fortunes and misfortunes.

Normlessness and Conflict of Norms

Associated with the disaffection, dissatisfaction, disengagement, and other forms of alienation of individuals from the constrictive and frustrating state of affairs in the status quo, there occurs a progressive weakening of existing norms that previously insured the run of social life along established channels. The greater the tensions and strains from the motivational base that affect the individuals (from famine, unemployment, unequal treatment, and denial of self-determination over one's own affairs by a dominant party), the greater are their puzzlement, doubts, disillusionment, and breakdown of faith in existing rules and norms, both formal and informal. This pro-

558   Social Psychology

gressive weakening may reach the point of normlessness, with resulting collapse of the normative system.

As noted in several contexts, doubting, much less shedding the values or norms which have been ingrained as personal beliefs in the self system, is psychologically disturbing—even in the face of rising aspirations to get loose from one's misery and frustrations. The conflict between ingrained values and identifications pulling in one direction and aspirations to be rid of their restraints arouses severe ego-tensions (Chapter 17). This psychological state of normlessness or conflict of norms is conducive to *heightened suggestibility*.

Individuals caught in value conflict or the ambiguity of normlessness become more susceptible to solutions proposed by others, especially alternatives coming from people in the same boat as themselves or from a leadership that they believe is on the same side. The tendency toward psychological patterning becomes operative in accentuated degree (Proposition 6).

The heightened suggestibility is further increased by increased fluidity or lack of structure in the surroundings—for example, during wartime, crisis, or economic depression when the times are "out of joint" (Proposition 10). Thus there are psychological bases for the frequent observation that persons swept up in a social movement are highly "suggestible."

SEARCH
FOR NEW ALTERNATIVES

Instigated by the motivational base, alienated from the prevailing state of things and normative anchorages, torn between dysfunctional norms and aspirations for a better life, individuals are thrown into a state of restlessness and personal crisis. They are left with the tensions of their misery, deprivation, or frustration without firm moorings or anchorages. Their whole sense of the stability of the self-image is disturbed or shattered, along with certainty and structure of the social world in which they live. The state of normlessness, the state of being torn by value or norm conflict is painful and not to be endured for long.

The psychological state thus engendered

sets individuals in motion to search for ways to re-establish a social world for themselves that is stable, predictable, less prone to traumatic and unexpected turmoils than the world of crisis they are in. Of course, what has been stated here is often treated in the literature in terms of the disruption of equilibrium and restoration of equilibrium, utilizing analogies to the return to a steady state after disruption of homeostasis or return of water to its level after a flood. Therefore, a word of comment on such models is in order.

Note on Equilibrium Models. In the case of human events such as disruptions created by social movements, the general equilibrium model has a grain of truth. But, in considering the disruption of stability and moves toward stability in human interactions during crisis, social movements, or revolution, the analogies leave out what perhaps are the most significant aspects psychologically. There are particular characteristics in the processes of stability, disruption of stability and re-establishment of a new stability in the course of human movements that make it mandatory to conceptualize them on the level of human events.

People who are restless, alienated, and searching do not seek relief and security at any price. The disrupted ties and values are not restored to their original state, as is the case with the homeostatic process or water levels. Stability has to be re-established at a new level of the rising aspirations that contributed to the upset in the first place. There is, in brief, a problem crying for resolution. The alternatives of successful social movements emerge eventually as a body of measures that aim to re-establish stability through removing the roots of the problem, or transforming social conditions which it diagnoses as the "causes." In other words, stability can be re-established only by changing or destroying what originally produced the initial instability. Whether movement or counter-movement, the emerging "solution" is not merely return to stability but, in some degree, re-establishment of stability on new terms at a level defined by the adherents' claims and aspirations.

Meanwhile, the conflict, normlessness, and resulting sense of lost identity leave the person up in the air—without anchorages or caught betwixt and between. As discussed in Chapter 17, the individual cannot remain up in the air in confusion indefinitely. He actively seeks guideposts and paths that appear to lead to clear and friendly grounds.

Search and the Motivational Base. In proportion to the intensity and scope of the motivational base, the person's capacity to endure this state of being up in the air is reduced. Seeing others in the same boat and interacting with them (at times intensely with all of the differential effects on his experience and behavior that are produced by interaction focused on a significant common problem), he is likely to act directly in concert with them to protest his plight, which is quickly seen as a common predicament. For example, if the motivational base is hunger among people formerly above the starvation level, their interaction quickly turns to protest and direct collective action to do something about their gripes. Thus, in the early phases of a movement broadly based on deprivation, collective action in the form of protests or looting arises sporadically, not in just one locality but across the board throughout the whole territory as persons gripped with hunger or fear turn toward those nearest them who also suffer.

Many examples occurred during the Great Depression of the 1930s in the United States. The following are typical of news stories from *The New York Times* appearing during the early years of the crisis (Shannon, 1960):

OKLAHOMA CITY, *Jan. 20* (AP).—A crowd of men and women, shouting that they were hungry and jobless, raided a grocery store near the City Hall today. Twenty-six of the men were arrested. Scores loitered near the city jail following the arrests, but kept well out of range of fire hose made ready for use in case of another disturbance.

The police tonight broke up a second meeting of about one hundred unemployed men and arrested Francis Owens, alleged head of the "Oklahoma City Unemployed Council," who was accused of instigating the raid.

Before the grocery was entered, a delegation of unemployed, led by Owens, had demanded of City Manager E. M. Fry that the authorities furnish immediate relief. Owens rejected a request by Mr. Fry for the names and addresses of the "Unemployed Council," said to number 2,500 men and women, both white and Negroes.

. . .

"It is too late to bargain with us," the leaders shouted, as they stripped the shelves.

MINNEAPOLIS, *Feb. 25* (AP).—Several hundred men and women in an unemployed demonstration late today stormed a grocery and meat market in the Gateway district, smashed plate glass windows and helped themselves to bacon and ham, fruit and canned goods.

One of the store owners suffered a broken arm when he was attacked as he drew a revolver and attempted to keep out the first to enter.

One hundred policemen were sent to the district and seven persons were arrested as the leaders.

However, not all motivational bases of social movements are so immediate, irresistible, and pressing as physical deprivation. Nor are the appropriate alternatives for action always so immediately clear-cut. Thus the search for solutions depends on the available avenues, including the opportunity to interact collectively, as well as on the variety of values, ideas, or ideologies current at the time. For example, the historic bus boycott in Montgomery, Alabama in 1955 would have been unthinkable only a few decades earlier, in part because it would have met immediate repression. Proceeding on the forward surge of dissatisfaction and rising expectations of Negro citizens, through the vehicle of organized groups (churches and civil-rights organizations), the Montgomery bus boycott became feasible because the Negro citizens, who composed 75 percent of bus passengers, could see a rent in the status quo *outside* of Montgomery. At the national level, the moral support and sympathy of powerful segments of the population restrained the hand of violent reaction.

Convergence on Bill of Gripes and Platform of Changes: The Ideological Base

A broad motivational base engulfing a large number of individuals—arousing unrest, alienation, and weakening of norms— is necessary but not sufficient for the patterning of a social movement, as we have seen. The interaction of individuals sharing the common motivational base within the bounds of face-to-face relations results in local formations (secret or public) in different localities, with local expressions of collective protest or outbursts.

Such local formations and events are signals of the shape of things to come, unless the arousal is simply a temporary phenomenon or repression is total. For example, one of the important beginnings in the rise of the American labor movement was the growth of the Order of the Knights of Labor, which initially consisted of "local assemblies," each meeting held *in secret* in Philadelphia of the 1870s and in small numbers, out of fear of being "victimized." "Eventually a 'general assembly' came into existence, which elected officers and a general executive board to supervise the Order" (Pelling, 1960, p. 64). A similar sequence was true of movements of even larger scope, culminating eventually in revolutions or the founding of a new nation. In all of them, before the movement was crystallized, there were sporadic outbursts and local formations.

The pattern of a social movement consists of much more than a series of sporadic and spontaneous flare-ups in different localities, uncoordinated to one another (Heberle, 1951, pp. 7, 411). There has to be a convergence on a bill of gripes and a platform of changes advocated, namely:

1. A bill of gripes about the state of things as they are, sooner or later to be crystallized in short-cut verdicts or slogans (in the American Revolution: "No Taxation Without Representation" and "Resistance to Tyranny is Obedience to God"). Such verdicts or slogans capture in short-cut dictums the analysis of the cause(s) of the ills.

2. The formulation of the premises and rationale of the movement with a platform of changes advocated, and an action strategy to be followed in bringing about the changes. Various aspects of this positive side are also formulated as dictums and slogans (for example, "United We Stand, Divided We Fall," "All Power to the Soviets," and "Liberty, Equality, and Fraternity").

Together, these two convergences constitute the ideological base of the movement. The pattern of a social movement then takes shape in several phases through the convergence, *in time,* of the *motivational base* and the *ideological base.* By and large, the formulators of the ideological base are those alienated intellectuals (or those alienated persons who are *more* inclined toward the analysis of ideas) who throw their lot with those who share the motivational base more directly.

The existence of the premises for a social movement (self-determination of people, consent of the governed, the right to equality, or economic sufficiency) is not sufficient for the motivational and ideological bases of a movement to converge. The basic premises may have been within the covers of books neatly catalogued in libraries for years. Ideas have to be brought to bear on ongoing concerns of people in concrete terms of the particular time and place.

Thus, those who give all credit (or blame) to the ideology of a movement are just as wrong as those who see the motivational base as the single "cause." The premises have to be translated into forms that have relevance to ongoing actualities in the form of short-cut pronouncements and dictums that are acceptable crystallizations of the protest and the changes needed. Only then can the ideological base serve to crystallize common attitudes, a delineation of "we" from "they," and action strategies that grip participants as necessities—things that *have* to be done. This is the intellectual task, but an intellectual task that is performed only by persons who have completely identified themselves with the movement, staking everything they have with it. The greater the divergence of the advocated changes from the prevailing state of things, the greater are the demands for changes in the self-identity of individual participants.

The growth of the emerging movement is associated with the differentiation of statuses, roles and tasks within it—that is, with organizational solidification across the board rather than merely locally. The resulting hierarchy among the participants that belong is the organizational structure of the movement, so cogently emphasized by Heberle (1951).

Exacting demands for performance, for personal sacrifice, and for disciplined participation in various activities develop proportional to the risks that are involved for the fate of the movement and the membership. Such demands may be so exacting that, not infrequently, the weak-in-heart drop out of the movement. Again, proportional to the risks involved, the margin of tolerance for *deviation* within the movement becomes narrowed. In other words, the latitude of acceptable behavior for members in so many respects (including ideas) narrows in proportion to the risks that membership entails. This may be at the basis of the "intolerance" noted by so many observers within movements in dealings with wavering and wayward members. Typically, such "intolerance" is found in movements struggling at great odds against the existing system.

Multifaceted Activities, Including Collective Action, Are Parts of the Pattern

As the movement gains momentum and acquires a differentiated structure (organization), activities become multifaceted and deliberate, and sporadic flare-ups are less frequent—giving their place to planned or staged actions. Even though direct collective action may be the essential strategy that a movement is priming itself for (toward bringing about its avowed changes), a movement does not engage in collective encounters day in and day out. This is true whether the collective action is nonviolent and legal, massive demonstrations designed to put pressure on authorities or to influence the ballot, or consists of riots and other violent means outside legal bounds.

A great deal of a movement's activities at this phase may consist of office work (membership rolls, preparing pamphlets or papers), study circles, discussion groups, training, recruiting, and so on. The tactics followed in open collective action episodes, their violent or nonviolent character, their defiant or moderate character, are parts of the pattern and make sense only with reference to it. At this stage, the frequency, timing, and character of collective actions are typically planned deliberately. This planning and the execution of collective action may not be an easy undertaking.

Of course, at any phase, there are instances of collective outbursts that are not planned, but are precipitated by relatively minor incidents that serve as triggers. At times, such incidents are directly provoked by the other camp or counter-movements. At other times, it becomes difficult to identify who started what. Threatened by interpartisan antagonism—each camp committed in dead earnest to the glorification of its stand—neither side can be kept under control.

Within the movement, the actions taken in collective encounters are, in turn, often the focus of controversy. The sharing of goals advocated by participants in a movement does not imply that there is uniformity on the routes to be followed in their attainment. As a rule, factions develop in every movement which, in terms of the spectrum of positions that it can tolerate, range from moderate to extremist. Most frequently, these factions involve ideological differences (again within the movement's spectrum) linked to differences in strategy and action.

Movement and Counter-Movement

Whether the changes advocated are evolutionary reform(s) in some sphere(s) of social life or more drastic revolutionary change (national independence or transfer of power from one class to another), no social movement has a smooth path. As a vehicle for change, every social movement is countered by opposition.

For example, during the Great Depression of the 1930s, labor won "a right to organize and bargain collectively through representatives of their own choosing" through passage of the National Industrial Recovery Act. But, "the passing of the Act was followed by a large increase in company unions, which were clearly established with the purpose of preventing the growth of the independent unions" (Pelling, 1960, p. 160).

The growth of interpartisanship promoted by a social movement inevitably constitutes a challenge to the establishment, whether it is a business organization, church, or government. The loyalty of partisans in the movement is, indeed, a challenge to established authority, and is recognized as such through attempts to weaken the movement, discourage loyalty to it, or through active repression. In his account of the growing power of the Indian National Congress as a movement before World War II, Nehru (1941) noted that the interpartisan conflict and the hardening of the government's position in the face of challenge was a process that had more to do with relative power than with any particular personalities involved:

This vague sense of a dual authority growing in the country was naturally most irritating to the [British] Government. The sense of conflict grew, and we could feel the hardening on the side of Government. . . . A legend grew up that the new Viceroy was a hard and stern person and not so amenable to compromise as his predecessor. Many of our politicians . . . do not realize that the broad imperial policy of the British Government does not depend on the personal views of the Viceroys. The change of Viceroys, therefore, did not and could not make any difference, but, as it happened, the policy of Government gradually changed owing to the development of the situation. [The Government] had the idea that they had added to the Congress influence and Gandhiji's prestige by dealing with him almost as an equal . . . the Government stiffened its back and tightened its hold . . . .. (p. 206).

In the case of movements advocating more drastic changes, counter-movements acquire a more repressive and merciless character. In this process, the less-committed participants of the movement drop out. Through these twin events, however, the self-identity of those who remain with the hard-core of the movement becomes highly sharpened. Probably the excesses that social movements sometimes engage in through words or through the staging of collective action episodes, as well as the severity of the reprisals engaged in as they become successful, may be accounted for at least partly in terms of the tribulations that the devoted participants have gone through as targets of counter-moves in their arduous course.

For example, by the 1770s the movement for independence in the American colonies had gained such momentum that it could not be retracted. It would subside only after positive gains. "During the winter of 1774–1775, the 'menaces of blood and slaughter'

which reverberated through the New England countryside became increasingly ominous. . . . if the British troops ventured far from Boston, they might well expect a warm reception from the Yankees" (Miller, 1943, p. 398).

It was in this setting that the outbreak of collective violence awaited a relatively minor incident, which came at Lexington and Concord in 1775. The identity of the side that fired the first shot is still not certain. In the tense atmosphere, given a few moments, either side might have fired first. So widespread was the colonists' resentment of British counter-moves that the crisis might well have occurred at another spot and on another day, wherever the aroused antagonists faced each other.

The Springs of Collective Violence and Other Differential Effects

Collective interactions, especially encounters between two camps divided already by the lines of antagonism and deadly serious opposition, often involve acts, either heroic or bestial, which the individuals (committed as they are) would not even contemplate if they were not parts of an interaction episode within the movement. Even though there are brave men and cruel men, such out-of-the-ordinary episodes frequently involve risks and deeds that no one would choose to engage in if he were to calculate the pros and cons in isolation. Because the participants are already identified as members in a pattern with motivational directionality, the behavior of members is profoundly affected by collective interaction involving fellow members, particularly in a clash with antagonists.

Such differential effects of collective interaction episodes at the peak of a social movement have been noted by many writers, especially by Le Bon in his dramatic descriptions, as we have seen. Most traditional accounts of such actions contain more verdicts on the actions than explanations. Le Bon's notion of a return to barbarism during revolutions simply does not fit the facts, as we shall see. Freud (1922) contended that the behaviors in crowds, at which Le Bon had recoiled, required no special explanation at all. He had already decided that men had a storehouse of bestiality, repressed in the unconscious and only waiting for release by a situation that stripped away the thin veneer of culture. He stated this position very clearly in the following words:

From our point of view we need not attribute so much importance to the appearance of new characteristics. For us it would be enough to say that in a group the individual is brought under conditions which allow him to throw off the repressions of his unconscious instincts. The apparently new characteristics which he then displays are in fact the manifestations of his unconscious, in which all that is evil in the human mind is contained as a predisposition. We can find no difficulty in understanding the disappearance of conscience or a sense of responsibility in these circumstances (1922, pp. 9–10).

There is a serious flaw in Freud's analysis, in addition to the fact that collective interaction episodes may and do produce heroic and generous acts as well as the excited forms of violence to which he referred. These accentuated, extraordinary behaviors, whether for good or for evil, have antecedents. The individuals have already taken the fateful step of becoming part and parcel of a movement. They have commitments to the movement and the changes that it proposes. They have sworn to others that they will march together to the bitter end. They would not be human beings if they did not become more suggestible, more excited, more daring, more destructive or sacrificial, as the case may be, under these circumstances than when they were in the run-of-the-mill routine of their daily lives.

If, as we have seen, interaction episodes in the peaceful atmosphere of a psychological laboratory can produce differential effects on behavior (Chapter 6), it is not at all necessary to seek for entirely different explanations of collective interaction, especially when the individuals face crises and a highly fluid situation. It is in such circumstances that new properties of behavior emerge. Thus, the ensuing behavior is *emergent,* not a *regression* phenomenon.

The accentuated differential effects on behavior during collective interaction acquire proper significance when evaluated relative to their antecedents and in relation to their consequences. The changes ad-

vanced by the vandalism of the Boston Tea Party or the rowdy storming of the Bastille were turning points in man's conception of himself throughout the world since then, providing peoples with formulas and values in their struggles to achieve free self-determination and human dignity without masters over their heads.

PARTICIPANTS IN COLLECTIVE ACTIONS OF A SOCIAL MOVEMENT

It is not always easy to choose neutral terms in describing collective behavior: What the public and the establishment call a *riot* is a *frustration reaction* to sympathizers. In this instance, it is easy to see that one term refers to the immediate short-term disruption and damage while the other refers to long-term background of the event. However, the extreme forms of collective action—such as protests, riots, and revolutions—are not matters that can be viewed with detachment. They are praised or damned, glorified or debunked, not only by actual partisans of one or another side in the conflict, but also by the general public and by writers on the topic.

Writers sympathetic to a movement that carries out extreme forms of collective action tend to view them as spontaneous, popular outbreaks of downtrodden, oppressed, or victimized people. Writers viewing the same events from the side of the established order regard them as outcomes of planned conspiracy on the part of a small, even tiny minority of unbalanced agitators and neurotic fringe. The historian Brinton summed up these different views as they apply to writings on revolutions:

To sum the matter up in a metaphor: the school of circumstances regards revolutions as a wild and natural growth, its seeds sown among tyranny and corruption, its development wholly determined by forces outside itself or at any rate outside human planning; the school of plot regards revolutions as a forced and artificial growth, its seeds carefully planted in soil worked over and fertilized by the gardener-revolutionists, mysteriously brought to maturity by these same gardeners against the forces of nature. Actually, we must reject both extremes, for they are nonsense, and hold that revolutions do grow from seeds sown by men who want change, and that these men do a lot of skillful gardening; but that the gardeners are not working against nature, but rather in soil and in a climate propitious to their work; and that the final fruits represent a collaboration between men and nature (Brinton, 1965, pp. 85–86).

The theoretical issues raised by the polar perspectives of the "spontaneity" vs. "conspiracy" doctrines are important in social psychology. They amount to raising the question of whether people who engage in collective action are merely responding to their intense motives, on the one hand, or are merely (innocently, but by the same token rather stupidly) dupes of unscrupulous and even unbalanced manipulators. For this reason, the serious study of the participants, their composition, and <u>their actions prior to great collective outbreaks is important</u> for social psychology.

More sober study of *who took part* in the great collective outbreaks during the French Revolution and subsequent uprisings in Paris gave an altogether different picture of the participants than that given in the descriptions by authors such as Le Bon, whose descriptions were drama-filled verdicts from the viewpoint of the horrified elite. What is described as a mob or a crowd during such historical events is not a faceless natural force like a tornado or hurricane. It is composed of human individuals in search of more viable alternatives than their present predicament, not merely at the moment of collective action. They have been raising problems in their minds and have already been exchanging notes with one another, frequently with active efforts to do something about their plight in less dramatic forms, organizing themselves to this end.

This conclusion is based on an illuminating survey by Tilly (1964) of recent research by modern historians of the French Revolution who utilized modern techniques of social analysis. On the basis of this survey, Tilly concludes that "neither the theory nor the findings of any of the authors give much reinforcement to the *elitist* emphasis on the release of inherently violent tendencies of the masses through the disintegration of the controlling elite" (p. 120).

The conclusions in Tilly's survey are based on elaborate historical research unearthing the motivational basis of unrest, the background of participants, the immediate precipitators of outbursts and their locations, and the participants in the collective actions of the French Revolution and subsequent revolutionary events in Paris. They necessitate revision of romantic notions about collective action still framed in the image of Le Bon.

In order to appreciate the contrast between the established facts and Le Bon's fancy, the following passage by Le Bon can serve to recall his views of the French Revolution:

Conclusion

The facts of the Revolution teach us . . . that <u>a people freed from social constraints, the foundations of civilization and abandoned to its instinctive impulses, speedily relapses into its ancestral savagery</u> (1913, p. 329).

Here we can give only a few representative generalizations from the facts collected by historians of the French Revolution who have used modern tools of social analysis and demography. As presented by Tilly, these facts show that the <u>collective actions in Paris—far from being merely impulsive flare-ups—had steady directionality from a widespread motivational base and from previous political enlightenment, kindled by the inheritance of ideas from Rousseau and the *Philosophes*</u> in meetings and local assemblies.

Motivational Base. It becomes clear from the evidence that there was a widespread motivational base and sharpening political conciousness conductive to collective action in time. Analysis of prices and income in France revealed a rising trend from about 1733 to the early nineteenth century, but with significant fluctuations, "the most serious of the eighteenth century reaching exactly its maximum at the fateful time of July, 1789," <u>producing conditions</u> that "squeezed the <u>workers and small peasants unmercifully</u>" while profiting those <u>already rich in land and commerce (p. 104).</u> Thus, at the time of the outbreaks, "the popular revolt of the spectacular revolutionary days from 1789 to the Year III <u>surged from anguish about daily bread</u>" (B. Lefebvre as quoted by Tilly, p. 114). The focus of many major outbursts of collective action concerned <u>questions of subsistence, price</u>

control, rapid increases in bread prices, or decreased supply.

Description of the motivational base of great upheavals in terms of economic variables does not complete the picture from a social-psychological viewpoint, as well expressed by C. E. Labrousse:

Deeply felt—like every movement, like every acute misfortune—by a considerable number of affected persons, crisis and depression influence the judgments and attitudes of large human collectivities. But that influence works in an already-constituted psychological setting. It affects a kind of sensitivity, a mentality, an ideology. The fact of the crisis is perceived, in the last analysis, through a social psychology already in existence. . . . In the last analysis, the study of such crisis is a chapter in the study of social psychologies —one of the great tasks of tomorrow's history (Labrousse, 1956, as quoted by Tilly, 1964, p. 106).

Participants. The picture of the participants in collective interaction is scarcely that of the rabble depicted by Le Bon. Tilly concludes: "If the unemployed and the occupants of rooming houses sometimes figured in insurrections, homeless men, criminals and men without any settled occupation were rare indeed among the rebels" (p. 119). Ecological analysis of the sections of Paris that were scenes for the most militant actions revealed the following: "The revolutionary neighborhoods, in short, contained little people, many of them familiar with want, but many of them also skilled and established in their trades and businesses" (p. 112).

Specifically, in the storming of the Bastille on July 14, 1789, a date henceforth celebrated as the official landmark of the French Revolution, the crowd was scarcely composed of the "scum" and the "rabble" pictured by Le Bon. According to George Rudé's evidence: " . . . there was a tiny number of bourgeois. . . . The rest . . . are almost all small tradesmen, artisans, and wage-earners. Of these, about two-thirds are small workshop masters, craftsmen, and journeymen drawn from almost thirty petty trades; the remainder are engaged in manufacture, distribution, building, the professions, and general trades" (Rudé, 1959, as quoted by Tilly, 1964, p. 118).

Political and Organizational Preparation. From the evidence it becomes clear that the Paris outbreaks were not merely "spontaneous" nor "unconnected with their political context" (Tilly, p. 119). There has to be convergence in political awakening, self-consciousness, the formulation of a bill of gripes, and a vision of an alternative course of action for massive collective action to materialize.

"The shortage of bread mobilized a population already politically conscious, active and organized . . . and they were far from the most desperate or miserable segment of the population . . . they responded to the *presence* of misery more than to their own misery" (Tilly, p. 115). Thus, in this case, "the presence and pressure of desperate masses" served to arouse "the politically alert portions of the population to extreme actions" (p. 115).

The closer look by scholars points to the fact that the outbursts of great scope and intensity were the culmination of meetings, protests, and political activity already underway on a more restricted scope at a more local level.

The great outbursts grew from the more usual concourses of the population—meetings in the markets, sessions at the inn, orderly political demonstrations, and so on—which were transformed into violent affairs by extraordinary tensions, by what Rudé calls panic-fear, and by conscious promotion. The little people developed increasingly definite political ideas as the early Revolution advanced; they chose their leaders and stated their grievances in terms of those ideas. The channels through which the insurrectionary word circulated were essentially the same as those followed by the routine forms of revolutionary indoctrination (pp. 119–120).

From the vast amount of material evaluated in the works he reviewed, Tilly draws a general conclusion as to the nature of collective action of significant proportions:

Disorders they may have been. Aberrations they were not. The violent popular actions of the Revolution . . . expressed the heightened hopes and fears of ordinary men and women, and came into existence through approximately the same mechanisms and milieux that brought ordinary men and women into other forms of political activity (p. 120).

Actual and Potential Participants. In controversies about the nature of great social movements that attempt or achieve revolutionary changes, question is almost always raised about the proportion of the population that is actually involved as supporters of the change. Concentrating on the organized part of the movement and its leaders alone, it is often easy enough to show that they constitute only a small fraction of the population. Such concentration provides, thereby, grounds for a *conspiracy* notion. By counting instead at the time of great collective actions, the *spontaneous uprising* theory can often be supported.

An accurate assessment of the extent of popular involvement in a social movement requires a time perspective, in addition to head counts of active, organized adherents and participants in collective action at a given time. Such perspective also helps in understanding why, at any given time, the participants in collective action may include individuals who have not previously been directly active in the social movement.

Estimates of popular participation in a social movement have to include assessment of the number of people who are disenchanted, dissatisfied, and alienated as prompted by the motivational base of the movement. The scope of the motivational base, as well as the skill of the movement in recruiting and the fear of repressions from counter-movements, are pertinent to the questions of how widespread the actual or potential support for a movement is at one point in time.

In discussing recruitment and attrition in revolutionary movements, the political scientist Karl Deutsch (1964) provided a pertinent illustration:

A well known example of differential rates of recruitment is taken from the American War of Independence of 1775–1783. It has been estimated that roughly one-third of the Colonial population supported the Patriots in that conflict; another one-third sympathized with the Loyalists; and the last one-third was neutral. Although the two main factions were thus evenly matched, the Patriots produced 400,000 enlistments in the course of the conflict, while the Loyalists produced only 50,000 or one-eighth the rate of their opponents (p. 105).

While the British certainly could and did contend that the initial outbreaks signaling the Revolution were a minority affair and the doings of "agitators," the perspective of time reveals a social movement capable of winning wide support and participation. Needless to say, this question is also related to the activities of counter-movements. For long years, the history of many nationalist movements in a number of countries involved "abortive" revolutionary attempts by small numbers who were crushed by determined repression.

The Role of Leadership

An aspect in the controversy about the *conspiratorial* vs. *spontaneous* staging of collective action in social movements is the controversy over the relative roles of leadership and the rank and file. Here, too, the proponents of the Great Man Doctrine advocate that movements and turning points of history were the creations of heroes or charismatic leaders, set apart in a class of their own and distinct from the usual run of humanity. On the other hand, those sympathetic to changes, especially of revolutionary form, view collective action as feats of popular mass movements with a coloring of spontaneity, in which leaders are merely fortunate to have been present.

As we have seen, a social movement of any proportion cannot succeed in bringing about changes, especially of a revolutionary order, without having appropriate leadership. The emergence of leadership(s) is part of the growth of a movement. Leadership cannot be imposed from outside arbitrarily, no matter how skillful and cunning the pretenders. But, in every instance, leadership of great movements and of the collective actions they staged was contingent on the presence of a widespread motivational base, which *is* the essential precondition for the rise of both the movement and its leadership.

Thus, like other participants of a movement, the leaders, too, are products of the same motivational base, widespread unrest, and disenchantment. While they may not have been directly affected by the same conditions as the rank-and-file, they too share their alienation from the established order. Thus the rise to leadership in a movement is contingent upon the potential leader throwing in his lot with those affected by the motivational base (which is the necessary but not the sufficient condition for the rise of a social movement, as stated earlier).

The rise of a social movement beyond the restricted scope of local protests and assemblies is contingent upon analysis of the ills touching its scattered beginnings, formulation of the overall changes that are needed, and the strategies to be followed—building an organization that coordinates the localities affected and providing short-cut slogans as guides for action.

Fulfillment of these leadership functions in a social movement requires *intellectual preparation* which may, indeed, be lacking in sufficient degree among those directly affected by the motivational base. Clearly, a potential leader must be out-of-the-ordinary in those attainments and skills required for mobilizing and coordinating the movement. However, sheer intellectual preparation and organization skills are not sufficient for attainment of leadership in a social movement. Such leadership is more than technical performance and more than intellectual acumen. It is essential that the potential leader be alienated by the existing scheme of things and, more important, that he be willing to break with it and throw his lot with those directly affected, with all of their fortunes and misfortunes.

Therefore, leaders of great movements have come from the widest variety of backgrounds—rich and poor, previously well known and unknown, well-educated and (in formal terms) poorly educated, successful and apparent "failures," and possessed of a wide variety of individual personalities and skills (Brinton, 1965, pp. 95–120). Such a diversity of individuals is possible only because leaders are as much creations of the movement, its motivational base, and its temper at a particular time, as they are creators of the movement. And they are both.

Leadership has to be responsive to the unrest and the momentum attained among the rank-and-file at a given time. Their decisions as to the timing of moves, and planning collective action and other activities are as much affected by the state of the movement's pattern and the responsiveness of the rank and file as by any of their own ideas or whims. Genuine and prolonged leadership of a social movement involves understanding of the sacrifice and risk by the rank-and-file who participate, not through any official directives but through growing identification with the movement and its aims. This understanding regulates the decision-making of leaders.

Leaders who brought their movements to successful culmination in social reforms or establishment of new governments have keener insight into their responsibility as part of a movement than those writers who place the leadership and the rank-and-file into independent categories. For example, in the American revolutionary movement of the 1770s, the timing of the Declaration of Independence was as much a response to the impatience of the colonists up and down the Atlantic coast as a calculated decision on the part of the leaders of the various colonies who sat in the Continental Congress: "Strictly speaking, the movement for the break with Great Britain was spreading upward from the colonies to the Continental Congress, rather than downward to the colonies from the Congress" (Beard and Beard, 1944, p. 106).

Nor did the leaders in the Continental Congress simply *sense* the impatience of their constituents: For example, Joseph Hawley sent a letter to Samuel Adams from Massachusetts, dated April 1, 1776, which included the following report: "The People are now ahead of you, and the only way to prevent discord and dissension is to strike while the iron is hot. The People's blood is too hot to admit of delays. . . . All will be confusion if independence is not declared immediately" (Miller, 1943, p. 485). Considering the slowness of communication and transportation in those days, the July Declaration can be considered fairly prompt response to such reports as this one.

A more recent example of the responsiveness of leadership to the rank-and-file was given by Nehru (1941) in describing Gandhi's role as leader of the civil disobedience movement of the 1930s and the following decade. The Indian national movement took on an organized form in the 1880s, with the founding of the Indian National Congress by upper-middle-class Indians with the aid of a British civil servant. During the next half-century, the movement "spread to the lower middle classes and became a power in the land" (p. 204). However, weight of the rural masses was not felt until the 1930s, during Gandhi's civil disobedience campaign.

The civil disobedience movement of 1930 happened to fit in, unbeknown to its own leaders at first, with the great world slump in industry and agriculture. The rural masses were powerfully affected by this slump, and they turned to the Congress and civil disobedience. . . . The British government, like most governments, I suppose, has an idea that much of the trouble in India is due to "agitators." It is a singularly inept notion. India has had a great leader during the past fifteen years who has won the affection and even adoration of her millions and has seemed to impose his will on her in many ways. . . . [however] . . . It was Gandhi's chief virtue as a leader that he could instinctively feel the pulse of the people and know when conditions were ripe for growth and action (p. 205).

Social Movements, Counter-Movements, and Social Change

Throughout this chapter, we have emphasized in several contexts that the rise of a social movement encounters opposition as soon as it is seen as a threat to the establishment or to those outside of the establishment who are dead set against the changes it proposes. In fact, there is evidence that organized repression of a social movement is more likely to occur when the movement has gone beyond its initial phases and has gathered some momentum.

The rise of an actual counter-movement is, like that of any social movement, a process occurring over time. In fact, counter-movements that arise to maintain the existing order of things or to suppress trends toward evolutionary or revolutionary changes can be analyzed as social movements, as indicated in our definition of social movements (pp. 543–545). Counter-movements do have a motivational base, in that they seek to maintain privileges and power vested in the prevailing order or some segment of it, or to seize power in the interests of some segment of the population. Their bill of gripes pertains to the threat of other movements and/or the way the threat is being handled by the powers that be. Their platforms represent strengthened or "purified" versions of the existing order, or return to the values of an earlier time. They, too, stage collective actions, and develop organization and leadership. Furthermore, they often have the added leverage of appeals to existing stereotypes, prejudices, and, in some cases, of the support of legal and political power, either overt or covert. The fascist movement in Italy, the Nazi movement in Germany, and the Falangist movement in Spain were examples of counter-movements that became successful, at least for the time, in their attempts to gain power.

In view of the common features in the analysis of the rise of social movements directed toward humanitarian principles in seeking change and of the rise of counter-movements, the reader has a perfect right to ask the social psychologist the obvious question: Is it not necessary to differentiate among social movements in terms of the values they profess and the goals they seek? The answer, in our opinion, should be "yes." This is the reason that we have repeatedly stressed that the long-term consequences of a social movement on attitudes and self-identity must be included in an adequate analysis of the movement.

The analysis of long-term consequences of a social movement involves, however, questions of social, political, and ethical evaluation that far exceed the scope of social-psychological analysis. For example, such questions involve the value placed on human life. As social psychologists who value human life and who define it as co-extensive with the human species, we believe that some tentative criteria can be proposed for assessing, in a time perspective, the consequences of collective actions in a social movement as well as the eventual success or defeat of the movement's aims. As one looks back at counter-movements such as the Nazi and Fascist movements, he cannot help but see that their appeals, and the changes advocated and accomplished were in the interests of a special segment of humanity with entrenched and vested interests, at the expense of much of the rest of humanity. Their effects on attitudes and self-identity of participants were to rationalize self-glorifying superiority to the rest of humanity.

In time perspective, the following criteria

may help us in assessing the consequences of a social movement for humanity and upon the attitudes and self-identity of those who share its impact:

How compatible are the advocated changes with widening the circle of human beings who can share the benefits of the changes? How compatible is the move-ment's positive platform with a widening sense of self-identity that includes all humanity in the benefits proposed? Conversely, how restrictive will the success of the movement be for the rest of humanity? How restrictive is its definition of humanity to which its benefits will apply?

References

Abelson, R. P., Aronson, E., McGuire, W. J., Newcomb, T. M., Rosenberg, M. J., and Tannenbaum, P. (Eds.), 1968. *Cognitive Consistency*. Chicago: Rand McNally.

Abt, L. E., 1950. In L. Bellak and L. E. Abt (Eds.), 1952. *Projective Psychology*. New York: Knopf.

Adams, H. F., 1912. Autokinetic sensations. *Psychol. Monogr., 59*, 32–44.

Adams, J. B., 1960. Effects of reference group and status in opinion change. *Journ. Quart., 37*, 408–412.

Adams, R., 1937. *Interracial Marriage in Hawaii*. New York: Macmillan.

Adams, S., 1938. Analysis of verb forms in the speech of young children and their relation to the language learning process. *J. exp. Educ., 7*, 141–144.

Adrian, E. D., 1954. Science and human nature. *Science, 120*, 679–684.

Allport, F. H., 1924. *Social Psychology*. Boston: Houghton Mifflin.

Allport, F. H., 1933. *Institutional Behavior*. Chapel Hill: Univer. of North Carolina Press.

Allport, F. H., 1934. The J-curve hypothesis of conforming behavior. *J. soc. Psychol., 5*, 141–183.

Allport, F. H., 1962. A structuronomic conception of behavior: Individual and collective: I. Structural theory and the master problem of social psychology. *J. abnorm. soc. Psychol., 64*, 3–30.

Allport, G. W., 1935. Attitudes. In C. Murchison (Ed.), *Handbook of Social Psychology*. Worcester, Mass.: Clark Univer. Press, 798–844.

Allport, G. W., 1943. The ego in contemporary psychology. *Psychol. Rev., 50*, 451–478.

Allport, G. W., 1954. Historical background of modern social psychology. In G. Lindzey (Ed.), *Handbook of Social Psychology*. Vol. I. Reading, Mass.: Addison-Wesley, 3–56.

Allport, G. W., and Kramer, B. M., 1946. Some roots of prejudice. *J. Psychol. 22*, 9–39.

Allport, G. W., and Postman, L. J., 1965. The basic psychology of rumor. In H. Proshansky and B. Seidenberg (Eds.), *Basic Studies in Social Psychology*. New York: Holt, Rinehart and Winston, 47–64.

American Council on Education, 1932. *The Story of Weights and Measures*. Washington: Achievements of Civilization, No. 3.

American Council on Education, 1933. *Telling Time Throughout the Centuries*. Washington: Achievements of Civilization, No. 5.

Anastasi, A., and Foley, J. P., Jr., 1949. *Differential Psychology*. New York. Macmillan.

Anderson, R. C., 1963. Learning in discussions: A resumé of the authoritarian-democratic studies. In W. W. Charters, Jr., and N. L. Gage (Eds.), *Readings in the Social Psychology of Education*. Boston: Allyn and Bacon, 153–162.

Aronson, E., Turner, Judith A., and Carlsmith, J. M., 1963. Communicator credibility and communicator discrepancy as determinants of opinion change. *J. abnorm. soc. Psychol., 67*, 31–37.

Asch, S. E., 1940. Studies in the principles of judgments and attitudes: II. Determination of judgments by group and ego standards. *J. soc. Psychol. SPSSI Bull., 12*, 433–465.

Asch, S. E., 1946. Forming impressions of personality. *J. abnorm. soc. Psychol., 41*, 258–290.

Asch, S. E., 1956. Studies of independence and conformity: I. A minority of one against a unanimous majority. *Psychol. Monogr. 70*, No. 9.

Associated Press, 1965. Whistling language in Turkey. *Columbus* (Ohio) *Dispatch*, June 16, 7 A.

Atkins, A. L., Deaux, Kay, and Bieri, J., 1967. Latitude of acceptance and attitude change: Empirical evidence for a reformulation. *J. Pers. soc. Psychol., 6*, 47–54.

Atkinson, J. W. (Ed.), 1958. *Motives in Fantasy, Action and Society*. Princeton, N. J.: Van Nostrand.

Ausubel, D. P., 1952. *Ego Development and the Personality Disorders*. New York: Grune & Stratton.

Ausubel, D. P., 1954. *Theory and Problems of Adolescent Development*. New York: Grune & Stratton.

Ausubel, D. P., 1962. Implications of preadolescent and early adolescent cognitive development for secondary school teaching. *High School J. 45*, 268–275.

Ausubel, D. P., 1965. Psychological acculturation of modern Maori youth. In M. Sherif and Carolyn W. Sherif (Eds.), *Problems of Youth: Transition to Adulthood in a Changing World*. Chicago: Aldine, 110–128.

Avigdor, Rozet, 1952. The development of stereotypes as a result of group interaction. Ph.D. thesis, New York University.

Baker, G. W., and Chapman, D. W., 1962. *Man and Society in Disaster*. New York: Basic Books.

Bakke, E. W., 1959. Concept of social organization. In M. Haire (Ed.), *Modern Organization Theory*. New York: Wiley.

Baldwin, J. M., 1895. *Mental Development in the Child and the Race*. New York: Macmillan.

Bales, R. F., 1950. *Interaction Process Analysis: A Method for the Study of Small Groups*. Reading, Mass.: Addison-Wesley.

Bales, R. F., 1953. The equilibrium problem in small groups. In T. Parsons, R. F. Bales and E. A. Shils, *Working Papers in the Theory of Action*. New York: Free Press.

Bales, R. F., 1965. Task roles and social roles in problem solving groups. In I. D. Steiner and M. Fishbein (Eds.), *Current Studies in Social*

Psychology. New York: Holt, Rinehart and Winston, 321–332.

Bandura, A., and Walters, R. H., 1963. *Social Learning and Imitation.* New York: Holt, Rinehart and Winston.

Barber, T. X., and Calverley, D. S., 1964a. Empirical evidence for a theory of "hypnotic" behavior: Effects of pretest instructions on response to primary suggestion. *Psychol. Rec.* **44**, 457–467.

Barber, T. X., and Calverley, D. S., 1964b. An experimental study of "hypnotic" (auditory and visual) hallucinations. *J. abnorm. soc. Psychol.* **68**, 13–20.

Barber, T. X., and Glass, L. B., 1962. Significant factors in hypnotic behavior. *J. abnorm. soc. Psychol.,* **64**, 222–228.

Barker, R. G., 1963. On the nature of the environment. *J. soc. Issues,* **19**, No. 4, 17–38.

Barker, R. G., and Wright, H. E., 1954. *Midwest and Its Children: The Psychological Ecology of an American Town.* New York: Harper & Row.

Barnard, C. I., 1948. *The Functions of the Executive.* Cambridge, Mass.: Harvard Univer. Press.

Barnett, H. G., 1953. *Innovation: The Basis of Cultural Change.* New York: McGraw-Hill.

Barringer, H. R., Blanksten, G. I., and Mack, R. W. (Eds.), 1965. *Social Change in Developing Areas.* Cambridge, Mass.: Schenkman.

Bartlett, F. C., 1932. *Remembering: A Study in Experimental and Social Psychology.* New York: Cambridge Univer. Press.

Barton, R. F., 1930. *The Half Way Sun.* New York: Brewer and Warren.

Bass, B. M., 1960. *Leadership, Psychology and Organizational Behavior.* New York: Harper & Row.

Bauer, R. A., 1964. The obstinate audience: The influence process from the point of view of social communication. *Amer. Psychologist,* **19**, 319–328.

Beals, A. R., 1962. Pervasive factionalism in a south Indian village. In M. Sherif (Ed.), *Intergroup Relations and Leadership.* New York: Wiley, 247–266.

Beals, R., 1953. Past and present trends in acculturation study. In A. L. Kroeber (Ed.), *Anthropology Today.* Chicago: Univer. of Chicago Press, 621–641.

Bean, C. H., 1932. An unusual opportunity to investigate the psychology of language. *J. genet. Psychol.,* **40**, 181–202.

Beard, C. A., and Beard, Mary R., 1930. *The Rise of American Civilization.* Vol. I. New York: Macmillan.

Beard, C. A., and Beard, Mary R., 1944. *A Basic History of the United States.* New York: New Home Library.

Beaver, A. P., 1932. The initiation of social contacts by preschool children. *Child Develpm. Monogr.,* **7**.

Beck, D., and Nebergall, R. E., 1967. Relationship between attitude neutrality and involvement. Paper presented at the Annual Meeting of the Speech Association of America, Los Angeles.

Beebe-Center, J., 1932. *Pleasantness and Unpleasantness.* Princeton, N. J.: Van Nostrand.

Bell, G. D., 1963. Processes in the formation of adolescents' aspirations. *Social Forces,* **42**, 179–195.

Bell, W., 1965. Urban neighborhoods and individual behavior. In M. Sherif and Carolyn W. Sherif (Eds.), *Problems of Youth.* Chicago: Aldine, 235–264.

Bem, D. J., 1967. Self-perception: An alternative interpretation of cognitive dissonance phenomena. *Psychol. Rev.,* **74**, 183–200.

Benedict, Ruth, 1942. *Race and Cultural Relations, Problems in American Life,* No. 5. Washington: National Education Association.

Bennett, L., Jr., 1966. Black power. *Ebony,* September, 25–27 ff.

Benoit-Smullyan, E., 1944. Status, status types and status interrelations. *Amer. sociol. Rev.,* **9**, 151–161.

Berelson, B., and Janowitz, M., 1966. *Reader in Public Opinion and Communication.* New York: Free Press.

Berelson, B., Lazarsfeld, P. F., and McPhee, W. N., 1954. *Voting: A Study of Opinion Formation in a Presidential Campaign.* Chicago: University of Chicago Press.

Berg, I. A., and Bass, B. M. (Eds.), 1961. *Conformity and Deviation.* New York: Harper & Row.

Berko, Jean, 1958. The child's learning of English morphology. *Word,* **14**, 150–177.

Berkowitz, L., 1962. *Aggression: A Social-psychological Analysis.* New York: McGraw-Hill.

Berne, E. V. C., 1930. An experimental investigation of social behavior patterns in young children, *University of Iowa Studies in Child Welfare,* **4**, No. 3.

Berry, M. F., and Eisenson, J., 1945. *The Defective in Speech.* New York: Appleton-Century-Crofts, 277–278.

Biddle, B. J., and Thomas, E. J. (Eds.), 1966. *Role Theory: Concepts and Research.* New York: Wiley.

Bieri, J., 1967. Attitudes and arousal: Affect and cognition in personality function. In Carolyn W. Sherif and M. Sherif (Eds.), *Attitude, Ego-involvement and Change.* New York: Wiley, 178–200.

Bieri, J., Atkins, A. L., Briar, S., Leaman, R. L., Miller, H., and Tripodi, T., 1966. *Clinical and Social Judgment: The Discrimination of Behavioral Information.* New York: Wiley.

Biesheuvel, S., 1958. Methodology in the study

of attitudes of Africans. *J. soc. Psychol.* **47**, 169–184.

Binet, A., 1900. *La Suggestibilité.* Paris, Schleicher frères.

Bird, C., 1940. *Social Psychology.* New York: Appleton-Century-Crofts.

Bitterman, M. E., 1965. The evolution of intelligence. *Scient. Amer.*, **212**, No. 1, 92–100.

Black, C. E., 1966. *The Dynamics of Modernization: A Study in Corporate History.* New York: Harper & Row.

Blake, R. R., and Brehm, J. W., 1954. The use of tape recording to simulate a group atmosphere. *J. abnorm. soc. Psychol.,* **49**, 311–313.

Blake, R. R., Helson, H., and Mouton, Jane S., 1957. The generality of conforming behavior as a function of factual anchorage, difficulty of task, and amount of social pressure. *J. Pers.,* **25**, 294–305.

Blake, R. R., and Mouton, Jane, S., 1962. The intergroup dynamics of win-lose conflict and problem-solving collaboration in union-management relations. In M. Sherif (Ed.), *Intergroup Relations and Leadership.* New York: Wiley.

Blake, R. R., and Mouton, Jane S., 1965. Loyalty of representatives to ingroup position during intergroup competition. In H. Proshansky and B. Seidenberg (Eds.), *Basic Studies in Social Psychology.* New York: Holt, Rinehart and Winston, 702–705.

Blake, R. R., Shepard, H. A., and Mouton, Jane S., 1964. *Managing Intergroup Conflict in Industry.* Houston: Texas, Gulf Publishing Company.

Blau, P. M., and Scott, W. R., 1962. *Formal Organizations: A Comparative Approach.* San Francisco: Chandler.

Bleuler, M., and Bleuler, R., 1935. Rorschach's ink-blot test and racial psychology: Mental peculiarities of Moroccans. *Charact. & Pers.,* **4**, 97–114.

Blumer, H., 1946. Social movements. In A. M. Lee (Ed.), *New Outlines of the Principles of Sociology.* New York: Barnes & Noble, Ch. 22.

Blumer, H., 1957. Collective behavior. In J. B. Gittler (Ed.), *Review of Sociology.* New York: Wiley, Ch. 5.

Bochner, S., and Insko, C. A., 1966. Communicator discrepancy, source credibility and opinion change. *J. Pers. soc. Psychol.,* **4**, 614–621.

Bogardus, E. S., 1924–25. Social distance and its origins: Measuring social distances. *J. appl. Sociol.,* **9**, 216–308.

Bogardus, E. S., 1947. Changes in racial distances. *Int. J. Opin. Attit. Res.,* **1**, No. 1, 55–62.

Bogdonoff, M. D., Klein, R. F., Back, K. W., Nichols, C. R., Troyer, W. G., and Hood, T. C., 1964. Effect of group relationship and the role of leadership upon lipid mobilization. *Psychosom. Med.* **26**, 710–719.

Bonner, H., 1959. *Group Dynamics: Principles and Applications.* New York: Ronald Press.

Boring, E. G., 1942. *Sensation and Perception in the History of Experimental Psychology.* New York: Appleton-Century-Crofts.

Boring, E. G., 1946. The perception of objects. *Amer. J. Physics,* **14** (March–April), 99–107.

Bovard, E. W., Jr., 1948. Social norms and the individual. *J. abnorm. soc. Psychol.,* **43**, 62–69.

Bovard, E. W., Jr., 1951. Group structure and perception. *J. abnorm. soc. Psychol.,* **46**, 398–405.

Bovard, E. W., Jr., 1953. Conformity to social norms in stable and temporary groups. *Science,* **117**, 361–363.

Braine, M. D. S., 1963. The ontogeny of English phrase structure: The first phrase. *Language,* **39**, 1–13.

Braine, M. D. S., 1967. Paper presented to Seminar on Verbal Behavior, The Pennsylvania State University.

Brinton, C., 1965. *The Anatomy of Revolution.* Englewood Cliffs, N.J.: Prentice-Hall (PB: Vintage, Random House, rev. ed.)

Brock, T. C., and Balloun, G. L., 1967. Behavioral receptivity to dissonant information. *J. Pers. soc. Psychol.,* **4**, 413–428.

Brock, T. C., and Becker, L. A., 1965. Ineffectiveness of "overhead" counter-propaganda. *J. Pers. soc. Psychol.,* **2**, 654–660.

Bronfenbrenner, U., 1967. The split level American family. *Saturday Review,* October 7, 60–66.

Brown, J. D. (Ed.), 1967. *The Hippies.* New York: Time, Inc.

Brown, R., 1954. Mass phenomena. In G. Lindzey (Ed.), *Handbook of Social Psychology.* Vol. II. Reading, Mass.: Addison-Wesley, 833–873.

Brown, R., 1957. Linguistic determination and the part of speech. *J. abnorm. soc. Psychol.,* **55**, 1–5.

Brown, R., 1958. *Words and Things.* New York: Free Press.

Brown, R., 1965. *Social Psychology.* New York: Free Press.

Bruner, J. S., 1957. On perceptual readiness. *Psychol. Rev.,* **64**, 123–152.

Bruner, J. S. (Ed.), 1966. *Studies in Cognitive Growth.* New York: Wiley.

Bruner, J. S., and Taguiri, R., 1954. The perception of people. In G. Lindzey (Ed.), *Handbook of Social Psychology.* Vol. II. Reading, Mass.: Addison-Wesley.

Borgatta, E. F., and Cottrell, L. S., 1955. On the classification of groups. *Sociometry,* **18**, 409–422.

Buchanan, W., and Cantril, H., 1953. *How Nations See Each Other: A Study in Public Opinion.* Urbana: Univer. of Illinois Press.

Buck, P. H., 1938. *Ethnology of Mangarena.* Honolulu: B. P. Bishop Museum Bull. No. 157.

Bugental, J. F. T., and Zelen, S. L., 1949–50. Investigation into the "self-concept:" I. The W-A-I Technique. *J. Pers.,* **18**, 483–498.

Buss, A. H., and Portnoy, N. W., 1967. Pain tolerance and group identification. *J. Pers. soc. Psychol.* **6**, 106–108.

Cameron, W. B., 1966. *Modern Social Movements.* New York: Random House.

Campbell, A., Converse, P. E., Miller, W. E., and Stokes, O. E., 1960. *The American Voter.* New York: Wiley.

Campbell, D. T., 1950. The indirect assessment of social attitudes. *Psychol. Bull.,* **47**, 15–38.

Campbell, D. T., 1958. Common fate, similarity and other indices of the status of aggregates of persons as social entities. *Behavioral Sci.,* **3**, 14–25.

Campbell, D. T., 1963. Social attitudes and other acquired behavioral dispositions. In S. Koch (Ed.), *Psychology: A Study of a Science,* Vol. 6. New York: McGraw-Hill, 92–172.

Campbell, E. Q., and Pettigrew, T. F., 1959. Racial and moral crisis: The role of Little Rock's ministers. *Amer. J. Sociol.,* **64**, 509–516.

Campbell, J. D., 1967. Studies in attitude formation. In Carolyn W. Sherif and M. Sherif, *Attitude, Ego-involvement and Change.* New York: Wiley, 7–25.

Cantril, H., 1940. *The Invasion from Mars.* Princeton: Princeton University Press (PB: Torchbook 1966; New York: Harper & Row.)

Cantril, H., 1941. *The Psychology of Social Movements.* New York: Wiley.

Cantril, H., 1944. *Gauging Public Opinion.* Princeton: Princeton Univer. Press.

Cantril, H., 1946. The intensity of an attitude. *J. abnorm. soc. Psychol.,* **41**, 129–135.

Cantril, H., 1963. A study of aspirations. *Scientific Amer.,* **208**, No. 2, 41–45.

Cantril H., 1965. *The Pattern of Human Concerns.* New Brunswick, N. J.: Rutgers Univer. Press.

Caplow, T., 1964. *Principles of Organization.* New York: Harcourt, Brace & World.

Carmichael, L., 1948. Growth and development. In E. G. Boring, H. S. Langfeld, and H. P. Weld (Eds.), *Foundations of Psychology.* New York: Wiley.

Carmichael, L., Hogan, H. P., and Walter, A. A., 1932. An experimental study of the effect of language in the reproduction of visually perceived forms. *J. exp. Psychol.,* **10**, 214–229.

Carmichael, S., and Hamilton, C. V., 1967. *Black Power: The Politics of Liberation in America.* New York: Random House (PB: Vintage, Random House.)

Carpenter, C. R., 1964. *Naturalistic Behavior of Nonhuman Primates.* University Park: Pennsylvania State Univer. Press.

Carroll, J. B., 1939. Determining and numerating adjectives in children's speech. *Child Develpm.,* **10**, 214–224.

Carter, J. H., 1952. Military leadership. *Military Rev.,* **32**, 14–18.

Carter, L. F., 1953. Leadership and small group behavior. In M. Sherif and M. O. Wilson (Eds.), *Group Relations at the Crossroads.* New York: Harper & Row.

Cartwright, D., 1965. Influence, leadership and control. In J. G. March (Ed.), *Handbook of Organizations.* Chicago: Rand McNally.

Cartwright, D., and Zander, A., 1960, 1968. *Group Dynamics: Research and Theory.* (2nd and 3rd ed.) New York: Harper & Row.

Cattell, R. B., 1951. New concepts for measuring leadership in terms of group syntality. *Human Relat.,* **4**, 161–184.

Cattell, R., and Stice, G. F., 1954. Four formulae for selecting leaders on the basis of personality. *Human Relat.,* **7**, 493–507.

Cattell, R. B., and Wispé, L. G., 1948. The dimensions of syntality in small groups. *J. soc. Psychol.,* **28**, 57–78.

CBS Reports, 1966. Black Power, White Backlash, September 27.

Centers, R., 1952. The American class structure: A psychological analysis. In G. E. Swanson, T. M. Newcomb, and E. L. Hartley (Eds.), *Readings in Social Psychology.* New York: Holt, Rinehart and Winston.

Chamberlain, A. F., and Chamberlain, I. C., 1904. Studies of a Child: I. *Pedagog. Sem.,* **11**.

Chapanis, N. P., and Chapanis, A., 1964. Cognitive dissonance five years later. *Psychol. Bull.,* **61**, 1–22.

Chapman, D. W., and Volkmann, J., 1939. A social determinant of the level of aspiration. *J. abnorm. soc. Psychol.,* **34**, 225–238.

Chapman, D. W., 1962. In G. W. Baker and D. W. Chapman (Eds.), *Man and Society in Disaster.* New York: Basic Books.

Chomsky, N., 1959. Review: *Verbal Behavior* by B. F. Skinner. *Language,* **35**, 26–58.

Chomsky, N., 1965. *Aspects of the Theory of Syntax.* Cambridge, Mass.: M.I.T. Press.

Chomsky, N., and Halle, M., 1968. *The Sound Patterns of English.* New York: Harper & Row.

Chowdry, K., and Newcomb, T. M., 1952. The relative ability of leaders and non-leaders to estimate opinions of their own groups. *J. abnorm. soc. Psychol.,* **47**, 51–57.

Christie, R., 1954. Authoritarianism re-examined. In R. Christie and Marie Jahoda (Eds.), *Studies in Scope and Method of "Authoritarian Personality."* New York: Free Press, 123–193.

Christie, R., and Garcia, J., 1951. Subcultural variation in authoritarian personality. *J. abnorm. soc. Psychol.,* **46**, 457–469.

Christie, R., and Jahoda, Marie (Eds.), 1954.

Studies in the Scope and Method of "The Authoritarian Personality." New York: Free Press.

Clark, H., 1916. The crowd. *Psychol. Monogr.,* **49**, 311–313.

Clark, J. P., and Tifft, L. L., 1966. Polygraph and interview validation of self-reported deviant behavior. *Amer. sociol. Rev., 31*, 516–523.

Clark, K. B., 1940. Some factors influencing the remembering of prose material. *Arch. Psychol.,* No. 253.

Clark, K. B., 1965. *Dark Ghetto.* New York: Harper & Row.

Clark, K. B., and Clark, M. K., 1947. Racial identification and preference in Negro pre-school children. In T. M. Newcomb and E. L. Hartley (Eds.), *Readings in Social Psychology.* New York: Holt, Rinehart and Winston.

Clark, R. E., 1965. Differential association and reference group theory. Unpublished manuscript, The Pennsylvania State University.

Clarke, P., and James, J., 1967. The effects of situation, attitude intensity and personality on information seeking. *Sociometry, 30*, 235–245.

Clemmer, D., 1940. *The Prison Community.* Boston: Christopher.

Coffin, T. E., 1941. Some conditions of suggestion and suggestibility: A study of certain attitudinal and situational factors influencing the process of suggestion. *Psychol. Monogr.,* No. 241.

Coleman, J. S., 1961. *The Adolescent Society.* New York: Free Press.

Coleman, J., Katz, E., and Menzel, H., 1966. *Medical Innovations: A Diffusion Study.* Indianapolis: Bobbs-Merrill.

Coleman, J., Menzel, H., and Katz, E., 1959. Social processes in physician's adoption of a new drug. *J. Chron. Disease, 9*, 1–19.

Cook, P. H., 1942. The application of the Rorschach test to a Samoan group. *Rorschach Res. Exch., 6*, 51–60.

Cook, S. W., and Harris, R. E., 1937. The verbal conditioning of the galvanic skin reflex. *J. exp. Psychol., 21*, 202–210.

Cook, S. W., and Selltiz, Claire, 1964. A multiple-indicator approach to attitude measurement. *Psychol. Bull., 62*, 36–55.

Cooley, C. H., 1902. *Human Nature and the Social Order.* New York: Scribner.

Cooley, C. H., 1909. *Social Organization.* New York: Scribner.

Coombs, C. H., 1952. *A Theory of Psychological Scaling.* Ann Arbor: Univer. of Michigan Press.

Coombs, C. H., 1967. Thurstone's measurement of social values revisited forty years later. *J. pers. soc. Psychol., 6*, 85–91.

Cope, L., 1919. Calendars of the Indians north of Mexico. *Univer. of Calif. Publ. in Amer. Archaeol. and Ethnol., 16*, 137.

Coser, L., and Rosenberg, B., 1964. *Sociological*

Theory: A Book of Readings. New York: Macmillan.

Cowles, J. T., 1937. Food-tokens as incentives for learning by chimpanzees. *Comp. Psychol. Monogr., 14*, No. 5.

Croner, M. D., and Willis, R. H., 1961. Perceived differences in task competence and asymmetry of dyadic influence. *J. abnorm. soc. Psychol., 62*, 705–708.

Crutchfield, R. S., 1955. Conformity and character. *Amer. Psychologist, 10*, 191–198.

Dalton, M., 1955. In W. F. Whyte, *Money and Motivation.* New York: Harper & Row, Chapter 6.

Dashiell, J. F., 1930. An experimental analysis of some group effects. *J. abnorm. soc. Psychol., 25*, 190–199.

Davies, J. C., 1962. Toward a theory of revolution. *Amer. sociol. Rev., 27*, No. 1, 5–19.

Davis, K., 1947. Final note on a case of extreme isolation. *Amer. J. Sociol., 52*, 432–437.

Davis, K., and Warner, W. L., 1937. Structural analysis of kinship. *Amer. Anthrop., 39*, 291–313.

DeFleur, M. L., and Westie, F. R., 1958. Verbal attitudes and overt acts: An experiment on the salience of attitudes. *Amer. sociol. Rev., 23*, 667–673.

DeNike, L. D., and Spielberger, C. D., 1963. Induced mediating states in operant conditioning. *J. verbal Learning and verbal Behav., 1*, 339–345.

de Schweinitz, K., Jr., 1964. *Industrialization and Democracy. Economic Necessities and Political Possibilities.* New York: Free Press.

De Soto, C. B., and Bosley, J. J., 1962. The cognitive structure of a social structure. *J. abnorm. soc. Psychol., 64*, 303–307.

Delf, G., 1961. *Jomo Kenyatta: Towards Truth about the "Light of Kenya"* Garden City, N.Y.: Doubleday.

Deutsch, K. W., 1964. External involvement in internal war. In H. Eckstein (Ed.), *Internal War: Problems and Approaches.* New York: Free Press, 100–110.

Deutsch, M., and Collins, M. E., 1951. *Interracial Housing.* Minneapolis: Univer. of Minnesota Press.

Diab, L., 1963 a. Factors affecting studies of national stereotypes. *J. soc. Psychol., 59*, 29–40.

Diab, L., 1963 b. Factors determining group stereotypes. *J. soc. Psychol., 61*, 3–10.

Diab, L., 1965 a. Studies in social attitudes: I. Variations in latitudes of acceptance and rejection as a function of varying positions on a controversial social issue. *J. soc. Psychol., 67*, 283–295.

Diab, L. N., 1965 b. Studies in social attitudes: II. Selectivity in mass communication media as a function of attitude-medium discrepancy. *J. soc. Psychol., 67,* 297–302.

Diab, L. N., 1966. Reaction to a communication as a function of attitude-communication discrepancy. *Psychol. Rep., 18,* 767–774.

Diab, L. N., 1967. Measurement of social attitudes: Problems and prospects. In Carolyn W. Sherif and M. Sherif (Eds.), *Attitude, Ego-involvement and Change.* New York: Wiley, 140–158.

Diaz-Guerrero, R., 1965. Sociocultural and psychodynamic processes in adolescent transition and mental health. In M. Sherif and Carolyn W. Sherif (Eds.), *Problems of Youth.* Chicago: Aldine, Ch. 7.

Diebold, J., 1959. *Automation: Its Impact on Business and Labor.* Washington, D.C.: National Planning Assoc. Planning Pamphlet No. 16.

Dinneen, F. P., 1967. *An Introduction to General Linguistics.* New York: Holt, Rinehart and Winston.

Dinneen, F. P., 1969. Linguistics and the social sciences. Chapter 14 in M. Sherif and Carolyn Sherif (Eds.), *Interdisciplinary Relations in the Social Sciences.* Chicago: Aldine.

Dodd, S. C., 1935. A social distance test in the Near East. *Amer. J. Sociol., 41,* 194–204.

Dollard, J., *et al.,* 1939. *Frustration and Aggression.* New Haven: Yale Univer. Press.

Doob, L. W., 1948. *Public Opinion and Propaganda.* New York: Holt, Rinehart and Winston.

Dubin, R., 1962. Leadership in union-management relations as an intergroup system. In M. Sherif (Ed.), *Intergroup Relations and Leadership.* New York: Wiley, 70–91.

Dubin, R., and Dubin, Elizabeth R., 1965. Children's social perception: A review of research. *Child Develpm., 36,* 829–838.

DuBois, W. E. B., 1935. *Black Reconstruction in America.* New York: Russell & Russell.

Dukes, W. F., and Bevan, W., Jr., 1951. Accentuation and response variability in the perception of personally relevant objects. *J. Pers., 20,* 457–465.

Durkheim, E., 1933. *The Division of Labor in Society.* New York: Macmillan (PB: Free Press, Macmillan, 1964.)

Durkheim, E., 1938. *The Rules of the Sociological Method.* New York: Free Press.

Durkheim, E., 1951. *Suicide: A Study in Sociology.* New York: Free Press. (Translated from French by G. Simpson.)

Eagley, Alice H., 1967. Involvement as a determinant of response to favorable and unfavorable information. *J. pers. soc. Psychol. Monogr., 7,* No. 3, Part 2, 1–15.

Edwards, A. L., 1946. A critique of "neutral items" in attitude scales constructed by the method of equal-appearing intervals. *Psychol. Rev., 53,* 159–169.

Edwards, A. L., 1957 a. *Techniques of Attitude Scale Construction.* New York: Appleton-Century-Crofts.

Edwards, A. L., 1957 b. *The Social Desirability Variable in Personality Assessment and Research.* New York: Holt, Rinehart and Winston.

Edwards, A. L., 1961. Social desirability or acquiescence in the MMPI? A case study with the SD scale. *J. abnorm. soc. Psychol., 63,* 351–359.

Edwards, A. L., and Walker, J. N., 1962. Relationship between probability of items endorsement and social desirability scale value for high and low groups on Edwards' SD scale. *J. abnorm. soc. Psychol., 64,* 458–460.

Edwards, L. P., 1927. *The Natural History of Revolution.* Chicago: Univer. of Chicago Press.

Einstein, A., and Infeld, L., 1951. *The Evolution of Physics.* New York: Simon and Schuster.

Eisenberg, P., and Lazarsfeld, P. F., 1938. The psychological effects of unemployment. *Psychol. Bull., 35,* 358–390.

Eisenstadt, S., 1966. Sociological aspects of political development in underdeveloped countries. In I. Wallerstein (Ed.), *Social Change: The Colonial Situation.* New York: Wiley, 572–582.

Eisman, Bernice, 1959. Some operational measures of group cohesiveness and their interaction. *Human Relat., 12,* 183–186.

Elbing, A. O., 1962. An experimental investigation of the influence of reference group identification on role playing as applied to business. Ph.D. thesis, University of Washington, Seattle.

Elkin, F., 1946. The soldier's language. *Amer. J. Sociol., 51,* 414–422.

Emerson, R., 1960. *From Empire to Nation: The Rise of Self-Assertion in Asian and African Peoples.* Cambridge: Harvard Univer. Press.

Eriksen, C. W., and Hake, H. W., 1957. Anchor effects in absolute judgments. *J. exp. Psychol., 53,* 132–138.

Etzioni, A., 1964. *Modern Organizations.* Englewood Cliffs, N.J.: Prentice-Hall.

Evans, R. M., 1948. *An Introduction to Color.* New York: Wiley.

Faris, R. E. L., 1953. Development of the small group research movement. In M. Sherif and M. O. Wilson (Eds.), *Group Relations at the Crossroads.* New York: Harper & Row.

Faris, R. E. L., 1962. Interaction levels and intergroup relations. In M. Sherif (Ed.), *Intergroup Relations and Leadership.* New York: Wiley, 24–47.

Faris, R. E. L., 1967. *Chicago Sociology—1920–1932.* San Francisco: Chandler.

Faunce, W. A., 1958. Automation in the automobile industry: Some consequences for inplant social structure. *Amer. sociol. Rev., 23,* No. 4, 401–407.

Faunce, W. A., 1960. Automation and the automobile worker. In W. Galenson and S. M. Lipset (Eds.), *Labor and Trade Unionism: An Interdisciplinary Reader.* New York: Wiley, 370–379.

Feather, N. T., 1967 a. Level of aspiration and performance variability. *J. pers. soc. Psychol.,* **6**, 37–46.

Feather, N. T., 1967 b. A structural balance approach to the analysis of communicator effects. In L. Berkowitz (Ed.), *Advances in Experimental Social Psychology.* New York: Academic Press, 99–165.

Fehrer, Elizabeth, 1952. Shifts in scale values of attitude statements as a function of the composition of the scale. *J. exp. Psychol.,* **44**, 179–188.

Feldman, R. A., 1968. Interrelationships among three bases of group integration, *Sociometry,* **31**, 30–46.

Feldman, S. (Ed.), 1967. *Cognitive Consistency.* New York: Academic Press.

Fenchel, G. H., Monderer, J. H., and Hartley, E. L., 1951. Subjective status and the equilibration hypothesis. *J. abnorm. soc. Psychol.,* **46**, 476–479.

Fendrich, J. M., 1967. A study of the association among verbal attitudes, commitment and overt behavior in different experimental situations. *Soc. Forces,* **45**, 347–355.

Ferguson, L. W., 1935. The influence of individual attitudes on construction of an attitude scale. *J. soc. Psychol.,* **6**, 115–117.

Festinger, L., 1947. The treatment of qualitative data by scale analysis. *Psychol. Bull.,* **44**, 149–161.

Festinger, L., 1957. *The Theory of Cognitive Dissonance.* New York: Harper & Row.

Festinger, L., 1963. The theory of cognitive dissonance. In W. Schramm, *The Science of Human Communication.* New York: Basic Books.

Festinger, L. (Ed.) 1964. *Conflict, Decision and Dissonance.* Stanford: Stanford Univer. Press.

Festinger, L., Schachter, S., and Back, K., 1950. *Social Pressures in Informal Groups.* New York: Harper & Row.

Fiedler, F., 1968. Personality and situational determinants of leadership effectiveness. In D. Cartwright and A. Zander (Eds.), *Group Dynamics.* 3rd ed. New York: Harper & Row, 362–380.

Fillenbaum, S., 1961. How fat is fat? *J. Psychol.,* **52**, 133–136.

Fishbein, M. (Ed.), 1967. *Readings in Attitude Theory and Measurement.* New York: Wiley.

Fisher, S., and Cleveland, S. E., 1958. *Body Image and Personality.* Princeton, N.J.: Van Nostrand.

Fisher, S., and Lubin, A., 1958. Distance as a determinant of influence in a two-person social interaction situation. *J. abnorm. soc. Psychol.,* **56**, 230–238.

Flament, C., 1959 a. Modèle stratégique des processus d'influence sociale sur les jugements perceptifs. *Psychol. française,* **4**, 91–101.

Flament, C., 1959 b. Ambiguité du stimulus, incertitude de la réponse et processus d'influence sociale. *Année psychologique,* **59**, 73–92.

Foster, G. M., 1962. *Traditional Cultures and the Impact of Technological Change.* New York: Harper & Row.

Fraisse, P., 1963. *The Psychology of Time.* New York: Harper & Row.

Frank, J. D., 1944. Experimental studies of personal pressure and resistance: I. Experimental production of resistance. *J. gen. Psychol.,* **30**, 23–41.

Frank, J. D., 1963. *Persuasion and Healing: A Comparative Study of Psychotherapy.* New York: Schocken Books.

Frazier, F., 1957 a. *The Negro in the United States.* (rev. ed.) New York: Macmillan.

Frazier, F., 1957 b. *Black Bourgeoisie.* New York: Free Press.

Freedman, J. L., 1964. Involvement, discrepancy and change. *J. abnorm. soc. Psychol.,* **69**, 290–295.

Freedman, J. L., 1965. Preference for dissonant information. *J. pers. soc. Psychol.,* **2**, 287–289.

French, D. H., 1962. Ambiguity and irrelevancy in factional conflict. In M. Sherif (Ed.), *Intergroup Relations and Leadership.* New York: Wiley, 232–246.

Frenkel-Brunswik, Else, 1949. Intolerance of ambiguity as an emotional and personality variable. *J. Pers.,* **18**, 108–143.

Freud, S., 1922. *Group Psychology and the Analysis of the Ego.* London: Hogarth.

Freud, S., 1927. *The Ego and the Id.* London: Hogarth.

Freud, S., 1930. *Civilization and Its Discontents.* London: Hogarth.

Freud, S., 1950. *Collected Papers.* London: Hogarth, Ch. 25.

Fritz, C. E. and Marks, E., 1954. The NORC studies of human behavior in disaster. *J. soc. Issues,* **10**, No. 3, 26–41.

Fritz, C. E., and Mathewson, J. H., 1957. *Convergence Behavior in Disasters: A Problem in Social Control.* Washington, D.C.: National Research Council Publication 476.

Fromm, E., 1955. *The Sane Society.* New York: Holt, Rinehart and Winston.

Garner, W. R., 1966. To perceive is to know. *Amer. Psychologist,* **21**, 11–19.

Getzels, J. W., 1963. Conflict and role behavior in the educational setting. In W. W. Charters, Jr., and N. L. Gage (Eds.), *Readings in the Social Psychology of Education.* Boston: Allyn and Bacon, 309–318.

Gibb, C. A., 1947. The principles and traits of leadership. *J. abnorm. soc. Psychol.,* **42**, 267–284.

Gibb, C. A., 1950. The sociometry of leadership in temporary groups. *Sociometry, 13*, 226–243.

Gibb, C. A., 1954. Leadership. In G. Lindzey (Ed.), *Handbook of Social Psychology,* Vol. II. Reading, Mass.: Addison-Wesley.

Gibb, C. A., 1968. Leadership: I. Psychological aspects. In D. L. Sills (Ed.), *Internat. Encyclopedia of Soc. Sci., 9*, 91–101. New York: Macmillan and Free Press.

Gibson, J. J., 1953. Social perception and the psychology of perceptual learning. In M. Sherif and M. O. Wilson (Eds.), *Group Relations at the Crossroads.* New York: Harper & Row.

Gibson, J. J., 1960. The concept of the stimulus in psychology. *Amer. Psychologist,* **15**, 694–703.

Gibson, J. J., 1967. *The Senses Considered as Perceptual Systems.* Boston: Houghton Miffiin.

Gilbert, G. M., 1950. Stereotype persistence and change among college students. *J. abnorm. soc. Psychol.,* **46**, 245–254.

Gilchrist, J. C., Ludeman, J. F., and Lysack, W., 1954. Values as determinants of word-recognition thresholds. *J. abnorm. soc. Psychol.,* **49**, 423–426.

Glaser, D., 1956. Criminality theories and behavioral images. *Amer. J. Sociol.,* **61**, 433–444.

Glass, L. B., and Barber, T. X., 1961. A note on hypnotic behavior, the definition of the situation and the placebo effect. *J. nerv. ment. Dis.,* **132**, 539–541.

Glixman, A. R., 1965. Categorizing behavior as a function of meaning domain. *J. pers. soc. Psychol.,* **2**, 370–377.

Goffman, E., 1959. *The Presentation of Self in Everyday Life.* Garden City, N.Y.: Doubleday.

Goffman, E., 1967. *Interaction Ritual.* Chicago: Aldine.

Goldman, I., 1937. Competitive and cooperative habits among the Zuni Indians of New Mexico. In M. Mead (Ed.), *Cooperation and Competition Among Primitive Peoples.* New York: McGraw-Hill.

Goldstein, K., and Scheerer, M., 1941. Abstract and concrete behavior: An experimental study with special tests. *Psychol. Monogr.,* **53**, 1–31.

Goldstein, N. F., 1948. *The Roots of Prejudice Against the Negro in the United States.* Boston: Boston Univer. Press.

Golembiewski, R. T., 1962. *The Small Group: An Analysis of Research Concepts and Operations.* Chicago: Univer. of Chicago Press.

Goodman, M. E., 1952. *Race Awareness in Young Children.* Reading, Mass.: Addison-Wesley.

Gottschaldt, K., 1955. Gestalt factors and repetition. In W. D. Ellis (Ed.), *A Source Book of Gestalt Psychology.* New York: Humanities Press, 109–135; London: Routledge.

Gottschalk, L. R., 1929. *The Era of the French Revolution, 1715–1815.* Boston: Houghton Mifflin.

Gouldner, A. W., 1954. *Patterns of Industrial Bureaucracy.* New York: Free Press.

Graham, D., 1962. Experimental studies of social influence in simple judgment situations. *J. soc. Psychol.,* **56**, 245–269.

Grice, H. H., 1934. The construction and validation of a generalized scale designed to measure attitudes toward defined groups. *Bull. Purdue Univer.,* **25**, 37–46.

Green, E. H., 1933. Group playing and quarreling among pre-school children. *Child Develpm.,* **4**, 302–307.

Greenberg, P. J., 1932. Competition in children: An experimental study. *Amer. J. Psychol.,* **44**, 221–248.

Greer, S. A., 1955. *Social Organization.* Garden City, N.Y.: Doubleday.

Gross, N., Mason, W. S., and McEachern, A. W., 1958. *Explorations in Role Analysis: Studies of the School Superintendent.* New York: Wiley.

Group for Advancement of Psychiatry, 1964. *Psychiatric Aspects of the Prevention of Nuclear War.* New York: 104 E. 25th Street.

Guest, D., 1963. *Marxist Philosophy.* London: Lawrence and Wishart, (new ed.). Letter from F. Engels to J. Block, September 21, 1890.

Guetzkow, H. S., and Bowman, P. H., 1946. *Men and Hunger: A Psychological Manual for Relief Workers.* Elgin, Ill.: Brethren Publishing House.

Guilford, J. P., 1931. Racial preferences of a thousand American university students. *J. soc. Psychol.,* **2**, 179–204.

Guillaume, P., 1927. Les débuts de la phrase chez l'enfant. *J. de Psychol., 24*.

Guttman, L., 1947. The Cornell technique for scale construction. *Educat. & Psychol. Measmt.,* **7**, 247–280.

Haire, M., 1954. Group dynamics in the industrial situation. In A. Kornhauser, R. Dubin, and A. M. Ross (Eds.), *Industrial Conflict.* New York: McGraw-Hill, 373–385.

Haire, M. (Ed.), 1959. *Modern Organization Theory.* New York: Wiley.

Haller, A. O., and Butterworth, C. E., 1960. Peer influences on level of occupational and educational aspirations. *Soc. Forces, 38*, 289–295.

Hallowell, A. I., 1941. The Rorschach method as an aid in the study of personalities in primitive societies. *Charact. & Pers.,* **9**, 235–245.

Hallowell, A. I., 1942. Some psychological aspects of measurement among the Saulteaux. *Amer. Anthrop.,* **44**, 62–77.

Hallowell, A. I., 1951. Cultural factors in the structuralization of perception. In J. H. Rohrer and M. Sherif (Eds.), *Social Psychology at the Crossroads.* New York: Harper & Row.

Halloran, J. D., 1967. *Attitude Formation and*

Change. Leicester, England: Leicester Univer. Press.

Hammond, K. R., 1948. Measuring attitudes by error choice: An indirect method. *J. abnorm. soc. Psychol., 45,* 38–48.

Hanfman, Eugenia, 1963. Social structure of a group of kindergarten children. In W. W. Charters, Jr., and N. L. Gage (Eds.), *Readings in the Social Psychology of Education.* Boston: Houghton Mifflin, 123–125.

Hansche, J., and Gilchrist, J. C., 1956. Three determinants of the level of aspiration. *J. abnorm. soc. Psychol., 53,* 136–137.

Harcum, E. R., 1967. Parallel functions of serial learning and tachistoscopic pattern perception. *Psychol. Rev., 74,* 51–62.

Hare, A. P., 1952. A study of social interaction and consensus in different sized groups. *Amer. sociol Rev., 17,* 261–267.

Hare, A. P., 1962. *Handbook of Small Group Research.* New York: Free Press.

Harris, D. B., 1963. *Children's Drawings: A Measure of Intellectual Maturity.* New York: Harcourt, Brace & World.

Hartley, E. L. (See also Horowitz, E. L.), 1946. *Problems in Prejudice.* New York: King's Crown Press.

Hartley, E. L., 1951. Psychological problems of multiple group membership. In J. Rohrer and M. Sherif (Eds.), *Social Psychology at the Crossroads.* New York: Harper & Row.

Hartley, E. L., 1967. Attitude research and the jangle fallacy. In Carolyn W. Sherif and M. Sherif (Eds.), *Attitude, Ego-involvement and Change.* New York: Wiley, 88–103.

Hartley, Ruth E., 1957. Personal characteristics and acceptance of secondary groups as reference groups. *J. Indiv. Psychol., 13,* 45–55.

Hartley, Ruth E., 1960. Norm compatibility, norm preference, and the acceptance of new reference groups. *J. soc. Psychol., 52,* 87–95.

Harvey, O. J., 1953. An experimental approach to the study of status relations in informal groups. *Amer. sociol. Rev., 18,* 357–367.

Harvey, O. J., 1956. An experimental investigation of negative and positive relations between small groups through judgmental indices. *Sociometry, 14,* 121–147.

Harvey, O. J., 1966. System structure, flexibility, and creativity. In O. J. Harvey (Ed.), *Experience, Structure and Adaptability.* New York: Springer, 39–65.

Harvey, O. J., 1967. Conceptual systems and attitude change. In Carolyn W. Sherif and M. Sherif (Eds.), *Attitude, Ego-involvement and Change.* New York: Wiley, 201–226.

Harvey, O. J., Hunt, D. E., and Schroder, H. M., 1961. *Conceptual Systems and Personality Organization.* New York: Wiley.

Harvey, O. J., and Rutherford, Jeanne, 1958.

Gradual and absolute approaches to attitude change. *Sociometry, 21,* 61–68.

Harvey, O. J., and Sherif, M., 1951. Level of aspiration as a case of judgmental activity in which ego-involvements operate as factors. *Sociometry, 14,* 121–147.

Hayes, C., 1951. *The Ape in Our House.* New York: Harper & Row.

Hayes, D. P., 1964. Item order and Guttman scales. *Amer. J. Sociol., 70,* 51–58.

Hebb, D. O., 1966. *A Textbook of Psychology* (rev. ed.). Philadelphia: Saunders.

Heberle, R., 1951. *Social Movements: An Introduction to Political Sociology.* New York: Appleton-Century-Crofts.

Hechinger, F. M., 1967. A black identity. *The New York Times,* October 29, Section E, 9.

Hechinger, F. M., 1967. In H. E. Salisbury (Ed.), *The Soviet Union: The Fifty Years.* New York: Harcourt, Brace & World.

Heidbreder, E., 1945. Toward a dynamic psychology of cognition. *Psychol. Rev., 52,* 1–22.

Helson, H., 1959. Adaptation level theory. In S. Koch (Ed.), *Psychology: A Study of a Science.* Vol. I. New York: McGraw-Hill.

Helson, H., 1964 a. Current trends and issues in adaptation level theory. *Amer. Psychologist, 19,* 26–38.

Helson, H., 1964 b. *Adaptation Level Theory: An Experimental and Systematic Approach to Behavior.* New York: Harper & Row.

Hemphill, J. K., 1961. Why people attempt to lead. In L. Petrullo and B. M. Bass (Eds.), *Leadership and Interpersonal Behavior.* New York: Holt, Rinehart and Winston, 201–215.

Hersey, J., 1946. *Hiroshima.* New York: Knopf.

Herskovits, M. J., 1949. *Man and His Works.* New York: Knopf.

Higham, T. M., 1951. The experimental study of the transmission of rumor. *Brit. J. Psychol.* (general section), *42,* 42–55.

Hill, V. T., 1952. The spread of reaction of insecure and "normal" individuals in the autokinetic situation. University of Oklahoma.

Himmelweit, Hilde, 1950. Frustration and aggression: A review of recent experimental work. In T. H. Pear (Ed.), *Psychological Factors of Peace and War.* New York: Philosophical Library, 159–192.

Hinckley, E. D., 1932. The influence of individual opinion on construction of an attitude scale. *J. soc. Psychol., 37,* 283–296.

Hinckley, E. D., and Rethlingshafer, D., 1951. Value judgments of heights of men by college students. *J. Psychol., 31,* 257–296.

Hirota, K., 1953. Experimental studies of competition. *Jap. J. Psychol.* (1951), *21,* 70–81. (*Psychological Abstracts* [1953], *27,* 351.)

Hocart, A. M., 1912. The "psychological interpretation of language." *Brit. J. Psychol., 5,* 267–279.

Hoffman, E. L., Swander, D., Baron, S. H., and Rohrer, J. H., 1953. Generalization and exposure time as related to autokinetic movement. *J. exp. Psychol., 46*, 171–177.

Hofstätter, P. R., 1957. *Gruppendynamik: die Kritik der Massenpsychologie.* Hamburg, Germany: Rewohlt.

Holbrook, S. H., 1946. *Iron Brew: A Century of American Ore and Steel.* New York: Macmillan.

Hollander, E. P., 1961. Emergent leadership and social influence. In L. Petrullo and B. M. Bass (Eds.), *Leadership and Interpersonal Behavior.* New York: Holt, Rinehart and Winston, 30–47.

Hollander, E. P., Julian, J. F., and Haaland, G. A., 1965. Conformity process and prior group agreement. *J. pers. soc. Psychol., 2*, 852–858.

Hollander, E. P., and Willis, R. H., 1967. Some current issues in the psychology of conformity and nonconformity. *Psychol. Bull., 68*, 62–76.

Hollingshead, A. B., 1949. *Elmtown's Youth.* New York: Wiley.

Holmberg, A. M., 1946. The Siriono: A study of the effect of hunger frustration on the culture of a semi-nomadic Bolivian Indian tribe. Ph.D. thesis, Yale University.

Holt, R. R., 1945. Effects of ego-involvement upon levels ·of aspiration. *Psychiatry, 3*, 299–317.

Holtzman, W. H., 1961. *Holtzman Inkblot Tests.* Austin: Univer. of Texas Press.

Holtzman, W. H., 1965. Cross-cultural research on personality development. *Human Develpm., 8*, 65–86.

Holyoke, G. J., 1893. *The Rochdale Pioneers.* New York: Scribner.

Homans, G. C., 1950. *The Human Group.* New York: Harcourt, Brace & World.

Hood, W. R., and Sherif, M., 1955. Appraisal of personality-oriented approaches to prejudice. *Sociol. & soc. Res., 40*, 79–85.

Hood, W. R., and Sherif, M., 1962. Verbal report and judgment of an unstructured stimulus. *J. Psychol., 54*, 121–130.

Hopkins, T. K., 1964. *The Exercise of Influence in Small Groups.* Totawa, N.J.: The Bedminster Press.

Horowitz, E. L., 1936. The development of attitudes toward Negroes. *Arch. Psychol., No. 194.*

Horowitz, E. L., and Horowitz, Ruth E., (See also Hartley, E. L., and Hartley, Ruth E.), 1938. Development of social attitudes in children. *Sociometry, 1*, 301–308.

Horowitz, Ruth E., 1939. Racial aspects of self-identification in nursery school children. *J. Psychol., 7*, 91–99.

Horrocks, J. E., 1963. *The Psychology of Adolescence.* Boston: Houghton Mifflin.

Hovland, C. I., 1959. Reconciling conflicting results derived from experimental and survey studies of attitude change. *Amer. Psychologist, 14*, 8–17.

Hovland, C. I., Harvey, O. J., and Sherif, M., 1957.

Assimilation and contrast effects in reactions to communication and attitude change. *J. abnorm. soc. Psychol. 55*, 244–252.

Hovland, C. I., Janis, I. L., and Kelley, H. H., 1953. *Communication and Persuasion.* New Haven: Yale Univer. Press.

Hovland, C. I., and Pritzker, H. A., 1957. Extent of opinion change as a function of amount of change advocated. *J. abnorm. soc. Psychol., 54*, 257–261.

Hovland, C. I., and Sherif, M., 1952. Judgmental phenomena and scales of attitude measurement: Item displacement in Thurstone scales. *J. abnorm. soc. Psychol., 47*, 822–832.

Hovland, C. I., and Weiss, W., 1951. The influence of source credibility on communication effectiveness. *Public Opin. Quart., 15*, 635–650.

Hull, C. L., 1920. Quantitative aspects of the evolution of concepts: An experimental study. *Psychol. Monogr., 28*, No. 123.

Hunt, J. L., and Pringle, A. G., 1943. *Service Slang.* London.

Hunt, W. A., 1941. Anchoring effects in judgment. *Amer. J. Psychol., 54*, 395–403.

Hyman, H. H., 1942. The psychology of status. *Arch. Psychol., No. 269.*

Hyman, H. H., and Sheatsley, P. B., 1947. Some reasons why information campaigns fail. *Publ. Opin. Quart., 11*, 412–423.

Hyman, H. H., and Sheatsley, P. B., 1964. Attitudes toward desegregation. *Scient. Amer., 211* (July), 2–9.

Inhelder, Bärbel, and Piaget, J., 1958. *The Growth of Logical Thinking from Childhood to Adolescence.* New York: Basic Books.

Inhelder, Bärbel, and Piaget, J., 1964. *The Early Growth of Logic in the Child.* New York: Harper & Row.

Ittelson, W. H., 1960. *Visual Space Perception.* New York: Springer.

Ittelson, W. H., and Cantril, H., 1954. *Perception: A Transactional Approach.* New York: Doubleday.

Jackson, J., 1965. Structural characteristics of norms. In I. D. Steiner and M. Fishbein (Eds.), *Current Studies in Social Psychology.* New York: Holt, Rinehart and Winston, 301–309.

Jacobs, R. C., and Campbell, D. T., 1961. The perpetuation of an arbitrary tradition through several generations of a laboratory microculture. *J. abnorm. soc. Psychol., 62*, 649–658.

Jahoda, G., 1961. *White Man.* London: Oxford Univer. Press.

Jahoda, Marie, and Warren, A., 1966. *Attitudes: Selected Readings.* Baltimore: Penguin.

James, W., 1890. *The Principles of Psychology.* New York: Holt, Rinehart and Winston.

Jamous, H., and Lemaine, G., 1962. Compétition entre groupes d'inégales ressources: Expérience dans cadre naturel, premier travaux. *Psychologie franç.* **7**, 216–222.

Janis, I. L., 1962. Psychological effects of warnings. In G. Baker and D. W. Chapman (Eds.), *Man and Society in Disaster.* New York: Basic Books, 55–92.

Janis, I. L., and Field, P. B., 1959. Sex differences and personality factors related to persuasibility. In C. I. Hovland and I. L. Janis, *Personality and Persuasibility.* New Haven: Yale Univer. Press, Ch. 3.

Janis, I. L., and King, B. T., 1954. The influence of role playing in opinion change. *J. abnorm. soc. Psychol.,* **49**, 211–218.

Jenkins, W. O., 1947. A review of leadership studies with particular reference to military problems. *Psychol. Bull.,* **44**, 54–87.

Jennings, Helen H., 1950. *Leadership and Isolation. A Study of Personality in Inter-personal Relations.* (2nd ed.). New York: McKay.

Jespersen, O., 1923. *Language, Its Nature, Development and Origin.* New York: Holt, Rinehart and Winston.

Johnson, C. S., 1941, 1967. *Growing up in the Black Belt: Negro Youth in the Rural South.* New York: Schocken Books.

Johnson, D. M., 1955. *The Psychology of Thought and Judgment.* New York: Harper & Row.

Johnson, H. H., 1966. Some effects of discrepancy level on responses to negative information about one's self. *Sociometry,* **29**, 52–66.

Johnson, H. M., 1960. *Sociology: A Systematic Introduction.* New York: Harcourt, Brace & World.

Jones, E. E., and Aneshansel, Jane, 1965. The learning and utilization of contravaluant material. In H. Proshansky and B. Seidenberg (Eds.). *Basic Studies in Social Psychology.* New York: Holt, Rinehart and Winston, 39–47.

Jones, L. W., 1965. The new world view of Negro youth. In M. Sherif and Carolyn W. Sherif (Eds.), *Problems of Youth: Transition to Adulthood in a Changing World.* Chicago: Aldine.

Jones, L. W., and Long, H. H., 1965. The Negotiation of Segregation in Ten Southern Cities. Nashville: Race Relations Department of the American Missionary Assn., Fisk University (mimeographed).

Jordan, N., 1964. The mythology of the non-obvious—autism or fact? *Contemporary Psychol.,* **9**, 141–142.

Jourard, S. M., and Secord, P. F., 1955. Body-cathexis and the ideal female figure. *J. abnorm. soc. Psychol.,* **50**, 243–246.

Kamano, D. K., and Drew, Janet E., 1961. Selectivity in memory of personally significant material. *J. gen. Psychol.,* **65**, 25–32.

Kaplan, B., 1954. A study of Rorschach responses in four cultures. Cambridge, Mass.: *Papers of the Peabody Museum of American Archaeology and Ethnology,* Harvard University, CLII, No. 2.

Kaplan, B., 1961. Cross cultural use of projective techniques. In F. L. K. Hsu (Ed.), *Psychological Anthropology.* Homewood, Ill.: Dorsey Press, Ch. 8.

Katz, Daniel, and Allport, F. H., 1931. *Students' Attitudes.* Syracuse, N.Y.: Craftsman Press.

Katz, Daniel, and Braly, K., 1932. Racial stereotypes of one-hundred college students. *J. abnorm. soc. Psychol.,* **28**, 280–290.

Katz, David, 1950. *Gestalt Psychology.* New York: Ronald Press.

Katz, E., 1965. The two-step flow of communication: An up-to-date report on an hypothesis. In H. Proshansky and B. Seidenberg (Eds.), *Basic Studies in Social Psychology.* New York: Holt, Rinehart and Winston, 196–209.

Katz, E., and Feldman, J. J., 1962. The debates in light of research: A survey of surveys. In S. Kraus (Ed.), *The Great Debates.* Bloomington: Indiana Univer. Press, 173–223.

Katz, E., and Lazarsfeld, P. F., 1955. *Personal Influence: The Part Played by People in the Flow of Mass Communications.* New York: Free Press.

Kelley, H. H., 1950. The warm-cold variable in first impressions of persons. *J. Pers.,* **18**, 431–439.

Kelley, H. H., 1952, 1965. Two functions of reference groups. In G. E. Swanson, T. M. Newcomb, and E. L. Hartley (Eds.), *Readings in Social Psychology* (rev. ed.), and H. Proshansky and B. Seidenberg (Eds.), *Basic Studies in Social Psychology.* New York: Holt, Rinehart and Winston.

Kelley, H. H., Condry, J. C., Jr., Dahlke, A. E., and Hill, A. H., 1965. Collective behavior in a simulated panic situation. *J. exp. soc. Psychol.,* **1**, 20–54.

Kelley, H. H., Hovland, C. I., Schwartz, M., and Abelson, R. P., 1955. The influence of judges' attitudes in three methods of scaling. *J. soc. Psychol.,* **42**, 147–158.

Kelley, H. H., and Shapiro, M. M., 1954. Conformity to group norms. *Amer. sociol. Rev.,* **19**, 667–677.

Kelley, H. H., and Thibaut, J. W., 1954. Experimental studies of group problem solving and process. In G. Lindzey (Ed.), *Handbook of Social Psychology.* Reading, Mass.: Addison-Wesley, 735–785.

Kellog, W. N., and Kellog, L. A., 1933. *The Ape and the Child.* New York: McGraw-Hill.

Kelman, H., 1950. Effects of success and failure on "suggestibility" in the autokinetic situation. *J. abnorm. soc. Psychol.,* **45**, 267–285.

Kerrick, Jean S., and McMillan, D. H., 1961. The effects of instructional set on the measurement of attitude change through communication. *J. soc. Psychol.,* **53**, 113–120.

Ketchum, J. D., 1965. *Ruhleben: A Prison Camp Society.* Toronto, Canada: Univer. of Toronto Press.

Key, V. O., Jr., 1960. The politically relevant in surveys. *Public Opin. Quart.,* **24** (Spring) 54–61.

Keys, A., Brozek, J., Henschel, A., Mickelsen, O., and Taylor, H. L., 1945. *Experimental Starvation in Man.* Laboratory of Physiological Hygiene, University of Minnesota.

Kidd, J. S., and Campbell, D. T., 1955. Conformity to groups as a function of group success. *J. abnorm. soc. Psychol.,* **51**, 390–393.

Killian, L. M., 1952. The significance of multiple-group membership in disaster. *Amer. J. Sociol.,* **57**, 309–317. Also in H. Proshansky and B. Seidenberg, 1965, 505–510.

Killian, L. M., 1962. Leadership in the desegregation crisis: An institutional analysis. In M. Sherif (Ed.), *Intergroup Relations and Leadership.* New York: Wiley, 142–166.

Killian, L. M., 1968. *The Impossible Revolution? Black Power and The American Dream.* New York: Random House.

Killian, L. M., and Grigg, C., 1964. *Racial Crisis in America: Leadership in Conflict.* Englewood Cliffs, N.J.: Prentice-Hall.

Kilpatrick, K. P. (Ed.), 1952. *Human Behavior from the Transactional Point of View.* Hanover, N.H.: Institute for Associated Research.

King, B., and Janis, I., 1956. Comparison of the effectiveness of improvised vs. non-improvised role playing in producing opinion change. *Human Relat.,* **9**, 177–186.

King, M. L., Jr., 1964. *Why We Can't Wait.* New York: Signet.

King, M. L., Jr., 1964. Letter from Birmingham's jail. In B. Daniel (Ed.), *Black, White and Gray.* New York: Sheed & Ward, 62–80.

King, M. L., Jr., 1968. The role of the behavioral scientist in the civil rights movement. *Amer. Psychologist,* **23**, 180–186.

Kintz, B. L., Delprato, D. J., Metter, D. R., Persons, C. E., and Scheppe, R. H., 1965. The experimenter effect. *Psychol. Bull.,* **63**, 223–232.

Kiray, Mübeccel B., 1964. *Ereğli.* Ankara, Turkey: State Planning Organization.

Klineberg, O., 1950. *Tensions Affecting International Understanding.* New York: Social Science Res. Council Bull. 62.

Klineberg, O., 1954. *Social Psychology* (rev.). New York: Holt, Rinehart and Winston.

Klineberg, O., 1964. *Human Dimension in International Relations.* New York: Wiley.

Klineberg, O., 1965. The place of social psychology in a University. In O. Klineberg, and R. Christie (Eds.), *Perspectives in Social Psychology.* New York: Holt, Rinehart and Winston.

Klapper, J. T., 1960. *The Effects of Mass Communication.* New York: Free Press.

Klapper, J. T., 1967. Mass communication, attitude stability and change. In Carolyn W. Sherif and M. Sherif (Eds.), *Attitude, Ego-involvement and Change.* New York: Wiley, 297–310.

Klein, G. S., and Schoenfeld, N., 1941. The influence of ego-involvement on confidence. *J. abnorm. soc. Psychol.,* **36**, 249–258.

Koffka, K., 1922. Perception: An introduction to Gestalt-theorie. *Psychol. Bull.,* **19**, 531–585.

Koffka, K., 1935. *Principles of Gestalt Psychology.* New York: Harcourt, Brace & World.

Kohlberg, L., 1963. Moral development and identification. In National Society for Study of Education, 62nd Yearbook: *Child Psychology.* Chicago: Univer. of Chicago Press.

Köhler, W., 1929. *Gestalt Psychology.* New York: Liveright.

Köhler, W., 1938. *Dynamics in Psychology.* New York: Liveright.

Kornhauser, A., and Sheatsley, P. B., 1961. Questionnaire construction and interview procedure. In Claire Selltiz, Marie Jahoda, M. Deutsch, and S. W. Cook (Eds.), *Research Methods in Social Relations* (rev.). New York: Holt, Rinehart and Winston, 546–587.

Koslin, B. L., 1966. Personal communication.

Koslin, B. L., Haarlow, R. N. Karlins, M., and Pargament, R., 1968. Predicting group status from members' cognitions. *Sociometry,* **31**, No. 1, 64–75.

Koslin, B. L., Waring, P. D., and Pargament, R., 1965. Measurement of attitude organization with the "own category" technique. Prepublication report, Princeton University (mimeographed).

Krasner, L., Ullmann, L. F., Weiss, R. L., and Collins, Beverly J., 1961. Responsitivity to verbal conditioning as a function of three different examiners. *J. clin. Psychol.,* **17**, 411–415.

Krech, D., Crutchfield, R. S., and Ballachey, E. L., 1962. *Individual in Society.* New York: McGraw-Hill.

Kroeber, A. L., 1919. On the principle of order in civilization as exemplified by changes of fashion. *Amer. Anthropologist,* **21**, 235–263. (Bobbs-Merrill Reprint Series in Social Science A-137.)

Krugman, H. E., 1966–7. The measurement of advertising involvement. *Publ. Opin. Quart.,* **30** (Winter), 583–596.

Kubany, A. J., 1953. A validation study of the error-choice technique using attitudes on national health insurance. *Educ. & Psychol. Measmt.,* **13**, 157–163.

Kuhn, M. H., and McPartland, T. S., 1954. An empirical investigation of self-attitudes. *Amer. sociol. Rev.,* **19**, 68–76.

Külpe, O., 1904. Versuche über Abstraktion. *Bericht über den I. Kongress für experimentelle Psychologie,* 56–68.

Labrousse, C. E., 1956. Panoramas de la crise. In C. E. Labrousse (Ed.), *Aspects de la crise et de la depression de l'economic française au milieu du XIXe siecle*. La Roch-sur-Yon: Imprimerie Centrale de l'Ouest.

La Fave, L., 1961. Humor judgments as a function of reference groups: An experimental study. Ph.D. thesis, University of Oklahoma (Dissert. Abstr., **22**, 1284).

La Fave, L., and Sherif, M., 1968. Reference scale and placement of items with the Own Categories Technique. *J. soc. Psychol.*, **76**, 75–82.

La Fave, L., Szczesiak, R., Yaquinto, J., Adler, B., 1963. Connotation as a supplemental variable to assimilation-contrast principles in psychosocial scales. Fuller report of paper presented at the Annual Meeting of the American Psychological Association, Philadelphia (mimeographed).

Lambert, W. E., Libman, Eva, and Poser, E. G., 1960. The effect of increased salience of a membership group on pain tolerance. *J. Pers.*, **28**, 350–357.

Lang, Olga, 1946. *Chinese Family and Society*. New Haven: Yale Univer. Press.

LaPiere, R. T., 1934. Attitudes versus action. *Soc. Forces*, **13**, 230–237.

Larimer, G., 1966. Social judgment approach to the investigation of French and English Canadian attitudes. Paper presented at the Annual Meeting of the Eastern Psychological Association, New York.

Lawrence, P. R., Bailey, J. C., Katz, R. L., Seiler, J. A., Orth, C. D., Clark, J. U., Barnes, L. B., and Turner, A. N., 1961. *Organizational Behavior and Administration. Cases, Concepts and Research Findings*. Homewood, Ill.: Dorsey Press.

Lazarsfeld, P. F., Berelson, B., and Gaudet, Hazel, 1948. *The People's Choice*. New York: Columbia Univer. Press.

Le Bon, G., 1895. *The Crowd*. London: T. Fisher Unwin, 1914 edition. New York: Viking Press, 1960 edition.

Lee, A. M., 1955. *Fraternities Without Brotherhood*. Boston: Beacon Press.

Lee, A. M., and Humphrey, N. D., 1943. *Race Riot*. New York: Holt, Rinehart and Winston.

Leeper, R. W., 1948. A motivational theory of emotion to replace "emotion as disorganized response." *Psychol. Rev.*, **55**, 5–21.

Lefcourt, H. M., and Ladwig, G. W., 1965. The effect of reference group upon Negroes' task persistence in a biracial competitive game. *J. pers. soc. Psychol.*, **1**, 668–671.

Leibowitz, H. W., 1965. *Visual Perception*. New York: Macmillan.

Lenneberg, E. H., 1967. *Biological Foundations of Language*. New York: Wiley.

Leuba, C. J., 1933. An experimental study of rivalry in young children. *J. comp. Psychol.*, **16**, 367–378.

Levine, J., and Butler, J., 1953. Lecture vs. group decision in changing behavior. In D. Cartwright and A. Zander (Eds.) *Group Dynamics: Research and Theory*. New York: Harper & Row.

Levine, J. M., and Murphy, G., 1943. The learning and forgetting of controversial material. *J. abnorm. soc. Psychol.*, **38**, 507–517.

Levine, R., Chein, I., and Murphy, G., 1942. The relation of the intensity of a need to the amount of perceptual distortion. *J. Psychol.*, **13**, 283–293.

Lewin, K., 1935. *Dynamic Theory of Personality*. New York: McGraw-Hill.

Lewin, K., 1947, 1965. Group decision and social change. In H. Proshansky and B. Seidenberg (Eds.), *Basic Studies in Social Psychology*. New York: Holt, Rinehart and Winston, 423–436.

Lewin, K., 1948. *Resolving Social Conflicts*. New York: Harper & Row.

Lewin, K., Dembo, T., Festinger, L., and Sears, P. S., 1944. Level of aspiration. In J. McV. Hunt (Ed.), *Personality and the Behavior Disorders*. New York: Ronald Press.

Lewin, K., Lippitt, R., and White, R. K., 1939. Patterns of aggressive behavior in experimentally created "social climates." *J. soc. Psychol.*, **10**, 271–299.

Lewin, K., Lippitt, R., White, R. K., 1965. An experimental study of leadership and group life. In H. Proshansky, and B. Seidenberg (Eds.), *Basic Studies in Social Psychology*. New York: Holt, Rinehart and Winston, 523–537. Also in G. E. Swanson, T. M. Newcomb, and E. L. Hartley (Eds.), 1952. *Readings in Social Psychology*. New York: Holt, Rinehart and Winston.

Lewis, M. M., 1936. *Infant Speech*. New York: Harcourt, Brace & World.

Lewis, M. M., 1948. *Language in Society, the Linguistic Revolution and Social Change*. New York: Social Sciences Publishers.

Lewis, M. M., 1963. *Language, Thought and Personality in Infancy and Childhood*. New York: Basic Books.

Lewis, O., 1942. The effects of white contact upon Blackfoot culture. *Monogr. Amer. Ethnolog. Soc.*, **6**.

Life, 1963. The point of no return for everybody—Automation: its impact suddenly shakes up the whole U.S. July 19, 68A–88.

Likert, R., 1932. A technique for the measurement of attitudes. *Arch. Psychol.*, No. 140.

Lincoln, C. E., 1961. *The Black Muslims in America*. Boston: Beacon Press.

Lindesmith, A. R., and Strauss, A., 1950. Critique of culture-personality writings. *Amer. Sociol. Rev.*, **15**, 587–599.

Lindesmith, A. R., and Strauss, A. L., 1956, 1968. *Social Psychology* (2nd and 3rd eds.). New York: Holt, Rinehart and Winston.

Lindgren, E. J., 1938. An example of culture contact without conflict. *Amer. Anthropologist,* **40**, 605–621.

Lindsey, Almont, 1942. *The Pullman Strike.* Chicago: Univer. of Chicago Press.

Lindzey, G., 1961. *Projective Techniques and Cross-Cultural Research.* New York: Appleton-Century-Crofts.

Linton, R. (Ed.), 1940. *Acculturation in Seven American Indian Tribes.* New York: Appleton-Century-Crofts.

Linton, R., 1945. *The Cultural Background of Personality.* New York: Appleton-Century-Crofts.

Lippmann, W., 1922. *Public Opinion.* Baltimore: Penguin.

Lipset, S. M., and Bendix, R., 1959. *Social Mobility in Industrial Society.* Berkeley: Univer. of California Press.

Lomax, Louis E., 1962. *The Negro Revolt.* New York: New American Library.

Lorenz, K., 1963. *On Aggression.* New York: Harcourt, Brace & World.

Los Angeles Times, 1965. Protest march canceled..September 3, p. 3.

Lott, A. J., and Lott, Bernice E., 1965. Group cohesiveness as interpersonal attraction: A review of relationships with antecedent and consequent variables. *Psychol. Bull.,* **64**, 259–309.

Lowie, R. H., 1925. *Primitive Society.* New York: Liveright.

Lowin, A., 1967. Approach and avoidance: Alternate modes of selective exposure to information. *J. Pers. soc. Psychol.,* **6**, 1–9.

Luchins, A. S., 1945. Social influences on perception of complex drawings. *J. soc. Psychol.,* **21**, 257–273.

Luchins, A. S., 1950. The stimulus field in social psychology. *Psychol. Rev.,* **57**, 27–30.

Luchins, A. S., 1960. Influence of experience with conflicting information on reactions to subsequent conflicting information. *J. soc. Psychol.,* **51**, 367–385.

Luchins, A. S., and Luchins, Edith H., 1955. On conformity with true and false communications. *J. soc. Psychol.,* **42**, 283–305.

Luchins, A. S., and Luchins, Edith H., 1961. On conformity with judgments of a majority or an authority. *J. soc. Psychol.,* **53**, 303–316.

Luchins, A. S., and Luchins, Edith H., 1963 a. Effects of order of evidence on social influences on judgment. *J. soc. Psychol.,* **61**, 345–363.

Luchins, A. S., and Luchins, Edith H., 1963 b. Half views and the autokinetic effect. *Psychol. Rec.,* **13**, No. 4, 415–444.

Luria, A. R., 1961. *The Role of Speech in the Regulation of Normal and Abnormal Behavior.* New York: Liveright.

Luria, A. R., 1965. *Higher Cortical Functions in Man.* New York: Consultants Bureau.

Luria, A. R., 1966. *Human Brain and Psychological Processes.* New York: Harper & Row.

Lynd, R. S., and Lynd, Helen M., 1937. *Middletown in Transition.* New York: Harcourt, Brace & World.

McCarthy, Dorothea, 1946. Language development in children. In L. Carmichael (Ed.), *Manual of Child Psychology.* New York: Wiley (rev. ed., 1954).

McClelland, D. C., 1965. N achievement and entrepreneurship: A longitudinal study. *J. pers. soc. Psychol.,* **1**, 389–392.

McClelland, D. C., Atkinson, J. W., Clark, R. A., and Lowell, E. L., 1953. *The Achievement Motive.* New York: Appleton-Century-Crofts.

Maccoby, Eleanor E., 1965. The choice of variables in the study of socialization. In I. D. Steiner and M. Fishbein (Eds.), *Current Studies in Social Psychology.* New York: Holt, Rinehart and Winston, 56–68.

McCord, F., 1948. The formation of group norms. *J. soc. Psychol.,* **27**, 3–15.

MacCrone, I. D., 1937. *Race Attitudes in South Africa.* London: Oxford Univer. Press.

McGehee, W., 1940. Judgment and the level of aspiration. *J. gen. Psychol.,* **22**, 3–15.

McGranahan, D. V., 1936. The psychology of language. *Psychol. Bull.,* **33**, 178–216.

McGuire, W. J., 1962. Persistence of the resistance to persuasion induced by various types of prior belief defenses. *J. abnorm. soc. Psychol.,* **64**, 241–248.

McGuire, W. J., 1968. Consistency as a key to cognitive structure. In R. P. Abelson *et al* (Eds.), *Cognitive Consistency.* Chicago: Rand McNally.

McGuire, W. J., 1969. Nature of attitudes and attitude change. In G. Lindzey and E. Aronson (Eds.), *Handbook of Social Psychology.* Second Ed. Reading, Mass.: Addison-Wesley.

MacLeod, R. B., 1965. Foreword and postscript. In J. D. Ketchum, *Ruhleben: A Prison Camp Society.* Toronto, Canada: Univer. of Toronto Press.

MacNeil, M. K., 1965. Norm change over subject generations as a function of arbitrariness of prescribed norms. Master's thesis, University of Oklahoma. One of the series directed by M. Sherif with N.S.F. support.

MacNeil, M. K., 1967. Power of status in norm formation under differing conditions of group solidarity. Ph.D. thesis, University of Oklahoma.

McNemar, Q., 1946. Opinion—attitude methodology. *Psychol. Bull.,* **43**, 289–374.

McNickle, D'Arcy, 1937. Indian and European: Indian-white relations from discovery to 1887. *Ann. Amer. Acad. Pol. Soc. Sci.* **311**, 1–11.

Malcolm X, 1964. *The Autobiography of Malcolm X*. New York: Grove Press.

Malcolm X, 1965. *Malcolm X Speaks*. New York: Grove Press.

Maier, N. F., and Schneirla, T. C., 1963. *Principles of Animal Psychology*. (PB: New York: Dover, rev. ed.)

Malinowski, B., 1922. Argonauts of the Western Pacific. London: Routledge.

Malinowski, B., 1930. The problem of meaning in primitive languages. In C. K. Ogden and I. A. Richards, *The Meaning of Meaning*. New York: Harcourt, Brace & World.

Malinowski, B., 1945. *The Dynamics of Social Change: An Inquiry into Race Relations in Africa*. New Haven: Yale Univer. Press.

Manheim, H. L., 1960. Intergroup interaction as related to status and leadership differences between groups. *Sociometry*, **23**, 415–427.

Manis, M., 1960. The interpretation of opinion statements as a function of recipient attitude. *J. abnorm. soc. Psychol.*, **60**, 360–364.

Mann, R. D., 1959. A review of the relationship between personality and performance in small groups. *Psychol. Bull.*, **56**, 241–270.

March, J. G., 1954. Group norms and the active minority. *Amer. sociol. Rev.*, **19**, 733–740.

March, J. G. (Ed.), 1965. *Handbook of Organizations*. Chicago: Rand McNally.

March, J. G., and Simon, H. A., 1958. *Organizations*. New York: Wiley.

Marks, E., 1943. Skin color judgments of Negro college students. *J. abnorm. soc. Psychol.*, **38**, 370–376.

Marks, E. S., 1949. The undecided voter. In F. Mosteller, H. Hyman, P. J. McCarthy, E. S. Marks, and D. B. Truman (Eds.), *The Pre-election Polls of 1948: Report to the Committee on Analysis of Pre-election Polls and Forecasts*. Soc. Sci. Res. Council Bull; **60**, 263–289.

Marquis, D. P., 1941. Learning in the neonate: The modification of behavior under three feeding schedules. *J. exp. Psychol.*, **29**, 263–281.

Marx, K., 1964. The notion of alienation. Excerpted from *The German Ideology: The Political-Economic Manuscript* and *Economic Studies from Marx's Notebook*. In L. A. Coser and B. Rosenberg (Eds.), *Sociological Theory: A Book of Readings*. New York: Macmillan.

Masuoka, J., 1936. Race preference in Hawaii. *Amer. J. Sociol.*, **41**, 635–641.

Mathiez, A., 1929. *The French Revolution*. New York: Knopf.

Mausner, B., 1953. Studies in social interaction: III. Effect of variation in one partner's prestige on the interaction of observer pairs. *J. appl. Psychol.*, **37**, 391–394.

Mausner, B., 1954 a. The effect of prior reinforcement on the interaction of observer pairs. *J. abnorm. soc. Psychol.*, **49**, 65–68.

Mausner, B., 1954 b. The effect of one partner's success in a relevant task on the interaction of observer pairs. *J. abnorm. soc. Psychol.*, **49**, 557–560.

Mausner, B., 1960. The effect of instructed bias on judges in a Thurstone scale construction. Graduate School of Public Health, University of Pittsburgh (mimeographed).

Mead, G. H., 1913. The social self. *J. Philos.*, 374–380.

Mead, G. H., 1934. *Mind, Self and Society: From the Standpoint of a Social Behaviorist*. Chicago: Univer. of Chicago Press.

Mead, Margaret, 1933. The primitive child. In C. Murchison (Ed.), *Handbook of Child Psychology*. Worcester, Mass.: Clark Univer. Press.

Mead, Margaret (Ed.), 1937. *Cooperation and Competition Among Primitive Peoples*. New York: McGraw-Hill.

Meenes, M. A., 1943. A comparison of racial stereotypes in 1935 and 1942. *J. soc. Psychol.*, **17**, 327–336.

Melton, A. W., 1956. Present accomplishments and future trends in problem solving and learning theory. *Amer. Psychologist*, **11**, 278–281.

Meltzer, H., 1939. Group differences in nationality and race preferences of children. *Sociometry*, **2**, 86–105.

Merei, F., 1949. Group leadership and institutionalization. *Human Relat.*, **2**, 23–29.

Merker, F., 1904. *Die Masai*. Berlin: Dietrich Reimer.

Merrill, M. H., 1964. The constitution and civil rights. *Sooner Magazine*. (Norman: Univer. of Oklahoma Assn.) March, 10–13.

Merton, R. K., 1946. *Mass Persuasion*. New York: Harper & Row.

Merton, R. K., 1949. Patterns of influence: A study of interpersonal influence of communications behavior in a local community. In P. F. Lazarsfeld and F. N. Stanton (Eds.), *Communications Research, 1948–1949*. New York: Harper & Row, 180–219.

Merton, R. K., 1957. *Social Theory and Social Structure* (rev. ed.). New York: Free Press.

Merton, R. K., 1960. The ambivalences of Le Bon's *The Crowd*: Introduction to *Compass* edition of G. Le Bon, *The Crowd: A Study of the Popular Mind*. New York: Viking.

Miligram, S., 1963. Behavioral study of obedience. *J. abnorm. soc. Psychol.*, **67**, 371–378.

Milgram, S., 1965. Some conditions of obedience and disobedience to authority. In I. D. Steiner and M. Fishbein (Eds.), *Current Studies in Social Psychology*. New York: Holt, Rinehart and Winston, 243–262.

Miller, H. P., 1964. *Rich Man, Poor Man*. New York: Thomas Y. Crowell, 1–13 and 37–55.

Miller, G. A., 1956. The magic number 7 plus or minus 2. *Psychol. Rev.*, **63**, 81–97.

Miller, G. A., 1962. *Psychology: The Science of Mental Life.* New York: Harper & Row.

Miller, J. C., 1943. *Origins of the American Revolution.* Boston: Little, Brown.

Miller, J. C., 1948. *The Triumph of Freedom.* Boston: Little, Brown.

Miller, N., 1965. Involvement and dogmatism as inhibitors of attitude change. *J. exp. soc. Psychol.,* **1**, 121–132.

Miller, W., and Ervin, Susan, 1964. The development of grammar in child language. In Ursula Bellugi and R. Brown (Eds.), *The Acquisition of Language. Monogr. Soc. Res. Child Devel."opm., 29*, No. 1, Serial No. 92.

Montagu, A., 1951. *Statement on Race.* New York: Abelard-Schuman.

Moore, B., 1955. Educational facilities and financial assistance for graduate students in psychology: 1955–56. *Amer. Psychologist,* **10**, No. 1, 1–21.

Moreno, J. L., 1953. *Who Shall Survive?* (rev. ed). Boston: Beacon Press.

Morland, J. K., 1966. A comparison of race awareness in northern and southern children. *Amer. J. Orthopsychiat.* **36**, No. 1, 22–31.

Morrow, E. F., 1963. *Black Man in the White House.* New York: Coward-McCann.

Moscovici, S., 1967. Comunication processes and the properties of language. In L. Berkowitz (Ed.), *Advances in Experimental Social Psychology.* New York: Academic Press, 225–270.

Mouzelis, N. P., 1967. *Organization and Bureaucracy: An Analysis of Modern Theories.* Chicago: Aldine.

Munsterberg, H., 1923. *On the Witness Stand: Essays on Psychology of Crime.* New York: Boardman.

Murphy, G., 1947. *Personality: A Biosocial Approach to Origins and Structure.* New York: Harper & Row.

Murphy, G., 1953. *In the Minds of Men.* New York: Basic Books.

Murphy, G., and Hochberg, J., 1951. Perceptual development: Some tentative hypotheses. *Psychol. Rev., 58*, 332–349.

Murphy, G., and Murphy, Lois B., 1931. *Experimental Social Psychology.* New York: Harper & Row.

Murphy, G., Murphy, Lois B., and Newcomb, T. M., 1937. *Experimental Social Psychology.* (2nd ed.) New York: Harper & Row.

Murphy, Lois B., 1937. *Social Behavior and Child Personality.* New York: Columbia Univer. Press.

Murray, H. A., 1938. *Explorations in Personality.* New York: Oxford.

Murray, H. A., 1943. *Thematic Apperception Test Manual.* Cambridge, Mass.: Harvard Univer. Press.

National Advisory Commission on Civil Disorders, 1968. *U.S. Riot Commission Report.* New York: Bantam Books.

Neal, A. G., and Rettig, S., 1967. On the multidimensionality of alienation. *Amer. Sociol. Rev.,* **32**, 54–64.

Nehru, J., 1941. *Toward Freedom.* New York: John Day. (PB: Boston: Beacon, 1958.)

Nettler, G., 1957. A measure of alienation. *Amer. Sociol. Rev., 22*, 670–677.

Neugarten, Bernice L., Moore, John W., and Lowe, J. C., 1965. Age norms, age constraints and adult socialization. *Amer. J. Sociol., 70*, 711–717.

New York Times, The. August 9, 1952, 11.

Newcomb, T. M., 1943. *Personality and Social Change.* New York: Holt, Rinehart and Winston.

Newcomb, T. M., 1948. Attitude development as a function of reference groups. In M. Sherif, *An Outline of Social Psychology.* New York: Harper & Row.

Newcomb, T. M., 1950. *Social Psychology.* New York: Holt, Rinehart and Winston.

Newcomb, T. M., Koenig, L. E., Flacks, R., and Warwick, D. P., 1967. *Persistence and Change: Bennington College and Its Students after Twenty-five Years.* New York: Wiley.

Newcomb, T. M., Turner, R. H., and Converse, P. E., 1965. *Social Psychology.* New York: Holt, Rinehart and Winston.

Newman, E. B., 1948. Perception. In E. G. Boring, H. S. Langfeld, and H. P. Weld (Eds.), *Foundations of Psychology.* New York: Wiley.

Newsweek, 1962, 59. April 30, 66–67.

Newsweek, 1965. August 30, 19.

Nixon, R. M., 1964. L. B. J. should debate on TV. *Saturday Evening Post,* June 27, 12–14.

Nkrumah, K., 1961. *I Speak of Freedom.* New York: Praeger.

Norfleet, B., 1948. Interpersonal relations and group productivity. *J. soc. Issues,* **4**, 66–69.

North, R. C., 1962. International conflict and integration: Problems of research. In M. Sherif (Ed.), *Intergroup Relations and Leadership.* New York: Wiley, Ch. 8.

North, R. C., *et al.,* 1963. *Crisis and Crises.* Stanford Today Series, **1**, No. 4.

Nurmi, R., 1966. Judging weight under group pressure. *Scandinavian J. Psychol.,* **7**, No. 1, 31–33.

O'Donovan, D., 1965. Rating extremity: Pathology or meaningfulness? *Psychol. Rev., 72*, 358–372.

Ogburn, W. F., 1964. *On Culture and Social Change: Selected Papers.* Chicago: Univer. of Chicago Press.

Olmstead, J. A., and Blake, R. R., 1955. The use of simulated groups to produce modifications in judgments. *J. Pers., 23*, 335–345.

Olver, Rose R., and Hornsby, Joan P., 1966. On equivalence. In J. S. Bruner (Ed.), *Studies in Cognitive Growth.* New York: Wiley, 68–85.

Opler, M. K., 1940. The Southern Ute of Colorado. In R. Linton (Ed.), *Acculturation in Seven American Indian Tribes.* New York: Appleton-Century-Crofts, 119–206.

Oppenheimer, R., 1956. Analogy in science. *Amer. Psychologist,* **11**, 127–135.

Orne, M. T., 1959. The nature of hypnosis: Artifact and essence. *J. abnorm. soc. Psychol.,* **58**, 277–299.

Orne, M. T., 1960. Antisocial behavior and hypnosis: Problems of control and validation in empirical studies. (Paper presented at Colgate Symposium on Hypnosis.) In G. H. Estabrooks (Ed.), *Hypnosis: Current Problems.* New York: Harper & Row, 137–192.

Orne, M., 1962. On the social psychology of the psychological experiment, with particular reference to demand characteristics and their implications. *Amer. Psychologist.* **17**, 776–783.

Orne, M. T., 1965. Demand characteristics and their implications for real life: The importance of quasi-controls. Paper presented at the Annual Meeting of the American Psychological Association, Chicago.

Orne, M. T., and Evans, F. J., 1965. Social control in the psychological experiment: Antisocial behavior and hypnosis. *J. Pers. soc. Psychol.,* **1**, 189–200.

Orne, M. T., and Scheibe, K. E., 1964. The contribution of nondeprivation factors in the production of sensory deprivation effects: The psychology of the "panic button." *J. abnorm. soc. Psychol.,* **68**, 3–12.

Osgood, C. E., 1962. *An Alternative to War or Surrender.* Urbana: Univer. of Illinois Press.

Osgood, C. E., Suci, G. J., and Tannenbaum, P. H., 1957. *The Measurement of Meaning.* Urbana: Univer. of Illinois Press.

O.S.S. Assessment Staff, 1948. *Assessment of Men.* New York: Holt, Rinehart and Winston.

Page, M. M., and Dahlke, A. E., 1965. Awareness in the classical conditioning of verbal behavior. Paper presented at the Annual Meeting of the Southwestern Psychological Association, Oklahoma City.

Park, R. E., 1949. *Race and Culture.* New York: Free Press.

Park, R. E., and Burgess, E. W., 1921. *Introduction to the Science of Sociology.* Chicago: Univer. of Chicago Press.

Parsons, T., 1960. *Structure and Process in Modern Societies.* New York: Free Press.

Parsons, T., Bales, R. F., and Shils, E. A., 1953. *Working Papers in the Theory of Action.* New York: Free Press.

Parten, M. B., 1932. Social participation among pre-school children. *J. abnorm. soc. Psychol.,* **27**, 243–269.

Parten, M. B., 1933. Social play among pre-school children. *J. abnorm. soc. Psychol.,* **28**, 136–147.

Parten, Mildred, 1950. *Surveys, Polls and Samples: Practical Procedures.* New York: Harper & Row.

Paul, J., and Laulich, J., 1963. *In Your Opinion: Leaders and Voters' Attitudes on Defense and Disarmament.* Vol. I. Clarkson, Ontario: Canadian Peace Research Institute.

Pearl, A., 1965. Youth in lower class settings. In M. Sherif and Carolyn W. Sherif (Eds.), *Problems of Youth: Transition to Adulthood in a Changing World.* Chicago: Aldine, 89–109.

Pelling, H., 1960. *American Labor.* Chicago: Univer. of Chicago Press.

Pelz, Edith B., 1965. Some factors in "group decision." In H. Proshansky and B. Seidenberg (Eds.), *Basic Studies in Social Psychology.* New York: Holt, Rinehart and Winston, 437–443.

Peterson, R. C., and Thurstone, L. L., 1933. *Motion Pictures and Social Attitudes of Children.* New York: Macmillan, 24–25.

Pettigrew, T. F., 1964. *A Profile of the Negro American.* Princeton, N.J.: Van Nostrand.

Piaget, J., 1928. *Judgment and Reasoning in the Child.* New York: Harcourt, Brace & World.

Piaget, J., 1930. *The Child's Conception of Physical Causality.* New York: Harcourt, Brace & World.

Piaget, J., 1932. *The Moral Judgment of the Child.* London: Routledge.

Pierson, D., 1942. *Negroes in Brazil.* Chicago: Univer. of Chicago Press.

Pintner, R., and Forlano, G., 1937. The influence of attitude upon scaling of attitude items. *J. soc. Psychol.,* **8**, 39–45.

Pishkin, V. 1963. Experimenter variable in concept identification feedback of schizophrenics. *Percept. Mot. Skills,* **16**, 921–922.

Pollis, N. P., 1964, 1967, Relative stability of scales formed in individual, togetherness and group situations. (Ph.D. thesis, University of Oklahoma.) *Brit. J. soc. clin. Psychol.,* **6**, 249–255.

Porter, L. W., and Lawler, E. E., III, 1965. Properties of organization structure in relation to job attitudes and job behavior. *Psychol. Bull.,* **64**, 23–51.

Postman, L., and Murphy, G., 1943. The factor of attitude in associative memory. *J. exp. Psychol.,* **33**, 228–238.

Powell, F. A., 1962. Open- and closed-mindedness and the ability to differentiate source and message. *J. abnorm. soc. Psychol.,* **65**, 61–63.

Powell, F. A., 1966. Latitudes of acceptance and rejection and the belief-disbelief dimension: A correlational comparison. *J. pers. soc. Psychol.,* **4**, 453–457.

Prado, W., 1958. Appraisal of performance as a function of the relative ego-involvement of children and adolescents. Ph.D. thesis, University of Oklahoma.

Preyer, W., 1890. *The Mind of the Child: Part II. The Development of the Intellect.* New York: Appleton-Century-Crofts.

Priest, R. F., 1966. Election jokes: The effects of reference group membership. *Psychol. Rep.,* **18**, 600–602.

Proshansky, H., 1943. A projective method for the study of attitudes. *J. abnorm. soc. Psychol.,* **38**, 383–395.

Proshansky, H., and Seidenberg, B. (Eds.), 1965. *Basic Studies in Social Psychology.* New York: Holt, Rinehart and Winston.

Prothro, E. T., and Melikian, L., 1952. Social distance and social change in the Near East. *Sociol. soc. Res.,* **37**, 3–11.

Pyle, E., 1945. *Here Is Your War.* New York: Harcourt, Brace & World.

Pyles, Marjorie K., 1932. Verbalization as a factor in meaning. *Child. Developm.,* **3**, 108–113.

Radcliffe-Brown, A., 1922. *Andaman Islanders.* Cambridge, England: Cambridge Univer. Press.

Radcliffe-Brown, A., 1941. The study of kinship systems: Presidential Address. *J. Royal Anthrop. Inst. of Great Britain and Ireland,* **71**, Parts I and II.

Rafferty, F. T., 1962. Development of a social structure in treatment institutions. *J. nerv. ment. Dis.* **134**, 263–267.

Rafferty, F. T., 1965. Group organization theory and the adolescent inpatient unit. In M. Sherif and Carolyn W. Sherif (Eds.), *Problems of Youth: Transition to Adulthood in a Changing World.* Chicago: Aldine.

Ram, P., and Murphy, G., 1952. Recent investigations of Hindu-Muslim relations in India. *Human Organization,* **11**, 13–16.

Rand, M. A., 1967. An empirical comparison of Sherif's social judgment approach and Festinger's dissonance theory at their points of contrast: Ego-involvement and discrepancy of communication. Ph.D. thesis, University of Oklahoma.

Razran, G. H. S., 1935. Conditioned responses: An experimental study and a theoretical analysis. *Arch. Psychol.,* No. 191, 118.

Reich, J., and Sherif, M., 1963. Ego-involvement as a factor in attitude assessment by the own categories technique. Norman: University of Oklahoma (mimeographed).

Remmers, H. H., 1934. Generalized attitude scales—studies in social psychological measurements. *Bull. Purdue Univ.* **25**, 7–17.

Remmers, H. H., 1960. *Manual for the Purdue Master Attitude Scales.* Lafayette, Ind., Purdue Research Foundation.

Rhine, R. J., 1967. Some problems in dissonance theory research on information selectivity. *Psychol. Bull.,* **68**, 21–28.

Richardson, L. F., 1950. Statistics of deadly quarrels. In T. H. Pear (Ed.), *Psychological Factors of Peace and War.* New York: Philosophical Library.

Riecken, H. W., 1962. A program for research on experiments in social psychology. In N. F. Washburne (Ed.), *Decisions, Values and Groups.* New York: Pergamon Press.

Riley, Matilda, W., 1963. *Sociological Research: I. A Case Approach.* New York: Harcourt, Brace & World.

Rivers, W. H. R., 1924. *History of Melanesian Society.* Vol. I. Cambridge, England: Cambridge Univer. Press.

Rivers, W. H. R., 1926. *Psychology and Ethnology.* London: Routledge.

Rodgers, H. L., Jr., 1968. Reference groups as determinants of the judged credibility of political figures and their position on issues. M.A. thesis, The Pennsylvania State University, 1968.

Roethlisberger, F. J., 1945. The foreman: master and victim of double talk. *Harvard Bus. Rev.,* **23**, 283–298.

Roethlisberger, F. J., and Dickson, W. J., 1939, 1961. *Management and the Worker.* Cambridge, Mass.: Harvard Univer. Press. (PB: Wiley Science Series; New York: Wiley.)

Rogers, E. M., 1962. *Diffusion of Innovations.* New York: Free Press.

Rohrer, J. H., Baron, S. H., Hoffman, E. L., and Swander, D. V., 1954. The stability of autokinetic judgments. *J. abnorm. soc. Psychol.,* **49**, 595–597.

Rokeach, M., 1960. *The Open and Closed Mind.* New York: Basic Books.

Rokeach, M., 1968. A theory of organization and change within value-attitude systems, *J. soc. Issues,* **24**, 13–33.

Rorer, L. G., 1965. The great response style myth. *Psychol. Bull.,* **63**, 129–156.

Rose, A., 1948. *The Negro in America: A Condensation of an American Dilemma.* New York: Harper & Row.

Rosenbaum, M., and Blake, R. R., 1955. Volunteering as a function of field structure. *J. abnorm. soc. Psychol.,* **50**, 193–196.

Rosenberg, M., 1965. *Society and the Adolescent Self-Image.* Princeton, N. J.: Princeton Univer. Press.

Rosenberg, M., 1967. Psychological selectivity in self-esteem formation. In Carolyn W. Sherif and M. Sherif (Eds.), *Attitude, Ego-Involvement and Change.* New York: Wiley, 26–56.

Rosenthal, A. M., and Gelb, A., 1965. *The Night the Lights Went Out.* New York: New American Library.

Rosenthal, R., 1964. Experimenter outcome-orientation and the results of psychological experiments. *Psychol. Bull.* **61**, 405–412.

Rosenthal, R., 1966. *Experimenter Effects in Behavioral Research.* New York: Appleton-Century-Crofts.

Rosenthal, R., and Fode, K. L., 1963. Psychology of the scientist: V. Three experiments in experimenter bias. *Psychol. Rep., 12*, 491–511.

Rosenzweig, S., 1944. *Psychodiagnosis.* New York: Grune & Stratton.

Rosnow, R. L., 1965. Bias in evaluating the presidential debates: A "splinter" effect. *J. soc. Psychol., 67*, 211–219.

Ross, S., and Harmon, Jacqueline J., 1965. Educational facilities and financial assistance for graduate students in psychology: 1965–66. *Amer. Psychologist, 20*, No. 1, 67–90.

Roth, J. A., 1963. *Time Tables: Structuring the Passage of Time in Hospital Treatment and Other Careers.* Indianapolis: Bobbs-Merrill.

Rubin, E., 1921. *Visuell wahrgenommene Figuren: Studien in Psychologische Analyse.* Kobenhavn: Gyldendol.

Rudé, G., 1964. *The Crowd in History* (English translation). New York: Wiley.

Russell, J. G., and Sherif, Carolyn W., 1966. Reference groups of foreign students in the United States and the priority of their problems. Norman, Oklahoma: Institute of Group Relations (mimeographed).

Saenger, G., 1953. *The Social Psychology of Prejudice.* New York: Harper & Row.

St. Petersburg Times, 1966. Tampa Negro leaders warn bi-racial group of unrest. September 24, 12 B.

Salusky, A. S., 1930. Collective behavior of children at a preschool age. *J. soc. Psychol., 1*, 367–378.

Sampson, E. E., and Insko, C. A., 1962. Cognitive consistency and performance in the autokinetic situation. ONR Project Report, December (mimeographed).

Sampson, S. F., 1961. Historical review and critical appraisal of the reference group concept in psychology and sociology. M.A. thesis, University of Oklahoma.

Sampson, S. F., 1968. The effects of selected social relationships on the resolution and maintenance of dissensus in the autokinetic situation. Paper presented to the Annual Convention of the American Sociological Association, Boston, Mass. Based on Crisis in the Cloisters: A Sociological Analysis. Ph.D. thesis, Cornell University, 1968.

Sanford, R. N., 1936. The effects of abstinence from food upon imaginal processes: A preliminary experiment. *J. Psychol., 2*, 129–136.

Sanford, R. N., 1937. The effects of abstinence from food upon imaginal processes: A further experiment. *J. Psychol., 2*, 145–159.

Sapir, E., 1921. *Language. An Introduction to the Study of Speech.* New York: Harcourt, Brace & World.

Sapir, E., 1929. The status of linguistics as a science. *Language, 5*, 207–214.

Sargent, S. S., and Smith, M. W. (Eds.), 1949. *Culture and Personality.* New York: Wenner-Gren Foundation.

Sargent, S. S., and Williamson, R. C., 1966. *Social Psychology.* New York: Ronald Press.

Sayles, L. R., 1952. A case study of union participation and technological change. *Human Organization, 11*, 5–15.

Schneirla, T. C., 1946. Problems in the biopsychology of social organization. *J. abnorm. soc. Psychol., 41*, 385–402.

Schneirla, T. C., 1951. The "levels" concept in the study of social organization in animals. In J. H. Rohrer and M. Sherif (Eds.), *Social Psychology at the Crossroads.* New York: Harper & Row, 83–120.

Schneirla, T. C., 1956. Interrelationships of the "innate" and the "acquired" in instinctive behavior. In *L'Instinct dans le comportement des Animaux et de l'Homme.* Paris: Masson et Cie, 387–452. (Also in Maier, N., and Schneirla, T., 1963, 555–579.)

Schneirla, T. C., 1966. Behavioral development and comparative psychology. *Quart. Rev. Biol., 41*, 283–302.

Schramm, W. (Ed.), 1963. *The Science of Human Communication.* New York: Basic Books.

Schramm, W., and Carter, R. F., 1959. Effectiveness of a political telethon. *Publ. Opin. Quart., 23*, 121–126.

Schranger, S., and Altrocchi, J., 1964. The personality of the perceiver as a factor in person perception. *Psychol. Bull., 62*, 289–308.

Scott, J. P., 1953. Implications of infra-human social behavior for problems of human relations. In M. Sherif and M. O. Wilson (Eds.), *Group Relations at the Crossroads.* New York: Harper & Row.

Scott, J. P., 1958. *Aggression.* Chicago: Univer. of Chicago Press.

Scott, J. P., 1969. Biological basis of human warfare: an interdisciplinary problem. In M. Sherif and Carolyn W. Sherif, (Eds.), *Interdisciplinary Relationships in the Social Sciences.* Chicago: Aldine.

Scott, T. H., Bexton, W. H., Heron, W., and Doane, B. K., 1959. Cognitive effects of perceptual isolation. *Canadian J. Psychol., 13*, 200–209.

Sears, D. O., 1965. Biased indoctrination and selectivity of exposure to new information. *Sociometry, 28*, 363–376.

Sears, D. O., and Freedman, J. L., 1965. Effects of expected familiarity with arguments upon opinion change and selective exposure. *J. pers. soc. Psychol., 2*, 420–426.

Sears, R. R., 1960. The growth of conscience. In I. Iscoe and H. Stevenson (Eds.), *Personality Development in Children*. Austin: Univer. of Texas Press.

Sears, R. R., Maccoby, Eleanor E., and Levin, H., 1957. *Patterns of Child Rearing*. New York: Harper & Row.

Secord, P. F., 1959. Stereotyping and favorableness in the perception of Negro faces. *J. abnorm. soc. Psychol., 59*, 309–315.

Secord, P. F., and Backman, C. W., 1964. *Social Psychology*. New York: McGraw-Hill.

Secord, P. F., Bevan, W., and Katz, Brenda, 1956. The Negro stereotype and perceptual accentuation. *J. abnorm. soc. Psychol., 53*, 78–83.

Secoy, F. R., 1953. Changing military patterns of the great Plains (17th Century through early 19th Century). *Monographs of the American Ethnological Society*. Locust Valley, N.Y.: J. J. Augustin.

Seeleman, V., 1940. The influence of attitude upon remembering of pictorial material. *Arch. Psychol.,* No. 258.

Seeman, M., 1959, 1964. On the meaning of alienation. (*Amer. sociol. Rev., 24*, 783–791.) In L. A. Coser and B. Rosenberg (Eds.), *Sociological Theory: A Book of Readings*. New York: Macmillan.

Segall, M. H., Campbell, D. T., and Herskovits, M. J., 1966. *The Influence of Culture on Visual Perception*. Indianapolis: Bobbs-Merrill.

Segall, M. H., 1965. Anthropology and psychology. In O. Klineberg and R. Christie (Eds.), *Perspectives in Social Psychology*. New York: Holt, Rinehart and Winston, 53–74.

Sells, S. B. (Ed.), 1963. *Stimulus Determinants of Behavior*. New York: Ronald Press.

Selltiz, Claire, Jahoda, Marie, Deutsch, M., and Cook, S. W., 1961. *Research Methods in Social Relations* (rev.). New York: Holt, Rinehart and Winston.

Selltiz, Claire, Edrich, H., and Cook, S. W., 1965. Ratings of favorableness of statements about a social group as an indicator of attitudes toward the group. *J. Pers. soc. Psychol., 2*, 408–415.

Selvin, H. C., 1960. *The Effects of Leadership*. New York: Free Press.

Seward, Georgene, 1946. *Sex and the Social Order*. New York: McGraw-Hill.

Sewell, W. H., 1963. Some recent developments in socialization theory and research. *Annals Amer. Acad. Pol. soc. Science, 349*, 163–181.

Shafer, B. C., 1955. *Nationalism, Myth and Reality*. New York: Harcourt, Brace & World.

Shannon, D. A. (Ed.), 1960. *The Great Depression*. Englewood Cliffs, N.J.: Prentice-Hall.

Shaw, M. E., 1962. *Annual Technical Report, 1962*. Gainesville: Univer. of Florida. (Cited in Fiedler, 1968.)

Shaw, M. E., and Wright, J. M., 1967. *Scales for the Measurement of Attitudes*. New York: McGraw-Hill.

Sherif, Carolyn W., 1947. Variations in judgment as a function of ego-involvement. Paper presented at the Annual Meeting of the Eastern Psychological Association, Atlantic City.

Sherif, Carolyn W., 1961. Established reference scales and series effects in social judgment. Ph.D. thesis, University of Texas.

Sherif, Carolyn W., 1963. Social categorization as a function of latitude of acceptance and series range. *J. abnorm. soc. Psychol., 67*, 148–156.

Sherif, Carolyn W., and Jackman, N. R., 1966. Judgments of truth by participants in collective controversy. *Publ. Opin. Quart., 30*, 173–186.

Sherif, Carolyn W., and Sherif, M. (Eds.), 1967. *Attitude, Ego-involvement and Change*. New York: Wiley.

Sherif, Carolyn, W., Sherif, M., and Nebergall, R. E., 1965. *Attitude and Attitude Change: The Social Judgement-involvement Approach*. Philadelphia: Saunders.

Sherif, M., 1935. A study of some social factors in perception. *Arch. Psychol.,* No. 187.

Sherif, M., 1936. *The Psychology of Social Norms*. New York: Harper & Row. (PB: Torchbook, 1966, Harper & Row.)

Sherif, M., 1937. An experimental approach to the study of attitudes. *Sociometry, 1*, 90–98.

Sherif, M., 1948. *An Outline of Social Psychology*. New York: Harper & Row.

Sherif, M., 1951. Experimental study of intergroup relations. In J. H. Rohrer and M. Sherif (Eds.), *Social Psychology at the Crossroads*. New York: Harper & Row, 388–426.

Sherif, M., 1960. Some needed concepts in the study of attitude. In J. Peatman and E. J. Hartley (Eds.), *Festschrift for Gardner Murphy*. New York: Harper & Row.

Sherif, M., 1963. Social psychology: Problems and trends in interdisciplinary relationships. In S. Koch (Ed.), *Psychology: A Study of a Science*. Vol. 6. New York: McGraw-Hill, 30–93.

Sherif, M., 1966. *In Common Predicament: Social Psychology of Intergroup Conflict and Cooperation*. Boston: Houghton Mifflin. (British ed.: *Group Conflict and Cooperation: Their Social Psychology*. London: Routledge, 1967.)

Sherif, M., 1967. The psychology of slogans. *In Social Interaction. Process and Products*. Chicago: Aldine.

Sherif, M., 1967. *Social Interaction. Process and Products: Selected Essays*. Chicago: Aldine.

Sherif, M., 1968. Self concept. In *New International Encyclopedia of Social Sciences*. Vol. 14. New York: Macmillan and Free Press.

Sherif, M., and Cantril, H., 1947. *The Psychology of Ego-involvements*. New York: Wiley. (PB: Wiley Science Series, 1965; Wiley.)

Sherif, M., and Harvey, O. J., 1952. A study in

ego functioning: Elimination of stable anchor- ages in individual and group situations. *Sociometry,* **15**, 272–305.

Sherif, M., Harvey, O. J., White, B. J., Hood, W. R., and Sherif, Carolyn W., 1961. *Intergroup Conflict and Cooperation: The Robbers Cave Experiment.* Norman: Institute of Group Relations, University of Oklahoma.

Sherif, M., and Hovland, C. I., 1953. Judgmental phenomena and scales of attitude measurement: Placement of items with individual choice of number of categories. *J. abnorm. soc. Psychol.,* **48**, 135–141.

Sherif, M., and Hovland, C. I., 1961. *Social Judgment: Assimilation and Contrast Effects in Communication and Attitude Change.* New Haven: Yale Univer. Press. (PB: Yale U.P., 1966.)

Sherif, M., and Sherif, Carolyn W., 1953. *Groups in Harmony and Tension.* New York: Harper & Row. (Octagon, 1966.)

Sherif, M., and Sherif, Carolyn W., 1956. *An Outline of Social Psychology* (rev. ed.) New York: Harper & Row.

Sherif, M., and Sherif, Carolyn W., 1963. Varieties of social stimulus situations. In S. B. Sells (Ed.), *Stimulus Determinants of Behavior.* New York: Ronald Press, 82–105.

Sherif, M., and Sherif, Carolyn W., 1964. *Reference Groups: Exploration into the Conformity and Deviation of Adolescents.* New York: Harper & Row.

Sherif, M., and Sherif, Carolyn W. (Eds.), 1965. *Problems of Youth: Transition to Adulthood in a Changing World.* Chicago: Aldine.

Sherif, M., and Sherif, Carolyn W., 1967 a. Group processes and collective interaction in delinquent activities. *J. Res. in Crime and Delinquency,* January, 43–62.

Sherif, M., and Sherif, Carolyn W., 1967 b. Conformity-deviation, norms and group relations. In M. Sherif, *Social Interaction: Process and Products (Selected Essays).* Chicago: Aldine.

Sherif, M., White, B. J., and Harvey, O. J., 1955. Status in experimentally produced groups. *Amer. J. Sociol.,* **60**, 370–379.

Sherman, M., and Henry, T. R., 1933. *Hollow Folk.* New York: Crowell.

Sherman, Susan R., 1967. Demand characteristics in an experiment on attitude change. *Sociometry,* **30**, 246–261.

Shevky, E., and Bell, W., 1955. *Social Area Analysis.* Stanford, Calif.: Stanford Univer. Press.

Shibutani, T., and Kwan, K. M., 1965. *Ethnic Stratification: A Comparative Approach.* New York: Macmillan.

Shneidman, E., 1965. Projective techniques. In B. Wolman (Ed.), *Handbook of Clinical Psychology.* New York: McGraw-Hill, 489–521.

Siegel, Alberta E., and Siegel, S., 1957, 1965. Ref-

erence groups, membership groups, and attitude change. *J. abnorm. soc. Psychol.,* **55**, 360–364. (Reprinted in H. Proshansky and B. Seidenberg [Eds.], *Basic Studies in Social Psychology,* 1965. New York: Holt, Rinehart and Winston, 225–230.)

Silver, J. W., 1964. *Mississippi: The Closed Society.* New York: Harcourt, Brace & World.

Simmel, G., 1902. The number of members as determining the sociological form of the group (translated by A. W. Small). *Amer. J. Sociol.,* **8**, 1–46.

Simpson, G., 1963. *Emile Durkheim.* New York: Crowell.

Sinha, D., 1952 a. An experimental study of a social factor in perception: The influence of an arbitrary group standard. *Patna Univer. Journal.,* Jan.–April (reprint).

Sinha, D., 1952 b. Behavior in a catastrophic situation: A psychological study of reports and rumours. *Brit. J. Psychol.,* **43**, 200–209.

Smelser, N. J., 1959. *Social Change in the Industrial Revolution.* Chicago: Univer. of Chicago Press.

Smelser, N. J., 1962. *Theory of Collective Behavior.* New York: Free Press.

Smith, E. W., 1920. *The Ila-Speaking Peoples of Northern Rhodesia.* Vol. II. New York: Macmillan.

Smith, F., and Miller, G. A., 1966. *The Genesis of Language: A Psycholinguistic Approach.* Cambridge, Mass.: M.I.T. Press.

Smith, M. B., 1968. The self and cognitive consistency. In R. Abelson *et al.* (Eds.), *Cognitive Consistency.* Chicago: Rand McNally.

Smith, M. B., Bruner, J. S., and White, R. W., 1956. *Opinions and Personality.* New York: Wiley.

Smith, M. E., 1926. An investigation of the development of the sentence and the extent of vocabulary in young children. *Univer. of Iowa Studies in Child Welfare* (Iowa City), **3**, No. 5.

Sodhi, Kripal Singh, 1953. *Urteilsbildung in Sozialen Kraftfeld.* Göttingen: Verlag für Psychologie.

Southern School News, May, 1962, 2, 3, 5.

Southwick, C. H., 1955. Regulatory mechanisms of house mouse populations: Social behavior affecting litter survival. *Ecology,* **36**, 627–634.

Southwick, C. H., 1967. An experimental study of intergroup agonistic behavior in Rhesus monkeys (Macaca mulatta). *Behavior,* **28**, 182–209.

Spencer, B., and Gillen, F. J., 1927. *The Arunta: A Study of a Stone Age People.* New York: Macmillan.

Sperling, H. G., 1946. An experimental study of some psychological factors in judgment. Master's thesis, New School for Social Research. Summarized in S. E. Asch, 1952. *Social Psychology,* Englewood Cliffs, N.J.: Prentice-Hall, 487–490.

Spielberger, C. D., and DeNike, L. D., 1962. Operant conditioning of plural nouns: A failure to replicate the Greenspoon effect. *Psychol. Rep.,* **11**, 355–366.

Spielberger, C. D., and DeNike, L. D., 1966. Descriptive behaviorism versus cognitive theory in operant conditioning. *Psychol. Rev.,* **73**, 306–326.

Srinivas, M. N., 1966. *Social Change in Modern India.* Berkeley: Univer. of California Press.

Star, Shirley A., and Hughes, Helen McG., 1950. Report of an educational campaign: The Cincinnati plan for the United Nations. *Amer. J. Sociol.,* **55**, 389–400.

Star, Shirley A., Williams, R. M., Jr., and Stouffer, S. A., 1965. Negro infantry platoons in White companies. In H. Proshansky and B. Seidenberg (Eds.), *Basic Studies in Social Psychology.* New York: Holt, Rinehart and Winston.

Stern, B. J., 1939 (From the original document quoted by Stern in *The Family and Cultural Change.*) *Amer. sociol. Rev.,* **4**, 199–208.

Stern, R. M., 1964. Long-term observation of the autokinetic illusion: Frequency and direction of movement. *Percept. & Mot. Skills,* **18**, 825–830.

Stern, W., 1910. Abstracts of lectures on the psychology of testimony and on the study of individuality. *Amer. J. Psychol.,* **21**, 270–282.

Stevenson, H. W., and Allen, Sara, 1964. Adult performance as a function of sex of experimenter and sex of subject. *J. abnorm. soc. Psychol.,* **68**, 214–216.

Stogdill, R. M., 1948. Personal factors associated with leadership. *J. Psychol.,* **25**, 35–71.

Stogdill, R. M., 1959. *Individual Behavior and Group Achievement: A Theory, The Experimental Evidence.* New York: Oxford Univer. Press.

Stogdill, R. M., 1962. Intra-group-Intergroup theory and research. In M. Sherif (Ed.), *Intergroup Relations and Leadership.* New York: Wiley, 48–65.

Stone, L., 1966. Theories of revolution. *World Politics,* **18**, No. 2, 159–172.

Stone, W. F., 1967. Autokinetic norms: An experimental analysis. *J. pers. soc. Psychol.,* **5**, 76–81.

Stonequist, E. V., 1937. *The Marginal Man.* New York: Scribner.

Stouffer, S. A., 1955. *Communism, Conformity and Civil Liberties.* Garden City, N.Y.: Doubleday.

Stouffer, S. A., et al., 1950. *Measurement and Prediction.* Vol. IV of *Studies in Social Psychology in World War II.* Princeton, N.J.: Princeton Univer. Press.

Stouffer, S. A., Suchmann, E. A., DeVinney, L. C., Star, S. A., and Williams, R. M., Jr., 1949. *The American Soldier.* Vol. I. *Adjustments During Army Life.* Princeton, N.J.: Princeton Univer. Press. Stouffer, *et al.,* 1949, Vol. II.

Strauss, A., 1953. Concepts, communication and groups. In M. Sherif and M. O. Wilson (Eds.), *Group Relations at the Crossroads.* New York: Harper & Row.

Stricker, L. J., Messick, S., and Jackson, D.N., 1967. Suspicion of deception: Implications for conformity research. *J. pers. soc. Psychol.,* **5**, 379–389.

Strodtbeck, F. L., Simon, Rita J., and Hawkins, C., 1965. Social status in jury deliberations. In I. Steiner and M. Fishbein, *Current Studies in Social Psychology.* New York: Holt, Rinehart and Winston, 333–342.

Sullivan, H. S., 1947. *Conceptions of Modern Psychology.* Washington: William A. White Psychiatric Foundation, 2nd ed.

Sumner, W. F., 1906. *Folkways.* Boston: Ginn.

Sussman, M. B., and Weil, W. B., 1960. An experimental study on the effects of group interaction upon the behavior of diabetic children. *Int. J. soc. Psychiatry,* **6**, 120–125.

Sutherland, E. H., 1947. *Principles of Criminology.* 4th ed. Philadelphia: Lippincott.

Sykes, G. M. (Ed.), 1965. *Guide to Graduate Departments of Sociology.* Washington, D.C.: American Sociological Association.

Taguiri, R., and Petrullo, L., 1958. *Person Perception and Interpersonal Behavior.* Stanford, Calif.: Stanford Univer. Press.

Tajfel, H., 1957. Value and the perceptual judgment of magnitude. *Psychol. Rev.,* **64**, 192–204.

Tajfel, H., 1959. The anchoring effects of value in a scale of judgments. *Brit. J. Psychol.,* **50**, 294–304.

Tajfel, H., 1969. Social and cultural factors in perception. In G. Lindzey and E. Aronson (Eds.), *Handbook of Social Psychology.* 2nd ed. Reading, Mass.: Addison-Wesley.

Tajfel, H., and Wilkes, A. L., 1963. Salience of attributes and commitment to extreme judgments in the perception of people. *Brit. J. soc. clin. Psychol.,* **2**, 40–49.

Tajfel, H., and Winter, D. G., 1963. The interdependence of size, number and value in young children's estimates of magnitude. *J. genet. Psychol.,* **102**, 115–124.

Talland, G. A., 1954. The assessment of group opinion by leaders and their influence in its formation. *J. abnorm. soc. Psychol.,* **49**, 431–434.

Theodorson, G. A., 1953 a. Elements in the progressive development of small groups. *Soc. Forces,* **31**, 311–320.

Theodorson, G. A., 1953 b. Acceptance of industrialization and its attendant consequences for the social pattern of non-western societies. *Amer. sociol. Rev.,* **18**, 477–484.

Theodorson, G. A., 1957. The relationship between leadership and popularity roles in small groups. *Amer. sociol. Rev., 18*, 58–67.

Thomas, E. J., and Fink, C. F., 1963. Effects of group size. *Psychol. Bull., 60*, 371–384.

Thomas, W. I., and Znaniecki, F., 1918. *The Polish Peasant in Europe and America.* Chicago: Univer. of Chicago Press.

Thompson, H. S., 1967. *Hell's Angels: The Strange and Terrible Saga of the Outlaw Motorcycle Gangs.* New York: Random House.

Thrasher, F. M., 1927. *The Gang.* Chicago: Univer. of Chicago Press.

Thrasher, J. D., 1954. Interpersonal relations and gradations of stimulus structure in judgment variation. *Sociometry, 17*, 228–241. (Complete report in Ph.D. thesis with same title, University of Oklahoma, 1954.)

Thurnwald, R., 1932. The psychology of acculturation. *Amer. Anthrop., 34*, 557–569.

Thurstone, L. L., 1929. Theory of attitude measurement. *Psychol. Rev., 36*, 222–241.

Thurstone, L. L., and Chave, E. J., 1929. *The Measurement of Attitude.* Chicago: Univer. of Chicago Press.

Tilly, C., 1964. Reflections on the revolutions of Paris: An essay on recent historical writing. *Soc. Problems, 12*, No. 1, 99–121.

Time, 1962. April 30, 79, 45–46.

Time, 1963. May 24, 39.

Tittler, B. I., 1967. The relationship between attitude change and ego-involvement and its relevance to sex differences in attitude change. Master's thesis, The Pennsylvia State University.

Toch, H., 1965. *The Social Psychology of Social Movements.* Indianapolis: Bobbs-Merrill.

Tomkins, S. S., 1947. *The Thematic Apperception Test.* New York: Grune & Stratton.

Torgerson, W. S., 1958. *Theory and Methods of Scaling.* New York: Wiley.

Tresselt, Margaret E., 1947. The influence of amount of practice upon formation of a scale of judgment. *J. exp. Psychol., 37*, 251–260.

Tresselt, Margaret E., 1948. The effect of the experiences of contrasted groups upon the formation of a new scale of judgment. *J. soc. Psychol., 27*, 209–216.

Tresselt, Margaret E., and Volkmann, J., 1942. The production of uniform opinion by nonsocial stimulation. *J. abnorm. soc. Psychol., 37*, 234–243.

Triandis, H. C., and Triandis, Leigh M., 1965. Some studies of social distance. In I. Steiner and M. Fishbein (Eds.), *Current Studies in Social Psychology.* New York: Holt, Rinehart and Winston, 207–216.

Tuchman, B. W., 1965. Developmental sequence in small groups. *Psychol. Bull., 63*, 384–399.

Tuckman, J., and Kleiner, R. J., 1962. Discrepancy between aspiration and achievement as a predictor of schizophrenia. *Behavioral Sci., 7*, 443–447.

Tuddenham, R. D., 1961. The influence upon judgment of the apparent discrepancy between self and other. *J. soc. Psychol., 53*, 69–79.

Turk, H., 1961 a. Instrumental values and the popularity of instrumental leaders. *Soc. Forces, 39*, 252–260.

Turk, H., 1961 b. Instrumental and expressive ratings reconsidered. *Sociometry, 24*, 76–81.

Turk, H., Hartley, E. L., and Shaw, D. M., 1962. The expectation of social influence. *J. soc. Psychol., 58*, 23–29.

Turk, Theresa, and Turk, H., 1962. Group interaction in a formal setting: The case of the triad. *Sociometry, 25*, 48–55.

Turner, R. H., 1964. *The Social Context of Ambition.* San Francisco: Chandler.

Turner, R. H., and Killian, L. M., 1957. *Collective Behavior.* Englewood Cliffs, N.J.: Prentice-Hall.

United Nations Educational, Scientific and Cultural Organization (UNESCO), 1967. *Apartheid: Its Effects on Education, Science, Culture and Information.* Paris: Imprimeries Reunis de Chambery.

U.S. National Advisory Commission on Civil Disorder, 1968. *Report* (Kerner Report), New York Times Co. (paperback).

U.S. Bureau of the Census, 1967. Current Population Reports. Series P–60, No. 53, December 28, 4.

Unsigned article, 1947. I play for Toscanni. *This Week Magazine,* March 16, 1947, 20.

Upshaw, H. S., 1962. Own attitude as an anchor in equal-appearing intervals. *J. abnorm. soc. Psychol., 64*, 85–96.

Van Gennep, A., 1908, 1960. *The Rites of Passage.* Chicago: Univer. of Chicago Press.

Van Riper, C., 1947. *Speech Correction. Principles and Methods.* Englewood Cliffs, N.J.: Prentice-Hall.

Vaughan, G. M., 1963. The trans-situational aspect of conformity behavior. *J. Pers., 32*, 335–354.

Vaughan, Kathryn R., 1961. A disguised instrument for the assessment of intergroup attitudes. Master's thesis, Texas College of Arts & Industries.

Veblen, T., 1899. *The Theory of the Leisure Class.* New York: Macmillan.

Verba, S., 1961. *Small Groups and Political Behavior.* Princeton, N.J.: Princeton Univer. Press.

Vernon, M. D., 1962. *A Further Study of Visual Perception.* Cambridge, England: Cambridge Univer. Press.

Vidulich, R. N., and Kaiman, I. P., 1965. The effect of information source status and dogmatism upon conformity behavior. In I. D. Steiner and M. Fishbein (Eds.), *Current Studies in Social*

Psychology. New York: Holt, Rinehart and Winston, 294–300.

Vinacke, W. E., 1961. The investigation of concept formation. *Psychol. Bull.,* **48**, 1–31.

Volkmann, J., 1936. The anchoring of absolute scales. *Psychol. Bull.,* **33**, 742–743.

Volkmann, J., 1951. Scales of judgment and their implications for social psychology. In J. H. Rohrer, and M. Sherif (Eds.), *Social Psychology at the Crossroads.* New York: Harper & Row.

Voth, A. C., 1947. An experimental study of mental patients through the autokinetic phenomenon. *Amer. J. Psychiat.* **103**, 793–805.

Vigotsky, L. S., 1939. Thought and speech. *Psychiatry,* **2**, 29–54.

Vigotsky, L. S., 1962. *Thought and Language.* New York: Wiley.

Wainwright, J. M., 1945. *General Wainwright's Story* (R. Considine, Ed.). Garden City, N.Y.: Doubleday.

Walden, D., 1960. The contemporary opposition to the political and educational ideas of Booker T. Washington. *J. Negro History,* **45**, No. 2, April, 103–115.

Wallerstein, I., 1966, *Social Change: The Colonial Situation.* New York: Wiley.

Wallon, H., 1933. *Les Origines du Caractère chez l'Enfant.* Paris: Presses Universitaires de France.

Wallon, H., 1946. *Les Origines de la Pensée chez l'Enfant.* Tome I. Paris: Presses Universitaires de France.

Walster, Elaine, and Festinger, L., 1962. The effectiveness of "overheard" communications. *J. abnorm. soc. Psychol.,* **65**, 395–402.

Walter, N., 1955. A study of effects of conflicting suggestions upon judgment of the autokinetic situation (Ph.D. thesis, University of Oklahoma, 1952). *Sociometry* **18**, 138–146.

Walters, R. H., Marshall, W. E., and Shooter, J. R., 1960. Anxiety, isolation and susceptibility to social influence. *J. Pers.,* **28**, 518–529.

Wapner, S., and Alper, Thelma G., 1952. The effect of an audience on behavior in a choice situation. *J. abnorm. soc. Psychol.,* **47**, 222–229.

Wapner, S., Werner, H., Ajuriaguerra, J., Cleveland, S. E., Fisher, S., Critchley, M., and Witkin, H. A., 1965. *The Body Percept.* New York: Random House.

Warden, C. J., 1924. The relative economy of various modes of attack in the mastery of the stylus maze. *J. exp. Psychol.,* **7**, 243–275.

Ware, Caroline F., 1935. *Greenwich Village.* Boston: Houghton Mifflin.

Warner, W. L., and Lunt, P. S., 1941. *The Social Life of a Modern Community.* New Haven: Yale Univer. Press.

Warren, R. P., 1956. *Segregation: The Inner Conflict in the South.* New York: Random House.

Watts, A. F., 1944. *The Language and Mental Development of Children.* London: Harrap.

Webb, E. J., Campbell, D. T., Schwartz, R. D., and Sechrest, L., 1966. *Unobtrusive Measures: Nonreactive Research in the Social Sciences.* Chicago: Rand McNally.

Webb, S. C., and Chueh, Janet, 1962. The effect of role taking on the judgment of attitude items. Paper presented at the Annual Meeting of the American Psychological Association, St. Louis (mimeographed).

Webb, W. P., 1936. *The Great Plains.* Boston: Houghton Mifflin.

Weick, K. E., 1967. Promise and limitations of laboratory experiments in the development of attitude change theory. In Carolyn W. Sherif, and M. Sherif (Eds.), *Attitude, Ego-involvement and Change.* New York: Wiley, 51–75.

Weick, K. E., 1968. Systematic observational methods. In G. Lindzey and E. Aronson (Eds.), *Handbook of Social Psychology* (rev.). Reading, Mass.: Addison-Wesley.

Weir, Ruth H., 1962. *Language in the Crib.* The Hague: Mouton.

Weksel, W., and Hennes, J. D., 1965. Attitude intensity and the Semantic Differential. *J. Pers. soc. Psychol.,* **2**, 91–94.

Wertheim, W. F., 1956. *Indonesian Society in Transition: A Study of Social Change.* The Hague: W. von Hoeue.

Wertheimer, M., 1958. Principles of perceptual organization. In D. C. Beardslee, and M. Wertheimer (Eds.), *Readings in Perception.* Princeton, N.J.: Van Nostrand, 115–135.

Wever, E. G., and Zener, K. E., 1928. Method of absolute judgment in psychophysics. *Psychol. Rev.,* **35**, 466–493.

White, B. J., 1960. The relationship of concept availability to contrast effects in judgment. Ph.D. thesis, University of Oklahoma.

White, L. A., 1942. On the use of tools by primates. *J. compar. Psychol.,* **34**, 369–374.

White, L. A., 1948. The definition and prohibition of incest. *Amer. Anthrop.,* **50**, July–September, 416–435. (Bobbs-Merrill Reprint Series in Sociology, S-310.)

White, R. W., 1944. Interpretation of imaginative productions. In J. McV. Hunt (Ed.), *Personality and the Behavior Disorders.* Vol. I. New York: Ronald Press, 214–251.

Whittaker, J. O., 1958. Effects of experimentally introduced anchorages upon judgments in the autokinetic situation. Ph.D. thesis, University of Oklahoma.

Whittaker, J. O., 1963. Opinion change as a function of communication-attitude discrepancy. *Psychol. Rep.,* **13**, 763–772.

Whittaker, J. O., 1964. Cognitive dissonance and the effectiveness of persuasive communications. *Publ. Opin. Quart.,* **28**, 547–555.

Whittaker, J. O., 1964. Parameters of social influence in the autokinetic situation. *Sociometry,* **27**, 88–95.

Whittaker, J. O., 1965. Attitude change and communication-attitude discrepancy. *J. soc. Psychol.,* **65**, 141–147.

Whittaker, J. O., 1967. Resolution of the communication discrepancy issue in attitude change. In Carolyn W. Sherif and M. Sherif (Eds.), *Attitude, Ego-involvement and Change.* New York: Wiley, 159–177.

Whorf, B., 1940. *Science and Linguistics. Technology Rev.,* **42**, No. 6. (Cambridge, Mass.: M.I.T.)

Whyte, W. F., 1943. *Street Corner Society.* Chicago: Univer. of Chicago Press.

Whyte, W. F., 1943. A slum sex code. *Amer. J. sociol.,* **49**, 24–31.

Whyte, W. F., *et al.,* 1955. *Money and Motivation: An Analysis of Incentives in Industry.* New York: Harper & Row.

Whyte, W. F., 1961. *Men at Work.* Homewood, Ill.: Dorsey Press.

Whyte, W. F., and Gardner, B., 1945. Problems of the foreman. *J. appl. Anthrop.* Special issue, Spring.

Wiener, M., 1958. Certainty of judgment as a variable in conformity behavior. *J. soc. Psychol.,* **48**, 257–263.

Wilensky, H. L., 1966. Mass society and mass culture. In B. Berelson, and M. Janowitz (Eds.), *Reader in Public Opinion and Communication.* 2nd ed. New York: Free Press, 293–327.

Williams, Juanita H., 1964. Conditioning of verbalization: A review. *Psychol. Bull.,* **62**, 383–393.

Williams, R. M., Jr., 1960. *American Society: A Sociological Interpretation.* (rev. ed.) New York: Knopf.

Williams, R. M., Jr., 1964. *Strangers Next Door.* Englewood Cliffs, N.J.: Prentice-Hall, Inc.

Wilner, D. M., Walkley, R. P., and Cook, S. W., 1952. Residential proximity and intergroup relations in public housing projects. *J. soc. Issues,* **8**, 45–69.

Wilson, A. B., 1959. Residential segregation of social classes and aspirations of high school boys. *Amer. sociol. Rev.,* **24**, 836–845.

Witkin, H. A., *et al.,* 1954. *Personality Through Perception: An Experimental and Clinical Study.* New York: Harper & Row.

Wolf, W., 1956. *Essentials of Psychology.* New York: Grune & Stratton.

Wolfe, J. B., 1935. Effectiveness of token-rewards for chimpanzees. *Comp. Psychol. Monogr.,* **13**, No. 60.

Woodworth, R. S., and Schlosberg, H., 1954. *Experimental Psychology.* New York: Holt, Rinehart and Winston.

Wright, Q., 1949. Modern technology and the world order. In W. F. Ogburn (Ed.), *Technology and International Relations.* Chicago: Univer. of Chicago Press, 174–198.

Wylie, Ruth, 1961. *The Self Concept. A Critical Survey of Pertinent Research Literature.* Lincoln: Univer. of Nebraska Press.

Yarrow, Marian R., and Campbell, J. D., 1963. Person perception in children. *Merrill-Palmer Quart.,* **9**, 57–72.

Yarrow, Marian R., Campbell, J. D., and Yarrow, L. J., 1965. Interpersonal dynamics in racial integration. In H. Proshansky and B. Seidenberg (Eds.), *Basic Studies in Social Psychology.* New York: Holt, Rinehart and Winston, 657–669.

Yerkes, R. M., 1943. *Chimpanzees: A Laboratory Colony.* New Haven: Yale Univer. Press.

Yerkes, R. M., and Nissen, H. W., 1939. Prelinguistic sign behavior in chimpanzees. *Science,* **89**, 585–587.

Yinger, M., 1965. *A Minority Group in American Society.* New York: McGraw-Hill (Social Problem Series).

Young, W., 1968. Statement made over NBC television. January 12, 1968.

Youniss, R. P., 1958. Conformity to group judgments in its relation to the structure of the stimulus situation and certain personality variables. Phd. thesis, The Catholic University of America.

Zajonc, R. B., and Burnstein, E., 1965. The learning of balanced and unbalanced social structures. *J. Pers.,* **33**, 153–163.

Zaleznik, A., Christensen, C. R., and Roethlisberger, F. J., 1958. *The Motivation, Productivity and Satisfaction of Workers: A Production Study.* Boston: Harvard Univer. Press.

Zangwill, O. L., 1938. A study of the significance of attitude on recognition. *Brit. J. Psychol.,* **28**, 12–17.

Zavalloni, Marisa, and Cook, S. W., 1965. Influence of judges' attitudes on ratings of favorableness of statements about a social group. *J. pers. soc. Psychol.,* **1**, 43–54.

Zeaman, D., 1946. Assessment of interpersonal relations through autokinetic technique. Personal communication.

Zeligs, R., and Hendrickson, G., 1933–34. Racial attitudes of 200 sixth-grade children. *Sociol. & Soc. Res.,* **18**, 26–36.

Zeligs, R., and Hendrickson, G., 1933–34. Checking the social distance technique through the personal interview. *Sociol. & Soc. Res.,* **18**, 420–430.

Zimbardo, P. G., 1960. Verbal ambiguity and judgmental distortion. *Psychol. Rep.,* **6**, 57–58.

Zinn, H., 1964. *SNCC: The New Abolitionists.* Boston: Beacon, 19–20.

Zorbaugh, H. W., 1929. *The Gold Coast and the Slum.* Chicago: Univer. of Chicago Press.

Indexes

Index of Names

(Also consult References, pp. 573 ff.)

Index of Subjects

607